MEMOIRS OF A TORY RADICAL

Also by Nigel Lawson

The Power Game (with Jock Bruce-Gardyne)
The Nigel Lawson Diet Book
An Appeal to Reason: A Cool Look at Global Warming

NIGEL LAWSON

MEMOIRS OF A TORY RADICAL

An abridgement of *The View from No.11*
With a new concluding chapter

First published in Great Britain in 1992 by Bantam Press as *The View from No. 11*

This revised edition published in 2010 by
Biteback Publishing Ltd
Westminster Tower
3 Albert Embankment
London
SE1 7SP

ISBN 978-1-84954-047-6

10 9 8 7 6 5 4 3 2 1

A CIP catalogue record for this book is available from the British Library.

Set in Garamond by SoapBox
Printed and bound in Great Britain by TJ International Ltd, Padstow, Cornwall

To my children

CONTENTS

FOREWORD

This book is a half-length abridgement of *The View from No.11*, originally published in 1992, to which has been added a new concluding chapter. It is not an autobiography, but a ministerial, and in particular a Chancellorial, memoir. In other words, it excludes all that is most important in life. But politics and political office do matter, particularly when they are about more than office for its own sake. That was certainly the case with the Thatcher era, and with my part in it.

If this book is not an autobiography, neither is it an essay in the higher economic scholasticism. Although I have been heavily involved in economic policy and have sought to come to terms with rival economic ideas, I have done so as a politician rather than as an economist. But no account either of the Conservative Government of the 1980s or of the work of a modern Chancellor of the Exchequer can make sense without an explanation of the economic thinking that lay behind so many of the key decisions that were taken.

When I started this book I drafted it in strict chronological order, describing the events of 1979–89 as they happened. This certainly conveyed the reality of a Minister's, and in particular a Chancellor's life, with so many different problems and issues jostling to be addressed at one and the same time. But it soon became clear that this real-life treatment would make the story all but incomprehensible. I have therefore compromised between the chronological approach and dealing with one subject at a time. As a result, some of the key conclusions emerge early on in the book. I have, however, liberally sprinkled dates to enable the reader to follow what was happening when.

Although the book is an account of the period, and of my part in it, as I saw it and see it, and in that sense is inevitably subjective, I have sought to be both accurate and fair. Should any inaccuracies have none the less inadvertently crept in – for I did not keep a diary – I apologise; but I would be surprised if they alter the account in any material way.

The original edition of this book was virtually completed before the turmoil in the foreign exchange markets of mid-September 1992, which led to the departure of sterling from the European exchange rate mechanism. While nothing that has happened since has caused me to resile from the view I took of the ERM as Chancellor, it has of course been overtaken by events with the coming of the Euro. That and other topics are covered in the new concluding chapter, which was written in August 2010.

Many readers may be particularly interested in the dramatic events leading up to my resignation as Chancellor in October 1989, recounted in part five of the book. But I would direct the reader's attention to the first four parts, which are intended to shed some light on the working of British government. Most books about how decisions are taken in government tend to be written by academics or journalists: indeed, as a journalist many years ago, I co-wrote one myself. This, book gives the view from the inside. A further reason for directing readers to the first three parts is that many of the central policies of the Thatcher era were formulated at a very early stage, and remained in place thereafter. Thus some of the main discussion of the issues, and even of personalities, occurs in these parts.

This edition of the book has been produced with the invaluable assistance of Christopher Collins of the Margaret Thatcher Foundation, to whom I am very grateful.

EDITOR'S PREFACE

This abridged version of *The View from No.11* has been prepared from the first edition published in autumn 1992 and comprises just over 50 per cent of the original 1100 page text.

No general attempt has been made to update the original, which would have made little sense: *The View from No.11* was written as a memoir, not a text book.

Nigel Lawson has added a few dozen footnotes where the text seemed to require contemporary comment: these begin '[2010 note]' to distinguish them from footnotes in the original. And he has written a new concluding chapter of reflections from the perspective of 2010.

In places, new material has been drafted to facilitate the process of condensation (typically, bridging sentences to allow cuts), but where that has been done, care has been taken not to alter the sense of the original. And it has been a firm principle throughout the business of editing that any hostages to fortune in the original should be left unransomed.

Entirely omitted are the final part of the 1992 book, 'The Abiding Legacy' (which the new closing chapter replaces), as well as seven annexes reproducing some key documents and statistics.

From the main body of the text, much material on international economic diplomacy has gone, although not where it impacted significantly on domestic policy, as in the case, for example, of the Plaza and Louvre accords or European Monetary Union.

Many smaller cuts have been made at the level of sections, paragraphs, even sentences, intended to omit material of secondary interest without reshaping the book as a whole. It is hoped that almost everything belonging to the central story remains in the present text and that its powerful narrative force remains undiminished.

For those anxious to examine the original alongside the abridgement, it can be found online at *www.margaretthatcher.org*, the website of the Margaret Thatcher Foundation. Over time many hundreds of the documents on which the book is based will also appear there, selected from the official archives of the

Treasury and No. 10, as well as from the private papers of Lady Thatcher and Lord Lawson, among many others.

Christopher Collins
Edinburgh, October 2010

PART ONE

FOUNDATIONS

CHAPTER ONE

FORMATIVE YEARS

Beginnings · Early Beliefs · Economic Evolution

BEGINNINGS

By way of very brief personal background, I was born on 11 March 1932 into a comfortable Hampstead household, complete with nanny, cook and parlourmaid. My father was a tea merchant, the proprietor of a small but successful firm in the City of London and my mother's father was the wealthy senior partner of a firm of stockbrokers. My family was not an especially political one. When the war ended I was sent to Westminster School, where my father had been educated. Unlike many public schools, Westminster is a worldly place. My main intellectual interest then was mathematics, in which I won a scholarship to Christ Church, Oxford, in 1951. I had intended to read law, but was dissuaded by a distinguished former Law Officer, Sir John Simon, who advised me that the study of law at Oxford was a poor preparation for the bar, which at that time I was contemplating as a future career. So, like many others, I read Philosophy, Politics and Economics (PPE), specialising in philosophy, partly because of a natural affinity between mathematics and philosophy.

Oxford philosophy was much influenced at the time by the school of Linguistic Analysis, and I became fascinated by it. It was in many ways an arid school, being concerned solely with the logical elucidation of every proposition. But it trained its practitioners to think clearly and identify nonsense, however dressed up, which was not a bad training for politics. Philosophy satisfied my taste for theory: my interest in economics lay in its practical application to policy. Economic policies cannot be chosen just by references to the eternal verities. Too much depends on the circumstances of time and place. Moreover, if there are any such verities, they are probably of the non-technical, uncomfortable kind listed in Kipling's *The Gods of the Copybook Headings*:

In the Carboniferous Epoch, we were promised Abundance for all,
By robbing selected Peter to pay for collective Paul:
But, though we had plenty of Money, there was nothing Money could buy,
And the Gods of the Copybook Headings said: 'If you don't work you die'.

My extra-mural interests were not primarily political. Much has been made of a taste for poker, but it is an interest shared by many undergraduates and I have not played since I left Oxford. I acted, without great distinction, fenced, skied (for the University second six) and went to a large number of parties. I never spoke at the Oxford Union, nor did I bother to join the University Conservative Association. This was mainly because my contemporaries in the acting set were rather more amusing than those in the political set. I did join a somewhat decadent high Tory dining club, the Chatham, where a large amount of mulled claret was consumed and the invited speakers tended to be Tory mavericks like Leo Amery, Bob Boothby and 'Hinch' Hinchingbrooke. My only serious political involvement was with the Strasbourg Club, which was devoted to the then unfashionable cause of European union, and of which I became president.

After (somewhat to my surprise) getting a first, and two years' national service with the Navy, where I was lucky enough to be given my own command (a motor torpedo-boat), in the summer of 1956 I joined the staff of the *Financial Times,* where my contemporaries included Andrew Shonfield, William Rees-Mogg, Michael Shanks, Samuel Brittan and Jock Bruce-Gardyne. The choice was wholly fortuitous. Having been rejected by the Foreign Office, I thought of journalism as an alternative way of becoming involved in public affairs. The FT was at that time the only national newspaper which did not insist on preliminary apprenticeship in the provinces, and took untrained graduates straight from Oxford or Cambridge.

I stayed there a little over four years, as feature writer, industrial reporter, oil correspondent, features editor, and finally chief writer of the Lex column, and learned a great deal, under the remarkable editorship of Gordon Newton, before leaving to become the first City Editor of the newly formed *Sunday Telegraph*. I always endeavoured in my columns to discuss economics in a manner intelligible to the layman. Although I probably failed more often than not, it was mainly for this reason that Oliver Poole, the chairman of the *Financial Times* and joint chairman of the Conservative Party, offered me in 1963 a post in the office of the Prime Minister, Harold Macmillan, to help him with his political speeches.

Macmillan resigned almost immediately on health grounds. I stayed on throughout the premiership of Sir Alec Douglas-Home, who claimed to understand economics only by using matchsticks. This was a characteristically modest assessment of his talents, and I came to admire Alec enormously. Working for the Prime Minister allowed me a unique glimpse of politics and government from the centre. After some seven years as a critical observer of the nation's economic management, proximity to the exercise of power sharpened the urge to test my criticisms in practice. I felt I ought to get out on the field and play.

Not wishing to be a backroom boy, however eminent, I declined the Directorship of the Conservative Research Department after the 1964 general election and at the end of 1965 I was appointed editor of the *Spectator* in succession to Iain Macleod, where I stayed for the next four and a half years. I was sacked by the then proprietor, who wished to control editorial policy himself, while I was away contesting (unsuccessfully) the then Labour seat of Eton and Slough in the 1970 general election. I was selected in 1972 as prospective Conservative candidate for Blaby in Leicestershire, a new and very much more promising constituency in the heart of England, between Leicester and Rugby. Confident of electoral success, I took up a research fellowship at Nuffield College, Oxford later that year. I completed there much of my share of the work which culminated in the book I published with my old friend Jock Bruce-Gardyne in 1976, *The Power Game*. It examined four major political decisions and among its conclusions was the proposition that 'So often it is pure hazard which tips the scale of decision in the end'. I was eventually elected Member of Parliament for Blaby in February 1974, on the eve of my forty-second birthday.

EARLY BELIEFS

Although my parliamentary career started late, my political recollections go back to the immediate post-war years. I suppose nowadays nobody of any significance calls himself or herself a socialist, except between consenting adults in private, without at least a twinge of embarrassment. That was decidedly not the case when my political views were formed. The Attlee Labour Government that had swept into office with a landslide majority in 1945 was proud to call itself socialist, and determined to build a new socialist Jerusalem in Britain. After all, had not the war been won thanks to an unprecedented co-ordination of national activity by State planning and State control? Surely this formula would prove just as triumphant in winning the peace – particularly since the old hierarchical order had been swept aside by a new spirit of egalitarianism symbolised by the ration book and the queue.

For Churchill's Conservatives, the war had not been about that at all. It was a victory not for State planning and State control, but for the forces of freedom; and the spirit that had welded the nation together had been not egalitarianism but patriotism. It was to this interpretation that I was instinctively attracted, but I watched with interest how the new Labour Government – the first peacetime government of which I was politically conscious – set about its task.

The experience confirmed all my prejudices. For a country that felt it had won the war, the economic failure of the Attlee years was a national humiliation. But the failure was more than just economic. It seemed to me that in every respect the socialism the Labour Government was seeking to put into practice went against the grain of human nature – not least its Utopian disregard of original sin or of what Anthony Quinton has called 'man's moral and intellectual imperfection'.

Anyone imbued with a sense of this imperfection was no more likely to be attracted by the anarcho-capitalism later to be fashionable in some extreme free-market circles, especially in the United States, in the 1970s and 80s, than by post-war ideas of reconstructing society from Whitehall. But the latter have been the practical threat during my adult lifetime. Both are types of Utopianism which overlook the dependence of political, personal and economic freedom alike on the tradition of an ordered and orderly society. As Edmund Burke said to the voters of Bristol, liberty 'not only exists along with order and virtue but ... cannot exist at all without them'.

Order in turn is dependent on a very unfashionable virtue, the recognition of duly constituted authority, order, rank and precedence. It is, of course, an error to attribute to a dramatist the words of his characters. But Shakespeare was clearly preoccupied with the problems of legitimate authority and the need for it. He had no illusions about the imperfections of those all too often likely to be at the top – 'a cur's obeyed in office'. Nor was he lacking in sympathy for those at the bottom: for instance, Lear's reference to 'poor naked wretches' with 'houseless heads and unfed sides'. But to destroy authority does not increase compassion and understanding. In the words of Ulysses in *Troilus and Cressida*:

> Take but degree away, untune that string
> And hark! what discord follows; each thing meets
> In mere oppugnancy.

Many modern political thinkers have queried whether this essentially pre-capitalist ordered structure is in fact compatible with capitalism. The Austrian-American economist and sociologist, Joseph Schumpeter, writing in the early 1940s, emphasised the paradox that:

> Capitalism creates a critical frame of mind which, after having destroyed the moral authority of so many other institutions, in the end turns against its own; the bourgeois finds to his amazement that a rationalist attitude does not stop at the credentials of kings and popes but goes on to attack private property and the whole scheme of bourgeois values ... From the fact that criticism of the capitalist order proceeds from a critical attitude of mind, i.e. from an attitude which spurns allegiance of extra-rational values, it does not follow that rational refutation will be accepted. Such refutation may wear the rational garb of attack, but can never reach the extra-rational driving power and that always lurks behind it. Capitalist rationality does not do away with sub-or super-rational impulses. It merely makes them get out of hand by removing the restraint of sacred or semi-sacred tradition.

Schumpeter believed that capitalism would be destroyed by its cultural and political – not its alleged economic – contradictions. Similar fears have been expressed more recently by American writers such as Irving Kristol and Daniel Bell.

The outcome has often seemed a pretty close-run thing. But in the end Schumpeter underestimated the ordinary wage and salary earner, who has been better able to see through Utopian pretensions than many so-called intellectuals. (The post-war years have also seen the rise of a conspicuously successful form of capitalism in Japan and in the newer industrial countries of the Far East, which owes little to Western rationalism or extreme individualism.)

But the most striking practical victory of capitalism, which Schumpeter, who died in 1950, could hardly have foreseen, was the disintegration of the collectivised economies of the former Soviet Union and Eastern and Central Europe – a rare example of an historical experiment testing a theory to destruction. Post-Communist rulers have, with varying degrees of success, tried to pick up the pieces after the disintegration of a socialism which lacked both liberty and order and which was held together in its last years only by cynicism and corruption.

I cannot of course claim to have foreseen these momentous events in observing post-war England. But my instinctive suspicion of creeping socialism was reinforced by all I saw of the Labour Government of 1945–51. Yet despite the fact that, within little more than six years, the Attlee Government had been voted out of office, battered by economic failure and exhausted of ideas, it proved to have set the political agenda for the next quarter of a century. It may have been defeated at the polls, but it had captured the moral high ground. The two key principles for which it stood, big interventionist government and the drive towards equality, remained effectively unchallenged for more than a generation.

There is another aspect of the post-war consensus about which I have always had misgivings – the downgrading of nationalism. As early as 1967 I wrote in a *Spectator* series, 'A Tract for The Tories':

> Today 'nationalism' is out of fashion among the opinion-formers. Thanks to a superficial misreading of history, it is accused of having been responsible for two world wars and has widely come to be regarded as a political sin of the first magnitude, fortunately found only in such antiquated and obsolete figures as General de Gaulle. In fact the real danger comes from ideologies not nationalism; for while a nation may properly respect the nationhood of others, an ideology knows no frontiers ...
>
> Once [the Tories] lose their claim to be, in the fullest sense, the 'national party', they are left, as they are in danger of being left today, either as the party of the 'individual' – a noble but to most people an austere and forbidding creed – or else as the party of the middle classes, which condemns them to a permanent minority.

All this had to change. It is to Margaret Thatcher's great credit that she, at last, successfully challenged this debilitating post-war consensus. True, by 1979 the tide of ideas was flowing her way. But tides still have to be caught.

ECONOMIC EVOLUTION

If my political perspective was formed early on, my approach to economic policy, at least in one important respect, took longer to evolve. While always a firm believer in the market economy and the enterprise culture, it took some time for me to recognise that this needed to be set within a firm framework of financial discipline if inflation was to be suppressed. This was partly because I had been brought up as a Keynesian (my economics tutor at Oxford had been Keynes's pupil and biographer, Roy Harrod), and the Keynes of the *General Theory* displayed, to say the least, a distinctly cavalier attitude to inflation. But it also stemmed from the fact that during the 1950s and the 1960s Britain's inflation rate averaged a shade under 4 per cent, and except at the very end of that period showed no sign of acceleration. When it rose above 5 per cent in 1969, it was the first time that this had occurred for fourteen years.

For some time, therefore, I wrongly took relatively low and nonaccelerating inflation for granted. Ironically, in the light of subsequent events, I failed to appreciate the importance of the discipline that was being exerted by the Bretton Woods fixed exchange-rate system. But when inflation did start to take off at the end of the 1960s and the early 1970s, my perspective quickly changed. It was clear to me that the overriding object of macroeconomic policy must be the suppression of inflation. Moreover, unlike the conventional wisdom of the time embraced by pretty well the entire economic establishment and even (then) by Margaret Thatcher – I was equally clear that incomes policy, of which I had been publicly and consistently critical right from the start, was no solution.

So by the time I entered the House of Commons in 1974, the views I had arrived at, and which I continue to hold today, could be summarised in terms of two interconnected reversals of the post-war conventional wisdom. The first is the conviction that the recipe for economic success is the greatest practicable market freedom within an overall framework of firm financial discipline – precisely how that discipline is best applied being essentially a second-order question, though important, and one which was to prove surprisingly explosive. This is in stark contrast to the approach that culminated in the débâcle of the 1970s, in which an ever-increasing erosion of market freedom was accompanied by the progressive abandonment of financial discipline.

The second reversal is that which I made the theme of my Mais Lecture as Chancellor in 1984. That is to say, instead of seeking to use macroeconomic (i.e. fiscal and monetary) policy to promote growth and microeconomic policy (of which incomes policy was a key component) to suppress inflation, the Government should direct macroeconomic policy to the suppression of inflation and rely on microeconomic (or supply-side) policy, such as tax and labour market reform, to provide the conditions favourable to improved performance in terms of growth and employment.

Of course, there is more to it than that, as will become apparent later on. But that was, and is, the essence of it.

CHAPTER TWO

MEMBER OF PARLIAMENT

New Boy · Prime Minister's Questions · Advent of Margaret Thatcher
Opposition Whip · Preparation for Office

NEW BOY

The general election of February 1974, which brought me into the House of Commons as Member of Parliament for Blaby with a comfortable 12,000-plus majority, also ushered in a Labour Government with no overall majority. It was obvious that Harold Wilson, once again (somewhat to his surprise) Prime Minister, would soon call another election, in an attempt to repeat his success of the 1960s, when after scraping in very narrowly after thirteen years of Tory Government in October 1964 he dissolved Parliament and won by a landslide in March 1966.

Having drafted, with some misgivings, the Tory manifesto for the February election, I was asked, along with my old friend Douglas Hurd (who had entered the House with me) and one or two others, to help Ted Heath to cobble together a platform to avert this disaster. The outcome was a somewhat bizarre appeal, but the main objective was achieved. A re-run of 1966 was averted. Labour won the October 1974 election with an overall majority so narrow that they were constantly fighting for survival and, with the normal attrition of by-election defeats, were eventually forced to call an election at a time not of their choosing, having been defeated on a 'no confidence' motion on the floor of the House of Commons in March 1979 – the first time this had happened for over half a century.

Losing manifestos have only one home: the scrapheap. But that of October 1974 was to prove an unfortunate exception. Ted had put his former Education Secretary, Margaret Thatcher, in charge of housing policy, with a policy group, of whom I was one, to assist her. This was my first experience of working with Margaret, and I was impressed by her vigour and energy. While almost all her former Cabinet colleagues – the great exception being her economic mentor, Keith Joseph – were demoralised by ejection from office, she went to work with a will. As a result, of the few specific pledges in the manifesto, hers stood out. The centrepiece was an undertaking, first to reduce the rates by transferring the cost of teachers' pay to the central exchequer, and subsequently to abolish domestic rates altogether, 'replacing them by taxes related to people's ability to pay'.

The abolition of domestic rates was highly controversial within the party, both within the policy group and at the wider back-bench meeting subsequently convened, not least because no-one had the slightest idea what the replacement tax would be. But at least it was fully, indeed passionately, discussed, and – subject to what the alternative might prove to be – probably secured majority support. That could not be said about the second major pledge in the housing field. This was inserted by Margaret at the last moment, though clearly with Ted's approval. To my horror, I discovered that we had pledged ourselves to reduce mortgage rates, then 11 per cent, to 9.5 per cent forthwith, and to cap them at that level in perpetuity.

Unlike the pledge to abolish domestic rates, which was to rise from its grave to haunt the Tory Government years later, the economic nonsense of a 9.5 per cent mortgage cap was well and truly destined for the scrapheap. Indeed, during the entire eleven-and-a-half-year Thatcher premiership, the mortgage rate only once went as low as 9.5 per cent, and then for only three months. But it did provide an early demonstration of Margaret's devotion to the cause of the home-buyer, irrespective of the economic consequences; and, as a result, her antipathy to high interest rates. Her detestation of inflation was genuine enough; but while willing the end, she was repeatedly reluctant to embrace the means.[1]

But to come back to my own story: I had entered the House of Commons rather later and rather better known than most new Members. This meant, to those on the Labour benches, and some on the Conservative benches, too, that I needed to be taken down a peg. I was soon made aware that the House of Commons is like a school, in which the new boys are expected to show all the humility of new boys, irrespective of whether or not they have achieved anything before passing through its portals.

[1] [2010 note] The release of the Prime Minister's official files for 1979 stirred a faint memory of mine. In fact the idea of a mortgage cap was not quite killed off by the October 1974 defeat: spooked by stories in the Sunday press of 24 June 1979 that mortgage rates were set to rise, Margaret made a determined effort to revive it that summer, demanding that the Treasury use the contingency reserve to hold rates at 11.75 per cent. I was present at a meeting on 4 July in which she urged a government loan to the Building Societies. This found no takers, but with some reluctance we did agree to put pressure on the Societies to hold off an early increase in mortgage rates (Michael Heseltine and myself doing the honours). Of course, the pressure became public and did little to improve the government's credentials for monetary discipline, a fact we were to rue in November when a gilt strike forced a 3 per cent increase in interest rates, the largest one-day rise before or since.

PRIME MINISTER'S QUESTIONS

In other words, I had to establish myself in parliamentary terms from scratch. It clearly made sense to specialise in economic policy, but I felt I needed to do more than that. The obvious answer was to specialise in Prime Minister's questions, too. As radio listeners were subsequently to discover, this plays, somewhat noisily, to a packed House for a quarter of an hour every Tuesday and Thursday. For a new Opposition back-bencher, the opportunity to practise his parliamentary skills by asking awkward questions of the Prime Minister of the day had obvious attractions, even if with a Prime Minister as experienced as Harold Wilson it was something of a high-risk occupation. Fortunately, I had been studying Wilson closely for over ten years, first as special assistant to the then Prime Minister, Alec Home, in 1963–64, when Wilson was Leader of the Opposition, and subsequently as a journalist, during his first premiership.

As a result, I had come to understand him rather better than most Tory Members and to know his weaknesses, which enabled me (according to Wilson's own later account) to become his most effective questioner on the Tory side, though he suffered even more at the hands of his own Labour colleague, the defiantly left-wing mining MP, Dennis Skinner, with whom I established an unprincipled informal collaboration. When Wilson surprisingly resigned in March 1976 I found his successor, Jim Callaghan, very much harder to deal with, and rather lost interest in this particular art-form. But by then I had already established a parliamentary reputation of sorts.

There are some who affect to believe that Prime Minister's questions are little more than a silly game, and nothing to do with the serious business of politics, let alone statesmanship. Certainly, the questioning does not even pretend to be a search for information. But what it does provide is a continuous public examination of the character and competence of the Prime Minister of the day; and I have never known a Prime Minister who did not take it very seriously indeed.

Specialising in economic policy meant a number of things. I spoke in economic debates and in particular Budget debates (I had made my maiden speech appropriately enough on All Fools' Day 1974, during Denis Healey's first Budget debate). I got myself on to the standing committee on successive Finance Bills, where the Bill that enacts the Budget is subjected to clause-by-clause, line-by-line scrutiny. I became a member (in the place of my dear friend Jock Bruce-Gardyne, who sadly lost his seat to a Scottish Nationalist in the second 1974 election) of the then General Sub-Committee of the Expenditure Committee, the precursor of today's Select Committee on the Treasury and

Civil Service. I also joined the *ad hoc* select committee set up by the Labour Government under the chairmanship of Douglas Jay to recommend the form that the Wealth Tax to which they were committed should take; an exercise which the Tory members of the committee, well led by Maurice Macmillan, were eventually and with no little elegance to abort.

After the October 1974 election Ted Heath made the somewhat bizarre decision effectively to split the position of Shadow Chancellor in two, giving the job of the front legs of the pantomime horse to Robert Carr and that of the back legs to Margaret Thatcher. Her principal remit was to lead the assault on Labour's promised second 1974 Budget, the main purpose of which was to introduce a swingeing attack on inherited wealth (including family businesses) in the shape of the Capital Transfer Tax. The battle was effectively joined at the committee stage, where I found myself working with her once again, and got to know her rather better. It was an exercise in which the ability to master detail she had acquired as a lawyer stood her in good stead.

Interestingly, of the fifteen Tories on the standing committee of that Finance Bill, no fewer than nine were to become Cabinet Ministers during the Thatcher years: apart from Margaret herself, there were David Howell, Norman Lamont, John MacGregor, Tony Newton, Cecil Parkinson, Peter Rees, Nicholas Ridley and myself. We were an effective team. It was, indeed, in the middle of that committee stage that Margaret was elected Leader of the Conservative Party. And happily, as Chancellor under her premiership, I was able to transform the economically and socially damaging Capital Transfer Tax into a broadly acceptable Inheritance Tax.

When Margaret Thatcher defeated Ted to become leader in February 1975 it was more a rejection of Ted – on personal and political grounds alike – than a positive endorsement of her, at least so far as the majority of her parliamentary colleagues were concerned. As one of the few, at that time, who broadly shared her political and (in particular) economic thinking, I was greatly relieved. The Conservative Party badly needed a new approach, and she clearly meant to provide it. Owing largely to her background, perhaps, Margaret was thankfully free of that middle-class guilt that had made most leading politicians, of both parties, who had received expensive private educations, ashamed of quality, embarrassed by capital and tolerant of the excesses of organised labour.

ADVENT OF MARGARET THATCHER

Margaret instinctively realised the need to regain the moral as well as the practical initiative from collectivism. In this she was strongly fortified by the writings of the economist and philosopher Friedrich Hayek. Although Hayek's popularity was largely confined to non-mainstream bodies like the robustly free-market Institute of Economic Affairs, his warnings conformed very closely to recent British experience. He had given advance notice of the evils of socialism and central planning in *The Road to Serfdom*, a book first published in Britain in March 1944 and dedicated ironically to 'the socialists of all parties'. Hayek's development of the concept of a spontaneous natural order provided a strong philosophical underpinning for the market, not least by demonstrating that our understanding of the nature of society and the economy is too partial to admit economic management by the state.

Economic planning was both impossible and unnecessary. Individual agents acting on incomplete information could none the less operate a market economy by means of the price mechanism. This was a much more efficient means of transmitting consumer wants and needs than the vast bureaucracies of Whitehall and the nationalised industries, as I had argued for nearly twenty years. Above all, Hayek also opened up for the first time since the war the possibility of a morally superior political conception to that of socialism, by elevating private actions above public direction and dismissing 'social justice' as both vague and arbitrary. These were all ideas which, like Margaret Thatcher, I had nursed, without much articulation, since I had left Oxford; and they fitted naturally with my subsequent realisation that the fundamental defect of the British economy was not a shortage of demand but a failure of supply.

At a more down-to-earth level, Margaret was unusual, for a Tory leader, in actually warming to the Conservative Party – that is to say, the party in the country, rather than its Members of Parliament. Certainly, that had not occurred for many years. Harold Macmillan had a contempt for the party, Alec Home tolerated it, Ted Heath loathed it. Margaret genuinely liked it. She felt a communion with it, one which later expanded to embrace the silent majority of the British people as a whole. What was initially an unusual and rather endearing trait was eventually to become part of the hubris that led to her nemesis.

After a little while I had the good fortune to be asked by her to be part of a small team of back-benchers – known to the Press subsequently as the 'Gang of Four' – who joined her each Tuesday and Thursday to discuss the best line of attack and the best form of words for her to use during Prime Minister's questions. The other members of the team were Norman Tebbit, Geoffrey Pattie and George Gardiner. Norman, whose populist manner and street-fighter approach to parliamentary debate concealed from most observers at the time his shrewd political judgement, was particularly good at this. He, Margaret and I, while all quite different personalities, had a very similar approach to both politics and policies, and cemented an alliance that was to last well into our time as Cabinet colleagues.

OPPOSITION WHIP

As it happened, I did not remain on the back benches for too long, though the manner of my leaving them was somewhat astonishing. In November 1976 the Chief Whip, Humphrey Atkins, invited me to join the Opposition Whips' Office. A more unlikely Whip would have been hard to imagine even though my only two rebellions had been in Ted's time, when I had voted against government financial assistance to the Chrysler motor car company and against the Healey mini-Budget of July 1974 which *inter alia* reduced the rate of VAT from 10 per cent to 8 per cent – when in each case the official Opposition line had been to abstain. In the Conservative Party at any rate, any new nominee for the Whips' Office requires the endorsement of all the existing Whips: a single blackball excludes. I am not sure which was the more surprising: to have been suggested in the first place, or to have been universally accepted. In any event, having established that, as an Opposition Whip, I would still be free to speak in the House, I accepted.

During my year in the Whips' Office, I was able to learn a fair amount about parliamentary tactics and procedure, and perhaps even more important, about my parliamentary colleagues. But my main achievement as a Whip was of a somewhat freelance nature. From the moment I first entered Parliament in 1974, in Finance Bill after Finance Bill, I had been campaigning for the indexation of the tax system in general, and of the personal allowances in particular, so as to prevent the system from being insidiously subverted by inflation without parliamentary approval of any kind.

Following the 1977 Budget, I became the Opposition Whip on the standing committee on the Finance Bill. Astonishingly, the Government had carelessly included among the Labour back-benchers on the Committee two – Jeff Rooker (who understood what he was doing) and Audrey Wise (who may not have done) – who were sympathetic to the indexation of personal allowances, as a means of preventing those on low incomes from being dragged into the tax net simply by virtue of inflation. As soon as I discovered that, I arranged with Rooker to co-ordinate tactics.

I also went to see Geoffrey Howe, whom Margaret had made Shadow Chancellor, to let him know that there was a real chance of inflicting a serious defeat on the Government and getting the principle of the indexation of the tax system on to the statute-book. He was initially more attracted to the former than the latter, fearing it might tie his hands as Chancellor – though he could also see that, for a party pledged to reduce the burden of income tax, preventing inflation from increasing it by stealth made sense.

In practice, of course, there was (rightly) no way in which a future Chancellor's hands could be completely tied, since he had the unfettered right to propose each year whatever level of allowances he saw fit; but I suggested that this could be made clearer by amending the Rooker-Wise 'automatic' indexation amendments to provide an explicit procedure for the Government to seek parliamentary approval to override the indexation provisions in any given year. This satisfied him, and he suggested we should forthwith see Margaret, who he feared would be difficult to persuade, given her general prejudice against indexation of all kinds.

Happily, she eventually agreed to the course I proposed; and by some careful manoeuvring I was able to secure the Government's defeat in committee by a majority of one. Rather than risk the humiliation of a further defeat on the floor of the House, the Government conceded without a fight at the Report stage, the final stage of the Bill; and the indexation of the personal tax allowances thus reached the statute-book. One of our first acts in Government was to tidy up and extend this legislative innovation.

The following November, after an eventful year as a Whip, I was asked by Margaret to become an Opposition Treasury spokesman, under Geoffrey Howe. He remained a close friend and colleague for the rest of my relatively short time in Opposition and considerably longer time in Government.

A fine mind, intellectual conviction, courage, integrity, tenacity, resilience, great courtesy allied to almost ruthless ambition, more than made up for a somewhat colourless public personality (although he was far from colourless in private) and lacklustre parliamentary performances. Although in no sense an economist, his experience of trying to implement the absurdities of a statutory prices and incomes policy as Minister for Consumer Affairs in the Heath Cabinet, coupled with his liberal principles in the true sense of the word, meant that there was a ready meeting of minds. Very much a lawyer, he is a glutton both for work and for detail, and needs remarkably little sleep.

This is something he shares with Margaret; but in other respects they could scarcely be more different. For him politics is about being reasonable, and persuasion a matter of patient education. My manner, too, is very different from Geoffrey's, but I never felt his to be a sign of weakness, as she clearly did. Curiously, in the light of subsequent events, our only significant policy difference was over Europe, where the drift towards a United States of Europe was something that I viewed with deep foreboding, but which Geoffrey manifestly did not.

PREPARATION FOR OFFICE

As a Shadow Treasury spokesman, I inevitably became more deeply involved in the preparations we made for office, which Margaret had initiated as soon as she had become Leader in 1975. For me, this meant chiefly the unprecedentedly detailed and thorough work we did to identify the scope for public expenditure savings. This was something that had been unwisely neglected during our previous period of Opposition in the sixties, as a result of which, when the Heath Government took office in 1970, nothing at all was done in that vital first hundred days, and when it did get round to it, it did too little.

By contrast, between 1975 and 1979, not only did a Shadow Treasury team, ably assisted by the Conservative Research Department, and in particular by Adam Ridley, who had been a member of the Central Policy Review Staff (CPRS: the so-called think-tank) during the Heath Government, scrutinise every Government spending programme, but a Shadow public expenditure round was then conducted with the various Shadow spending Ministers. I myself chose to concentrate on housing where, unlike many other areas of public expenditure, there is a flourishing private sector alternative to public provision, to which more and more people aspire; and with the invaluable assistance of Mark Boleat, now Director General of the Building Societies Association, I was able to produce a paper identifying very substantial savings indeed.

On the tax side, in which I was also involved, rather less preparation was done, since the principal difficulty was not so much identifying the course we wished to steer but securing the public expenditure savings which would enable us to embark on it. Nevertheless, the little we did do was done with meticulous thoroughness, thanks largely to Arthur Cockfield, the former Inland Revenue official (he claimed to have been the inventor of PAYE – Pay As You Earn) who had been tax adviser to the then Chancellor, Tony Barber, during most of the Heath Government and was recalled by Margaret for the purpose. We looked into the theoretically attractive idea of a wholesale switch from an income tax to an expenditure tax system, and had a long session with Professor James Meade, its foremost exponent, but (in my view rightly) shrank from the upheaval and practical problems that would have been involved.

Looking back, however, while we were right to concentrate on the public expenditure side, where the political battle is toughest, we should perhaps have done more work than we did on tax reform. But that said, the programme of tax reform we did in the event carry out was no small achievement.

A bigger error, in hindsight, was to do so little work in Opposition on the conduct of monetary policy – not least because this was where the official Treasury was weakest and the Bank of England was little better. That monetary policy was the weapon with which we would slay the dragon of inflation was not in doubt. Lingering dissensions within the Conservative Party discouraged too obvious and explicit attention to monetary strategy and tactics, as well as an anxiety to avoid giving hostages to fortune. We also assumed too readily that the task was essentially one of applying with conviction the approach that a reluctant Labour Government had had forced upon it by the International Monetary Fund (IMF). When it all turned out to be much more complicated than that, far too much time had to be spent in Government in hacking a path through the jungle. Maybe even if we had done the work, we would not have emerged with the right answer. But it would have been less difficult, and certainly far less damaging, to have addressed the key issues far more thoroughly than we did, and reached a measure of agreement on them, in the relative tranquillity of Opposition.

Alongside the official preparations for Government, there was the parallel and highly secret 'Stepping Stones' exercise, conducted under the aegis of Keith Joseph at the Centre for Policy Studies. The convenor of this work, in which I was also among those involved, was John Hoskyns, a former army officer turned computer expert, who was fired by a determination to save Britain from seemingly inexorable decline. He had offered his services to Keith after losing faith in Harold Wilson, and was to become the first head of Margaret Thatcher's Number 10 Policy Unit before resigning in despair. His insistence on a coherent long-term strategy, his freshness of approach and his readiness to think the unthinkable were invigorating, though perhaps at times removed from political reality. I cannot recall the 'Stepping Stones' papers having much practical influence in Government except in so far as they helped to maintain the momentum for a radical reform of trade union law.

I made the most of my period in Opposition, the first five years of my time in the House of Commons, learned a great deal and contributed what I could.

But it was a dismal and depressing experience to live through the failures of the seventies. In one sense so close to the centre of events, yet wholly unable to influence them. The cliff-hanging one-vote defeat of the Labour Government on a confidence motion on Wednesday, 28 March 1979 came as a blessed deliverance.

Only one thing remained to be done before Parliament was dissolved for the election which we were widely expected to win. Denis Healey had prepared a Budget for the following Tuesday, 3 April. This could no longer be delivered. Instead a very brief Finance Bill had to be introduced to enable those taxes that have to be enacted by Parliament afresh each year, notably income tax, to continue in being until the first Budget of the new Parliament, after the general election.

Geoffrey and I met Denis Healey and his Chief Secretary, Joel Barnett, in the Chancellor's room in the House of Commons, to agree the contents of his holding Bill. There was only one minor point of contention. Should the personal allowances remain unchanged in money terms, as would hitherto have been correct, or should they – following the enactment of 'Rooker-Wise' – be indexed? Hoist by my own petard, Geoffrey and I were obliged to compromise: the Bill would index the allowances, but the extra money would not reach the voters' pockets until after the election on 3 May. In fact, it is unlikely in the extreme that the Inland Revenue could have beaten the 3 May deadline even if we had not made this stipulation. In any event, it was Labour's last throw: the general election of May 1979 produced an overall Conservative majority of forty-four and the start of my ten years as a Minister in the Thatcher Government.

Almost fifteen years after I had first resolved to 'get out on the field and play' I was at last about to do so. But outside the small world of parliamentary politics there was no great sense that the whole nature of the game was about to change. Jim Callaghan's warning during the election that a Thatcher Government was 'too big a gamble for the country to take' was dismissed by most commentators as routine electioneering, but he understood very well that the moral and intellectual tide was against him. On the eve of the election he confessed to his political adviser, Bernard Donoughue, that the Attleeite settlement that had dominated politics since the war had probably run its course:

> You know there are times, perhaps once every thirty years, when there is a change in politics. It then does not matter what you say or what you

do. There is a shift in what the public wants and what it approves of. I suspect there is now such a sea change – and it is for Mrs Thatcher.

CHAPTER THREE

PRESENT AT THE CREATION

A New Course · Financial Secretary · The official Treasury
The 1979 Inheritance · The Underlying Malaise

A NEW COURSE

It is difficult to convey the excitement of those first few weeks in office – the most exciting of my political life. It is a thrill for any politician to become a Minister for the first time – certainly a Treasury Minister. It is a particular thrill to do so at the start of a new Government, with a comfortable majority in the House of Commons.

Of course, the Private Office's deft organisation of the mundane details of one's personal routine, the car and the driver, the politeness and deference, are all very agreeable. And at the Treasury, in particular, the standard of the (usually prompt) submissions in response to any ministerial query is impressively high. But the real sense of excitement came from being part of a team that had come to office determined to set an entirely new course for the economy and indeed for the country. This was no slogan: we meant it, and we had been preparing for it with exceptional thoroughness.

Even the traditionally cynical Civil Service was quick to recognise that something genuinely new was happening. I recall David Hancock, then a particularly able Treasury official, and subsequently Permanent Secretary to the Department of Education and Science, writing to me in August 1980, referring to us as 'what seems to me to be the most radical government we have had since the war – radical in the sense of making a break with what has gone immediately before'. And in a book published in 1982, Leo Pliatzky, a former Second Permanent Secretary to the Treasury and Permanent Secretary to the Department of Trade, wrote that,

> The Conservative Government elected in May 1979 was more than just another change of Government; in terms of political and economic philosophy it was a revolution.

I also recall his expressing, in an earlier radio interview, astonishment – not to say shock and horror – for a different reason: he complained that economic policy was being determined by Ministers (instead of, presumably, by Treasury officials). Although the voluble and innovative Pliatzky was not a typical Civil Servant, in both cases he accurately reflected the Whitehall view of the new Government.

FINANCIAL SECRETARY

But all that lay a little way ahead when the telephone rang at my home in my Leicestershire constituency on the morning of Saturday, 5 May 1979, two days after the election. It was Number 10 on the line: the Prime Minister wished to speak to me. I warmly congratulated her on her splendid victory and then she got down to the matter in hand. 'I want you to go to the Treasury,' she said. 'I have made Geoffrey Chancellor and John Biffen Chief Secretary. I would like you to be ... ' there followed a disconcerting pause, which I broke by suggesting 'Financial Secretary?' 'Yes, that's right,' she replied.

I was greatly relieved. I had been a front-bench Opposition spokesman for only the previous eighteen months. She could easily have given me something less. Financial Secretary to the Treasury, the number three job in the most powerful Government Department, both of whose top two jobs are of Cabinet rank, was the most I had hoped for.

Geoffrey Howe had, of course, been Margaret's Shadow Chancellor in Opposition and he and I had worked closely together in preparing for Government. John Biffen was a somewhat surprising choice as Chief Secretary: I had expected the job to go to John Nott, who had been a Minister of State at the Treasury in Ted Heath's Government, and had made no secret of wanting it. Instead, Nott became Secretary of State for Trade. Later, his frustrated ambition for the Chancellorship soured his relations with Geoffrey Howe and ultimately led him to quit politics altogether in favour of a very successful and lucrative stint as chairman of the merchant bankers, Lazards.

The job of Chief Secretary, invented by Harold Macmillan in the early sixties to relieve the Chancellor of what had become an unbearable load, is to ensure that public expenditure is kept under control. It requires unceasing vigilance to that end, and an ability and appetite to master detail.

That was not John Biffen's forte, and his was not to prove a successful appointment. But John was then quite close to Margaret, thanks largely to his record of opposition to Ted Heath, and at that time she may not have had the fullest understanding of the role of Chief Secretary.

Geoffrey's first and simplest task was the allocation of duties among his ministerial team. John Biffen's responsibility – public expenditure – went automatically with the job of Chief Secretary, so what this meant was the allocation of the rest between myself and the two Treasury Ministers of State, Peter Rees in the Commons and Arthur Cockfield in the Lords. Normally, the Financial Secretary's main responsibility is those taxes that are collected by the Inland Revenue – generally speaking, direct taxation – and the Department of Inland Revenue itself; but although taxation interested me greatly, it was clear that with two eminent tax experts as his two Ministers of State, they had a far better claim to deal with taxation than I did. Fortunately, Geoffrey had a collegiate approach to Budget-making, which I sought to emulate when I became Chancellor: so I was able to be involved in tax when it mattered most, while avoiding the chore of having to approve and sign the replies to the huge volume of MPs' letters on constituents' tax complaints that the Chancellor of the Exchequer receives.

More important, I was able to secure the portfolio of other duties I most wanted. These included in particular monetary policy – at the very heart of our new economic approach – with which went the banks, the building societies, the Department of National Savings and exchange control, whose abolition I had advocated in the last article I had written before the election; privatisation (then known, quaintly, as 'disposal of assets'), a brand new responsibility on which I was particularly keen, and which has remained in the Financial Secretary's bailiwick ever since; and the European Community Budget.

My responsibility for monetary policy was something I took particularly seriously, and I inaugurated a system of monthly meetings to assess the state of play with officials from the Treasury and Bank of England under my chairmanship. The position of the Bank in those days was somewhat paradoxical. While it regarded monetary policy as very much part of its own bailiwick, not to be usurped, it believed in it far less than the new Government did. The key figure of Kit McMahon, later Deputy Governor, who was by training a professional economist, was an unreconstructed neo-Keynesian; and even the Governor, Gordon Richardson, impressively leonine in appearance, believed that his main job was to warn the Government of the day to curb its Budget deficit and to encourage it to be firm on pay.

Another very different perspective arose from my appointment as Britain's 'Budget Minister' (for that was what, in Community parlance, my devolved responsibility for the European Community Budget – which had previously lain with Joel Barnett – was called). This involved regular trips to Brussels to attend meetings of the Budget Council (the Council of Budget Ministers) and haggle interminably over the minutiae of the Community Budget, visits which gave me an early insight into the reality of EC membership: the cumbersome and jargon-ridden nature of its proceedings, the self-conscious moral authority of the Commission, and above all the intensity and dominance of the Franco-German axis, which our Labour predecessors had ineffectually tried to counter by developing a high-spending alliance with the Italians.

Somewhat embarrassingly, Geoffrey also asked me to assist John Biffen with public expenditure control. This was ostensibly because I had been heavily involved in the work we had done on this in Opposition, but it also reflected Geoffrey's doubts about John. Understandably, spending Ministers were less than overjoyed, when they came to negotiate their spending programmes bilaterally with the Chief Secretary, to find me sitting alongside him, asking the awkward questions he had refrained from posing.

All in all, it gave me an exceptionally heavy burden for a non-Cabinet Minister; but apart from the public spending chore, it was what I wanted; and fortunately I am physically robust.

I was rather less fortunate with my room, having been automatically allocated that of my Labour predecessor, Bob Sheldon. But I discovered too late that the charming oak-panelled sanctuary traditionally occupied by the Financial Secretary had been allowed by Sheldon to pass to the Minister of State, and had accordingly been allocated to Peter Rees.

The room which I had inherited was in every way inferior, other than size. I decided to civilise it as best I could by acquiring some pictures from the Government Picture Collection, run by the admirable Wendy Baron. This was easier said than done: first pick went to our Embassies abroad, with Ministers having to make do with what was left; and the Financial Secretary quite properly had to wait until the Cabinet had made its choice. Eventually I managed to secure an imposing portrait of an undistinguished but long-serving eighteenth-century Chancellor of the Exchequer, Henry Pelham, resplendent in his gold and black Chancellorial robe, and an Ernest Proctor nude entitled 'The Judgement of Paris' to cheer things up a little.

THE OFFICIAL TREASURY

The official Treasury is a very fine institution indeed. I remember being at a cocktail party with Leo Pliatzky very early on, when he said he was sure I was enjoying the Treasury. 'They are the praetorian guard', he said. A good phrase, true, and how they see themselves. I had known the Treasury for a long time so its denizens' generally very high quality of intellect and pride in their job (despite the policy demoralisation in the closing period of the outgoing Labour Government) was no surprise to me. It was a real pleasure to work with them.

Nevertheless it was clear that our policies did not commend themselves to more than a very small number of Treasury officials. The official Treasury recognised that the old policies had failed – indeed, they were almost shell-shocked by the scale of that failure, whose nadir had been the sterling crisis of 1976, when the UK had had to be humiliatingly bailed out by the IMF. Pliatzky, the senior Treasury official in charge of public expenditure in 1976, later wrote of that episode that it was 'difficult to express what an anxious and worrying time that was'. However, they had little faith in any alternative. They welcomed our determination to curb public expenditure: economic fashions come and go, but the one constant belief at the heart of the Treasury, which governs its thinking on much else too, is its mission to stand firm against the desire of politicians of all parties and the whole of the rest of Whitehall to devise new ways of increasing Government spending. But monetarism was seen by most of them, not least by the Permanent Secretary, Douglas Wass, as at best an intellectually interesting variety of mumbo-jumbo to which lip-service probably had to be paid to appease the financial markets.

In principle they welcomed a government that knew its mind, after the drift and ultimately the death-wish of the outgoing administration: but like the commentators in the Press, they had little doubt that we would abandon the policies on which we had embarked, not least the rejection of incomes policy, before very long. The only argument was whether the U-turn would occur in six months' time or whether it would take as long as a year for the Thatcher Government to introduce an incomes policy.

The indispensable element of the revolution which so astonished Whitehall was Margaret Thatcher herself. She had set out from the very beginning as a Prime Minister who knew her own mind, and led from the front from the word go. But in those days she had no Number 10 bunker to envelop her, nor did she yet feel wholly self-sufficient. She considered the Treasury to be *her* Department. Of her four predecessors as Tory Leader and Prime Minister, Eden was a Foreign

Office man through and through, Macmillan deeply distrusted the Treasury, which he regarded as deflationary and responsible for the depression of the thirties, Douglas-Home was in the Eden mould, and Heath sought (improbably) to model himself on Macmillan.

But at a time when most of the Party and indeed most of her Cabinet were still 'wet', it was the Treasury that Margaret ensured was 100 per cent 'dry' and on whose support she relied. (The terms 'wet' and to a lesser extent 'dry' were important defining terms in those days. The term 'wet' was originally coined by Margaret Thatcher for those Tories who had no stomach for the fight ahead, but was later self-consciously endorsed by the paternalist wing of the party. The word 'dry' came more slowly and hesitantly into circulation to indicate the opposite of 'wet'.) Partly for that reason, partly thanks to the relationship forged in Opposition, she frequently asked me to see her about something that had cropped up, and very occasionally I would take the initiative and seek a meeting. All this was distinctly unusual for a Minister who was not even in the Cabinet. But the relationship, although close, had no social dimension to it. There may have been some rare exceptions, but in general that was not her style.

THE 1979 INHERITANCE

During any election, officials prepare briefs to cater for the possibility of the incumbent government being defeated, binding them in red if the Opposition is Labour and blue if it is Conservative. The blue plastic folder which greeted Treasury Ministers in May 1979 confirmed in much greater detail the rather gloomy assumptions we had made in Opposition. The main difference was that the prospect for inflation was far worse than we had expected. Nevertheless the new Conservative Government, unlike some preceding incoming administrations, made little play with the misfortunes of its inheritance. An over-emphasis on how bad things are only weakens external and internal confidence, to no good purpose. Even from a partisan point of view it is a pointless tactic. For once an election has been won, there is little gain to be had from gloating over the other party's misfortunes. But the main reason for the lack of speeches on the horrors of the 1979 inheritance was simply that we were so busy with our own agenda that we had little time for such exercises. The economic sickness we set out to cure went far deeper than the state of the conjuncture in May 1979.

Nevertheless a short retrospect on the economy as it was in the spring of 1979 should help to put the policies of the new Government in perspective. The most uncontroversial fact about 1979 is that it was a peak year of a business cycle, like

1973 before it and 1988 or 1989 after it. Another indisputable feature is that, for all Labour's rhetorical emphasis on manufacturing, manufacturing output had in fact fallen in absolute terms, since its 1973 peak. It did not regain and overtake that earlier level until 1987, during my own period as Chancellor. It is not unduly partisan to suggest that the 1979 boom was disappointingly weak from an output point of view, while severe in the degree of inflationary pressure it piled on a fragile economy with high inflationary expectations.

This pessimistic diagnosis was subsequently reinforced by the Treasury's analysis of the slow-down in the underlying trend of output.[2]

The Labour Government had been forced to curb monetary growth and public sector borrowing and spending as a result of the sterling crisis which culminated in the IMF loan of 1976. Partly as a result of that squeeze, and partly because of a temporary dampener imposed by pay ceilings, average annual headline inflation had fallen from 24.2 per cent in 1975 to 8.3 per cent in 1978. But the respite was short-lived, and by April 1979 the annual increase in the retail price index (RPI) was back in double figures and clearly accelerating. In the latest six months the annualised rate was already 12.3 per cent (excluding seasonal foodstuffs). The increase in the oil price, following the deposition of the Shah of Iran, was about to push up the headline inflation rate still further. As Alec Cairncross, a former Chief Economic Adviser to the Government, has subsequently written,

> There were those in America, Germany and elsewhere who hoped that a changed Britain would emerge, phoenix-like, from the [1976] crisis, free from past illusions and able to hold to a steady line of policy ... But there was little change of heart in the Labour Party. The Prime Minister might denounce public spending as a way of coping with depression, but he was prepared to back a PSBR [public sector borrowing requirement] of not less than £9 billion. The Chancellor had every intention of restoring the cuts when it seemed safe to do so and the PSBR was back above £9 billion by 1978/79, Labour's last year in power.

Denis Healey, the Labour Chancellor, had indeed taken the opportunity of sterling's recovery following the IMF agreement to boost public sector spending and borrowing once again. Between 1977/78 and 1978/79 the public sector

[2] The Treasury has estimated that the trend growth of non-North Sea output fell from 2.75 per cent per annum in 1964–73 to only 0.5 per cent per annum in 1973–79 before recovering to around its earlier rate in 1979–89.

borrowing requirement rose from £5.4 billion to £9.3 billion, that is to say from 3.5 to 5.25 per cent of GDP, despite the economic upturn, which should have led to public sector borrowing falling as a share of GDP. A further increase to £10 billion or £11 billion (over 6 per cent of GDP) was forecast by Treasury officials for the financial year 1979/80 – equivalent in 1992 terms to a PSBR of getting on for £40 billion at the peak of the economic cycle.[3]

As Andrew Britton records in his authoritative account of the period, 'The possibility of an early general election was given increasing weight in the conduct of economic policy ... The most difficult problem was the negotiation of an acceptable deal with the trade unions on pay and prices.' Pay policy had already been in deep trouble from the start of the so-called Phase Three in July 1977. The White Paper of 1978 called for a 5 per cent pay norm (in a year when inflation was running at 8 per cent) which was bound to be widely disregarded, and duly was, with a nine weeks' strike at Ford Motors in the autumn ending with a much-publicised 17 per cent pay rise. By the time we took office in the spring of 1979, earnings in manufacturing were rising at an annual rate of 13 per cent and in the whole economy by 15 per cent. The Labour Government still attempted to impose modified versions of its norm on the public sector. Strikes against these attempts led to the notorious 'winter of discontent', when the dead were left unburied, and the final crumbling of the Government.

The outgoing Labour Government did take one other decision, albeit a negative one, whose fateful importance was not widely recognised at the time: not to join the Exchange Rate Mechanism (ERM) of the European Monetary System (EMS). This duly came into being, with the participation of all the member states of the European Community except Britain, in March 1979, two months before Labour left office.

THE UNDERLYING MALAISE

What worried me more than the 1979 conjuncture was the long-term decline of the British economy, and the climate of defeatism this engendered. This had its origins well before the 1974–79 Labour Government, but the debility reached an acute stage during its period in office.

For the Western world as a whole, the post-war golden age had finally come to an end after the first oil price explosion of 1973/74, triggered off by the Yom Kippur War between Israel and Egypt. Even during the golden age there had

[3] [2010 note] That sum is equivalent to around £90 billion today.

been growing concern in Britain as our growth rate, although not greatly different from that of the United States, lagged well behind that of the rest of Europe and Japan. Over the six years from the cyclical peak of 1973 to that of 1979, which as it happens broadly corresponded with Labour's period of office, the British economy all but stopped growing altogether. Excluding North Sea Oil, to provide a true measure of underlying performance, the average annual rate of growth over that period was a half of one per cent.

However, if the deterioration in Britain's growth performance was bad enough, the deterioration on the inflation front was even worse. The average annual rate of inflation had risen, seemingly inexorably, from 3.5 per cent under the Conservative Governments of 1951 to 1964, to 4.5 per cent under the first Wilson administration, to 9 per cent under Heath and to 15.5 per cent under the Labour Government of 1974 to 1979. By the time Margaret Thatcher became Prime Minister, the British economy was trapped in the cycle of low growth and high inflation which economists called 'stagflation'; and mainstream Keynesianism was intellectually and politically bankrupt of solutions to it. Even the normally staid Bank of England, in its March 1978 *Bulletin*, gave way to a despair that was rapidly becoming endemic:

> The United Kingdom has long been a country where productivity grew relatively slowly; but ... the United Kingdom's performance has in the last five years become even poorer ... If the will were there, productivity could clearly be transformed. The consequences of failing to arrest this country's industrial decline are likely to become more pressing and obvious as time goes on. Now condemned to very slow growth, we might later even have to accept, if present trends continue, declines in real living standards.

Trade union power, which had been greatly enhanced by the war, was entrenched in the sixties and seventies both by legislation and by the involvement of trade union leaders in economic planning and incomes policies. Profits, not surprisingly, sank. The real rate of return on capital invested in British industry (excluding the North Sea) declined according to official estimates from an average of 10 per cent during the period 1964/73 to an average of 5.5 per cent during the period 1973/79. 'Profit' had become a dirty word, and 'capitalist' a term of abuse, as income tax rose under Labour to a top rate of 83 per cent on earned income and 98 per cent on investment income. Management, ground between the upper and nether millstones of government interference and trade union power, had all but ceased to manage. Instead, the energetic ones tramped the corridors of Whitehall in search of subsidies, and the less energetic took to the golf course.

But it went deeper than that. The 'winter of discontent' in 1978–79, had shown the ugly face of trade unionism and raised, once again, the question first asked during the miners' strike of 1974: had Britain become ungovernable? Indeed Labour Ministers had secured considerable high-level American support in the seventies by warning that the election of a Conservative Government would lead to uncontrollable civil unrest and the risk of a far-left Government rising to power on its back.

By 1979 Britain was pitied abroad and mired in an all-pervasive defeatism at home. This was the culmination of trends that had begun long before the Labour Government of 1974–79, but which by the end of that period had become pathological. That was what we set out to reverse.

CHAPTER FOUR

RESTORING INCENTIVES AND REMOVING EXCHANGE CONTROL

An Early Budget · The New Fiscal Strategy · Tax Reform: The First Steps
The Attack on Public Spending · Currency Freedom at Last
Abolition in Retrospect

AN EARLY BUDGET

Margaret Thatcher and her economic team decided in Opposition that if there were a May election in 1979, there would be a new Budget on 12 June, Arthur Cockfield having demonstrated that this was the earliest practicable date. Geoffrey Howe informed Treasury officials of the plan as soon as we took office.

We were determined not to repeat the mistake of the Heath Government, which had come into office in June 1970, but did nothing on the economic front until October of that year, when it announced an inadequate public expenditure package for the following financial year. There was no Budget until April 1971, by which time the Government was already being driven by events and felt the need to respond to the surge in unemployment. We decided in Opposition that we would introduce a Budget as soon as we possibly could and that it would contain both the main tax changes we had prepared and a major assault on public spending – *starting with the year in progress.*

We also resolved that our first Budget should make a decisive start to the process of reducing the deficit, and to do so entirely by cutting Government spending. A quick start was made possible by the detailed work we had done in Opposition. Plans for public spending cuts had been agreed with Shadow Ministers in the summer of 1978 when the election had looked likely that autumn; and these plans were updated by the Shadow Treasury team in time for the actual election of May 1979.

We had come to office at a time when the UK economic cycle had peaked and was about to turn down – as for that matter was the world economy – and it would have been much easier to have deferred our attack on the deficit (and indeed on inflation via higher interest rates). But we consciously decided to press ahead, because deferment can become a way of life. Had the necessary action been postponed, the momentum would have been lost and, so, too, much of the new Government's credibility (or rather, the credibility it was seeking to build).

Right from the start, too, we attached the first importance to specific tax measures. For we were engaged not only in the battle against inflation, but also, and in parallel, on supply-side[4] measures to improve economic performance. We were clear that a significant reduction in income tax was needed to restore incentives. But given the Budget constraint, this inevitably meant a large increase in Value Added Tax (VAT), and hence in the Retail Prices Index (RPI), at a time when UK inflation was already soaring and sharply rising oil prices were about to have a further adverse effect on the RPI. Again, it would have been much easier to have deferred the tax switch; but if we had not made it then it would never have happened at all, and we had decided that it must. We could console ourselves that we were paying a short-term price for a lasting gain: in the longer run, you no more cause inflation by raising indirect taxes than you cure it by providing subsidies.

In short, in the macroeconomic and microeconomic fields alike, we made a conscious decision to forge ahead without delay despite the unpropitious nature of the conjuncture. In retrospect I still believe that this decision was absolutely right and of the first importance.

THE NEW FISCAL STRATEGY

We came to office at a bad time in many ways. On top of the underlying rise in inflation, there was superimposed a new world oil price explosion, to which was added the purely domestic shock imposed by pay awards as high as 26 per cent for public sector workers, recommended by the Clegg Commission on Pay Comparability. This body had been established by the outgoing Government to quell the Winter of Discontent, with a promise to honour its conclusions whatever they might be. Unfortunately during the election campaign Margaret had felt obliged to match this unwise commitment.

[4] The term 'supply side' was invented by economists long before we came to office as a deliberate contrast to the emphasis on regulating demand which had dominated so much of post-war economic policy. The expression was used by left-wing economists who believed intervention and Government support would improve performance, as well as free-market ones who rested their hopes on improving the performance of markets. Margaret Thatcher hated the expression 'supply side', but neither she nor anyone else came up with anything better.

Despite this discouraging background we decided to press on with our radical fiscal plans. For if we had waited for a good moment to make them, the opportunity would have slipped from our grasp.

The overall framework was determined by our decision to make a significant start on cutting the PSBR (the Budget deficit). Our aim was to reduce from £9.25 billion, or 5.25 per cent of GDP, in Labour's last year, 1978/79, to £8.25 billion or 4.5 per cent of GDP in 1979/80. The 1979/80 outlook, however, was for a PSBR of some £10 billion to £11 billion, depending on the economic assumptions made. Unreconstructed Keynesians might have argued that, on the contrary, the situation called for a stimulus and an even higher PSBR. But right from the beginning we had set our face against this sort of fine-tuning. As for simply allowing the PSBR to rise as a result of the lower tax revenues and higher spending (on unemployment benefit and the like) caused by the recession, without any deliberate stimulus: this would have been perfectly acceptable had the PSBR not been far too high to start with.

We thus had a gap of up to £3 billion to bridge, even without taking account of our own tax measures. As our income tax reductions would cost around £4 billion, we had a sum of nearly £7 billion to find. Clearly we had to curb public spending. The expenditure position we inherited was unacceptable both in its absolute level and also in the growth which was planned. It is always difficult to cut public expenditure once the financial year is under way – Joel Barnett, Labour's Chief Secretary, had declared it to be impossible – and by the time we took office the year was already several weeks old. But it had to be done.

As a signal, within days of taking office, Margaret Thatcher appointed Derek Rayner of Marks & Spencer to head an Efficiency Unit within the Cabinet Office. Incoming Conservative Governments usually tend to be over-optimistic about the scope for 'eliminating waste' – a pledge which is always more popular than specific spending cuts. Such elimination was always likely to have only a marginal impact on the spending totals, although perhaps rather more impact on the psychological climate.

But our main hope of making an early dent in public expenditure was an emergency squeeze on cash limits, starting in the current (1979/80) financial year. Initially Anthony Rawlinson, Treasury Second Secretary in charge of public expenditure, recommended a cut in cash limits of 1.5 per cent. This proposal went up via John Biffen and Geoffrey to Margaret, who rightly dismissed it out of hand as inadequate. Eventually we ended up with overall reductions of 3 per cent in manpower budgets, expected to save over £1 billion. Geoffrey also managed to find over £1.5 billion of specific economies by trimming the plans of the nationalised industries, by cutting so-called 'industrial support' and a whole rag bag of other measures. In addition, a target of £1 billion was set for 'asset disposals'. The largest contribution was to come from a sale in the Government's shareholding in British Petroleum, a measure to which Labour could hardly object very strongly as it had already resorted to it in 1977.

In total our public expenditure cuts would save £4 billion in the fiscal year that had just started. This was a good deal less than required to finance our income tax changes and make a start in reducing public borrowing. So the centrepiece of the Budget had to be a massive switch from direct to indirect taxes. In the event our tax changes were broadly neutral. (They brought in £0.5 billion in a full year but actually cost £1 billion in 1979/80.) Our intention was to start the process of cutting the PSBR below what Denis Healey had planned, although in the event it overshot to very nearly £10 billion.

TAX REFORM: THE FIRST STEPS

We resolved on the switch to indirect tax at the first ministerial meeting I ever attended, called by Geoffrey Howe on the morning of 9 May to discuss Budget strategy. The new Government had inherited from Labour two rates of VAT: a higher rate of 12.5 per cent charged on so-called luxury items like petrol, boats and caravans and a lower rate of 8 per cent on everything else. We consolidated them into a single rate of 15 per cent, where it was to remain for over a decade.

In 1979 the near doubling of VAT to 15 per cent was a contentious decision. It added 3.5 to 4 per cent to the RPI at a time when inflation was resurgent, oil prices were rising and the workforce, which had become accustomed to link its annual pay increases to headline inflation, was chafing under the frustration of four years of incomes restraint. Not only the Labour Party, but even a number of economically sympathetic commentators, such as the London Business School and Samuel Brittan in the *Financial Times*, argued that the increased rate would fuel inflationary expectations, give a fillip to the gathering wage explosion and increase the unemployment cost of reducing inflation.

Margaret Thatcher herself was at first fearful of the 15 per cent VAT rate, even though the manifesto had clearly promised a switch from income tax to VAT, partly because it was a bigger switch than she had in mind and partly because of the initial RPI effect. (Throughout her time she was acutely sensitive to any administrative decisions that affected the RPI, although this was not enough to deter her from the Poll Tax.) But Geoffrey persuaded her that if we did not grasp this nettle in the first Budget it would never be grasped at all.

There was some discussion of the shape of our income tax cuts. Geoffrey Howe, Arthur Cockfield and I had agreed in Opposition that the first Budget should raise VAT to 15 per cent to finance the cut in the top rate of income tax from 83 per cent to 60 per cent, plus either a dramatic cut in the 33 per cent basic rate or a smaller, but still sizeable cut to 30 per cent (at which it had stood under the Heath Government) plus a worthwhile real increase in the personal allowances. Geoffrey eventually opted for the latter course. In addition, the threshold for the Investment Income Surcharge, the 10-15 per cent additional income tax payable on income from savings, which penalised many older people in particular, was raised almost threefold. The cut in the top rate of income tax was massive, but did no more than bring the UK rate into line with the European average.

Contrary to popular mythology, Geoffrey Howe did not pledge the Government to a 25 per cent basic rate of income tax, but set it out more as an aspiration: 'Our long-term aim should surely be to reduce the basic rate of income tax to no more than 25 per cent.' It was to take nine years before I, as his successor, was able to realise this aspiration.

The pressure of time meant that all the more detailed tax changes we had in mind had to be left until the 1980 Budget. But we had nevertheless succeeded in producing a substantial Budget in forty days and forty nights. It was rapturously received by our supporters on the back benches. The Opposition was still too demoralised by its election defeat to mount any serious attack on it, even though the change in the method of uprating pensions (described below) and the higher rate tax cuts were both anathema to Labour.

THE ATTACK ON PUBLIC SPENDING

The most controversial decision announced in the 1979 Budget was the repeal of the Labour Government's legislatively enshrined formula for uprating pensions. Under this formula they were increased each year in line with prices or earnings, whichever rose faster. We decided to switch to straightforward indexation in line with prices.

As earnings normally rise faster than prices, Labour's commitment was an expensive one, which it then did its best to evade. In 1976, when, following a steep rise, inflation was expected to fall, Labour changed from an historic to a forecast basis for annual upratings, saving a huge sum of money by somewhat shabby means. It then saved further sums by consistently under-forecasting inflation and earnings increases.

The very large 19.5 per cent increase in pensions announced by Geoffrey in his 1979 Budget, together with 17.5 per cent increases in other benefits, was designed to compensate for Labour's most recent under-forecast and to soften the blow of the change in the form of indexation. But even in the new form the forecast basis was manifestly still unsatisfactory, and we eventually and rightly switched back to the historic basis. The politically brave decision to change the pensions formula was a critical part of regaining control of public expenditure and evidence, too, of a government that took the long view rather than seeking merely short-term expedients.[5]

As soon as the Budget was out of the way, we started work on further reductions in public expenditure, with John Biffen conducting our first annual public expenditure round. His habit of concluding bilateral discussions with spending Ministers by proposing that they split the difference soon became rather too well known for the Treasury's comfort. The outcome, the Public Expenditure White Paper of November 1979, containing the new plans for the year ahead, 1980/81, was probably more important for its sentiments than its contents. Its opening sentence – 'Public expenditure is at the heart of Britain's present economic difficulties' – caused some consternation among officials accustomed to less robust prose in government publications. It aimed to stabilise public spending by a mixture of higher prescription charges, savings in transport, housing and education expenditure, and by additional 'asset disposals'. It was disappointing to find that, with social security spending rising as unemployment rose sharply, cuts of £3.5 billion merely left overall public spending unchanged. The White Paper's stated goal of reducing public expenditure as a proportion of GDP proved impossible to achieve in recession. But at least it did establish a certain austere flavour. In the summer of 1979 I minuted Geoffrey Howe:

> To plan public expenditure before the required growth is available to support it would ensure that, in the event, growth of output does not

[5] [2010 note] This highly controversial and hugely important public expenditure saving endured not merely throughout the Thatcher and Major Conservative Governments, but also throughout the subsequent 13 years of the Blair/Brown Labour Governments. Unwisely, however, despite having inherited a fiscal deficit even worse than that of 1979, the Conservative–Liberal Democrat coalition that took office following the inconclusive general election of 2010 committed itself to restoring from April 2011 the pre-1979 formula of uprating pensions annually in line with prices or earnings, whichever rose faster, with the added guarantee that the increase would never be less than 2.5 per cent, irrespective of what happened to prices and earnings.

> take place. Public expenditure cannot any longer be allowed to precede, and thus prevent, growth in the private sector.

Or as Geoffrey had put it more succinctly in his Budget speech, 'Finance must determine expenditure, not expenditure finance.' As soon as the ink was dry on the interim White Paper of November 1979, we conducted a thorough review of Government spending over a three-year period. The results were set out in our second and fuller public expenditure White Paper, experimentally published on Budget Day, 26 March 1980. This expressed the Government's hope 'not merely to halt the growth of public expenditure but progressively to reduce it' by 4 per cent in volume terms over the four years to 1983/84. The main reductions shown in the inherited programmes were in subventions to nationalised and private industries, in housing and in education. There were also further tentative gestures towards privatisation. While this overall hope was, of course, never realised, had we not started with the determination to make actual cuts, we might never have succeeded in the more modest but virtually unprecedented aim of reducing public spending as a proportion of the national income.

CURRENCY FREEDOM AT LAST

The 1979 Budget had contained an important relaxation of exchange control. I had long been convinced that exchange control should be abolished altogether and had already urged (with the due caution proper to my new responsibilities) 'a substantial relaxation of exchange control' in my 'maiden speech' as an Opposition Treasury spokesman on 10 November 1977.

The context at that time was the prospect of a substantial improvement in the oil sector of Britain's overseas trade balance, which inevitably had implications for the rest of the balance of payments. What is often overlooked is that the one certainty about the overall balance of payments is that, like the balance sheet of a company, it has to balance: it is what is known as an accounting identity. If one sector of the current account, in this case oil, shows a sharp improvement, there will either have to be an offsetting deterioration in the rest of the current account, which is largely composed of trade in manufactured goods – the mechanism by which this occurs would normally be a rise in the exchange rate – or else an offsetting deterioration in the capital account, which could be brought about by an outflow of capital. It was clear that a relaxation of exchange control might help create such an outflow; while in the longer term the capital invested overseas would yield a useful stream of foreign exchange in the years ahead as North Sea oil gradually ran out.

I had another opportunity to return to the charge in a Press article, which appeared on 20 April 1979 in the middle of the election campaign and which argued the case for exchange control abolition. There was no mention whatever of the subject in the manifesto and I was anxious to put down a clear marker before we took office. I cleared the principle with an apprehensive but fundamentally sympathetic Geoffrey Howe – then Shadow Chancellor. Howe himself agreed about the desirability of abolition but did not yet share my view about doing it as soon as possible. Nor had Margaret been squared.

At that time Britain operated the most restrictive exchange control regime of any major industrialised country. It had been imposed as a temporary measure at the outbreak of the Second World War in 1939, and maintained ever since. People had lived with exchange control for so long that it was not in any real sense an issue: it was a fact of life; and there was considerable nervousness that any raising of the topic by the Conservative Opposition might lead to a run on the pound for which the Tories might be blamed.

Nevertheless, when we came to office it was very clear that officials, irrespective of their own views, expected us to abolish exchange control. This was partly because they attached more authority to my article than it deserved, but even more because most of the top people at the Bank of England – especially those responsible for administering exchange control – actively wanted to see it go, with the support of some, although not a majority, of the official Treasury. Against this background and in the knowledge of my views, Geoffrey Howe asked me to look at the pros and cons of exchange control abolition, and the timescale, assisted by a team of Treasury and Bank officials. I had no doubt that, with sterling buoyed up by a combination of its petro-currency status and growing international confidence in the sound monetary policies of the new Government, early and complete abolition was not only achievable but economically necessary.

Abolition was none the less a radical and highly controversial step. It was impossible to predict the scale of the capital outflow which might result; but the pent-up demand for overseas portfolio investment in particular suggested it would be large. Labour, after all, had insisted on retaining exchange controls in the expectation that without them capital would flee the ramshackle British economy. Abolition was bound to be a leap in the dark. Fortunately, perhaps, neither I nor the Treasury or Bank officials concerned focused our attention at the time on the important practical consequences abolition was to have for the conduct of monetary policy.

Geoffrey Howe, for understandable reasons, favoured a cautious, step-by-step approach. In particular, he – and I – saw the first step, taken in the Budget in June, as dipping a toe into the water to test the temperature and see how the financial markets reacted. Hence the limited nature of the relaxation package announced in the Budget, which left controls on overseas portfolio investment more or less untouched. The reaction caused no problems and the following month Geoffrey accepted a recommendation of mine to make a modest start on the portfolio side.

Finally, on 4 October 1979 I minuted Geoffrey Howe, arguing that we should now move to complete abolition. After careful analysis, I and my Bank/Treasury team were satisfied that there was no coherent halfway house. Conditions in the currency markets could scarcely have been more propitious. 'I do not believe that the abolition of controls will make a fundamental difference to the exchange rate,' I wrote in my minute. The strength of the pound owed far more to the oil factor and to the soundness of our policies than to exchange controls.

After taking him through our report in painstaking detail, I persuaded him – somewhat nervously – to agree. Once he was convinced, he in turn persuaded an even more hesitant Margaret Thatcher.

Much later on in a lecture in 1991, he himself subsequently described the process in these terms:

> First, the ending of Exchange Control. I count this as one of the most important achievements of my Chancellorship – and certainly the most fraught with worry ... It still stands as the only economic decision of my life that caused me to lose a night's sleep. But it was right.

When the decision was put to Cabinet (at the eleventh hour, to ensure secrecy), Ministers were taken completely by surprise; but the only open opponent was Michael Heseltine, then the Environment Secretary, who argued that people would abuse their unaccustomed freedom, and buy villas in the south of France rather than invest in productive assets at home. Geoffrey made his historic announcement to the House of Commons on 23 October. Even the day before, the dollar premium (at which the limited pool of foreign exchange for portfolio investment changed hands) was still around 20 per cent: a remarkable tribute to our success in avoiding any hint of a leak. The Bank of England had a special tie designed, in which the Bank's traditional Britannia emblem was flanked with the laconic inscription 'EC 1939/1979'. Geoffrey and I were each presented with one, and as Chancellor I always made a point of wearing mine on Budget Day.

The Labour Party was predictably hostile to the decision, Denis Healey calling it 'reckless, precipitate and doctrinaire'. The Liberals, on the other hand, endorsed the decision warmly. Enoch Powell, then sitting as an Ulster Unionist, simply said 'Is the Chancellor aware that I envy him the opportunity and privilege of announcing a step that will strengthen the economy of this country and help to restore our national pride and confidence in our currency?' So did I.

A more considered if markedly less orthodox Labour reaction was given in the House of Lords on 17 November, by Harold Lever, the millionaire financial expert who had been a member of the Wilson and Callaghan Cabinets. Lever welcomed 'the end of this exchange control, which has served no useful purpose, and the abolition of which could be a considerable encouragement to a great trading, insurance and banking nation like our own' and which was 'not even a useful machinery for protection against a run on sterling'.

ABOLITION IN RETROSPECT

By October 1979, the pound was rising strongly under the influence of oil, 'the Thatcher factor', and our relatively tight monetary policies. And in the short run, my hunch that the relaxation of exchange controls would not lead to any softening of the exchange rate was quickly proved correct. The Bank of England estimated that the relaxation of exchange controls led to an outflow of £1 billion in the third quarter of 1979, and around the same in the fourth quarter, much of it representing no more than the early repayment of outstanding liabilities. The pound scarcely paused at all. Indeed, between 1979 and 1981 the strength of sterling subjected the British economy to a tight financial squeeze of astonishing power and effectiveness. At the same time, the consequent capital outflow led to a significant rise in the UK's net stock of overseas assets – although the official statistics in this area are, regrettably, almost worthless.

From a wider perspective it is hardly possible to overstate the critical importance of our decision. Politically it was the first significant increase of market liberalisation undertaken by the Thatcher Government. It marked the start of a process of deregulation which has embraced the world in general and the European Community in particular. Industrially, by enabling UK firms to invest where they liked, it ensured that investment in the UK would yield a worthwhile return – the economy had to compete. Without it the City would have been hard put to remain a world-class financial centre.

Abolition also greatly affected the practical conduct of monetary policy, making direct controls on UK lending institutions – even if desired – largely ineffectual. In addition, as part of a worldwide move (in which it played an influential role) towards freedom of capital movements, it changed the entire international financial and economic environment in ways that I discuss in a later chapter. Finally, it was an important blow for freedom – not least so far as the notorious foreign travel allowance was concerned.

The abolition of exchange control in 1979 was also another nail in the coffin of those who believe that major changes should be made only on a bipartisan basis; that is to say, only when there is a consensus. On that basis we would still have had exchange control today. As it was, by defying the consensus, we not only brought about an important and successful change, but moved the consensus, in due course, too. Coupled with the highly controversial tax and public spending changes announced in the Budget earlier in 1979, it constituted the most radical first year of any new Government within living memory; and no praise is too high for Geoffrey Howe's courage and determination in seeing it through.

CHAPTER FIVE

BLOOD, TOIL, TEARS AND SWEAT

The Coming of Monetarism · The Honeymoon Ends · Pay Freeze Rejected
Search for a Treasury Guru · The Sharp End · Obstinacy and Bare Knuckles ·
Sterling Climbs in Earnest · A Retrospect on Sterling · Thatcherism in Zurich

THE COMING OF MONETARISM

The 1979 Budget was important not only as a tax-reforming Budget. It was also the first major statement of the new Government's economic policy. This became known by the single word 'monetarism', although in fact that was only part of the story. The core of monetarism, as its name suggests, is the proposition that inflation is a monetary phenomenon. Rapid and continuous inflation is not due to excessive pay settlements, world commodity price movements or disappointing productivity trends. All these things may precipitate an initial upward movement of prices and pay; and they may increase the unemployment cost of curbing inflation. But prices and wages cannot carry on chasing each other ever upwards unless a sufficiently easy money policy accommodates the process.

The process linking money and inflation has never been better described than by the great eighteenth-century Scottish philosopher and political economist David Hume, who wrote as long ago as 1752:

> Though the high price of commodities be a necessary consequence of the increase of gold and silver, yet it follows not immediately upon that increase; but some time is required before the money circulates through the whole state, and makes its effects be felt on all ranks of people. At first, no alteration is perceived; by degrees the price rises, first of one commodity, then of another, then of another; till the whole at last reaches a just proportion with a new quantity of specie which is in the kingdom. In my opinion, it is only in this interval or intermediate situation, between the acquisition of money and rise of prices, that the increasing quantity of gold and silver is favourable to industry.

The setting of an annual target for the growth of the money supply had already been inaugurated by Denis Healey, Chancellor in the previous Labour Government, essentially to propitiate the IMF and the financial markets. The definition of money the Treasury had then chosen was £M3, pronounced Sterling M-three (roughly speaking, cash plus bank deposits of all kinds). But simply to continue with 'unbelieving monetarism' à la Healey was clearly out of the question. Some degree of shock treatment was essential if inflationary expectations were to be wrenched down.

This was implicit – although I was never quite sure how far Geoffrey recognised this – in our decision to announce in the 1979 Budget a slight reduction in the £M3 target we had inherited, despite the fact that inflation was rising and that we had raised nominal GDP still further through the increase in VAT. This made the £M3 target very tough indeed, implying an actual fall in the real money supply (i.e. after allowing for inflation). Indeed, had we raised interest rates sufficiently to stand a chance of hitting that target – which would have meant raising them by much more than we did: perhaps by as much as Paul Volcker, the chairman of the Federal Reserve Board, subsequently raised rates in the US – the shock would have been even greater than that which British industry did in fact suffer.

None the less, we took the new £M3 target seriously. It was in order to try to meet it that Geoffrey had announced in his 1979 Budget speech an increase in interest rates from the 12 per cent we had inherited in May 1979 to 14 per cent – the highest they had been since the sterling crisis of 1976, when the Labour Government had been obliged to seek assistance from the IMF. But this time we were doing it when sterling was strong and rising.

Douglas Wass, the Treasury Permanent Secretary, was keen to demonstrate that he could give effective backing to a policy that he did not at heart support. For he was above all anxious to prevent the politicisation of the higher Civil Service. Indeed, like other 'unbelieving monetarists', he was sometimes more unyielding in his advice than our genuine intellectual supporters, no doubt for the best of motives. In July 1979, he gave a valid warning in a memorandum to Geoffrey Howe, of the dangers of a backlash against policies which were 'relatively strange to a British audience' and whose long-term nature was not understood. Geoffrey responded with a public relations exercise which had some limited success.

THE HONEYMOON ENDS

But the battle had only just begun. I minuted Geoffrey at the end of August 1979:

> Now that the (hundred day?) honeymoon is over, and at least until the fruits of our policies show up (which will not be for some time yet), they will attack us whatever we do; for 'primitive monetarism' if we continue on our present course and for weakness, U-turns and general Heath/Barber recidivism if we do not. There is no way in which we can avoid being attacked, whatever we do: we must be guided by the reflection that it is better to be attacked for the right policies than the wrong ones and concentrate on getting our own message across, *for which purpose incidentally, 'primitive' language is essential: nothing else will be understood.* [Italics added.]

After approving the emphasis on the need to adjust expectations to reality and the disaster that would follow any change of course, I argued the need for,

> a third note that really must be struck along with the other two, a note of confidence and above all of hope; the message that there is indeed light at the end of the tunnel. This is absolutely vital, not least if we are to maintain a reasonable degree of business confidence over the difficult eighteen months that lie ahead. But of course it goes wider than that. Churchill may have told the British people that he had nothing to offer them but blood, toil, tears and sweat; but that was not strictly true. There was something else he offered them: the promise of victory – and that was why they followed him.

Striking this note was not made any easier, however, by the fact that by early November 1979 £M3 was growing at an annualised rate of 14 per cent, well above the top of our target range. Confidence in the financial markets was fragile, making it a constant struggle to sell sufficient gilt-edged stock to finance the Budget deficit outside the banking system; and the deficit itself was running above forecast.

Accordingly, Geoffrey announced on 15 November a package of measures designed to rein back both the Budget deficit and monetary growth. The collection of Petroleum Revenue Tax was advanced two months, which the oil industry could well afford with North Sea production and prices both at record heights. To enable the Bank of England to sell sufficient gilts to finance the burgeoning PSBR, the Bank of England's Minimum Lending Rate was raised by three percentage points to 17 per cent, the biggest single interest rate increase ever announced, which took nominal short-term rates to an all-time record level.

Excuses could have been found for avoiding such an unpopular package. In particular, as indeed was soon to occur, we could have pointed to the rise in the exchange rate as evidence of an effective policy tightening.[6] But it was time for primitive signals. Whatever our hopes for the future, underlying inflation – and not just the RPI – was still rising. The labour market was still very tight – unemployment, which normally lags the economic cycle, continued to fall until the last quarter of 1979 – and over the winter of 1979/80 there were long and bitter strikes in the steel and engineering industries. We thus had to demonstrate in the clearest possible way our commitment to the monetary approach to inflation and a degree of obstinacy in its pursuit. However, a gesture to the anxieties aroused by high interest rates – not least on Margaret's part – was the announcement by Geoffrey on the same day of his intention to publish a Green Paper on methods of monetary control.

PAY FREEZE REJECTED

The honeymoon was indeed over. By the late summer of 1979 the economy had passed its peak, even though the recession proper did not begin until 1980. Inflation measured by the RPI seemed to be moving inexorably upwards, boosted by the impact of rising oil prices, the pay explosion and our switch from income tax to VAT. Meanwhile businessmen were beginning to complain of the triple squeeze from high interest rates, rising pay costs and a rising exchange rate. Above all, there was a widespread lack of understanding, even among the business community, of the extent of our break with the old consensus, while Press commentators were free with predictions of an imminent 'U-turn'.

There were recurrent rumours about the reimposition of pay policy. Margaret Thatcher was somewhat ambivalent and, unlike me, had supported the idea of an incomes policy in the past. In his autobiography, Garret Fitzgerald, a reliable witness, recalls a conversation he had with her at a Bilderberg meeting in Turkey in 1975, when she was Leader of the Opposition and he was Ireland's Foreign Minister. She had learned a good deal from the discussions, she told him, 'for example the inadequacy of the money supply approach, because so much had to be done by way of supportive action to make the money supply work. If

[6] Moreover, contrary to what our critics allege, we were well aware of the deficiencies of £M3 or any other specific indicator of monetary conditions, and we pointed out at the time the elements of distress borrowing in the growth of credit and money.

inflation were very high an incomes policy was necessary, but there should be a statutory policy only for a very short time'.

Thankfully, on this occasion she rejected the idea, but others did not. Jim Prior, the Employment Secretary, was arguing in Cabinet for a public sector pay norm, an idea which in May 1980 gained the support of John Hoskyns, the head of the Number 10 Policy Unit. I derided the proposal in a minute to Geoffrey as a 'well trodden route to disaster', divorcing pay from market conditions and politicising the wage-bargaining process. The only practical effect of this climate was to make the unions determined to secure the largest possible pay settlements before any clampdown occurred.

SEARCH FOR A TREASURY GURU

By a stroke of good fortune the post of Chief Economic Adviser to the Treasury (who was also Head of the Government Economic Service, and thus theoretically responsible for all the economists throughout Whitehall) fell vacant at the end of 1979. Fred Atkinson, who was due to retire, was an amiable and shrewd, if laid-back, economist, who was curious about our new approach, but knew that he was not the person to take the Treasury into a new era.

My own view was that the job could be done effectively only by somebody who sympathised with the new beginning initiated after the election, but who understood more mainstream ways of thinking and could command the respect of Treasury economists. Well before the 1979 election I had come to the conclusion that the best bet was probably Terry Burns, the young Director of the Centre for Economic Forecasting at the London Business School, and had invited him to lunch at the Garrick Club to sound him out. He was clearly both sympathetic to our thinking and interested in the job. He was also already a member of the Treasury's Academic Panel. After much discussion and consultation, Geoffrey Howe accepted my strong recommendation that he should be appointed. Terry was only thirty-six when he arrived at the Treasury in early 1980 and his appointment was greeted with the rave notices that the British reserve for the very young and the very old. The appointment proved a great success, tarnished only by his failures in the forecasting area in the late 1980s and early 1990s – the very area, ironically, where he had originally made his academic reputation. He subsequently rose (well after my resignation as Chancellor) to be Permanent Secretary to the Treasury.[7]

[7] [2010 note] Following Labour's victory at the 1997 general election he rapidly fell out with the new Chancellor, Gordon Brown, and agreed to retire the following year to the safe haven of the House of Lords.

Burns was soon forgotten by the media in the flurry of excitement created by Margaret Thatcher's decision to appoint Alan Walters as her personal economic adviser at the beginning of 1981. Outsiders never really understood the difference between the Burns and Walters posts. Burns was a very senior Treasury official, whereas Walters was a freely floating personal Number 10 adviser. Walters' declared view was that it was best for an adviser in either position not to stay too long – he suggested not more than four years. Regrettably, he did not see fit to follow his own advice when he returned to Number 10 in 1989.

THE SHARP END

To business and industry what mattered at this time was the fact that the economy was in recession and that they were being crucified by a sharply rising exchange rate. Moreover the general gloom was deepened by an unprecedentedly sharp rise in unemployment. For if the severity of the squeeze in output was fully foreseen by the Government, the size of the accompanying rise in unemployment came as a shock. Whereas employers had reacted to previous recessions by holding on to labour as long as possible, the squeeze of the early 1980s led to a blitz on overmanning. The long-standing relationship between output and jobs, used in Treasury forecasting, was shattered (as most forecasts and relationships tend to be when they are really needed by policy-makers).

The total loss of output between the cyclical peak in the second quarter of 1979 and the recession low point in the first quarter of 1981 was 5.5 per cent. Employment, however, fell from its peak of 23.1 million in the fourth quarter of 1979 to a low point of 21 million in the first quarter of 1983, a drop of nearly 10 per cent. The rise in recorded unemployment was even greater. It more than doubled in 1980 and 1981, to reach 2.3 million at the end of 1981, and then continued to climb, at a slower pace, for the best part of the next five years. The manpower squeeze was especially severe in manufacturing, where more than 2 million jobs, corresponding to 14 per cent of total employment, were lost.

The human and political costs were obviously large. The other side of the story, however, was a long overdue and badly needed onslaught on decades of overmanning, which paved the way for a remarkable improvement in productivity, especially in manufacturing. There was both an immediate recession spurt and a longer-term improvement. Partly as a result, the annual increase in unit wage costs plunged from 22 per cent in 1980 to 9 per cent in 1982 and 4 per cent in 1983. As Professor Geoffrey Maynard put it in a book which deserves to be better known:

> By refusing to accommodate rising costs and poor productivity with exchange rate depreciation, macro-policy imposed pressure on industry to raise productivity, lower costs and generally move its product up market. Many firms, whose managements were often vociferous in their criticism of government exchange rate policy, subsequently achieved productivity improvements and product upgrading to an unprecedented extent.

The management revolution was due not only to the exchange rate squeeze and the move to higher nominal interest rates, but also to the end of the era of incomes policy and to the widespread impression that the Thatcher Government, unlike its predecessors, would not bail out loss-making firms at the first political outcry – or indeed at all. The policy thus both established the Government's counter-inflationary credentials and at the same time reinforced management's newly rediscovered right to manage. The squeeze was relaxed only when there were clear signs that it had done its job.

I believe that we gained far more than we lost in microeconomic terms – i.e. quite apart from the beneficial effects for inflation – from the higher exchange rate. Of course, there were real costs as well as benefits. But as I have already indicated, a shock *was* needed if attitudes were to change. Overall, so far from losing our industrial base, our industrial base emerged from the fire more productive, more efficient, more competitive in the best sense, and very much better managed. This was the so-called 'leaner and fitter' effect – even though I was hardly the person to use at least the first part of that metaphor.[8]

The unfinished task was to create the conditions in which the productivity improvements could be reflected in greater total output, as well as higher output per head. In any case, once the cultural change had been largely secured, the case for continuing the shock treatment was very much weaker. Hence the relaxation of the squeeze in the course of 1981 and the shift to what Geoffrey Howe called in October 1982 (when I was no longer in the Treasury) 'flexibility without laxity'.

OBSTINACY AND BARE KNUCKLES

A good deal of obstinacy was needed to persevere with our chosen course. Many Press commentators could scarcely contain their impatience to see a U-turn.

[8] [2010 note] On this topic, to which I turned my attention after leaving office, see *The Nigel Lawson Diet Book* (1996).

Industrialists could not, of course, be expected to enjoy what was happening. I remember travelling the country as Financial Secretary and addressing meetings of businessmen, sometimes on governmental and sometimes on Conservative Party occasions, and receiving an almost universally hostile reception when it came to the questioning. The main theme was invariably how the Government was crucifying British industry with the high exchange rate and how it clearly did not understand the consequences. This experience, incidentally, was probably the origin of the myth that the Thatcher Government generally, and I in particular, were hostile to manufacturing industry and considered it of little importance.

Not only was the honeymoon with business well and truly over, but for a time divorce was in the air. Maurice Hodgson, the chairman of ICI, visited Margaret in October 1980 to warn her that the company would make a third quarter loss for the first time in its history; and Michael Edwardes, the chairman of British Leyland (subsequently to change its name to Rover Group), proclaimed that if the Government 'cannot find a way of living with North Sea oil, then I say: leave the bloody stuff in the ground'. This phase culminated in a widely publicised attack on the Government at the CBI's annual conference in November 1980, which passed a motion critical of Government policy on interest rates, on exchange rates and on public spending. It was there that Terence Beckett, the newly installed Director-General, hit the headlines by declaring:

> We have got to take the gloves off and have a bare knuckle fight [with the Government] because we have to have an effective and prosperous industry ... Our short-term needs are clear. We have got to have a lower pound, lower interest rates and a reduction in the National Insurance surcharge.

All this was too much for five of the CBI's most substantial member companies, which promptly resigned from the organisation. At a subsequent Number 10 meeting between Margaret and a somewhat chastened Terry Beckett, the CBI Director-General explained that industry loved her after all.

The complaints from industry about the strength of sterling were all the more strident because the discipline was not one to which they had been accustomed. For most of post-war history, the movement of sterling had been persistently and unequivocally downwards. Indeed British policy-makers, viewing the periodic struggles of German governments to keep down a rising Deutschmark were inclined to react in terms of the New York Jewish idiom, '*I* should have such problems'.

The first intimation that such problems could occur even in Britain came after the Labour Government's deal with the IMF in 1976. The resulting return of confidence led in the following year to the unfamiliar spectacle of a strengthening pound. Sterling's movements at this time are best tracked by means of the so-called sterling index, which is a trade-weighted average of the exchange rate against various currencies. (The sterling D-Mark rate came into its own rather later.) The 1977 upsurge was not in retrospect that large and the pound regained little more than half the ground lost in the 1976 crisis. But the rise was enough to alarm the Treasury's Permanent Secretary, Douglas Wass, who was a strong believer in a 'competitive' pound.

The authorities used both intervention and lower interest rates to stem the rise. MLR was slashed dramatically, from 14 per cent at the beginning of 1977 to 5 per cent in October of that year. After that Denis Healey, acting on Gordon Richardson's advice, uncapped the pound – the only time (according to his memoirs) that he overruled Wass. The Labour Government's worries about a rising pound were, however, all too short-lived. MLR had to be increased several times in the course of 1978 to prevent sterling falling too far, and again in January 1979.

STERLING CLIMBS IN EARNEST

It was only after that, that the pound began its more dramatic rise. By election day, 3 May 1979, sterling was still below where it had been before Labour's crisis negotiations with the IMF. After the Conservative victory, sterling began to take off, with only a temporary relapse in the closing months of 1979 when Paul Volcker's arrival at the Fed led to the imposition of a fierce monetary squeeze in the US.

By the end of January 1981 the pound was more than 20 per cent higher than it had stood on election day. Many commentators prefer to look at estimates of the real exchange rate, i.e. taking into account inflation, which at that time was significantly higher in Britain than in major competitor countries. On the basis of relative producer prices, the real appreciation of sterling at its peak was some 30 per cent. (A real appreciation of nearly 50 per cent can be obtained on the basis of IMF unit labour costs, but the realism of that particular index is open to question.)

Our decision to do nothing to prevent the pound's rise, despite the complaints of businessmen, was a deliberate one. At the end of August 1979, to the astonishment of Treasury officials, I wrote to Geoffrey Howe:

> So far from wishing to do anything to lower the exchange rate, I believe that the strong pound is the biggest thing we have going for us. Not only is it an integral part of our anti-inflation policy, but any attempt to weaken it would quickly lead to a very serious loss of confidence in our resolve to stick to that policy. We must have expectations working for us and not against us: that is fundamental. Thus it is even, I believe, unwise to hint that we are unhappy at the strength of the pound.

Not wishing to appear too outrageous, I added that 'a rapidly and inexorably rising pound would be another matter, but that is neither the reality nor the prospect.' Like almost everyone else, I failed to see how far the pound would eventually rise and how long its strength would persist.

Anyone who can explain why the exchange rate moves as it does under a floating regime would be able to predict future movements and thus become a multi-millionaire, which I am not. Nor, incidentally, are those who claim to have a simple monetarist explanation of exchange rate behaviour. But looking back, not entirely with hindsight, on the huge rise of sterling in 1979/80, three factors almost certainly played a part:

1. *The Thatcher Effect*: by this I mean financial market confidence in the new Government with its stern new approach.
2. *The Oil Effect:* in other words the belated recognition of sterling as a petro-currency at a time when oil prices were rising sharply, following the Iranian Revolution and the outbreak of the Iran–Iraq war.
3. *The Carter Effect:* this last is often forgotten in the UK; but the Carter Presidency, especially towards the end, forfeited the confidence of the world's financial markets with disastrous consequences for the dollar. When Ronald Reagan was elected in November 1980, and inaugurated the following January, the market's attitude to the dollar changed completely.

While we were in no doubt about the policy that we wished to pursue, we were in two minds over the pace at which it was sensible to seek to squeeze inflation out of the system. Geoffrey's instinct was for a policy of gradualism. But the big question was the severity of the first step. I was conscious that while too great a shock could cause unnecessary dislocation to the economy, it was also true that too gradualist a start would do nothing to change expectations – which was urgently needed – and would dissipate much of the benefit of having a new Government in place plotting a new course for the economy.

A RETROSPECT ON STERLING

The question is whether, with hindsight, there was a preferable alternative to the policy we pursued; an alternative that would have squeezed inflation out of the system without the high exchange rate which put such pressure on the internationally traded sector of the economy and on manufacturing in particular.

Excessive pay increases played a large part in the employment squeeze. Private sector expectations took some time to adjust to the new climate, quite apart from the knock-on effects of Clegg, VAT and oil prices already mentioned. It is easy to say that the sterling overshoot was deeply damaging; and certainly it seems to sit awkwardly with my later advocacy of the ERM as a desirable measure of exchange rate stability.

But in the early 1980s, after the false trails that had led to the debacle of the previous decades, some degree of shock treatment was needed, and the exchange rate provided it. Moreover inflation generally in the Group of Seven was too high and too variable to make exchange rate stability a credible objective at that time.

The rise in the pound can be divided into two phases. There was the surge from the beginning of 1979 to the autumn of 1980. Although this was neither planned nor intended, we were able to use it to achieve both our counter-inflationary objectives and the necessary improvement in industrial efficiency. Then there was the further rise to the peak at the end of 1980 and the beginning of 1981. This was a clear example of overshooting and is the type of counter-productive movement which should ideally be combated either by a system of international exchange rate management or in a regional system like the exchange rate mechanism of the EMS. If either such system had been in working order, it might have been possible to maintain existing interest rates while using co-ordinated international intervention to offset currency overshooting. But no such international system existed, while the ERM had been established for only a year, and sterling was in any case not part of it.

It was, of course, right to reduce interest rates as clear evidence arrived of progress in reducing inflation and, as far as the international position – which was dominated by the Fed's tight money drive – allowed. But Alan Walters' attempt, with the enthusiastic support of Margaret Thatcher, to hurry the process by using the 1981 Budget to reduce interest rates, was not in those terms a great success. Base rates, which stood at 14 per cent on the eve of that Budget, were cut to 12 per cent in its wake. That was just below the rate of inflation, then 12.75 per cent. Within six months MLR had to be jacked up to 14 per cent to fight off the downward pressure on the pound; and by the beginning of October it was up to 16 per cent. It was not until the end of February 1982 that it came below 14 per cent again and not until July of that year that it was back to 12 per cent – by which time inflation was down to 8.5 per cent and falling fast.

THATCHERISM IN ZURICH

As Financial Secretary, I was inevitably deeply concerned with these monetary issues. I was also well aware of the need to provide some answer to the angry clamour of businessmen and their supporters in the Press and elsewhere for a lower exchange rate, without admitting too explicitly that we were relying on the high exchange rate to squeeze inflation out of the system. My major speech to the Zurich Society of Economics on 14 January 1981, has to be seen against this political background. At the same time, I was concerned that the word 'monetarism' – even when correctly used and not treated simply as a hate word – was an inadequate description of the Government's policy. Indeed it was Keith Joseph, Margaret Thatcher's economic mentor and the John the Baptist of monetarism within the Conservative Party, who had entitled his 1976 Stockton lecture 'Monetarism is not enough'. He pointed out there the need for it to be accompanied by measures that would improve economic performance by the encouragement of enterprise at all levels. This became the party line, reflected in the 1979 manifesto and in numerous speeches.

I spent some time trying to make the twin strands more explicit and coherent. One reason for the confusion was that the anti-inflation macro policy produced results sooner than the enterprise-inducing micro policy did; but the misunderstandings went deeper still. It was largely to clear up this confusion that I entitled my Zurich speech 'Thatcherism in Practice'. This was, so far as I was aware at the time, the first ever use of the term 'Thatcherism' to describe our policies. (I later discovered that it had been used by the recherché, and now defunct, publication *Marxism Today* before we had even taken office in 1979, but no-one had taken any notice.)

The speech caused something of a stir. Michael Foot, then Leader of the Opposition, seized on my admission that we had 'so far, on balance, increased the real burden of taxation overall'. But in general it was well received, both by the more serious commentators, as the first detailed and coherent account of the Government's economic policy, and by Margaret Thatcher. I have to confess, however, that I gave an advance copy of the speech to Geoffrey very late in the day, giving him little practical opportunity to suggest any changes.

'Thatcherism' is, I believe, a useful term, and certainly was at the time. No other modern Prime Minister has given his or her name to a particular constellation of policies and values. However it needs to be used with care. The wrong definition is 'whatever Margaret Thatcher herself at any time did or said'. The right definition involves a mixture of free markets, financial discipline, firm control over public expenditure, tax cuts, nationalism, 'Victorian values' (of the Samuel Smiles self-help variety), privatisation and a dash of populism.

A subsequent formulation of the Government's supply-side policy objective which I was to use frequently and which was also much used by Margaret was the recreation of the 'enterprise culture' in the UK. The model in this case was the United States – although that country had in turn derived it from the vigorous enterprise culture of Victorian England and Scotland, and developed it further. As far as I know the 'enterprise culture' was my coinage and the 'dependency culture' was Margaret Thatcher's.

Be that as it may, the point here was that we were seeking not simply to remove various controls and impositions, but by so doing to change the entire culture of a nation from anti-profits, anti-business, government dependent lassitude and defeatism, to a pro-profit, pro-business, robustly independent vigour and optimism. I was later to be castigated for creating a climate of excessive optimism. There may be some truth in this – corrections tend to overshoot – but correction in this direction was badly needed. I remain in no doubt that a necessary precondition of economic success is a fundamental business optimism based on self-belief and the will to succeed. Defeatism, the characteristic of pre-Thatcher Britain, is invariably self-fulfilling.

The Zurich speech was also highlighted by the British Press because of its hint that the forthcoming Budget might have to be a tough one. In fact, much of the speech – inevitably, in view of the supposedly expert audience – was devoted to explaining in some detail why British monetary policy remained tight despite the misfortunes of our headline monetary target. More important was my declaration that 'to have abandoned the fight against inflation on the grounds that the world recession and the transformation of sterling into a petro-currency provided sufficient problems to be getting on with, would have been a dereliction of duty which we had no intention of committing.' But the most important contribution of the speech was putting the monetary exposition side by side with an account of the deeper cultural changes we were trying to encourage.

CHAPTER SIX

THE MEDIUM TERM FINANCIAL STRATEGY

The Origins · What It Said and Why · Borrowing Targets · The Abiding Legacy
A Personal Postscript

THE ORIGINS

Looking back on these events from the perspective of the early 1990s, Geoffrey Howe generously told the Institute for Fiscal Studies:

> There emerged the rigorous discipline of the Medium Term Financial Strategy, and for that we owe a great deal to the clear-sighted tenacity of its chief draftsman, Nigel Lawson. The MTFS, too, was not instantly applauded by the Bank of England nor in Number 10, where the then incumbent had little enthusiasm for what she described as 'graph paper economics'. I have no doubt, in retrospect, about the overriding need for such a device.

During our period in Opposition, I had developed the idea of a stabilisation programme extending several years ahead to replace the short-term and unbelieving monetarism of Denis Healey. I set out my thinking in a *Times* article published on 14 September 1978 in the following terms:

> The time has come for a wholly new approach to economic policy in Britain. The overriding need is for a long-term stabilisation programme to defeat inflation, recreate business confidence and provide a favourable climate for economic growth. At the head of such a programme must lie a firm commitment to a steady and gradual reduction in the rate of growth of the money supply, until it is consistent with our best guess at a potentially sustainable rate of economic growth. Only in this way can inflation be wrung out of the system. But this alone is not enough ... An

> equally important part of a long term stabilisation plan has to be a reduction in the present Budget deficit ... Indeed, something akin ... to the old balanced Budget discipline needs to be restored: the secret of practical economic success, as overseas experience confirms, is the acceptance of known rules. Rules rule: OK?

I wrote this article when I did because, like everyone else, I expected an election in the autumn of 1978. (Indeed the Liberals had left the Lib-Lab Pact in the summer of that year on that clear understanding.) I was therefore anxious to put the idea into circulation before the campaign began. As luck would have it, the article appeared in print just after Jim Callaghan had announced the postponement of the election until 1979. The piece still achieved its purpose. Geoffrey Howe, then Shadow Chancellor, was impressed by the argument and in particular the sentence 'Rules rule: OK?'

But neither he nor I had any time to address ourselves to the MTFS until the June 1979 Budget was out of the way. I then suggested to him that we should have a stabilisation plan along the lines of my *Times* piece. Geoffrey agreed and asked me to work it out with the help of Peter Middleton, then an Under Secretary and the closest approximation to a monetarist the official Treasury could produce, and Adam Ridley, Geoffrey Howe's own senior political adviser who had earlier been a Treasury official. We set to work, and the result was the Medium Term Financial Strategy.

I had hoped the MTFS would be introduced at the time of the November 1979 interim Public Expenditure White Paper. This would have been possible as the main outlines had already been worked out within the Treasury by then. But because of internal opposition we had to be content with a Treasury Seminar attended by outside experts, including Terry Burns who argued forcefully in favour of the idea.

John Biffen, the Chief Secretary, was characteristically opposed to the whole concept, believing that governments should never impale themselves on hooks in this way, since it reduced their room for manoeuvre as circumstances changed. That of course was the point of the whole exercise. The MTFS was intended to be a self-imposed constraint on economic policy-making, just as the Gold Standard and the Bretton Woods system of exchange rates had been in the past, and the ERM came to be for most European Community countries in the 1980s.

John felt so strongly about it, however, that he wrote personally to Margaret setting out his objections to the MTFS, which understandably annoyed Geoffrey when he got to hear of it. Douglas Wass, too, was unenthusiastic about the MTFS and sought to neuter it.

WHAT IT SAID AND WHY

The actual text of the first MTFS in the 1980 Red Book is still worth reading, as it is often misrepresented even in academic commentaries. It started off with the Government's determination to 'bring down the rate of inflation and to create conditions for a sustainable growth of output and employment'. To that end it would 'progressively reduce the growth of the money stock' and 'pursue the policies necessary to achieve this aim'. It established a target range of 7–11 per cent growth for £M3 for 1980/81 and set out a path, declining by 1 per cent each year to reach a range of 4–8 per cent by 1983/84. The precise targets for the intervening years would be decided at the time. Right underneath the first table, and at the very beginning of the whole section was a crucial footnote which read: 'The way in which the money supply is defined for target purposes may need to be adjusted from time to time as circumstances change.' But it suited our critics to pretend it was not there. There followed Paragraph 3, which enunciated the central doctrine:

> Control of the money supply will over a period of years reduce the rate of inflation. The speed with which inflation falls will depend crucially on expectations both within the UK and overseas. It is to provide a firm basis for those expectations that the Government has announced its firm commitment to a progressive reduction in money supply growth. Public expenditure plans and tax policies and interest rates will be adjusted as necessary to achieve the objective. At the same time, the Government will continue to pursue policies to strengthen the supply side of the economy by tax and other incentives, and by improving the working of the market mechanism.

The document also set out the Government's intention of making a substantial reduction over the medium term in the PSBR as a percentage of GDP. It added that the relationship between the PSBR and the growth of the money supply was not simple, being affected by the economic cycle, the rate of inflation, the structure of taxation, public spending and much else.

In the early years, and especially when the MTFS was first launched, Press and political attention was focused chiefly on the 'implied fiscal adjustment' line in the key table. This was Treasury jargon for tax cuts, and was the difference between projected revenue and expenditure after allowing for stated public borrowing objectives. Our 1980 projections suggested that, despite the tough times we were going through, there would be scope for tax cuts in the last two years of the parliament, 1982/83 and 1983/84, as indeed there proved to be. The Press saw this as the central purpose of the MTFS: to keep the potentially mutinous troops – especially in the House of Commons – quiescent with a promise of jam tomorrow. And it probably did serve that useful purpose at that time. This was not, however, what the MTFS was really about.

I do not, of course, claim intellectual paternity of the idea of a medium-term financial strategy. Several economists (including Terry Burns and Alan Budd in the October 1977 London Business School Economic Outlook) had suggested something similar. But I was responsible both for introducing the idea into the political arena and for getting it past the watering-down instincts of permanent officials.

The purpose of the MTFS was to confirm and consolidate the complete change of direction on which we had embarked. In the first place it was explicitly medium term. So far from believing that there was any short-term mechanical link between financial policy and inflation, we were sure that a financial approach would work only if we persisted in it year in, year out; and that progress would not be in a straight line. In the second place, we wanted to signal a shift from a real to a nominal framework for macroeconomic policy. This sounds something of a mouthful. But at the time I tried to spell out its meaning in simple terms in my 1980 lecture, *The New Conservatism*:

> The distinctive feature of our medium-term financial strategy, which differentiates it from the so-called national plans of other times and other places, is that it is confined to charting a course for those variables – notably the quantity of money – which are and must be within the power of governments to control. By contrast, governments cannot create economic growth. All the instruments which were supposed to do this have succeeded only in damaging the economy and have ultimately broken in the hands of the governments that sought to use them.

So far as inflation was concerned, the twofold error of previous Governments had been the commitment to full employment, come what may, and the false teaching of the neo-Keynesian economic establishment that the route to full employment was ever more monetary (and fiscal) expansion. Too many monetarists spoiled their case by making it all sound much too easy and by failing to recognise the political realities. They tended to treat monetary growth as if it were an autonomous prime cause of inflation, as if Governments foolishly over-expanded the money supply simply out of ignorance or sheer perversity. This was, of course, nonsense. Previous Governments may have lacked backbone, and held a self-defeatingly limited idea of the range of the politically possible. But their actions, however mistaken, were the result of political pressures rather than caprice. An important part of the point of the MTFS was to commit the Government to resisting such pressures in the future.

BORROWING TARGETS

Most political discussion concentrated, not on the arcana of monetarism, but on the more widely comprehensible figures in the MTFS showing a declining path for public sector borrowing up to 1983/84. The object of this was three-fold. First, it was a way of bringing expenditure and revenue together. Second, it was important that the PSBR objective for the coming year should not stand alone, but should be seen as part of a medium-term programme for reducing it to a low proportion of GDP. Third, it was believed at the time that a declining PSBR would enable our monetary objectives to be reached without 'excessive reliance on high interest rates'. Or as I put it in a speech in January 1980:

> Too high a PSBR requires either that the Government borrows heavily from the banks, which adds directly to the money supply; or, failing this, that it borrows from individuals and institutions, but at ever increasing rates of interest which place an unacceptable squeeze on the private sector.

Later I became sceptical of the link between Budget deficits and interest rates in a world of free capital movements. Even in 1980, I had my doubts about how strong the link really was. But in so far as a link existed, it could only be in the direction the Treasury alleged.

Getting the Government to commit itself to declining deficits was not only a way of disciplining Chancellors – of putting them on a hook; it was also a way of disciplining the Cabinet in its capacity as a bevy of spending Ministers. Moreover the promise of low interest rates if the MTFS was followed was an important *ad feminam* argument to persuade Margaret (and subsequently

Cabinet colleagues) to accept the MTFS. Although initially highly sceptical, Margaret was brought round by Geoffrey by the argument that the MTFS would be (a) a powerful weapon against spending Ministers and (b) an influence for lower interest rates. Her opposition turned out to be not nearly as deep-seated as that of the Bank of England, which wanted to retain complete and unfettered discretion over monetary policy.

A number of senior Treasury officials were worried by the apparently smooth declining path of the PSBR in the Strategy. They feared that we were so anti-Keynesian that we failed to realise that Government borrowing could not decline in a recession. In the end, the Red Book made it very clear that the smooth path was illustrative. I pointed out in a well-reported speech in January 1980, even before the MTFS was launched, that the actual path of decline was likely to be 'stepped', falling in normal years and remaining level in recession years.

In further speeches then, and subsequently as Chancellor, I consistently drew a distinction between the effect of the business cycle on the PSBR, which should not be a cause for alarm or for action of any kind, and the activist use of the PSBR in an attempt to dampen the cycle, which should be firmly eschewed. The conceptual distinction could not be clearer; yet it is something the Treasury Select Committee and many others never seemed to understand, despite my many attempts to explain it. The original discipline of a declining PSBR, and the subsequent discipline of a balanced Budget, which I introduced as Chancellor, have both to be understood over the economic cycle as a whole. This is sometimes described as 'allowing the automatic stabilisers to come into play'; but never by me. For the description begs the whole question of whether fiscal surpluses and deficits have any serious capacity to stabilise or destabilise the economy in the first place. In my opinion they do not – indeed if they did, the 1981 Budget would most certainly have been seriously destabilising, as the notorious 364 economists wrongly predicted.

The true consideration has nothing whatever to do with short-term 'stabilisation'. It is that tax policy needs to be seen in a medium-term, not to say long-term, supply-side context. In other words, taxes should be changed (reduced or reformed or both) in order to improve economic performance. Unnecessary fluctuations in tax levels are inimical to economic performance and undermine any benefits of reduction or reform by casting doubt on the durability of the change. By the same token, taxes should be reduced only if the reduction can be sustained – which means that they need to be justified not by the vagaries of the economic cycle, but by the underlying level and trend of Government spending.

Tax changes should be made only if they are for the better, and if they are for the better they should not be undone. In other words, once the position has been reached where the long-term fiscal objective – in my view a balanced Budget when the economy is growing at its sustainable trend rate – has been attained, then the revenue shortfall that occurs as a result of a recession should neither be made good by tax increases nor augmented by 'Keynesian' tax reductions designed (vainly) to counter the recession. Precisely the same applies, in reverse, to the revenue surplus that occurs as a result of a boom.

THE ABIDING LEGACY

'The best laid schemes o' mice an' men/Gang aft a-gley.' The MTFS was not fulfilled in any literal sense, at least not on the monetary side. The liberalisation of financial markets which we had ourselves launched changed the meaning of the monetary aggregates and made them much more difficult to predict and control. The original 1980/81 monetary target was heavily overshot. So, less heavily, was that for 1981/82; and the objectives for the subsequent two years were met only after the targets had been raised, and then by somewhat artificial means (the technique known as 'overfunding'). The target definitions of money were also changed in subsequent years.

Nevertheless, in terms of its fundamental aims, the MTFS succeeded. I remember a meeting I had with senior Treasury officials shortly before the 1980 Budget, when we were finalising the MTFS for publication. One of them asked me if I cared to write down what I thought inflation would come down to over the period. Never one to resist a challenge, I scribbled down an illustrative path, culminating in 5 per cent in the final year (1983/84). Inflation at the time of our discussion stood at virtually 20 per cent. With the exception of Terry Burns, they all thought I had taken leave of my senses, although of course they did not put it quite so bluntly. In fact, inflation turned out to be slightly below 5 per cent in 1983/84.

There can be no doubt that the MTFS came to play a central role in the Government's economic policy. We could not have kept the show on the road, particularly in the early days, when the majority of the Cabinet were 'wets', without it. In particular the controversially tight 1981 Budget, discussed in the next chapter, would never have been introduced had it not been for the MTFS.

Even a highly critical witness such as Christopher Allsopp (a Bank of England economist at the time) conceded in a 1991 post mortem:

> There appears to be a widespread agreement that macroeconomic policy should concentrate on providing a stable and stabilising nominal environment which is conducive to the control of inflation and within which supply-side improvements are most likely to be successful. This, it may be argued, is the abiding legacy of the medium-term financial strategy.

The fiscal side of the MTFS wore better than the monetary side. Until the late 1980s, the Government came as close to fulfilling its forward objectives for the PSBR as can be expected in an uncertain world. After that the departures from target were initially in the favourable direction of Budget surplus and debt repayment, with some erring in the opposite direction in the early 1990s.

A PERSONAL POSTSCRIPT

In the New Year's Honours list for 1981 I was made a Privy Councillor. This is the most parliamentary of all honours, enabling the recipient to graduate from being an honourable Member to a Right honourable Member. It comes automatically on promotion to the Cabinet: for Ministers outside the Cabinet it is rather more selective. I went on 18 February 1981 to Buckingham Palace to be sworn in by the Queen. The ceremony is as brief as it is bizarre, requiring the recipient to progress to the monarch by a complex mixture of bowing, walking and kneeling at specified intervals. The procedure is so complicated that the Clerk of the Council, then Sir Neville Leigh, was in the habit of arranging a rehearsal beforehand.

However, it soon became clear that my Privy Councillorship was a consolation prize. For on 5 January 1981, Margaret Thatcher announced her first Cabinet reshuffle, in which John Biffen was moved from being Chief Secretary to Secretary of State for Trade. The need for a new Chief Secretary was not in dispute; but it came as a great blow to me that Leon Brittan – hitherto a young Minister of State at the Home Office with no previous experience of economics or finance – was brought in and promoted to the job above my head. The first I heard of the news was when I received a telephone call in my constituency just before the public announcement was made. Geoffrey Howe was not even in town when I returned to London the following day, having an urgent appointment in Ireland.

Although Leon was a close friend of Geoffrey (and Elspeth) Howe, who was very glad to have him at the Treasury, the main sponsor of his promotion was undoubtedly Willie Whitelaw, who was not only Home Secretary but effectively deputy Prime Minister and for whose political feel Margaret had at that time considerable respect. Willie was at that time determined both to advance his protégé at the Home Office and to block my path to the Cabinet. Subsequently, Willie and I were to become close colleagues and good friends; but that was not the case then, when I underestimated him and he distrusted me.

No-one, of course, has any pre-emptive right to any particular job. But having worked round the clock for the best part of two years, I did not rush back to full-time office duties in the first working week of the New Year, an indulgence which was described by some as 'sulking', although in fact I was determined not to sulk, and simply needed a few days to get over it. Instead, I took an early opportunity of letting Margaret know directly of my disappointment.

No doubt sensing how I might be feeling, she kindly invited Thérèse and myself to Sunday lunch at Chequers on 18 January. Apart, of course, from Denis, no-one else was there. It was Thérèse's first close encounter with Margaret, to whom she took an instant liking which never waned – although she was somewhat taken aback when, very early on in the proceedings, Margaret cautioned her to be very careful never to repeat anything from the privileged conversations she was about to hear. In fact, the conversation between Margaret and me over lunch, although friendly and moderately indiscreet – with Denis making his usual blunt interjections of the kind subsequently made familiar to a wider public through the 'Dear Bill' column in *Private Eye* – was pretty inconsequential.

After lunch she whisked me off to the small room she used as her study, leaving Denis to entertain Thérèse in their cosy, chintzy, television room. Thérèse later told me that after about a minute's politesse, he said, 'Why don't you read the newspapers, dear' and promptly fell asleep in his armchair. Meanwhile, in the course of our discussion *à deux*, Margaret assured me that she intended to put me in the Cabinet in her next reshuffle. Suddenly, there was a tremendous hullabaloo, which turned out to be a false fire alarm. Margaret and I carried on with our talk, but Thérèse was rushed by the staff to the safety of the communications room by the front door and left there on her own. She found herself in a small room full of elaborate telecommunications equipment, including the hotline to the US President. She was sorely tempted to pick it up and see what happened, but refrained.

When the time came to leave, we had first to wait on the front steps while every fire engine in Buckinghamshire screeched round the circular drive and, discovering that their arrival was unnecessary, out again. On the way home I told Thérèse what Margaret had said. I was well aware that the undertaking she had given me, although undoubtedly sincere, was vulnerable to the hazards of political life, as all such undertakings are. But I left Chequers feeling rather better than I had on arrival.

Meanwhile, Leon's move brought me some practical benefit. For as soon as he had run himself in I was able to turn over to him all the public expenditure work I had been doing, which he was fully capable of handling himself and which I should never have had to assume.

CHAPTER SEVEN

1981 – A TIGHT AND CONTROVERSIAL BUDGET

Origins of the 1981 Budget · Taxing the Banks · Biting the Tax Bullet
The Fiscal Arithmetic · The Political Row · The Economic Row
Inflation Starts to Fall

ORIGINS OF THE 1981 BUDGET

The 1981 Budget defiantly raised the tax burden in a recession and provoked a notorious letter of protest to *The Times* from 364 economists. Yet its success in turning round sentiment and as a prelude to more than eight years of economic growth made it in retrospect seem climacteric. As a result there has been some myth-making and attempts to claim the credit. It is worth setting the record straight.

The Government did not set out with the deliberate intent of making a dramatic doctrinal challenge to economic orthodoxy or to the political faint-hearts in its own ranks. The 1981 Budget was essentially a response to the fiscal difficulties which had emerged in the financial year 1980/81. As that year progressed it became clear that the Budget deficit as measured by the PSBR was running well ahead of the £6 billion target set the previous March and embodied in the MTFS. By November 1980 it was apparent that the deficit would be at least £11.5 billion; and the eventual out-turn was £12.5 billion or 5.25 per cent of GDP (equivalent to some £30 billion in early 1990s terms).

Roughly half the overrun, which was largely on the public expenditure side, could be attributed to the recession. Although, in output terms, no deeper than forecast, it was accompanied by a much greater than expected rise in unemployment, and hence spending on social security benefits. It was also having a much more severe effect on the finances of the nationalised industries than had been predicted. But a good deal was also due to weaknesses in our system of public expenditure control.

In the circumstances it was clear that the forthcoming public spending round would need to be a very tough one. At the July 1980 Cabinet meeting on public expenditure, Geoffrey secured the agreement of Cabinet to a substantial reduction in the so-called public expenditure planning total for 1981/82. But when it came to the autumn public expenditure round of bilateral discussions between the Treasury and spending Ministers, the specific savings needed to achieve this overall reduction were not forthcoming. And even where they were, the success was short-lived. Patrick Jenkin, the Social Services Secretary, responsible for the biggest budget of all, argued that the only means by which he could find the savings demanded of him by the Treasury was by abandoning the annual uprating of pensions in line with inflation, an offer John Biffen, the Chief Secretary, gratefully accepted. The decision was subsequently overturned by Cabinet, as Patrick had no doubt expected it would be.

This was an object lesson to Treasury Ministers in a standard spending Minister's ploy: the political boomerang offer. Subsequently, when I became Chancellor, I made a point of warning each of the four Chief Secretaries that served under me about it and of the importance of securing savings that would not be too politically difficult for Cabinet to swallow – not to mention the *sine qua non* of getting Margaret fully signed up before the matter ever went to Cabinet.

The public spending round for 1981/82 was particularly hard fought. Its final resolution required no fewer than three Cabinet meetings in the first half of November 1980, the first two of them devoted to nothing else. In the end, Geoffrey had to settle for an overall reduction, achieved principally by squeezing cash limits, of only half the figure the Cabinet had agreed in July. The outcome was manifestly inadequate, especially in view of the deteriorating fiscal position for 1980/81 and, in consequence, the steadily worsening outlook for 1981/82.

The position was clearly unacceptable, on a number of levels. The private sector, hard hit by the recession and the rising exchange rate, was increasingly resentful that the public sector appeared to be getting off relatively lightly – an argument with which Treasury Ministers had considerable sympathy. Quite apart from the manifest unfairness, the public sector was felt to be 'crowding out' the private sector: the precise reverse of what the Government had entered office to bring about. The argument was that high public spending, resulting in high public borrowing, pushed up interest rates, which in turn choked off private sector investment.

In retrospect I believe we overstated that effect. Short-term interest rates, which (apart from the level of stocks) have little direct bearing on private investment anyway, are determined not by the scale of the PSBR but by the needs of the Government's anti-inflation policy. Long-term interest rates, which have a direct impact on equity yields and thus on private investment decisions, are determined by the balance of supply and demand in the capital market. As the capital market was becoming increasingly a single global market, the public borrowing of any one country – with the important exception, because of its sheer size, of the United States – had a correspondingly diminished effect.

But the crowding-out thesis was in any case only part of the story. Another consideration which carried considerable weight, not least with the official Treasury at that time, was the belief that the burden needed to be shifted from companies, hard hit by high interest rates and a high exchange rate, to individuals, who benefited from the high exchange rate – provided they were in work. Yet a further important factor was that the Government's credibility in the financial markets clearly depended greatly on the extent to which it was seen to be taking the newly published MTFS seriously. And with the wayward behaviour of £M3, it was all the more important that the fiscal side of the MTFS – the declining path for public borrowing – should be observed.

Finally, of course, it was no bad thing to demonstrate to the Cabinet colleagues and to the country alike that failure to curb public spending, on which the Government had set such store, would mean higher taxes. Thus it was that on 24 November 1980, for the first and only time, the Thatcher Government came close to introducing a mini-Budget of the kind that had characterised the Healey Chancellorship and which we had resolved to eschew. Geoffrey Howe announced a percentage point increase in employees' National Insurance Contributions from 6.75 per cent to 7.75 per cent, to take effect from 1 April 1981. It was true, of course, that National Insurance Contribution rates were, for administrative reasons, always reviewed and announced in the autumn. But on this occasion Geoffrey also announced a new Supplementary Petroleum Duty (SPD) of 20 per cent of the gross return of each field to take effect from 1 January 1981, an impost which it was felt the prosperous North Sea oil industry could well afford. Each of these measures was expected to bring in an extra £1 billion in 1981/82.

To soften the blow the Government had announced three days earlier a £245 million package to increase various employment subsidies and launch a Community Enterprise programme. Less happily, there were further increases in aid to hospitalised enterprises in the state sector, notably British Leyland and British Steel, and in the External Financing Limits of the nationalised industries generally. On 24 November itself, MLR was reduced from 16 to 14 per cent.

The November measures had their expected favourable effects on financial confidence. Nevertheless the PSBR overrun continued unabated. As we embarked on the preparation for the 1981 Budget, it was clear that further increases in taxation would be required. The only question was how much, and where the burden should fall.

TAXING THE BANKS

Apart from North Sea oil, there was one other sector of the economy that was doing well while business and industry in general suffered: the banks. This was largely because, in those days, the banks enjoyed a substantial 'endowment' income from money kept in current accounts on which no interest was paid. Clearly the higher the level of lending rates, the greater this endowment income became.

In the circumstances, and somewhat in conflict with our non-interventionist philosophy, we decided to ask the banks to take over the responsibility for financing a proportion of the Government's fixed-rate export credit scheme. This would involve the banks in assuming a financial liability which they could well afford. But the main attraction to the Treasury was that it would 'score' as a reduction in public expenditure. Whether it ought to score in purely economic arithmetic was beside the point at a time when a Government was fighting to maintain confidence in its budgetary strategy during the worst post-war recession to date and in the face of disaffection in its own ranks.

Geoffrey accordingly asked me, as Financial Secretary with delegated responsibility for the banks, to negotiate an agreement along these lines. I duly held a meeting at my room in the Treasury with Jeremy Morse, chairman of Lloyds Bank, in his capacity as chairman of the Committee of London Clearing Banks, at which I argued that, in return for their acquiescence, the banks, whose reputation among the hard pressed business community was not particularly favourable, would be able to promote themselves as public spirited and patriotic citizens helping the UK exporter. But I was not so naïve as to believe that this not particularly juicy carrot would suffice without some sort of stick as well, and accordingly agreed with Geoffrey that, if all else failed, we would have to impose some sort of additional taxation on the banks.

In a series of meetings, Morse insisted that there was no way the banks could justify to their shareholders taking over the financing of fixed-rate credit to exporters. I hinted that the alternative would be some form of special tax on the banks. Morse, assuming that I was bluffing, declared that that would be the lesser evil, since the banks would not have any problems with their shareholders in that event. For good measure, however, he wrote to Margaret to complain about this threat – a singularly pointless exercise, since Margaret had no love for the banks, regarded Morse himself as a neo-Keynesian 'wet', and had been kept fully on side by Geoffrey about the work I had asked Treasury officials to do on a scheme to extract a contribution from the banks towards solving the pressing PSBR problem.

A once-for-all bank levy of 2.5 per cent of the value of non-interest bearing bank deposits on the eve of the Budget was duly announced as part of the 1981 Budget on 10 March, to bring in some £400 million of additional revenue. It caused some disquiet on our own benches, notably on the grounds of retrospection. This was the least valid objection of all. For if the date on which the levy was based had been later, it would have been a simple matter for the banks to decide to pay a modest rate of interest on current accounts, even on a purely temporary basis, thus reducing the yield from the levy to zero. Happily, there was only one resignation on the issue, that of Tim Renton, at the time PPS to John Biffen. As for the other bank chairmen, their anger at the Government was matched by their criticism of Morse for mishandling the situation on their behalf: it appeared that he had told them of the fixed-rate export credit proposal, but they had not been aware of the likely alternative.

BITING THE TAX BULLET

Even with this source of revenue on top of the one percentage point increase in National Insurance contributions and the new Supplementary Petroleum Duty, the prospective PSBR gap remained a yawning one. Geoffrey believed in a collegiate approach to Budget making, holding a series of meetings with the other Treasury Ministers as well as his top Treasury, Inland Revenue and Customs and Excise officials and the special advisers present. We were determined not to reverse the income tax cuts we had introduced in 1979, but felt that VAT at 15 per cent was as high as it could go. With businesses hard hit by recession, there was no question of any increase in Corporation Tax: instead some modest reliefs were required. We were thus left with the excise duties on alcoholic drinks, tobacco, petrol and derv, all of which we decided to increase by double the amounts required to keep pace with inflation.

But as Budget meeting followed Budget meeting, it became clear that this was not enough. In an atmosphere of mounting gloom, the economist then responsible for the Treasury's short-term forecasting would give his latest estimate of the current year's PSBR and his latest forecast of the PSBR for 1981/82. Each set of figures he produced was worse than the previous one. Towards the end of February when the final Budget decisions had to be taken, the prospective PSBR for 1981/82, even taking into account the increase in National Insurance contributions, but before any Budget measures, was forecast to be £14 billion. Not only was the sheer size alarming; but it meant that the PSBR was still rising at time when the Government's policy, newly enshrined in the MTFS, was to bring it down substantially.

Meanwhile, at a meeting at Chequers in January, Geoffrey Howe had warned Margaret of the serious deterioration in the public finances and of his sombre conclusion that he would have to do whatever was necessary to get the 1981/82 PSBR down to at most some £10 billion. She was not amused. She was even less amused in February, when he informed her that the picture was even worse and that he would have to raise taxes in the forthcoming Budget by £3.5 billion. She convened a meeting at Number 10, at which her new personal economic adviser, Alan Walters, who had taken office at the beginning of the year, was also present. Walters strongly supported Geoffrey's analysis, adding that, in his view, the increase in taxation should if anything be even larger – say £4 billion. Margaret responded angrily that she had not been elected to put up taxes; but eventually and with a heavy heart agreed to a Budget that would increase taxation on the scale recommended both by her Chancellor and her economic adviser, on the clear understanding that this would permit a significant reduction in interest rates.

To bridge the gap that remained even after the substantial real increase in the excise duties, it was clear that we would have to bite the bullet and raise the burden of income tax. But we remained – rightly – determined not to reverse the 1979 cut in the basic rate. This meant acting on the personal allowances. Initially it looked as if we could meet our target by confining the increase in the allowances to half that required by the indexation formula. But as the forecasts deteriorated, it became apparent that we would not be able to increase the allowances at all for 1981/82.

As the main architect of the indexation provisions, I had no hesitation in supporting this course of action. Indeed I volunteered to take the Finance Bill clause setting aside indexation of the personal allowances through the committee stage on the floor of the House myself, which I duly did. Although Michael Foot and others called for my resignation, I had little difficulty in reminding the House that the whole purpose of my Amendment to the Rooker-Wise Amendment in 1977 (already described in Chapter 2) had been to make it clear that indexation, although the presumption, was not automatic. Under the pre-1977 system the maintenance of the existing allowances for a further year in unchanged cash terms would have required no Finance Bill legislation whatever. It was only because of the Rooker-Wise-Lawson Amendment that the Government had to come out in the open and treat the non-indexation of the allowances as a tax increase, raising £2 billion of additional revenue, and could no longer increase the tax burden by stealth.

THE FISCAL ARITHMETIC

The overall increase in taxation on the fully indexed basis nowadays employed, although not at that time, was £4.5 billion. Adding back the increase in employees' national insurance contributions, the increase was well over £5 billion or around 2 per cent of GDP, equivalent to some £12 billion in terms of the early 1990s. The projected effect was to reduce the PSBR from the then estimated 6 per cent of GDP in 1980/81 to 4.25 per cent of GDP, or £10.5 billion, in 1981/82. In the event, the out-turn was considerably better, at £8.5 billion. We thus more than achieved our target. If we had had more accurate forecasts, we might well have done less, and not felt it necessary to freeze the personal allowances. But this might have been a mixed blessing. For the Budget might then not have made the salutary public impact that it did, and our long-term aim of sharply reducing the Budget deficit might have taken longer to achieve.

THE 1981 BUDGET

Figures are on an indexed basis

Estimated PSBR outcome, 1980/81	£13.5b*
Expected PSBR, 1982/82 before Budget measures	£14.5b
Effect of Budget measures:	
- *Non-indexation of income tax allowances & thresholds*	-£1.9b
- *Increase in Excise Duties above indexation*	-£1.2b
- *Oil tax increases & other*	-£1.2b
- *Expenditure changes*	+£0.3b
Total impact of Budget	-£4.0b
Forecast PSBR, 1981-82	£10.5b
Actual outcome	£8.6b
	*(final outcome £12.5b)

THE POLITICAL ROW

To introduce a tax-raising Budget on this scale in the depth of the recession was inevitably highly controversial. At the Cabinet of Tuesday, 10 March, at which Geoffrey unveiled the Budget to his colleagues, he was roundly attacked by the usual wets: Jim Prior, Peter Walker, Ian Gilmour – all of whom subsequently claimed that they had toyed with the idea of resignation. Margaret knew full well that the Cabinet would be a difficult one and had armed herself with a concession – in future there would be a pre-Budget discussion of Budget strategy in January or February of each year, and there would be a further Cabinet discussion of economic policy each July, in advance of the annual spending round. These innovations were duly implemented and no doubt Jim Prior, in particular, felt he had gained something of value. But from my own experience as Chancellor I can confirm that these concessions in no way derogated in practice from the sovereignty of the Chancellor of the day over the Budget, subject only to the need to carry the Prime Minister with him.

Among our own back-benchers, the focus of discontent was on the specific measures rather than on the economic doctrines supposedly violated by the Budget. Somewhat surprisingly they homed in on the increase in the duty on petrol. Advised by Michael Jopling, the Chief Whip, that we would have difficulty in getting the relevant Finance Bill clause through the House, we decided to offer a limited concession. We would go ahead with the petrol duty increase as proposed – we needed the money – but we would make the far less costly sacrifice of confining the increase in the duty on fuel for diesel engined road vehicles ('derv') to no more than that required to keep pace with inflation. We argued that this concession would have a directly beneficial impact on business costs. At the same time Geoffrey austerely made it clear that he would have to recoup the revenue lost by the derv concession elsewhere, which he duly did by moving an amendment to increase the tobacco duty still further, adding a further 3 pence, making an extra 17 pence in all, to a packet of twenty cigarettes. Such is the success of the anti-smoking lobby that the tobacco duty is the one tax where an increase commands more friends than enemies in the House of Commons. Thus was the back-bench rebellion against the 1981 Budget overcome, without any alteration whatever to the overall Budget arithmetic.

THE ECONOMIC ROW

The most memorable reaction to the 1981 Budget came not from the world of elected politicians, but from academics, in the shape of a round-robin letter signed by no fewer than 364 economists (one for every day in the year save Christmas day). Its text, published in *The Times* of 30 March 1981 read:

> We who are all present or retired members of the economic staff of British universities, are convinced that:
>
> - There is no basis in economic theory or supporting evidence for the Government's belief that by deflating demand they will bring inflation permanently under control and thereby introduce an automatic recovery in output and employment;
> - Present policies will deepen the depression, erode the industrial base of our economy and threaten its social and political stability;
> - There are alternative policies;
> - The time has come to reject monetarist policies and consider which alternative offers the best hope of sustained recovery.

The statement was prepared and circulated in the universities by two Cambridge economics professors, Frank Hahn and Robert Neild, on 13 March. The signatories included five former chief economic advisers to the Government – Robert Hall, Alec Cairncross, Bryan Hopkin, Kenneth Berrill, and Terry Burns' immediate predecessor, Fred Atkinson.

Their timing was exquisite. The economy embarked on a prolonged phase of vigorous growth almost from the moment the letter was published. So far from launching the economy on a self-perpetuating downward spiral, the Budget was a prelude to eight years of uninterrupted growth and left our economic critics bewildered and discredited.[9] It brought public borrowing back on track, and rescued the fiscal side of the MTFS. The one achievement it did not secure was the one that Margaret Thatcher and in particular Alan Walters had seen as its *raison d'être*: the 2 per cent cut in interest rates (to 12 per cent the day after the Budget). This had to be reversed within six months and interest rates were raised a further two percentage points to 16 per cent in October of the same year, to halt a run on the pound.

In the course of time the 1981 Budget came to be seen almost as a political equivalent of the Battle of Britain: the Thatcher Government's finest hour; its

[9] Output touched bottom in the first quarter of 1981; and in the year to the first quarter of 1982, real GDP began its recovery, rising by 1.8 per cent. In the eight years 1981–9 it grew by an average of 3.2 per cent per annum. (The turning point in employment came a little later, in the first quarter of 1983, and in unemployment not until the third quarter of 1986.) The figures are average estimates of GDP at constant factor cost. Back series for quarterly data are taken from the Annual Supplement to *Economic Trends*.

most widely acknowledged success and a turning point in its political fortunes. Hence the myth-making and attempts to claim the credit.

But the truth is beyond dispute. As Geoffrey was later to declare in his 1991 IFS Lecture:

> There has sprung up a myth about the paternity of those difficult Budget judgements, the implication being that the 1981 Budget was somehow 'made in No. 10' against Treasury advice. Those Budget judgements were in fact fashioned by the Chancellor of the Exchequer with the help of Treasury Ministers and on the strength of Treasury advice.

INFLATION STARTS TO FALL

What really mattered, of course, was that the policy was working. The RPI, in its customary way, moved in fits and starts. Its year-on-year increase reached a peak of 21.9 per cent in May 1980. It then fell sharply to 16.9 per cent in July when the VAT increase dropped out of the annual comparison, and then more gradually to 13 per cent in January 1981 and 12 per cent in April. It fluctuated around that level during the rest of 1981 before plunging decisively to 5 per cent by the end of 1982.

Other indicators gave a smoother picture of what was happening. Producer output price inflation peaked at 14 per cent in 1980 and was down to 9.5 per cent in 1981 and 7.7 per cent in 1982. Average earnings moved in line with this, falling from a peak annual increase of over 20 per cent in 1980 to 13 per cent in 1981 and 9.5 per cent in 1982. The battle against inflation was being won.

CHAPTER EIGHT

'THERE IS NO ALTERNATIVE'

Making the Case · High Unemployment For Ever?
Funny Money' & The Civil Service Strike · Fresh Faces
The European Community Budget · The Dawn of the EMS

MAKING THE CASE

The case for the Government's economic policy was frequently summarised (not least, in derisory terms, by its opponents) by the acronym TINA, 'There is no alternative'. The sentence was actually Geoffrey's, but was soon attributed by the media to Margaret Thatcher, for whom it became almost a nickname. And indeed it encapsulated an important truth. I did try, however, to go beyond this and embark on a vigorous attempt to sell the 1981 Budget to a hostile Press and economic establishment.

The first and simplest point I had to make was that we were not perversely ignoring the effects of the recession. We were budgeting for a deficit of £3 billion above that implied by the MTFS: that £3 billion was our best estimate of the recession effect. But over half the threatened overrun was due to other factors, such as increased restructuring expenditure on British Steel and British Leyland. We could allow the recession to alter the time profile of the declining deficit we had set ourselves, but not to abandon the objective altogether, which we would have done if we had taken the easy way out and tried to attribute every aspect of the public expenditure overrun to some indirect effect of the recession.

My most substantial defence of the 1981 Budget was a lecture to a largely hostile audience at the Institute of Fiscal Studies (IFS) on 23 March. Part of what I had to say was inevitably defensive. We had been pursuing a tight financial policy to reduce inflation. But the Budget did not make it any tighter. The tax increases were necessary to pay for the rising share of public spending in GDP which we had not yet succeeded in reversing. Paying higher taxes to finance higher spending could not be considered deflationary, however unpalatable it was to a Conservative Government.

But my principal point was that it was monetary policy which was the main Government influence on domestic demand, and we had no intention of allowing our monetary stance to be such as to lead output to spiral downwards. The main influence of the fiscal stance was on the pattern of domestic demand – in particular, the balance between public spending and private spending – rather than on its level. In a sentence which proved more prophetic than I might have wished, I asked, 'Is there any reason to believe that demand will fall if we replace lower public sector borrowing by higher private sector borrowing?'

The basic reason for being concerned about the Budget balance is the old adage: 'If you borrow too much you are in trouble' – whether you are a private individual, a company or Her Britannic Majesty's Government. At the very least, the higher the debt burden, the higher will be the future tax burden in servicing it. In particular, if debt increases faster than the national income, a debt trap is likely to occur in which the Government has to borrow ever more, simply to service the interest on past debts. In practice governments have nearly always inflated their way out of persistent and excessive deficits; in other words, they have defaulted by the back door.

HIGH UNEMPLOYMENT FOR EVER?

The real academic venom was directed not so much against the Budget as against the notion of tight financial policies to reduce inflation. The House of Commons Treasury Committee was then and subsequently the home of model-based, technically advanced analysis, taking place in an intellectual time warp. The Committee's advisers accepted, superficially and reluctantly, that there might be no long-term trade-off between inflation and unemployment. But they sought to rescue the inflationist argument by attempting to quantify the short-term cost of moving from a higher to a lower rate of inflation in terms of the number of man years of unemployment involved. The Committee argued that to get inflation down by 1 per cent required, over a four-year period, a cumulative loss of output of 4 per cent and the equivalent of a year's additional unemployment for 650,000 people. As such mechanistic do-it-yourself formulae have remained in vogue, especially among the Eastern seaboard academics in the United States, it is perhaps worth repeating the refutation contained in my 1981 IFS speech, in which I employed the *reductio ad absurdum* method which can be particularly illuminating:

> Take first the so-called inflation/unemployment trade-off. If a lasting fall in the rate of inflation of about 1 per cent per annum can be achieved at

a cost of 650,000 man-years' unemployment, presumably this calculation can equally well be reversed and thus provide us with a simple way of curing unemployment if only we are prepared to accept the higher inflation involved. Let us see what this would imply in practice. The Public Expenditure White Paper assumes an average unemployment rate of 2.5 million in 1981/82 and 2.7 million in 1982/83 and 1983/84. This level might imply a cumulative unemployment figure of about 10 million over four years. Suppose that we wished to have no more than a cumulative level of 4 million unemployed over the next four years; that is an average of 1 million. The solution, according to the Treasury Committee's ready-reckoner, is simple. All we need to reduce unemployment by 6 million over this period is 9 per cent higher inflation for ever ... Who can possibly take this sort of nonsense seriously, particularly when we recall that the crucially important feature of the past quarter of a century is the way in which inflation and unemployment, under successive governments, have steadily and inseparably risen?

In the 1960s the UK had an inflation rate of about 3.5 per cent; during the lifetime of the 1974–79 Labour Governments this had risen to an average of 15 per cent per annum. At the same time unemployment rose from a level of under 0.5 million in the early 1960s to an average level of 1.25 million in the period of the last Government. Now we learn that apparently all that was preventing us from avoiding this deterioration in unemployment was a failure to let inflation rise still higher. Does it surprise you that we have got into our present difficulties of high inflation and high unemployment when we have a significant group of people who believe in such magic?

It is claimed by the proponents of these ideas that the calculations are based on the Treasury model. It just goes to show how careful you have to be when handling a model.

None of this is to deny that there is a painful transitional cost in reducing inflation, which can however be reduced by clarity and credibility in macroeconomic policy and by specific measures to improve the working of the labour market. The extent of the cost depends on specific circumstances, and is thus particularly difficult to predict. But the important point is that it is not a lasting cost. The question asked in every recession by gloom-mongers and associated sceptics, not least businessmen, is 'Where will the growth come from?' (During the recession of the early eighties, this tended to take the allied form, 'Where will the jobs come from?', which became a constant refrain. However, in a world of unmet wants, increased productivity implies the capacity for increased output, rather than enforced idleness; so the two questions are much the same.) In my IFS lecture I dutifully gave the Treasury forecasters' answer, which was reduced savings, less destocking and some world economic upturn, which on this occasion turned out to be not too bad a prognosis. But I was provoked to the following outburst:

> Behind the prevailing scepticism lies the usually unspoken assumption that no economic recovery is ever possible other than by a conscious act of demand management by an expansionist government. This view, which is remarkably widely and deeply held, is not merely economic nonsense – implying as it does that the economy in general and the labour market in particular is incapable of adjusting to changing conditions, and that market forces are not merely blunted by the imperfections of the real world: but that they don't operate at all. It is also, and much more obviously, historical nonsense. If neo-Keynesian demand management were the necessary condition of economic growth, we would all still be living in caves and wearing woad, instead of listening to lectures at the centrally heated Charing Cross Hotel. I am, needless to say, making no value judgement here.

'FUNNY MONEY' AND THE CIVIL SERVICE STRIKE

The task of controlling public expenditure was also greatly complicated by the way in which spending was planned, and in particular by the way in which it accounted for inflation. Programmes for a series of years ahead were planned in the prices of the starting year. The jargon term was 'constant' or 'survey' prices, which eventually became known as 'funny money'. The theory was that this enabled spending Departments to plan resources – the number of teachers or doctors employed, or the number of miles of motorway built – without worrying about inflation. In fact 'funny money' meant that public expenditure was bound to get out of control.

The previous Labour Government had itself been forced to introduce a system of 'cash limits' in 1976, although this applied to a limited number of programmes and volume planning continued alongside it. When we came into office we decided to build on this system and switch to planning wholly in cash terms. The change was made and announced on Budget Day, 1981, forcing

Ministers to justify demands for extra cash rather than receiving the money automatically if inflation overran forecasts.

Not everything can be done by methodology. An important element in the increase in public expenditure in the early years was the surge in public sector pay which resulted from the recommendations of the Clegg Commission, which the Government had unwisely committed itself to implementing in full. The total public sector pay bill in 1980/81 rose by a quarter over the previous year, an increase twice as large as in the private sector. The resulting additional volume of taxation placed a burden on the private sector at a time when it was already hard pressed. Moreover, while the Treasury does have control over pay in the Civil Service, its influence over pay in the rest of the public sector, in particular in the nationalised industries and in local government, is almost non-existent, depending on the blunt instrument of overall cash controls and the Government's willingness to hold to them. My own preference was to demonstrate unequivocally our commitment to cash limits by resisting a public sector strike successfully. In August 1979 I remarked in a minute to Geoffrey that 'A successful stand taken at an early stage (the ground will need to be carefully chosen) is essential.' An opportunity did not arise until 1981.

In February of that year the Council of Civil Service Trade Unions, which represented 513,000 Civil Servants, rejected a final pay offer of 7 per cent (which could be accommodated within the official 6 per cent cash limits) and threatened to strike. On 9 March, there was a one-day walkout at airports, social security offices and other Government centres. A campaign of selective strikes continued until the end of July, making it the longest industrial dispute since the General Strike of 1926. The bitterness was undoubtedly exacerbated by our commitment to reduce Civil Service manpower by 100,000 within five years, and a general sense that the Thatcher Government was hostile to the public sector and all who worked in it. The strike's organisers concentrated their efforts on preventing Inland Revenue and VAT staff getting to work, in a deliberate attempt to wreck the public finances. Some £1 billion of tax went temporarily uncollected, costing millions in interest charges; and some VAT payments were lost forever. The costs of the strike were reduced by the commendable response of British business which, at a very difficult time, made a tremendous effort to pay its tax bills to those Inland Revenue offices that remained open, and despite the strike the 1981/82 PSBR turned out better than forecast. The unions eventually settled in July for a pay increase of 7.5 per cent and the promise of an inquiry into the Civil Service system of pay determination.

Christopher Soames, who as Lord President was the Minister responsible for the Civil Service, was very unhappy about the Government's stand and made known his view that the dispute could have been settled for 7.5 per cent several weeks earlier. But even if this was so – and it was impossible to be sure – it ignored the beneficial demonstration effect of the Government's tough stance. My own view, stated in a speech at the time, was that:

> One obvious and major cause of unemployment has been the success – if that is the right word – of some union leaders in pushing wage costs above the level that companies can afford to pay ... There are welcome signs that in private industry the vital lesson is being relearned. It is less clear that the message has got through to the public sector where the illusion still persists that the Government has some inexhaustible crock of gold.

The result of the strike was a victory for economic sanity. The Government was not seriously damaged and many of the strikers lost a great deal of money. But even today Britain's wage inflexibility remains the biggest avoidable cause of unemployment.

FRESH FACES

Despite the lesson of the 1981 Budget and the advent of cash planning the battle for public expenditure control was still far from won. Public spending, unlike most other key aspects of economic policy, is genuinely a joint Cabinet responsibility. There was little chance of real progress so long as the Cabinet, despite incremental changes, was a visible descendant of the Shadow Cabinet Margaret had inherited from Ted Heath.

The first of the promised Cabinet discussions of economic strategy duly took place on 17 June 1981, but it did not go well. Geoffrey presented a paper warning of 'a long and difficult haul' and stressed that it was vital not to ease up on public expenditure. 'Reflation – like import controls and incomes policy – is no answer to the real problems of the economy.' After the meeting at least six Cabinet sceptics made it known that they would resist any further curbs on Government spending. Soon afterwards there was extensive rioting in several of Britain's inner cities, including the Toxteth area of Liverpool, Southall in London, and parts of Manchester. These followed similar disturbances in Brixton in April and provided ammunition to supporters of the 364 economists who asserted that the Government's economic policy threatened the 'social and political stability' of the nation.

The riots unnerved many in the Cabinet; and when Geoffrey presented his annual public expenditure proposals to Cabinet at two meetings on 21 and 23 July, he received an exceptionally hostile response to his call for further curbs. Quintin Hailsham likened Geoffrey to Herbert Hoover, the American President during the onset of the Great Depression. Peter Carrington, Ian Gilmour, Jim Prior, Francis Pym and Peter Walker made less apocalyptic, but no less disparaging noises. Geoffrey's critics even included two members of what was thought to be Margaret's ultraloyalist breakfast group, John Biffen and John Nott.[10] Margaret and Geoffrey found themselves backed only by Keith Joseph, the Industry Secretary, and of course Geoffrey's number two at the Treasury, Leon Brittan, the Chief Secretary.

Margaret closed the discussion with the promise to resume it after the summer recess: but the meeting was a severe jolt for her. The result, as Jim Prior put it, was not 'a fresh examination – it was fresh faces'. Margaret Thatcher reshuffled the Cabinet before Parliament returned in the autumn, and I entered it as Secretary of State for Energy.

THE EUROPEAN COMMUNITY BUDGET

There was one particular public expenditure issue that was still unresolved when I left the Treasury in September 1981. This was the vexed question of Britain's contribution to the Community Budget. My own direct involvement in the issue was less than my official responsibility for the EC Budget would suggest. The size and nature of that Budget was largely determined by the Common Agricultural Policy (CAP) and to a lesser extent by initiatives agreed at Heads of Government level. The role of the Budget Ministers and of the EC Budget Commissioner was confined to the details of non-farm spending programmes and the implementation of guidelines largely agreed at a higher level.

The Labour Government had favoured almost every conceivable increase in non-agricultural spending, as a potential gain for Britain. It did not take me long to stop officials briefing me along these lines. It would have made no sense to be striving to curb Government spending at home while boosting it at EC level. Moreover a very large increase in Community spending was required to

[10] In the early years Margaret held a weekly economic breakfast meeting with a small number of like-minded Cabinet colleagues. The regular attenders were Geoffrey Howe, Keith Joseph, John Biffen and John Nott.

achieve only a small net flow of funds, if any, to Britain. So I was extremely selective in the expenditure increases I supported.

The big issue was the strategic one, handled at Heads of Government level. The Treasury had made a study of the costs and benefits of EC membership. The need to pay more than world prices for food imports was a real cost to the British economy over and above the direct budgetary drain. But we decided to focus on the latter as it was itself a substantial sum and one that was quantifiable without any scope for argument. Had we sought to base our claim on the overall cost, we might have got bogged down in interminable controversies over what world prices would have been in the absence of the CAP. The issue was difficult enough without that.

The budgetary drain arose because Britain received only a tenth of Community agricultural expenditure, which accounted for nearly two thirds of its total Budget, while contributing a fifth of the Community's tax revenue. Our high level of agricultural imports and extensive trade with the rest of the world meant that our net contribution to the Community Budget was far higher than our economic performance warranted. Britain, although at that time seventh in terms of GDP per head, was the largest net contributor to the Community Budget. Indeed, the UK and Germany were the only net contributors: all the others were net recipients.

The European Commission was reluctant to admit the cost of our net contribution even though it was readily calculable; but the Treasury estimated that, without adjustment, it would run at around £1 billion in 1980 which, as I remarked to the House of Commons, was 'manifestly and massively inequitable'. The Foreign Office, however, was unhelpful and defeatist. Peter Carrington, the Foreign Secretary, went so far as to tell the French that 'the net contribution problem was ultimately of our own making in the sense that we were not running our economy properly'. Fortunately, it was an issue on which Downing Street, rather than the Foreign Office, led.

Armed with Treasury briefing, Margaret launched her unforgettable campaign to 'get our money back'. At a memorable European Summit in Dublin at the end of November 1979, she rightly rejected an offer of only £350 million despite appeasing advice from the Foreign Office. Her efforts were made all the harder by the close relationship between the French President Giscard d'Estaing and the German Chancellor Helmut Schmidt; but the root of the problem was that, to the extent that the UK contributed less, others would have to contribute more, and behind the pious protestations that we were being un-Communautaire it was this they found unpalatable.

It appeared at first as if Paris and Bonn thought we were complaining about the effect on the balance of payments, which was indeed adverse. But this was clearly not the case at a time of an almost embarrassingly strong pound. Once they grasped the budgetary nature of our complaint, the French haughtily accused us of the infamous crime of seeking a *juste retour* from the Community instead of being content with the profounder benefits of membership.

My own involvement in the issue arose mainly from the Treasury's role in briefing the Prime Minister rather than my specific job as, in Community terms, the UK's Budget Minister. I had minuted Geoffrey early on that 'sooner or later we have to be prepared to be bloody-minded (that is Gaullist) in the pursuit of our objective, and even before that to let it leak out both to our partners and to Parliament that we are prepared to be bloody-minded.'

It soon became clear the only serious threat we could make was to withhold our contributions to the Community Budget altogether. Under the joint guidance of the Treasury and the Law Officers, a Bill was prepared on a contingency basis to provide the legal backing for such a move and the modalities that would be employed. In the event, while we discreetly let it be known that the option of withholding was being considered, the Bill was never published, let alone introduced.

A considerable advance on the Dublin offer was secured at meetings in Luxembourg and Brussels in the spring of 1980, where rebates were negotiated for 1980 and 1981 worth £1,570 million in all. This success was due entirely to the obstinacy of Margaret Thatcher who was reluctant to accept even this improved offer, although she did in the end. She was right in thinking that this agreement, which went only up to the end of 1981, did not mark the end of the matter. A third rebate of £476 million for 1982 was later secured, accompanied by a Community commitment to find a permanent solution. This was finally concluded at the Community Summit in Fontainebleau in June 1984, where Britain won a £600 million rebate for that year plus an automatic formula for refunds on subsequent years. If Margaret's bloody-mindedness was the essential ingredient, the successful outcome owed a good deal to the skill of the lean and cerebral Michael Butler, Britain's Ambassador to the Community, whose understanding of the nuts and bolts of Community law and practice was as impressive as his unflagging zeal in carrying out his remit.

There was, however, a negative aspect to Margaret's triumph. Although the quality improved later on, the poor advice given by the Foreign Office over the Community Budget in 1979 and 1980 reinforced Margaret Thatcher's instinctive distrust of that Department; and the wetness of the diplomatic service became a perpetual theme in her thinking. Moreover the outcome of the Budget negotiations persuaded her that it always paid to be bloody-minded in dealings with the Community. This was to prove increasingly counterproductive in practice. Nor did it help when I sought to interest her in sterling's membership of the Exchange Rate Mechanism (ERM) of the European Monetary System (EMS).

THE DAWN OF THE EMS

By the summer of 1981, I had become persuaded of the case for making the discipline of the ERM, rather than targets for domestic monetary aggregates, the prime determinant of monetary policy and hence of the conduct of the battle against inflation. In Opposition I had written in support of the idea of Britain's full EMS membership, but with a 6 per cent margin, in place of the normal 2.25 per cent. This was a concession which Italy had negotiated at the start in 1979 and which both Spain and Britain were to obtain when they eventually joined the EMS in 1989 and 1990 respectively. But when I joined the Government in 1979, inflation was rising so fast that I felt that the best bet for the time being was to concentrate on domestic monetary policy and leave sterling to market forces.

But two years later, with inflation on the way down, I had changed my mind. On 15 June 1981, I sent Geoffrey a long note, arguing that 'we should take advantage of our forthcoming presidency [in the second half of 1981] to join the EMS.' It was a conclusion I had reached with some misgivings. As I wrote:

> This is in many ways a second best course. Financial discipline is essential for the conquest of inflation; and there are two forms which financial discipline can take. It can be a self-imposed explicit monetary discipline, or a partly externally imposed exchange rate discipline ... I have no doubt that ideally a straightforward monetary discipline is superior. But we are now getting into that phase, which will become increasingly evident as the election approaches, when the political pressures for relaxation of monetary discipline will start to mount. This raises the question of whether, in practice, we may not be able to enforce and maintain a greater degree of effective financial discipline if we were to embrace the exchange rate discipline, for all its imperfections. This is particularly apposite given that those of our colleagues who are most likely

> to be pressing for relaxation of monetary discipline, are those who are keenest on the UK joining the EMS. In other words, we turn their sword against them. Essentially what this would mean is tying the pound to the German Mark ... You will not be surprised to know that I have very mixed feelings about the course I have sketched out. At the end of the day the argument rests on political judgement.

The colleagues I had in mind were the Cabinet sceptics who even before the fateful July Cabinet meeting had made known their opposition to further public spending curbs and who were equally opposed to a firm monetary policy.

My advice was rejected on a number of grounds. It was argued that stability against the dollar was more important to British industry than stability against European currencies, an objection the force of which was somewhat weakened by the fact that stability against the dollar was not on offer; and that the prevailing sterling exchange rate against the Deutschmark was in any case too high a rate at which to join. More fundamentally, at that time Geoffrey, as well as Margaret, was still committed to the idea of an exchange rate determined by the free play of market forces. (While I became convinced of the merits of the ERM on hard-headed politico-economic grounds, Geoffrey's conversion derived initially from his Europeanism.)

Meanwhile, my own conviction of the case for the ERM was becoming steadily firmer. In the last memorandum I wrote to Geoffrey as Financial Secretary, on 14 September 1981, the day I joined the Cabinet as Energy Secretary, I pointed out that we were receiving 'increasing evidence of the weakness of £M3 as a reliable proxy for underlying monetary conditions, without any greater confidence being able to be attached to any of the other monetary aggregates. This clearly strengthens the case for moving over to an exchange rate discipline.' I left before I got a reply. But it was perhaps fitting that I should have joined the Cabinet secure in the same conviction that carried me out of it just over eight years later.

The issue did not come to a head until well after I returned to the Treasury as Chancellor in June 1983. There was an important Prime Ministerial meeting on the EMS in the Cabinet Room of Number 10 on 22 January 1982, while I was at the Department of Energy, although I did not come to hear of it until some time afterwards. Geoffrey at that time was not in favour of joining – indeed, he became fully convinced of the case for membership only after he became Foreign Secretary a year and a half later. At the 1982 meeting, he could see the attraction but was worried that the ERM might conflict with domestic monetary policy.

He also sympathised with industry's view that the prevailing exchange rate (of around DM4.30) was too high a level at which to join. His most percipient objection (from the viewpoint of the committed European he always was) was that people might be turned off the whole European Community ideal if the ERM were, rightly or wrongly, held responsible for high British interest rates – which indeed happened after Britain eventually joined in 1990.

The principal supporter of the ERM at the time was the Governor of the Bank of England, Gordon Richardson. He correctly pointed out that the evolution of monetary policy under the Thatcher Government already indicated the need for a clearer role for the exchange rate, for which the ERM provided the right – and indeed the only practicable – framework. He was also afraid that the pound would depreciate outside the system. Unfortunately the post-Richardson Bank wavered in subsequent years, and at some key moments retreated into muttering that the timing was wrong.

Margaret summed up along lines that were to become increasingly familiar. She was not convinced of the advantages of the EMS and was worried about the loss of 'freedom to manoeuvre'. She conceded that the case would be stronger once British inflation and interest rates were closer to German levels (but when they were she found other objections). She concluded that the Government should maintain the existing position of being (supposedly) ready to join 'when the time is ripe'.

PART TWO

CABINET MINISTER

CHAPTER NINE

ON BECOMING A SECRETARY OF STATE

Member of Cabinet · Life as a Minister · Cabinet Meetings
The Falklands Cabinets · The Thatcher Style · The Abuse of Information
Consent of the Victims · The Department of Energy

MEMBER OF CABINET

The most important event, for me, of my time as Financial Secretary had been my marriage to Thérèse (with whom I had been living since the beginning of 1979) in October 1980, three months after my divorce from Vanessa whom I had married in 1955. Shortly afterwards Thérèse became pregnant and asked me if I would like to be present at the baby's birth. This unexpected suggestion took me by surprise, being of a generation for whom this was not customary, but I readily assented. I had not witnessed the birth of any of my five previous surviving children, and this was in all probability my last chance of an exciting new experience.

However, as the due date approached, it was clear that there was a real risk that when the baby arrived I would be away at Strasbourg addressing the European Parliament in my capacity as President of the Budget Council (the UK held the Community Presidency at that time). Thérèse's gynaecologist kindly solved this dilemma by offering to induce the birth a few days early. Accordingly on 10 September 1981, with me in rapt – and I hope helpful – attendance, Emily was born. Thérèse was characteristically brave throughout the process.

In the event, I never did get to make my carefully prepared speech to the European Parliament. For four days after Emily was born, on 14 September, Margaret decided to purge the Cabinet of most of the 'wet' opponents of her economic policies, having already signalled her intentions by dismissing in January 1981 Norman St John Stevas, the Leader of the Commons, whose wit tended to get the better of his discretion, and effectively demoting the lugubrious Francis Pym from Defence Secretary to Leader of the Commons in his place. Out went the amiable Secretary of State for Education, Mark

Carlisle, the sour number two at the Foreign and Commonwealth Office, Ian Gilmour (with the Foreign Secretary, Peter Carrington, in the Lords, Margaret had considered it necessary for the FCO to have a Cabinet Minister in the Commons as well), and the old-guard Leader of the House of Lords, Christopher Soames. Peter Thorneycroft, another distinguished representative of the old guard, was relieved of the Party Chairmanship: he had shortly before admitted to 'rising damp' and had written to Margaret to urge a change of economic course.

Margaret clearly considered Carlisle and Gilmour politically incapable of causing trouble on the backbenches, and the more heavyweight Soames and Thorneycroft constitutionally incapable of doing so as members of the House of Lords. Those wets whom she feared might cause trouble on the backbenches – notably Peter Walker at Agriculture, Michael Heseltine, only semi-wet anyway, at Environment, and the demoted Francis Pym she left in place; although Jim Prior was moved from Employment Secretary to the backwater of Northern Ireland Secretary. The affable but short-fused Heathite squire, Prior, made the mistake, when rumours of the impending move reached his ears, of letting the *Observer* know that he would sooner resign from the Government than be moved from his present post. When Margaret called his bluff and he accepted the Northern Ireland job, the episode effectively destroyed his standing as a significant political force.

The moral I drew from this was that resignation threats should not be lightly made, and if they are made, they should be made in private and must be in earnest. A threat withdrawn in the face of Prime Ministerial resolution fatally undermines the Minister concerned. Moreover, a serious resignation threat should be made with the probability in mind that it will have to be implemented and the Minister concerned out of office for a long time, if not for ever. If this personal fate is accepted, a resigning Minister can occasionally hope that his resignation will have some long-term effect. It is also probably salutary for Prime Ministers to be reminded from time to time that, while Cabinet colleagues may not be the equals that constitutional mythology makes out, they cannot be taken for granted either.

The four newcomers in 1981 were Janet Young as Leader of the Lords, Norman Tebbit as Employment Secretary, Cecil Parkinson as Party Chairman, in the Cabinet as Paymaster General, and myself as Energy Secretary, this last post made vacant by the move of David Howell to Transport Secretary as part of a long sequence of changes arising from the departure of Mark Carlisle.

Janet, an old friend of Margaret's, likeable, brisk, with a distinguished career in local government behind her, was the only woman Margaret ever appointed to Cabinet. She never really made her mark and was dropped from Cabinet less than two years later. Norman Tebbit, Cecil Parkinson and myself, all committed Thatcherites, despite our very different characters, were to play larger and longer roles in the Thatcher Government.

Thus it was that in September 1981, two years and four months after taking office as Prime Minister, Margaret Thatcher at last secured a Cabinet with a Thatcherite majority. And after just over seven years in the House of Commons, I was a member of that Cabinet. It was a tremendous stroke of luck, and an equal privilege. Margaret herself very soon remarked – I think it was at the second Cabinet meeting after the reshuffle, but it may even have been the first – how much more agreeable the discussions were than they had been before the reshuffle.

Certainly, despite the Government's unpopularity, the spirit in Cabinet when I first joined it was excellent. Among most of us then was a clear sense of being bound together in a common endeavour, in which we believed, and of mutual trust. Those who had doubts concealed them. And Margaret herself, although she led from the front – that was always her style, and nothing wrong with that – had by that time developed neither the delusion of self-sufficiency nor the distrust of any colleague who was not a yes-man which were in time to make her so difficult and to contribute so much to her downfall.

LIFE AS A MINISTER

Becoming a member of the Cabinet is in some ways like joining the first eleven (though the actual numbers were precisely twice that). But the most important difference from being a Minister outside the Cabinet is that of having one's own Department to run and the responsibility for taking the initiatives and solving the problems that fall within its sphere. Since I enjoy taking decisions, it was a great pleasure for me to have my own show to run, even though any major decision clearly required the endorsement of my Cabinet colleagues in general and of the Prime Minister in particular.

Thanks in particular to the brilliant *Yes, Minister* series of television programmes, most people are aware that British Ministers are treated with great servility to their face, and looked after hand and foot while on duty, but are also more overworked than their counterparts in most other countries. Moreover, all official support is suspended once a Minister is deemed to be engaged on private

– or heaven forbid – party political work. Departments may stretch a point and allow a Minister's driver to pick him up after a private dinner in London, so that he can come home to his boxes more quickly; but this indulgence does not apply in his constituency. He will have a driver and a private secretary to accompany him if he opens a factory; but if his next engagement is a speech to his local party, he will have to make his own transport arrangements.

A Cabinet Minister's workload is in any case generally much heavier than that of lesser Ministers. This is a burden with which some new Cabinet members at first find it difficult to cope. The danger then is that they solve the problem by becoming the creature of their officials. This danger did not arise in my case, since my workload as Energy Secretary was no greater than it had been as Financial Secretary, who probably carries the heaviest workload of any Minister outside the Cabinet. It is also true that being Energy Secretary (or so it seemed to me in retrospect after I became Chancellor) is only a part-time job.

The demands made by the various Cabinet posts vary enormously. Apart from the Premiership itself, which is *sui generis* – carrying as it does not only awesome responsibility but a workload that varies enormously according to the way in which the incumbent chooses to exercise that responsibility – the heaviest load and toughest job is generally agreed to be that of Chancellor. That was certainly the view of Jim Callaghan, who held all three great offices of State – Chancellor, Home Secretary and Foreign Secretary – before becoming Prime Minister: I remember him telling me as much when we were chatting one sparkling November morning, waiting to take up our places on the politicians' side of the Cenotaph on Armistice Day early on in my time as Chancellor. The best job, short of Prime Minister, was in his view Foreign Secretary: 'It's a doddle' he told me, advising me to make that my ambition.

CABINET MEETINGS

The least important aspect of Cabinet membership, certainly in Margaret Thatcher's time, were the Cabinet meetings themselves. The imprimatur of Cabinet was taken seriously, and there were occasional Cabinet meetings that really mattered, such as those that concluded the annual public expenditure round. But in general and for good reason, key decisions were taken in smaller groups – either the formal Cabinet Committees, of which the most important (such as the Overseas and Defence Committee and the two main economic policy Committees, Economic Strategy, which seldom met, and Economic Affairs, which met a great deal) were, like the Cabinet itself, chaired by the

Prime Minister; or at still smaller informal meetings of Ministers which she would usually hold in her study upstairs. The Cabinet's customary role was to rubber stamp decisions that had already been taken, to keep all colleagues reasonably informed about what was going on, and to provide a forum for general political discussion if time permitted.

Thus, as Chancellor, I used to look forward to Cabinet meetings as the most restful and relaxing event of the week. This was all the more so since, by long tradition, Cabinet starts with a discussion of parliamentary affairs, initiated by the Leader of the House of Commons, followed by a discussion of Foreign Affairs, led by the Foreign Secretary. There then follows whatever specific items may be on the agenda for discussion. Towards the end of her long stint as Prime Minister, Margaret introduced a third regular item, Home Affairs, in which any colleague who had any important information to impart on the home front was expected to launch forth. But though the importance of the subject would have fully justified a weekly report by the Chancellor under the heading Economic Affairs, I was quite content to leave it to others to propose this break with tradition, which happily none of them did.

Perhaps they assumed that any Chancellor's report would be as uninformative as the Foreign Secretary's routine dissertation on foreign affairs, which could be delivered with elegance and wit, yet seldom revealed anything that was not already well known to the attentive newspaper reader. Indeed, during Geoffrey Howe's time, unkind colleagues would take to listening to the news bulletin just before Cabinet met, and embarrassing him by asking for his assessment of some reported new development overseas on which he had not had time to be briefed, not even as to whether the development had in fact occurred.

A normal Cabinet meeting has no chance of becoming a grave forum of statesmanlike debate. Twenty-two people attending a two-and-a-half hour meeting can speak for just over six and a half minutes each on average. If there are three items of business – and there are usually far more – the ration of time just exceeds two minutes, if everyone is determined to have his say. Small wonder then that most Ministers keep silent on most issues or confine themselves to brief but pointed questions or observations.

Given the nature of Cabinet meetings, anyone who was inclined to talk too much would need to have something interesting to say if he was not to forfeit the sympathy of his colleagues and the patience of the Prime Minister. That exceptionally nice man, Patrick Jenkin, was one who fell into this trap. As Energy Secretary, and a new and junior member of Cabinet, I usually succeeded in restraining my natural inclination to air my views; subsequently, as Chancellor, I naturally took a fuller part in Cabinet discussions, but still less than I did at other meetings at which decisions were actually taken.

THE FALKLANDS CABINETS

The limitation of general discussion at Cabinet meetings became clear during the Falklands War in the spring and early summer of 1982, when Margaret introduced the practice of holding a second weekly Cabinet meeting in addition to the normal Thursday one. The conflict was, of course, the dominant event of 1982, and wholly preoccupied all our thinking while it lasted. Throughout the critical weeks of May and June, there was a full Cabinet meeting every Tuesday after the daily War Cabinet. The Chiefs of Staff were present and, although sensitive military matters were not discussed, it was possible always to gauge the balance of the conflict. It was at the special Tuesday Cabinet meetings that we discussed the various peace proposals put forward by the American Secretary of State, Al Haig, and the United Nations Secretary General, Javier Perez de Cuellar, during the weeks before the landings at San Carlos Bay.

I was convinced from a very early stage in the conflict that the various diplomatic manoeuvrings would amount to nothing and that it would be necessary to retake the islands by force, and said as much. This view may not have been universally shared. In any event, had the Galtieri junta accepted the British proposal of 20 May to place the islands under the indefinite jurisdiction of the United Nations, it is possible that the recall of the Task Force would have commanded a majority in Cabinet. Very foolishly it did not do so. As a result, there was no dissension within Cabinet throughout the war, even if one or two members may have nursed private doubts.

THE THATCHER STYLE

Whether before Cabinet or the more effective smaller meetings, Margaret, who appeared to need only four hours' sleep a night, always did her homework on the subjects for discussion, almost as if she were about to sit an examination. In general this was a desirable characteristic, but it could lead to time-wasting attempts to show off her mastery of detail, at the expense of the main business in hand.

Some of the time saved through her economy of sleep was devoted to what was frequently her first appointment of the day: the visit of her hairdresser. She was convinced that her authority – in a world in which a woman's appearance is always a subject of comment, a man's only occasionally – would be diminished if she were not impeccably turned out at all times. She was probably right – and certainly this was one aspect of her with which the great mass of women voters could readily identify, however much it may have been derided in NW1.

Another and most attractive aspect of her femininity was the instant note (sometimes accompanied by flowers) sent to Thérèse when she was ill or had any problems. These notes were topped and tailed by Margaret in the early days, and written completely by hand when I became Chancellor and we were her next-door neighbours.

The practice of taking important decisions in smaller groups and not in Cabinet itself can clearly be taken too far, particularly if the groups are too small; but it makes obvious sense. Not only is twenty-two an unwieldy number for a good discussion, but Ministers whose interests lie elsewhere are unlikely to have informed themselves sufficiently to make a worthwhile contribution. Moreover, a Cabinet meeting is nowadays a highly visible and almost public affair. The Press and TV all know when Ministers arrive for it, and when they leave. Any unusually prolonged discussion thus leads inevitably to stories of splits, dissension and disarray, with attempts (occasionally assisted by the participants themselves) to identify who stood where. Thus meetings of Cabinet Committees or *ad hoc* groups, at times that are neither regular nor announced, with a membership that was not then revealed – indeed their very existence used not to be officially admitted – are a more effective way to conduct business. (These special committees alternate between being called 'MISC' and 'GEN' at each change of Prime Minister.)

I have no doubt, however, that the best arrangement is for the Prime Minister of the day to develop an Inner Cabinet, which would be joined by appropriate additional participants to discuss specific issues. Key issues should initially be discussed by the Inner Cabinet alone. This is something that Margaret at one point, as I shall record later, came very near to doing, but never in fact did.

THE ABUSE OF INFORMATION

Instead she sought to fragment any dissident voices. What had started off as a justified attempt to make effective decisions in small and informal groups degenerated into increasingly complex attempts to divide and rule. More and more, decisions were effectively taken in very small groups in which she had hand-picked the balance of membership to ensure the outcome she sought. Her conduct of meetings also became increasingly authoritarian. Some of her predecessors, such as Harold Macmillan, would allow other colleagues to have their say before summing up and stating a conclusion. Margaret on the other hand, when there was an issue on which she had already formed a firm view, would start with an unashamedly tendentious introduction of her own, before inviting the responsible and sometimes cowed Minister to have his say. Thus what began as a method for the most expedient conduct of business ended as a means of getting her own way irrespective of the merits or political costs.

This was not her only mode. In some ways far more irritating was her behaviour when her strongly held general views were not sufficient to reach a conclusion on difficult and complex detailed issues. She could then become unbelievably discursive, sounding off at random on various aspects of the matter, and generally going round in circles getting nowhere, reaching agreement only on the time and date of the next meeting. Broadcasting and education (where, however, she was not wholly to blame) were two cases in point. To busy Ministers seeking to get matters decided this was the most frustrating of all. Margaret, of course, was equally busy; but, presumably, being the star turn at these meetings was compensation enough. Eventually, after I became Chancellor, I took to offering to chair meetings of the key Ministers involved, in between her meetings, as the only way of making progress – I did this, with her full knowledge and consent, both over the Government's proposals for the development of broadcasting and over the year-long review of the health service.

CONSENT OF THE VICTIMS

Why did the colleagues allow her to govern in the way she did? While spinelessness or careerism may be adequate explanation in the case of some, it will not do for all. And belief in her infallibility was even more narrowly shared. Of course all Prime Ministers are in a position of great power, so long as they can retain the office; and she was a particularly formidable Prime Minister who, over the years – she became, after all, the longest-serving Prime Minister this century – had acquired considerable experience.

But beyond this, her method of Cabinet Government was accepted because in many ways it was highly convenient to her colleagues. Most Cabinet Ministers, particularly after a longish period in government, tend to be preoccupied with fighting their own battles and pursuing the issues that matter within their own bailiwick, and lose interest in the wider picture. Most of the time it is comforting for them to feel that all they need to do is strike a deal with the Prime Minister, and not have to bother overmuch about persuading their other colleagues. (And if they are fighting the Prime Minister on an issue that means a great deal to them, all the more reason to concentrate on that.) It was noticeable that, towards the end, those colleagues who most bemoaned the lack of collective discussion of issues outside their own departmental field were busy making private bilateral deals with Margaret over issues within their own departmental responsibility.

Finally, if less important, was the fact that she was in practice at her best in bilaterals and other small gatherings. The larger the numbers, the greater her tendency to play to the gallery, either showing off her own knowledge on the subject or rounding, in a profoundly embarrassing way, on some hapless colleague whom she felt either bullyable by nature or objectively in a weak position at a particular time. Geoffrey Howe was a favourite victim.

Different Prime Ministers have different personal characteristics. But *mutatis mutandis*, I suspect that any Prime Minister so long in office is likely to develop much along the lines she did – which, to repeat, was far from inconvenient to individual Ministers most of the time – unless they have the wisdom to prevent it by the creation of a genuine Inner Cabinet.

THE DEPARTMENT OF ENERGY

By 1981 none of this pathology was apparent. Meanwhile, newly installed as Energy Secretary, my main problem, with which fortunately I had enough adrenalin to cope, was that for my first six months in Cabinet Emily did not allow me a single night's uninterrupted sleep.

The Department of Energy could more aptly be described as the Department of Nationalised Industries. Within its purview lay three of the great industries nationalised by the Labour Governments of 1945 to 1951 – coal, gas and electricity – and the British National Oil Corporation (BNOC), created by Attlee's successors of the 1970s. All this meant that energy was also an important economic department, and so much more congenial to me than, say, the Department of Health and Social Security would have been. In fact, energy issues had become dangerously remote from economic policy. The nationalised industries then accounted for over a tenth of national output and over a sixth of total UK fixed investment. Characterised by weak management and strong unions, and untainted by market forces, they epitomised in an extreme form the problems of the British economy. Yet no government had found a satisfactory means of dealing with them.

Harold Wilson and Jim Callaghan had used the Department of Energy for the purpose of isolating its Secretary of State, the increasingly left wing Tony Benn. Callaghan distrusted Benn so deeply that he denied him access to virtually all sensitive Cabinet papers. This inevitably starved Benn's officials of influence as well and had completely destroyed the Department's morale.

Within less than two years of the Conservatives' return to office, morale, which had begun to improve with the departure of Benn and the restoration of normal relations with Number 10, was once again badly bruised. This time the cause was the débâcle of February 1981, when Margaret overruled David Howell, whom she had appointed Energy Secretary when the Government was first formed in 1979, and decided on a quick but abject surrender to the National Union of Mineworkers (NUM) over pit closures rather than face a confrontation which she felt the NUM were bound to win.

While my new officials professed to be glad to see me there, those who expected their Secretary of State to embark vigorously on the promotion of an energy policy were disappointed, as I did not believe in any such animal. I saw myself, quite simply, as having three main tasks: to bring to a successful conclusion the long struggle with the miners' union that had begun so disastrously in the last days of the Heath Government and, following February's climbdown, was now likely to be exacerbated by the growing power of the militant would-be revolutionary Arthur Scargill; to pursue Britain's interests in the international politics of oil; and privatisation, which represented a continuation of work on which I had been deeply involved in the Treasury and was to continue as Chancellor.

Meanwhile, before getting the right policies and priorities in place, and securing the official support I required, there was one other matter which had to be dealt with. On becoming Energy Secretary I inherited a fine large room on the second floor (the traditional ministerial floor throughout Whitehall) of Thames House on Millbank, overlooking the river. But the furniture – which had been chosen by Tony Benn and left unchanged by David Howell – was an appalling example of the airport lounge school of decor. I recall with particular displeasure the armless tubular steel easy chairs, covered in an exceptionally hairy off-white fabric. I lost no time in replacing the lot – and for good measure put in pride of place on one of the walls the large eighteenth-century portrait of Henry Pelham which I had had in my room at the Treasury. I needed an environment in which I could work without being assaulted by ugliness on all sides. And there was no harm, either, in letting the Department know right from the start that they had not merely a new Secretary of State, but a new broom.

CHAPTER TEN

COAL

The Initial Retreat · Preparing for Conflict · Mobilising Against Scargill
Increasing Endurance · The Great Head-hunt · A Famous Victory

THE INITIAL RETREAT

Margaret Thatcher's brief to me when she appointed me Energy Secretary in September 1981 was succinct. 'Nigel,' she said, 'we mustn't have a coal strike.' At the forefront of her mind was the half-truth, firmly believed in by the NUM, the media and most Conservative MPs, that it was the miners who had brought down the last Conservative Government in 1974; and the débâcle of the previous February had scarred her quite badly.

It was indeed a humiliating episode. David Howell had recognised from the start that the massive losses being incurred by the National Coal Board could be stemmed only by the closure of unprofitable pits. He had hoped to make this acceptable to the miners by offering 'social' grants and investment in new coalfields; and the 1980 Coal Industry Act, which guaranteed the Coal Board some £600 million a year in new investment for three years, was the centrepiece of this strategy.

But the strategy started to fall apart almost from the moment the Act was on the statute-book. As the recession bit, the demand for coal declined, but the output-obsessed Coal Board carried on producing as if nothing had happened. The result was a mountain of unsold coal, which was later to prove a blessing, but which at the time presented the Coal Board with a huge additional financing cost.

Throughout the Autumn of 1980 the Coal Board chairman, Derek Ezra, had warned David Howell that the market for coal had collapsed, and that unless still more public money was forthcoming, pit closures would be inescapable. David duly conveyed this to Margaret and other interested colleagues, and Ezra undertook to broach the matter with the NUM, promising David that he would in no circumstances mention a specific number of pits to be closed.

Yet no sooner had the meeting between the Coal Board and the mining unions ended on 10 February 1981, than a 'hit list' of plans to close between twenty and fifty pits was in the public domain. There were strong suspicions within the Department that someone in the upper echelons of the Coal Board had colluded with the NUM in revealing the number of pits to be closed. Arthur Scargill, then leader of the Yorkshire area NUM, had warned the meeting that closures 'could lead to one thing only – confrontation'. The wily Joe Gormley, then President of the NUM, had used the pressure from his left to threaten a national ballot on strike action.

Unofficial strikes soon started in the South Wales and Kent coalfields, the areas likely to be most affected, and all the signs were that a strike would be solid. John Moore – my parliamentary Under-Secretary of State and the minister responsible for coal – was keen to make a fight of it. David was unsure. Margaret was not keen at all. She, rightly, felt that coal stocks at the power stations were insufficient to be sure of winning a prolonged strike, and promptly if less than heroically withdrew her support for the closure plans. Willie Whitelaw, Peter Carrington and especially Jim Prior, who fancied himself in touch with trade union thinking, were further worried that a coal dispute would spread to steel and the railways, the coal, steel and railway unions having announced the renewal of the old so-called 'Triple Alliance' to resist retrenchment in any one of the three nationalised industries with strikes in the others.

The climbdown was a severe embarrassment to Energy Ministers and officials. They had all privately assured the Coal Board, the NUM and the Press that the Government would resist a strike. The only redeeming feature of the decision to back down was the speed with which it was taken. The episode was over within a week of the 'hit list' leak, and before the media had really got their teeth into the story, but the surrender terms were even worse than they need have been. The Government undertook not only to relax the NCB's borrowing limits still further in order to keep the unprofitable pits open; but also to make the nationalised steel and electricity industries abandon their practice of buying a quantity of cheaper imported coal and rely exclusively on British coal instead. It was, to all intents and purposes, the formula that had been advocated by Arthur Scargill at the February meeting with the Coal Board, when he called for a 'complete ban on imports and for [further] subsidisation of home coal production.' It was the first time the Thatcher Government had been defeated by militant trade union power.

As Energy Secretary, I was determined that, if I had anything to do with it, it would never happen again.

This was an issue that had begun to preoccupy me well before Margaret appointed me to the job. I became convinced that the problems of the coal industry could not be resolved without the decisive defeat of the militant arm of the NUM, even if that meant facing up to a strike, for which we would need to be properly prepared. In April 1981, while still Financial Secretary, I minuted Geoffrey Howe:

> Our original aim was to build a successful, profitable coal industry independent of government subsidies; to de-monopolise it and ultimately open it to private enterprise ... Then the events of February 1981 showed beyond any reasonable doubt we will make no progress towards our aim until we deal with the problem of monopoly union power.

This conclusion was not immediately drawn elsewhere. In the winter of 1980–81 the Prime Minister invited the Central Policy Review Staff (CPRS), popularly known as the think-tank, then newly headed by an Imperial Chemical Industries (lCI) director on secondment, Robin Ibbs, to analyse the nationalised industries. Its report was delivered at the end of July 1981. In the case of coal it advised a continuation of the failed policy of offering new investment in return for pit closures. At the Treasury I read the paper with a mounting sense of disbelief. It was already apparent that Joe Gormley would be succeeded as miners' leader by Arthur Scargill. 'The problem is essentially a political one, centring around industrial relations in general and outmanoeuvring Arthur Scargill in particular ... [Yet] all that is really being claimed is that if large quantities of additional public money are poured into the industry this might persuade the NUM to agree more readily to pit closures in the long run,' I wrote to Geoffrey Howe after reading it. Within a few weeks I was charged with the responsibility for dealing with this problem.

PREPARING FOR CONFLICT

On John Moore's advice, the first pit I visited was in Scargill's heartland rather than my own territory of Leicestershire. I chose Kellingley in North Yorkshire, where I went underground in July 1982, and I did not visit the Leicestershire coalfield until I went to Bagworth colliery in September. These occasions were rather like a State visit. Accompanied by two of my officials, I was met at Doncaster station by the station master, sporting a bowler hat, who ushered us towards a motorcade of Stalinist dimensions, compered by the area manager, which conveyed us to a local hotel for a slap-up dinner with the pit managers. After dinner, and fortified by a large quantity of alcohol, they gave me their views of the industry's problems, notably Arthur Scargill, and how the Government had mishandled things. Next morning the motorised cavalcade sped us to Kellingley colliery, where I donned a miner's overalls and helmet and descended the shaft in the company of the pit deputies and overseers.

A miner's job is dirty, difficult and dangerous; but it has its attractive side, too. For one thing, detailed supervision is impossible underground, and the teams of miners working the seam enjoy a degree of independence unknown in any factory job. Miners are also – or were then – one of the last bastions of old-world courtesy. Whenever we came across a group of resting miners huddled in a corner of the long tunnel leading to the coal face we were wished a cordial and totally non-deferential 'good morning'. And a miner feels he is doing a real man's job – often reinforcing his macho image of himself by choosing to work semi-naked and in some cases even spurning the eye-protection that modern coal-cutting machinery, which sends splinters of coal flying in all directions, clearly requires.

I was then photographed emerging from the pit with a suitably blackened face. There followed a meeting with the local representative of the NUM, who said that investment in the pit was inadequate, that wages were too low and that management disregarded safety in pursuit of productivity. These lamentations were followed by an ample lunch, after which we boarded the train back to London, and I was promised a traditional miner's lamp (which turned out to be the slightly superior version carried by pit foremen as a badge of office) as a memento of my visit. It was quite a show, designed to persuade me that Kellingley was run by honest people doing a difficult job in trying circumstances, and that it was therefore a deserving home for public money.

It was on that visit to Kellingley that I first met Michael Eaton, who was then the Coal Board's North Yorkshire area manager. His blunt common sense and articulacy impressed me, and I was not surprised that he was subsequently plucked from North Yorkshire to play a key role on the presentational side during the coal strike of 1984–85. Unfortunately he and Ian MacGregor did not hit it off and the arrangement was not a success.

Meanwhile, on the coal front, I subordinated almost everything to the overriding need to prepare for and win a strike. It was not that I was seeking one. But it was clear that Arthur Scargill was, and I was determined that he should lose it when it came.

The débâcle of February 1981 left massive financial and managerial problems which could not be resolved without his defeat. When I became Energy Secretary, the Coal Board had the biggest External Financing Limit (EFL) – the amount of public money annually injected in loans and grants combined – of any nationalised industry. At £1,117 million, it was more than the EFLs for British Steel and British Telecom combined. Another £800 million was pledged to a huge programme of investment in new pits. Total subsidies to the industry, in the form of social, operating and deficit grants amounted to £550 million a year – or some £1.5 million a day, or £5 for every tonne of deep-mined coal or £35 a week for every member of the Coal Board's workforce. The February setback had forestalled any immediate hope of stemming the financial haemorrhage. Instead of trading new investment for old pit closures, as planned by David Howell, the Government was now committed to subsidising old pits as well as investing in new ones.

MOBILISING AGAINST SCARGILL

When Arthur Scargill succeeded Joe Gormley as President of the NUM in April 1982 – with the support of 70 per cent of the miners who voted – a strike became inevitable. Scargill was a self-confessed class-war revolutionary, uninterested in rational discussion about the future of the industry. He first came to prominence during the 1972 coal strike as the leader of the so-called flying pickets who descended on the Saltley coke depot, where their behaviour led to a disastrous police withdrawal. After the 1974 strike, which was widely seen as having brought down the Heath Government, he told the *New Left Review* that the Transport and General Workers Union (TGWU) 'had a contractual arrangement with the working class and if they didn't honour that arrangement we'd make sure, physically, that they did. For we would have thrown their lorries and everything else into the dyke.' Thus violence was legitimate even against other trade unionists.

As NUM President-elect and subsequently as President he toured the country agitating ceaselessly for a strike; yet he never won a national ballot in favour of one (despite having engineered a change in the Union's constitution reducing the required majority from 55 per cent to anything over 50 per cent). This was not for want of trying. During my time as Energy Secretary the NUM polled its members no fewer than three times on strike action, over pay in January 1982, over pay and pit closures in October 1982, and over pit closures in March 1983. On the first occasion 45 per cent voted for a strike: on the second and third occasions the figure fell just below 40 per cent. It was these three failures that persuaded Scargill to call a strike, in the spring of 1984, without a national ballot; and it was his failure to hold a national ballot which in turn caused the Midlands miners – the most moderate in the union – to feel justified in carrying on working.

Although I had met Scargill on a number of occasions at television studios over the years, I did not meet him formally until immediately after he was elected President of the NUM, when I invited him to come and see me at the Department. He duly turned up, in April 1982, flushed with his overwhelming success in the presidential ballot. I had been warned that he always carried a tape recorder in his jacket pocket, so I was prepared to be more than usually guarded in what I said. I need not have worried, since he was determined to do almost all the talking himself. He spouted the most amazing nonsense, garnished liberally with spurious statistics 'proving' how even the least productive British pits were highly economic by comparison with their heavily subsidised competitors abroad. It was an extraordinary meeting, at which it became quite clear to me that Scargill's concept of the truth was heavily influenced by what he found it convenient to believe. After he had left I told my officials that there was no way we could do business with him.

At the end of March that year Joe Gormley, the outgoing NUM President, had also come to the Department to say farewell and let me know what he thought of his successor. Joe had deliberately stayed in his post longer than his colleagues had envisaged, so as to ensure that by the time he stepped down the formidable if somewhat unsubtle President of the Scottish NUM and former chairman of the Communist Party of Great Britain, Mick McGahey, was too old (under union rules) to succeed him. Gormley had little more time for Arthur Scargill than he had for Mick McGahey. He described Scargill to me as an astute tactician but a poor strategist, committed to subverting the Government. Age and experience, he thought, might mature him. It proved a forlorn hope.

Gormley, who had outsmarted the Heath Government in 1973–74 and humiliated the Thatcher Government in February 1981, was able in the end to redeem himself. The strike ballot of January 1982, engineered by Scargill in the twilight months of the Gormley presidency, looked as if it would be a close-run thing. And, at that time, we were still not adequately prepared for a strike. Joe, with all the authority of President of the NUM, was prevailed upon to write an article in the *Daily Express* of 13 January, on the eve of the ballot, advising his members to vote against strike action. It may well have been this that denied Scargill his majority. Certainly, it cannot have done any harm. I later persuaded

Margaret to offer Gormley a peerage, the first – and probably the last – time that a Conservative Government had ennobled a President of the NUM.

The NUM was not the only trade union with a part to play in any miners' strike, but Scargill's political posturing and unpopularity among his trade union colleagues made it difficult for him to build a coalition with other unions – notably those involved in the critically important power industry. I was careful to court John Lyons, the general secretary of the Electrical Power Engineers' Association (EPEA), whom I had got to know quite well in Opposition. (Indeed, he had given my son Dominic his first job, in the union's research department, in 1978.) He was a moderate with little time for Scargill, or the TUC, which had thwarted his plans to enlarge his union. Even so, representing as it did the skilled engineers and junior managers in the power stations, the power of his union was immense. His members were fully capable of closing down the power stations by themselves, as indeed they had demonstrated in Northern Ireland during the Ulster Loyalist strike of 1974. Equally, if they were prepared to co-operate with the army, they could keep the power stations going even if the other power unions decided to strike. Although a Labour man himself, Lyons told me that the majority of his members voted Conservative. But that did not mean that they could be taken for granted.

Fortunately, I was also on good terms with Frank Chapple, the brave and tough Cockney leader of the industry's principal union, the Electrical, Electronic, Telecommunications and Plumbing Union (EETPU). Chapple, who detested Scargill, was at one with me in longing for a Coal Board management capable of standing up to him. It was Frank who probably gave me the best advice about the chairmanship of the Coal Board. 'Get someone who's not afraid of Scargill,' he said, after we had been discussing the matter over dinner *à deux* at my home one evening: 'Most businessmen will tell you they're not, but in their hearts they are.' The 'Chapple test' was one good reason why I went for Ian MacGregor.

INCREASING ENDURANCE

The overriding need in preparing for a coal strike was to increase substantially power station endurance – that is, the length of time the power stations could continue to meet the nation's needs in the event of a complete cessation of coal production in the UK. Preferably, too, adequate endurance should be secured without recourse to the three-day week that had featured so prominently and so unhappily in the coal strike of 1974.

Fortunately, the country's coal stocks were unusually high. By December 1981 total coal stocks, largely at the pithead, amounted to 43 million tonnes, the highest level since the late 1960s, when the country's demand for coal was considerably greater. The hard part was shifting the coal from the pitheads to the power stations. This could scarcely be left to be done during a strike, since the quantities involved were too large and the picketing problem introduced too much uncertainty. On the other hand, in advance of a strike, coal stocks could not be moved secretly, since the trains which ferried the coal to the power stations were as visible as the piles of coal themselves.

David Howell had begun the process of shifting the coal to the power stations, in a deliberately low-profile way, and had instituted the practice of the Central Electricity Generating Board (CEGB) reporting weekly to both the Department of Energy and Number 10 on the level of power station coal stocks and other relevant information. But it was all too clear when the February 1981 showdown occurred that they were insufficient to withstand a prolonged strike, and by the time I arrived in September the position was little better. I accordingly asked officials to commission from the CEGB, as quickly as possible, a detailed and costed plan for increasing power station coal stocks, laying in extra supplies of the ancillary chemicals required in electricity generation, transporting coal by road rather than rail, and for conserving coal by increasing the amount of electricity generated by oil-fired power stations.

The most complicated part of this was probably the ancillary chemicals, where nothing at all had so far been done. Modern power stations cannot operate on coal alone. They need fuel oil to start the combustion process and carbon dioxide to cool their giant turbines. Other chemicals – oxygen, hydrogen and chlorine – are also required. Some of these could readily be stockpiled at the power stations in adequate quantities. Others could not, because of their short shelf-life, requiring them to be replenished during the course of a strike. Contingency plans would need to be made to fly these in by helicopter, a feasible operation given the relatively small quantities required, and potential helicopter landing sites were identified within the perimeter of every power station. I had not forgotten that the blockade of chemicals was one of the main causes of the power cuts of the 1970s.

The CEGB report was produced by the end of 1981, and going over it carefully with my key officials I put a proposal to a meeting with Margaret and other senior colleagues in February the following year recommending a dramatic acceleration in the build-up of power station coal stocks. For security reasons, I said nothing about the chemicals, feeling in any event that it was within my ministerial responsibility, without a need for collective discussion, to require the necessary contingency plans to be drawn up. This I duly did, and in due course was proudly shown by Walter Marshall, the newly appointed chairman of the CEGB, a meticulously detailed plan, complete with photographs of the helicopter landing sites that had been identified.

Meanwhile, the February meeting with the colleagues was by no means plain sailing. Jim Prior, in particular, speaking with the authority of a former Employment Secretary, considered my proposals dangerously provocative and likely to cause a strike. I conceded that a rapid build-up of coal stocks to the unprecedented levels I proposed (essentially the maximum the power stations could physically contain) would be a very high-profile policy. But I argued that, so far from provoking a strike, it would actually act as a deterrent, since the miners would know that, if they did vote for a strike, it would inevitably be a long one. Jim was also concerned that the railwaymen would refuse to carry the coal and go on strike themselves, supporting the miners under the terms of the Triple Alliance. In fact, there had been an unsuccessful train-drivers' strike in January 1982, and when they returned to work they were only too happy to recoup their lost earnings by working overtime transporting coal to the power stations.

But with Margaret's wholehearted backing, I secured the go-ahead, and pretty soon the so-called 'merry-go-round' – that part of the railway system dedicated to the transport of coal to power stations – was operating twenty-four hours a day, seven days a week. As a result power station coal stocks rose steadily, to 52.3 million tonnes in 1982 and 58 million tonnes in 1983, with a corresponding increase in power station endurance.

Indeed, Margaret was so keen that I found myself – much to the Treasury's relief – successfully resisting further suggestions of her own, such as the conversion of all coal-fired power stations to dual-firing (coal and oil), which would not only have been inordinately expensive but would have come to fruition beyond the timescale within which we were likely to be faced with a strike. She also set up an *ad hoc* committee of senior officials, initially under the Deputy Secretary to the Cabinet, Robert Wade-Gery, an outstandingly clever and likeable Wykehamist from the Foreign Office, subsequently our High Commissioner to India, to monitor the evolution of power station endurance and make recommendations, which I welcomed.

THE GREAT HEAD-HUNT

The top management of both the CEGB and the Coal Board were clearly crucial to the successful prosecution of a miners' strike. Fortuitously, the chairmanships of both organisations became available during my time as Energy Secretary.

For the CEGB I eventually opted for Walter Marshall, who was then running the UK Atomic Energy Authority. He was a brilliant scientist and had a strong commercial instinct, although he was not really interested in the financial side at all for which he had little feel. But I needed someone to keep the power stations running in the event of a coal strike, and meanwhile to co-operate to the full with the Government in the preparations to withstand a strike. On both counts Marshall came up trumps. I knew, of course, that in addition to his scientific and technological ingenuity Marshall had the motivation, since at an earlier stage in his career he had been Chief Scientist at the Department of Energy and had been sacked by Benn, with whom he had fallen out over nuclear policy. So he had no affection for Benn's friend and ally, Scargill.

Opinionated, articulate, with a caustic wit, the large and shambling Marshall was, although very much his own man and no courtier, greatly admired by Margaret. This was partly because he was a passionate advocate, as was she, of nuclear power – which is why I had little difficulty in persuading her that he should be CEGB chairman despite the fact that he was not a businessman.

Marshall's commitment to nuclear power, incidentally, and his readiness and ability to take on the anti-nuclear lobby, although not the main reason why I had chosen him, was at that time an undoubted plus – not least because it relieved me of much of the burden of making the case in which I still believed.

He set to work with great zest and obviously enjoyed devising plans to smuggle essential chemicals into the power stations. Where I failed was in finding a top-class finance director for the CEGB which it badly needed. I made sure there was no shortage of financial expertise among the part-time members of the CEGB. David Howell had brought in Eric Sharp, then chairman of Cable and Wireless, on this basis, and I persuaded Dick Giordano, then Chief Executive of British Oxygen (BOC) to join him. But that was no substitute.

The managerial inadequacies of the CEGB, however, were as nothing compared with those of the Coal Board. It was the archetypal public corporation, where genuine business management was almost unknown. The pits around the country were run on a joint basis by mining engineers, who were unversed in management, and the local representatives of the NUM – the precise balance of power varying with the individuals concerned, although the greater cohesion of the NUM tended to give it the upper hand most of the time. As I had discovered on my visit to Kellingley, there was an *esprit de corps* between men and management in the coal industry, derived from the genuine need for teamwork and mutual support in the dangerous business of extracting coal. That was all very well, but neither management nor unions were much interested in either the costs of production or the demand for coal.

At the Coal Board's Hobart House headquarters in London, its chairman seldom lost an opportunity to warn the Government that any provocative action might bring the miners out on strike. The Board was also suffused with the paternalist, corporatist mentality of the post-war settlement. 'All I did deliberately was to seek the maximum area of agreement. That applied both within the management and with the union,' was how Derek Ezra, Coal Board chairman from 1972 to 1982, characterised his management style. He had in practice accepted the extraordinarily powerful role in the industry's affairs assumed by the NUM, the running of the industry to the NUM, which he relied on Gormley to control, and appeared to see himself chiefly as a super-salesman for the industry. Throughout Whitehall and Westminster, the Coal Board was known as 'the Derek and Joe show'. And just in case the management – prompted perhaps by the Government of the day – did make the occasional attempt to manage, Hobart House was riddled with NUM moles who would quickly report the offence to Gormley. It was scarcely surprising that productivity was lamentable and the losses astronomic. This was no basis either for turning the industry round, or for confronting Scargill.

Although the lugubrious Ezra was still only fifty-three when his second five-year term expired in 1982, I decided not to offer him a third term. He was not at all surprised. He had originally been appointed chairman by Heath in 1972, which his conduct during the 1973–74 strike soon demonstrated to have been a big mistake, and was less surprisingly reappointed by Benn five years later.

Discussion about Ezra's successor had begun long before his contract actually expired, but no compelling names had turned up. Finally I fastened on Ian MacGregor, the highly effective chairman of British Steel. Quite apart from the toughness and business skills that he had demonstrated he possessed in that job, he knew the coal industry well, having been chairman of the Amax Corporation in the US, which had substantial coal mining interests. There was no risk of his running scared of Scargill.

I then had to persuade Margaret. This was far from easy. Patrick Jenkin, then Industry Secretary, understandably wanted to keep Ian at steel, and he was strongly backed by Geoffrey – the Chancellor is always consulted on nationalised industry chairmanships, and of course has to agree the salary. Margaret had a high regard for Ian, but she told me that he was doing such a good job at steel that he should not be moved, and that in any case his appointment to coal would be highly provocative: Ian was widely seen as an overpaid, over-aged, ruthless American whose main achievement at British Steel had been to slash the workforce. Eventually I secured her hesitant agreement, pointing out, first, that Ian had virtually completed the job he had been sent to do at British Steel, and that there was an excellent successor in his deputy, Bob Scholey, who could now pick up the baton; second, that the really big challenge now was coal, and we should put our best man in the biggest job; and, third, that while a coal strike sooner or later was highly likely, a strike simply as a result of the appointment of MacGregor was not on the cards.

Ian MacGregor eventually agreed to take the job in February 1983, after prolonged negotiations over his remuneration. We eventually settled for the Coal Board chairman's then salary (£58,325) plus a £1.5 million fee payable to Lazard Frères, New York (in which Ian was a partner) in compensation for the loss of his services for another three years. The fee was a tidy sum, but its public presentation was eased considerably by its exact correlation with the amount the Coal Board was losing each day. Ian eventually took over as chairman of the Coal Board in September 1983, three months after the election, by which time I had become Chancellor.

The news of his likely appointment leaked several months earlier, and the reaction showed that Margaret's fears were by no means peculiar to her. There were gales of protest in the Press. Large numbers of Tory back-benchers predictably panicked. Some, mesmerised by the end of the Heath Government in 1974, told me I had lost us the election. When I came to make my Statement to the House on 28 March 1983, the Whips were in a state of terror. They need not have been – as they had the grace to admit to me afterwards: it went very well.

The leak came, it seems, from 10 Downing Street. If it was a last-ditch attempt by someone close to Margaret to prevent Ian from getting the job, it backfired. The leak took much of the sting out of my announcement to the House. Nor were Labour able to make too much of the fact that Ian MacGregor was seventy years old, as he was only a few months younger than Michael Foot, the then leader of the Labour Party who, as I reminded the House, was 'seeking even more onerous responsibilities' at the forthcoming election.

A FAMOUS VICTORY

By the time the coal strike was called in March 1984, I was Chancellor of the Exchequer. Indeed the strike began effectively the day before my first Budget, when on Monday, 8 March, NUM leaders gave official sanction to strikes in Yorkshire and Scotland against pit closures and similar actions planned elsewhere. This was done without a strike ballot: the left-wing majority on the NUM executive insisted, however dubiously, that Rule 43 of the union allowed for a strike without a ballot. The plan was, of course, to get the militant areas out first, and then get them to intimidate the moderate areas into following suit. Even Martin Adeney and John Lloyd, in their standard book on the strike, concede that 'the preparation of the no-ballot option is one example of the premeditation with which the NUM leadership approached the strike'.

It also, of course, reflected their fear, after the failure of the three previous ballots, that if they did hold a strike ballot they would once again lose it. But what took me by surprise was not Scargill's decision to have a strike without a ballot – it had been clear for some time that he was determined to have one, come what may. The surprise was his astonishingly inept decision to start one in the spring, with the summer months, when coal consumption is at its lowest, immediately ahead. This inevitably greatly eased the power station endurance problem, which we had identified from the start as the key to winning any strike.

Margaret immediately set up a high-powered Cabinet Committee, Misc 101, under her chairmanship, to determine the Government's response to the strike as it evolved, while being careful not to usurp the role of the Coal Board against whom the strike had ostensibly been called. The committee met every week throughout the year-long strike – if necessary more than once – and at particularly critical moments there would be informal smaller meetings in her study upstairs. Misc 101 itself was a pretty large committee: in addition to Willie Whitelaw and myself, it included Peter Walker, my successor as Energy Secretary, Leon Brittan, then Home Secretary and responsible for the police, Michael Havers, the Attorney General, who provided legal advice, Michael Heseltine, then Defence Secretary, and a number of others. She also sought to set an example to us all by ostentatiously rushing around Downing Street turning off unnecessary lights.

The violent tactics used by the NUM pickets reopened the issue of 'Who governs Britain?' first raised in the 1974 election. Scargill himself had declared in his first presidential address to the NUM: 'Every trade unionist has to be determined to defy the law and to render it ineffective.' The physical intimidation of the many miners who wanted to work, and of the lorry drivers taking coal to the power stations, plumbed new depths.

Thanks to Scargill's folly in starting the strike in the spring, by the time the winter of 1984–85 came the striking miners had already foregone their wages for six months. With the Nottinghamshire pits running at full production, the winter came and went without making much of a dent in the massive coal stocks we had ensured that the power stations possessed. Thus it was hardly surprising that the striking miners had little stomach for enduring the long wait until the winter of 1985–86 – particularly since Scargill had falsely assured them that we would not be able to survive the previous winter. Both before and during the conflict, Scargill refused to accept that any mine was uneconomic and insisted that every pit must stay open as long as there was any coal at all to be extracted, irrespective of the fact that the costs of extraction far exceeded the market value of the coal. Having, as he thought, seen the miners bring down the Heath Administration in 1974, he was confident he could repeat the feat ten years later with the Thatcher Government.

He was, of course, totally mistaken. But it would have been a much more close-run thing if the Midlands miners had not carried on working. Another factor in the successful resistance to the strike was the encouragement given by Leon Brittan to the police to uphold the law and not retreat as they had done during the 1972 strike – notably at the Saltley coke depot. Walter Marshall, too, deserves credit for the technological ingenuity he showed in increasing the amount of electricity generated from a given quantity of coal. The fact that the Cabinet remained united at all times in its determination to see the strike through to a successful conclusion was clearly of the first importance.

The firmness of MacGregor throughout the strike vindicated my choice of him as Coal Board chairman, although he was pretty hopeless at public relations. In one bizarre episode he fled from journalists who discovered him in a hotel, departing down the back staircase and trying to conceal his face behind a plastic bag. Fortunately, public relations was one thing that Peter Walker was good at. After a much predicted and long-delayed drift back to work, the strike finally came to an end exactly a year after it had begun, when an NUM delegate conference voted to return to work on 5 March 1985.

Although we were able to ensure that power supplies were wholly unaffected, the year-long strike inevitably inflicted considerable short-term economic damage. During the financial year 1984/85 it reduced output, worsened the balance of payments, exacerbated unemployment, increased public expenditure and borrowing, and undermined the pound. The effects were felt especially in the currency markets. The strike, which was very newsworthy, was widely reported abroad – unlike most events in the UK – and inevitably affected international confidence in sterling. As usual, overseas observers knew nothing of the true state of affairs: they simply recalled the outcome of the previous UK miners' strike. They were also surprised – and therefore worried – by the duration of the strike. The miners' strike was thus partly responsible for sharp increases in interest rates in both the summer of 1984 and the early days of 1985 when the pound fell sharply on the foreign exchanges.

This was not the only adverse effect. Although manufacturing output (which excludes coal) continued to grow vigorously during 1984, industrial production as a whole came to a virtual standstill and recorded GDP growth fell back sharply. Both the coal industry and its two main customers – the electricity industry, which consumed three quarters of the coal mined in Britain, and the steel industry which consumed another fifth – were then state owned, which meant that the impact of the strike on their costs and revenues fed directly into the public finances. The largest single cost was the additional expense of burning oil rather than coal at the power stations, but the Treasury had also to meet the cost of commissioning lorries to transport coal from the working pits to the power stations.

The miners' strike thus made 1984/85 the only year in my Chancellorship in which there was substantial overspending. The public expenditure planning total was exceeded by over £3.5 billion in 1984/85, two thirds of the overspend being attributable to the strike. In the same financial year the strike added £2.75 billion to the Public Sector Borrowing Requirement.

These one-off costs did not in any way colour my attitude towards the strike. It was essential that the Government spent whatever was necessary to defeat Arthur Scargill. Inevitably, however, any robust Government language was deliberately misinterpreted. Margaret Thatcher's famous reference in a speech to the 1922 Committee in which she referred to the hard core of Scargillite activists as 'the enemy within' was a case in point. Labour politicians, from Michael Foot downwards, deliberately seized on it as a slur on the mineworkers as a whole. In fact, we were careful throughout to make it clear that we had nothing against the miners themselves. Those who continued to work were portrayed as heroes (and behind the scenes a considerable amount of private money was raised to help them resist the Scargillite intimidation to which they were subjected) and the strike was always referred to as a coal strike rather than a miners' strike.

Adeney and Lloyd, writing from a left of centre perspective, are clear enough:

> Few episodes in the Thatcher Government's life went so well as its handling of the miners' strike. It won its main objective: it faced out the weightiest constitutional challenge it was likely to face on the UK mainland ... and it wholly secured the right to make the coal industry – and thus any other industry, since that was the strongest bastion of non-market production – profitable and market oriented.

The miners' strike was the central political event of the second Thatcher Administration. Just as the victory in the Falklands War exorcised the humiliation of Suez, so the eventual defeat of the NUM etched in the public mind the end of the militant trade unionism which had wrecked the economy and twice played a major part in driving elected governments from office – James Callaghan's in the aftermath of the Winter of Discontent in 1979 no less than Edward Heath's in 1974.

Both as a Leicestershire Member and as a former Energy Secretary it gave me no pleasure to see ordinary decent miners suffer (on whichever side of the barricades) and be humiliated. But the responsibility for this clearly lay with those who sought to subvert normal trade unionism to serve extraneous revolutionary aims. And although, with Scargill a pathetic and discredited figure, the coal industry since the strike has shrunk dramatically as it has come to terms with economic reality, sooner or later this was unavoidable.

As Adeney and Lloyd point out, the Government's victory owed a great deal not only to the careful preparations we had made but also to the lessons learned from the Heath episode. Although there was no doubt on whose side the Government was, it remained throughout an industrial dispute. Neither the Prime Minister, nor any other Minister, held any meetings with the NUM. The Government steered clear of the talks that did take place, the details of which were left to the Coal Board (though at critical moments Ian MacGregor was of course made aware of the Government's views). There was not even the shadow or hint of an incomes policy to inflame the situation, or lead other unions to rally to Scargill's support.

There was one disappointment for the Government at the time. During the course of the strike we had been languishing in the opinion polls, even though public opinion was overwhelmingly anti-Scargill. That was hardly surprising; but we did expect that victory would bring a political bonus in terms of our poll ratings. It did nothing of the sort. The British people were relieved the strike was over, and promptly turned their attention to other things. But at a more profound and lasting level, the political gain was immense. It was a gain not just for the Government, but for the country as a whole.

CHAPTER ELEVEN

PRIVATISATION 1: THE JEWEL IN THE CROWN

The Coming of Privatisation · Origins and Myths
Nationalisation: The Experiment that Failed · Mules are not Zebras
Wider Ownership · A Low-key Start

THE COMING OF PRIVATISATION

> Privatisation has been the most striking policy innovation since 1979 ... It also represents the Jewel in the Crown of the Government's legislation programme, around which all shades of Tories can unite. The idea has been taken up, and copied, with explicit acknowledgement of the British influence, not only by other industrialised countries, but also by the Third World countries.

So writes Peter Riddell, a leading political journalist who is no Thatcherite, but whose book on the period has far more to say on the substance of policy than better-known works which have concentrated on the nature of Margaret Thatcher's personality. If Riddell had gone to press slightly later, he would have included the ex-Communist countries of Central and Eastern Europe and indeed the Republics of the former Soviet Union among the emulators.

By the 1992 general election, about two thirds of the formerly State-owned industries in the UK had been transferred to the private sector. Some forty-six major businesses, employing some 900,000 people, had been privatised.[11]

The expertise about privatisation that Whitehall and the City have, sometimes painfully, acquired in the process became a lucrative source of invisible earnings. Libraries could be filled with the books and reports written on the subject. What I can give in this book is an account of the origins of the idea, of

[11] [2010 note] By 1997 the figure had reached 1.02m.

the thinking behind it, and of how the initial difficulties were tackled. Not the least of those initial difficulties was the fact that, to all intents and purposes, it had never been done before. This is remarkably rare in Whitehall. Whenever a Minister has what he thinks is a new idea, the chances are that it is nothing of the sort. His officials dust down the relevant departmental dossier, and off they go. But with privatisation there was no departmental dossier to dust down. Officials had to start from a blank sheet – an almost unheard-of experience. But they went to work with a will, and the good ones, who were very good indeed, soon found that while pioneering was hard work, it was actually much more enjoyable than re-treading a well trodden path.

First, however, a note on the semantics. Privatisation means almost the same thing as denationalisation. 'Almost' because industries such as the telephone service, which had always been in the State sector, and thus never been through a process of nationalisation in the first place, were transferred to the private sector. Partly for this reason and partly because most of us felt denationalisation did not sound positive enough, the process came to be officially described as 'privatisation'. The word was, to the best of my recollection, David Howell's invention. It is an ugly word – and Margaret disliked it so much that for some time she refused to use it. But none of us could come up with anything better; and as this word, or quite literal translations of it, is now used from Siberia to Patagonia, we may as well stick to it.

A further terminological point is that privatisation essentially means the transfer of control of a whole industry or firm from the State to the private sector. The sale of a minority stake which still leaves the organisation concerned under State control is emphatically not privatisation.

Another borderline case is contracting out and franchising, where State-controlled organisations cease to carry out a particular activity and award a contract to a private firm instead. Obvious examples are municipal refuse collection or hospital laundries. But, to repeat: the essence of privatisation is the transfer of the ownership and control of enterprises from the State sector to the private sector.

ORIGINS AND MYTHS

The limited and low-key reference to denationalisation in the 1979 manifesto has led many commentators, even Peter Riddell, to suppose that privatisation was not part of our original programme and emerged as an unexpected development into which we stumbled by happy accident. They could not be more mistaken. The exiguous references in the 1979 Conservative manifesto reflected partly the fact that little detailed work had been done on the subject in Opposition; partly that the enthusiasts for privatisation were Keith Joseph, Geoffrey Howe, John Nott, David Howell and me, rather than Margaret herself; and, perhaps chiefly Margaret's understandable fear of frightening the floating voter. But privatisation was a central plank of our policy right from the start. In Geoffrey Howe's first Budget Speech, less than six weeks after we had first taken office in May 1979, he referred (in a passage which I helped to draft) to a review

> of the scope for reducing the size of the public sector. It is already clear that the scope for the sale of assets is substantial. Such sales not only help in the short term to reduce the PSBR. They are an essential part of our long-term programme for promoting the widest possible participation by the people in the ownership of British industry. This objective – wider public ownership in the true meaning of the term – has implications not only for the scale of our programme but also for the methods of sale we shall adopt.

Geoffrey went on to announce that assets sales of some £1 billion would be made in 1979/80 of which the biggest single contribution would come from the sale of part of the Government's holding in BP, bringing it well below the 51 per cent at which it then stood. This was a simple operation, carried out in November, which raised £290 million. It needed no legislation: the shares were already quoted on the Stock Exchange, and the previous Labour Government had inadvertently paved the way with its 1977 BP share sale. So the official Opposition could hardly complain with much conviction. Although the sale was not in fact a true privatisation, since despite the majority Government stake, BP had always been run as a private sector company and had always been classified as being in the private sector, it clearly pointed the way.

In my 1980 lecture, *The New Conservatism*, I went a little further, saying:

> We have also embarked on a major programme of privatisation of the state-owned industries, of which British Aerospace and British Airways will be among the first candidates ... Throughout this exercise we are anxious to see the widest possible spread of private shareholding – so that the so-called public sector industries really do belong to the public – including in particular employee shareholding.

Meanwhile, immediately after the 1979 election, Margaret had set up a sub-committee of the main Economic Committee to explore candidates for privatisation. It was chaired by Geoffrey Howe as Chancellor, and both John Biffen as Chief Secretary and I as Financial Secretary were members of it. It was unique for a Cabinet Committee to have no fewer than three Treasury Ministers in it, and it no doubt reflected Margaret's lack of confidence in most of the rest of her first Cabinet.

Not only was privatisation opposed tooth and nail by Labour, but the Liberals (and the Liberal-Social Democrat 'Alliance' while it existed) sought to demonstrate their moderation by being opposed to privatisation and nationalisation with equal vehemence. This was a curiously conservative attitude (with a small 'c') to the boundary between the State and private sectors of industry for politicians who sometimes sought to portray themselves as radical to take. According to Roy Jenkins, on innumerable occasions, this stance was dictated by a distaste for the damage done by so-called 'pendulum politics', under which successive Labour and Conservative Governments reversed their predecessors' acts, and industries were deprived of all stability as they allegedly oscillated to and fro between the State and the private sectors.

His argument would have been more impressive had it borne any correspondence to historical reality. In fact, with the arguable exception of steel in 1951, when the incoming Churchill Government had declined to complete the nationalisation embarked on in the twilight months of the Attlee Government, and the industry was thus spared that fate until the advent of the Wilson Government of the sixties, the motion had been not that of a pendulum, but of a one-way street – with the story prior to the Thatcher Government being one of ever-growing State ownership.

But devoid of principle and historical accuracy alike, the Liberal position accurately reflected the views of the British people. Opposed to nationalisation, they were scared by privatisation. In advance of every significant privatisation, public opinion was invariably hostile to the idea, and there was no way it could be won round except by the Government going ahead and doing it. Then, when the scare stories which had been so luridly peddled by the Opposition about the consequences of a particular privatisation in prospect were proved to be unfounded, the private sector status of the industry concerned became accepted as a fact of life.

This demonstrated, to my satisfaction at least, that while in an ideal world a Government would always persuade the people of the wisdom of a policy before implementing it, in practice that is often not possible, and becomes simply a recipe for inaction.

NATIONALISATION: THE EXPERIMENT THAT FAILED

The climate after the Thatcher Governments was very different. Even economists who originally supported nationalisation in the West were to be found advising ex-Communist countries on how to privatise as quickly as practicable. There were, naturally, setbacks and disappointments in countries without any recent tradition of private enterprise and the culture that sustains it. The ultimate goal is more likely to survive intact if we remember why the experiment of State ownership failed and do not simply treat privatisation as an unthinking article of faith.

My own most extensive early statement was made in a talk I gave in Oxford, on 23 September 1982. I had been provoked during the debates on the privatisation of Britoil by the confusion between the State and the nation, which implied that no enterprise could be truly British unless it were owned by the State. (I also, incidentally, found it perverse to use the term 'public sector' to describe a part of the economy where, as often as not, the State posted a notice to potential competitors saying 'private: keep out'.)

I began by recalling the reasons put forward for nationalisation by the Attlee Government of 1945–51 at the time. These were:

1. The improvement of industrial relations
2. The promotion of full employment
3. The gain in productivity from the removal of absentee ownership
4. The efficient regulation of monopolies (which were in themselves considered superior to 'wasteful competition')
5. The replacement of short-term profit maximisation by wider national and social priorities

There is no longer any need to labour the failure of nationalisation to achieve these objectives. But the reasons I gave in 1982 may still be of interest.

The nationalised industries, so far from improving industrial relations, proved the source of the biggest threat to industrial peace – doubtless because of the combination of centralised union power and recourse to the bottomless public purse. On full employment I observed that 'while nationalisation has enabled some industries to postpone job losses for a time, the resulting overmanning has usually proved unsustainable and the eventual job losses consequently greater.'

As for short termism versus national priorities, I pointed out that governments 'enjoy no unique hotline to the future'. But I went on to make the less obvious point that governments may well have more power in practice to influence the behaviour of the private sector by legislation (not least tax legislation) than they do that of supposedly State-controlled concerns. 'We have created industrial baronies not truly accountable to anyone – Parliament, Government, shareholders or the marketplace.'

But I concentrated more on the productivity and monopoly issues, speaking at a time when the rate of return on capital in the nationalised industries as a whole was negative. I was at the time particularly impressed by the findings of Richard Pryke, from whom I had commissioned an article when I was editor of the *Spectator* in 1966. He had just resigned from the Cabinet Office where he had worked under Tommy Balogh. He remained a champion of the nationalised industries in a book published as late as 1971. But he then began to develop doubts and, in the late 1970s, he brought out a fresh work which came to the conclusion that nationalised industries had performed less well than their private enterprise counterparts.

Nor was the failure due solely to the monopoly nature of some State industries. For Pryke also made a detailed study of three non-monopoly concerns – British Airways, British Rail sea ferries and the once all-too-familiar appliance retailing outlets of British Gas and the Area Electricity Boards – which established that they had used capital and labour less effectively than their private counterparts, and were operating at a loss. The reasons Pryke gave for his findings remain fundamental. As I put it at Oxford, 'What public ownership does is to eliminate the threat of takeover and ultimately of bankruptcy, and the need, which all private undertakings have from time to time, to raise money from the market.'

The regulation of monopoly argument was, and is, perhaps the most insidious of all. For the belief that State ownership or regulation can be an effective substitute for competition leads governments to exaggerate the irreducible amount of natural monopoly and neglect ways of introducing competition. This brought me to what might be called the 'sub-text' of my speech, designed to answer the many faint-hearts in the Cabinet and Whitehall who believed that reforming public sector monopolies could be an alternative to privatising them.

Most damaging of all was the inevitable *politicisation* of nationalised industries. While governments find it hard to exercise strategic control over their industrial empire, the temptation to indulge in short-term interference in everything from prices and salaries to the placing of new plant in marginal constituencies is almost irresistible. The effect on nationalised industry management is equally bad: accommodating government or placating pressure groups becomes more important than commercial results.

MULES ARE NOT ZEBRAS

At the time of my 1982 speech the nationalised industries accounted for over a tenth of total national output and more than a seventh of total fixed investment, and employed a workforce of some 1.75 million. For some private industries they were the only domestic customer; for some consumers the only suppliers. Yet no government, of either party, had found a satisfactory basis for running them. This was not for want of trying. 'The stream of White Papers, studies and reports has been unending,' I pointed out. 'Yet the problems have remained, more acute than ever.'

As my old friend Patrick Hutber used to say, you can no more make a State industry imitate private enterprise by telling it to follow textbook rules or to simulate competitive prices, than you can make a mule into a zebra by painting stripes on its back. There is no equivalent in the State sector to the discipline of the share price or the ever-present threat of bankruptcy. It is a commonplace of post-Communist economies that price reform is insufficient without introducing effective property rights to provide managers with an incentive to respond the right way. The same applies, albeit to a lesser degree, to the nationalised industries in Western mixed economies.

Of course, there are professional groups, such as doctors and academics, or members of the armed forces, who perform their tasks from a sense of vocation and not just for the financial rewards. This is excellent as far as it goes. But it is dangerous to press such non-profit motivation too far. A manager of a steel plant or an oil company needs much clearer day-to-day market signals to do his job effectively than does a surgeon or a musician. But, even in the non-profit-making sectors, as we have seen in education and health, it is important to have the right structure of incentives and rewards.

One of the key messages of my Oxford speech, directed in particular at my own colleagues, was that reform of the nationalised industries was no substitute for returning them to the private sector. One of the detailed reformist documents I had in mind was the Central Policy Review Staff (CPRS) report on the nationalised industries, commissioned by Margaret from its director Robin Ibbs and circulated in the summer of 1981. Its authors imagined that it was possible to transform the relationship between the Government and the nationalised industries. Its recommendations included defining strategic objectives for each nationalised industry; smaller boards dominated by outsiders; the establishment of 'Business Groups' within the sponsoring department headed by executives on secondment from the private sector; regular efficiency audits; and closer monitoring by government. This whole approach seemed to me to be fundamentally mistaken.

Only the Treasury exerted any external discipline over the nationalised industries, through its imposition of External Financing Limits (EFLs) in the annual spending round. The industries complained – with good cause – that the Treasury was obsessed with financial at the expense of commercial objectives. The sponsoring Departments for their part, always sensitive to the charge of surrendering to the Treasury, tended to side with their charges – something the 'Business Groups' proposal vainly was intended to cure.

The adoption of another of the CPRS recommendations demonstrated the limitations of trying to improve the efficiency of the nationalised industries without a change of ownership. At the beginning of 1982, the Treasury tried to formalise its relations with the nationalised industries by asking Departments to agree written policy objectives with them. These 'policy letters' would be signed by the Secretary of State and the chairmen of the industries for which he was responsible, and would be published by way of a written answer in Hansard.

Given the political sensitivity of nationalised industry spending and investment, however, this was easier said than done. In the case of coal, in particular, where pit closures could provoke a strike at any time, it was clearly dangerous to publish anything but the blandest list of overall objectives.

In arguing the need to break up and genuinely privatise the large public utilities, I was originally in quite a small minority. Early efforts were directed at schemes to enable the nationalised public utilities to borrow directly from the public. The most notable example of this was the abortive 1982 plan for a British Telecom 'Buzby Bond'. The failure of these attempts to square the circle helped to swing Whitehall opinion behind privatisation. I found it striking that the Treasury officials who worked in the Department's PE (Public Enterprise) division, whatever their political views and whatever the views on State-owned industries with which they had begun, nearly all ended up convinced that nationalisation did not work and in practice was positively harmful.

Since the case for privatising the so-called natural monopolies like gas, electricity and water is so rarely understood by the public and even by academics,

I was subsequently driven to write a note to Nicholas Ridley in March 1989, in connection with water privatisation, summarising the case in terms which applied beyond water:

1. All experience shows that businesses are more efficient and successful in the private than in the public sector;
2. The water and sewerage industry is a business like any other;
3. A quarter of the industry is already in the private sector;
4. Of course it will need regulation – to protect the consumer as it is a natural monopoly and for environmental reasons (purity of water etc.) – but it is far better for the State's responsibility to be clearly confined to that of regulator rather than to have the existing conflict of interest when it is both regulator and producer;
5. Even though water is a natural monopoly, the privatised water industry will still face (a) competition for capital in the private sector, and (b) a published daily share price – a comment on performance and a powerful spur to management;
6. Privatisation not only widens share ownership (desirable in itself) but increases employee share ownership, which previous privatisations show leads to further improved performance.

Nick was, of course, totally committed to water privatisation. But the arguments that he and his number two, Michael Howard, were then using to try to convince a hostile parliamentary and public opinion did not, in my judgement, get to the heart of the matter.

WIDER OWNERSHIP

Although the primary aim of the privatisation programme was to improve the performance of the former State-owned industries, there was a substantial spill-over benefit in the opportunities it provided for widening share ownership.

The references in Geoffrey Howe's first Budget Speech to 'the widest possible participation by the people in the ownership of British industry' was, of course, an extension of the Tory theme, central at least since Anthony Eden's day, of the creation of a property-owning democracy – which had hitherto been interpreted almost exclusively in terms of home-ownership.

I spelt out some of the reasons at the first Maurice Macmillan Memorial Lecture which I gave in June 1985:

> Those who, in the nineteenth century, argued the dangers of a mass democracy in which a majority of the voters would have no stake in the country at all, had reason to be fearful. But the remedy is not to restrict the franchise to those who own property: it is to extend the ownership of property to the largest possible majority of those who have the vote. The widespread ownership of private property is crucial to the survival of freedom and democracy. It gives the citizen a vital sense of identification with the society of which he is a part. It gives him a stake in the future – and indeed, equally important, in the present. It creates a society with an inbuilt resistance to revolutionary change.

Giving details of the decline of individual share ownership and the drift towards the institutions, I went on to remark:

> Institutional investors are certainly powerful. But I give away few political secrets when I say that Governments are likely to be more concerned by the prospect of alienating a mass of individual shareholders than they are by the lobbying of half a dozen investment managers.

The Thatcher Government introduced a number of measures to encourage share ownership. But in practice the biggest boost was provided by privatisation. Many commentators made the wholly erroneous assumption that, since I was a Treasury Minister, my interest in privatisation could only be in the proceeds, and my only policy the maximisation of the proceeds. In fact I was much more concerned about improving the UK's dire economic performance and thus was always on the side of introducing competition and a tough regulatory regime where no competition was practicable, despite the fact that either would reduce proceeds. There was no difference here between officials and myself. What *is* true is that I believed in selling the shares rather than in literally giving them away, a superficially attractive policy that bristles with practical difficulties.

In fact no-one was keener than I to achieve the widest possible distribution of shares in the privatised businesses both to small shareholders in general and to their employees in particular, who in most cases were able to acquire shares on favourable terms. The most spectacular case of employee share ownership occurred in the relatively modest privatisation of National Freight in early 1982 where there was a management-worker buy-out, suggested by the management and welcomed by Norman Fowler, then Transport Secretary. But even in the larger flotations employee shares were invariably a major feature. In the case of British Telecom (BT) no fewer than 96 per cent of the eligible workforce took up shares: the average was 90 per cent. The proportion of the adult population owning shares rose from 7 per cent in 1979 to 25 per cent ten years later. This was not enough to reverse the long-term decline in the proportion of shares held by private individuals rather than institutions – a worldwide trend – but it remains a change of the first importance.

In addition to its many objective virtues, there was also a clear political motive behind promoting the wider share ownership of the privatised companies. For the more widely the shares were spread, the more people who had a personal stake in privatisation, and were thus unlikely to support a Labour Party committed to renationalisation. And if this forced Labour to abandon its commitment to renationalisation, so much the better. For our objective was, so far as practically possible, to make the transfer of these businesses to the private sector irreversible.

A LOW-KEY START

Because of its responsibility for public finance, and because it had been specifically given the task by Margaret Thatcher, the Treasury was the lead Department in charge of co-ordinating the whole privatisation programme. When I was made Financial Secretary in 1979, I persuaded Geoffrey Howe to give me privatisation as a specific delegated responsibility which has remained with the Financial Secretary ever since. Later, as Energy Secretary, I pushed through the privatisation of Britoil, the former British National Oil Company (BNOC), at that time (1982) the largest privatisation the world had ever known; and of course on becoming Chancellor in 1983, I was automatically in overall charge of the entire privatisation programme. But it was while I was at Energy, with direct responsibility for more major nationalised industries than any other Minister, that I was able to give the greatest proportion of my time to the subject; and it is convenient to deal with it in this section of the book.

Initially it proved something of a struggle to get the privatisation programme off the ground. David Howell was invited by the Treasury to submit plans for the sale of parts of the British Gas Corporation and the British National Oil Corporation (BNOC) nearly three weeks before the 1979 Budget. But obstacles developed. We eventually raised just under £1 billion from asset sales in 1979/80, although in a somewhat curious way, most of it coming from forward sales of BNOC oil.

In the following two financial years, 1980/81 and 1981/82, the scale of privatisation was relatively modest, not least because the original plan to privatise British Airways, the legislation for which was on the statute-book by November 1980, had to be shelved because of the world recession. Even so, we managed to privatise some well-known firms which should never have been in the State sector. The principal public flotations during those two years were Cable & Wireless, British Aerospace, and Amersham International. In addition, Fairey Engineering, Ferranti, National Freight, International Aeradio and British Rail Hotels were sold.

These were concerns already operating in competitive markets.

When I became Energy Secretary in September 1981, I found myself directly responsible for a larger industrial empire and was able to take action myself to get the privatisation programme moving faster. My announcement in October 1981 of the privatisation of the oil-producing assets of both BNOC and British Gas amounted to a substantial extension of the established programme of privatising State-owned sections of the enterprises. But I became increasingly convinced of the merits of taking privatisations beyond the competitive sector into the realm of the giant monopoly public utilities. For me, this meant the privatisation of British Gas and the entire electricity supply industry, the two main State-owned monopolies supervised by the Energy Department.

Among these early privatisations, the Energy Department had responsibility for Amersham International. This was an interesting little company, which was in the State sector simply because it had, under the name of the Radiochemical Centre, been a spin-off from the government nuclear research establishment, the Atomic Energy Authority. Its business was the manufacture of radioactive isotopes for use in medicine, a field in which the only other company of any significance in the world was by that time a wholly owned subsidiary of the US chemical-based giant, DuPont. This sale, supervised by John Moore, was already at an advanced stage when I became Energy Secretary and the only important issue that remained to be decided was the pricing.

Nicholas Ridley, who had succeeded me as Financial Secretary to the Treasury, had wanted to offer the shares for sale not at a fixed price, as is customary in the UK, but by auction (technically known as the tender method). I had no objection in principle to the idea, having pioneered the issue of gilt-edged stock by tender when I was Financial Secretary myself, and Amersham, as the only company in its field, was unusually difficult to price. But I was anxious to use the issue to promote wider share ownership, and I had little doubt that this required a fixed-price offer, since small shareholders would have no idea what to bid in an auction and would be put off altogether. The advisers to the Amersham sale – Rothschilds advising the Government and Morgan Grenfell advising the company – were also divided on the matter. Nick and I agreed that the only way to resolve the matter was to invite Geoffrey Howe, as Chancellor, to adjudicate; and a meeting was arranged at Number 11 between the three of us. To Nick's amazement and disgust, Geoffrey – after having us put the respective cases – came down in favour of a fixed-price offer.

Since it is impossible to predict with any great precision either the demand for a new share issue or still less the state of the market when dealings in it begin (normally at least a fortnight after the offer price has been agreed with the underwriters of the issue) it is more a matter of luck than of judgement if the fixed price for any new issue turns out to be exactly right. Thus fixed-price issues invariably prove to be either underpriced or overpriced. In the latter case, when the bulk of the shares are left with the underwriters, the issue is always described in the financial Press as a 'flop', whereas the former case, when the issue is oversubscribed and goes to a premium, is described as a 'success'. There is thus a general tendency for issues to be deliberately slightly underpriced.

Unfortunately, in the case of Amersham, the merchant bank advisers who fixed the price – in those early days we did not equip ourselves, as we did later, with an independent adviser on pricing – overdid the underpricing by an embarrassingly wide margin. As a result, the £71 million issue was no less than twenty-four times oversubscribed, and shot to a premium of some 35 per cent when dealings began. This led to an enormous political storm, with Labour accusing the Government of ripping off the taxpayer and deliberately selling State assets on the cheap to its friends in the City. Nick Ridley understandably felt wholly vindicated, and I was acutely embarrassed. I felt obliged to announce an inquiry into what had gone wrong – not that there was any mystery about it.

In retrospect, the serious underpricing of Amersham, although in no sense deliberate, may have been no bad thing. The enormous publicity given to the profits enjoyed by subscribers to the issue conveyed the clear message to the general public that investing in privatisation issues was a good thing. As for the general question of fixed price versus tender, it is significant that experience has led the Government to make fixed-price offers the norm for its privatisation issues. But at the time I felt deeply humiliated, and resolved that the next privatisation for which I was responsible, namely Britoil, would have to be a tender. Whatever happened, I could not afford a second Amersham.

CHAPTER TWELVE

PRIVATISATION 2: THE BIRTH OF POPULAR CAPITALISM

A Revolution Briefly Announced · Compressing British Gas · No 'People's Stake' BNOC into Britoil · The British Telecom Breakthrough

A REVOLUTION BRIEFLY ANNOUNCED

On 19 October 1981, in my first appearance as Energy Secretary, I announced to a surprised House of Commons the privatisation of the entire oil-producing businesses of both BNOC and the British Gas Corporation, and subsequently other parts of British Gas, together with the removal of the Corporation's 'unique statutory rights over the purchase of gas and its sale to the industry in particular' and the conversion of its pipeline network into a common carrier. To maximise the dramatic effect, I had kept the announcement deliberately brief. I was able to expand on it in the Debate on the Address the following month.

My November speech contained two declarations which set the tone for the approach to privatisation that I was to pursue throughout my time in Government. The first was the general slogan: 'The Conservative Party has never believed that the business of government is the government of business.' The second drew the inescapable conclusion: 'No industry should remain under State ownership unless there is a positive and overwhelming case for it so doing. Inertia is not enough. As a nation we simply cannot afford it.'

Meanwhile, my October announcement had pleased our own side and plunged the Labour Party into one of its customary frenzies. Replying for the Opposition, Merlyn Rees, then Shadow Energy Secretary, committed a future Labour Government to renationalise the oil assets at the sale price, presumably in part a vain attempt to frustrate the privatisation, although it had of course to be prominently recorded in the prospectus. Even this did not go far enough for Tony Benn, the former Energy Secretary, then seeking to reshape the Labour Party in his own image, who threatened to renationalise the industry without any compensation at all. Apparently Benn's departure from the Party line provoked a resignation threat from Rees. The Conservative benches had been on the defensive for so long over unemployment and the economy that they were hugely cheered by Labour's obvious discomfiture.

The Bill to give my proposal legislative effect was published on 17 December 1981. At its heart was the biggest privatisation hitherto attempted, anywhere in the world. I had originally sought two Bills in the 1981/82 session, one to deal with BNOC and the other with the British Gas Corporation, but Cabinet ruled that there was legislative time only for one, and I was obliged to put both sets of measures into a single Bill – which I was more than content to do.

COMPRESSING BRITISH GAS

For most of my period at the Department of Energy, the chairman of the British Gas Corporation, Denis Rooke, was my most formidable opponent. A large, craggy, overbearing, man, he has been described by normally reticent retired senior Civil Servants in language that I cannot reproduce in a book designed for family reading. He dominated British Gas and regarded the Energy Department as the principal obstacle to his plans for the gas industry, and indeed for the economy as a whole, treating Ministers and officials alike with a mixture of distrust, dislike and contempt. David Howell had unaccountably missed the only opportunity to replace him when his contract came up for renewal in 1980; so I was stuck with him.

Rooke had entered the gas industry in the 1950s when it was moribund, and he had seen it transformed from the Cinderella of the energy market into the most popular source of domestic power. To break the Corporation up in any way was a negation of his life's work, and he opposed efforts to do so at every turn.

I tried to outflank him by appealing over his head to his Board of Directors, with whom power technically resided; and in December 1981 I called a meeting of the entire Gas Corporation Board at the Department to see if any of them were amenable to reason; but they appeared to be quite overawed by Rooke. After that meeting I decided to make some changes on the Board. I appointed three eminent businessmen as non-executive directors – men who could not be pushed around by anyone. They also kept me better informed than my officials were usually able to do.

Although there was no reason for British Gas to be in the oil business at all, it had acquired substantial minority stakes in a number of North Sea oil fields and a half share in Britain's biggest onshore oilfield, at Wytch Farm in Dorset, which it had discovered, but which was operated by the owner of the other half share, BP. David Howell, using his powers under the Heath Government's Gas Act of 1972, had required British Gas to dispose of its interest in Wytch Farm in June 1981. Rooke did everything he could to resist, but I persisted. It was obviously impossible to float Wytch Farm as a separate entity on the stock market, so the Department held an auction. Although a number of companies and consortia were interested, the outcome was most unsatisfactory.

The detailed information about Wytch Farm, which potential bidders required in order to decide whether and how much to bid, had to be supplied by British Gas; and extracting this proved very much more difficult than extracting the gas itself. As a result, when the auction closed, the prices offered were so low that I could not have justified the acceptance of any of the offers to the Public Accounts Committee.

Undeterred, I invited all the bidders to reconsider their offers, but not before I had acquired more adequate information from British Gas. On 30 March 1983, I called the entire Gas Corporation Board to the Department to complain about what had been going on, which I documented in detail. Several directors expressed considerable surprise and concern when they discovered what had been happening. Wytch Farm was not finally sold until well after I had left the Department.

Rooke was scarcely more co-operative during the preparation for the privatisation of British Gas's offshore oil interests. These eventually became Enterprise Oil, which was floated on the Stock Exchange in June 1984, and named after the Act which had made its privatisation possible. Thanks to Rooke's foot-dragging, I was just about to sign the instruction to him, under the terms of the Oil and Gas (Enterprise) Act, to dispose of the oil assets when the 1983 election was called. Constitutional propriety required that any further action be delayed until the outcome of the election was known.

Rooke clearly hoped that the election would bring a more compliant Secretary of State, but I was determined to have the last word if I possibly could. I therefore signed the letter to enforce the disposal before leaving the Department for the campaign trail, and gave it to my private secretary for safekeeping, with instructions to destroy it if we lost the election, but to send it on, on receipt of a telephone call from me, if we won. I duly telephoned him the day after the election, and the letter was sent. It turned out to be my last act as Energy Secretary: the following day I became Chancellor of the Exchequer.

My successor as Energy Secretary was Peter Walker, whose views on the privatisation of British Gas were as different from mine as was his attitude on most other issues. Indeed, my former officials told me it was almost as if there had been a change of Government.

After the election Margaret held a series of meetings at Number 10 to agree on the best way of privatising British Gas. My strong preference was to break up the corporation both regionally and into separate gas and appliance businesses before privatising it. It would have reduced the proceeds of the sale, but I judged competition a more important consideration than maximising government revenue. Peter was totally opposed to anything of the kind. As he records in his autobiography, he maintained that 'The breaking up of the corporation was lunacy ... I wanted a powerful British company which could compete around the world.'

This, of course, precisely echoed the views of Rooke, who was vehemently opposed to the dismantling of the Corporation, and whom Walker describes as 'the best nationalised industry chairman I have met'. Rooke had originally been passionate in his opposition to gas privatisation in any shape or form. It was only later, when it became clear that the Government was determined to privatise British Gas, that he fell back on his second line of defence: his insistence on the retention, intact, of the existing monopolistic and integrated gas industry.

Meeting followed meeting; but despite Margaret's support for the competitive route, we were getting nowhere. Meanwhile, time was running out. Eventually, after yet another wasted meeting I asked Peter to come next door with me to Number 11: I had a suggestion to make. I told him that I would agree to privatisation *en bloc* provided he undertook to go ahead post haste with the privatisation of British Gas without further ado. He promised to do so, feeling that he had won a great victory. When, at the next Number 10 meeting, Margaret learned of the deal, she no doubt felt I had gone soft, however relieved she was that the problem had been resolved. But I reckoned that this had become the only way privatisation would occur during the lifetime of that parliament.

As it was clear that Margaret was not prepared to move Peter, which would have been the only way around the impasse, I would have to rely on the regulatory authority, after privatisation, to introduce competition. This was to be the Office of Gas Supply (Ofgas), with a regulatory regime based on that devised for British Telecom and described later in this chapter, except that the price control based on the formula RPI-x+y, where y represented the world oil price. (As for x, this was to rise from 2 per cent at the outset to 5 per cent in 1991.) But its remit would extend far beyond the relatively simple matter of price control. There is still much to play for.

NO 'PEOPLE'S STAKE'

But to return to my time as Energy Secretary. Far and away the most important privatisation I secured during that time was that of BNOC. This had been set up by the Labour Government in 1976 to explore for, produce, refine and distribute oil from the North Sea. It accounted for some 7 per cent of total North Sea oil production. It also had the right, by a system of participation agreements, to buy up to 51 per cent of all UK North Sea oil, whoever produced it, and bring it onshore. This gave BNOC a predominant position in the purchase and trading of North Sea oil, even though nine tenths of it was produced by private sector companies, and in practice the BNOC offer price was, not surprisingly, kept close to the world market price. The Corporation was also equipped with an extensive list of privileges. It was exempt from Petroleum Revenue Tax, guaranteed access to interest-free funds, and enjoyed preferential rights in the licensing of new oil fields. It was also, along with British Gas, guaranteed the right of first refusal of any North Sea assets sold to third parties by private companies. This combination of preferential treatment and tax-subsidised competition had deterred some exploration and development by the private sector.

The 1979 manifesto promised to review all of BNOC's activities. The Corporation was made liable to PRT in Geoffrey's first Budget; and it was progressively stripped of most of its other privileges. It should really have been privatised well before I became Energy Secretary; but at the time such a radical step seemed fraught with political difficulties. It had an articulate chairman and board who were wholly opposed to privatisation. But the main constraint was presentational.

The usual lack of enthusiasm for State ownership was reinforced in the public mind by the feeling that North Sea oil was a unique national asset which should remain strictly under national political control. Despite the fact that the private sector already accounted for the vast bulk of North Sea oil output, it was difficult to find a way of privatising BNOC without succumbing to the charge that the Government was relinquishing ownership of a priceless national treasure to speculators, foreigners or multinationals. Indeed the main reason for David Howell's hesitancy was Margaret's acute sensitivity that privatisation of BNOC's operating arm implied that Britain would somehow lose control of part of her oil. She rejected a number of BNOC privatisation options on these grounds at an important meeting of the Economic Committee of the Cabinet in March 1980.

Prevented by Margaret from mounting a full-frontal assault, David Howell had concentrated his efforts on preparing the ground by installing a pro-privatisation chairman, Philip Shelbourne, with a City background – and, somewhat less constructively, on abortive plans for a so-called 'People's Stake' in North Sea oil. There have, of course, been various plans to hand over 'free' to all citizens a tradeable security entitling them to either all or part of government North Sea oil revenues, and – a completely separate proposal – to make a free gift of BNOC and other privatisation shares to all citizens instead of selling them for cash. Because the word 'oil' occurred in both, the two proposals were frequently confused. The first idea was put forward by Samuel Brittan and Barry Riley of the *Financial Times* and the second by Samuel Brittan on his own. The first idea had nothing to do with BNOC, and the second would have applied to all privatisation issues. Moreover the first idea, although the more ingenious of the two, failed to address the issue of the ownership of BNOC.

Whatever may be necessary in ex-Communist countries which need to privatise a large proportion of their industry rapidly in the face of a barely existing domestic capital market, the give-away idea had no real supporters in the Thatcher Government, least of all me, as I made clear to Samuel Brittan from the beginning. The reason was put very succinctly two centuries ago by Thomas Paine, the author of *Rights of Man* and hardly a right-wing figure: 'What we obtain too cheap, we esteem too lightly.' David Howell's idea, however, which he launched with a great fanfare in his speech at the 1980 Party Conference, was neither of these. What it amounted to was in effect a National Savings Certificate whose return would be linked to the value of Britain's North Sea oil output. Although a fair amount of work was done on it, I must confess that I could see little merit in it. As I argued at the time, there is no substitute, either industrially or politically, for full-blooded privatisation.

BNOC INTO BRITOIL

The putative North Sea oil bond died a natural death. On becoming Energy Secretary I decided that the political damage Margaret feared could be minimised if BNOC were split in two, with the exploration and production business, where the value was, privatised, and the trading business, together with the participation agreements on which it was based, remaining for the time being at least in the State sector.

Assembling the best official team the Department could provide, led by an exceptionally able Under Secretary, Richard Wilson (he subsequently became

Cabinet Secretary), I set to work to direct the separation of the oil assets from the trading arm of BNOC, the preparation of a suitably capitalised Britoil balance sheet and the writing of a prospectus. The name 'Britoil' was not in fact my choice. I would have preferred 'British North Sea Oil', but Philip Shelbourne was wedded to 'Britoil' since he wanted to convert it, post-privatisation, to a global oil company rather than one confined to the North Sea. This he eventually did, to some extent, via a series of purchases which failed either to strengthen the company, or to impress the markets, and left it vulnerable to the takeover which a few years later occurred.

In preparing Britoil for privatisation, Ministers and officials alike were in uncharted territory. Even though we chose to sell only 51 per cent of the company in the first instance, it was still the biggest transfer of assets from the State to the private sector yet attempted. When we began work in the autumn of 1981, the Government's experience of privatisation consisted of 51 per cent of British Aerospace and Cable and Wireless, neither of which sales exceeded £300 million in value, whereas 51 per cent of Britoil was worth around twice that amount. Moreover both British Aerospace and Cable and Wireless were straightforward Companies Act companies – as was Amersham International, whose bitter-sweet flotation preceded the Britoil offer for sale, whereas BNOC was a fully-fledged Morrisonian public corporation. The sheer size of the issue was also felt to be somewhat daunting. Both the Bank of England and Warburgs, the Department's financial advisers, were deeply worried that the equity market would be unable to absorb such a large amount of stock, especially in view of the campaign of vilification which preceded the sale.

Part of that vilification was caused by the fear that, once privatised, the company would fall into foreign hands; and it became politically imperative to find an answer to this. I recalled from my brief time as 'Lex', the stock market columnist of the *Financial Times*, in 1959/60, the curious voting structures I had occasionally come across (and invariably inveighed against), which enabled the owners of a very small slice of the equity to exercise quite disproportionate power. Inspired by this, I devised the so-called 'golden share', a special share which would be retained by the Government after privatisation, and which would enable it to prevent control of the company from falling into unsuitable hands. (The term 'unsuitable' had to be used, rather than 'foreign', to avoid falling foul of Community law; but everyone knew what it was likely to mean.)

The 'golden share' has since become a standard feature in privatisation issues, but in the early days both Philip Shelbourne and Rothschilds, whom he had brought in as advisers to BNOC, maintained that shackles of any sort on a free market in the shares of the privatised company would make the flotation more difficult. In this they were mistaken. However, we did not get the precise design of the Britoil golden share right, which was to prove awkward later on; but the details could be and were amended in subsequent privatisations: it was the concept that mattered.[12]

The Labour Party inevitably made the Oil and Gas (Enterprise) Bill the focal point of their parliamentary opposition that session, obliging me to ask the business managers to introduce a guillotine motion, putting a limit to the time available for debate, in March 1982. The Press, too, as with most subsequent privatisations, was largely hostile, right up to the launch. So at the start, were many of our own back-benchers.

But the political difficulties were at least familiar ones: not so the technical problems that had to be overcome. Being a public corporation, it had first to be converted into a Companies Act company, and given an appropriate balance sheet. This was eventually achieved, not without a prolonged argument with Philip Shelbourne, who wished the new company to carry no debt at all on its books. I was less successful in my search for a high flyer from the oil industry to appoint as Chief Executive of Britoil – partly because of Labour's renationalisation pledge. In the end I had to give up the search, as time was running out, and had to content myself with persuading BNOC's senior oilman to delay his impending retirement, and appointing three heavyweight non-executive directors whose clear remit was to find a new Chief Executive as soon as possible after privatisation.

The biggest technical problem of all, however, was devising a wholly new method of sale. Following the Amersham affair, I had decided that Britoil would be not a fixed-price offer but a tender, which would be underwritten at the minimum tender price. Both Shelbourne and Rothschilds, the company's financial advisers, were opposed to this unfamiliar technique. But Warburgs, the Department's financial advisers, considered it a perfectly viable proposition, and with Margaret's full concurrence we set to work to devise a novel form of tender designed to avoid the danger, which had led me to oppose the tender for Amersham, of deterring the small investor.

What we came up with was a tender in which anyone who applied for shares, if they were uncertain as to what price to bid, could simply write in the box

[12] [2010 note] In 2003 the European Court of Justice ruled illegal the British Government's golden share in the British Airports Authority, restricting – although not altogether eliminating – the use of this device.

the words 'striking price' – which meant that they undertook to subscribe for the shares at whatever price emerged from the tender process. The application form itself was completely redesigned to make it simpler and clearer than in any previous share offer, whether by the Government or the private sector; and the fact that payment was by instalments, with the first instalment set at a fixed price, meant that despite the tender the investor knew exactly what cheque to send with his application. Finally, to encourage the genuine small shareholder, as against the 'stag' who applied in the hope of selling at a quick profit as soon as dealings in the shares commenced, I introduced (in addition to the employee share scheme customary in privatisation issues) a 'small shareholder bonus', under which any small shareholder who retained his shares for three years would receive an additional allocation of shares, on a one-for-ten basis, free.

I finally agreed the minimum price for the tender with David Scholey, Warburg's chairman, in early November 1982, after consulting Dundas Hamilton, a distinguished stockbroker whose firm had no connection with the issue, and whom I had formally appointed the Government's independent adviser on pricing. This was the first time this appointment, which was to be repeated in most of the subsequent large privatisations, had been made. It was, quite simply, designed to provide an extra line of defence against a possible investigation by the parliamentary watchdog, the Public Accounts Committee (PAC), the most powerful of all the select committees, which was by this time becoming restive at the apparent underpricing of privatisation issues and consequent loss to the taxpayer.

On 10 November the underwriting of the issue was quickly and successfully completed. That night I said to my weary officials, 'Well done. Whatever happens now, Britoil has been privatised.' What did happen then, however, was something wholly unexpected. Over the critical weekend before the closing date for applications for the issue a fortnight later, Sheikh Yamani, the Saudi Oil Minister, then at the height of his power and prestige, gave an interview to an obscure Kuwaiti newspaper in which he expressed gloom about the future course of the price of oil. This was soon all over the wires. The oil price duly dipped, and sentiment about the Britoil flotation abruptly deteriorated. The issue was badly undersubscribed, with the underwriters being left with some 70 per cent of the shares, and dealings opened at a marked discount. In standard City parlance, the issue was 'a flop'.

But it was certainly no disaster. My old friend Godfrey Chandler, of Cazenoves, than whom there is no wiser observer of the City scene, wrote to me aptly describing the issue as 'a successful disappointment'. Britoil had been privatised. The momentum of the Government's overall privatisation programme was in no way impeded. Although the tender method used for the sale had not been the cause of the undersubscription, it had certainly not helped, and fixed-price offers, or some variant of them, became accepted as the norm for future privatisations. There was one further silver lining to this particular cloud. The PAC, in its scrutiny of privatisation, had been developing the theory that it was wholly unnecessary for the Government to have its share sales underwritten – influenced to some extent by Labour claims that this was simply a way in which the Tories lined the pockets of their friends in the City. After Britoil, little more was heard from the PAC of this canard.

Of the remaining 49 per cent of Britoil, one per cent had to be retained to distribute to those qualifying for the small shareholder bonus, and the other 48 per cent was disposed of in a successful offer for sale to the general public in August 1985. By that time all the political agitation had abated, and it was no longer necessary to pay lip-service to the idea that Britain's oil security depended on the state retaining the rump of BNOC as a trading arm. Peter Walker, with my support, initially merged it with the Government's long-standing strategic pipeline system to form the Oil and Pipeline Agency (OPA). In due course the oil trading operation, which was nothing but an intermittently embarrassing (and potentially costly) irrelevance, was quietly abandoned.

THE BRITISH TELECOM BREAKTHROUGH

With the transfer of Britoil to the private sector, the privatisation programme was now gathering pace. But the cause of wider share ownership had yet to be greatly advanced. Britoil, even without Yamani's ill-timed (and some thought deliberate) intervention, was in any case not the right vehicle for the breakthrough. The general public are interested primarily in holding shares in companies they know and of which they are regular customers. The ideal vehicle was now at hand, in the shape of the telephone giant, British Telecom.

This had emerged through a number of stages. Originally, both the post office and the telephone system were, anomalously, a single government department staffed by Civil Servants and headed by a Minister known as the Postmaster General. The Wilson Labour Government of the 1960s, prompted by the then head of the Civil Service, William Armstrong, had separated them and converted them into two Morrisonian public corporations.

Shortly after we returned to office in 1979 Keith Joseph, as Industry Secretary, energetically set about breaking the British Telecom monopoly by fostering the birth of a partial competitor, Mercury Communications, owned principally by the newly privatised Cable and Wireless. Then, in 1982, his successor at Industry, Patrick Jenkin, announced that British Telecom was to be privatised. A Bill was duly introduced, but it had not completed its passage when the 1983 general election was called, and it was reintroduced in the subsequent parliament by the new Secretary of State for the (once again) merged Department of Trade and Industry, Norman Tebbit.

The length of time all this took was not wasted. When we first examined the nationalised British Telecom we discovered that, in true East European style, the corporation had not the faintest idea which of its activities were profitable and which were not, let alone any finer points of management accounting. All this clearly had to be changed. A new chairman, George Jefferson, was brought in from the private sector and charged with the task of putting this right and otherwise preparing the corporation for privatisation.

Our original preference had been to split up British Telecom so as to increase the competition in this fast-growing and capital-hungry industry which the birth of Mercury had begun. But Jefferson was insistent that his empire should remain intact. As it was, the trade unions representing its workforce – like all nationalised industries, it was totally unionised – were bitterly opposed to privatisation and were making all manner of threatening noises. We felt that we could scarcely afford to have the management against us as well, if we were to achieve a successful privatisation.

But the sale of even 51 per cent of British Telecom as a single entity meant a flotation far larger than any that had previously been contemplated. I vividly recall a small private dinner party held in the penthouse suite of the Dorchester Hotel by Kenneth Corfield, then chairman of Standard Telephones and Cables (STC) in honour of the unusually named American, Rand Araskog, chairman of the US telephone monopoly, ITT, which was about to be broken up under US anti-trust legislation.

Araskog naturally showed an interest in our plans for British Telecom, and views were sought from those present, who, myself apart, were all captains of industry and pillars of leading City merchant banks. With the exception of Martin Jacomb from Kleinworts, which had been retained by the Government to advise on the sale, each and every one of them roundly declared that the privatisation was impossible: the capital market simply was not large enough to absorb it.

Needless to say, we went ahead, with Norman Tebbit in the lead, until he was severely injured by the IRA bomb which caused such devastation at the Grand Hotel, Brighton, during the Conservative Party Conference of October 1984. As Chancellor, I then took over for the last lap, and British Telecom was privatised by means of a fixed-price offer for sale in November 1984.

The final discussions involved, among other things, the regulatory regime that was to be put in place. This again was breaking new ground: British Telecom was the first more or less monopoly public utility to be privatised, and such animals clearly cannot be permitted to exploit that position. An independent State-owned agency, the Office of Telecommunications (Oftel) was set up to oversee the industry; and the key element in the regime was the rule that the company could increase its charges each year by no more than RPI-x; representing the rate of inflation for the previous year less a percentage designed to reflect the industry's scope for increasing efficiency. This formula, which had been devised by Professor Stephen Littlechild, was originally envisaged as a rough-and-ready short-term solution to the problem; but in practice it has endured and been used as the basis of the regulatory regimes for all the privatised public utilities.

It is undoubtedly greatly superior to the system used in the United States, the home of privately owned public utilities, where the regulatory regime is based on limiting the permitted return on capital, which inevitably leads to the inflation of costs of all kinds. By contrast, the price-based UK system means that the utilities can increase their profits only by reducing their costs. In the case of British Telecom, there was a major argument as to how big the x-factor should be, with the company (supported by Norman Tebbit) arguing for 2 per cent, while I wanted 4 per cent. Inevitably, we eventually compromised on 3 per cent.[13]

Another innovation of the Telecom privatisation – and once again something hitherto unknown to the City – was the launch of a two-stage advertising campaign, particularly on television, designed to stimulate public interest in the share sale. Prior to the offer, this took the form of intensified corporate advertising; once the offer was launched, it advertised the offer itself – without, of course, going so far as to advise people to buy the shares.

[13] [2010 note] The formula remains intact in areas where BT is judged to retain significant market power – a power that has been greatly eroded, not least by the development of a highly competitive market in mobile telephony, itself an objective of policy. At times the x-factor has stood as high as 13 per cent, helping to drive down the real price of fixed-line calls to consumers by more than 70 per cent since privatisation.

The outcome of the offer for sale in November 1984 was a success that not only confounded our critics but exceeded even our own expectations. The price valued the total sale at almost £4 billion, to be paid in instalments over two financial years. It was comfortably oversubscribed. By tilting the allocation of shares in favour of the small investor we succeeded in almost doubling the number of Britons who owned shares overnight. Altogether some two million people, or 5 per cent of the adult population of the United Kingdom, bought shares in British Telecom, half of them applying for no more than 400 shares. As I put it at the time:

> The successful sale of British Telecom ... reveals a vast and untapped yearning among ordinary people for a direct stake in the ownership of British enterprise. Investment in shares has begun to take its place, with ownership of a home and either a bank or building society deposit, as a way for ordinary people to participate in enterprise and wealth creation. We are seeing the birth of people's capitalism.

'People's capitalism' was my own coinage. Margaret Thatcher liked the idea, but not the precise formulation, which she thought sounded Communist, reminding her of expressions like 'people's republic'. She amended it to 'popular capitalism', and thus modified it became part of the stock-in-trade of Conservative speech-making from that moment on.

CHAPTER THIRTEEN

PRIVATISATION 3: THE PROGRAMME REACHES A CLIMAX

Privatisation Gathers Pace · Hot Water · The Nuclear Blight

An Assessment of Privatisation

PRIVATISATION GATHERS PACE

The great success of the British Telecom privatisation opened the way to the privatisation of the next public utility, British Gas. As Energy Secretary, I had secured Margaret's agreement to include in the 1983 manifesto a somewhat cautious pledge to seek 'means of increasing competition in, and attracting private capital into, the gas and electricity industries'. I have recorded a little earlier on how my plans for making competition in the gas industry were frustrated, but the attraction of private capital on a massive scale was almost effortlessly achieved, assisted by the 'Don't tell Sid' (and subsequently 'Tell Sid') advertising campaign, which caught on to such an extent that for a time small shareholders became known as 'Sids'.

Unlike the Telecom sale, a full 100 per cent of British Gas was successfully offered for sale in December 1986, raising £5.4 billion, payable in instalments, with the allocation of the oversubscribed offer tilted in favour of the small shareholder, thus increasing still further the proportion of British adults holding shares, if only in one or two privatisation issues. This again took place while I was Chancellor, with overall responsibility for the privatisation programme, day-to-day supervision of which I delegated to my Financial Secretary, John Moore. John went about his task with missionary zeal, something the City establishment was distinctly short of. 'But John,' the head of one broking house exclaimed to him, 'we don't want all those kind of people owning shares, do we?'

British Airways, which was eventually sold for £900 million in February 1987 was financially a very much smaller privatisation than Gas. But it caused far more trouble than any other. It was originally intended to be the first privatisation of all, and the enabling legislation was introduced as early as November

1979, and completed its passage through Parliament without any difficulty. It was then that the problems began. The airline industry is notoriously cyclical, and British Airways' profits were very badly hit by the world recession of the early eighties.

This would not have mattered so much in the United States, where airline shares are well known on the stock market and their cyclical nature fully understood. But in the UK no publicly quoted airline share existed, and the Government had no practical choice but to defer the issue until the recovery phase was firmly established. Meanwhile the rugged, astute, and politically aware industrialist John King – later Lord King, and rightly one of Margaret's favourite businessmen – was brought in as chairman in 1981, and with the indispensable assistance of his excellent Chief Executive, Colin Marshall, set about doing the remarkable job of transferring British Airways from one of the world's least efficient major airlines to one of its most efficient. The massive overmanning, characteristic of almost all nationalised aviation, was drastically eliminated, and with the minimum of trouble from the trade unions; peripheral businesses were disposed of; unprofitable routes were discontinued; the airline's marketing strategy was greatly improved; and productivity was increased in every aspect of the business.

This dramatic transformation, incidentally, is an example of the difficulty of quantifying the great improvement in industrial efficiency that privatisation invariably brings. It occurred while British Airways was still a nationalised industry, yet it would not have happened at all had it not been for the prospect of privatisation. Had he not been able to take the airline into the private sector John King would never have accepted its chairmanship in the first place; and even if he had been prevailed upon to do so, he would never have embarked on the massive and difficult task of turning the company round as he did. Nor, equally, even if he had tried to do so, would the unions have been nearly as acquiescent had they felt that the bottomless purse of the State would always be there to shield them from the rigours of economic reality and the need to make a profit. This is a story that was repeated time after time, if not on so dramatic a scale, throughout the privatisation saga.

Frustratingly, however, no sooner had the airline emerged from the rigours of the recession than it encountered a new and even more formidable obstacle to privatisation. During the seventies the ebullient cockney, Freddie Laker, had built up the independent airline he had created, Laker Airways, into a serious competitor to the established scheduled airlines, not least on the transatlantic route. At the start of the recession Laker Airways went out of business altogether. The creditors of the failed airline, however, claimed that it was not the recession that had caused its collapse, but an illegal conspiracy by the established airlines to do Laker down.

Given the appallingly cartelised nature of the airline business (at that time throughout the world, and still, lamentably, within Europe), and the psychology and business methods that cartels invariably manifest, this was probably true. Moreover, unlike the US airlines involved, the nationalised British Airways, in the best bureaucratic tradition, had kept a note of every telephone conversation its senior officers held. Not surprisingly, the creditors filed a civil action in the US courts against all the airlines allegedly involved, including British Airways.

There was no way the company could now be floated with this open-ended financial liability hanging over its head, which clearly would have had to be fully disclosed in the prospectus. A prior out-of-court settlement was the only answer. English lawyers were a cross I learned to bear during my time as a Minister, but the complications they cause are as nothing compared with their American opposite numbers. Eventually, after a seemingly interminable delay, unbelievable complexity, and numerous meetings of the relevant Cabinet Committee over which Margaret presided, a satisfactory out-of-court settlement was reached, and the long-awaited green light could be given for the privatisation of British Airways.

The flotation itself, the last of the 1983–87 parliament, was embarrassingly successful, being no less than eleven times oversubscribed. As in many previous privatisation issues, more than 90 per cent of the workforce subscribed for shares in the company. This had been an encouraging feature of most privatisations, and would continue to be. The trade union leaders would condemn the privatisation with bell, book and candle, and enjoin their members not to touch it with a bargepole; and their members would take not the slightest notice of them.

HOT WATER

The tide of ideas was now flowing strongly in favour of the market economy, and nothing illustrated this better than the Government's increasingly ambitious privatisation programme. With telecommunications and gas now safely in the private sector, we turned our attention to the two remaining giant public utilities, water and electricity, starting with water, the purest natural monopoly of all. The water industry was also the first multiple privatisation, with the ten regional water companies eventually being floated separately but simultaneously in November 1989.

The story began, however, as far back as the beginning of 1985. The nationalised regional water authorities were becoming increasingly restive about Treasury control of their ambitious investment plans and its insistence that they should earn a return that would finance those plans, which meant both cutting costs and raising prices. Roy Watts, the chairman of the largest authority, Thames Water, started to campaign publicly against the Government – unacceptable behaviour on the part of a nationalised industry chairman – and an ugly anti-Treasury mood began to emerge on the back benches. Fortunately, Watts had also made it clear that he favoured privatisation, as a means of escape from Treasury control (a view not shared by most of the other Water Authority chairmen), and this seemed to me the ideal solution.

I discussed the matter with my old friend Ian Gow, then a Minister of State at the Department of the Environment under Patrick Jenkin, with special responsibility for the water industry, and a long-standing enthusiast for the privatisation programme. I encouraged him to drop the following broad hint, the wording of which I had agreed with him, in a Commons debate on 7 February 1985:

> In our manifesto, we promised to transfer nine public sector businesses to independent ownership. The transfer of water authorities, which form a natural monopoly, presents special problems, not least because of their regulatory functions. Nevertheless, my Right Honourable Friends and I will be examining the possibility of a measure of privatisation in the industry.

Within no time, privatisation of the water industry had become firm Government policy, and announced as such. But it was out of one frying pan into another, for the proposal immediately aroused more hostility among our own back-benchers than any other privatisation, before or since.

The initial privatisation plans for water were published in the form of a White Paper in February 1986 by Kenneth Baker, who had succeeded Patrick Jenkin as Environment Secretary in Margaret's 1985 reshuffle, when Patrick was dropped from the Government altogether. They assumed that the various water authorities would simply be privatised as they stood. This reflected the strongly expressed views of the Water Authority chairmen, whose belief in the integrity of their empires was absolute. But it had little objective merit and served only to maximise back-bench opposition. Not that these empires were of long standing.

They had been created by the Heath Government's 1973 Water Act, of which the author was the then Environment Secretary, Peter Walker.

The 1973 Act had introduced the concept of 'integrated river basin management', and set up ten statutory water authorities, each responsible for the full range of activities connected with a single river basin such as the Thames or the Severn-Trent. This meant, as Ian Gow had warned, that their functions included regulatory and environmental matters like water conservation, controlling beach and river pollution, land drainage, flood prevention and fishing rights as well as the core business of supplying water and sewerage services (which latter had previously been the responsibility of the local authorities).

Talking to back-benchers shortly before the House rose for the 1986 summer recess, it was clear to me that most of the objections to privatisation on our own benches stemmed not from distress at the transfer of the core businesses of water and sewerage to the private sector, but from concern about the regulatory and environmental aspects, notably nature conservation and the defence of anglers' rights, about which they were receiving a large number of letters. England is a nation of anglers.

In the summer of 1986, Keith Joseph, to whom Margaret had been devoted ever since they had made common cause during the dark days of Opposition in 1974, left the Government at his own request and was replaced as Education Secretary by Kenneth Baker. To the horror of the environmentalists in the Party, she made Nick Ridley Environment Secretary in succession to Ken Baker.

Nowadays it is probably the Environment Secretary who has the most important of the second division posts. Certainly, given the fact that he is responsible for the relationship between central and local government, his impact on public expenditure is considerable. Ken Baker's every instinct was to spend, spend, spend – a weakness mitigated only by the good humour with which he would normally retreat from the impossible positions he initially adopted. Nick Ridley, by contrast, was a firm believer in strict public expenditure control. He seemed to me, as he did to my then Chief Secretary, John MacGregor, with whom I discussed the matter after Margaret had consulted me, the best man for the job, and I duly told her so. I also thought, wrongly as it turned out, that Nick, as a former Treasury Minister much involved with taxation, would see the political dangers in the Poll Tax which had eluded Ken Baker.

What Nick did recognise pretty soon was that the Baker plan for water privatisation was a non-starter. To the concern of my officials, who had pencilled the proceeds from water privatisation into their financial planning, he warned me that he proposed to tell Cabinet that the flotation would have to be postponed until after the election. I could not but agree.

We then discussed the way forward, and had little difficulty in agreeing that, despite the devotion of the Water Authority chairmen to the doctrine of integrated river basin management, the obvious route was to privatise the water and sewerage business and hive off the regulatory and environmental responsibilities into a separate State-owned National Rivers Authority. Treasury officials were initially very unhappy at the idea of creating a new quango, and had nightmares about the numbers it would employ and the public expenditure it would incur. But these were practical problems of a kind that the Treasury, after all, had some experience of addressing. What was manifestly absurd – despite the fact that it had been the practice hitherto – was that the regulator and the regulated should be one and the same entity.

In due course, and in good time for the election, Nick announced the Government's revised proposals for water privatisation; and despite opposition jeers at what they claimed was a U-turn, our back-benchers warmly approved the change and all seemed set fair for a flotation as soon as the Bill reached the statute-book in the new parliament. Public opinion, however, remained overwhelmingly hostile, with opinion polls regularly recording a 75-80 per cent majority opposed to water privatisation. Perhaps the British shared the Chinese belief – which has meant that even in that citadel of private enterprise, Hong Kong, the business of water supply remains in Government hands – that water, like air, is a divine element, and not a matter for commerce.

If so, it showed a remarkable lack of touch with reality. Most of the original waterworks were private, and operated under private Acts of Parliament, and they were only gradually taken over by the municipalities. Even after the 1973 Water Act, a quarter of Britain's water supply remained in the hands of twenty-nine private water companies, whose customers were perfectly content. In France, which ever since Colbert has countenanced far greater involvement by the State in the economy than Britain, the water industry was almost wholly in the private sector. Indeed, there was some embarrassment ahead of the flotation when a number of the smaller UK private water companies were gobbled up by the giant French water combines. Nick eventually decided to halt the traffic, making it clear he would refer any bid worth more than £30 million to the Monopolies and Mergers Commission.

The privatisation programme had now been going long enough for us to face public hostility, even on this unusual scale, with equanimity. What we had not bargained for was the more serious problem of the European Commission, which almost on the eve of the flotation decided to take the Government to the European Court for non-compliance with an absurd Community Drinking Water Directive of 1980 – the Government had agreed to it in the very early days when we were somewhat less experienced in the ways of the Commission – which demanded quite unnecessary standards of purity. Needless to say, no other major Community member country had complied either; but they were not in the process of writing prospectuses which would have to spell out and quantify all contingent liabilities, whereas we were.

Eventually a settlement was reached; but it meant that the companies would have to commit themselves to a massive investment programme, financed partly by an expensive injection of public money prior to the flotation and partly by higher charges to water consumers after it. This solved the last remaining problem. Eventually, in December 1989, a few weeks after I had resigned from the Government, and almost five years after Ian Gow's original intimation, all ten new-style regional water companies were simultaneously and successfully sold to the public, raising more than £5 billion in an issue that, overall, was comfortably but not excessively oversubscribed. As with the other public utilities already privatised, a regulatory agency was simultaneously put in place – in this case the Office of Water Supplies, or Ofwat – to scrutinise the industry and prevent it exploiting its monopoly, with a similar regulatory regime based on the Littlechild price-control formula.

Willie Whitelaw, who stood next to me during the Cabinet Secretary's reading of the Queen's Speech at Margaret's traditional ministerial dinner at Number 10 on the eve of the opening of the new parliament in June 1987, muttered that the Government would get into a great deal of trouble over the privatisation of water. He clearly had grave doubts as to whether we were politically wise to go ahead with it at all. I replied that, in my opinion it was electricity, not water, that was going to be the difficult one. So it proved.

Most of the problems with water were presentational rather than fundamental. Once it was clear that the regulatory and environmental responsibilities would remain in the public sector, the success of the privatisation never looked seriously at risk.

THE NUCLEAR BLIGHT

My forebodings about electricity were largely based on the fact that whereas water, although the more emotive of the two, was essentially a simple industry, electricity was very much more complex. But I do not claim to have foreseen all the hazards that did come to light. I had started the ball rolling, with the passage of the Energy Act, making the national grid a common carrier and abolishing the statutory prohibition on private generation for sale, and the Coopers and Lybrand report on electricity privatisation, during my last months as Energy Secretary in 1983. But my successor, Peter Walker, took the matter little further. There were one or two meetings on the subject under Margaret's chairmanship in early 1987 but it was clear that Peter was more anxious to maintain secrecy about what he was up to in this field than to make progress.

To mollify me and impress Margaret that he was serious, he arranged for a Treasury official to join his team; but it was not until Cecil Parkinson became Energy Secretary in June 1987 that preparations for the privatisation of electricity began in earnest. Electricity generation was at the time the responsibility of twelve area electricity boards. It was clearly sensible to privatise the latter first; and there were obvious similarities between the ten regional water utilities and the twelve area electricity utilities.

Floating the distribution companies threw up some very intricate problems, to which after much technical debate we managed to agree a relatively simple and, above all, effective solution. But the real obstacle to the privatisation of the electricity industry was elsewhere, in the field of generation, and in particular the economics of nuclear generation. The full horrors of this did not, however, become apparent until preparations for the sale were well advanced. There was no inkling of them when, on Saturday, 14 September 1987, Margaret held a day-long meeting at Chequers for Cecil and his officials to present their plans. Newly restored to the Cabinet after four years in exile, Cecil was anxious both to please the Prime Minister and to secure her support. His plan to transfer ownership of the National Grid from the CEGB to a new company jointly owned by the twelve distribution companies was patently sensible. The National Grid was effectively the marketplace for electricity. As long as it remained in the control of the CEGB, which supplied 95 per cent of the electricity transmitted by it, there was little prospect of independent generating concerns breaking into the market. The privatisation of the National Grid, and the concentration of purchasing power in the hands of independent distributors free to buy electricity from the cheapest source, was much more likely to encourage the emergence of private electricity generators.

The two contentious issues which emerged at the Chequers meeting in September 1987 both concerned the future of the CEGB. The key question was whether to privatise it whole or to break it up first; and, if so, into how many parts. The second (and related) question was whether or not to include in the sale the nuclear power stations operated by the CEGB in England and Wales and by the South of Scotland Electricity Board (SSEB) in Scotland. At that stage there seemed no compelling reason for excluding the nuclear power stations from privatisation – after all, something like half the nuclear power stations in the world were in the private sector – but this conclusion had implications for the break-up of the CEGB. Cecil was convinced, and convinced Margaret, that, in order to be sure of securing the planning permissions necessary to implement a continuing programme of nuclear power station construction, the private sector company owning them must be of real substance, with proven expertise in this particular field.

This led him to conclude that all the CEGB's nuclear power stations would need to be kept within a single generating company which, to be saleable to potential investors, would have to own a large number of non-nuclear power stations as well. This in turn implied a company so large that there was room for only one other private sector generating company to be created out of the old CEGB. This was the origin of what were known in Cecil's original White Paper of 25 February 1988 as 'Big G' and 'Little G', subsequently privatised, in March 1991, as National Power and PowerGen. The twelve regional electricity distribution companies – or 'distcos' – had already been successfully privatised in December 1990, and with the privatisation of Scottish Electricity in May 1991 the exercise was complete.

Or, at least, as complete as it could be. For right to the end, the nuclear problem cast a blight on the exercise. Initially, this took the form of Walter Marshall, the great nuclear power enthusiast and chairman of the CEGB, threatening to resign if the CEGB were broken up. Walter was confident that Margaret would not allow Cecil to lose him: Cecil, to his credit, stood his ground and Walter duly went. Then the economics of nuclear power, on analysis, proved to be such that no private sector company would ever build a nuclear station without some artificial inducement, and a fossil fuel levy had to be introduced. Finally, the nuclear power stations had to be removed from the privatisation altogether, and the whole of the Government's nuclear power station building programme put on ice, as the financial and economic truths which State ownership had successfully concealed from successive Governments were at last exposed in the run-up to privatisation.

AN ASSESSMENT OF PRIVATISATION

The success of the Conservative Government's pioneering privatisation programme is accepted throughout the world. But it is only right to note some of the criticisms that have been levelled closer to home.

The first and least central criticism is that the fees paid to the Government's professional advisers and to the financial institutions as underwriters have been too high – and that where shares were firmly placed with the institutions in advance of the public offer the terms on which this was done were too generous. To the extent that this is valid, and it became progressively less true as we gained in experience, we developed new techniques – one of which, 'clawback', under which the more successful an issue was, the more the institutions had to surrender their allotments to the general public, I can claim to have devised myself. Privatisation was an exercise in which Government found itself a financial innovator to an extent which is rare indeed.

A second criticism is that shares were offered to the public at prices that were less than could have been secured, in order to promote widespread share ownership. To this I would reply: 'Yes, and quite right too.' While the interests of the taxpayer had to be given adequate weight, the maximisation of proceeds, despite what many commentators said, was never the main objective. To quote Pliatzky:

> The objective of raising money for the Exchequer by these disposals, which later became an important by-product of the privatisation programme, played no part in the Conservatives' hostility to nationalisation, and little or no part in the gathering impetus of its drive for privatisation ... The prime motives for privatisation were not Exchequer gain but an ideological belief in free markets and a wider distribution of private ownership of property.

Wider share ownership was an important policy objective and we were prepared to pay a price for it – although this price declined as our techniques developed over time.

A third and related criticism is potentially more serious. This focuses not on Government revenues but on investor attitudes. Many well-disposed critics in the City and elsewhere have said that the process by which people apply for privatisation issues, are allotted a fraction of what they bid for, and then immediately sell the proceeds at a profit, gives them a false idea of the nature and function of both capitalism and the stock market. While it would be unrealistic to expect all shareholders to abjure the chance of a quick profit, what is striking is how long term many millions of shareholders have been. In some of the largest and most popular issues, such as gas and electricity, for example, more than half the new investors were still holding their stock at the time of writing.

Yet another criticism, which was very much in vogue at one time with the Treasury Select Committee and other less august commentators, is that the Government, in classifying privatisation receipts as 'negative expenditure', was in effect cooking the books and – perhaps even more seriously – deceiving itself in this way to an extent that adversely affected the conduct of macroeconomic policy. Despite Harold Macmillan's jibe about making ends meet by selling the family silver, I believe there is nothing in this whatever. I made a point of publishing figures for both Government spending and the Public Sector Borrowing Requirement on two bases: one with the benefit of privatisation proceeds, and the other without. No-one could possibly claim to have been misled; nor, needless to say, was there any self-delusion on the part of the Government. Any other presentation would have involved a major upheaval to no purpose.[14]

As it was, in fact, so far from flattering the public finances, the main consequence was probably to shed unwarranted doubt on what was by any standards a remarkable fiscal achievement. But that is for another chapter.

Probably the most serious criticism is that the Government concentrated too much on ownership and not enough on competition. This is the main charge made by John Kay in his studies with various co-authors. It reflects the standard mainstream economists' party line that it is only competition that matters and not ownership. This ignores both the theoretical importance of property rights and the practical experience of countries moving away from centrally controlled economies. Indeed, in a sense Kay comes to the same conclusion. His recipe for success is a combination of competition and privatisation, so that there are both market disciplines and personal incentives for the managers of the concerns in question.

The difference between mainstream economists and the Government of which I was a member was about what to do as a second best in cases where a high degree of competition was not an immediate option, partly because of the

[14] It has been argued that the proceeds of council house sales, which are also classified as negative expenditure, should similarly be stripped out of the public expenditure figures. Certainly the 'right-to-buy' programme, under which some 1.7 million local authority houses and flats were sold to sitting tenants between April 1979 and March 1992 for a total of over £24 billion, was a form of privatisation – indeed, it was the earliest form of privatisation. It is equally true that the there was no concealment; the figure for local authority receipts from council house sales was always separately identified and published annually. But the argument for a different treatment in the public accounts is even weaker in this case, not least because gross capital investment in public sector housing (which is of course classified as public expenditure) regularly exceeded the receipts from council house sales.

natural monopoly characteristics of some public utilities, notably water, partly for supposed technological reasons, as in British Telecom, and partly as a result of political obstacles, as in the case of British Gas. I believed that it was important to privatise as much as possible as quickly as possible; and this would itself set up pressures for more competition and other structural changes.

It is, for instance, difficult to believe that Mercury would have been able to challenge BT, if the latter had remained a conventional public utility and had not been forced to allow competition initially as a direct consequence of legislation and subsequently by the independent regulator the Government put in place. Similarly, no conventional sponsoring department would have had the power to force BT to replace within a few months its vandalised public telephone boxes in the way that Bryan Carsberg, the head of Oftel, was able to do with the threat of further competition in the background.

The very issues which Kay is so keen to explore, such as contracting out and the form of relations between public utilities and Government, have come out into open debate in a way that simply did not occur when the industries were publicly owned monopolies and were assumed by definition to be acting in the public interest.

His main empirical finding is that all State-owned corporations improved their productivity remarkably in the 1980s, whether they were privatised or not. But that is scarcely surprising. It was the process of preparing State enterprises for privatisation, and the prospect of privatisation, that initially enabled management to be strengthened and motivated, financial disciplines to be imposed and taken seriously, and costs to be cut as trade union attitudes changed. Without the privatisation programme none of the improvement identified by Kay would have happened. Neglect of the economic consequences of ownership is every bit as ideological as the neglect of competition, even if some British economists have difficulty in taking this on board.

But there remains another, more difficult, question about the State sector of the economy. The majority of public sector workers were never in the nationalised industries, but in the public services such as health, education and government itself, in particular local government. Although we were successful in reducing the number of Civil Servants and hiving off some government activities, there were never any plans for the wholesale transfer of the public services to the private sector – even though that could theoretically have been combined with continued public financing. How is this large and important sector of the economy, where the services provided (unlike those of the old

State-owned industries) are largely free at the point of use, to be made more efficient and more responsive to public demand, and to provide better value for money? There is no easy answer.

PART THREE

THE VIEW FROM NUMBER 11

CHAPTER FOURTEEN

BECOMING CHANCELLOR

A Bland and Excellent Manifesto · The General Election of 1983
The Call Comes · An Unusual Politician · The 1983 Reshuffle

A BLAND AND EXCELLENT MANIFESTO

By spring 1983, the Government was already on an election footing. After trailing in the opinion polls since the middle of 1980, the successful prosecution of the Falklands War had transformed the Conservative Party's re-election prospects. An upturn in the Government's fortunes had begun in the final months of 1981, as the recovery from the recession began to be apparent; and the Argentine surrender of 14 June 1982 secured it an unassailable lead. The 'Falklands Factor', the shambolic state of the Labour Party under the leadership of Michael Foot, the burgeoning economic recovery and the sharp fall in inflation all argued for an early general election. The reason why the so-called Falklands Factor was so powerful, and lasted so long, was that it was more than a military victory: it symbolised and reinforced the image of the Government, and of Margaret in particular, as tough, resolute and different from previous wishy-washy governments right across the board, not least in economic policy.

At the beginning of 1983, I was invited by Margaret to join the committee, chaired by Geoffrey Howe, whom she had charged with overseeing the drafting of the election manifesto. The committee members – Geoffrey, Norman Tebbit, David Howell and myself, plus Ferdinand Mount, then head of the Number 10 Policy Unit, and a writer of considerable style, to do the actual drafting – sifted the reports of various policy groups for items to include. A myth has grown up, which even Margaret came to believe, that the 1983 manifesto was too bland, that it lacked firm policy commitments and contributed to a lack of sense of direction during the 1983–87 parliament. This fashionable view could not be more mistaken.

The 1983 manifesto was ideal for a Government whose policies and general approach were unusually clear and inevitably well known, as of course was its record. The bad manifesto was its much less well-written 1987 successor, replete with policy initiatives that had not been properly thought through. Had it not been for the strength of the economy, the 1987 manifesto would have been a disaster; as it was, it was merely an embarrassment.

THE GENERAL ELECTION OF 1983

By the spring of 1983 there was a widespread feeling in the Cabinet, which Margaret on the whole shared, that if the local election results on 5 May were encouraging, we should go to the country without further ado. Headline inflation had fallen from over 20 per cent in the middle of 1980 to 12 per cent at the end of 1981 and 5 per cent in the early spring of 1983, and Geoffrey was worried that it would be rising again by the autumn. Margaret canvassed the opinions of her Cabinet colleagues in small groups. I was in a minority in arguing that Labour was in such a mess, with an unelectable leader, left-wing policies which the country would never stomach, and suffering badly from the Social Democrat defection, that we would win whenever the election was held, particularly with the economy recovering well and inflation low; and that an early election would merely trim a year from our term of office for no good reason.

But Margaret was superstitious. May 1979 was lucky for her and she wanted an early summer poll again; but waiting until May or June 1984, the last possible date, would leave the Government at the mercy of events. In retrospect I was probably wrong to counsel delay. The bird in the hand argument is so persuasive that it was right to go in June 1983. Margaret had already sensibly resisted the siren voices who had urged her to hold a 'khaki' election in the immediate wake of the Falklands victory in 1982. Her view was that a Government should always wait until the final year of the quinquennium, but once there should go as soon as it is confident it will win – a maxim that it is hard to fault.

This was the first election I had fought as a Cabinet Minister, which meant that instead of spending my time in my own Blaby constituency I spent most of it visiting marginal constituencies throughout the country, but I did not play a prominent role in the campaign. The potentially difficult issue for us was unemployment. Using today's definitions, unemployment had risen from 1.1 million in the spring of 1979 to nearly 2.4 million at the end of 1981. Although output began to recover in that year, unemployment continued to rise, although at a slower rate, and reached nearly 2.8 million in the second quarter of 1983. Hitherto the conventional wisdom was that rising unemployment on this scale would mean certain disaster for the party in office.

This did not occur in 1983 for a mixture of reasons. The electoral potency of the trend of unemployment was always chiefly that it was a good indicator of the general sense of economic well-being. But unemployment caused by the end of decades of overmanning (unemployment on the job) at a time when the economy was manifestly improving and the living standards of those in work rising was a different matter altogether. Moreover the electorate at least half believed the official Conservative line (as in 1992) that the UK recession the country had suffered was essentially part of a world recession.

None the less, anxious to rebut the gloom-mongers who were predicting that unemployment would go on rising for ever, I was rash enough to venture in a speech at Moorsholm, Cleveland, that 'next year there is every prospect that unemployment would start to fall'. I added that I was talking as a former economic journalist and that this was in no sense an official prediction.

I was not wrong about the underlying forces. Employment indeed started to recover early in the second quarter of 1983. What I failed to foresee was that most of the increase in jobs over the next three years would consist of women newly drawn into the labour force, chiefly in the service industries, rather than re-employment of the men who had lost their jobs in the great shake-out in manufacturing. My qualified prediction was thus wrong as well as rash: recorded unemployment did start to fall again, but not until 1986.

The most important event in the campaign for me was probably a joint press conference given at Conservative Central Office towards the end by Patrick Jenkin, the Industry Secretary, Leon Brittan, then Chief Secretary of the Treasury, and myself. It was quite clear that the Press and others present, not least Margaret, would be watching our relative performance with particular interest. For while none of us had played a prominent part in the campaign, we were generally regarded as the three main contenders for the job of Chancellor if, as was widely expected, Geoffrey Howe moved over to the Foreign Office after the election. Fortunately, I acquitted myself reasonably well. However, I was conscious that Patrick was comfortably the front runner. He himself expected the job both because of his seniority – he had been Chief Secretary in the Heath Government – and his long established friendship with Geoffrey Howe. He had not realised how much he had irritated Geoffrey by his public lobbying for industrial support after he had succeeded the aggressively free-market Keith Joseph as Industry Secretary in 1981 – and in any event neither of these qualifications would weigh very heavily with Margaret, whose decision it would be.

The Conservative victory on 9 June 1983, by a landslide margin of 144 seats, was the largest majority any party had secured since 1945. In my own constituency of Blaby my majority rose to over 17,000, and my share of the vote increased for the third election in succession. The election had been held in the customary way on a Thursday: it was not until the following Saturday morning that I was telephoned at home in Stoney Stanton by Robin Butler, the Prime Minister's Principal Private Secretary, asking me to call on the Prime Minister at Number 10. Unable to locate my ministerial driver, I took a taxi from Euston to Downing Street, where Margaret unexpectedly offered me the Chancellorship.

THE CALL COMES

I was delighted to be offered the job, and phoned Thérèse as soon as I could to tell her the news. She was doing the ironing at the time and was so taken aback that she burned a hole in my shirt. At last, I had the opportunity to put my own economic ideas into practice. The whole of my previous professional life had been in effect a preparation for what – quite apart from its intrinsic importance – is in practice the number two job in the Government.

I had, however, greatly enjoyed Energy. Moreover, there was a great deal more to do – gas privatisation and electricity privatisation, to name but two of the tasks that lay ahead, not to mention the coming confrontation with Scargill – and I would not have wished to leave it for anything else on the domestic front. Indeed, in many ways my short stay at Energy gave me more pleasure than any other job I have had before or since, although I did occasionally experience a feeling of frustration at the inability to make more of a public impact in the job. I have always had an ambivalent attitude to the show business aspect of politics, being both attracted to it and repelled by it.

Now, however, I had been given the one job in Government which I had always coveted. But it was sad to leave the friends I had made among the officials at Energy and I threw a farewell party for them in the State Room at Number 11.[15] Ian Gillis, my splendid Chief Information Officer at Energy, came up to me. I knew exactly what he was thinking, and got in first. 'You are going to say that no Prime Minister but Margaret Thatcher would ever have given me this job, aren't you?' He was. Ian was probably right. Unlike Geoffrey, who had always been seen as a safe pair of hands, I was a controversial choice, despite my generally acknowledged economic expertise, by no means a politically safe

[15] Number 11 Downing Street, next door to Number 10, is the official residence of the Chancellor of the Exchequer.

choice, somewhat irreverent, and scarcely an establishment figure. Although at fifty-one I was of a fairly standard age for Chancellors, I was unusually junior in political terms. I had been in the House of Commons for little over nine years and in the Cabinet for only twenty-one months. Margaret, more than any other Prime Minister, was unafraid of controversy, and generally devoid of the instincts and thought processes of the establishment.

Her admirable radicalism, however, stopped short with matters of personal deportment. As I left her study at Number 10 she gave me only one piece of advice. This was to get my hair cut, which I was then accustomed to wearing rather long. The story started to circulate long before anyone could possibly have known it to be true. I was at that time too grateful and overwhelmed to do anything than make the earliest convenient appointment with my barber.

AN UNUSUAL POLITICIAN

As Chancellor, I was inevitably propelled into the political spotlight, and was widely regarded as a most unusual kind of politician – indeed as not much of a politician at all. Margaret to some extent shared this conventional view of me, with two qualifications. She never regarded me as a political liability to the extent that she did Nicholas Ridley whom, for that reason, she never made Chancellor despite her great affection for him and a closer affinity of views. She may also have half-consciously thought that appointing someone who was technically proficient, but without any political base of his own, would enable her in effect to be her own Chancellor. If so, she was mistaken.

Margaret saw in me one who shared to some extent both her own strengths and her own weaknesses. According to the parliamentary sketchwriter Edmund Pearce: 'Lawson has never bothered to please ... but the arrogance derives from a belief that markets, banks, the whole apparatus of capitalism are good things and not to be excused nervously or given PR treatment as deserving a small measure of tolerance.' Much the same, with the same degree of exaggeration, could have been said of her. But she did not of course suppose that I had anything like her own rapport with the British people.

The attribute that Margaret thought we both lacked she called 'presentation'. This was largely the ability to appear smooth on television, while putting across the Government's policies. A particularly effective exponent of this was Cecil Parkinson, Party Chairman during the 1983 general election, who shortly afterwards fell victim to the Sarah Keays affair. Margaret had originally promised Cecil the Foreign Office after the election. Because of the Keays complication, of which he had told her in confidence, she felt obliged to make him Trade and Industry Secretary instead. But within four months Press exploitation of the scandal forced her to drop him altogether. I had done my best to persuade her to keep him, which she did as long as possible. Despite Cecil's tendency to exchange gossip with the Press, it was a sad loss. Unfortunately, when he at last returned to the Cabinet, in my old post of Secretary of State for Energy in 1987, much of the old sparkle had gone.

But while I was no great shakes at 'presentation', certainly as Margaret used the term, neither was I the non-political technocrat of the lobby columnists' imagination. There are two qualities in particular, that the complete politician should possess. First he should appear stupider than he is (or be cleverer than he appears). The obvious example of this is Willie Whitelaw. Secondly he should appear to be less of a politician than he really is. The first of these assets confers the enormous advantage of being underestimated; the second that of being trusted, since the British distrust politicians almost as much as they do cleverness. At least I could claim the second of them.

As Chancellor I found this a mixed blessing. The big gain – especially when there is no independent Central Bank and the Chancellor is responsible for monetary policy – was that the financial markets were less likely to be suspicious of me than of an obviously political Chancellor, something from which Denis Healey had suffered. The partially offsetting disadvantage was that Cabinet colleagues were too ready to assume that I was always voicing an official Treasury view. For example, when I argued that the Poll Tax would be a political disaster, one of the reasons – although not the main one – why this cut so little ice was that colleagues were too ready to assume that my real objection was a Treasury fear that the Poll Tax would lead to increased public spending.

A further political quality is being good with people, and with back-bench colleagues and the Press in particular. This is the aspect at which I was worst. I suppose I am not sufficiently gregarious by nature. But although not gregarious, I am too ready to speak my mind, when engaged, without pausing to consider the likely consequences – or even on occasion without considering whether I may indeed be wrong. It may have been these defects which made Willie Whitelaw for so long determined to keep me out of high office, although happily his view subsequently changed.

Another obvious requirement for any senior politician is being good at the despatch box – from which Ministers and Opposition front-benchers speak. Here I was very uneven. Although no natural orator, I was effective in

Opposition. Although good at thinking on my feet, as a Minister I would tend to give distinctly lacklustre performances when I was not particularly interested and did not make a great effort. But on the really big or challenging occasions, I could usually be counted on to turn in a pretty reasonable performance.

A parallel dimension is being good on television. Here again my record was patchy. When the adrenalin was not flowing I tended to be dull and to speak in bursts that were too fast to comprehend, interspersed with awkward pauses while I searched for the right word. But when the stakes were high enough and the adrenalin was flowing I could be effective, as for example my performances when I was belatedly fielded during the 1987 election campaign or my post-resignation interview with Brian Walden in 1989.

Those who write about politics tend to be concerned with the visible side: that is, what a politician says in public and what is said about him. But to my mind the most important yet most overlooked dimensions of being a politician are the least visible. These range from being a loyal and reliable colleague to being a fertile source of workable political ideas and able to make correct political judgements – that is to say what both the short-term and long-term consequences are likely to be of a particular course of action or turn of events; what the public will accept at a particular time and what it will not; or how best to present a particular policy, irrespective of who will be making the speeches.

Effective political judgement, moreover, involves thinking more or less simultaneously on two levels: assessing both the likely short-term electoral consequences and the longer-term political consequences where political ideas become more important. These range from how to entrench – that is to say, render unlikely to be reversed – a particular policy, to how to affect the longer-term political climate. This sort of strategic and tactical thinking was probably my strongest suit, even if I was sometimes less successful in persuading others of my judgement. By contrast, Margaret's well-advertised gut instincts were not always a satisfactory substitute for a considered strategy, as both the disastrous Poll Tax and her counterproductive handling of the European issue amply demonstrated.

Nevertheless, one way and another, my political shortcomings were sufficient to ensure that I was most unlikely ever to be elected Party Leader and thus Prime Minister. Realising this, I lacked the ambition and directed energy it takes to spend the necessary time in cultivating back-benchers with this object in mind – which was, of course, itself one of my main political shortcomings. Indeed I surprised a number of close observers – perhaps even disappointed a few friends and supporters – by publicly disclaiming all ambition for the top job when my standing was at its peak during the year following the general election of 1987.

I did not feel that I suffered greatly as Chancellor through not being a candidate for Number 10, although I know that others thought differently. On the one hand my actions did not excite the suspicions among my Cabinet colleagues aroused by those known to be motivated by personal ambition. On the other hand I had no faction on whose support I could rely in political conflicts, especially with Margaret. In other words, there was no future in being a Lawsonite.

There are many different kinds of politician, and most are probably needed. A paragon who combines the advantages of all and the drawbacks of none is unlikely to exist – and, if he did, he would almost certainly be impossible to live with.

THE 1983 RESHUFFLE

My own elevation was part of a much wider Cabinet reshuffle. The outgoing Foreign Secretary, Francis Pym, a gloomy Heathite, had never been an admirer of Margaret's (nor she of him) and he finally sealed his fate with a remark in the election campaign warning of the undesirability of a large Conservative majority. He was succeeded by Geoffrey Howe. Margaret saw Geoffrey as a patient and determined negotiator, with no strong views of his own; and Geoffrey himself, who still cherished Prime Ministerial ambitions, strongly supported by his formidable wife Elspeth, wanted to widen his experience. (I afterwards discovered, incidentally, that Geoffrey had unequivocally backed me for Number 11 rather than Patrick Jenkin.) A surprise elevation was that of Leon Brittan to be Home Secretary at the unusually early age of forty-four.

There was a pattern to the reshuffled Cabinet. Willie Whitelaw, who best represented the old Tory tradition, became Deputy Prime Minister and Leader of the Lords. Quintin Hailsham, then well into his seventies, but still a force, remained Lord Chancellor and a sparkling representative of continuity with the past. The three main Offices of State, however, were held by Geoffrey, Leon and myself, who were politicians of a different mould. We were all convinced supporters of Margaret's new brand of Conservatism. But in our different ways we had come to these beliefs through reason and experience, rather than through the sort of gut instinct that so powerfully animated her. We did not have Margaret's instinctive identification with the interests of the upper working and lower middle classes as she conceived them; nor were we part of her inner circle. Nor were we able to make up for her oratorical deficiencies. But we did have a capacity for clear thinking and hard work, a profound interest in policy, a toughness and an ability to deal with the higher Civil Service in their own language. She thus saw no threat at that time to her own position.

Press commentators tended to group Leon and myself very much together at the time, even though we were personally far from close. This may have been partly because we were both Jewish – as was Keith Joseph, a genuine confidant of Margaret's who remained at Education, and David Young, who the following year was given a peerage and elevated to the Cabinet as Minister without Portfolio. As I subsequently told Kenneth Harris of the *Observer:* my parents were 'certainly Jewish, not orthodox, but it was something they took for granted, and something I took for granted. I've frequently been puzzled – not peeved or irritated, simply puzzled – by the way this is focused on.' There has been much speculation about the unusually large proportion of Ministers of Jewish origin in Margaret's Cabinets, but no generally accepted explanation. I cannot solve the riddle either; although it certainly demonstrated that there was not the faintest trace of anti-Semitism in her make-up: an unusual attribute.

CHAPTER FIFTEEN

ALL THE CHANCELLOR'S MEN

Finding the Right Ministers · Prayer Meetings
The Changeover of the Mandarins · Surprise Choice for the Bank

FINDING THE RIGHT MINISTERS

Finding the right ministerial team was a demanding business. When Margaret saw me on the Saturday after the election to offer me the Chancellorship, she told me of her intention to make Peter Rees Chief Secretary. I had my reservations about his suitability for this particular job, but not having expected the Exchequer I had not come to Number 10 armed with an alternative candidate of my own. A convivial, dapper lawyer and son of a distinguished Welsh General, 'Tiger' Rees, Peter was a bon vivant whose gastronomic tastes were well indulged by his wife Anthea, at the time quite a chum of Thérèse's and a superb cook. He was however – perhaps because he yearned for the good life – not as well catered for in the Treasury as in his previous post, which involved a considerable amount of travel, which he loved. The no-frills hard grind of Chief Secretary was not quite his cup of tea. His very convincing portrayal of a dog while playing charades, at one of our pre-Budget meetings at Chevening, became a legend in Treasury circles.

Professionally Peter's forte was tax. As a former highly successful silk at the Revenue bar, he was an expert cross-examiner rather than a burner of the midnight oil. Margaret had chosen him because we had worked well together in both Government and Opposition, he had already had experience as a Treasury Minister and more recently had been a successful Minister of Trade. Never having been a Treasury Minister herself, she tended to regard all Treasury jobs below Chancellor as virtually interchangeable, and did not realise the special combination of qualities required for the control of public spending. I made sure that his successors as Chief Secretary were colleagues I had personally earmarked for their suitability for the job.

Nick Ridley, my successor as Financial Secretary, was still *in situ*. Although we were at that time firm friends and comrades-in-arms of long standing, he had been in the House considerably longer than I had, and understandably did not relish serving under me. He was depressed, too, by the thought that, having been left in place during Margaret's big 1983 post-election reshuffle, his last chance of entering Cabinet had eluded him. Unexpectedly, both these problems soon passed. Within a few months the resignation of Cecil Parkinson had led indirectly to a Cabinet vacancy as Transport Secretary, which Nick filled.

I had persuaded Margaret to let me bring John Moore with me from Energy to become Economic Secretary to the Treasury. When Nick Ridley departed. John was the obvious choice for promotion to Financial Secretary; his successor as Economic Secretary was Ian Stewart who had once been Parliamentary Private Secretary to Geoffrey Howe and knew the Treasury well. Ian and I had known each other for a very long time, since we did our National Service in the Navy together in the 1950s. He did an excellent job piloting both the Building Societies' Act of 1986 and the Banking Act of 1987 through all their stages in the House of Commons.

Finally there was Barney Hayhoe, the Minister of State I had inherited from Geoffrey. Although our economic views were very different, this presented no problems while he was at the Treasury, which he had joined in October 1981 as Minister of State in charge of the Civil Service, as a result of the Treasury's absorption of the short-lived Civil Service Department. Margaret appointed him Minister of Health, under Norman Fowler, in 1985. In that much more exposed post his limitations became more apparent; and a year later Margaret gave him the sack, thus ending his ministerial career. This greatly embittered him; and thereafter, despite the fact that our relations at the Treasury had been excellent, his voice was always prominent in the attacks on my Chancellorship from our own side.

At least I had no problems over my choice of Parliamentary Private Secretary (PPS). Mark Lennox-Boyd, who had been with me continuously since the latter part of my time as Financial Secretary, and had been planning to move on, agreed to stay with me when I became Chancellor.

PRAYER MEETINGS

On the whole we had a very happy and relaxed team at the Treasury. I continued Geoffrey Howe's practice of holding a 'prayer meeting' on Monday, Wednesday and Friday mornings. In my time the congregation consisted of Ministers (including the Treasury Whip for the time being), special advisers, PPSs, and the head of the Economic Section of the Conservative Research Department. The object was to have a political discussion of current policy issues without the inhibiting presence of officials. To some extent it was the counterpart of the weekly meeting of the PCC – the so-called Policy Co-ordinating Committee – where senior Treasury officials met to discuss current policy issues without the inhibiting presence of Ministers. The most obvious difference was that a note of the matters discussed at each prayer meeting, although not of the views expressed or conclusions reached, was circulated to the Treasury mandarinate. That way, even if the conversation was private, they did at least learn what was on Ministers' minds. Not that it was impossible for the Chancellor to learn what was exercising PCC, should the need arise.

Prayer meetings were not the only ones that took place without officials present. I always made it clear that I would be happy to see any Minister or special adviser privately, should there be something on his mind that he did not wish to put down on paper or otherwise expose at that stage. And, starting with John MacGregor, who arrived in 1985, I held a regular weekly tête-à-tête with the Chief Secretary of the day. The one issue that I did not discuss even on these intimate occasions was that of my differences with Margaret over the exchange rate during the latter part of my Chancellorship – although I did talk it over with one or two, including Peter Brooke, subsequently an outstanding Northern Ireland Secretary, but for most of the time one of my Treasury Ministers and sometime Chairman of the Party, a man whose judgement I respected and whose discretion could be utterly relied on. I was, of course, well aware that Margaret herself was less discreet. But this was a matter that was highly market-sensitive as well as politically explosive; and I saw no advantage in taking any further risks on that front.

Like previous Chancellors, I held a weekly meeting with the Permanent Secretary, in my case Peter Middleton, which was essential to the proper running of the Department. My Principal Private Secretary would be present as a note-taker, except occasionally when we were discussing sensitive issues of personal moves within the official Treasury. I also instituted a weekly tête-à-tête with the Chief Economic Adviser, Terry Burns. I hoped in this way to free him of any inhibitions he might have felt in front of other officials or Ministers. Equally I was able to test out my own economic ideas before I was ready to have them circulate throughout the Treasury.

It was sometimes thought that I relied on Terry too much for the interchange of economic ideas. Certainly, I had a high regard for him. But I do not believe there is much in the charge. In the first place, there were others within the Treasury with whom I could and did exchange economic ideas – notably Peter Middleton and my long-serving Press Secretary, Robert Culpin. Among outsiders, and admittedly subject to the inevitable constraints imposed by the need for secrecy, I regularly exchanged ideas with that doyen of economic commentators, my old friend Samuel Brittan. Then, in 1986, I formed a group of outside economists of differing views – soon dubbed by my officials the 'group of independent outside economists', or 'Gooies' – to discuss the key issues with me on a confidential basis twice a year at Number 11. (There are those who would argue that that was when the conduct of economic policy began to go wrong. Even if that were so – and I discuss this in subsequent chapters – it would on the whole be unfair to argue *post hoc ergo propter hoc.)*

Nor is it right to overlook the written word. I remember talking to a visiting American Professor of Politics of some distinction, who observed that ministerial life was far too busy to allow senior politicians any time to think. 'What you guys need is a sabbatical,' he declared. 'We do have sabbaticals in our system,' I replied. 'We call it Opposition. And I've had enough of it.' But I did make a point of using part of the summer holidays each year as a time for thinking, including reading the economic literature on a subject that seemed to me particularly important at the time – provided that it was written in English and not in algebraic symbols.

Finally, of course, I was not devoid of the capacity to develop economic ideas of my own – even though the commentators tend to assume that that is the copyright of professional economists. A good example of that is the labelling of my 1988 IMF speech on the balance of payments as the 'Burns Doctrine'. Certainly I discussed it thoroughly with Terry, who was his usual constructive self. But it would be wholly wrong to saddle him with the responsibility for that 'doctrine', or any other 'doctrine' for that matter.

There are some who feel that, notwithstanding all that, a modern Chancellor needs to equip himself with a professional economist of acknowledged standing as his own full-time personal economic adviser, someone who can take on the Treasury's economic establishment on their own terms: in essence the role that Nicky Kaldor played under two successive Labour Governments, during the Chancellorships of Jim Callaghan, Roy Jenkins and Denis Healey. Healey's own verdict on the experiment, as contained in his autobiography, could scarcely be more damning, and I have to agree with him. A Chancellor who really needs a 'personal' economic adviser has got the wrong man as Chief Economic Adviser, and should be able to change him.

THE CHANGEOVER OF THE MANDARINS

As I left Margaret's first-floor study in Number 10 on that Saturday in June 1983, the first person to congratulate me on my appointment as Chancellor was Robin Butler, whom I knew well as a former Treasury official, but who at that time was the Prime Minister's Principal Private Secretary (he was later to reach the top of the tree as Secretary to the Cabinet and Head of the Home Civil Service). He told me how pleased he thought the Treasury officials would be. I learned subsequently that the senior mandarins in Great George Street had discussed during the election campaign whom they would like to see as Chancellor and that I had emerged as their choice by quite a wide margin. I was not at all sure that this was entirely a good thing; but officials seemed to like a Minister who knew his own mind, enjoyed discussion and used the resources of the Department to the full. David Lipsey wrote in *The Sunday Times* of 19 June 1983: 'With Lawson they look forward to a kind of Denis Healey Mark II, with all the excitements of life in an intellectual rough house.'

It was also on the Saturday, shortly after my trip to Number 10, that I was telephoned by Peter Middleton, the recently appointed Permanent Secretary to the Treasury. I asked him to come and see me next day at Stoney Stanton. The Sunday turned out to be a beautiful summer's day and we spent most of it in the garden going over the whole range of Treasury issues. So when I arrived back in Great George Street on the Monday, to a warm welcome from officials, I had already been well briefed, and had had the opportunity to indicate my own priorities and concerns.

Peter Middleton was a man of outstanding ability, with whom I had worked closely on the formulation of the Medium Term Financial Strategy (MTFS) during my time as Financial Secretary. He was also an unorthodox choice, having ascended the Treasury hierarchy from Sheffield University and the Central Statistical Office. He had been a very skilful Press Secretary to both Tony Barber and Denis Healey before shrewdly specialising in monetary policy.

All Permanent Secretary appointments have to be approved by the Prime Minister of the day, but the importance of the Treasury is such that Margaret took a particularly keen interest in the Wass succession. Within the Treasury, the consensus was that none of the Second Permanent Secretaries were right for the job and that the choice lay between two up-and-coming Deputy Secretaries, David Hancock and Peter Middleton. Hancock would almost certainly have won in a Treasury vote. I have no idea what his politics were. But the majority of Treasury officials, as indeed of Whitehall generally, saw themselves for want of a better description as social democrats. David Hancock certainly fitted that picture, however he actually voted. Discreet, civilised, knowledgeable in the ways of the Treasury and very Oxbridge, he was very much the mandarin's mandarin. He had been immensely sceptical of George Brown's Department of Economic Affairs and the National Plan and was probably almost as sceptical of Tory radicalism. He was not the official who said in a public lecture that the good Civil Servant should 'avoid the last ounce of commitment', but it was not hard to imagine his making the remark.

He was clearly not Margaret's type. In her eyes, the choice lay between Middleton and the Second Permanent Secretary in charge of Public Expenditure, Anthony Rawlinson, for whom she had a soft spot. He was not only the best looking – in a tall, wiry, matinée idol way something that always cut a great deal of ice with her. He was also the one undoubted Tory of the three.

Geoffrey, however, strongly favoured Middleton, as did Leon Brittan, then Chief Secretary – and as I made clear I did, too, when Margaret consulted me informally in the voting lobby at the House one evening. Rawlinson, who had been a reserve for the Everest team and was sadly killed in a mountaineering accident in 1985, lacked the imagination and the intellectual firepower required. Eventually, Margaret came to the same conclusion. Not yet fifty when he was appointed, Middleton, although lacking Rawlinson's good looks, had many of the other qualities she admired. He was not only an enthusiast for monetary policy. He strongly believed in supporting the Government of the day – for instance in not thrusting an incomes policy down the throat of a Conservative Government which happened to be dead against the idea. Moreover his interpretation of the constitution was essentially Prime Ministerial, believing that all other Ministers and officials should toe the line. Margaret was also impressed by his support against the Foreign Office in the campaign to 'get our money back' from the European Community, and rightly regarded him as a doer and not just a talker.

A northern grammar school boy who had never been fully accepted as a member of the establishment, Middleton had none the less succeeded in rising to the top of the establishment-conscious mandarinate, even though he was disappointed in his ultimate ambition to become Cabinet Secretary and Head of the Home Civil Service. Although I always enjoyed his quickness, his intelligence, and his political sensitivity, and Thérèse got on particularly well with him, he and I were somewhat wary of each other. He worked very hard for me for over six years, and in many ways I could not have asked for anyone better; but I was never sure that his habit of cultivating the Press, which he had acquired during his years as the Chancellor's Press Secretary, was always helpful. A good Civil Servant, who has to serve with equal commitment Ministers of all types and of both political parties, has to become to some extent all things to all men; but in Peter's case this characteristic was particularly highly developed. Nevertheless, he was an outstanding Permanent Secretary to the Treasury.

Middleton and Burns worked very closely together, got on very well together, and formed a formidable partnership, rarely disclosing their differences in front of me. But the combination of the practical problems of technical monetarism and pressure of work made Middleton in some ways more like a traditional Treasury Permanent Secretary than might have been expected, taking the lead in discussions with lawyers, juggling with top-level appointments and keeping – as he saw it – the peace between Ministers. He was 'turned-on' most by the interface with the City, where he eventually ended up. He was at his best as a troubleshooter, taking a grip of a complex specific issue in a way few others could have done.

The official whom a Minister sees most is not of course the Permanent Secretary but his Principal Private Secretary. I had inherited in that post a Foreign Office official who had for some years been on secondment to the Treasury, John Kerr, who had been chosen by Geoffrey Howe. He was an amazingly lively and quick-witted character, whose love of plots and intrigue outdid any politician I have ever worked with. He worked extremely hard, but often could not be tracked down in the evenings, even though he had not officially packed up at the office. He was usually to be found at Number 10, picking up the latest gossip. These feats of over-assiduousness were faults on the right side, and John Kerr was one of the best Principal Private Secretaries I had during my time as Chancellor.

SURPRISE CHOICE FOR THE BANK

At least as important as the change at the top of the Treasury was that at the Bank of England. Although he was already sixty-seven years old and had served two terms as Governor, Gordon Richardson was disappointed not to be offered a third term. Although a sound, even stern, anti-inflationist by his own lights, he regarded the sometimes crusading radicalism of the Thatcher Government with ill-concealed distaste, which was more than fully reciprocated by Margaret. He is reported to have remarked: 'She is canine; I am feline.'

There was therefore little astonishment that she appointed a new Governor but some surprise at his identity. Six months before I went to Number 11 in December 1982 she announced that it would be an outsider – Robin Leigh-

Pemberton, then chairman of the National Westminster Bank. He took up his post in July 1983, a month after I had taken up mine. Although he was not initially widely respected within the Bank and at first had no great authority there, officials at both Great George Street and Threadneedle Street increasingly grew to like him. Unlike Richardson, he did not insist on controlling every aspect of the Bank's activities himself. This pleased senior Bank officials and made him a very much easier Governor with whom to work, both for me and for the Treasury as a whole.

Both Robin and I were keen to improve the rather prickly relationship that had developed between the Bank and the Treasury under Richardson. One of the first things we did was institute a regular monthly lunch to discuss areas of current or potential difficulty, and to compare notes on our views of monetary conditions. These lunches, held alternately at Robin's elegantly furnished gubernatorial flat in New Change and in the Soane dining room at Number 11, and attended only by my Principal Private Secretary as note-taker, allowed us to defuse a number of potential problems before they could cause trouble.

CHAPTER SIXTEEN

A JOB WITH FEW FRIENDS

The Switchback · Range of Duties · The Finance Ministers' Trade Union
Steering the Economy · A Spending Squeeze

THE SWITCHBACK

In my first house of Commons speech as Chancellor, on 29 June 1983, I remarked that 'I am keenly conscious that few Chancellors of the Exchequer have left office with their reputations enhanced.' I could have added that these few had mostly stayed only a short time. The exception was my predecessor, Geoffrey Howe, who had four years in the post and to whom I paid tribute in that speech.

Part of the reason is that, more than other Ministers', the Chancellor's stock tends to follow a switchback course, and he is more likely to depart, for whatever reason, in a trough than at a peak. In my case I started with the usual honeymoon from my appointment in June 1983 to the summer recess of that year – a honeymoon, however, interrupted by a major embarrassment over some leaked spending cuts. Then came a poor, though not disastrous patch, from my rather indifferent 1983 Party Conference speech until my rapturously received first Budget in 1984.

But the glow lasted only a few months after which there was a very lean period, including my 1984 Conference speech (the least well received of the series) the nadir of which was probably the sterling crisis of early 1985, to my first enthusiastically received Conference speech, that of 1985. This triggered a steady climb back, leading to my really strong and supposedly 'unassailable' phase, which lasted from the 1986 Budget to the summer recess of 1988, when it was interrupted by an unexpectedly large deterioration in the trade figures. Finally there was a steady decline from the summer of 1988 until my resignation in October 1989, when the genuine problems of reducing inflationary pressure and the resulting unpopular rises in interest rates to a very high level were compounded by a prolonged conflict between Margaret and myself over the management of sterling.

RANGE OF DUTIES

Before going into these events it is worth saying something about the job of the Chancellor of the Exchequer. It is an absorbing one, a difficult one, at times a frustrating one; but it is also a particularly demanding one. We are unusual in Britain in that the Chancellor has responsibility for taxation, for the control of public expenditure and for the whole of monetary policy, including interest rates and the management of sterling.[16]

In other countries these jobs are normally divided up – for example, in the United States. But despite the very heavy demands it makes on the Chancellor, the concentration of responsibilities for the most part makes good sense. For public expenditure and taxation are after all two sides of the same coin. They are the income and expenditure sides of the State's budget. The coherence of policy is improved when they are in the same hands.

Monetary policy, however, is a different matter, and I eventually came to the conclusion that it would be best handled by an independent but accountable central bank, at arm's length from Government, on the lines of the German Bundesbank or the US Fed. Nevertheless the monetary side of things was of special interest to me, probably more so than to many other Chancellors, I had specialised in it during my time as Financial Secretary, and it lay at the heart of the Government's economic policy.

Less well known, perhaps, is the fact that the Chancellor has his finger in pretty well every pie in Government. This follows partly from his responsibility for Government spending and partly from tradition. As a result, he can exert a significant influence on policies which are announced by other Ministers and which the public does not associate with the Treasury at all.

The Chancellor, if he proceeds with care and caution, can affect the content and not merely the cost of other Ministers' policies and, in a limited number of carefully selected areas, generate the ideas which decisively influence the direction of Government policy. Indeed, as I shall later describe, I played a significant part in both the health and education reforms of the late eighties. But at the end of the day the basis of the Chancellor's influence is in his control over finance.

This is exemplified by the long-standing rule that any Minister who has a proposal to put before Cabinet must first submit it to the Treasury. He can of course take it to Cabinet even if the Treasury disagrees; but in that case there has

[16] [2010 note] Since then, the Chancellor has been rightly relieved of the responsibility for monetary policy. This is discussed in the new final chapter below.

to be a paragraph in his Cabinet paper, written by the Treasury, which sets out the nature of the Treasury's disagreement and the reasons for it.

This influence is acquired at a price. For it inevitably ensures that both the Treasury as a Department and the Chancellor as an individual are regarded by most of the rest of the Government as the enemy. A Chancellor who is doing his job properly has few friends. That is one reason why it is of vital importance to the successful conduct of Government that there is an extremely close and special relationship between the Chancellor of the day and the Prime Minister. They do not have to be cronies or soul mates, but they do have to be on the same wavelength. This was the case with Margaret Thatcher and myself for very many years. When that harmony came to an end I took the view that it was impossible to do the job effectively and therefore it was better not to do it at all.

There is another, less substantial but probably better known, way in which the British system differs considerably from others, even from the French. That is, the extraordinary ritual we have on Budget Day. Going round the world I was surprised to find that almost all the people I met had seen photographs of Thérèse and myself outside Number 11, with the old battered Gladstone Budget box brandished in my hand. If truth be told, my opposite numbers in other governments were secretly envious of the British Budget.

In this country Press and academic commentators are predictably cynical. They describe it as a ridiculous survival, a foolish ritual and a meaningless tradition. That is not how I see it. Quite apart from the fact that it can be fun, it seems to me no bad thing that for one day in the year the attention of the entire nation should be focused on the national economy and on the issues involved.

THE FINANCE MINISTERS' TRADE UNION

There is one consolation for unpopularity among one's colleagues at home. This is that other Finance Ministers around the world are in a very similar position. They too, if they are doing their job properly, have few friends among their own colleagues. As a result, there readily grows up a quite remarkable degree of camaraderie among the Finance Ministers of the various developed countries. For almost the only political friends they have are each other, and they are soon on Christian name terms.

I became particularly close to the long-serving German Finance Minister, Gerhard Stoltenberg, a tall, silver-haired man of total integrity, who subsequently became Defence Minister until he had to resign under something of a cloud. Gerhard and I used to ring each other up regularly to compare notes. On matters of mutual interest he would tell me on a strictly personal basis what was happening in the German Cabinet and I would let him know on the same basis, confident that it would go no further, the state of play in our own Cabinet.

More than mutual sympathy was involved. I recall one occasion when Gerhard telephoned me to discuss a projected European space venture he was seeking to resist within the German Cabinet. His opponent, as usual, was the seemingly perpetual German Foreign Minister, Hans-Dietrich Genscher, from the Free Democrat part of the ruling coalition, who held the job continuously from 1974 until his surprise resignation in 1992. Genscher, a man addicted to 'European' gestures and used to having his own way, had claimed in Cabinet that Germany had no choice but to support the proposal, irrespective of the cost, since the British had caved in to French pressure and if Germany were not to go along, too, it would find itself out on a limb, which would be intolerable. I was able to reassure Gerhard that Genscher was making it all up; that in fact we were resolute in our opposition to the project and would remain so. This enabled him to treat Genscher's intervention with the scepticism it deserved.

There were a number of occasions of this kind. In many ways I was sorry for Gerhard, who, despite the success of the German economy, had a tough time politically. This was an almost inevitable consequence of coalition politics, which follow from proportional representation. The Prime Minister of the day, in this case Helmut Kohl, always tended in any dispute to back the leader of his coalition partner, who posed no threat to him, against his own senior party colleagues, whom he saw as political rivals.

Since the Germans were our natural allies over so many issues within the European Community, it was unfortunate that my own relationship with Stoltenberg was not mirrored by Margaret's with Kohl. Whereas the Socialist President of France, François Mitterrand, was able to score a hit with her by treating her as a woman, Kohl's clumsiness served only to reinforce her pathological hostility to Germany and the Germans which in the end came to dominate her view of the European Community. Things might have been better, curiously enough, had the gloomy and highly intelligent Social Democrat leader, Helmut Schmidt, remained in office: Margaret had a considerable respect for him – as he had for her, to the extent that he was capable of holding a high opinion of any other politician.

STEERING THE ECONOMY

The economic situation I inherited from Geoffrey was one of resumed growth, following the quite severe recession of 1980/81 and inflation down to an underlying rate of some 5 per cent. But these generally satisfactory trends did not mean that everything was coming up roses when I first became Chancellor. Unemployment was high and still remorselessly rising; and although the pace of the rise had been gradually slowing down from the peak increase of some 800,000 in 1981, recorded unemployment did not start to fall, from a figure of well over 3 million, until three years after I had moved into Number 11.

Moreover the forecasts were extremely gloomy, not merely for future years but even for the course of events in 1983. The National Institute for Economic and Social Research (which has since improved) expected a complete standstill in output that year. The official statisticians were little better, understating what had recently happened, let alone what was likely. When the year 1983 was over, they reported that growth had been 2 per cent – a figure that has since been raised to 3.8 per cent in subsequent revisions – a sign of the statistical problems with which Chancellors have to struggle. At the same time the Treasury expected a rise in inflation towards the end of 1983 (this had been Geoffrey's main argument for holding the election in June rather than October), which happily did not occur.

During most of my time as Chancellor, I was assaulted by two groups of critics. The first and larger group wanted me to expand demand to absorb the unemployed: their recommended method was increased public spending. More sophisticated economists of this school argued that unemployment was above the supposed equilibrium rate consistent with stable inflation. The other, less vociferous, critics wanted an even tighter policy, designed to eliminate inflation altogether in short order although they rarely spelled out what that would mean in terms of interest rates, pressure on profits and a still tighter labour market squeeze.

For my own part, I have always been extremely suspicious of analysis in terms of output gaps or equilibrium rates of unemployment. They are in practice extremely nebulous magnitudes; and estimates are contradictory and subject to huge variations, even when made by the same economist. I decided to try to keep the economy on a steady path, concentrating on a stable monetary framework as expressed by the MTFS, and not attempting to manage output and employment from the Treasury. The only concession I made to the clamour to 'do something' about unemployment was that I was content to make progress slowly towards the declared ultimate aim of 'zero inflation' – well defined by Alan Greenspan, the Fed chairman, as a state of affairs when the rate of inflation has ceased to be a factor in business calculations – rather than try for a quick kill. I saw my main macroeconomic task as that of keeping steady downward pressure on inflation in the face of international and domestic disturbances and pressures.

One practical warning against departing from the MTFS approach, certainly in the stimulatory direction the Press and the Opposition were urging on me, was that the growth in average earnings per head stopped declining in 1983 and remained astonishingly stable at around 7.5 per cent a year up to and including 1987. Pay increases do not in themselves cause inflation, but they can be part of the transmission mechanism and are an important indicator of how much progress is being made.

For my first five years as Chancellor, up to the middle of 1988, I appeared to be broadly succeeding in achieving my objective. Total national output, as measured by real GDP, grew by an average of between 3 and 4 per cent a year – somewhat faster than was sustainable in the long run but (at least until the end of the period) reasonable after the deepest post-war recession to date. At the same time inflation over the five years averaged not much more than 4 per cent a year (as measured by the Retail Prices Index excluding mortgage interest payments).

It was only then that it became clear how dubious an indicator unemployment had turned out to be of the gap between output and capacity, and of how that gap was changing. From the middle of the 1980s some other indicators, such as the CBI capacity survey, had been suggesting a very different picture, with capacity utilisation high and increasing.

Sticking to a steady path did not, regrettably, mean putting the economy on auto-pilot and relaxing. On the contrary, a Chancellor's life is a never-ending struggle against destabilising forces. Many of them are day-to-day pressures which come and go. But beyond these I decided to give priority to dealing with three major problems: how to improve the labour market by supply-side reforms, which – *pace* the expansionists – was the only lasting way of making inroads on unemployment; the problem of the monetary indicators which were not doing a good job in providing a stable financial framework; and keeping public expenditure to our chosen path. The first problem was long term and involved other Departments besides the Treasury. The second, or so it seemed to me when I took over as Chancellor in June 1983, could wait for a few months.

But the public expenditure problem was staring me in the face, and was right at the heart of the Treasury's traditional responsibilities.

A SPENDING SQUEEZE

Indeed the urgent difficulty I faced on entering Number 11 was a very worrying surge in public expenditure. If uncorrected it would have meant increases in taxation or borrowing – or both. The pressure stemmed from the usual tendency to enter into new public spending commitments in the run-up to an election, coupled with an unwise decision made by Cabinet in the autumn of 1982 to encourage the nationalised industries and local authorities to increase their capital spending. The view was that, given the persistence of high and rising unemployment, the Government should listen more seriously to the demands from the construction industry for more capital investment. Margaret herself had been of this view, and had personally written to the local authority associations and nationalised industry chairmen on 2 November 1982 urging them to make 'full and proper use of the sums we have allocated to capital'.

In theory she was simply trying to persuade them to shift the balance from current to capital spending, and bring forward the use of sums already agreed. But I thought it an unwise invitation and said as much in Cabinet as Energy Secretary. Quite apart from the fact that investment of any sort is valuable only if it produces a worthwhile return, I was concerned at the signal Margaret's message was bound to convey that the period of public spending stringency was over.

To make matters worse, the spending forecasts on which Margaret's uncharacteristic and ill-advised exhortations were based turned out to be false, as she was duly furious to discover. In the autumn of 1982 the Treasury had predicted that the public sector would underspend significantly in the then current financial year, 1982/83. It need not have worried. As usual, there was a last-minute spending spree by Departments anxious to use up their allocations. Alas, the temporary weakening of Treasury control spilled over into the following financial year, 1983/84, and threatened to push the Budget deficit some £3 billion above target.

This upsurge in part reflected a change in the psychological climate. There was a feeling not only among back-benchers and the Press, but even among some officials in the Treasury and Bank of England, that, with inflation back well into single figures, the focus of policy should switch to the conquest of unemployment. Unaccustomed to the idea of any Government holding to a steady course for any length of time, it was felt to be inconceivable that the policies of the first term would be continued in the second. I was most emphatically not of that view, as I made clear to those journalists who interviewed me at the time. I did not believe that there was any trade-off to be obtained from a relaxation in the struggle against either inflation or excessive public spending and borrowing.

In my first speech to the House as Chancellor, on 29 June 1983, the final day of the debate of the first Queen's Speech of the new parliament, I declared that I intended to 'maintain rigorous control of public sector borrowing ... [which] in turn requires firm control of public expenditure, otherwise there will be no room for significant tax cuts throughout the lifetime of this parliament'. On public spending I said 'there is no scope for relaxation this year, next year or in any year ... I stand ready to take action if our objectives are endangered.' But if I was to disabuse my colleagues (and indeed the commentators) of the idea that there had been a change in policy priorities, I had to make an early and dramatic move to wrench prospective public spending for 1983/84 back towards our original objective. Embarrassing though it was so soon after the general election, once I had revealed to Margaret the full horror of the Treasury's Summer Forecast[17] of the PSBR I had little difficulty in persuading her of the need for an emergency package of spending cuts. The Opposition were bound to claim that this justified their allegations during the campaign that we had a 'hidden agenda' of further public spending cuts; but I could readily demonstrate that all I was seeking to do was to get back as close as I could to the figures we had already published.

This would not be easy. With the financial year already in progress, I had to resort to the blunt instrument of a 2 per cent squeeze on general cash limits and a 1 per cent squeeze on the pay element. Most of this resulted in relatively modest cuts in specific programmes. But I needed to do more with defence, where the overrun threatened to be greatest. At a tense meeting between Margaret, Michael Heseltine, then Defence Secretary, and myself at Number 10, I managed to secure agreement on a £240 million cut in the defence budget.

The overall package came to £1 billion, half representing genuine savings and the other half a further sale of BP shares, to be held in September. Although the genuine savings were less than half of one per cent of total public expenditure

[17] Treasury economists carried out three full-scale forecasts a year: the Winter Forecast, which was published on Budget Day, the Autumn Forecast, which was published in the Autumn Statement, and the Summer Forecast, which was not published at all.

they nevertheless had a profound psychological effect, reminding colleagues that the tight grip on public expenditure would not be relaxed simply because inflation had come down and unemployment was continuing to rise. They also set a new baseline for future years, which was particularly valuable in controlling the defence budget, since at that time the policy was to increase defence spending by 3 per cent a year in real terms, in accordance with the NATO guidelines.

As I explained in a Press interview: 'if we had done nothing this would have given the false impression that we no longer cared about what was happening to public spending and borrowing'. This was hardly an attitude which I had any wish to encourage, not least because public expenditure, partly as a result of inherited commitments, had risen by 3.5 percentage points as a proportion of GDP during the first three years of a supposedly ferocious Thatcher Government.

CHAPTER SEVENTEEN

THE TAMING OF LEVIATHAN

The Nuts and Bolts of Spending Control · General Principles
A Science That is Not There · A Cabinet Riot · The Green Paper
The 1983 Spending Round · The 1984 Round and the Brighton Bomb
The Row Over Student Grants · The 1985 Round – Leviathan Tamed
A Defence Concordat · 1986 – The Pre-Election Round

THE NUTS AND BOLTS OF SPENDING CONTROL

The control of public expenditure might not seem the most gripping aspect of economic policy, let alone of Government as a whole. Yet without it the successful conduct of economic policy, and indeed of Government itself is impossible.

One of our first decisions when we took office in 1979 was to review, each year, the spending plans for the next three years. Previously, the Treasury had worked to a four-year time horizon; but the fourth year was so speculative that we decided to drop it. In any event, it is inevitably the year immediately ahead that is the main focus of attention. A more fundamental issue than the length of the planning period is the choice that has to be made between negotiating spending programmes individually (virtually guaranteeing an excessive total) or setting a guideline for the totality of public spending, an 'envelope', agreed in advance by Cabinet. The latter approach, which we adopted from the start, is clearly superior.

The round started in earnest with a meeting of the Cabinet in early July, at which the Chief Secretary presented a paper setting out in stern and measured tones the current public expenditure picture and trends, and recommending guidelines for the coming year. This was accompanied by a paper from the Chancellor setting out the general economic context, drawing out the tax implications, and urging colleagues to accept the Chief Secretary's recommendations. With varying enthusiasm, they would do so.

Cabinet agreement on the overall guideline was followed by bilateral discussions between the Chief Secretary and spending Ministers. Ministers taking part in the bilateral meetings were expected to agree the departmental totals in considerable detail, and the measures needed to secure any savings. The bilaterals started pretty soon after the July Cabinet; and after a break for the summer holidays, they resumed in September and continued right up to and usually during the Party Conference in October.

It was virtually unheard of for agreement with any spending Minister to be reached after one bilateral; there would invariably be a second and, if it was likely to prove productive, a third. It was a matter of virility for some spending Ministers, egged on by their officials, to put in bids well above anything remotely consistent with the overall envelope agreed by Cabinet. There were always Press reports of excess bids inspired by talkative spending Ministers, activities unhelpful to the Government and to them personally, since they never got what they asked for. Some politicians simply have a compulsion to leak, even when they have nothing to gain from it.

If an agreement could not be reached bilaterally, the Chief Secretary would discuss with the Chancellor, who of course saw all the papers, how best to resolve it. There were basically three options, all of which were used on different occasions in my time. The Chancellor might have a private meeting with the spending Minister, with no officials present, to agree a compromise. Alternatively, where large sums and major policy issues were involved, the Prime Minister might hold a meeting with the Chancellor, Chief Secretary, and the particular spending Minister involved, usually with no officials other than a Number 10 note-taker present.

The third option was to leave it to the Star Chamber, which – if required – would start work immediately after the Party Conference in October, to resolve the remaining disputed issues. 'Star Chamber' was the popular name for an *ad hoc* Cabinet Committee first set up in 1982 to adjudicate unresolved issues between the Treasury and spending Ministers, named with gallows humour after a royal court in Tudor and Stuart times famous for its severity and intolerance. Its first chairman was Willie Whitelaw, who continued in the role until his resignation through illness in January 1988. Needless to say, he worked closely with the Treasury.

The Star Chamber had very little time, even sitting four days a week, to get everything buttoned up in time for the final public expenditure Cabinet, which was in those days usually held in the first half of November immediately prior to the Autumn Statement. It was thus important that it was not given too many outstanding programmes to resolve: five would be the absolute maximum. On the other hand, it would be foolish to set up the Star Chamber just to resolve one remaining programme – and difficult for the Star Chamber, too, which would be unable to do its main job of weighing up the relative merits of the cases put by different spending Ministers, and allocating the sum that remained between them. There would thus be heavy pressure on a sole spending Minister still in dispute to settle. That pressure would be exerted either by the Chancellor or by the Prime Minister with the Chancellor present.

The threat to activate the Star Chamber was always present and was intended to act as a deterrent to bloody-minded spending Ministers. Margaret and I would decide on its composition. Willie was an excellent chairman, not least because one of his doctrines was that the cause of good government required that the Treasury did not suffer many defeats. The fact, too, that by the time I had become Chancellor we were on good personal terms did no harm either.

Following Willie's enforced departure, and given Margaret's profound hostility to Geoffrey Howe which ruled him out, the chairmanship went to less obvious colleagues – first to Cecil Parkinson and after John Major took over, to John Wakeham. This did not matter as much as it might have done, since during my time it never had to swing into action during the post-Willie phase, neither in 1988 nor 1989. Ironically, this was partly since some colleagues settled prior to the Star Chamber because they were not prepared to submit themselves to the arbitration of a tribunal to whose chairman they were unwilling to defer.

The rest of the members had to be very carefully chosen. We would look for around four of them, in addition to the Chief Secretary and also the Chief Whip, who, as with the Cabinet itself, is not officially a member but who sits in and speaks if invited to do so by the chairman. The four would ideally consist of three public spending hawks and one public spending dove, thus ensuring that while both wings of the Cabinet and the Party were represented, the balance was sound. Membership of the tribunal was, in fact, quite sought after, partly because it was enjoyable in itself to sit in judgement on one's colleagues. Only those who had settled were eligible for the role, so I could sometimes persuade a colleague to settle early with the incentive that, if he did, he would be asked to go on the Star Chamber. The most effective members in my day were, in their very different ways, Norman Tebbit and Kenneth Clarke.

Cabinet would meet to conclude the whole process in early November. Finally, the Chancellor would announce the decisions agreed in the Autumn Statement, an innovation of Geoffrey Howe's in 1982.

GENERAL PRINCIPLES

How much of our income should be spent privately as individuals or families or via voluntary organisations; and how much should be spent collectively through the State? The Government, of course, apart from relatively insignificant receipts from a few properties it owns, has no income of its own other than what it raises compulsorily by taxation or through the deferred form of taxation known as borrowing.

There is clearly no grand principle which will yield an answer in terms of a specific percentage of the national income as the appropriate level for public spending. There are some goods identified by economists as 'public goods', for which it is either technically difficult to charge or which are jointly provided to many beneficiaries. Standard examples are defence and the police. Others include lighthouses and parks (which benefit all those who look at them, even if they do not enter them). There is also a generally accepted case for raising public funds to relieve poverty and provide for the needs of the sick and disabled which many economists misleadingly describe as 'redistribution'.

These objectives, however, can only be a general guide. They still leave the most important issues a matter of opinion. Whether a good is a public one or not is often a matter of degree. There is a 'public good' element in basic education, as the benefit from a literate body of citizens spills over to others. Higher and vocational education tends inevitably to involve the State because of the difficulties young people face in borrowing on their own security. There is also the problem that the benefits of training spill over from the employer who undertakes the training to his rival who poaches the workers. On the other hand there are private enterprise security organisations, and the police charge for keeping order at pop concerts. Where to draw the line is a political more than a technical issue. Moreover, even if there were universal agreement on the proper scope of State provision, this would still not determine how much should be spent on these agreed objectives.

There was one basic principle which guided my own efforts. Much writing on social choice and welfare economics implicitly assumes that all income belongs in the first instance to the State, and is then allocated by the State to individuals. Hence the Labour fury at the cuts in the higher tax rates in my 1988 Budget, which led to the temporary suspension of the House. The Tory belief should be the opposite one: that income or property belongs to the people who earn it or who have legitimately acquired it; and that a case has to be made for taxing it away. When the trumpets and drums are silent, and the last revisionist tract is off the Press, this is the abiding rift which still remains between Left and Right.

With that principle in mind, real world Tory politicians have to start off from where they find themselves: from existing structures, institutions, beliefs, political pressures and (sometimes unwelcome) manifesto commitments. Nevertheless, despite these handicaps, it is possible, with difficulty, to reduce public expenditure as a share of GDP. Where previous Conservative governments (with the rather special exception of a few years in the early 1950s, when defence spending was greatly reduced following the end of the Korean War) had merely succeeded in slowing down the seemingly inexorable onward march of the State, the Thatcher Government, by single-minded determination, succeeded in reversing it.

The following figures, all of which are after allowing for inflation, show that the Cabinet's public expenditure machinery was indeed able to discriminate between rival spending claims.

% CHANGE IN REAL TERMS 1979/80 TO 1989/90

GDP	+23.3
General Government Expenditure	+12.9
of which	
Law and Order	+53.3
Employment and Training	+33.3
Health	+31.8
Social Security	+31.8
Transport	-5.8
Trade and Industry	-38.2
Housing	-67.0

The first three specific programmes listed above were clear Government priorities (although it must be said that the very high figure for law and order was swollen by the excessively generous formula for determining police pay we had inherited from the last days of the Callaghan Government). Social Security was not. But we had pledged ourselves to maintain most of the main benefit levels in real terms. Beyond this, social security expenditure was largely demand determined, reflecting the steady growth in the pensioner population, the alarming rise in the number of one-parent families, the greatly increased take-up of means-tested benefits (promoted by unofficial claimants' groups, who advised their 'clients' how best to exploit the system, rather like tax accountants at the other end of the income scale), and to a lesser extent the growth in unemployment.

At the other end of the scale, the run-down in transport, trade and industry and housing reflected the fact that they contained a large element of subsidy which it was Government policy to phase out. In addition, the standard accounting treatment ensured that the sale of council houses greatly reduced the figures for housing. The differences also reflect the general principle that State spending can more easily be cut back in those areas where there is a readily available private sector alternative. This explains, too, why Government expenditure on training, despite its rise over the decade as a whole, was allowed to fall towards the end of the period as company profitability recovered, and Government schemes were developed which involved substantial private sector funding.

A SCIENCE THAT IS NOT THERE

There was one recurring criticism of our public spending system, which was made from time to time by (among others) the Treasury Select Committee, which is based on a misunderstanding. It is argued that there ought to be an explicit and rational method for deciding priorities between rival claims on the public purse. Unfortunately there is no such science upon which we can draw. Even the economists' method of looking for the highest return at the margin does not work well here.

How, for example, do you decide objectively between building a new hospital, recruiting more policemen, increasing British Rail's investment programme or providing the local authorities with more money to spend on schools – which in any event you cannot ensure is all spent on schools, let alone determine what the schools do with the money? There should be nothing surprising here, since the same applies to how we decide our own personal spending priorities. All the time we are choosing between a more expensive holiday, a new hi fi, restaurant meals or a new overcoat. But the process is scarcely an objective or scientific one.

Thus public spending is more like personal spending than it is like corporate expenditure. This is not very remarkable, given the high proportion that is either current expenditure on goods and services or transfer payments, rather than investment: the latter makes up only 10 per cent of general government expenditure. Moreover, even in the investment sector the greater proportion is in public services which provide no cash return.

There are of course techniques such as cost–benefit analysis. These can to some extent be used to decide priorities within particular sectors of spending programmes: for example, where, if anywhere, a third London airport should be built; or priorities within the road programme; or the various investigations of where to put the rail link for the Channel Tunnel. As these examples show, not even studies such as these can avoid emotively charged assumptions and judgements. But they can at least help to organise information coherently. Attempts to use this technique to make comparisons between sectors – say military expenditure and the Health Service – are in practice a waste of time.

Just as revealed choice in the marketplace is a standard way of assessing consumer preferences, so the political marketplace is the only known method of making choices between different types of collective spending, or between the collective and private variety. Electoral choice has the disadvantage that the voter can choose only between two rival proclaimed policy bundles; he does not have the opportunity to make up his own bundles, as in a supermarket or other commercial market; which is an important reason why, other things being equal, private is preferable to collective provision. But within the public sector, the two-party system is a more subtle instrument for choice than the crude model suggests. Not only do parties offering unpopular bundles tend to stay out of office for long periods; but the political market works via changes of emphasis within the political parties as well as choices between them.

A CABINET RIOT

These reflections are not *a priori*. Towards the end of Geoffrey Howe's time as Chancellor, he made a serious attempt to produce a comprehensive review of how much public spending there should be and of what kind. The background was Geoffrey's very reasonable alarm about the implications of a Treasury study of public expenditure trends. The Cabinet accordingly authorised a survey of options by the Central Policy Review Staff – the so-called 'think tank'. The CPRS team was led by Alan Bailey, an official on secondment from the Treasury, who produced his report with an expedition rare in Whitehall – which may in part account for its political insensitivity.

Geoffrey's paper made grim reading. On a low economic growth projection, public expenditure seemed destined to remain at 47 per cent of GDP even in 1990; that is to say, still three percentage points higher than in Labour's last year. On a more optimistic growth projection, it might come down to just below 40 per cent by that year. Indeed this is exactly the ratio it did reach.

However Geoffrey and his advisers considered the optimistic projections unrealistic – if only because history showed that public spending tended to rise faster at a time of more rapid growth. Unfortunately, the implications of the pessimistic scenario did not bear contemplation. Taxation would have to rise to 45 per cent of GDP, even if the PSBR were not eliminated. The paper pointed out that this implied either a basic rate of income tax of 45 per cent or a single rate of VAT of 25 per cent, in place of both the zero rate and the then standard rate of 15 per cent.

It was in this context that Geoffrey brought in the CPRS paper, which canvassed various options, such as education vouchers in place of 'free' state schools; an increase in the pupil-teacher ratio; the replacement of part of the National Health Service (NHS) by compulsory private health insurance; and the cancellation of the Trident missile programme. This sounded like a Radical Right manifesto, but its inspiration was mainly Treasury-inspired arithmetic. Geoffrey certainly did not recommend all or any of these specific proposals, but urged the need for a new and fundamental study of public expenditure, with further exploration along the lines identified by the CPRS.

The result was the nearest thing to a Cabinet riot in the history of the Thatcher administration. Geoffrey's other and perfectly reasonable request – that no new spending commitments should be made, and that Ministers should avoid repeating old pledges that would otherwise expire – was not even properly discussed.

The episode played into the hands of the 'wets'. They not only managed to get the CPRS report shelved at the meeting; but made sure that its contents were leaked to the *Economist*, which obligingly described it as 'dismantling huge chunks of the welfare state'. Horrified articles duly appeared in the *Guardian* and the 'heavy' Sunday papers. Margaret, who in those pre-Poll Tax days knew how to beat a necessary retreat, was forced to state publicly that the Government had no intention of pursuing any of the options in the CPRS paper. It was this episode that formed the foundation of Labour allegations of a 'secret manifesto' in the 1983 election; and a full text of the CPRS report was released by the then Shadow Chancellor, Peter Shore, in the closing days of the campaign.

Although I strongly supported Geoffrey's emphasis on the need to curb the growth of public spending, and indeed achieved this during my own time as Chancellor, his September 1982 initiative was surprisingly maladroit for so experienced and cautious a politician. Had I still been at the Treasury I would certainly have counselled against it. As it was, his misjudgement (which Margaret, to say the least, had done nothing to restrain) was probably a product of his habitual overestimate of his colleagues' and opponents' desire to be educated and of their readiness to respond to patient reasoning. Fortunately, little real harm was done. Indeed, the only casualty was the CPRS, which within a year Margaret, still smarting from the September 1982 episode, had disbanded for good.

THE GREEN PAPER

When I returned to the Treasury as Chancellor in June 1983, I discovered that it was all set to return to the charge. A Green Paper was in preparation, designed to demonstrate the nature of the long-term public expenditure problem and to encourage discussion of the consequences and possible remedies. It was based on a trawl of the spending Departments' own estimates of what they felt they would need to spend in the year ahead on the basis of current policies; and the idea was that these figures should be duly published to illustrate the scale of the problem.

This looked like yet another own goal, and I quickly put a stop to it. It seemed to me painfully obvious that public exposure of the various Departments' spending aspirations would give the figures a legitimacy that would make savings harder, not easier, to achieve. I decided instead to produce a Green Paper of a significantly different kind, and briefed one of my best officials, Michael Scholar, on what I wanted. He did an excellent job.

The Green Paper was published on Budget Day, March 1984 under the title *The Next Ten Years: Public Expenditure and Taxation into the 1990s*. It incorporated the published plans for public spending up to 1986/87, which projected a roughly unchanged spending total after allowing for inflation. This assumption was projected forward without departmental detail until 1988/89. Beyond that, it declared, there would be a margin for choice.

The Green Paper began, however, by quantifying some disturbing trends in the previous twenty years. In that period the UK's real national income had increased by about 50 per cent, but public expenditure had grown by 90 per cent. Taxes to pay for it already took up two fifths of GDP and were set to increase further if the trend were not halted and reversed. It was no consolation to Britain that other industrial countries experienced similar trends.

It then went on to discuss spending pressures in different sectors in terms that would repay rereading today. Its central message was that 'It is in the nature of the public services that demands are literally limitless, because they are not restrained by the price mechanism which forces those making demands to balance them against costs.' The Government would transfer provision to the market 'where possible and sensible' – no hostages to fortune here. Charges would be considered to limit demand. 'But over a wide range of services the only means of controlling costs is for the Government to limit the supply.' The so-called 'underfunding' of public services, in the sense of the Government having to say 'no' to demands for funds, is nothing more than an inescapable fact of life.

The Paper then spelled out the tax consequences of alternative spending trends, concluding that 'Government and parliament must reach their judgement about what public expenditure in total can be afforded, then contain programmes within that total'. In the past 'spending decisions, taken issue by issue, have steadily raised the burden of total spending without regard to what taxpayers will tolerate or the consequences for incentives and growth'. In advance of its publication there had been mounting demands from the House of Commons Select Committee on the Treasury and others for the Government to produce a Green Paper on the long-term public expenditure issue, as a basis for a great public and parliamentary debate. Characteristically, as soon as the Green Paper was published the Committee lost interest in the subject. The absence of political own goals must have come as a great disappointment.

THE 1983 SPENDING ROUND

Largely as a result of the row which followed the leak of the 1982 CPRS report, the Government had effectively abandoned the attempt to secure tax cuts through real reductions in public spending, a policy formulation that had always been designed more to create a badly needed new climate than as a prosaic description of the likely outcome. I decided to switch to a new and more realistic objective which I put to the Treasury and Civil Service Select Committee just before Christmas 1983: holding the level of public spending steady in real terms while the economy grew. I subsequently refined it further to a slower rate of growth for public spending than the sustainable growth rate of the economy as a whole, with the result that public expenditure would steadily decline as a share of GDP.

Meanwhile, I referred to the concerns about public spending in my first Party Conference speech, in October 1983. Indeed, the main theme of the economic debate was that we faced a stark choice between a rigorous control of public spending and increases in taxation. As it was, the need to curb Government borrowing had caused the overall burden of tax to climb from 34.75 per cent of GDP in 1978/79, Labour's last year, to 38.75 per cent in 1982/83 (excluding oil revenues in each case). Although there were one or two calls from the floor for higher public expenditure to 'reflate' the economy, my emphasis on the need to restrain public expenditure before we could consider tax cuts echoed the mood of most of the speakers.

I listed some of the long-term pressures for higher public spending. 'They come from the ageing of the population, the development of costly technologies, the lobbying of vested interests, the innate desirability of many of the forms of public expenditure, the inherent desire of all bureaucracies to expand their empires, and the failure to recognise that what is provided free still has to be paid for.'

At an evening fringe meeting Ian Gilmour predictably attacked what he described as 'housewife economics', saying that the party had won the election in spite of its economic policies rather than because of them, describing potential cuts in social security spending as 'an affront to common sense' and calling for outright reflation and an incomes policy. John Biffen, the Leader of the House, appeared on *Weekend World* the Sunday before the Conference began, and unhelpfully asserted that the Tory Party had a very well-established tradition of the protective role of the State, and that 'very often means an expensive role'. As John Biffen had not previously been a 'wet', the media invented a new type of Cabinet split, between the consolidators and the radicals; but the fevered atmosphere of 1981 was not rekindled, and the prevailing mood at the Conference was clearly in favour of curbing public expenditure to finance tax reductions.

THE 1984 ROUND AND THE BRIGHTON BOMB

In the end, the plans approved by Cabinet for my first full financial year, 1984/85, were close to the declared objective of holding public expenditure steady in real terms: we agreed an increase of less than a half a per cent after expected inflation. In the event, the Planning Total was exceeded by some £3.5 billion and rose by 3 per cent over the previous year after allowing for inflation, but the overshoot was overwhelmingly caused by the extra public spending incurred in resisting the miners' strike, above all to the extra borrowing by the coal and electricity industries. Needless to say, unlike the unfortunate events of the two previous years, this represented no loss of control of public expenditure, but was the result of a policy decision in wholly exceptional circumstances, and one that was fully justified.

At the time this emerged, however, I had been going through a bad patch, which caused the overshoot to be seen in a worse light than it warranted. The

1984 Party Conference will always be remembered as the occasion of the Brighton bomb, when the IRA attempted to murder the Prime Minister and the entire Cabinet, and came very close to succeeding. Five of those staying at the Grand Hotel, the Party's Conference headquarters, were killed, and two of my close colleagues, Norman Tebbit and John Wakeham, were badly injured. Although I was among the majority to emerge unscathed, it was a night of devastation which I shall never forget.

The previous day I had made the worst Party Conference speech of my career, and failed to secure a standing ovation. Since a Chancellor's authority depends to a considerable extent on his political standing, and since the media take their cue to a considerable extent from the Conference's response to a Minister's speech – it is almost the only occasion outside the House of Commons where the impact of a speech on those present actually matters – this was a very bad mistake. It was not that the speech was a poor one in itself; but it was far too cerebral for a Party Conference and I delivered it in far too perfunctory a manner. My first Budget, earlier that year, had gone down so well that I felt I did not really need to bother much with my Conference speech. It was not a mistake I was to make a second time.

THE ROW OVER STUDENT GRANTS

The Autumn Statement which followed shortly afterwards, in November 1984, was not a great success either, but for a very different reason. The main event was a huge row which blew up over student grants. Keith Joseph had become Education Secretary in 1981, as part of the reshuffle which brought me into the Cabinet as Energy Secretary, with a personal commitment both to university education and to the control of public spending. This led him to seek to finance extra spending on the universities by savings in the grants paid to parents for the cost of maintaining their children at universities. Under the system he had inherited, tuition fees were fully paid by the State, in other words the UK taxpayer, for all students, whether British or from overseas, irrespective of their parents' income. The cost of student maintenance, however, was theoretically the parents' responsibility; but so far as the UK students were concerned, means-tested grants were available to defray the cost, ranging from a minimum grant for comfortably-off parents to a grant that covered the full cost of student maintenance for the poorest parents.

The first change Keith made, in 1982, was to end the practice of asking the UK taxpayer to finance the tuition cost of overseas students: instead, these would have to be financed either by the overseas students themselves or by their own governments. This common-sense move aroused howls of protest both from the universities themselves and from the Labour Opposition. Since then, the number of overseas students at UK universities has continued to grow, and the change has long since ceased to be an issue: indeed, it is impossible to conceive of any future Government, of whatever political colour, choosing to reverse it.

But at the time, coming on top of our refusal to exempt the universities from the public spending stringency that we imposed on the rest of the public sector, it led to a seething hostility towards the Thatcher Government within the universities. The most striking manifestation of this was Oxford University's unprecedented decision to vote down the granting of an honorary degree to Margaret Thatcher, a courtesy which had been denied to no previous Oxford-educated Prime Minister. As an Oxford man myself, I was deeply embarrassed by this petty and boorish act. Since it was essentially all about money, I decided that the appropriate response was to consign to the waste-paper basket all the glossy appeals for funds I subsequently received from the university. Following my resignation as Chancellor, I was happy to accept the chairmanship of the Leicester University Development Committee, which exists to appeal for contributions from private benefactors. Not only is their need greater than that of a wealthy university like Oxford, but their manners are better, too.

So far as UK students were concerned, Keith's policy in his first three spending rounds as Education Secretary – in 1981, 1982 and 1983 – was to agree to an increase in the minimum grant less than the rate of inflation. As he saw it, the rationale for this was clear. Not only was he diverting funds from student support – strictly speaking, the support of students' parents – to university support. He was also remedying an injustice, since the existing system was in effect taxing the parents of non-students, whose children's earnings in later life would be less, in order to subsidise the parents of students, whose children's earnings in later life would be greater. Moreover, by concentrating the real terms reduction on the minimum grant, he was reducing most the subsidy to the better off parents who received only the minimum grant. The poorest parents, by contrast, continued to receive the full grant.

But in 1984 Keith decided he needed to go further. The universities had convinced him that they urgently needed a substantial increase in their science research budgets. To finance this he agreed with Peter Rees, the Chief Secretary, both that the minimum maintenance grant paid to all parents, regardless of means, should be abolished; and more controversially, that better-off parents should pay a means-tested contribution towards the tuition fees as well.

When the Autumn Statement was published, along with the usual Departmental press releases filling out the details, on 12 November 1984, all hell broke loose. Keith was asked to appear before the back-bench Education Committee, where he robustly defended the changes, and was given a roasting. The back-benchers would have been up in arms anyway; but their fury was exacerbated by the fact that they had always suspected that Keith had no political judgement, a suspicion that was reinforced by an aside he dropped to the effect that the way ahead lay in students being partly financed via loans – as indeed was the norm in most of the rest of the civilised world.

The real problem was the people who would be hurt by the proposed changes. These were not the poor, who were fully protected, nor the rich, who could take the increased parental contributions in their stride, but the people in between. They were the people who comprised the bulk of the Party activists in the constituencies and, in particular, the local Party officers.

It soon became clear that we would not get the changes through the House of Commons, and that a tactical retreat was inevitable. Margaret held a meeting with Keith and myself at Number 10 on 5 December 1984 at which she asked us to sort something out between us. I asked Keith to come and see me at Number 11 the next morning. At that meeting I proposed to him that we should stand firm on the abolition of the minimum grant, but that we should drop the idea of seeking a parental contribution towards tuition fees. This would leave a shortfall of some £20 million, which I suggested we should split 50:50 – that is to say, I would give him an extra £10 million for his education budget from the Reserve, and he would reduce the proposed substantial increase in the science budget by £10 million. Keith agreed, and this did the trick. The revolt simmered down to containable proportions.

The next day, with characteristic courtesy, Keith dropped me a line in his own hand, thanking me 'for helpfulness at a crucial time – and for decisiveness'. But I had learned a lesson. Although both Margaret and I had of course known about the original settlement Keith had reached with Peter Rees, it had been buried away in the papers for the final public expenditure Cabinet in November, and had not been specifically drawn to the colleagues' attention. In all subsequent years I was careful to ensure that any politically controversial savings that had been agreed either in bilaterals or by Star Chamber were explicitly drawn to the attention of Cabinet.

THE 1985 ROUND – LEVIATHAN TAMED

There was, however, a much more serious shortcoming in the 1984 Autumn Statement. It rapidly became apparent that the overall public expenditure totals we had published for 1985/86 (and hence for the subsequent years) had been based on unrealistic assumptions and were thus far too low. I have never seen any virtue in living in cloud cuckoo land, not least because reality has an unfortunate habit of intruding at the most awkward moment. I eventually persuaded a very reluctant Margaret that the least bad course was to add a couple of billion pounds to the Reserve for each of the three survey years when it came to the Budget. It was profoundly embarrassing.

No sooner had that adjustment been made than a new threat to public expenditure control emerged from an unexpected quarter. Poor Keith Joseph, still smarting from the drubbing he had received over the student grants affair, decided that the heart of the problem was that Cabinet had never had a proper discussion of public expenditure priorities, and lobbied Margaret to hold one. He was supported by her then Principal Private Secretary, the normally sagacious Robin Butler, who should have known better, and she decided to go ahead as Keith had requested. I was distinctly cool. It seemed clear to me that, while in theory this was a wholly rational way of proceeding, in practice no spending Minister would agree that his own programme was a low priority, and each would seek to argue the reverse. Thus the only practical consequence could be a rash of new spending bids. All I succeeded in doing was persuading Margaret that the discussion should be held at Chequers, in the hope that colleagues would be less aggressive in a rural setting than they would be in Downing Street.

The priorities meeting duly took place at Chequers on Sunday, 23 June 1985, with Peter Rees giving a general presentation with charts, followed by a discussion round the table. Fortunately, although some colleagues, such as Peter Walker and John Biffen, argued the case for a more relaxed attitude to public expenditure altogether, it was less damaging than I feared. Needless to say, however, it served no constructive purpose and was never repeated.

Margaret did however make an important contribution to improved spending control in her Cabinet reshuffle of 2 September. This was to bring in my old friend John MacGregor as Chief Secretary in place of Peter Rees, whom she dropped from the Government altogether. In the same reshuffle Barney Hayhoe was moved from Minister of State at the Treasury where he was a relatively junior member of the four-strong team, to the much more exposed position of Minister of Health, to be replaced by another old friend, Ian Gow, subsequently murdered by the IRA. The strategic gain was the acquisition of John MacGregor whose appointment I had long urged on Margaret. I had known John since we had worked together on Alec Douglas-Home's speeches before the 1964 election. Quiet and undemonstrative, he is easy to underrate. He combined a social liberalism with a Scottish determination (all too rare in today's Scottish establishment) to keep a firm rein on the public purse, assisted by shrewd political judgement.

The 1985 expenditure round was in the end uneventful – which means it went well. The July public expenditure Cabinet simply reaffirmed the cash figure for 1986/87 that had been published at the time of the Budget. I was helped by the drop in inflation in the second half of 1985, associated in part with a falling oil price, which reconciled the spending Departments to their cash allocations. A more fundamental gain was the expiry, at long last, of the UK's pledge to NATO to increase defence spending by 3 per cent a year in real terms.

Growth on this scale had been a long-standing NATO aspiration, accepted in principle by all its member Governments, but in practice honoured more in the breach than in the observance. A unilateral pledge that the UK would meet this target had featured prominently in the manifesto on which we had fought and won the 1979 general election. As time passed, this commitment became increasingly irksome to a Government desperately trying to curb the growth of overall public spending; particularly since it was quite clear that our European NATO allies, who as it was spent far less on defence both absolutely and as a share of GDP than we did, had no intention of following suit.

So by the time of the 1983 election, this pledge was quietly dropped from the manifesto. With a Labour Party led by the old CND campaigner Michael Foot and aggressively committed to the cause of unilateral nuclear disarmament, there was no need for us to repeat the NATO pledge to pose convincingly as the Party of strong defence. This meant that the first Autumn Statement of the new parliament – my first, in November 1983 – could plan for the 3 per cent a year real growth, which we had scrupulously honoured since taking office in 1979, to come to an end in 1985/86. The new year that entered the plans for the first time, 1986/87, showed no real growth in defence spending at all.

This evolution had been eased, too, by the appointment of Michael Heseltine as Defence Secretary in January 1983, following the wayward John Nott's surprise decision to leave politics altogether. Contrary to his reputation, Michael (unlike, say, Peter Walker or Kenneth Baker) has never been an indiscriminate big spender, and he accepted without demur the dropping of the NATO pledge. He was also responsible, in 1984, for appointing Peter Levene as Chief of Defence Procurement – the first serious attempt by any Defence Secretary of either Party to get value for money.

A DEFENCE CONCORDAT

A further breakthrough was secured in the control of defence spending early in April 1986, following the resignation of Michael Heseltine over the Westland affair and his replacement by George Younger.

The defence budget is the largest programme of expenditure on 'goods and services' (as opposed to transfers like pensions) administered by a single Government Department. It is inherently difficult to control because, as with the health budget, thanks to the ever onward march of technological development, the cost of its hardware rises far faster than inflation generally. But on top of this there was a self-inflicted handicap. Hitherto Defence, unlike all other Departments, had operated a block budget – supposedly for reasons of national security. The Chief Secretary could negotiate with the Defence Secretary only over the total defence spending budget. There would be no discussion of individual items, which would not even be revealed.

Obviously there were exceptions. The Defence Secretary could not have complete carte blanche. Any major new procurement project would require Cabinet or Cabinet committee approval, which gave the Treasury an opportunity to probe its costs and those of alternatives. Any bid by the Defence Department for a slice of the Reserve in the course of a financial year would also need to be justified on its merits. Armed forces pay, too, was considered separately through the Pay Review Body. In addition, during the Falklands War, Falklands defence spending had to be put in a separate category, which continued for some time afterwards, given the need to fortify the islands. But despite the exceptions, the Defence allocation was essentially a block grant.

It was this system which at long last changed. Michael Heseltine had not been prepared to surrender the block budget which he had inherited, chiefly because he wanted to use the defence budget to implement a UK industrial policy, a notion that the Department of Trade and Industry (DTI) had largely and rightly abandoned. To the extent that overseas entanglements were inescapable, he wanted to see a European industrial policy. This, rather than defence considerations, was what really lay behind the Westland helicopter affair.

The sanctity of the defence block budget came to an end with the arrival of George Younger, which happily coincided with some outstanding promotions at the official level. Robin Butler moved from Number 10 to become Second Permanent Secretary at the Treasury in charge of public spending, very much at my instigation. The other key official was Clive Whitmore, another former Private Secretary to the Prime Minister, who had become Permanent Secretary at Defence.

All these moves paved the way for a hitherto unrecorded concordat between George Younger and John MacGregor, buttressed by a similar one between Whitmore and Butler. All of them deserve a share of the credit. The agreement laid down that Defence would henceforth open its books to the Treasury and allow the expenditure round to be conducted on an item-by-item basis. But the process would be very restricted. The only non-Defence individuals allowed to see them in the Treasury would be the Chancellor, the Chief Secretary, the Permanent Secretary, the Second Permanent Secretary responsible for public spending, and – operationally the key – one middle ranking Treasury official whose full-time job was vetting defence spending. That was quite enough.

The new defence arrangements could not of course be expected to make very much difference to the plans already agreed in the three-year programmes. But they almost certainly prevented the subsequent escalation which would otherwise have occurred.

One long overdue casualty of the defence economies was the UK-made Nimrod early warning aircraft, cancelled after massive cost overruns and delays and persistent operational shortcomings. Ironically, another item which did not in any sense leave the ground was the inordinately expensive Zircon spy satellite project.

This became something of a cause célèbre in January 1987 when details of it were procured by a left-wing investigative journalist called Duncan Campbell. He planned to broadcast them as part of a BBC Scotland television series, 'The Secret Society'. The Government managed to lean on the BBC to ban the programme. When Campbell published a *New Statesman* article instead, Margaret instructed Michael Havers, the Attorney General, to issue an injunction against him and every newspaper in the country. In a somewhat unfortunate blaze of publicity, the police raided the offices both of the BBC in Glasgow and of the *New Statesman* in London in an attempt to discover the source of his information. The irony lay in the fact that, well before all this blew up, I had succeeded in getting the Zircon project cancelled on grounds of cost.

In general, however, the security services, their establishments and their hardware, were one of the very few areas of public life virtually untouched by the rigours of the Thatcher era. Most Prime Ministers have a soft spot for the security services, for which they have a special responsibility. But Margaret, an avid reader of the works of Frederick Forsyth, was positively besotted by them.

1986 – THE PRE-ELECTION ROUND

The 1986 public expenditure round was the only one that John MacGregor saw through from beginning to end. The pre-election round is always the toughest of the series and John deserves a tribute for what was in reality an outstanding result. Yet it did not look like that; for I was obliged to announce in the Autumn Statement of November 1986 a Planning Total (excluding privatisation) for 1987/88 some £5 billion higher in cash terms than the figure previously published. This was intensely embarrassing to me, to John, and to our officials alike, and inevitably led to the accusation that I was engaging in a pre-election public spending bonanza.

In fact the previously published figure had once again been unrealistic; and the figure for which we settled represented only a minuscule real increase over the previous year. Indeed, the 1987/88 out-turn proved to be virtually identical to the previous year in real terms. This was a remarkable and almost unprecedented result in view of the electoral calendar.

Nevertheless, I felt it sensible to use the occasion of the 1986 Autumn Statement to change the presentation of the Government's public expenditure objective and provide a basis for making the whole process of spending control more realistic. I shifted the emphasis from the Planning Total to General Government Expenditure, and redefined the Government's public expenditure objective as ensuring that General Government Expenditure should continue to fall as a proportion of GDP – in the first instance, up to 1988/89.

The chief difference between General Government Expenditure and the Planning Total is that GGE includes debt interest. But the main point, as the ever-reliable Pliatzky explains, is that the Planning Total corresponds to no recognised statistical aggregate in general use outside the Whitehall process, while GGE corresponds much more with a common-sense view of what Government expenditure is, as well as with international conventions, and indeed had been the concept used in the Green Paper.

I none the less had to insist on the reformulation almost over the dead bodies of the Treasury mandarins, who seemed to feel that simply aiming at a falling share of GDP was selling the pass. Critics from the political Right also attacked me for being content merely to cut the public spending ratio rather than the absolute level of spending. They were not living in the real world.

The problem of public expenditure, as the Green Paper had clearly shown, was that in the past it had consistently risen faster than the growth of the economy as a whole – as indeed was the case in most other countries. The new target, if attained, would mark a fundamental change of trend. Moreover, unlike the previous practice of defining the goal each year in terms of a specific cash figure for the Planning Total, it was a logical rule rather than an arbitrary number. The logic, of course, is that public expenditure falling as a share of GDP is the necessary and sufficient condition for tax cuts. It was helpful, too, that the original 1979 manifesto pledge had explicitly been to reduce the share of national income taken by the State.

Some too-clever-by-half commentators, such as *Financial Times* leader writers, attempted to ridicule the idea, asking whether the ratio was intended to fall indefinitely. Once again, they were missing the point; namely that, in the absence of any such guideline, the public spending share tends to rise inexorably. As it was, the goal of reducing public spending as a share of GDP over the three years to 1988/89 was, as the Soviet planners used to say, 'overfulfilled'.

Indeed, it is noteworthy that during the period 1978/79 to 1983/84, when the Thatcher Government was supposedly trying to cut public spending, the ratio of public spending to GDP rose embarrassingly. During the following five years, when we had on paper a less ambitious objective, the ratio fell dramatically to the lowest since the mid-1960s – even excluding privatisation receipts. The fall in the public spending ratio from 1982/83, more or less continuously up to 1990/91, was something that had not been achieved under any government since the 1950s.

By the eve of the 1987 election, while the commentators and Opposition were trotting out their clichés about a pre-election give-away, the truth was that my objective of ensuring that total public spending should rise less rapidly than the economy as a whole was being comfortably achieved. I was helped in this both by the improved prospect for debt interest as the PSBR plummeted and by the strong growth of the economy. But although the state of the economic cycle undeniably helped, it is clear from the zero real growth of public spending that this was no mere cyclical phenomenon. Public spending was genuinely under firm control – unprecedentedly so.

CHAPTER EIGHTEEN

AN AGENDA FOR TAX REFORM

A Chance to Surprise · The Making of the Budget · A Memo to the Prime Minister · Only One Chancellor · Tax Objectives · The Tax Proportion · Lower Rates and Fewer Breaks · For and Against Neutrality · A Discouraging Fiscal Outlook

A CHANCE TO SURPRISE

The first Budget of a new Government is the greatest opportunity a Chancellor has to introduce sweeping changes, and Geoffrey Howe had seized his opportunity in June 1979 with gusto. The next best thing is the first Budget after an election in which the Government has been renewed in office, when a Chancellor once again has the opportunity to introduce reforms which might be difficult later on, either because they are too controversial or because it takes too long for their beneficial effects to become apparent before the next election. The timing of the 1983 election meant I had to wait the best part of a year before I could introduce a Budget of my own, but I was determined to make the most of the chance it provided.

Some Chancellors used to regard the Budget as a means of fine-tuning the economy. Others saw it more as a statement from the chairman of the board on the state of the economy. But I conceived its role rather differently: as an essential part of a long-term programme to improve economic performance.

Of course the Budget is not the only part of such a programme (nor always the principal part). Indeed I pressed for supply-side reforms of various kinds in the appropriate Cabinet committees, and in the course of planning public expenditure, as other chapters demonstrate. Privatisation, where as Chancellor I had the co-ordinating role, was something I was able to push particularly hard. But tax reform is the one major branch of supply-side reform which is unequivocally under the direct control of the Chancellor.

THE MAKING OF THE BUDGET

Work on the Budget would start in earnest as soon as the Autumn Statement was out of the way in November. 'Budget starters', as they are called, are generated in one of four ways. First, there are the main tax rates and allowances which, by statute, have to be fixed annually anyway. Second, there are the technical proposals put forward by the Inland Revenue to close loopholes or to fulfil undertakings already given or to rectify acknowledged defects in the tax system. Third, there are the ideas put forward by the Chancellor and other Treasury Ministers, by Cabinet colleagues and by senior officials. Finally, the Treasury receives an enormous number of Budget submissions from various interest groups during the run-up to the Budget, which are examined with care. Only a small minority of starters actually make it to the Budget, of course. Periodic culls reduce them, so that by the beginning of the Christmas recess serious planning can begin.

In our time the next step, in mid-January, was for Treasury Ministers and senior officials to gather for an intensive weekend of discussion and planning at Chevening, a fine Regency House in Kent, left to the government in the 1960s by the last Earl of Stanhope. Geoffrey Howe had inaugurated this practice in 1982. I found it helpful to continue it, though I was a little doubtful of his decision to invite spouses also, who inevitably found themselves neglected much of the time. On the Saturday evening there would be a snooker match between Ministers and officials, very much in a Gentlemen versus Players mode. Middleton and Burns took it seriously and brought their own cues. It was naturally expected that the officials would win, and mostly they did.

From Chevening the provisional shape of the Budget would emerge, on which detailed work would take place over the following months in groups chaired by Ministers, with lengthy weekly review meetings to take the big decisions. A 'scorecard' was kept of the emerging Budget, detailing the cost (or yield) of individual measures.

The general shape of the Budget should have been settled at least a month before the event, though the last day for changes could be surprisingly late – tobacco duties were altered at the last minute in 1984, and the basic rate of income tax in 1986. Work on the Budget speech would have to begin well before it reached final form.

Although with no ambition to be Prime Minister I spent rather less time than many of my colleagues in cultivating the back-benches, I was unusual in spending a good deal of time canvassing their views in advance of the Budget, more than any previous Chancellor. Treasury Ministers would see groups of ten for a drink, with me seeing the most senior, some of them individually. The mood varied with the state of the economy, but the effort was undoubtedly appreciated.

Unlike my post-war predecessors, and some of my successors, one important objective I set myself in my 1984 and subsequent Budgets was to confine the Budget to tax changes and rule out any new announcements, however politically attractive, on the public expenditure front. Public spending decisions having been taken in the previous autumn, and the plans announced in the Autumn Statement, it never seemed to me compatible with firm control of public expenditure to allow spending Ministers a second crack of the whip in the spring. I felt obliged to make a few rare exceptions to this rule, when unemployment was high and rising and special employment measures were called for; but on the whole I succeeded in getting the message accepted.

A MEMO TO THE PRIME MINISTER

The Budget preparations in 1984 followed pretty much the standard course, including an exceptionally hard-working but otherwise successful Chevening weekend in the first half of January. A few days later, on 19 January 1984, as a background to the specific measures I had in mind and of which I would shortly be informing her, I sent Margaret a fairly lengthy memorandum setting out the tax reform strategy I believed we should pursue during the course of the new parliament. Some of the thinking in it I have since modified in the light of experience, as subsequent chapters explain; but not the main thrust. It began as follows:

> TAX REFORM STRATEGY
>
> In addition to tax reduction, I believe that we should aim to make substantial progress in the field of tax reform during the life of this Parliament. I have in mind a programme of reform covering both personal and company taxation.
>
> *Personal Taxation*
>
> 2. The priorities here should be:
>   (i) to increase the scope for income tax cuts by continuing the process embarked on by Geoffrey Howe in his first Budget of switching some of the burden from income tax to VAT;
>   (ii) to improve incentives; and
>   (iii) to remove or reduce distortions.
> 3. (i) above should not be pursued by increasing the 15 per cent rate of VAT still further, but by broadening the base of the tax, bringing

into the VAT net some items at present zero-rated. Only half of all consumer spending is now subject to VAT. The need to have regard to the impact effect on the RPI in any one year points to the desirability of making gradual progress, starting this year. The political sensitivities are obvious, but I believe there is appreciable scope for action.

4. As to (ii) above, the priority here must be to increase personal tax thresholds. The married man's allowance has fallen as a percentage of average earnings from about 60 per cent in 1950 to just over 30 per cent today. The level of income at which people in this country start to pay income tax is well below that of our major competitors. A substantial increase in the thresholds would take many people out of the tax net altogether, ease the poverty and unemployment traps, and improve incentives. We also need to tackle the unsatisfactory 'kink' in the marginal rate of total deductions (income tax plus national insurance) in the present system, which starts at 39 per cent, then drops to 30 per cent, and then rises again to 40 per cent; and to improve the tax treatment of share option schemes. When we have raised the income tax threshold to a reasonable level, we can again turn our attention to the rates of tax.
5. So far as (iii) above is concerned, the present system runs completely counter to our fundamental philosophy by encouraging the institutionalisation of savings and discouraging share ownership by the individual. The specially favourable reliefs for life assurance are the obvious example, but we shall also need to consider, when Norman Fowler's review is complete, the tax privileges of the pension funds. On the other side of the coin, I should like to get rid of the investment income surcharge.

Business taxation

6. At the present time we suffer from an excessively high level of Corporation Tax (52 per cent) made to some extent tolerable by an extensive and somewhat capricious system of reliefs.
7. Our long-term objective should be to bring the corporation tax rate down to 30 per cent, which would remove the present distortion in the system against equity finance and in favour of loan finance. A gradual move in this direction could be financed for the most part

by a correspondingly gradual reduction in the generous allowances and reliefs which at present bias investment between different types of assets and between capital and labour.

8. I believe that over the lifetime of this Parliament we should aim to abolish, in stages, the first year allowance for plant and machinery and for industrial buildings. This would leave the annual writing down allowances of 25 per cent and 4 per cent respectively to take account of depreciation. We should make corresponding changes in the less important allowances. We should also abolish stock relief, now that the high inflation which made it necessary is behind us.
9. We are pledged to abolish the National Insurance Surcharge during the lifetime of this Parliament. I am considering the right timing.

The remainder of the note mentioned a review of all the various capital taxes and the need to reduce stamp duty, 'as a tax on mobility and a disincentive to wider ownership, as well as a threat to the survival of a strong central securities market in London'. The note ended, predictably, by saying the tax reform would be easier against a background of tax reduction, to reduce the number of losers from any change to politically tolerable levels. These reductions in turn depended 'on the most stringent control of public spending'.

I never expected Margaret to be as enthusiastic as I was about my proposed Corporation Tax reforms. This idea of tax neutrality – the removal of special reliefs for this, that or the other, discussed later on in this chapter – held no appeal for her. Indeed, she was constantly proposing new tax breaks of one kind or another, usually arguing that this was preferable to higher public spending, which I was just as constantly rejecting. None the less, she acquiesced without demur in the proposed switch from capital allowances to a lower rate of Corporation Tax, at least partly because the package contained other items on which she was keener.

A reduction in income tax clearly had more appeal; and she was prepared to go along with the principle of widening the VAT base to help pay for it. But when it came to the point, the extension of VAT to building alterations (too close to home ownership for her to feel comfortable with it) and hot take-away foods was as far as she was prepared to go. She was delighted by the amount by which I was able to raise the tax thresholds and did not object to postponing basic rate cuts. She shared my enthusiasm for abolishing the Investment Income Surcharge and for reducing stamp duty. She was less keen on abolishing the tax relief on life assurance premiums, and in subsequent Budgets was against taking any further moves to reduce fiscal privilege.

ONLY ONE CHANCELLOR

The nearest we came to a row in 1984 was over the involvement of Arthur Cockfield in the Budget preparations. Arthur had a long history of tax expertise, beginning his career with the Inland Revenue and serving as a tax adviser to the Conservatives in Opposition and Government, latterly as a Minister. At this stage Margaret was a great admirer of Arthur's and urged me to involve him fully in Budget discussions. For a number of reasons this was something I was not prepared to do, above all because there can be only one Chancellor of the Exchequer – a fact I could not see him recognising.

The confidant of my own choosing was Norman Tebbit. As Trade and Industry Secretary, he would inevitably face a lot of flak for the changes I was proposing in company taxes, which were likely to be opposed by virtually the whole business establishment. He was also the colleague in whom I was keenest to confide my fiscal strategy. I had formed a close working relationship with Norman, who had entered the Cabinet on the same day as I did, since the days of Opposition. Although our characters are very different, our political and economic instincts were not. It became a particularly useful alliance once I had assumed the lonely occupation of Chancellor and he had succeeded Cecil Parkinson as Secretary of State for Trade and Industry, the key economic Department outside the Treasury.

Indeed the alliance with Norman was the most effective and closest I formed in the 1983–87 parliament. As we shall see, he supported my November 1985 attempt to make sterling a full participant of the European Monetary System, before the issue had become entangled in political passions about 'Europe'. Even after his growing distance from Margaret contributed to his resignation in 1987 he continued to see me regularly at Number 11, although I had to be more careful about what I said. The fact that our relations sadly deteriorated after my resignation in 1989 and still more after Margaret's the following year is no reason to rewrite history.

Geoffrey Howe, of course, remained a close colleague and friend, and we continued to meet from time to time à deux. But his Foreign Office responsibilities left him little time for involvement in domestic matters. It was only after the 1987 election, when foreign and economic policy became intertwined on the European issue, that we were to see more of each other.

TAX OBJECTIVES

Right from the start, I devoted a great deal of time, thought and political capital to the question of tax reform. Moreover, despite the occasional carping of critics in the quality Press and elsewhere – partly because my reforms did not coincide with their preferences – I think it is fair to say that what I achieved, taking all six Budgets together, represented a coherent and substantial measure of reform.

Rather than presenting each of my Budgets as an isolated set of measures, it makes more sense to outline my approach to tax reform as it developed and place the individual Budgets in that framework.

My overriding purpose in reforming taxes was to improve the performance of the economy. In a nutshell the objectives were:

1. To leave people more of their own money so that they could choose for themselves what to do with it.
2. So far as was practical, to reduce marginal tax rates, so that an extra pound of earnings or profits was really worth having.
3. To see that, as a general rule, people's choices were distorted as little as possible through the tax system.
4. But to be prepared, when sensible, to promote tax reliefs designed to make the economy work better.
5. To ensure, so far as possible, that the tax system both was simple and acceptable (not least to married women).
6. To adopt an economic rather than a social approach.

Certainly the Government has a responsibility for health, education, and assisting those who for whatever reason lack normal earning power. But these responsibilities are best discharged by those Government Departments, like the Department of Social Security, that are explicitly in charge of the various aspects of the welfare state, rather than by complicating the tax system.

THE TAX PROPORTION

The Conservative Governments of 1979–92 cannot claim to have reduced the burden of tax as a proportion of GDP. Irrespective of whether North Sea revenues are included or not, the tax take was in fact a couple of percentage points higher in 1991/92 than it had been in 1978/79, the previous Labour Government's last year. This was understandably disappointing, but it arose as a result of the need to reduce the unsustainably large Budget deficit we had inherited from Labour, and its use as a debating point comes ill from the mouths of political opponents whose main complaint was that taxpayer-financed public spending was too low. Moreover, despite the inability to reduce the overall burden of taxation, a substantial measure of tax reform was carried out.

During my own time as Chancellor the proportion of GDP taken in taxes and social security contributions fell from 38.25 per cent in 1983/84 to 37.75 per cent in 1989/90, a decline of only a half per cent. Over the same period General Government Expenditure, excluding privatisation receipts, fell from 46.5 per cent to 40 per cent of GDP. As a result, the Public Sector Borrowing Requirement shifted from 3.5 per cent of GDP to a repayment of 0.75 per cent (again excluding privatisation proceeds). These numbers are hardly consistent with a charge of fiscal laxity or of failing to allow for the effects of the boom in the conduct of fiscal policy.

The main way in which we were able to leave people more choice was by switching the tax burden from income to spending – itself a 'savings incentive' seldom acknowledged. The big move here was of course Geoffrey Howe's switch from income tax to VAT in his first Budget (Chapter 4), in which I had been involved as Financial Secretary. The switch went further with the modest extension of the range of goods liable to VAT that I was able to announce in 1984. The further increase of VAT from 15 to 17.5 per cent by Norman Lamont in 1991 to reduce the severity of the Poll Tax, was theoretically a widening of choice; but it would have been far better not to have had to make it.

The Conservative Government was able in the end to reduce the basic rate of income tax to 25 per cent. Even if employees' National Insurance contributions, which were increased in Geoffrey Howe's time, are taken into account, there was an overall reduction in marginal tax rates for the generality of the population from 39.5 per cent to 34 per cent, five percentage points of which occurred while I was Chancellor. Some would argue that employers' contributions are passed on to employees in one form or another. On this basis, and including the National Insurance Surcharge, the marginal tax rate was 53 per cent in 1978/79, 50.5 per cent in 1983/84, and 44.5 per cent in 1989/90. This merely underlines the fact that marginal rates are still too high.

The reconciliation between a rising or at best stable tax share and the periodic lowering of income tax rates is only partly due to the switch to indirect taxes. Just as important is the property of the tax system known by the ugly name of fiscal drag. This is the tendency of tax revenues to rise faster than the national income, which has two aspects. First, the tax system is not price-indexed in its entirety. Second, even those parts of the system that are price-indexed are not earnings-indexed. The first aspect alone must be of the order of £2 billion a year.

This enables a Chancellor who can prevent public spending from rising faster than the economy as a whole to cut tax rates even when there is no real reduction in the tax burden. Equally, a Chancellor who wishes public spending to rise faster than the national income can, up to a point, do so without having to announce increases in tax rates – a process sometimes known euphemistically as 'using the fiscal dividend'.

A further reduction in the tax take amounting to some 2 per cent of GDP is estimated by the Treasury to have occurred between 1989 and 1992. Most of this fall was the automatic consequence of the recession, although the coming into force of independent taxation for married women has also had an effect. The key point, however, is that if my guideline that public spending should rise less rapidly than the economy as a whole is observed there will ultimately be scope for reducing not merely tax rates but the tax burden, too, over time.

The overall reduction in the total of the basic rate of income tax and employee's National Insurance contribution was part of a larger objective. For what really matters is whether, through a series of Budgets, a climate can be created in which people feel they are living in a country where tax rates are reasonably low and likely to come down further – a country where individuals and businesses are working less for the Government and more for themselves and their families, and for the causes they wish to support.

LOWER RATES AND FEWER BREAKS

For any given level of public spending, the ideal way of achieving lower marginal rates is not through fiscal drag (or, as the Americans call it, bracket creep) or even by switching to indirect taxes. It is by eliminating privileges and exemptions of all kinds. A good tax system should be broadly based, with low tax rates and few tax breaks. The reason for this is not merely the avoidance of economic distortions, although that itself is important. There is also the practical point that tax breaks are inevitably abused as methods of tax avoidance, which means that the general level of taxation has to be still higher to bring in the required revenue. Moreover, the granting of one tax break inevitably increases the political pressures for others.

The higher rates we inherited when we took office in 1979 were frequently not paid. The well-heeled and well-advised took great pains to avoid liability through the perfectly legal use of tax shelters of one kind or another; and the tax avoidance (its practitioners liked to call it 'tax planning') industry flourished as never before. Needless to say, reducing or eliminating tax breaks is never popular with those who benefit from them. Reform plans here and abroad have foundered on this rock more than once. But the principle is clear: as somebody once said, 'If you want the Government off your back, you have to get your hand out of its pocket.'

So long as this approach is persevered with there is a virtuous circle to be had. Reducing or eliminating tax breaks provides increased revenue which can be used to bring down tax rates. Lower tax rates themselves reduce the value of tax breaks. So it is then a little easier to reduce the privileges that remain. This in turn releases more money to reduce tax rates. So just as high tax rates tend to bring with them high tax breaks, lower tax rates go hand in hand with lower tax breaks. Moreover, as high marginal tax rates are brought down, taxpayers will be less inclined to pay expensive accountants to devise complex schemes to reduce their liability or to seek remuneration in non-cash forms. These are among the reasons why a reduction in high marginal tax rates can lead in practice to a significantly smaller loss of revenue than the simple arithmetic would suggest.

This is the true virtuous circle. Some critics have confused it with another kind of virtuous circle promoted by some wishful thinking ultra-Keynesians – and ultra-supply-siders. This is the notion that tax cuts, without any spending cuts or substitute source of revenue will so stimulate the economy that the Budget balance will improve, enabling further tax cuts to be made, and so on. In fact, of course, long before anything like that could happen, the economy would be subject to massive inflationary pressures, and interest rates would have to be raised or tax policy reversed at the cost of severe recession. While excess demand can occur by inadvertence, this spurious kind of virtuous circle was emphatically not part of my thinking.

FOR AND AGAINST NEUTRALITY

The trimming of allowances and reliefs was not only a matter of helping to find the revenue needed to pay for reductions in marginal rates. It was also intended to make the tax system more neutral. That is, to reduce the extent to which the tax system biases people's choices, by making it worth their while to spend or save in some ways rather than in others, purely for tax reasons.

The system we inherited in 1979 was not only badly biased, but biased in ways that could not fail to stultify the progress of the economy. It was biased against employment, biased against savings, biased against share ownership and biased against sensible business investment decisions.

There were three main biases against employment. First and most obviously there was the employers' National Insurance Surcharge, which Denis Healey imposed, and which Geoffrey Howe and I managed to get rid of entirely by 1984. Second, there was the bias against jobs inherent in the Corporation Tax system. In the form in which we inherited it, it provided tax subsidies for investment in capital equipment, even when more labour-intensive methods of production might be more economic. That was something I dealt with by the Corporation Tax Reforms of 1984. Third, National Insurance contributions acted as a deterrent to employers thinking of taking on lower paid and less-skilled workers. This was something I remedied in my 1985 and 1989 Budgets, which both made it cheaper to employ people on low earnings and allowed such people to keep more of what they earned.

I attacked the bias against savings by a number of measures, among them the abolition of the Investment Income Surcharge, the replacement of Capital Transfer Tax by the far less penal Inheritance Tax, and the launch of Personal Equity Plans (PEPs); while my Corporation Tax reforms were the principal way of removing the bias against sensible business investment suggestions.

Not only do many politicians, mainly although not exclusively in the Labour Party, want to restore some of these biases, so too do some industrialists, who identify the national good not with the long-term profitability, but with the short-term cash flow of their own companies. Nevertheless, while most departures from tax neutrality are simply concessions to pressure groups, there are some that would be justified even on the most elevated principles.

Economists since Adam Smith have known that there are some so-called spill-over costs and benefits which are not captured in a conventional market system. Where the distortions are large and straightforward the use of taxes or subsidies to encourage or discourage certain activities, by operating through the price mechanism, is a more attractive remedy than outright prohibition. This is the theoretical case for the deliberately high excise duties on alcohol and tobacco. The pioneer of theoretical welfare economics, A.C. Pigou, proposed a tax on smoking chimneys before the First World War, although successive governments in practice preferred rules about permissible emissions. Nowadays there is a revival of interest in pollution taxes of various kinds.[18]

[18] [2010 note] This whole issue has been given added importance by the emergence, since my time as Chancellor, of concern that man-made emissions of carbon dioxide might increase global temperatures to a dangerous extent. See the new final chapter – and, for a fuller discussion, my 2008/2009 book, *An Appeal to Reason: A Cool Look at Global Warming*.

The candidates for fiscal intervention which most attracted my attention, however, were in those grey areas where unimpeded market forces might in principle be sufficient but where the markets in question suffered from long years of ossification. To take the most significant examples, the labour market was notoriously rigid, while the market for private renting verged on the non-existent. Modest tax reliefs to complement our other policies to get these markets working better seemed to me well worth providing.

Well-directed tax reliefs can help to make the economy more flexible, adaptive and dynamic. That is why, for example, in my 1988 Budget I extended the Business Expansion Scheme (BES), a tax break introduced by Geoffrey Howe, to cover the provision of private rented accommodation.

The lack of privately rented housing in the UK was – and still is – a serious blemish which greatly inhibits mobility of labour. Nicholas Ridley rightly sought to tackle it through housing legislation. I judged it worth helping by offering a new tax incentive for a limited period of five years. For similar reasons I introduced tax relief on Profit Related Pay in 1987: again a desirable carrot to get more flexibility into the labour market. Interestingly, the biggest response to it came from small businesses, confirming that these are in many ways the spearhead of the enterprise culture.

But while some tax reliefs can play a worthwhile role, the general presumption against them means that, as time passes, every relief must be reviewed with a critical eye. Is this one still needed for the purpose for which it was devised? Is that one now being used more as a tax planning device than for its original purpose? Is the other one showing diminishing economic returns in relation to the amount of revenue forgone?

The process can be illustrated by reference to the Business Expansion Scheme. When we first came into office, new business formation was in the doldrums; and it was still difficult, if not impossible, for small or medium sized companies to raise venture capital. So Geoffrey Howe introduced the Business Start-up Scheme, which developed into the Business Expansion Scheme. That provided tax incentives which have helped substantially to promote new businesses, to the undoubted benefit of the economy as a whole.

Meanwhile the spread of the enterprise culture, fostered by this and other policies, brought about a dramatic growth in the venture capital industry, from almost nowhere to over £1 billion of investment a year at the beginning of the 1990s. Thus much of the original purpose of the BES scheme was fulfilled. I therefore took steps in my 1988 Budget to limit the amount any one company could raise through the scheme each year, so as to concentrate BES money on the smallest companies where the need still existed. Moreover in extending the scheme to private renting I explicitly limited the relief to five years, running out in 1993.

In 1992, Norman Lamont decided to bring the whole scheme to a close by the end of 1993. This could be justified on two quite separate grounds. In the first place, the UK had by then a venture capital industry equal to that of any in the world outside the US, so over the longer term the scheme was no longer needed. And in the second place, the early announcement of the ending of the tax break might, with luck, lead to a rush of applications to take advantage of this before the guillotine came down – a useful ephemeral boost at a time of recession when bank finance was less readily available.

A DISCOURAGING FISCAL OUTLOOK

Although there are obvious advantages for a Chancellor in introducing his first Budget in the first year of a new parliament, after a stunning election victory, in other respects the timing of the 1984 Budget was distinctly unpromising. The immediate PSBR prospect seemed to rule out any early start on tax reduction. Indeed if I was going to make any impact in my first Budget, it would be by reforming taxation rather than reducing it – although without the lubricant of tax reduction, tax reform was not going to be easy.

Despite the emergency public spending cuts in July 1983, it was still clear that the Public Sector Borrowing Requirement for 1983/84 would considerably exceed the £8.25 billion target set by Geoffrey Howe in his 1983 Budget. The Autumn Statement forecast had put it at £10 billion, and the eventual outcome was not far short of that at £9.75 billion, or 3.25 per cent of GDP – equivalent to some £20 billion in 1992/93 terms.

Net tax cuts did not therefore, as I put it in my public utterances that autumn 'look a lively prospect for 1984'. Indeed the 'fiscal adjustment', which I then had an obligation to publish, indicated the need for a modest increase in tax receipts; and I have recorded how it attracted the fiercest opprobrium from the self-appointed keepers of Conservative conscience in the tabloids, despite my warning of the tentative nature of the forecast.

In the end the fiscal outlook improved sufficiently for me to get away with a neutral Budget, in the sense of no significant net increase or decrease in the tax take for the coming financial year. But taking expenditure and revenue together, my aim was to reduce the PSBR.

In the event, the public finances were knocked badly off course by the cost of the miners' strike, and the deficit in 1984/85 came to over £10 billion. The strike, was effectively called only the day before the Budget, far too late to alter the forecast. But even if I had ventured a guess, which I was prepared to reveal, of how long the strike would last, and Treasury economists had had the opportunity to estimate the consequences for the PSBR, it would not have affected my Budget judgement. For the essence of the fiscal strategy was that it was a medium term one, which *inter alia* implied refraining from raising or lowering taxes in response to short-term shocks, whether these shocks were due to the economic cycle or any other cause.

CHAPTER NINETEEN

1984 – MY FIRST BUDGET

Strategy and Principles · The Reform of Business Taxation
The Results and a Postscript · VAT Vexations · An Unexpected Triumph

STRATEGY AND PRINCIPLES

In my Budget speech, I prefaced the tax measures with the declaration that 'this will be a radical, tax reforming Budget'. I went on to explain that the reforms were governed by two principles: 'First the need to make changes that will improve our economic performance over the longer term; second the desire to make life a little simpler for the taxpayer.' I rejected the notion of replacing the entire income-based tax system with an expenditure system. Even if such a root and branch change were desirable, 'it would, I believe, be wholly impractical and unrealistic'. My choice was the middle way: 'to introduce reforms, some of them far-reaching, within the framework of our existing income-based system'.

Even with this compromise approach I felt bound to utter the following warning:

> I am well aware that the tax reformer's path is a stony one. Any change in the system is bound, at least in the short term, to bring benefits to some and disadvantages to others. And the disapproval of the latter group tends to be rather more audible than the murmurings of satisfaction from the former.

This warning may have seemed otiose in March 1984 in view of the highly favourable reception the Budget received. But later events showed how necessary it was.

THE REFORM OF BUSINESS TAXATION

One popular and satisfying element in the Budget was that it included for the first time in living memory the complete abolition of a tax – indeed, of two, the

National Insurance Surcharge and the Investment Income Surcharge. Abolition is, of course, the ultimate simplification, and I sought to abolish a tax in every Budget. But the cornerstone of the 1984 Budget was the reform of business taxation. This was the area where my reforms were most radical and based on clear fiscal principles. These closely followed the lines I had set out in my reform memorandum to Margaret, which I reproduced in the previous chapter. Not only did I believe that the prevailing 52 per cent rate of Corporation Tax was too high, 'penalising profit and success and blunting the cutting edge of enterprise'; it was also the 'product of too many special reliefs, indiscriminately applied and of diminishing relevance to the conditions of today. Some of these reliefs reflect economic priorities or circumstances which have long vanished and now serve only to distort investment decisions and distort choices about finance.'

Although the details were inevitably complex, the basic thinking was quite simple. Because of a long prevailing belief that physical investment was good in itself, successive governments had tried to subsidise it in various ways. The subsidy applied more to manufacturing than to services; while investment in plant and equipment was more favourably treated than investment in buildings – not to mention investment in people.

The system I inherited was one of 'initial allowances'. In the case of industrial plant and machinery, 100 per cent of the cost could be written off immediately – that is, used to reduce taxable profits in the first year. The system was sometimes called 'free depreciation' and previous Ministers (of both Parties) had boasted that British incentives were the best in the world. It had proved wholly counterproductive. As I remarked at the time, 'We need investment decisions based on future market assessments, not future tax assessments.'

The new system of capital allowances which I announced – to come fully into effect in 1986/87 at the end of a three-year phased transition – was less artificial. Plant and machinery would in future qualify for annual tax allowances on a 25 per cent 'reducing balance' basis. This meant writing off 25 per cent of the cost in the first year, 25 per cent of the written-down value in the second year, and so on. For industrial buildings, which previously enjoyed a 75 per cent first-year allowance, the rate of write-off for tax purposes would be 4 per cent 'straight line' – i.e., 4 per cent of cost each year. The idea, in both cases, was to approximate to the rate of genuine commercial depreciation, erring on the side of generosity.

The quid pro quo was that the rate of Corporation Tax, levied on company profits, would be reduced in three successive stages to reach 35 per cent in

1986/87 – a lower rate than in almost any other competitor country including Japan. It was to remain there until Norman Lamont announced a further reduction, to 33 per cent, in his first Budget in 1991. At the same time I cut the small companies' Corporation Tax rate from 42 per cent to 30 per cent, equivalent to the basic rate of income tax, to which it has been linked ever since. The Inland Revenue had estimated that when these and the other changes to Corporation Tax had fully worked their way through, companies would on balance enjoy substantial reductions in their tax bills, for any given level of profits, since the reduction in the rate of Corporation Tax was a genuine remission, whereas the changes in capital allowances constituted not an increase in tax but merely bringing forward the date on which it became payable.

An incidental advantage of the switch was that it acted as a temporary investment incentive. This was useful in the early stages of an economic upturn, bringing forward investment to take advantage of the old system of capital allowances before they disappeared, the return on which would then be taxed at the new and lower rate.

But that was merely a beneficial side-effect. 'The more important and lasting effect', I argued, 'will be to encourage the search for investment projects with a genuinely worthwhile return, and to discourage uneconomic investment. It is doubtful whether it has ever been really sensible to subsidise capital investment irrespective of the true rate of return. But certainly, with over three million unemployed, it cannot make sense to subsidise capital so heavily at the expense of labour.'

Moreover, as I subsequently pointed out at the post-Budget meeting of the NEDC, the Corporation Tax reform removed the previous discrimination in favour of investment in hardware as against investment in either training or research.

An important subsidiary aim of my Corporation Tax reform, which I stated explicitly at the time, but which is frequently forgotten, was to narrow the gap between the main Corporation Tax rate and the basic rate of income tax. When I became Chancellor the gap was between 52 per cent Corporation Tax and 30 per cent income tax – a difference of 22 per cent. It was reduced to 5 per cent by the 1984 reforms. My subsequent reduction in the basic rate of income tax caused it to creep up again to 10 per cent, and Norman Lamont's two-point cut in Corporation Tax announced in 1991 brought it back to 8 per cent. While any gap at all is in principle undesirable, this is at least substantially less than it was before I embarked on the reform.

The reason why the gap matters is that companies have a choice between financing themselves via equity capital and financing themselves via debt. So far as the tax system influences their choice, it is because debt interest is offsettable against Corporation Tax whereas equity dividends are not. The latter are paid by the company net of income tax at the basic rate. Thus the greater the amount by which the Corporation Tax rate exceeds income tax, the greater the encouragement to debt finance. I was always worried about the financing of the corporate sector, since an excessive reliance on debt finance was bound to lead to an underlying weakness which would be exposed at times of economic pressure.

Tax is of course only one of many factors influencing the way in which businesses choose to finance themselves. I believe that a case can be made that the most malign consequence of the Black Monday Stock Exchange crash of October 1987 was that it killed the equity-raising market for at least a year and probably longer. This led to a massive switch to debt finance which in turn was one of the roots of the subsequent world recession, which was notably worse in the Anglo-Saxon world whose corporate sector is much more reliant on external finance. It may well be that the problem of corporate indebtedness would have been even worse without the 1984 reforms.

THE RESULTS AND A POSTSCRIPT

As I added in a mini-peroration to this section of the speech:

> These changes hold out an exciting opportunity for British industry as a whole: an opportunity further to improve its profitability, and to expand, building on the recovery that is already well under way. Higher profits after tax will encourage and reward enterprise, stimulate innovation in all its forms, and create more jobs.

This was a theme to which I returned in my winding-up speech on the Budget debate when I said:

> Under-investment has not been the problem. The problem has been the poor quality of so much of the investment, as measured by the return that it earns. I readily admit that my reforms will be bad for bad investment, but they will be good for good investment, because the lower rate of tax on the profits earned will stimulate investment in projects yielding a genuinely good return.

I concluded that 'The purpose of the reforms is to rehabilitate the role of profits in the British economy and in our national political debate'.

While it is always difficult to establish causality in political economy, the subsequent record is at least consistent with the hope I expressed then. Not only did business investment as a share of GDP rise to an unprecedented degree between 1984 and 1989, but even the subsequent trough in the depth of the recession of the early 1990s left business investment as a share of GDP still above the highest levels reached in the 1970s. More important, there was a parallel improvement in the profitability of investment, with the rate of return very nearly doubling between 1984 and 1989. Again, the subsequent decline during the recession of the early 1990s still left it well above the levels prevailing in the 1970s. The predictions of woe from the opponents of the change have been comprehensively confounded.

My decision to phase out first-year capital allowances did cause one hiccup just before the Budget. In 1981 Norman Tebbit, while Minister of State at the Department of Industry, had announced that Nissan, the Japanese car manufacturer, would establish an assembly plant in County Durham. Among the factors they had taken into consideration was the prospect of enjoying the 100 per cent first-year capital allowance, and the chairman of Nissan had a letter from Margaret alluding to this carrot. But by the time they came to build the plant these allowances would have disappeared under my Budget plans. If nothing had been done, Nissan might well have gone ahead anyway, and certainly the new tax regime brought a considerable amount of new inward investment by overseas companies attracted by the low Corporation Tax rate. But there would have been loud and embarrassing allegations of bad faith which it would have been hard to gainsay.

Norman Tebbit and I had to find a formula to get round this. Simply making Nissan exempt from the change would not only have caused a public row but would have rendered the Finance Bill 'hybrid', the term used for any Bill that seeks to legislate about a specific named entity rather than a general class of entities. This would have been a parliamentary nightmare, and was unthinkable. For hybrid Bills – which are few and far between – are required to undergo a different and much more protracted legislative process before reaching the statute-book, making it impossible to enact a hybrid Finance Bill in time for the tax changes to come into effect at the start of the new financial year.

We therefore had to devise a general alteration to the Bill which would have the effect of exempting Nissan, while exempting as little else as practicable. This took the form of exempting investment projects in development areas, provided they had already been firmly announced, from the phased withdrawal of capital allowances. Fortunately in this context, the language in which Finance Bills are drafted is so arcane as to bear little resemblance to the English language, and no-one spotted what this particular clause was really about. Had they done so, there might well have been an outcry, and certainly the battery of claims for special treatment I received from industries that felt particularly hard hit by it would have intensified. Meanwhile our Ambassador in Tokyo was able to assure the Nissan Board that its 100 per cent capital allowance was safe, irrespective of the 1984 Finance Act. Nissan was suitably discreet.

VAT VEXATIONS

VAT was in many ways a curious tax, falling as it did on little more than half of consumer spending. A flat-note tax on the whole of consumer spending would have been very much better, minimising or even eliminating the distortion created by the present system, avoiding the administrative problem of policing difficult borderlines, and either allowing the tax to be levied at a lower rate, or bringing in more revenue from the existing rate, which would finance a reduction in income tax.

The problem was an amalgam of history and timidity. VAT was introduced by the Heath Conservative Government in 1972 as the replacement for Purchase Tax, which had been imposed at various different rates on a fairly narrow range of goods. The then Chancellor, Tony Barber, unified the rate at 10 per cent and extended the coverage, but did not feel able to extend it universally. In particular, the massive areas of food, fuel, housing and transport were zero-rated. But inevitably, once there are some exclusions (and these were not the only ones) this generates pressure for others. On the whole, that pressure has been successfully resisted, although during the passage of the original Bill a Conservative back-bench rebellion, supported by the Opposition, forced the Government to zero-rate children's clothes and shoes, too.

The 1979 manifesto on which we were first elected stated quite openly our intention to shift some of the burden of taxation from income tax to VAT – but added a pledge that food, fuel, housing and transport would remain zero-rated. When, in subsequent elections, we sought to keep our options open, the Labour Party would immediately accuse us of planning to put VAT on food, which Margaret would instantly deny, and this would be followed by pledges about the other 'basics', too.

So when, in 1984, I sought to broaden the base of the tax, the scope was disappointingly limited. I looked first at food – for despite the pledge, the definition of food was not as obvious as it might seem. Restaurant meals, for example, had been liable to VAT since the tax was first introduced; and Labour's obsession with the evil of VAT on food had not prevented Denis Healey, in his first Budget in 1974, from extending VAT to chocolates (including chocolate biscuits), sweets, ice-creams, crisps and the like. I concluded that the best bet for a further extension was take-away foods, a suggestion I owed to Thérèse, since these were clearly competing against restaurant meals, bar snacks and the rest, which were already liable to VAT. As a fast-growing sector I felt they would provide a buoyant source of revenue.

The question then arose as to the borderline between those foods, and groceries, which were to remain zero-rated. I recall a lengthy submission from the Customs and Excise, proposing a detailed schedule of the various items that would be liable to VAT, and seeking ministerial guidance on such earth-shattering issues as the treatment of filled rolls. The whole thing was in danger of degenerating into Nabarro-like farce, until I ruled that we should cut the Gordian knot by confining the tax to hot take-away foods and drink, which were unmistakably different from groceries.

Thus arose the notorious imposition of VAT on fish and chips, about which the popular press went to town. The *Daily Mail*'s headline was typical: 'Nigel's give and take-away Budget'. I doubt if the highly publicised criticism of this measure did me any harm.

The second VAT extension I decided to make was on building alterations and improvements. The logic behind this – once again a fast-growing market which should therefore produce a buoyant source of revenue – was that, since its inception, building repairs and maintenance had been liable to VAT. But improvements and alterations were zero-rated, producing what the Customs and Excise found the most difficult of all the VAT borderlines to police. It is well known that members of the building trade are not the most enthusiastic payers of tax of any kind, and it was common practice for repairs to be invoiced as improvements in order to escape VAT.

The disappearance of this problem by the extension of VAT to improvements and alterations aroused much less excitement in the popular press, but a storm of protest from every conceivable organisation connected with the building trade. The heritage lobby, which had long cultivated support on the back benches for its case for assistance of one kind and another, was particularly vocal, too; and to head off an awkward rebellion I introduced an amendment retaining zero-rating for improvements and alterations to listed buildings.

I also planned, and had in the Budget until the very last moment, a third VAT extension – to newspapers and magazines (although not to books). But in what was scheduled as our final pre-Budget discussion Margaret advised against it. 'Look, Nigel,' she said, 'this is a wonderful Budget and you should get a wonderful reception. You don't want to spoil that by putting VAT on newspapers.' I told her I would reflect on what she had said. The next day I saw her again and told her I would take her advice, and raise the £200 million that VAT on newspapers would have brought in 1984 by an extra increase in the cigarette tax instead.

Had I decided to stand my ground on newspapers I could certainly have done so. That I did not is something I have regretted ever since. The opportunity never recurred: it is just the sort of thing that needs to be done, if it is done at all, by a new Chancellor in the first Budget of a new parliament. I had a second go with Margaret in the first Budget of the subsequent parliament in 1988; but by that time our relations had deteriorated and there was no way I could persuade her. With the benefit of hindsight, I have no doubt I could have got away with it in 1984. While the newspaper proprietors would have fumed, by no means all the newspaper editors would have allowed that to determine their reception of the Budget.

But at the time Margaret had used a shrewd argument. The Budget I had produced was a radical and highly controversial one. There was no guarantee that it would get the amazingly good reception it did. Not surprisingly I was obviously particularly keen that my first Budget should be thought a success. Moreover, it was emphatically my own Budget: in particular, the Corporation Tax Reform, which was its centrepiece, was entirely my own idea – although the Inland Revenue, once they learned what I wanted to do, gave me the most superb professional and technical support. Until her advice to drop VAT on newspapers, Margaret had gone along with everything I had proposed, even though much of it was very different from what she would have done in my place. Failing to extend VAT to newspapers in 1984 was, I believe, a mistake; but it is one for which I blame myself as much as I blame her.

The extra tax on cigarettes caused no political problem whatever. Such is the success of the anti-smoking lobby – whose intolerance even I, as a non-smoker, find intensely unattractive – that the tobacco duty is the one tax a Chancellor can increase and receive at least as much praise as execration for so doing. The only constraints are the risk of losing as much if not more revenue from people giving up smoking as is gained from those who continue to smoke – we are not quite there yet – and the immediate adverse effect on the RPI, which is particularly large.

So far as income tax was concerned, I left the basic rate unchanged and chose instead 'to use every penny I have to lift the level of tax thresholds'. The personal allowances were increased by more than twice the amount required by indexation, some 7 per cent in real terms. Around 400,000 people were taken out of tax altogether over and above the automatic effects of indexation. In presenting this I argued that 'it makes very little sense to be collecting income tax from people who are at the same time receiving means-tested benefits. Moreover low tax thresholds worsen the poverty and unemployment traps, so there is little if any financial incentive to find a better job or even any job at all.' This preference for raising personal allowances rather than reducing the basic rate was one I was later to abandon completely.

AN UNEXPECTED TRIUMPH

Much to my surprise, despite an appalling leak to the Press – one of the worst ever breaches of Budget security – and the absence of any significant net tax reduction, the tax-reforming Budget of 1984 was extremely well received. This became clear as soon as I had sat down after delivering the Budget speech. The Conservative benches erupted in a tremendous cheering and waving of order papers, and even some Opposition Members congratulated me on it privately afterwards. Jim Callaghan told Mark Lennox-Boyd, my PPS, that he thought it was the best constructed Budget speech he had listened to – leaving aside (he was quick to add) his own efforts between 1964 and 1967.

The excellent reception continued when I went upstairs for the customary Budget day meeting of the Party's Back-bench Finance Committee, whose chairman, William Clark, opened by describing my first Budget as 'one of the most imaginative we have had'. The two hundred or so Tory Members crammed into Committee Room 14 banged their desks enthusiastically. The Budget undeniably lifted Party morale, which had been somewhat dented since the election by a series of embarrassments over issues ranging from the resignation of Cecil Parkinson to the ban on trade unions at GCHQ. It was on the whole a difficult Budget to criticise. Terry Beckett, the Director General of the CBI found it hard to attack the withdrawal of first-year capital allowances in public, given the fulfilment of his long-standing wish to be rid of the National

Insurance Surcharge, which I had presented as part of the overall business package, although he wrote to me to protest. The CBI as a whole has remained opposed to my 1984 Corporation Tax reforms and has continued ever since to favour subsidies for capital spending, which they could well obtain from some future misguided Chancellor. Nevertheless, at the time a number of individual businessmen of distinction supported me; so, surprisingly, did the Engineering Employers Federation, which welcomed my Budget wholeheartedly.

It is probably true to say that nothing I have ever done has gone down quite so well as my first Budget in 1984. The political commentators were surprised that I did not make any attempt to use my Budget triumph as a foundation on which to build up support on the back benches. The explanation lay in my lack of ambition to be Prime Minister. With hindsight, however, I was short-sighted in failing to take the opportunity to try to build a solid block of support that would not fade away with any adverse turn of economic events – not because it might have led to higher things, but because it would have been helpful to me in the storms that lay ahead, not least in the difficulties I was to have with Margaret.

The 1984 tax changes helped to launch a worldwide wave of new thinking on tax reform. Indeed if privatisation was the Thatcher Government's prime claim to world leadership in economic policy-making, tax reform must surely come second. The corporate side of the US tax reform package of the mid-1980s was consciously based on my 1984 Budget; other countries have followed much the same path. I cannot recall any previous UK Government exercising this kind of leadership in economic ideas and their practical implementation in one field, let alone two.

CHAPTER TWENTY

1985 – INTERESTS AND INCENTIVES

An Anticlimax · The Reform of NICs · Civilisation in Danger
Home Dear Home · Nearly Taxing Consumer Credit

AN ANTICLIMAX

It was always obvious that, whatever it contained, my 1985 Budget would be an anticlimax after the extraordinary success of my first Budget in 1984. On that occasion, the Budget's contents far outstripped political and public expectations. A year later expectations were working the other way, with politicians and commentators anticipating a similar display of fiscal ingenuity.

Nor was the budgetary outlook so comforting that I could float off tax reform on a sea of tax reduction. After the Budget deficit overrun caused by the miners' strike I did not want to take any chances, and concluded that the fiscal priority must be to bring about a decisive break from the plateau of 3–3.25 per cent of GDP on which the Budget deficit had been stuck for the previous four years, to 2 per cent, or just over £7 billion in cash, in 1985/86, in line with the Medium Term Financial Strategy. Some revenue boost was likely from the rebound after the coal strike, but I did not wish to rely on it too much in advance. On the basis of Treasury forecasts, I could reduce taxation by only £700 million in the coming financial year (on the usual indexed basis), which became some £1.3 billion in a full year.

The objective of my Budget was 'to continue the fight against inflation and help create conditions for more jobs'. To this end I had agreed with Norman Fowler, then Social Services Secretary, a major reform of the National Insurance Contributions system. But that inevitably meant that the 1985 Budget lacked the simple impact that only a cut in the basic rate of income tax can secure. There was, however, another reason why the 1985 Budget was an anticlimax. This was that the majority of the reforms I had hoped to introduce were controversial changes that I had to abandon, for the most part because Margaret was not prepared to swallow them. They included extending the coverage of VAT to newspapers and children's clothes, confining mortgage interest relief to the basic rate, introducing a tax on consumer credit, and taxing pension lump sums.

THE REFORM OF NICs

The centrepiece of the 1985 Budget as I have indicated, was a reform of National Insurance contributions designed 'to cut the costs of employing the young and unskilled and to sharpen their own incentive to work at wages which employers can afford to pay'.

At that time National Insurance contributions for both employers and employees used to start at £35.50 a week at a flat rate of 9 per cent for employees and 10.45 per cent for employers. Unlike income tax, however, National Insurance contributions are levied not just on earnings beyond this level but, once the threshold is reached, on total earnings up to the so-called Upper Earnings Limit. In other words, while someone on £35 a week paid nothing, someone on £36 a week had to pay £3.24 (9 per cent of £36) in National Insurance Contributions: a considerable deterrent to earning the extra £1. Employers were similarly deterred from taking on low-paid labour, making it harder for the unskilled to find work.

I introduced instead a series of lower rate bands, starting at 5 per cent (for both employer and employee) before the full rates were reached. These reductions were paid for by abolishing the upper earnings limit for employers, while retaining it for employees. This did not affect the contributory principle, since it was the employee's contribution record that determined entitlement to benefit, and it avoided the enormous practical problems involved in abolishing the upper earnings limit for employees. I dimly sensed these in 1985, but the full force of them was brought home to me only when I contemplated taking this seemingly obvious and superficially attractive step in 1988.

On tax proper I was able to take reform only modestly forward in 1985. I abolished one further tax, the Development Land Tax, at a modest cost of £50 million in a full year. This had been intended to cream off soaring land values at a time of high taxation, but its practical effect at 60 per cent was to discourage the bringing forward of land for development. Moreover, its disappearance swept away another 200 pages of complex legislation. The main measure of interest to the general taxpayer was the increase in the income tax thresholds by 5 per cent more than the rate of inflation. This cost a little under £1 billion in a full year, somewhat less than the cost of 1p off the basic rate. I was also able to improve the indexation of Capital Gains for tax purposes.

But for the most part, 1985 was a steady-as-she-goes Budget. I was able to gain modest additional revenues by raising excise duties, especially on vehicles, by rather more than the rate of inflation. My only notable extension of VAT was to impose it on newspaper and magazine advertising, which brought in some £50 million, with the prospect of higher sums in future. I also changed the status of transactions between credit card companies and retailers from zero rating to exemption. This actually brought in some revenue because of the absence of tax deductibility.

CIVILISATION IN DANGER

The Budget was preceded by several unprecedented lobbying campaigns. Since my VAT extensions in the 1984 Budget, there was a feeling there would be further extensions and that the leading candidates would include books and newspapers. The publishing industry and various literati like Philip Larkin, Margaret Drabble and Antonia Fraser portrayed – under the slogan 'don't tax reading' – the extension of VAT to books as characteristic of Philistine Thatcherism. The House of Lords, where a number of university dons are to be found, staged an entire debate on the issue. In fact, the Great and Good could have saved their energies, because despite the fact that the vast majority of the 60,000-odd titles published in Britain every year are devoid of literary merit, I never had the slightest intention of extending VAT to books.

Even if I had been prepared to endure the hurricane of indignation, sales of books form such a small proportion of consumer expenditure that the relatively small and far from buoyant revenues raised would have made the game not worth the candle. Net home sales of books in 1990 were less than £500 million, suggesting net tax revenues of only £70 million. But as I told the House of Commons in the Budget speech: 'To have revealed this prematurely would not have stilled speculation; it would have merely concentrated it on those matters which were under consideration – a practice that no Chancellor, rightly, has sought to encourage.' While as a general rule this must be right, in retrospect it might have been better to have made an exception in this particular case.

The campaign against VAT on newspapers on the whole took the form of private pressure rather than public protest, although the President of the Newspaper Society publicly declared that a tax on newspapers represented the gravest threat to the freedom of the Press since stamp duty, which had been repealed in 1855. It was notable that two popular Conservative dailies, the *Mail* and the *Express*, attacked me fiercely over student grants and the taxation of pensions at the same time.

The two extensions I had in mind were newspapers and children's clothes. Unlike books, newspapers offered a very considerable source of revenue, but by 1985 the Government was trailing in the polls and Margaret was insistent that we could not afford to alienate the Press in this way. The zero-rating of children's clothes had become particularly anomalous, since it was based on size, with the result that small women escaped VAT and larger children (or, rather, their parents) paid it. But it was politically sensitive, and I decided that, while an extension to both newspapers and children's clothes was just about acceptable, picking on children's clothes alone was not. To prevent a recurrence of the campaigning from the various VAT interest groups, which had caused consternation among the back-benchers, I announced that I had no further extensions to the VAT base to make during the lifetime of that parliament.

HOME DEAR HOME

Margaret's diary that year did not allow us to have our usual pre-Budget discussion over dinner and we had to move the meeting to Number 10 at 8 o'clock on the evening of Sunday, 3 February – a good time to catch her when she returned from the weekend at Chequers. I argued that the fiscal encouragement to invest in houses was far too strong, diverting funds from outlets like shares, and contributed to the housing booms and busts from which Britain had suffered in the past and was to suffer again. It was also, of course, an incentive to borrow.

Mortgage interest relief was costly in terms of revenue, too. I had worked out a self-financing package, in which the savings from the withdrawal of higher-rate mortgage interest relief would be used to reduce the higher rates of tax to a level sufficient to compensate most higher-rate mortgage payers. Margaret argued that this was out of the question, since it would contravene our manifesto pledge to retain mortgage interest relief. Indeed she countered by pressing me to raise the mortgage interest relief ceiling from £30,000 to at least £35,000. I replied that the Manifesto commitment would be fully honoured by retaining mortgage interest relief at the basic rate. Indeed this would concentrate the relief more on the first-time buyer, which was presumably where the Government's intent lay, since the first-time buyer was unlikely to be a higher-rate tax payer. I added that I had no intention of making matters worse by raising the £30,000 ceiling.

In the event, the restriction of mortgage interest relief to the basic rate was implemented by Norman Lamont in the first Budget after Margaret's deposition from the premiership. Structural changes have to be made when the opportunity arises. But if this one had been made when I proposed it in 1985, it might have helped to moderate the residential property boom and enabled the Government to curb the inflationary surge at the end of the decade at lower rates of interest. By the time Norman made the change the property market was in serious decline and the short-term impact was to aggravate the recession.

NEARLY TAXING CONSUMER CREDIT

One of the hitherto untold stories of the Thatcher era is how near we came to imposing a tax on consumer credit. I began to think about this, in fact, soon after becoming Chancellor in 1983. A number of different considerations seemed to point in the same direction. First, under European Community law financial transactions are exempt from VAT. So there was a clear 'level-playing-field' argument for imposing some other tax on this particular service to the consumer. Second, I needed revenue to finance income tax cuts, and a tax on something as buoyant as consumer credit could be a useful source. And third, since the traditional direct controls on consumer credit had become unworkable following the abolition of exchange control, a consumer credit tax was the only available supplement to high interest rates in curbing excessive growth in this type of lending.

I got my officials to work up the various options and, at a meeting I held on 15 February 1984, it was provisionally agreed to announce in the 1984 Budget the following month that there would be a duty of 1 per cent a year on all outstanding consumer credit, to come into force from July 1985, so as to give time for the banks and others to reprogramme their systems as well as providing a period for consultation. It was reckoned that if all forms of consumer credit were covered by the new tax – including, crucially, mortgages – it would raise up to £500 million a year. Although the concept was a simple one, however, the implementation bristled with practical difficulties; and I decided to drop it for 1984 with a view to doing more work on the outstanding problems and including it in my 1985 Budget.

Officials pointed out that one-man businesses were likely to indulge in a fair amount of evasion of the tax, but as a Minister committed to promoting the enterprise culture, I felt it was something we could live with. I was far less happy with the Bank's insistence that there would have to be a sixteen-month gap between the announcement of the tax and its coming into effect, largely to give time for the consultation with the banks which they saw as essential. While

I understood their reasons, I did not relish the politics of the protracted public row which this would have guaranteed.

But the critical issue, as I saw it, was mortgages. Not only did lending on mortgages represent over 80 per cent of consumer credit, but if mortgages, in addition to their other tax advantages, were to be exempt from an otherwise general consumer credit tax, their share would be even greater. In other words, without the inclusion of mortgages the yield of a consumer credit tax would be so diminished that the game would not be worth the candle. With the details worked out, following a lengthy discussion at the annual pre-Budget brainstorming weekend of officials and Treasury Ministers at Chevening, and the practical problems solved at least to my satisfaction, I broached the new tax with Margaret in front of the 1985 Budget. She was hostile to the whole idea of introducing a new tax – a view which, in principle, I shared; but this seemed to me an exception. But on one issue she was adamant: there could be no question of a tax on mortgages. Given this veto, I lost interest in the idea, and dropped it from my 1985 Budget package.

My interest then revived with the start of the surge in consumer credit in the latter half of 1986, reinforced by the discovery I had made during a brief visit to Denmark that year, for an informal Ecofin, that the Danes had recently introduced a rough-and-ready consumer credit tax which seemed to be workable. At the Chevening meeting in January 1987 it was agreed to change the base of the earlier proposal and levy a 5 per cent tax on all consumer credit payments, with the exception of mortgage payments. Yet once again the Bank insisted that, with an announcement in the 1987 Budget, the tax could not be introduced until July 1988; and I decided to drop the whole idea without even bothering to put it to Margaret.

It admittedly would have looked odd to tax mortgage credit while at the same time continuing to give mortgage interest relief. But despite this presentational awkwardness, I believe that subsequent problems would have been less acute had I been able to introduce the comprehensive consumer credit tax I sought in the 1985 Budget, even if it had not come into effect until July 1986.

CHAPTER TWENTY-ONE

1986 – PRINCIPLES AND A PENNY OFF

The Oil Factor Again · How to Use a Small Sum · The Politics of a Penny off Basic Rate versus Thresholds · The Invention of PEPs · An Overall Assessment The Charities Package

THE OIL FACTOR AGAIN

The background to my 1986 Budget was mixed. Total national output (GDP) had risen the previous year by some 3.75 per cent, part of which represented the rebound from the coal strike. Despite this above average growth, unemployment was still rising. Inflation, happily, was coming down rapidly and averaged 3.4 per cent during 1986, the lowest for very nearly twenty years. It was to prove the lowest, too, of the Government's entire period of office.

But there was a snag in this very sharp drop. For, as with the similarly sharp drop in inflation in the rest of the world, it chiefly reflected the impact of the collapse in the oil price following Saudi Arabia's warning that it was no longer prepared to support the price in the world market by holding back its own production. Saudi Arabian light oil fell from around $27 a barrel in 1985 to $10 a barrel in the first quarter of 1986, thus more than reversing the explosion of 1979/80. Connoisseurs might have noted that my Budget speech was less sanguine on the supposed benefits to the UK of an oil price collapse than the Treasury's chapter on the economy in the Red Book.

Sterling had originally weakened somewhat, but had steadied after I increased base rates by one percentage point to 12.5 per cent in January, which I was able to reverse the day after the Budget. The testing time for the pound was to come later in the year. My main direct concern over the oil price, which dominated all our economic thinking at that time, was its effect on tax revenue. In fact, despite the loss of oil revenues, the PSBR for 1985/86 turned out at only £5.5 billion or 1.5 per cent of GDP, thanks to firm control of public spending coupled with buoyant non-oil revenue.

In deciding on the appropriate borrowing requirement for 1986/87 there were two conflicting considerations. The medium-term strategy of smoothing out the impact of shocks and fluctuations suggested that a higher PSBR should be allowed, to let the oil price effect be absorbed gradually. On the other hand the projected rise in privatisation proceeds argued for a lower figure. It seemed to me to be best to stick to the MTFS course, erring slightly on the side of caution. I accordingly aimed for a PSBR in 1986/87 of £7 billion, or 1.75% per cent of GDP.

My £7 billion target allowed me, on the forecast provided, to reduce taxation by £1 billion in 1986/87 on the usual indexed basis. In the end the outcome for that year was much better than I dared hope: a PSBR of £3.5 billion, or £8 billion excluding receipts from privatisation. This was so despite the oil price remaining depressed at around $10 a barrel for most of the financial year. Oil revenues in fact fell dramatically, from £11.5 billion in 1985/86 to £4.75 billion in 1986/87, even faster than the forecasters expected.

HOW TO USE A SMALL SUM

At the pre-Budget meeting at Chevening, electoral considerations began to loom. I toyed with the idea of giving myself more scope to cut income tax by exploiting the vagaries of the RPI and raising VAT to 16 per cent. Inflation would then appear to fall when the VAT rise dropped out of the index a year later, the probable election year, just as the effects of lower oil prices were falling off. In the end I felt that this would be too clever by half.

The clear consensus was to use any available scope we had to reduce income tax. The discussion was on whether to raise thresholds yet again or make a cut in the basic rate. The view at Chevening was that it was not worth cutting only a penny, taking it from the 30 per cent at which it had stood since Geoffrey's first Budget in 1979, to the somewhat bizarre figure of 29 per cent. It had to be two pence off, which would cost £2 billion in the coming financial year – or it would not be worth doing it at all. And it was hard to see, given the oil price fall, how we could possibly afford that sort of money.

But I continued to brood on it. In my usual pre-Budget note to Margaret on 13 February, I wrote:

> All in all, I believe we have reached a point where we have already done a great deal of what needed to be done on thresholds. Our next priority should be to reduce the basic rate. Once we have made significant reductions there, it will be time to look again at thresholds.

The pre- Budget Cabinet that month was steeped in gloom as a result of the sharp fall in oil revenues. At the final meeting of the overview group on the Budget a fortnight later, on 3 March, made up of Treasury Ministers, special advisers, senior Treasury officials and the chairmen of the Inland Revenue and the Customs and Excise, the consensus was still to do nothing on the basic rate.

However, immediately after the overview meeting, each of the three special advisers, Peter Cropper, Rodney Lord and Howard Davies, wrote to me privately to argue in favour of taking a penny off the basic rate, primarily for political reasons. It was characteristically the shrewd Peter Cropper who put his finger on the fact that the very silliness of the 29 per cent figure – which he knew was what had concerned me at Chevening – was a strength and not a weakness. For as he wrote:

> A reduction to 29 per cent would be seen as an unqualified commitment to cutting the burden of taxation. It would be ludicrous to stop with a basic rate of 29 per cent for more than a year or two: people will see that.

THE POLITICS OF A PENNY OFF

Although it was very late in the day, that convinced me; and I informed Margaret of my change of plan only eleven days before the Budget. She was delighted by the idea once I had reassured her that the overall Budget arithmetic was prudent.

Politically it proved a tremendous success. Here I was helped by the trap I had carefully laid for the Labour Party – and instant newshounds – in my Budget speech. Near the end I warned in pure Treasury-speak: 'Given the need for caution in the light of current circumstances, I do not have the scope this year for a reduction in the basic rate of income tax' – at this point I took a sip from the glass beside me, to give time for the predictable hoots of derision and *schadenfreude* from the Opposition benches, before continuing – 'beyond one penny in the pound'. The benches behind me erupted in triumphant cheers. I continued by saying that this represented 'the first cut in the basic rate of income tax since my predecessor took it down from 33 per cent to 30 per cent in 1979. So long as this Government remains in office, it will not be the last.'

The extraordinary impact of this modest reduction has to be seen against the political background. The year 1986 could not have opened worse. First Michael Heseltine resigned over Westland and then Leon Brittan. Margaret's position was shakier than at any time until the events which led to her downfall in 1990. Then came the one penny cut in the Budget in March, and the whole mood changed. Labour did not know what to do, so the Liberals decided to step into the limelight and divide the House against it. A predictable group of Labour rebels went into the Liberal lobby against the tax cuts, while the majority stuck to the Party line and limply abstained.

The 'penny off' allowed me to revive Geoffrey's 1979 aspiration of a basic 25 pence basic rate and make it sound more like a pledge. Margaret Thatcher, weakened by the Westland affair, was in no condition to oppose it, much as she disliked pledges of this kind. My main objective was to lock the Party into a publicly proclaimed tax objective, as a means of preventing the scope for future tax cuts from being eroded by public expenditure promises as the election approached.

But the last thing I wanted to do was to get the basic rate – as some backbenchers assumed – down to 25 per cent that parliament. I wanted to keep it as a manifesto pledge. But it had to be a realistic one; and at the rate of a penny off every seven years it was not realistic yet. It was the further twopence off in the 1987 pre-election Budget that immediately made it realistic.

There was a further political bonus from the 1986 penny. When I cut twopence off in 1987, Labour were determined not to be caught out by the Liberals again, and promptly decided to vote against the tax themselves. This was manna from heaven. No doubt they had taken at their face value (as indeed had the pundits) all the polls which showed a consistent and substantial majority in favour of public spending increases rather than tax cuts. Any politician with any understanding of the electorate, however, knows exactly what those particular polls mean.

There are large numbers of people in this country who have been conditioned to believe that it sounds better to say that they would like to see more money spent on worthy public services – however doubtful they may be about whether the worthy public services will improve as a result – than that they would like to receive a tax cut. But when it comes to casting a vote which might determine which of the two takes place, it is a different matter altogether. This was clearly demonstrated, to my complete lack of surprise, by the outcome of the 1987 general election. Yet, astonishingly, five years later, in the run-up to the 1992 general election, when the opinion polls once more predictably purported to show an overwhelming popular preference for increased spending on public services over tax cuts, both the pundits and the Labour Party were again taken in.

BASIC RATE VERSUS THRESHOLDS

The desire of a Conservative Chancellor, given the scope to do so, to reduce the burden of taxation was not surprising. Despite having entered office pledged to reduce taxes, we had in fact, because of the need to reduce the budget deficit first, felt obliged to endure a net increase in the tax burden to date. Nor was it surprising that the focus was on income tax: again, that had been our declared objective from the start. But there was a lively argument on the relative desirability of cutting the basic rate and raising thresholds.

On this my thinking had evolved. I had started as a 'threshold' Chancellor, and raised the personal allowances substantially more than indexation required in both of my first two Budgets, those of 1984 and 1985. I then changed my mind, and became convinced that it was better to concentrate on reducing the basic rate, a view I hold to this day.

In a sense, of course, I had always recognised the unique importance of the basic rate. During the 1981 Budget I had as, Financial Secretary, fully supported the decision not to index allowances at all, but would have been aghast at any increase in the basic rate. When I first became Chancellor, however, I was seduced by the fact that one could fine-tune the amount by which the allowances were increased, so as to add up, with other measures, to precisely the overall reduction in revenue I had decided was prudent. The basic rate, on the other hand, lacked that flexibility since it had to be cut by a penny at a time, and each penny off cost a substantial sum in lost revenue. This made the rest of the Budget-making process far more difficult. Yet at the same time it seemed implausible that a single penny off would have any significant effect on incentives – unlike the threshold increase, which would have a considerable impact (via the poverty and unemployment traps) on an admittedly very small number of people.

Against that, however, it became clear to me that the threepence off the basic rate that Geoffrey had been able to achieve in his first Budget, financed by a substantial rise in VAT, was not something that I could repeat. So unless I was prepared to cut a penny at a time, I would probably never get the basic rate down at all: great distances can be travelled in short steps, but not with no steps at all. Moreover, the more the scope for reducing the burden of tax was used up by increasing the allowances, the less scope there would be ever to act on the basic rate. I also suspected that incentives were affected not merely by the rate of income tax, but also by the direction in which people expected it to move. In other words, a reduction to x per cent, coupled with a sense that tax was on the way down, would create a more invigorating climate than an increase to x per cent coupled with a sense that tax was on the way up – even though in each case the basic rate was the same x per cent.

I was struck, too, by the fact that, whereas probably an overwhelming majority of taxpayers knew what the basic rate of tax was, it was doubtful if one in a hundred knew what their threshold was.

Moreover we had already raised tax thresholds by over 22 per cent in real terms since 1979, and by 1986 they were close to the international average. By contrast, there had been no change in the basic rate since the Government's first Budget. The combined marginal rates of Income Tax and National Insurance Contributions for the bulk of the population had fallen by a meagre half of one point since Labour were in office, from 39.5 per cent to 39 per cent, and our income tax rates were still, in general, higher than overseas.

The balance of the argument shifted still further following Norman Fowler's 1985 social security reform, which greatly reduced the effect of raising thresholds on the unemployment and poverty traps. For means-tested benefits were now to be paid on the basis of post-tax rather than the pre-tax earnings. Thus every pound by which I raised post-tax incomes by raising thresholds, would in future simultaneously reduce the entitlement to benefit. The high implicit marginal rate paid by the poorest households resulted in any event from the speed at which means-tested benefits (especially family credit, housing benefit and community charge benefit) were withdrawn as income rose, and tax changes were of comparatively trivial importance to this group.

Much the most important consideration, however, was that, if I wished to create a large constituency in favour of income tax reductions, as a counter to all the many vocal constituencies and pressure groups there always are for higher Government spending on everything under the sun, the last thing I wanted to do was to reduce the size of that constituency by taking people out of income tax altogether by raising thresholds. I was struck by the number of people who complained to me after the tax cut of 1986 that I had done nothing for them. These were people who did not pay income tax at all, many of them thanks to the large real threshold increases in my first two Budgets. All these considerations, but perhaps most of all the last, made a compelling case for concentrating on cutting the basic rate.

THE INVENTION OF PEPS

As in the previous year, much of my speech was devoted to unemployment and the labour market. With some reluctance, I decided to include in the Budget some public expenditure measures on this front. But in contrast to the previous year, they could be financed out of the Reserve; and there was no overall increase in the Government's expenditure plans. My most innovative, if tentative, proposal – at this point there was not even a Green Paper – was for tax relief for Profit Related Pay. I gave a warning that despite rising productivity, pay was rising still faster, and that as a result labour costs were increasing faster than was compatible with high employment. These warnings, and the crucial linkage of pay to jobs, were sadly lost from sight in the boom of the late 1980s. But they were all too well vindicated by subsequent events.

The reforms I had made to the taxation of savings in my 1984 Budget, and those I had been stopped from making in my 1985 Budget, had been chiefly concerned with levelling down the playing field for institutional savings. By 1986 I felt the time had come to focus more on levelling it up for at least one form of direct personal savings: wider share ownership. This led to the invention of Personal Equity Plans (PEPs) and their launch in the 1986 Budget. Under the PEP scheme anyone could invest a specified annual amount in UK equities, in a properly supervised 'plan', and escape all liability to income tax and capital gains tax on the investment made, provided the sum remained in the plan for a full calendar year. Indeed, there would be no need to report it to the Inland Revenue at all. PEPs were deliberately designed to augment the progress already made in widening share ownership through employee share schemes and the privatisation programme.

The scheme began in January 1987, with an investment limit of £200 a month or £2,400 a year. Once the year's qualifying period ended, investments could be realised without any penalty; but clearly the longer the investment remained in the PEP, the more the tax relief built up, and the greater the benefit. Anyone legally able to deal in securities could register as a PEP manager; but the investor himself could decide whether to use a plan in which he decided whether to make investment decisions himself, or one in which he delegated them to the PEP managers.

I was always very cautious about describing PEPs as savings incentives. Although I hoped they would encourage the growth of small savings, at a time when the personal savings ratio was falling away, I was well aware that they might simply divert money that would have been saved anyway, in National Savings for example. Any overall savings increase was a bonus over and above the main objective, an expansion in direct share ownership.

Initially, PEPs looked like being a great success. In their first year of operation a quarter of a million people invested £500 million in PEPs. But the Stock Exchange crash of October 1987, only ten months after their inauguration, dealt them a savage blow, and it became necessary to give them the kiss of life.

This took a number of forms: finding ways of reducing the burdens on the PEP managers so as to minimise the initially high management charges they levied; steadily increasing the permitted annual investment limit (by 1992 this stood at £6,000); and, most important of all, greatly enlarging the amount that could be invested in investment and unit trusts, where the big breakthrough came in my 1989 Budget.

This went against my original conception of PEPs as a means of encouraging direct popular investment in UK companies, with no institutional intermediary of any kind; but it was clear that the PEP scheme had to be promoted on a substantial scale, and it was only the Unit Trust companies that were prepared to do this.

As a result of all these improvements, PEPs, which at one point had seemed in danger of fizzling out altogether, went from strength to strength. By the end of 1990 over one million PEPs were in existence involving a total investment of some £3 billion, and the total was growing fast. Indeed the prospect of a Labour Government in the spring of 1992, and the risk of its bringing the PEP scheme to an end, led to a positive frenzy of PEP promotions and take-up.

CHAPTER TWENTY-TWO

FRAUD AND THE CITY

Divided Against Fraud · Reforming the Stock Exchange · Big Bang and After
The Johnson Matthey Débâcle · Strengthening Bank Supervision
A New Banking Act · The Role of the Bank of England · Reflections on Banking Supervision · How to Put Fraudsters Behind Bars

DIVIDED AGAINST FRAUD

It might seem surprising at first sight that a Government, and a Chancellor, so committed to deregulation, including financial deregulation, should have spent so much time over, and been so concerned with, financial regulation. Indeed, some have even seen it as a tacit admission that financial deregulation went too far. But this is to be confused by words. Financial deregulation in no way implies the absence of financial regulation for prudential purposes and for the prevention, so far as possible, of fraud. Economic freedom, as much as political freedom, is possible only within the framework of the rule of law.

Unlike most other finance ministries in the world, which have ministerial responsibility for the regulation of the financial sector, in Britain the responsibility was divided, with the Treasury having responsibility for the banks and building societies and the Department of Trade and Industry being responsible for the securities and insurance industries. This division was always a mistake, but it became increasingly nonsensical as the distinctions between financial institutions became increasingly blurred. The nonsense was compounded by the fact that the Bank of England, which keeps an eye on the entire financial sector, has the Treasury as its sponsoring Department.

Although I was never an empire builder, I minuted Margaret in March 1987, arguing the case for using the opportunity of the new Government she would be forming after the general election to follow international practice and common sense and consolidate responsibility for the entire financial sector in the hands of the Treasury, as soon as the forthcoming general election was behind us. Unfortunately Margaret, who was temperamentally averse to changes in the machinery of government, rejected my advice; and it was left to John Major to make this long overdue move after the 1992 general election.

My proposal to give overall departmental responsibility to the Treasury was based on the lessons of experience. For a number of reasons, I had been plunged into this particular corner of the Chancellor's bailiwick right from the moment I entered Number 11. One of the first worries Peter Middleton expressed to me after welcoming me as the new Chancellor in 1983 concerned the inadequacy of Whitehall's machinery for dealing with commercial fraud. He was absolutely right. He suggested that I might set up and chair an inter-ministerial group on the subject, which I readily agreed to do, with Margaret's acquiescence. As 'Lex' of the *Financial Times* in 1960, I had seen the exposure of financial skulduggery – in so far as the lawyers permitted me to engage in it – as a major part of my job, and had continued this intermittent crusade as City Editor of the *Sunday Telegraph* in 1961–63. I was thus fortunate in having some background knowledge of the subject, if of a somewhat mature vintage.

But the inter-ministerial group which I chaired in my room at the Treasury in 1983 and 1984 was a depressing if instructive experience. It soon became clear that a *sine qua non* of an effective Government response to financial fraud was the fullest co-operation between the various departments with responsibility in this area. That was not to say that the component parts themselves were adequate: they were not. But there was no need to make matters worse by a refusal to subordinate departmental *amour propre* to the common cause.

Yet that proved to be the case. The Department of Trade and Industry, with its wide-ranging regulatory responsibilities and the statutory power to initiate the most searching investigations into suspect companies, felt that it should head the combined Government effort. The Attorney General, to whom the Director of Public Prosecutions (DPP) and his Department reported, had no doubt that a consolidation of the Government's capability under any other auspices than his own would be grossly improper. And the Home Office, with responsibility for the police in general and the fraud squad in particular, and a strong sense of its high place in the Whitehall pecking order, was adamant that not an inch of its departmental turf should be surrendered.

Eventually, as a new Chancellor, the best I could secure was the setting up of the Fraud Investigation Group (FIG) as a new permanent body, backed by additional resources, to deal with serious cases of commercial and financial fraud. It would be located in the DPP's Department and would comprise accountants seconded from the DTI as well as lawyers. The Home Office promised that it would enjoy the fullest co-operation from the police. I minuted Margaret on 29 June to inform her of this modest proposal, which she endorsed. It was announced on 3 July 1984 and came into effect on 1 January 1985.

The FIG was eventually superseded on the recommendation of an official inquiry into the conduct of serious fraud trials chaired by Lord Roskill. Regrettably, Cabinet rejected what I regarded as the most important of Roskill's recommendations: the setting up of a special Fraud Trials Tribunal which would replace the normal trial by jury in particularly complex and serious fraud cases. Quintin Hailsham, the Lord Chancellor, and I appeared to be its only supporters, with the Government's law officers and the other lawyers in Cabinet – apart from Quintin – particularly hostile. Subsequent events have served only to reinforce my belief in the necessity for this reform.

Most of the other Roskill recommendations, however, were accepted by Cabinet, including the setting up of a new specialist Serious Fraud Office. This was eventually enacted in the 1987 Criminal Justice Act, and once it had been set up replaced the more modest FIG.

REFORMING THE STOCK EXCHANGE

My other early Chancellorial involvement in the broad area of financial regulation concerned the Stock Exchange. Shortly before we first took office in 1979 the Office of Fair Trading (OFT) had begun an investigation of the restrictive practices of what was then still known as the London Stock Exchange. As the investigations rumbled on, the Stock Exchange became increasingly alarmed. The end of the road could only be an inordinately expensive case before the Restrictive Practices Court, which it was bound to lose, and to have reform imposed upon it. In 1980, while I was Financial Secretary, Nicholas Goodison, the tall, urbane, civilised, effective and deceptively languid chairman of the Stock Exchange, called on the then Trade Secretary, John Nott, asking him to call off the OFT, for which he had ministerial responsibility, promising that the Stock Exchange would reform itself. John Nott refused to play. Goodison also saw Geoffrey, who was much more sympathetic, but pointed out that John Nott was the lead Minister in this field. This served only to reinforce Goodison's ardent support for the transfer of ministerial responsibility for the oversight of the securities industry to the Treasury.

When John Biffen replaced John Nott as Trade Secretary in January 1981 he unsurprisingly saw no reason to change what had become the departmental line.

But when Arthur Cockfield in turn replaced John Biffen in April 1982 he saw the sense in striking a deal, and began discussing with Geoffrey the form this might take. That was the state of play I discovered when I became Chancellor in June 1983, as did Cecil Parkinson who was appointed to the enlarged post of Trade and Industry Secretary at the same time. Moreover the matter had become urgent, with the first hearing of the OFT's action against the Stock Exchange scheduled to take place the following January.

Cecil came to see me about it immediately after the election, and told me he favoured a deal in which the Stock Exchange would be exempted by law from the ambit of the Restrictive Practices Act in return for an undertaking that it would reform itself. I told him I agreed, provided the reform was genuine and adequate. The Bank, of course, had been urging a deal along these lines right from the moment we took office in 1979. There was little to be said for long drawn out litigation, which in addition to its inordinate expense – the point which weighed heaviest with the Stock Exchange's own members – would in practice delay reforms which were urgently needed.

The specific restrictive practices included 'single capacity', which meant the enforced separation of the securities business between brokers, who were agents acting for their clients for a fixed commission, and jobbers, who made the markets and theoretically provided liquidity by holding lines of stocks and shares on their books; fixed minimum commissions; the insistence that brokers and jobbers should be independent and not part of any larger financial group; and the exclusion of foreigners from stock exchange membership.

The old system had many virtues, but in addition to being intellectually indefensible it had one fatal practical defect: it was woefully undercapitalised. As a result, while the City of London remained one of the world leaders – if not *the* world leader – across a whole range of financial markets, such as the foreign exchange market, in the securities market it was in danger of becoming a backwater.

Cecil asked me to help him to persuade Margaret of the need for the deal. He himself was not at his best, and in the strictest confidence he explained to me why. He was, at that time, totally preoccupied with the personal complications of the Sarah Keays affair, which was about to erupt into the public prints and eventually to force his resignation after only four months in his new job. When he told me of his problems I urged him not to resign; and when it had become public and the pressure began to intensify I urged Margaret not to yield to it. That was her instinct, too; but eventually she felt she had no option.

With Cecil in this state, I had to play a larger part than would normally have been necessary in getting the right decisions taken. This was notably the case at the key meeting held shortly after the election in Margaret's room at the House of Commons. Margaret was fearful of the politics of intervening at the eleventh hour to rescue the Stock Exchange from the embrace of the Restrictive Practices Court, leaving its would-be prosecutor, the Director-General of Fair Trading, angrily deprived of the quarry he had been patiently hunting for so long; and her misgivings were powerfully reinforced by Willie. There was no doubt that the politics were uncomfortable: the Labour Party would inevitably accuse us, as indeed they did, of rushing to protect our wealthy friends in the City who, it would be alleged, had financed our election campaign, while leaving manufacturing industry to face the full rigours of the law and the marketplace.

At that meeting I supported Cecil strongly, and for the reason I have indicated had to make most of the running myself. I argued that Cecil's proposal was right on the merits of the case, and that the politics could be ignored at the start of a new parliament, with the next election several years hence. Well before that, it would have become clear that the reforms on which we were insisting were genuine. Eventually, Margaret acquiesced.

BIG BANG AND AFTER

Cecil gave Goodison the green light on 1 July 1983, after which a period of intensive negotiation began, culminating in Cecil's statement to the House four weeks later. There were three key issues. First, whether Goodison would agree to the reforms we believed were essential. After some discussion, but without too much difficulty, he did. Second, whether he could persuade his members to agree to them. This was less straightforward, and Goodison showed considerable skill, patience and firmness over a prolonged period in achieving this. The third key issue was whether the changes should be phased in over a period or whether everything should happen at once, on a single day. This became known as the choice between the gradualist and the big bang approaches. Goodison felt that it was only by introducing all the changes in full overnight that he could be confident of securing his members' agreement. The Government concurred, and the chosen date was 27 October 1986 – subsequently to become known as 'Big Bang', a name which was also attached to the package of reforms itself and the far-reaching changes these reforms set in train.

The coming of Big Bang underlined the need, which had been identified during the early years of the Thatcher Government, for a new and improved regulatory framework for all aspects of the savings and investment industry. This eventually came into being in the shape of the 1986 Financial Services Act (FSA), and the various agencies set up under that Act. The FSA was based on the idea of what was somewhat misleadingly termed 'self-regulation'. It was in fact – necessarily – a fully statutory system; but the rules were made by the various so-called self-regulatory organisations (SROs) set up under the Act, manned by practitioners rather than bureaucrats, under the aegis of a Securities and Investment Board (SIB) on which practitioners were also represented. The system had been greatly influenced by the Gower Report on investor protection, which had been published in January 1984, and which *inter alia* sapiently observed that the level of supervision should not 'seek to achieve the impossible task of protecting fools from their own folly' – an observation of wide application which was sadly forgotten towards the end of the 1980s – but should rather 'be no greater than is necessary to protect reasonable people from being made fools of'.

The concept, in fact, was admirable; but what eventually emerged was something far more cumbersome and bureaucratic than I or, I believe, any of us in Government had ever envisaged. The fault lay largely in the rules promulgated by the SIB, under its first chairman, Kenneth Berrill, a somewhat peripatetic member of the Whitehall establishment. Norman Tebbit, who had succeeded Cecil Parkinson as Trade and Industry Secretary, had left the task of finding the first chairman of the SIB to the Governor, Robin Leigh-Pemberton; and Robin's first choice had been my old friend Martin Jacomb, founder-chairman of the investment bank BZW. Martin would have done the job very well; but he was too busy to take it on, agreeing only to serve as a member of the SIB, from which he resigned in frustration some two years later. One of the practical problems with practitioner-based regulation is that most of the ablest practitioners are too busy making money to be able to devote adequate time to the task of regulation. Perhaps that is why, despite the massive SIB rule book, the SROs did not always prove as vigilant against fraudsters as might have been hoped.

The dominant figure on the Berrill SIB, however, was neither Berrill himself nor Jacomb, but the deputy chairman, Mark Weinberg, a South African lawyer who had come to London and made a fortune by building up an innovative and highly successful life assurance business. When he was asked to take on the role of poacher-turned-gamekeeper the lawyer in him came very much to the fore, and played a large part in framing the excessively legalistic rule book that emerged. But the bankers and brokers who complained so bitterly were themselves partly to blame, by failing to make good use of the lengthy consultation period before the rules were promulgated.

THE JOHNSON MATTHEY DÉBÂCLE

The aspect of financial regulation which concerned me most was the supervision of the banks. Anyone who has read their Bagehot will be aware of the economic importance of banking and its effective supervision. The latter is not an easy task. If the supervisory authority were to be prepared to allow banks to fail as readily as governments should allow other unsuccessful or unlucky businesses to fail, this could lead to a major collapse of confidence throughout the banking system with devastating consequences for the economy as a whole. If, on the other hand, it were to ensure that no bank ever failed, this would inevitably encourage irresponsible and imprudent banking. Thus the supervisory authority has to be very careful both in deciding when to intervene and when not to intervene, and to keep banks on their toes by creating uncertainty as to whether it would intervene in any particular case.

It is essentially the acceptance that the Bank of England will, in appropriate circumstances, save banks (and thus their depositors) from the full consequences of insolvency, that creates the 'moral hazard' which makes it necessary for the banks in return to submit to a degree of official supervision unknown to other businesses. For the main – although not the only – task of bank supervision is to prevent banks from getting into a situation that is likely to lead to failure in the first place.

The event which was to focus my mind on it occurred at six o'clock in the morning of Monday, 1 October 1984. It was then that the telephone rang in the Number 11 flat and I found Peter Middleton on the line with the news that the Governor and Deputy Governor wished to see me before the markets opened about a banking matter. I agreed to see them at Number 11 at half-past seven. I asked Peter Middleton to come along too, and to bring Frank Cassell, the relevant Treasury Under Secretary, with him.

Robin and Kit McMahon duly arrived, and told me that Johnson Matthey Bankers (JMB), a bank of no great consequence, was on the brink of collapse. The problem was that its parent company was the prominent City bullion dealer, Johnson Matthey; and the difficulties of JMB were on such a scale that the Bank feared that, if nothing were done, they could bring down the parent company too. The Bank believed that this could create a crisis of confidence in the London bullion market as a whole, the most important gold market in the world, accounting for half of all world business in the metal. It did not want to see the centre of the world gold market decamp from London to, say, Zurich. It was also worried about the contagion spreading to other members of the small and select bullion market. It was particularly concerned about Samuel Montagu, since this was a subsidiary of the Midland Bank, already by then in a fragile state, and in no position to take a further knock.

The Bank had therefore decided, on the merits of the case, that JMB had to be rescued. The decisive factor, in the Bank's eyes, was the damage that might be done to the London bullion market were JMB allowed to fail: something that was not, strictly speaking, within the ambit of bank supervision – which is concerned with the protection of depositors and the probity and stability of the banking system – at all. Be that as it may, the Bank had tried to be midwife to a private sector rescue, but had failed. In particular, its discussions with the Bank of Nova Scotia, on which it had pinned great hopes, had finally broken down late the previous evening. There was now no alternative but for the Bank to take over JMB itself. Moreover, an announcement would have to be made when the markets opened that morning, at 8 o'clock.

This was something the Bank of England, as the supervisory authority for the banking system, was fully entitled to do if it felt it to be necessary: it did not require my authority or approval. The snag was the amount of money that might be required. The Bank was in the process of extracting financial contributions of one kind or another from JMB's parent company, Johnson Matthey; from Johnson Matthey's principal shareholder, the giant mining group Charter Consolidated; and from the clearing banks, the other members of the London gold market, and some merchant banks. Some of this was already in the bag, some was yet to be secured. But it was clear that a very large part of JMB's loan book was bad, and it was possible that the Bank – which proposed to acquire JMB for the token payment of a one pound coin – could be faced at the end of the day with a loss of up to £100 million. This was a very large sum in relation to the Bank's own free reserves, which it maintained for such purposes, and it might therefore require a guarantee from the Treasury to make good any shortfall from public funds.

If the news itself was unpalatable, the very late stage at which I was informed of it made it even worse. The crisis had evidently erupted the previous week, while I was in Washington for the annual Bank and Fund meetings, along with both Robin and Kit McMahon. Yet no-one had seen fit to mention it to me. Since then, the Bank had been working night and day to try and discover the facts, evaluate the situation, and effect a rescue; still without a single word to me. As a result, I was being given only a few minutes to decide whether or not to give an open-ended guarantee of taxpayers' money in support of a rescue about whose wisdom – as I made clear to Robin and Kit at the time, and subsequently in a minute to Margaret – I was far from convinced. I had to make up my mind with no time to secure the information on which to base a considered decision. In the circumstances, I had no option but to rely on the Bank's judgement. I protected my position so far as I could by emphasising that I could give no undertaking that the Treasury would be prepared to give a guarantee, should it be asked to do so; but if the Bank was prepared to go ahead on that basis, so be it.

Needless to say, it was and did, as soon as the meeting was over. I could have prevented it only by making it clear that in no circumstances would the Treasury make public funds available. Leaving the issue open, as I did, enabled the Bank to go ahead confident that, once the rescue was a *fait accompli*, there was no way in which the Government could fail to provide the Bank with funds if it were to need them. The only stroke of luck was that the House of Commons was still in recess and not due to reassemble for a further three weeks. This meant that I had time to mount an urgent investigation without being required to make a statement to the House before I had the evidence on which to form a view.

STRENGTHENING BANK SUPERVISION

It turned out that JMB had been founded in 1965, and had grown particularly rapidly in the early 1980s by lending very large sums to a small number of little-known Asian businessmen. The more I discovered about it the less surprising its collapse became – but by the same token the more inexplicable the Bank's failure, as the supervisory authority, to step in at a much earlier stage. But my interest was not in raking over the JMB issue as such: it lay in strengthening the system of banking supervision in the UK so that a débâcle of this kind was far less likely to occur in future. Moreover, while the implementation of bank supervision was strictly an autonomous matter for the Bank of England, in which I had an interest to the extent that it raised issues of economic or political importance, the legislative framework within which the Bank carried out its duties was inescapably my responsibility.

On 17 December 1984 I made a statement to Parliament announcing the setting up of a Committee to look into the UK system of bank supervision and make recommendations. Astonishingly, although the House had by that time been sitting for the best part of two months, the official Labour Opposition had never once raised the matter. The only remotely serious probing had come from the Opposition back benches, in the person of the austere left-wing xenophobe and conspiracy theorist, Denis Skinner, the maverick Member for the mining constituency of Bolsover – an accomplished parliamentarian with the best and quickest repartee in the House, and a better sense of where the Government was vulnerable than the whole of his Party's front bench put together.

It was clear, even without an inquiry, that the supervisory side of the Bank of England had badly fallen down on the job over Johnson Matthey, and its reputation had suffered as a result. Not wishing the Bank to be humiliated any further, I decided on an internal rather than a public inquiry, and asked the Governor, Robin Leigh-Pemberton, to chair the Committee. But I was careful to put on it a strong Treasury team headed by Peter Middleton, together with a distinguished commercial banker, Deryk Vander Weyer, a former deputy chairman of Barclays Bank and arguably the outstanding commercial banker of his generation.

It cannot be said that my concern for the Bank's problems was entirely reciprocated. In the questioning that followed my statement, the chairman of the powerful Public Accounts Committee, Bob Sheldon, asked me what the Bank's liability was in respect of JMB. I replied, truthfully as I thought, that apart from the £1 spent on the purchase of JMB, there was only the Bank's half share of a £150 million indemnity, but that it was too soon to say how much of that indemnity would be required. It was only subsequently that it came to light that on 22 November the Bank had placed a £100 million deposit with JMB, which it had subsequently converted into permanent capital. It emerged that this had been authorised by Kit McMahon while Robin was away in the Soviet Union, and no-one had seen fit to inform me of it. I felt badly let down, as I made clear when I learned about it. While it is true that at the end of the day the money was recovered, misleading the House, however inadvertently, is a serious business.

I published the report of the Committee on banking supervision on 20 June 1985, and made a statement to the House the same day. Also on the same day, the Bank published its annual report, which contained a special Annexe on the JMB débâcle, together with a press notice announcing that, through JMB, it would be suing the accountancy firm of Arthur Young, who had been JMB's auditors prior to its collapse, for substantial damages.

Certainly neither the Bank nor the auditors emerged well from the report. The supervisory side of the Bank had effectively disregarded all manner of danger signals – including the failure of JMB's representatives to turn up at meetings called by the Bank to discuss its accounts – and the auditors had performed little better. The company appeared to have lost no less than £248 million; yet its records were in such a state of disarray that it was extremely hard to discover the circumstances in which the bad loans had been made. Inevitably, the Leigh-Pemberton Committee's report recommended a substantial strengthening, in terms of quantity, quality and expertise, of the supervision division of the Bank of England; and this Robin agreed to put into effect without delay.

There was, however, in my view a structural problem, which the report perhaps understandably did not address, but which had and still has important implications. By tradition, the Bank of England had two principal tasks: the implementation of monetary policy, including funding and exchange rate policy, and the supervision of the banking system. In the monetary policy field it was the Chancellor who was responsible for taking the decisions, with the Bank providing him with advice before the event and conducting the necessary financial market operations after it; whereas in the area of bank supervision, responsibility lay fairly and squarely with the Bank of England. Yet despite the Bank's subordinate role in monetary policy and its leading role in bank supervision, the high fliers were all attracted to the former, much sexier side, while the humdrum but important bank supervision side was always in danger of becoming something of a backwater. This problem would take on a new dimension with an independent Bank, as I discuss later in this chapter.

A NEW BANKING ACT

While indicating the non-legislative changes it felt to be necessary, the report also recommended a significant strengthening of the statutory framework within which the Bank carried out its task. I therefore took the opportunity of my statement of 20 June 1985 to announce my intention of publishing a White Paper on Banking Supervision later that year with a view to the early introduction of a new Banking Bill. The White Paper was duly published in December 1985 and the Bill, which was to become the 1987 Banking Act, the following December. The Bill embodied all the legislative recommendations of the Leigh-Pemberton committee, but went a great deal further.

Until 1979, banking supervision in the UK had been conducted on an entirely informal and non-statutory basis, with the Bank relying on what was officially termed 'moral suasion', and more commonly 'the Governor's eyebrows', to secure its objectives. In the clubby City of the past this could be a formidable weapon. But the change in the composition of the City made it increasingly inadequate, as the secondary banking crisis of the early 1970s had demonstrated – and in any case a European Community directive required all member states to have bank supervisory legislation in place. Hence the Banking Act of 1979, the last piece of legislation the outgoing Labour Government had been able to put on the statute-book.

But the 1979 Act, which the 1987 Act was to supplant, was defective in a number of ways. The powers it gave the Bank were seriously inadequate, and I strengthened them very considerably in the 1987 Act. The new Act also made it, for the first time, a criminal offence to provide false or misleading information to the supervisory authority, which had occurred in the case of JMB. The 1979 Act had divided all deposit-taking institutions into two categories: banks and licensed deposit-takers. The powers it gave the Bank of England in respect of the supervision of banks were appreciably less than those given in respect of the supervision of licensed deposit-takers. This reflected an assumption that serious problems would arise only among those below the salt. It was significant that JMB was a recognised bank.

The Leigh-Pemberton committee recommended the abolition of this distinction, which the 1987 legislation duly enacted. Any sensible supervisor will know that he has responsibility for a whole spectrum of institutions. But the main effect of the artificial separation of them into two distinct categories, sheep and goats, was to disadvantage British licensed deposit-takers vis-à-vis their foreign competitors. This arose because UK licensed deposit-takers were not permitted to call themselves banks, whereas licensed deposit-takers that were the UK offshoots of overseas banks – such as, most notoriously, the Bank of Credit and Commerce International (BCCI), source of the next big banking scandal – *were* allowed by the Bank to call themselves banks.

But to my mind a much more important recommendation of the Leigh-Pemberton Committee – even if it did not go far enough – was that the iron curtain of confidentiality that separated bank supervisors from bank auditors should be replaced by 'a regular dialogue'. This was an attempt to address a two-way problem. The accountancy profession considered itself prevented by a duty of confidentiality to its client from passing any information to the bank supervisors; while the supervisors were effectively prevented by the terms of the 1979 Banking Act itself from passing information to the auditors.

Clearly, the interests of effective supervision made this double barrier a nonsense. My original plan was to lay a statutory duty on bank auditors to disclose relevant information to the bank supervisors. This was regarded with horror not merely by the accountancy profession but also by the Bank, who felt that all that was necessary was to enable bank auditors to disclose information to the bank supervisors if they felt it right to do so, by protecting them from any action for damages in such cases. Eventually, I reached a compromise with the Bank, agreeing, somewhat reluctantly, to accept the Bank's weaker formulation, but with the addition of a power for the Treasury to make regulations in effect requiring the auditors to disclose information to the regulators should this appear to be necessary.

THE ROLE OF THE BANK OF ENGLAND

The other key feature of the 1987 Act, which went well beyond the recommendations of the Leigh-Pemberton report, was the setting up of a Board of Banking Supervision, chaired by the Governor, but with a two-thirds majority of independent (i.e. non-Bank) members, in effect to oversee the Bank's execution of its supervisory duties and to give the Bank advice on difficult cases. The Bank remained technically free to reject the advice of the independent members; but should it do so it would be required to inform the Chancellor of the Exchequer. Moreover, the independent members would have the right to inform the Chancellor of the reasons for their advice – which seemed to me to ensure that the Bank was most unlikely to overrule the Board of Banking Supervision in practice.

The Bank found the whole idea of a Board of Banking Supervision along these lines particularly unattractive. In the end, however, Robin went along with it quietly when I pointed out that he should see it as a satisfactory way of meeting the arguments of those who wished to take the task of bank supervision away from the Bank of England altogether. He knew – because I had told him privately of her views – that I was referring to Margaret. I had, of course, kept her fully informed about the Johnson Matthey affair and its aftermath throughout, and discussed the issues with her. She was so incensed by the extent of the Bank's failure over JMB that she argued strongly that the task of bank supervision should be removed from the Bank of England altogether, and entrusted to a new agency set up for the purpose.

Objectively, Margaret was absolutely right. This sort of separation was the practice in a number of countries overseas, notably Germany, where bank supervision fell not under the Bundesbank in Frankfurt but under the quite separate Bundesaufsichtsamt für das Kreditwesen in Berlin. It would have been the best way of overcoming the problem I identified earlier in this chapter of bank supervision becoming something of a backwater. It would also have removed the inherent conflict of interest between the task of monetary policy and that of bank supervision, with the former requiring a stern unbending and single-minded stringency and the latter favouring a judicious laxity to prevent bank failures.

I none the less resisted Margaret's proposal, despite its innate good sense, for one practical reason. Under the UK arrangements, with monetary policy clearly in the hands of the Chancellor, it was the unfettered responsibility for banking supervision that, as I saw it, largely gave the Bank its authority in the eyes of the City and thus more widely. If that were removed, I feared that the standing and authority of the Bank, not least in the eyes of its peers around the world, would suffer greatly; and I did not believe this to be in the national interest.[19]

If, however, we were to move, as I strongly favour to an independent Bank of England, in the sense of responsibility for monetary policy, then it would indeed be right from every point of view to remove from it all responsibility for banking supervision, which would be entrusted to a separate agency created for that sole purpose. In my 1988 minute to Margaret recommending the creation of an independent Bank of England I proposed that 'The Bank would, at least for the time being, retain responsibility for supervising the banking system.' This was because I felt that to introduce a further upheaval at the same time as the others contained in my proposal – which included the transfer to the Treasury of responsibility for funding the Government's borrowing requirement – might be too much. This was probably a mistake.

REFLECTIONS ON BANKING SUPERVISION

There were two areas of potential weakness in the new framework which worried me during my own time in office, and which the 1987 Act itself was unable to address. The first concerned the relationship between the Bank of England and the law. I have already mentioned how up to 1979 the Bank had operated without any statutory framework at all, an arrangement of sadly but inevitably diminishing efficacy. I got the impression, even a decade later, that it had never fully come to terms with the task of taking tough supervisory decisions within a statutory framework. Whether it did not take sufficient high-level legal advice,

[19] This was the only difference between Margaret and myself over the 1987 Banking Act. The claim in Stephen Fay's book, *Portrait of an Old Lady*, that the Board of Banking Supervision and certain other aspects of the 1987 Act were included at Margaret's insistence and against my wishes, is mistaken.

or whether it took the wrong sort of legal advice, or whether it failed to grasp the interaction between the law and practical common-sense reality, I do not know. But on a number of occasions during my time, in a number of different fields, I found the Bank fearful of taking a particular course of action because of a misplaced fear of being successfully taken to court if it did.

A more serious shortcoming, however, lay in the worrying fragmentation and compartmentalisation of the various law enforcement agencies involved in the financial area in one way or another, to which I referred right at the start of this chapter, in the context of fraud. In my experience it is very rare indeed for there to be a major supervisory problem in which fraud is not involved. Even if the origins of the problem lie elsewhere, as they usually do, fraud is characteristically resorted to subsequently to conceal the scale of the difficulties that have arisen.

That is why, in my personal foreword to the 1985 White Paper on Banking Supervision, I observed that 'an important deterrent to financial fraud is effective supervision'. The Bank tended to see very much less of a connection between the two: regulatory supervision, for which it was responsible, was one thing; the extirpation of fraud, for which the police in the shape of the sadly inadequate fraud squad were responsible, was another. This compartmentalisation could lead the Bank to be surprisingly innocent: on the very day the White Paper was published, I answered a question in the House on JMB by saying, on the firm advice of the Bank, that 'no *prima facie* evidence of fraud has so far been uncovered' – something I subsequently bitterly regretted. It may have been strictly true at the time: that depends on what is held to constitute 'evidence'. But of course fraud was involved in the JMB affair.

The real mischief, however, in the mistaken compartmentalisation of supervision and the detection of fraud is the dangerous lack of effective liaison, and in particular the failure to exchange relevant information, between the supervisors and the fraud squad. Moreover, as I have already indicated, this failure to co-operate effectively and to exchange relevant information is by no means confined to the Bank of England and the police. As emerged in the BCCI case – a fraud on a massive scale which did not come to light until well after I had left office – a number of other law enforcement agencies, in the widest sense, were involved, including the Customs and Excise, the Inland Revenue, and even the security services; but for most of the time they might almost have been living on different planets. I do not deny the difficulties involved and safeguards required in the exchange of information between different law enforcement agencies. But the traditional compartmentalisation culture is a fraudster's benefit.

Remedying this is at least as important as improvements in international co-operation between the various bank supervisory authorities around the world, which was widely, and rightly, felt to be one of the lessons of the BCCI scandal. Indeed there is nowadays probably more co-operation between central banks in the UK and overseas, between the police in the UK and overseas, and between the tax authorities in the UK and overseas, than there is between the Bank of England, the fraud squad and the revenue Departments within the UK.

HOW TO PUT FRAUDSTERS BEHIND BARS

One final area where a different approach is, I believe, badly needed, is that of prosecution – although here, paradoxically, co-operation of a malign kind is part of the problem. The expensive, time-consuming and complex task of the investigation of fraud and financial skulduggery, sometimes of a highly sophisticated nature, loses much of its point if there is not a successful prosecution at the end of the day. Successful prosecutions, leading to criminal convictions and prison sentences, are the most effective deterrent to financial fraud. Equally, the absence of a criminal prosecution tends to promote suggestions, however ill-founded, of a government cover-up, and to lead to a degree of cynicism among the public at large.

For all these reasons I always felt that putting fraudsters behind bars should be an important objective of policy. In some areas the failure to achieve this was less serious than others. The unique dependence of banking on confidence and trust, coupled with the immense battery of powers given to the Bank of England by the 1987 Act, meant that successful banking supervision and effective deterrence – and indeed to some extent the punishment of wrongdoers – could sometimes be achieved without the need for a criminal conviction.

Outside the banking field, the exposure of skulduggery in a DTI Inspector's Report, written by a distinguished lawyer or accountant, and protected by privilege from the libel laws, could serve a useful purpose. That is, of course, once it was published: I found myself constantly battling against pleas from the Attorney General and Director of Public Prosecutions of the day that DTI Inspectors' Reports should be held back since their publication might prejudice a successful prosecution. This was a dubious proposition at the best of times, made even more absurd by the infrequency of the occasions on which, at the end of the day, the DPP ever felt he had sufficient evidence to mount a successful prosecution. Not that publication of a damaging Inspector's Report was a fool-proof stratagem. The measured and carefully documented report on Robert Maxwell in 1971, which all but branded him a crook, did not prevent him from re-emerging in the 1980s to practise his fraud and skulduggery on an even larger scale, assisted by the unbelievable credulousness of the banks. To repeat the dictum of the good Professor Gower in a different but germane context, no system can perform 'the impossible task of protecting fools from their own folly'. Unfortunately others got badly hurt too.

Returning to the question of prosecution, it was inevitable that a time of boom and optimism such as the second half of the 1980s should see an upsurge in financial fraud: hence my desire to see some high-profile fraudsters behind bars. Yet on more than one occasion this was prevented by foolishly allowing the best to be the enemy of the good. Under the English legal system, the two Revenue Departments are, very sensibly, independent prosecuting authorities: unlike other Departments, they do not need to go through the DPP to mount a case. Moreover, for obvious reasons, fraudsters tend to be averse to paying tax.

On more than one occasion during my time, the Inland Revenue was about to prosecute a leading fraudster for tax evasion – which, if successful, would have led to a prison sentence – only to be held back by the DPP who insisted that this would obstruct the process of securing the evidence required for a conviction for the fraud itself. At the end of the day, the DPP discovered that he did not, after all, have sufficient evidence to mount a prosecution – by which time, however, the Inland Revenue trail had gone cold. It should not be forgotten that the US authorities managed to jail the notorious gangster Al Capone only by prosecuting him for not paying his income tax. There is a clear lesson for us here, in the extirpation of financial fraud in an increasingly complex world.

CHAPTER TWENTY-THREE

MY MONETARY PRINCIPLES

'The British Experiment' · No Jobs-Inflation Trade-off · A Nominal Framework Exchange Rate Mechanism · Principles and Practices · Reaction to Shocks The Counter-revolution in Retrospect

'THE BRITISH EXPERIMENT'

Monetary policy resembles the detection of financial fraud only in its complexity.[20] This very complexity makes it all the more important to state the main principles without sinking in a sea of technicalities. My essential beliefs about money, jobs and inflation were outlined in Part I and there is no need to go through all the theory again. In brief, inflation is a monetary phenomenon. This does not mean to say that the quantity of money is easy to measure or that there is any simple relation between money and prices. The basic point is that if everybody had twice as much money to spend, the main result would be to drive prices upwards. Any beneficial effect on output and employment would be transitory, as David Hume explained more than two centuries ago.

Unfortunately there is a long and tortuous route from these home truths to devising a framework of monetary control for a modern economy. So, far from inheriting a smoothly working system of monetary control, the system I inherited was – through no fault of Geoffrey's – full of puzzles and confusions. In the chapter on the Medium Term Financial Strategy, I explained that, although the monetary targets were missed, the spirit of the strategy was observed, as a result of which inflation fell far more than our supporters – let alone our critics – would have believed possible; and that the framework was useful in resisting calls for 'reflation'. But there remained a problem both of how best to state our policy and how best to carry it out technically.

As soon as I became Chancellor, therefore, I asked the Treasury to carry out a full-scale review of internal and external monetary policy, including the

[20] [2010 note] Some of the questions raised in this chapter are updated and further discussed in the new concluding chapter.

exchange rate and membership of the ERM. I also thought it important to try to pick out the wood from the trees: that is, to state the underlying beliefs which united practitioners of the new approach and to avoid getting lost in technical disputes.

Accordingly I was delighted to accept an invitation from the City University Business School to give the fifth Mais Lecture in June 1984, in which I tried to lay down the basic principles behind the new approach to economic policy.

The title I chose was 'The British Experiment', which I described as providing increasing freedom for markets to work within a framework of firm monetary and fiscal discipline. The opposite approach of ever-more *ad hoc* interference with markets coupled with financial indiscipline had often been embarked upon simply 'because British governments believed that political and electoral pressure gave them no option'. The British experiment was at the same time a political one: 'to demonstrate that union power could be curbed and inflation eradicated within a democracy'.

The basic doctrine I sought to set out in the Mais Lecture was straightforward. It divided economic policy into two branches: macroeconomic policy – interest rates, exchange rates and Budget deficits; the matters which get Chancellors into the headlines – and microeconomic (or supply-side) policy – the whole range of detailed measures designed to influence specific aspects of economic behaviour. It then challenged what had hitherto been the conventional wisdom head-on, by reassigning the roles of these two arms of economic policy:

> The conventional post-War wisdom was that unemployment was a consequence of inadequate economic growth, and economic growth was to be secured by macroeconomic policy – the fiscal stimulus of an enlarged Budget deficit, with monetary policy (to the extent that it could be said to exist at all) on the whole passively following fiscal policy. Inflation, by contrast, was increasingly seen as a matter to be dealt with by microeconomic policy – the panoply of controls and subsidies associated with the era of incomes policy.
>
> The conclusion on which the present Government's economic policy is based is that there is indeed a proper distinction between the objectives of macroeconomic and microeconomic policy, and a need to be concerned with both of them. But the proper role of each is precisely the opposite of that assigned to it by the conventional post-War wisdom. It is the conquest of inflation, and not the pursuit of growth and employ-

> ment, which is or should be the objective of macroeconomic policy. And it is the creation of conditions conducive to growth and employment, and not the suppression of price rises, which is or should be the objective of microeconomic policy.
>
> ... The most important point to emphasise is that this Government is pursuing simultaneously both a macro and a micro policy, that the one complements the other, that the macro policy is unequivocally directed at the continuing reduction in inflation, with the ultimate objective of stable prices, and that the micro policy is equally wholeheartedly designed to make the economy work better and thus generate more jobs.

In reality, the distinction may not always be quite as clear-cut as this. In certain circumstances, which history suggests do not occur very often, macroeconomic policy could also play a role in supporting economic activity. This was a point I made, not in the Mais Lecture, but in some of my Budget speeches and one or two other speeches I made at the time. It was in reply to those who worried that, if pay settlements were to decline at a time of falling inflation, spending power would also decline and that a downward spiral of depression might be created. The prospect of a serious depression being threatened in this way is much more remote than it appears; but the answer I gave applied irrespective of the cause – namely, that a properly functioning monetary policy is a safeguard against cumulative depression as well as against inflation. With this caveat the assignment of macro policy to the defeat of inflation and micro policy to the promotion of conditions favourable to growth is both accurate and the heart of the matter.

NO JOBS-INFLATION TRADE-OFF

The Mais Lecture was also a product of its time. Its aim was to tackle the then common view that macroeconomic policy either had changed or should have changed to give more emphasis to growth and employment over reducing inflation. It was an example of the cultural and intellectual lag of so many British economists and economic journalists that these doctrines were regarded as startling and disturbing. In many other countries the criticism would have been that they were too obvious.

As I put it in the lecture, 'double-digit inflation never persisted long enough to become embedded in expectations or a part of our economic bloodstream.' Yet 'stable prices are a blessed condition, but one that we in this country have not experienced other than very fleetingly for fifty years.' To achieve it required 'fighting and changing the culture and the psychology of two generations'. Here a policy of gradualism was required – 'bearing down on inflation' in the Treasury jargon, and taking advantage of every opportunity to lock it in at lower rates. The failure to take advantage in this way of the opportunity presented by the oil price collapse was the real error of the mid-1980s, for which those who opposed joining the ERM at the right time must take their share of the blame.

At the time of the Mais Lecture, the mainstream view was that the Government had intentionally or by inadvertence produced high unemployment, which in turn had reduced wage demands, which in turn had reduced inflation. What in fact had happened was a tight monetary policy had brought down inflation, largely, although not exclusively, via the exchange rate. But this reduction in inflation had only gradually permeated through to wage settlements. Thus profits were under squeeze; and it was 'the slowness of wages to adjust that was such an important factor in the rise of unemployment'.

A NOMINAL FRAMEWORK

What I was seeking to do as Chancellor was to keep total spending in the economy rising rapidly enough to allow reasonable real growth in an environment of price stability. But, in contrast to earlier post-war concepts of full employment policy, we did not attempt to sustain output and activity in the face of rising prices. Such attempts nearly always came to grief, as the wiser Keynesians realised: which is why they began to call themselves 'reconstructed' Keynesians. The key is to abandon the attempt to set 'real' variables – objectives for real economic growth, full employment or whatever – and instead to define objectives in money terms.

There are many different ways of doing this. The way that has been used throughout most of human history has been to maintain a metallic standard, usually gold or silver. This is obviously not very sophisticated. But in a rough-and-ready way it worked astonishingly well. For instance there was virtually no trend either way in the British price level for about two and a half centuries after the accession of Charles II in 1660. In recent times, there have been four candidates. In no particular order, they are:

1. A nominal GDP objective;
2. A money supply target;
3. A price level objective;
4. An exchange rate objective.

Nominal GDP, as its name suggests, is fundamental to the idea of a nominal framework. It simply means the total amount of national income in money terms, without adjusting by a price index. It is also roughly equal to the total amount of national spending on goods and services, and to the total value of output produced. (If the balance of payments is moving into deficit, nominal GDP will understate total spending, as some spending spills over into imports or into goods diverted from exports. So there are other related concepts, which have sometimes appeared in the Red Book, such as domestic demand or domestic expenditure. But these are refinements of the general principle.)

The weakness of nominal GDP and its variants is that they are too far removed both from the instruments that the policy-maker has at his disposal and from the information available to him. Estimates of GDP, whether real or nominal, are not normally available until two or three months after the quarter to which they refer – and then there are three separate measures, which should be the same but seldom, if ever, are. They are also among the numbers most subject to revision. Both for statistical reasons, and because of the inherent variability of the economy, the path of nominal GDP will inevitably wobble in the short term. To try to iron out these variations, by some misguided fine-tuning exercise, is contrary to the whole idea of a nominal framework. Even if it were possible, it would not be desirable. For some variation in the movement of output and income is almost certainly a necessary safety valve. None of the earlier students of business cycles ever thought that quarter-to-quarter stability was either possible or desirable.

Moreover it is not obvious how to translate an objective for nominal GDP into the kind of decisions that policy-makers actually take, such as whether to move interest rates up and down and by how much. Any attempt to use nominal GDP too directly is far too dependent on fallible forecasting models. Its real use, which can be very important, is as a guide to the medium term.

It is less often realised that many of the same difficulties apply to money supply targets. In virtually all modern economies, the Central Bank operates through its control of short-term interest rates. But the relationship between interest rates and the money supply is as uncertain as is the relationship of the quantity of money, however controlled and defined, to either the price level or to nominal GDP.

I do not want to go to the other extreme. A money supply target, in a country where financial institutions and practices have been fairly stable, can be a very useful aid to policy, as for instance in Germany. But it can never be an automatic pilot. Judgement is always required; in selecting the monetary rule, in deciding how to enforce it, and in assessing when short-term departures in either direction are acceptable.

A direct price-level objective has the great advantage of simplicity. Indeed if it had been followed in most of the post-war period we would almost certainly have benefited. Just as the Romans used to say, 'if you want peace, prepare for war', there is something to be said for the maxim 'if you want high employment, concentrate on price stability'.

Again such a rule is not nearly as automatic as it looks. There are many different price indices – producer prices, consumer prices and commodity prices, all of which can be constructed in various different ways. In the case of the UK RPI, a rise of 1 per cent in short-term interest rates adds more than one third per cent to the RPI. It would be quite absurd for the authorities to respond to the mechanistic effect of their own tightening by tightening further. There are also obviously one-off events – such as the Gulf War – which have a temporary shock effect on the price level, to which it might be perverse to react.

A price-level rule works best when there is some authority removed from day-to-day political pressure, such as an independent central bank, which is free to choose its own method, but which is held strictly to account for the results achieved in terms of price stability. The purest model of this at the time of writing is the contract between the New Zealand Central Bank and the New Zealand Treasury. A more conventional version consists of the rule that applies to the Bundesbank, which gives price stability as the overriding aim – and, *subject to that*, the duty to support other aspects of government economic policy.

A simple price-level objective may be more dubious when there are powerful recessionary tendencies. In the modern world, with its wage and price rigidities, it is possible that an unnecessarily severe recession could occur without prices actually falling. The monetary authorities might find a nominal GDP guideline more helpful in telling them when they can support activity by reducing interest rates without running an inflationary risk.

EXCHANGE RATE MECHANISM

The final option on the list, an exchange rate objective, is the clearest from the operational point of view. The exchange rate is a price available day by day and minute by minute in the markets. The range of policy choice is limited to short-term intervention in the foreign exchange markets and interest rate changes. Moreover, being readily understood, an exchange rate rule also has enormous expositional advantages over nominal GDP or money supply objectives. The study of the money supply or even of nominal GDP is inevitably very much a minority activity. Everyone remotely concerned with business can on the other hand understand the idea that if costs increase too quickly, British goods will be priced out of foreign markets, imports will displace British goods at home and bankruptcies and unemployment will result. It does not take the Nobel Prize in economics to see that if sterling is tied to, say, the Deutschmark, the long-run movement of prices of internationally traded goods and services cannot be too different in the two countries.

But nothing is without problems. An exchange rate target requires an anchor country with reasonably stable prices to which the domestic currency can be tied. For a long time the US dollar admirably fulfilled this function; under the Bretton Woods system governments had the illusion that they were pursuing domestic full-employment policies, whereas in fact they were following some form of international monetarism. Germany has been a very useful anchor country within Europe.

Another problem is that of non-traded goods, whose price is not directly governed by an exchange rate link. This is much more important in relation to very large economies such as the US and Japan, where the external sector is relatively speaking much smaller and for whom periods of neglect of the exchange rate are at least a partial option, which is not the case for middle-sized European countries. If a country like Britain or France could achieve long-run stability in the prices of all the many goods and services which are, or potentially can be, subject to international competition, this will be as good an approximation to price stability as is necessary or likely in the real world. Nor is it possible for wages and prices in the non-traded goods sector to take off in the long run in a completely different direction.

A more fundamental objection is that, as a matter of logic, not every country can follow an exchange rate objective. The anchor country has to have some domestic objective, whether a price-level or money supply or a nominal GDP rule, or some mixture of these. Some technical monetarists, such as Alan Walters, produce this point triumphantly as if it demolished the case for an exchange rate link. But of course it does nothing of the sort. It is obvious that an exchange rate objective is monetarism at one remove; and that is indeed its attraction. The question is – or should be – a severely practical one: which form of monetarism is the least difficult to operate successfully? If a country such as Germany, because of its track record, the independence of its Central Bank and many other factors, has anti-inflationary credibility, pegging other European currencies to the Deutschmark clearly makes sense.

The point of membership of the ERM, which is the obvious choice for an exchange-rate-based policy in today's world, is not that the Bundesbank is able to run UK monetary policy better than the UK. It is, first, that, for a mixture of historical, cultural and institutional reasons, Germany is able to maintain a reasonable degree of price stability with less difficulty than other European countries; second, that recognising this, the financial markets attach greater credibility to a monetary policy based on adherence to the Deutschmark link than they do to one which lacks it – and without financial market credibility it is hard to make a success of any monetary policy; and third, that within the ERM, companies know that if they fail to control their costs they are unlikely to be saved from bankruptcy by devaluation, and both companies and individuals will lower their inflationary expectations and act accordingly, Moreover, so long as the ERM exists, for one Community country to refuse to join it is likely to be interpreted, however wrongly, as that country wishing to retain the right to devalue – from which the markets (and UK companies) will draw their own conclusions.

It is of course possible to combine a number of different intermediate goals. Treasury officials during my time liked to give some weight to all of them, for instance to look at both domestic monetary indicators and the movement of the exchange rate. While a case can be made for this, the most obvious objection to such a combination is the lack of clear guidance that it gives to businessmen and the public generally.

Needless to say, none of these options is some sort of automatic pilot: all need to be operated with judgement. But one thing is clear. When all is said and done they are alternative means to common objectives. We can all make mistakes. But to go on heresy hunts against those whose intermediate monetary objectives are different from one's own would be laughable, if it were not for the damaging effect of such scholastic controversies on the British politico-economic debate and on the supposedly common-sense Tory Party in particular. Indeed one day somebody will write the history of the Conservative Party in terms of its disruption by economic controversy, from the Corn Laws in the last century to Empire Free Trade in the early part of this century and fixed versus floating exchange rates in our own time.

PRINCIPLES AND PRACTICES

One of the greatest challenges I had when I became Chancellor was in putting over the logical structure of the Government's approach. Debate in the UK seems to swing between market and academic technicalities – which ultimately and quite rightly lead even the most diligent layman to switch off – and vague partisan slogans. Serious argument on policy principles is much more difficult to launch, as I realised when I overheard people coming out of the Mais Lecture complaining that I had not announced any specific measures. The logical point I found most difficult to ram home was the distinction between 'first-order' and 'second-order' decisions. By this I mean the difference between the principles of economic policy – first order – and the precise means by which these principles are implemented – second order. (The analogy is with first and second orders of magnitude in the physical sciences.)

The point I sought to make was that the choice between the various methods of specifying the nominal framework was second order. The big choice was whether to aim at output and jobs directly, as in the post-war interpretation of Keynesianism, or whether to focus on nominal variables, such as money flows and prices. All of us who opted for the second alternative were monetarists of sorts, and the civil wars which have broken out between the varying schools are absurd.

The choice between the various methods of achieving nominal objectives must vary between time and place. It is perfectly sensible to target the money supply in some countries and at some times, and to target exchange rates at others. At the international level, say that of the Group of Seven, nominal GDP might come more into its own – especially when there is a serious risk of deflation or contraction, perhaps through the weakness of the banking system.

REACTION TO SHOCKS

This brings me to one omission in the Mais Lecture, which I intended to tackle on a subsequent occasion, but never in the end got round to doing. That is the reaction to shocks.

In general, as I argued, the task of monetary policy is to ensure reasonable price stability; and the task of supply-side policy is to promote growth and employment. There can nevertheless be periods of shock, such as the collapse of the American banking system in 1931, when the assignment might differ. A more vigorous monetary policy then might have prevented or reduced the fall in prices that took place and thus have mitigated the severity of the Great Depression. But it would be pedantic to treat an anti-depression financial policy simply in terms of the price level. It should, rather, be aimed at maintaining the national income, *but still in nominal terms.*

I very much doubt if we are ever likely to return to an inter-war state of affairs in which we can forget about inflation altogether. But since the international debt problem of the early 1980s and the more general problems of banking and corporate indebtedness, which emerged a decade later, the possibility of a systemic collapse has been lurking in the background. Were it to become a more imminent threat, a large part of the preventative and curative policy would need to be in the field of banking supervision, lender of last-resort operations and the like. The complete divorce of banking and corporate expertise from macroeconomics, inside both the Treasury and the Bank, and among outside commentators too, is a cross that the policy-maker has to bear.

THE COUNTER-REVOLUTION IN RETROSPECT

Looking back from the vantage point of the 1990s, it is possible to simplify further the difference between the post-war approach to macroeconomic policy and the counter-revolution of the 1980s.

The new approach of the 1980s was concerned with nominal variables; that is, amounts stated in cash. It did not pretend to guarantee particular rates of growth or employment. It laid down a financial policy tight enough to prevent any outside events, such as oil price explosions or an outbreak of union militancy, from acting as an inflationary trigger. On the other hand, had the circumstances arisen, the counter-revolutionary approach was meant to be as vigilant as Keynes could have desired in fighting off any cumulative contraction of national or global income. A satisfactory counter-revolution does not just go back to the status quo ante, but incorporates what is of value in the intervening revolution.

Stated in this way, a nominal framework covers both the normal case when macroeconomic policy is concerned with containing inflation and the more exceptional episodes when it is concerned to stop deflation or depression. Where my thinking did develop was in a growing belief that many of these tasks could be more readily accomplished by co-operative action among the main industrial countries rather than by each country confining itself to putting its own house in order, as in the early Reagan-Thatcher version. Such co-operation does not in my view require a European, still less a world, federal state. But it would *inter alia* be facilitated if the central banks of the main participating countries were independent of day-to-day control by governments.

CHAPTER TWENTY-FOUR

'WHERE WILL THE JOBS COME FROM?'

Unemployment – Cause and Cure · Job Losses of the 1980s · Pay and Jobs
An American Example · Unions or Employers? · Government's Role
Restart In, Workfare Out · Jobs in Boom and Recession

UNEMPLOYMENT – CAUSE AND CURE

It follows from the thesis set out in the Mais Lecture that the promotion of jobs and employment is not the Treasury's principal responsibility. But it does not follow from that that either the Thatcher Government as a whole or I as Chancellor was indifferent to the problem of unemployment. Indeed, as I have already indicated, we were firmly committed to the view that the key to improved economic performance was allowing markets of all kinds to work better. It is a commonplace that one of the most serious weaknesses of the British economy – one that it shares with most other European countries, but that is small consolation – is the way in which the labour market operates.

The diagnosis and treatment of unemployment shares one feature in common with monetary policy. It attracts every variety of crank and purveyor of misbegotten schemes. The contrast is that the cranks have even greater popular appeal when talking about jobs; and many supposedly down-to-earth political and business leaders share the approach of these cranks.

Most popular discussion of unemployment is governed by the idea that there is a limited amount of work to be done and that the wonders of modern technology threaten to produce a chronic and increasing shortage of work. Samuel Brittan has revived the term 'lump of labour fallacy' for this belief. But a more accurate label would be the 'lump-of-output fallacy'. For it assumes there is a limited amount of goods and services to be produced and that, if anything happens to enable these goods to be produced by fewer people, the result will be unemployment – unless there is compulsory work sharing, forced reduction in hours, early retirement and so on.

British industry was substantially overmanned during the 1970s, especially in manufacturing; and the strains of structural change were greatly increased by the emergence into the open of this disguised unemployment. The resulting dislocation engendered the deepest pessimism about the ability of the market economy to restore high employment.

This pessimistic mood exhibited the tendency, common to both booms and recessions, of extrapolating existing trends indefinitely into the future. This was as true of the recession of the early 1980s, which was not only both deeper than previous post-war economic downturns, but more uneven in its impact, as it was to be of the more prolonged recession of the early 1990s. There were calls from all sides to cut the supply of labour by reviving military conscription and other equally drastic measures. Some particularly sensational soothsayers talked of the need to educate people for a life of perpetual leisure. Their line of reasoning was both fallacious and debilitating.

The question I was most frequently asked at this time was 'where will the new jobs come from?' This succeeded in combining the lump-of-output fallacy with the collectivist fallacy of supposing that some central planner can or should be able to predict the future pattern of output and employment, which in fact depends on the unforeseeable development of technology and taste interacting in thousands of different markets.

Nevertheless it was a question that was put to me everywhere, not least by industrialists; the assumption being that, unless I could tell them precisely where the new jobs would come from, they would not believe there would be any respite from ever-increasing unemployment. It was clear by the time I became Chancellor that growth had resumed and that recovery from the recession was in train. But the immediate impact of technological progress, the failure of pay to adjust, greater efficiency, and the determination of businessmen not to return to the overmanning of the past seemed to be remorselessly rising unemployment. This was held to demonstrate that we had entered a new era in which unemployment would not only be a permanent feature but would rise inexorably.

JOB LOSSES OF THE 1980S

The first half of the 1980s provided particularly fertile soil for nonsense of this kind. By the spring of 1984 the economy was in its third consecutive year of growth, but recorded unemployment was rising for the fifth year in succession. Although the number of people in work had been rising since March 1983, the official unemployment figures, on which attention had always been focused, did not even start to fall until the second half of 1986. This translated into very considerable political pressure which increased as 1984 wore on.

Among the many prominent adherents of the lump-of-output fallacy was Francis Pym, the disaffected former Foreign Secretary whom Margaret had dropped from the Government after the 1983 election. In 1984 he brought out a book, which became something of a bestseller, part of which was devoted to promulgating this fallacy. It advocated reductions in the working day and in the working week, longer holidays, earlier retirement and artificially long training periods to raise the age of entry into industry. Pym cited 'some industrialists' who expected unemployment to reach nine million by the end of the century.

Francis Pym was quite the gloomiest politician I have ever met. He would dilate in the watches of the night on how democracy was doomed and the world was racing to perdition. But his despair over the outlook for jobs was shared by others of an altogether jollier disposition. Hector Laing, for example, the long-serving paternalist chief of the successful food manufacturing group, United Biscuits, and a strong supporter of the Conservative Party, persistently lobbied Margaret and myself to adopt an 'imaginative scheme' he had devised to stimulate employment. At the same time the Labour Party was advocating solving the problem by a massive expansion of public sector, particularly local authority, employment.

Schemes for reducing the size of the working population and increasing the numbers of those dependent on them seemed to me to be particularly perverse. To advocate early retirement at a time when the Fowler review of social security was rightly beginning to focus on radical solutions to the problem of the huge demands that existing policies would place on the taxpaying workforce, in a world in which the population was steadily ageing, was manifest lunacy. In the long run it clearly made a great deal more sense to raise the retirement age, rather than to reduce it.

Although I successfully resisted most of the work-sharing nostrums, the climate of the times, coupled with official Treasury resistance to anything that added to public spending, did cause the postponement of one common-sense reform: the abolition of the pensioners' earnings rule, which I was to announce in my last Budget in 1989.

The background to all this agitation was the shake-out in manufacturing described in Chapter 6, which led to the loss of two million manufacturing jobs which obviously could not be absorbed overnight in the expanding service sector. There tends to be a special resonance about the word 'manufacturing', and the quality of debate over this was not helped by the prevailing confusion between manufacturing output and manufacturing employment. Given the appalling degree of overmanning with which we had started, weakness in manufacturing employment was in fact likely to be a necessary precondition of strength in manufacturing output, which clearly depended on improved competitiveness.

It is true that I did not even pay lip-service to the contemporary House of Lords report on manufacturing, which advocated deliberate Government preference for that sector; and I was attacked as being anti-manufacturing because I declined to label any sector of the economy as uniquely meritorious. Yet without any special State stimulus UK manufacturing productivity during my Chancellorship rose more than in any other comparable period within living memory, and UK manufacturing output rose more than in any comparable period for a very long time. By contrast, during the lifetime of the previous Labour Government manufacturing output had actually fallen. There has seldom been a greater gulf between rhetoric and reality.

PAY AND JOBS

The labour market is more complicated than most other markets. But it is still true that, as in other markets, the higher the price the smaller the volume sold. Other things being equal, higher pay means fewer jobs. I have to confess to taking a moderate relish in bringing home to people unpalatable truths, as I did in my speeches on jobs in the mid-1980s. A moment's reflection is all that is needed to grasp the simple truth that for employers, the total real wage bill (including social security contributions and the cost of meeting employment protection legislation) is a cost which, if they cannot recover it in their selling prices, they will strive to reduce by economies in manpower.

As a Government, however, we were handicapped in explaining these elementary relationships by decades of propaganda about a supposed wage-price spiral in which the evils of excessive pay were seen almost entirely in terms of inflation rather than unemployment. The true causal chain in the 1970s – the most inflationary decade the UK has ever suffered – was different. High wage awards led to unemployment, which Governments felt obliged to combat by 'reflating' – that is, increasing spending in the economy. It was this that led to inflation, which made British goods uncompetitive in world markets. This was then offset by a falling exchange rate. The falling pound gave inflation a further boost, which encouraged still higher wage awards. Hence the supposed vicious circle. But the heart of the matter was Government financial accommodation of excessive pay awards – whether this was seen in terms of internal accommodation through lax monetary policy or external accommodation through allowing sterling to depreciate.

In fact, the relationship between pay and jobs was blindingly obvious. But to many, especially in the world of opinion formers, it appeared outrageous, provocative or even just a personal hobby horse of my own. Above all, it was seen as politically motivated: an attempt by the Government to escape the blame for unemployment and to pin it on the trade unions instead, just as previous Governments had sought to blame the unions for inflation. (In fact it was employers, not unions, that I consistently claimed were primarily responsible for determining pay.)

To demonstrate that it was none of these things, I decided to publish in January 1985 a Treasury Paper entitled: *The Relationship between Employment and Wages: Empirical Evidence for the UK.* It had a yellow cover and the unusual byline 'Review by Treasury Officials'. This was, of course, a correct description, in that the Treasury had done no first-hand research of its own into the subject, and could only bring together the research that had been conducted by others. But the purpose of publishing a paper explicitly by Treasury officials was to demonstrate that there was nothing political or opportunist about it: it was an analytical, if unpalatable, statement of the economic facts of life. The fact that it appeared at all demonstrated how great a change there had been in the intellectual climate. In the 1970s, the then deputy head of the Economic Section of the Treasury, Geoffrey Maynard, had found his life made impossible for merely suggesting that excessive real pay had something to do with high unemployment.

The central numerical estimate of the Yellow Paper – hedged with countless conditions and qualifications – was that a change of 1 per cent in real wages would be associated with a change the other way in employment of some 0.5 to 1 per cent, equivalent to 110,000 to 220,000 jobs. One still finds this numerical relationship as the best available guess in many much later studies.

The big question, of course, is why real wages rose too rapidly. Cannot employers prevent this from occurring? One theory, associated with Professor Richard Layard, is that unemployment has to be high enough to moderate wage earners' otherwise unrealistic expectations: it is thus the attempt to obtain excessive real wages that is responsible for high unemployment. Economists on the 'radical right' such as Patrick Minford put most emphasis on the level of social security benefits as the key. For this produced a 'floor' which discouraged workers, displaced by union monopoly, from pricing themselves into work in the non-unionised sector. It also provided the floor above which collective bargaining took place. I was fiercely attacked early in my Chancellorship for merely alluding to this relationship. While this was part of the story, another factor was that employers expected inflation to be higher than it turned out to be, thus expecting wage rises to be eroded more than they were. I have no doubt that more deep-seated cultural factors were also at work.

AN AMERICAN EXAMPLE

It is often forgotten how frequently the ballooning US Budget deficit was held up by domestic critics as an example for the British Government to follow. The hope was that this would stimulate growth and employment in the UK. These sentiments were uttered at the very same time that the harmful effects of the US deficit became a subject of condemnation at one international meeting after another. The American Budget deficit was applauded in the US by the more extreme Reaganites and in the UK by their less comprehending camp followers, such as *The Sunday Times*, as a magnificent example of supply-side economics. It was also warmly espoused by the Labour Party as a good old-fashioned Keynesian demand stimulus. An astonishing number of people got drawn into praising the US deficit, including at one time even the Duke of Edinburgh.

There was some superficial evidence to support this view. American real GDP shot up by about 6 per cent in 1984, and although the Fed then reimposed the brakes, there were none of the 're-entry' problems that Britain and other countries customarily experienced in returning from an unsustainable to a sustainable rate of growth. Nor was there any notable re-acceleration of inflation in the US, which until 1989 rarely strayed outside the corridor of 3 to 4.5 per cent a year. Long-term bond yields, where the effects of deficit finance were supposed to show themselves first, rose in 1984 and then subsequently fell in the remainder of the 1980s to around 8 or 9 per cent – less than in the UK – even though the President and Congress never succeeded in seriously tackling the deficit.

The sharp rise in the dollar undoubtedly helped to contain inflation during the most rapid phase of American growth, however embarrassing it was for other countries and for US exporters. But the policy mix of currency appreciation, large budget deficits and tight monetary policy, which some purveyors of instant wisdom urged on us, was not sustainable for more than a short period. Competitive appreciation is almost as self-defeating as competitive depreciation.

The US experience did, however, strengthen my view that monetary rather than fiscal policy was the key counter-inflationary weapon. The main harm inflicted by the high US Budget deficits, which were not financed by 'printing money', was long term. The burden of Federal Government debt-service spending steadily rose, which was among the factors which made it difficult for the Americans to take the same lead after the collapse of Communism in Europe that they previously took in the Marshall Plan period that followed the collapse of Nazism.

In any case, as soon as Ronald Reagan had been re-elected as President in November 1984, the US Administration abruptly stopped defending the Budget deficit and accepted that it was its number one economic problem. This abrupt change of tune was signalled by Don Regan, and preceded his imminent replacement as Treasury Secretary by James Baker. President Reagan had always believed in a balanced Budget, and blamed the deficit on the spending proclivities of the Congress. He defended his refusal to close the gap by increasing taxes, as we had done in 1981, by arguing that under the US system, with its separation of powers, any extra revenue raised would only have been spent by Congress. While there may have been some truth in this, it was undoubtedly a highly convenient belief.

From the point of view of employment, the US Budget deficit was a red herring. A superior US employment record went back to well before its Budget deficit began to climb. In the ten years up to 1983, as I pointed out in the Mais Lecture:

> ... the total number of people in work in Western Europe has fallen. In the US over the same period the number of people in work has risen by over fifteen million. This sharp contrast has not been the product of macro policy. It has been almost entirely due to the more efficient, competitive, innovative and adaptive labour and goods markets in the United States. Over the past ten years, the workers of Western Europe have seen their real earnings rise by around an eighth; over the same period their American counterparts have been prepared to accept a small reduction in real earnings. Relatively free markets, the spirit of enterprise, and workers who prefer to price themselves into jobs rather than out of them, are a powerful engine of employment. There is indeed an important lesson to be learned from the American experience, but it has nothing to do with the deficit.

UNIONS OR EMPLOYERS?

When the Thatcher Government came to office in 1979, the most obvious influence in pricing workers out of jobs was union power. For all their protestations about unemployment, unions were primarily concerned with those workers who already had jobs and (in their judgement) were likely to retain them.

The issue is too often presented in Treasury documents and elsewhere in terms of broad national averages. But the demand for labour depends as much upon relative as on average real wages. Pay did not adjust sufficiently to occupational, sectoral and regional differences in the supply and demand for workers. The long-standing preference among trade unions for centralised pay bargaining and nationwide rates of pay is one reason why heavy unemployment in some areas during the 1980s coincided with labour shortages, particularly of skilled labour, in others. Moreover these shortages, by depressing overall output, further aggravated joblessness everywhere.

A reduction in union power was an important aim of Conservative policy even though it was couched in the language of checking abuses, democratising procedures and so on. Union power was duly reduced by a series of Acts covering strike procedures, picketing, the closed shop and much else. Just as important was facing up to a number of strikes, above all the 1984–85 coal strike, and providing police support for employers who stood up to intimidation, such as Rupert Murdoch at Wapping. The development of the less unionised service sector and the mushrooming of small firms all further served to weaken trade union influence. Its main redoubt is now the State sector.

As the 1980s wore on I became more and more convinced that employers rather than unions were responsible for pay settlements incompatible with high employment. British employers had a marked preference for cutting unit labour costs by cutting payrolls rather than by cutting pay rates. Like the trade unions, their concern was with their employees rather than with those who had left their employment, and they felt inhibited by guilt in taking a tough line on pay at a time when profits were rising rapidly and top managers were paying themselves substantial increases.

Labour market rigidity is a weakness in many European economies and not just the UK. The curious feature on this side of the Atlantic is that an employer who wishes to cut his labour costs evidently finds it easier to persuade his workforce to accept large-scale redundancies rather than to forego a pay rise – let alone to take a pay cut. This is in sharp contrast to the US, where the labour market is more flexible, both in terms of pay and of labour mobility. American employers are also much less inhibited than their UK counterparts either by rising profits or by their own pay levels when it comes to taking a firm line on wages.

GOVERNMENT'S ROLE

In a market economy and a free society it is plainly a matter for business and industry itself to determine rates of pay, which in turn in the long run determine the level of employment; and the responsibility of Government is essentially to provide the right overall economic climate. But there were some specific areas in which Government action was needed, and to a considerable (although incomplete) extent that action was taken.

One such area was that of the long-established statutory Wages Councils, which set minimum pay rates in certain low-pay industries. These were not, as I would have liked, abolished; but their powers were greatly limited and (outside agriculture) those under twenty-one were removed from their scope altogether. It is not surprising if unqualified and untrained youngsters find difficulty in getting started in the world of work, if the first rung of the ladder of employment is removed by law.

On other fronts, Geoffrey Howe early on made unemployment benefit taxable – a brave step politically, but essential if the 'why work?' problem was to be solved – while the National Insurance reforms in my Budgets of 1985 and 1989 made it more worthwhile both for people with a low earnings capacity to take a job and for employers to employ them. Again, Norman Fowler's social security reforms shifted the basis of means-tested benefits from pre-tax to post-tax incomes. This meant that, although the combined marginal rate of tax, National Insurance and benefit withdrawal could be very high (a necessary evil if benefits are to be concentrated on those whose need is greatest), at least it could not reach (and indeed exceed) 100 per cent as it could before. Another way in which the Social Security Act of 1985 helped was that early leavers from occupational pension schemes were entitled to take their pension rights with them to a new employer. This eliminated a major discouragement to job mobility.

RESTART IN, WORKFARE OUT

One of the most important innovations of the 1980s was at that time called the 'Counselling Initiative and Jobstart Allowance'. This was the brainchild of David Young, the new Employment Secretary, and was launched nationally after the success of local pilot projects. Every single person on the register who had been unemployed for more than a year was invited to an interview at the local Job Centre and offered either a job or a place on a training scheme. It paid those prepared to take a job paying less than £80 a week a temporary £20 a week 'Jobstart Allowance' to top up the wage. David Young generously records in his own memoirs that 'the Treasury' – meaning the Chancellor and Chief Secretary – 'gave me all I asked for, except that interviewing and counselling had to be called "Restart" and the allowance "Jobstart".'

Of all the schemes introduced by the Government, 'Restart' had the most marked effect on the unemployment figures. Over two million interviews were carried out each year. Of those who took the short course offered, 60 per cent were in – or about to start – a job within six weeks. Others found jobs unaided when faced with what they saw as the threat of a Restart interview; and there were those who decided they were not looking for work after all and left the register. The scheme not only helped those who were genuinely looking for work, but weeded out those who were not – either because they had decided to take early retirement, or because they were already hard at work in the black economy.

Both Margaret and I were also interested in developing a fully fledged 'workfare' scheme in which the unemployed would be required to work rather than to do nothing, by the simple device of making the payment of benefit conditional on participation in a 'workfare' scheme. This was an American idea, which was subsequently taken up by Michael Heseltine as part of his long-running campaign for the Party Leadership. Under the federal constitution of the United States, this is a matter which comes within the authority of the individual State – something the centralists of Brussels would doubtless regard with horror if it were proposed for Europe. As a result, it operates in some States and not others, and better in some than in others. But there is ample evidence that it can work very well, not only in economic terms but in human terms, too. A number of meetings were held, under Margaret's chairmanship; but unfortunately an alliance on the issue between Norman Fowler, as Social Security Secretary, and David Young, as Employment Secretary, produced so many alleged practical difficulties that the idea was dropped. It is surely time to pick it up again.

JOBS IN BOOM AND RECESSION

I was always convinced that, once economic growth had attained sufficient momentum, smaller businesses had started to grow rapidly, and confidence recovered, larger established companies would start to recruit again. This took longer than I had expected because of the slowness with which wages responded to market pressures. But after years in which many feared that nothing would reverse the upward trend, unemployment suddenly started to fall dramatically. It fell from over three million (on current definitions) in mid-1986 to 2.8 million at the end of that year, 2.3 million at the end of 1988, 1.8 million in 1989 and 1.6 million (or 5.6 per cent) at its low point in early 1990.

Unfortunately the boom proved unsustainably vigorous, which inevitably exacerbated the subsequent recession. Clearly some, although I do not believe all, of the earlier fall in unemployment was cyclical. But none of this in any way undermines the important pay-and-jobs link. No sensible exponent of that link denies that unemployment can fall in a boom or rise in a slump. The point is that the rigidities of the British pay culture (a) increase the cyclical fluctuations in unemployment and (b) raise the underlying level of unemployment over the cycle as a whole.[21]

There was, moreover, one important silver lining to the sharp rise in unemployment in the recession of the early 1990s. Productivity, after a brief pause, resumed its rapid increase, especially in manufacturing. Precisely because there was much less overmanning to reduce this time round, the gain was even more impressive than that achieved in the recession of the early 1980s. This strongly suggests that the reforms of the 1980s have indeed improved the economy's long-term growth potential.

[21] Some economists would say that during my period as Chancellor, unemployment started off above the so-called NAIRU and ended up below it. The NAIRU stands for the 'Non-Accelerating Inflation Rate of Unemployment'. But since we do not have much idea of what the NAIRU is, I do not find it a helpful concept. To give an example: there was in the 1970s a great deal of suppressed unemployment due to overmanning. When this came out into the open was there really a sudden increase in the NAIRU which would normally be interpreted as increased malfunctioning of the British labour market? Richard Layard attempts to cope with such dilemmas in his magnum opus by envisaging a whole family of NAIRUs – a short-to-medium-term one, which reflects such shocks, and a long-term one reflecting underlying economic behaviour. But even that can change. All of which confirms my instinctive suspicion of the whole concept.

CHAPTER TWENTY-FIVE

THE MYTH OF A MONETARIST GOLDEN AGE

Far From Plain Sailing · What is Money? · Monetary Policy Reviewed · Transactions Balances · Black Box Monetarism?

FAR FROM PLAIN SAILING

I have set out the purposes and limitations of monetary policy as I saw them when I became Chancellor in an earlier chapter. The difficult task was to find a practical form in which to embody these principles.

There is a myth that all was plain sailing in the conduct of monetary policy until I began shadowing the Deutschmark in 1987 – or at least until my announcement at the Mansion House of the suspension of the £M3 target in the autumn of 1985. The truth is very different. It was never plain sailing, neither in Geoffrey's time nor mine.

According to this myth, monetary growth was kept within its target range until the policy was wantonly abandoned in either 1985 or 1987 to launch an irresponsible boom. Indeed, this appears to be what many students are nowadays taught at university; and something like it has been adopted for political purposes by many commentators who are far from being monetarists, but are glad of any stick with which to beat the Government of that period. It is not hard to demonstrate that this convenient picture represents a tendentious rewriting of history and distortion of the facts. If there is to be any real understanding of this difficult but important aspect of policy, it is necessary to take the trouble to get at the truth.

The Thatcher Government took over the targeting of £M3 from its Labour predecessor and maintained a target range for this aggregate during its first seven or eight years in office. But, contrary to the myth of a monetarist golden age, the target was hit only twice – in Geoffrey's last year and in my first (1982/83 and 1983/84). In every other year it was overshot, usually by a wide margin. It was overshot despite a large increase in the target range by Geoffrey in 1982 and an even larger increase by myself in 1986, in one last attempt to make something out of the aggregate. The problems with it were already apparent as far back as 1980 when I was Financial Secretary, and have been explained in Part One of this book.

To recapitulate briefly: the poor performance of the original target aggregate £M3 (which consisted essentially of cash and bank deposits) and the consequent need to supplement it with other indicators, were not surprising in the light of the changes taking place in the financial markets as a result of deregulation. The abolition of exchange control had exposed the London financial market to international competition, while the Latin American debt crisis persuaded the banks that they would be better off at home, competing with the building societies for mortgage business for the first time. At the same time, the building societies, gradually breaking free from their interest-rate cartel, were beginning to compete aggressively with the banks for deposits. Both were offering increasingly generous terms in competing for the same business; yet £M3 did not even include building society deposits. As inflation tumbled and real interest rates turned positive, money was left with the banks not for spending purposes but to earn a worthwhile return. As a result of all these developments, the money statistics were constantly changing their meaning.

WHAT IS MONEY?

Doubts had arisen both about the relationship of £M3 to inflation, and about its appropriateness as a definition of money. In the first place, underlying inflation had plummeted from 16.5 per cent in the last quarter of 1979 to 6.75 per cent in the last quarter of 1982, despite a massive overshoot in monetary growth, as measured by £M3. In the second place, it was increasingly argued that the £M3 definition was too wide. As real interest rates rose, bank as well as building society deposits took on many of the characteristics of financial investments and were much more a home for savings than a means of spending. This school therefore advocated a move to so-called narrow money – that is, cash plus only those balances likely to be used in settling transactions. Some of the monetarists closest to Margaret Thatcher, such as Alan Walters and Patrick Minford, belonged to the latter group. And there was no-one more contemptuous of 'your M3' than Karl Brunner, the Swiss-American economist of whom Margaret was such an admirer.

In the light of all this, Geoffrey Howe decided to change the monetary target in his 1982 Budget (while I was at Energy), introducing two new target aggregates alongside £M3: a measure of broad money later known as M4 and the narrow aggregate, M1 composed of bank accounts bearing no interest. To his great delight, Geoffrey at last hit his targets – for all three aggregates – in 1982/83. But this was only after he had set a revised target range which, in the case of £M3, was nearly twice that laid down in the original MTFS.

Moreover, this success had been achieved in part by a device known as over-funding. Basically it meant the Government selling more gilt-edged securities than it needed to do to finance its own Budget deficit, in order to attract money that would otherwise have been left with the banks. It was a peculiarly British practice, being unknown in other countries, such as the US and Germany, and of questionable monetary significance.

In the light of all these problems, the Government had begun to place increasing reliance on other financial evidence, including in particular the exchange rate. Although it was not yet pursuing an exchange rate target, it had experienced the effective discipline exerted by a high exchange rate during the squeeze of 1980/81. That, indeed, is why, during my time as Financial Secretary, we had been rightly prepared to let £M3 overshoot its range. But it is fair to say that by the time I became Chancellor monetary policy had degenerated into a business of muddling through, with avowed targets bearing less and less relation to actual policy, and having declining influence on expectations.

MONETARY POLICY REVIEWED

Accordingly, when I first became Chancellor in June 1983, I asked Peter Middleton to organise a number of official papers on macroeconomic strategy, including a review of monetary policy, and in particular a review of whether or not we should join the ERM.

The ERM aspect was covered by a paper from Geoffrey Littler, the Second Permanent Secretary in charge of Overseas Finance, who was one of the very few senior Treasury officials at that time in favour of ERM membership. After recalling Margaret's earlier rejection of the idea in 1982 the paper went on to state that the climate for sterling's participation in the ERM was more favourable than it had been in recent years. It referred to the benefit that France had derived from ERM membership, and went on to argue that the case for sterling's participation would be strengthened if a number of conditions were satisfied.

First, the oil market should continue to be relatively settled; second, UK and German policies and economies should continue to converge; third, a clearer way should be seen through the negotiations currently going on over the Community Budget; and fourth, and most important, that the dollar should fall against the Deutschmark. The reasoning was that the dollar was at that time unrealistically high and that it was bound to – and indeed should – fall against the Deutschmark. But when it did, sterling would inevitably fall part of the way with it, making it difficult if not impossible to maintain its ERM parity.

The paper suggested that these conditions might well be fulfilled some time in 1984. In fact it took somewhat longer for the foreign exchange market condition to be fulfilled. The dollar continued its vertiginous rise and did not turn down until 1985. The paper concluded that, in the meantime, private discussions with the Germans about practical UK-German co-operation might be desirable to prepare for membership. I did in fact initiate such discussions, but that was some while later.

At the meeting I held in the summer of 1983 to discuss the ERM paper, the other Treasury mandarins were far less enthusiastic, not least because by that time considerable intellectual capital had been tied up in the existing domestically based policy. Nevertheless, they were well aware – and this had been amply covered in the papers on domestic monetary policy – that there were considerable uncertainties over causal relationships in domestic monetary policy.

The outcome of the review, which had of course been conducted in close collaboration with the Bank, was somewhat inconclusive. There was general disillusion with £M3, but no interest in Monetary Base Control. Here the Bank's hostility, coupled with the considered rejection in 1981, were decisive. Discomfited by the unsatisfactory nature of the outcome but still not entirely clear in my mind as to the best way ahead, I arranged a couple of private meetings in the summer of 1983 with Gordon Pepper, whom I had known for over a decade, and who was at that time the leading monetary analyst in the City.

Pepper was scornful of broad money and favoured going over to Monetary Base Control (MBC). He knew, however, that the Bank, which would have to operate MBC, was very hostile to it; and agreed that in those circumstances to impose it on the Bank would be asking for trouble. He saw some value in using M0, whose composition is essentially the same as that of the monetary base, as an indicator; but in general felt that nothing short of full-blooded MBC would do, a view that he has consistently reiterated since.

Pepper was particularly derisory of £M3. Its link with fiscal policy, which so much appealed to Treasury and Bank officials, was seen by him as a neo-Keynesian contamination of monetary policy. Pepper also claimed that the Bank favoured £M3 because its close links with the PSBR meant that any excessive growth in the aggregate could be attributed as much to failures of

Treasury as of Bank control. I pointed out that the official preference for £M3 was based not only on the link with fiscal policy, but also on the fact that during the Heath inflation it was the movement of £M3, rather than that of M1, which had provided the warning. Pepper replied that M0 had provided the earliest warning of all.

TRANSACTIONS BALANCES

Inside the official Treasury, Terry Burns was almost as sceptical as Gordon Pepper about the continued value of targeting £M3. But most officials were nervous about downgrading £M3, which was the only aggregate accepted by the financial markets. Indeed, both the City and the financial Press were incapable, at that time, of conceiving that 'money' could mean anything else – a form of myopia that is not wholly eradicated, even today. In the light of this, I was not yet willing to abandon broad money targets altogether, but insisted on having a separate target for narrow money – that is the kind of money that is actually used for settling transactions. Here I was at one with Alan Walters (who had by then left the Government service).

After some internal debate we chose M0 – to all intents and purposes cash. It was undoubtedly a primitive measure of money, but its track record showed an impressively stable relationship with Nominal GDP. I announced tentatively in my first Mansion House Speech, on 28 October 1983 that 'M0 could have a more important part to play in monitoring monetary conditions'.

BLACK BOX MONETARISM?

As the account I have just given shows, nearly all the reputable monetarist gurus – with the exception of the City analyst Tim Congdon – so far from urging broad money targets on me criticised me for giving too much influence to broad money in general and £M3 in particular. The enthusiasm of the hard-core monetarists for M0 was to some extent based on wishful thinking, since many of them hoped it would be a staging post to Monetary Base Control, even though I had made it clear that that was not what I had in mind. The problem, however, was that M0 went down very badly with City opinion and financial journalists; and the Bank of England initially treated the measure with open contempt. Non-monetarist and anti-monetarist economists (who are in a majority) found a M0 target even more absurd than monetary targets in general.

This was because it consisted overwhelmingly of notes and coins. Students had long been taught that cash was only the 'small change of the monetary system'. People find it hard to believe that the amount of spending had anything to do with people's supply of ready cash. If people needed more notes and coins they could always get them by drawing on their bank, building society, or Post Office savings accounts. There were complaints, too, that using M0 was what was termed a 'black box' form of monetarism. In other words, however good its track record as an indicator, there was no way in which M0 growth could be said to be the cause of inflation. An excessively large increase in M0 was no doubt a sign of inflationary pressure, but could not be the cause of it.

This objection missed the point. Had there been a monetary aggregate with a clear and predictable causal connection with inflation, I should certainly have used it. The whole problem was that no such aggregate existed.

It was clearly a disadvantage of M0 that it was not much of an advance indicator. Some of its strongest supporters claimed that it gave a very short lead. But I always regarded it as essentially an up-to-date contemporaneous indicator – which was a great deal better than the tardy and uncertain figures for Nominal GDP itself, even though by the time M0 was clearly signalling danger, the economy would already be experiencing inflationary pressures. A rather more serious shortcoming was the failure of M0 to give a true picture at one or two crucial points, notably in early 1988.

In time it became clear that the real problem with M0 was that it lacked street credibility. That meant that none of the feedback mechanisms were in operation. The achievement of the M0 target – or even its undershooting – had no great effect on inflationary expectations. Here it was at the opposite end of the spectrum to the exchange rate target, where the mechanisms at work are much more obvious and, so long as the official commitment is credible, the feedback is very powerful indeed.

CHAPTER TWENTY-SIX

THE STERLING CRISIS OF 1984/85

The Trauma of July 1984 · Ours Not to Reason Why · The July Hike Undone
The Ingham Run on the Pound · Damage Limitation, January 1985

THE TRAUMA OF JULY 1984

While M0 lacked credibility and thus the ability to influence the markets, the exchange rate manifestly had it. That in itself was reason enough to pay increasing attention to the exchange rate.

In my first year at Number 11 sterling had gradually fallen back somewhat from its pre-election peak, but it still remained above the low point of early 1983. Moreover, from early in 1984 the pound had levelled off against all major currencies apart from the dollar. So it was reasonable to speak in terms of a rising dollar rather than a falling pound. With underlying inflation moving gradually downwards from 5 per cent towards 4 per cent, I was content to leave base rates fluctuating around 9 per cent, where they had been since June 1983.

The first real trauma did not occur until July 1984. Three sources of upward pressure on base rates developed very suddenly. The combination of rapid growth in the US and anxiety about the continuing large Federal deficit led to a sharp rise in US short-term interest rates between May and July; and the dollar started on one of its upward spurts. The financial markets began to worry about the miners' strike and the threat of a national dock strike (which in the end proved short lived, starting in August and ending in September). Lastly, the money supply figures for June were erratically high and, in the prevailing nervous atmosphere, increased financial market anxieties. When the Bank of England made a 'technical adjustment in the profile of its bill dealing rates' on 25 June, it took the unusual step of making a statement saying that it saw no need on monetary policy grounds for a general increase in interest rates. Within a few days that statement had backfired.

On 5 July sterling fell sharply against all currencies, not just the US dollar, and I increased base rates up to 10 per cent. On 9 July, the dock strike was called and on 10 July the shock-horror money supply figures appeared. During those few days three-month market interest rates shot up to almost 12 per cent, as the money markets had anticipated that the Government would respond to events by raising interest rates to defend sterling. The markets' move steadied the pound, but left the 'authorities' (as the Treasury and the Bank are collectively known) with a level of market interest rates quite incompatible with 10 per cent base rates. There had of course been many previous occasions when sterling weakness had forced the Government to raise interest rates. But this occasion, when the market had acted first, was a disconcerting new experience, subtly different from past periods of pressure.

There was a feeling of impotence in the air at a meeting I held at the Treasury on Wednesday, 11 July. The Bank recommended accepting the rise in interest rates. Otherwise the credibility of monetary policy would be put into question and sterling would fall sharply. They pointed out that in the circumstances they were powerless to influence the market by the usual mechanisms. They therefore favoured a two-point rise in base rates to 12 per cent, which would have the bonus effect of allowing large sales of gilts to be made, thereby reducing £M3 growth.

The Treasury mandarins, however, were unhappy with the Bank of England's advice, on three grounds. First they did not like being dictated to by the foreign exchange market in this way. In particular, they feared that if we let the markets do this to us once, it would set a most undesirable precedent, and we would have lost control of interest rates altogether. Second, they did not believe there was any objective reason why interest rates should go any higher – indeed they would have liked on 'economic' grounds to see them lower. And third, they did not want to see the option of a lower pound, which on balance they regarded as the lesser evil, ruled out in this way.

I had of course warned Margaret of the likely need for a further rise in interest rates, and told her that I was holding a meeting with the Bank that morning to discuss the situation. Halfway through the meeting my office heard from Number 10 that Alan Walters was over on one of his occasional visits to London (he was by then living in Washington) and the Prime Minister would like him to join us. I replied that he was welcome to do so. When he arrived I asked him for his opinion and he suggested splitting the difference. He saw no monetary reason for an increase in interest rates, but because of the pressures from the US, he thought it might be right to go up by one percentage point. That seemed to me almost guaranteed to get the worst of both worlds, and would certainly fail to get funding restarted. I believed we had no option but to raise interest rates enough to regain control of the situation, as the Bank had recommended.

The Treasury mandarins reluctantly concurred. I fully understood their reluctance. I did not relish being dictated to by the money market any more than they did, and subsequently commissioned a paper on how we might regain control. But I had no doubt at the time that I had to bite the bullet. I then went to see Margaret, to give her the unwelcome news. She accepted it with ill grace, expressing the desire that we should get interest rates down again as soon as possible.

OURS NOT TO REASON WHY

There was still the problem of how to present the two-point rise, which I raised at the end of the meeting at the Treasury. The financial Press did not seem to realise what was novel about the situation and treated it as an old-fashioned sterling crisis. Yet in previous such crises the authorities had, or felt they had, a choice of three responses to pressure on the pound: intervention (i.e. the Bank of England buying sterling), letting the exchange rate take the strain, and raising interest rates. Given that choice, I would have liked to try intervention; Treasury officials would have preferred sterling to take some of the strain, at least initially. But as things were, we did not – as I saw it – have the luxury of a debate: the financial markets had already imposed their own rise in interest rates.

At that time it would have been difficult to justify, on the domestic grounds we customarily used, a rise which took real interest rates to their highest levels since the War. On the other hand, had we given pressure on sterling as the reason (which, as I have indicated, was in any case true only indirectly), it would have been an open invitation to the financial markets to repeat the episode. As the main event in the foreign exchange markets – then and for many months to come – was the seemingly irresistible rise of the dollar, which put downward pressure on all other currencies, it was unlikely to be long before another such occasion arose.

Inevitably, I discussed the background to the July interest rate hike in my Mansion House Speech of 18 October 1984. This was to be my last significant utterance as an unreconstructed parochial monetarist. I reiterated the standard Treasury line:

> It is the monetary aggregates that are of central relevance to judging monetary conditions and determining interest rates. That has always been our

> policy and it remains so. We take the exchange rate into account when its behaviour suggests that the domestic monetary indicators are giving a false reading, which they are not. Provided monetary conditions are kept under firm control, excessive movements, whether in the money or exchange markets in response to outside influences, will tend to correct themselves relatively quickly.

This line was a fiction even when I uttered it, as the exchange rate played a much larger part in policy than I was prepared to admit in public. But there was a genuine difficulty about any alternative presentation. The Commons Treasury Committee and others were continually asking Ministers and senior officials who came before it what our exchange rate policy was; and outside the ERM it was a very difficult question to answer. The idea of giving weight to the exchange rate as a factor in monetary policy decisions, but not having an exchange rate target, was extremely hard to put across. In late 1984, opinion veered between attributing to the Government a secret sterling target and believing that we were completely indifferent as to where the pound went.

THE JULY HIKE UNDONE

Meanwhile, the weeks following the July interest rate hike had seen a welcome calm return to the foreign exchange markets, and I was able to undo 1.5 points of the two-point rise, in stages, by the middle of August. Despite this reduction, throughout the autumn of 1984 the advice I continued to receive from both Treasury officials and the Bank of England was that monetary conditions remained tight, and that there was a convincing case for lower interest rates. Although I queried the advice at the time, I mistakenly accepted it, and authorised a further one percentage point reduction to 9.5 per cent, in two stages, in November. My misgivings were based partly on a general sense that we were being imprudent, but more particularly because sterling was continuing to slide – something to which I felt the Treasury mandarins gave too little weight.

Pressure for an increase in interest rates did not start to build up again until the publication on 11 December of another large and erratic increase in £M3 in November, this time attributable for the most part to a surge in personal borrowing to finance the massive oversubscription of the British Telecom flotation. This unsettled the market, and in the last few weeks of the year, ominously, the pound, which had hitherto suffered from the superdollar no more than any other currency, started to slide against other currencies, too.

In the middle of December, I decided to take a long weekend off and spend it with Thérèse and the children at a hotel on the Kent coast. Although it might seem rather odd to go to the seaside in December, the sea breezes on the beach were wonderfully invigorating and the children were able to swim in the indoor pool at the hotel. It was from the hotel that I telephoned Peter Middleton to tell him that I thought events in the foreign exchange markets were looking increasingly dangerous and that it might be necessary to raise interest rates. He replied that there was no need to worry and that I should concentrate on enjoying my brief holiday. I was soon to regret having allowed him to talk me out of an interest rate rise in this way. For the result was a larger increase than anything I had in mind a few weeks later. Although sterling stabilised before the markets closed for the Christmas holidays, it began to weaken again when trading resumed in January.

THE INGHAM RUN ON THE POUND

One of the most self-defeating aspects of the Thatcher regime was Margaret's excessive and increasing reliance on Bernard Ingham, her long-serving Press Secretary and personal confidant. A blunt, sometimes thuglike, xenophobic Yorkshireman, and inordinately proud of it, Ingham became a tremendous admirer and promoter of the Prime Minister and her activities; but he never escaped from his Labour background sufficiently to understand the market economy – still less to persuade others of its merit. He was only really at home with the tabloids – above all the *Sun* – and once rebuked a newly appointed Press Secretary of mine for wasting time lunching with a senior *Financial Times* writer, instead of cultivating those who really mattered.

At quite an early stage, Margaret decided that she had no time to read the newspapers during the week. Instead, Ingham would get into Number 10 very early each morning, go through the papers himself, and prepare her a crisply written press summary. This had a selection and a slant that was very much his own. It would usually start with the *Sun*, the paper he himself was closest to and which he had taught Margaret represented the true views of the man on the street. It was also the paper whose contents he could most readily influence. This led to a remarkable circularity. Margaret would sound off about something, Ingham would then translate the line into *Sun*-ese and feed it to that newspaper, which would normally use it. This would then take pride of place in the news summary he provided for Margaret, who marvelled at the unique rapport she evidently enjoyed with the British people.

In his own way, Ingham was an outstandingly competent and thoroughly professional operator; but his successes were obtained at a high price. Margaret Thatcher was promoted, but her political and economic beliefs were not – with the exception of a truculent chauvinism, which was originally a caricature of her views but eventually became almost indistinguishable from her own as she started to live up to her caricature. Moreover, his concept of promoting her included denigrating her Cabinet colleagues. This not only irked the colleagues, but was plainly unhelpful to the Government as a whole.

He was unhelpful in other ways, too. In private, Margaret was in the habit of letting off steam in a thoroughly indiscreet and intemperate way, going far beyond the rather attractive outspokenness that marked her utterances in public. Ingham frequently failed to discern the distinction, and relayed to a wide audience sentiments that should never have been given a public airing. His view of the relative importance of her political colleagues and himself was well illustrated by the story he himself told on television in the wake of her resignation in 1990. Margaret, in her last days at Number 10, was evidently bitterly lamenting how the Party had turned against her. 'Don't worry about *them*, Prime Minister,' he claimed to have told her, seeking to comfort her, '*We're* right behind you.' That his perspective could be so distorted as to say this in the final stages of a leadership election in which it was the colleagues ('them') who had the voting power, and the courtiers, on whose behalf he spoke, who had none, is in its way even more revealing.

There is no doubt that he served her with dog-like devotion for eleven long years. But he reinforced all her worst characteristics and, unwittingly, did her a profound disservice. Willie Whitelaw, seeing this clearly, several times sought to persuade her that the time had come to find a new Press Secretary, but she would never hear of it. Although it was the last thing Ingham wanted, he undoubtedly contributed to her downfall.

This digression may seem a long way removed from the currency turmoils of the winter of 1984–85. But alas it is not: the continuing upward surge of the dollar in the first few months of 1985 would have made life difficult for sterling in any event, but matters were made far worse by a self-inflicted wound suffered by the Government, thanks to Ingham.

There had been no intervention to support sterling in December and very early January. It seemed to me folly to squander our then very limited reserves against a strong adverse tide of sentiment. Unfortunately the pound was given a downward shove by a story in *The Sunday Times* (a paper to which the business world tends to pay exaggerated attention) on Sunday, 6 January 1985:

> According to the highest sources in Whitehall yesterday, Mrs Thatcher, supported by the Chancellor of the Exchequer, Nigel Lawson, is determined to maintain a 'hands off' policy even if the pound falls to parity (£1 = $1). Mrs Thatcher, according to the sources, believes the pound will eventually find its own level. The Government's decision last summer to raise rates to protect the pound is now officially regarded as a mistake, and not to be repeated.

The story came from Ingham, who was aware of Margaret's theoretical distaste for 'bucking the [foreign exchange] market' and her hatred of high interest rates, but had concocted out of them a false account not only of my views, but even of hers.

Although Margaret was in principle a free floater, she was in practice schizoid about the issue. She deeply disliked a falling pound, particularly against the dollar. Her fixation with the United States made her share to the full the conventional exaggerated attention accorded to the sterling/dollar rate. Anyone who thought she would be indifferent to a 'one dollar pound' did not know the lady. She was most definitely not Milton Friedman in drag.

Predictably, *The Sunday Times* story knocked sterling not only against the dollar, but against the Deutschmark and other currencies as well. A good set of money supply figures was set aside early the following week as the market concluded that the Government was unwilling to defend the pound. I protested strongly to Margaret and received an assurance from her that all future questions about sterling would not be answered by Ingham but would be referred to the Treasury. But I did not feel that words alone would be enough, and on Friday, 11 January, with the pound worryingly weak, I insisted on a 1 per cent rise in base rates from 9.5 to 10.5 per cent, in large part as a clear demonstration that *The Sunday Times* story was wrong. This action should have demonstrated to anyone at all *au fait* with monetary policy that the Government was indeed concerned with sterling. I went off to Chevening for the normal pre-Budget weekend on Saturday, 12 January, imagining that I had seen the end of the Ingham affair.

The newspapers arrived late at Chevening that Sunday; and my officials had failed to check on the early editions available in London on Saturday night. I was therefore taken completely by surprise when I was telephoned by an excitable Margaret Thatcher at Chevening early on the Sunday morning. She had heard on the BBC radio news a summary of the main stories in the early editions of the Sunday newspapers, several of which led with a report that the Government was prepared to let the pound fall as far as the currency markets cared to push it. *The Sunday Times* carried the story under the banner headline 'Thatcher Ready to Let £1 Equal $1'. Variations on the same theme appeared in other papers.

Margaret was horrified that I had not, as she saw it, done anything about the stories. I told Margaret that I was even more horrified that they had appeared in the first place. I also undertook to get my Press Secretary to speak to the BBC forthwith to let them have an authoritative denial of the story, which he did, and this was duly broadcast. What I did not know was that, in answer to questions following the previous Friday's lobby briefing for the Sunday papers, Ingham had totally undermined the interest rate rise in terms which were outrageous if he understood what he was doing, and totally improper and a breach of his earlier undertaking if he did not. He has himself admitted subsequently that he 'vehemently stated that the Government was not going to waste its reserves on supporting the pound'.

The following day I summoned Ingham to my study at Number 11 and gave him a roasting. He seemed subdued, and apologised. But Margaret, when I tackled her about it, flatly refused to believe that he was responsible for the Sunday paper stories. Indeed, at a party that very Monday evening she showed him around, saying 'He's the greatest'.

DAMAGE LIMITATION, JANUARY 1985

The Ingham story was the end of all hopes of a reflective weekend on the Budget. I left Chevening to return to Downing Street straight after lunch on Sunday to try and further limit the damage Ingham had done. Treasury press officers telephoned the daily newspapers to ensure that the Monday Press rebutted the Sunday stories, and indicated the Government's willingness to accept a further rise in base rates to defend sterling. Robin Leigh-Pemberton was away for the weekend; I arranged a meeting at six o'clock that Sunday evening with Eddie George, then the executive director of the Bank in charge of monetary policy.

It was obvious to both of us that, when the markets opened on Monday, the pound would come under very severe pressure, and that interest rates would have to be increased. I went next door to see Margaret at Number 10 at half past eight that same evening, and warned her that unless interest rates were raised quite sharply the pound would go into free fall. The thought of the pound dropping below one dollar had put the fear of God into her. The sterling/dollar rate touched a new low of $1.10 in the Far East before the London markets opened;

and the Bank unveiled a 1.5 per cent rise in its Minimum Lending Rate (MLR) to 12 per cent.

Nor did I rely on higher interest rates alone. After staying out of the foreign exchange markets in December the Bank of England, along with other central banks, intervened to support sterling, to the tune of a published $500 million of reserve loss in January and February combined. But neither the 12 January interest rate rise nor the intervention proved sufficient to halt the run on the pound. One worry was a weakening of the oil price, which seemed much lower than it was, given that the price was denominated in rising dollars.

On 28 January, with sterling still suffering from both Ingham and a weak oil price, and with uncertainty on the latter front compounded by an OPEC meeting starting that day, I authorised another 2 per cent increase in base rates to 14 per cent – the highest level for three years and a level they were not to attain again until May 1989. Nevertheless it was much less of a trauma than the 14 January increase – or even than the increase the previous July – largely because it was widely seen as the necessary completion of the 14 January rise.

I made no attempt to postpone the 28 January hike even though I had to appear before the Treasury Committee that very afternoon – something I normally enjoyed but on this occasion it made me feel uncomfortably like Daniel in the lion's den. In fact I came out of it reasonably well, mainly by explaining factually and carefully the nature of the turmoil in the currency markets.

But in less specialist circles the Government was seen to be very much on the ropes, and it was no surprise that Labour tabled one of their rare censure motions for debate on 31 January. Margaret opened and I wound up for the Government. Fortunately for us the Kinnock/Hattersley team took charge for Labour. (Roy Hattersley was then Shadow Chancellor, a post he was eventually obliged to relinquish to the more effective John Smith.) Kinnock's proposal for bringing back exchange control and 'taking power' to set interest rates at a low level carried little conviction.

Both Kinnock and Hattersley made the mistake of not seriously probing the monetary side (where Labour tends to be badly informed) and instead broadening their attack into a general indictment of the Government's performance and notably of the level of unemployment. But given the increasing signs that Scargill was about to lose the miners' strike, our back benches were solidly behind us, and it was not hard to see off the Opposition attack. According to the political correspondent of the *Daily Telegraph*, it was 'another dismal performance by Labour on a major Commons occasion'. We were very lucky.

CHAPTER TWENTY-SEVEN

ENTER THE ERM

Anglo-Saxon Attitudes · Ripe and Unripe Time · Tackling the Treasury
Tackling the Prime Minister · The Meeting of 13 February 1985
The ERM and the Election

ANGLO-SAXON ATTITUDES

The attentive reader who has followed the account of the sterling crises of 1984/85 will have noted that British monetary policy was in practice constrained by the sterling exchange rate. In other words, our decisions had many of the characteristics of an explicit exchange rate policy but without the advantages that might be derived from public commitment and organised international support.

Moreover, partly because of the surge in the dollar and partly because of the lag in political and financial attitudes, there was a danger of getting hooked on the wrong exchange rate, that with the dollar. Indeed, Margaret had been fleetingly attracted in the earliest days to a proposal by the financial journalist, successful businessman and *bon vivant*, Patrick Sergeant, that we should pursue a two-dollar pound policy. The sterling/dollar rate (known as the 'cable') remains important for financial transactions. But the rate against European currencies has long been much more important for trade – which means both for UK inflation and for international competitiveness.

This line of thought inevitably pointed to exploring once again the arguments for British membership of the Exchange Rate Mechanism (ERM) of the European Monetary System (EMS). The decision not to join it had probably been the most important decision taken by the last Labour Government during their final months of office. As a result, it had started without the UK, after two and a half months' delay, on 12 March 1979, two months before the Thatcher Government took office. A Green Paper published by the Treasury the previous November had sought to give a balanced statement of the case for and against membership. But in common with most British economists, the official Treasury was in fact hostile to joining.

Technically speaking, the UK *was* a member, and a founder member at that, of the EMS, since the Labour Government had bizarrely joined the system while abjuring the exchange rate stability that it was all about. What this meant was that the UK had agreed to a modest pooling of reserves, would take part in EMS realignment meetings, and would maintain sterling as a component of the European Currency Unit (Ecu) – which was then just a currency basket and played little role in stabilising exchange rates.

The heart of the system was of course the ERM. This had many complex paraphernalia; but in essence was a parity grid, giving a lower and upper margin of fluctuation of each member currency against every other. Although parities were formally stated against the Ecu, which the founding fathers vainly hoped would be the core of the system, governments and traders alike soon saw that the key range for every currency was between its upper and lower limit against the Deutschmark. It was *de facto* – although not *de jure* – a Deutschmark zone.

Labour's main fear in 1979 had been that membership would inflict an excessively high exchange rate for sterling, to the detriment of the economy as a whole. Whereupon, as is so often the case, the pundits were proved wrong as the pound soared outside the ERM – and the business and academic argument advanced in favour of membership became the need to put a cap on the pound. But there was also a political element, equally ironic in the light of subsequent events. In Andrew Britton's words, 'The attitude of the Labour Party to Europe was still (at best) ambivalent', and there was no enthusiasm 'for a commitment which might restrict the action of British Governments'.

RIPE AND UNRIPE TIME

As I have recorded earlier, I became convinced of the desirability of British membership of the ERM as Financial Secretary before I left the Treasury in September 1981. Although I returned as Chancellor in June 1983, the first serious meeting I convened in the Treasury on joining the ERM was on 11 January 1985. Why did I wait those nineteen months?

The answer is that I felt I had to wait for the right opportunity. During the whole of that period the dollar had been rocketing upwards; and it was this problem – on which the ERM had no bearing – which was the overwhelming focus of concern so far as the exchange rate and its impact on monetary policy was concerned. Nor was it going to be easy. Joining the ERM was a far bigger issue for a widely held currency like sterling than it was for any other European currency. The official Treasury had always been opposed, although it was subsequently to change. The predominant Bank of England view was also hostile, with the conspicuous exception of the new Governor, Robin Leigh-Pemberton, who had still to make his mark on the Bank. The opposition from officials would not have mattered had Margaret Thatcher been sympathetic. Indeed it might scarcely have continued to exist. But in view of her position the official attitude added to the difficulties. I had to wait until the time was ripe, to coin a phrase.

In other words, Margaret was the key. The manifest absurdity of the rise in the dollar in 1984 had started to shake her faith in the foreign exchange markets; and the traumatic nature of the pressure on the pound in early 1985 frightened her as similar events had frightened every previous Prime Minister. That was essentially what created the 1985 opportunity, as I saw it. This was reinforced by the shift in the American position in President Reagan's second term away from free floating: Margaret's eyes were always focused across the Atlantic.

Throughout my period as Chancellor the holidays were the only time I had to sit back and reflect on policy. It was during the Christmas and New Year break of 1984–85 that I came to the conclusion that the time had arrived for a serious attempt to join the ERM. This was partly because I had become increasingly concerned both with the weakness of sterling and with the continuing problems I was having with the conduct and presentation of a domestically based monetary policy.

TACKLING THE TREASURY

The first internal Treasury meeting I held on the ERM membership was on the fateful Friday, 11 January, the day before the Chevening weekend, the day when I raised base rates by one percentage point to protect the pound, and also the day that, unknown to me, Bernard Ingham was briefing the Press that the Government was happy to leave sterling to its fate. The case for buttressing the pound and firmly dispelling the increasing uncertainty over monetary policy was clear to me.

Nevertheless most of those I invited to the meeting, including both Ian Stewart, the Economic Secretary, and Peter Middleton and Terry Burns, were at that time still opposed to membership. The principal reservation that Treasury Ministers and officials voiced in public – for instance at the Commons Treasury Select Committee – centred on sterling's continuing, although diminishing, role as a petrocurrency and the possible destabilising effects on the ERM itself of the entry of sterling, which was much more widely traded than other member currencies. There was also the question of how well the ERM would in fact hold together once the pressure from a strongly rising dollar was lifted. (When the dollar rises, funds move out of all European currencies into the dollar; but when the dollar falls, funds tend to move out of the dollar preponderantly into Deutschmarks, thus putting a strain on ERM parities.)

These were, however, essentially questions of timing and tactics. The true objections of officials were different. In the first place, they felt that the Government – and they personally – had invested a great deal of intellectual capital in the existing monetary policy framework and were loth to abandon it; second, they were also loth to lose control (as they saw it) over the level of interest rates; third, they were keenly aware of Margaret's strong views; and fourth, the 'snake' episode had left some scars. (The 'snake' was an earlier ill-fated attempt to narrow the extent of exchange rate fluctuations among EC currencies. It had been agreed to by the Heath Government on 1 May 1972; but a massive run on the pound forced the UK to abandon it, in the most humiliating way, the very next month.)

After I had raised the matter, Peter Middleton moved fairly quickly from the anti-ERM camp and on to the fence: like many good Civil Servants, that was his instinctive position on most issues. Terry was slower to shift, because he was keen to try and operate a policy based on M0. At the Bank of England Eddie George also shifted, partly in deference to the Governor. While the subsequent thinking of Treasury officials moved steadily in what I regarded as the right direction, Eddie's thinking pursued a more volatile and erratic path – like the markets he loved to monitor with his portable pocket screen.

At any rate, the conclusion of the meeting of 11 January was that officials would examine the mechanics of ERM membership and also of contingency plans to increase the foreign exchange reserves. In the course of 1985 I gradually brought my officials around to my way of thinking on the ERM. Since in the end Civil Servants have to support their Minister, they had no real choice; but as far as I could see their conversion was genuine, if in some cases unenthusiastic.

I also raised the issue with Geoffrey, in his capacity as Foreign Secretary. He was anxious to join the ERM, not only to strengthen his political hand in Europe, but because he now shared my assessment of the economic attractions. Needless to say, confiding in him did not constitute a plot against Margaret. We were old friends and colleagues and discussed a variety of policy matters over the years. Rightly or wrongly, there was only one occasion when, under extreme provocation, four years later, we acted in concert to put pressure on Margaret.

It was clear that more intervention in the foreign exchange markets was going to be the order of the day. Such intervention would be required to sustain the pound within the ERM; it would be required as part of any G5 or G7 concerted intervention in the currency markets; and it would help with any informal and unannounced targeting of sterling. Ultimately the main instrument would have to be domestic monetary policy – that is, interest rates. But intervention could supplement the use of interest rates and minimise or even avoid their use in the face of purely temporary shocks and disturbances.

Intervention on a worthwhile scale requires the holding of substantial reserves of foreign currency. Largely as a result of a deliberate policy of repaying the foreign debts run up by the last Labour Government, which we had embarked on in 1979 when we were seeking to underline the new Conservative Government's wholly different approach to economic policy, the UK's gross official published reserves had fallen from $27 billion in 1980 to just under $16 billion at the end of 1984, of which less than $8 billion consisted of readily usable convertible currencies. British reserves were not only very much smaller than those of Germany, but only a little more than a third of those of either France or Italy. A submission made to me by Treasury officials on 21 December 1984, emphasised the inadequacy of the UK's reserves and recommended (probably on the advice from the Bank of England) a dollar bond issue to replenish them. This proved a timely initiative.

TACKLING THE PRIME MINISTER

The question of the reserves came up again at a meeting in Number 10 on 28 January 1985, held (at my request) to secure Margaret's approval of the final two-point increase in base rate to 14 per cent. After we had concluded the main business, Margaret reported that she had recently asked the Dutch Prime Minister, Ruud Lubbers, for whom she had a high regard, why, although the Netherlands was also a major energy producer (of gas rather than oil), it did not experience similar currency turbulence to Britain. His reply had been that ERM membership protected it, as changes in the parity were not expected by the foreign exchange market. Margaret concluded by herself asking me to look into the question of whether in present circumstances it was right for the UK to join the ERM.

Needless to say, I was happy to do so, and took the opportunity to raise the matter again at one of my regular weekly bilateral meetings with her on 3 February. I told her that there was growing interest both among our backbenchers and within the business community in the possibility of joining the ERM. The Government had always said that it would join when conditions were right, and I believed this was a question which should be considered before the Budget. I remarked that financial discipline, which was the key to bringing down inflation, could be provided by either monetary targets or a fixed exchange rate. We should choose between the two on practical grounds.

New arguments, I reminded her, were now being put forward in favour of the ERM. The financial markets were having difficulty in understanding the Government's position so far as the exchange rate was concerned, and the ERM would provide clearer rules of the game. Moreover, as there was now substantial support for ERM membership within the Conservative Party in the House of Commons, it would be helpful in future arguments about spending and borrowing if our back-benchers in effect faced a discipline of their own choice. I added that membership would have the additional advantage of moving attention away from the misleading sterling/dollar exchange rate. It would also help domestically, as £M3 was becoming increasingly suspect as a monetary indicator.

For once I took the opportunity myself of urging a Prime Ministerial seminar on the issue. I suggested that in addition to a Treasury team headed by me and a Bank team headed by Robin Leigh-Pemberton, both Geoffrey Howe, as Foreign Secretary, and Alan Walters should be invited. She agreed, and asked her private secretary, Andrew Turnbull, to set it up.

I held a further internal Treasury meeting on the subject on 8 February. With sterling still very weak, I was worried about declaring an intention to join the ERM at the time of the Budget, by then only some five weeks away. It seemed to me that it would be better to reach agreement in principle as soon as possible, with a view to making the announcement and joining the ERM in the summer, when I expected sterling to be stronger.

THE MEETING OF 13 FEBRUARY 1985

The ERM seminar duly took place at Number 10 on 13 February 1985, attended by the cast I had suggested, with the exception of Alan Walters, who was in America, and with the addition of John Redwood, then head of the Number 10 Policy Unit, and subsequently a middle-ranking Minister. I opened the meeting by making clear that I was not seeking agreement to enter the ERM then and there, with the pound still under pressure, and that we needed to re-establish a reasonable degree of confidence in the currency first if the move was to be credible. But the balance of argument had shifted markedly in favour of joining, which would make the maintenance of financial discipline easier, and the time was now very close when it would be right to do so.

Geoffrey said that he recognised that a decision had to be taken on economic rather than political grounds, but doubted if there were any insuperable problems. He accepted that current circumstances were not right, but thought that the UK should be looking for the first opportunity to join. Robin Leigh-Pemberton said that the Bank was looking more sympathetically at the arguments in favour. He agreed that current circumstances were not right, but the Bank leaned towards joining at some stage, although he added that Bank opinion was not unanimous.

In her summing up, Margaret chose to dwell on the consensus that now was not the right time to join, and ignored the majority feeling that the right time was not far off. Nevertheless, I felt that some progress had been made. This was not least because one of the pre-conditions for joining, identified at the meeting, had been an increase in the UK's foreign exchange reserves. Margaret was alarmed to discover how small our reserves were, compared with those of other major European countries, and she asked me to investigate ways of increasing them. Once they had been increased, she concluded, the question of joining the ERM could be looked at again.

Needless to say, I was more than happy to get on with the job of rebuilding the reserves, but for the time being this would have to wait. The following month I had a Budget to present, and there was a great deal of work to be done on it. After the Budget was out of the way, I got down to the reserves issue without further delay, raising without difficulty $2.5 billion on the international capital markets.

After a brief family holiday, I saw Margaret privately and pressed once again the case for ERM membership, indicating my opinion that with the reserves strengthened the time would be right for sterling to join. Margaret was sceptical, but indicated that her mind was not completely closed on the issue, and argued that it was for those who favoured joining to make their case. She suggested that we should have a further seminar towards the end of September, which I welcomed.

THE ERM AND THE ELECTION

I told my officials that, in preparing the Treasury's paper for the seminar – which should be done in close collaboration with the Bank – they should address two central questions: first, precisely why we believed that the time was right to join, and, second, how the decision to join could be most positively presented in public. I also told them that Margaret was particularly exercised about a problem that Alan Walters had put to her when she last discussed it with him. (Although Walters had no official post, and was an academic living in Washington, she remained in frequent contact with him: indeed, our Washington Embassy used to grumble about being instructed by Number 10 to send him confidential Government papers.)

The problem that Walters had posed at that time, and which so worried Margaret, was that if sterling were in the ERM it could seriously damage our chances of electoral success. The scenario he painted was one of a general election campaign in which an opinion poll showing Labour ahead, or even a sharply narrowing Conservative lead, would lead to a run on the pound, which would force us to put up interest rates then and there to defend the parity, thus making a Labour win certain.

As an argument against joining, I did not find this convincing. In the first place, a purely political and intrinsically transitory problem of this kind was just the sort of situation in which massive intervention would be warranted; and I had little doubt that the Germans, who had no wish to see a Labour Government in Britain, would be helpful. In the second place, a pre-election run on the pound was at least as likely to occur with sterling outside the ERM, and it was highly unlikely that the Government (as Walters clearly envisaged) would be content simply to sit back and let it happen, unabated.

Finally, if the worst came to the worst, and interest rates had to be increased in the circumstances envisaged, I did not feel that it would be too difficult to make the political point (a) that this demonstrated the world's conviction that a Labour Government would be an economic disaster and (b) that if this was what even the prospect of Labour in power could mean, then it was not hard to imagine how much worse the reality would be. Certainly, there was no evidence that the Labour Party ever imagined that it would be in their electoral interest to engineer a pre-election sterling crisis: quite the reverse.

Despite this, however, I thought it prudent to arm myself with a fallback position when dealing with this point at Margaret's seminar, and asked the ever ingenious Geoff Littler to let me have one. He replied with a submission suggesting what he was later to term the *congé*: when senior officials suggest something they consider faintly disreputable, they evidently feel that the French language adds tone and a cloak of respectability. The proposal was that the Government might *in extremis* formally declare that the pound would be allowed to float until polling day, and couple this announcement with 'a strong statement' that, on re-election, it would immediately restore sterling to the ERM at the previous parity.

This seemed to me a reasonable contingency plan if one were needed: our partners would not welcome the *congé*, but in practice they would be powerless to stop us; nor was it conceivable that, in the circumstances, they would refuse us readmission. It should be recalled that, at that time, not only did the Labour Party have no commitment to ERM membership, let alone to any particular parity, but its subsequent love affair with the European Community had not even begun. None the less, during the 1992 election campaign, by which time its position on Europe and the ERM had changed completely, there were still tremors in the foreign exchange market when it looked as if Labour might win; but the situation was successfully contained with only modest amounts of intervention.

While my officials were busy preparing the papers for the seminar, I had to fly to New York for a special meeting of the G5 at the Plaza Hotel, where on 21 September we signed the so-called Plaza Agreement to take concerted action to reduce the international value of the dollar, as described in Chapter 29. I was very happy with this timing. There was reason to hope that the Plaza Agreement, which marked in the most formal way a major change in US exchange rate policy, away from free floating and the doctrine that you cannot (or should not) 'buck the market', might, at least subconsciously, soften Margaret's resistance to sterling's ERM membership. On my return from Washington I saw her to debrief her fully, in the usual way, on the events at the Plaza Hotel, and found that this had indeed modified her scepticism about the ERM: she remarked to me that the agreement created a favourable prelude to ERM membership, should we decide to join. She proposed 30 September as the date for the forthcoming seminar.

CHAPTER TWENTY EIGHT

THE AUTUMN ASSAULT OF 1985

The Meeting of 30 September · The Meeting of 13 November
Secret Mission to Germany · Retrospect · If the UK had joined in November 1985 ...

THE MEETING OF 30 SEPTEMBER

There were about a dozen of us present round the Cabinet table at Number 10 for the seminar which started at 4 o'clock in the afternoon of 30 September, including all the key figures from the Treasury and the Bank of England. Geoffrey Howe was also present.

Margaret was flanked by Brian Griffiths, a former professor of economics at City University who had replaced John Redwood as head of the Number 10 Policy Unit, and by one of her private secretaries, David Norgrove, as a note-taker. Walters was in the United States and unable to attend. This was on balance a pity, since he was the only economist who influenced her and I would have welcomed the opportunity to meet his arguments head-on. Griffiths, by contrast, simply presented her with a pale echo of Walters' views in private and said little on occasions such as this.

I opened by speaking to the paper which I had circulated in advance. I pointed out that, since our previous discussion in February, the recovery of the pound on the foreign exchange markets and the replenishment of the reserves had disposed of the two main arguments against joining then. The overwhelming case for joining now was the desirability of reinforcing our anti-inflationary strategy. While this continued so far to be successful, the monetary indicators were proving increasingly difficult to interpret.

In the light of this, we were already having to place increasing weight on the exchange rate in the conduct of monetary policy, and joining the ERM would thus be seen as a natural development. It would undoubtedly strengthen our strategy in the eyes of the markets, it would make it clear to industry that they could not look to exchange rate depreciation to solve their difficulties, and it would create a helpful context for the Government's public expenditure decisions. While monetary conditions were at that time adequately tight, we were still facing problems of presentation and market psychology.

The Governor of the Bank, Robin Leigh-Pemberton, strongly supported me, claiming that the need to make subjective judgements about the interpretation of the monetary indicators, coupled with our resistance to the increasing pressure from the market to disclose an exchange rate 'target', were undermining the credibility of policy. Geoffrey pointed out the significance of the fact that both the Treasury and the Bank, who had for so long been sceptical of the merits of ERM entry, were now both unequivocally in favour of it. He added that it was clear that the exchange rate was already dominating economic decision-making, and he believed that joining the ERM would strengthen the MTFS by which he continued to set great store.

Margaret then responded. It was clear that she had been speaking to Walters since I had seen her on my return from Washington. She argued that an exchange rate discipline would increase interest rate volatility and would mean a much tighter monetary squeeze than any internal discipline. It would reduce the Government's room for manoeuvre (by which she meant its ability to reduce interest rates and let the pound depreciate) and might require unattractively high interest rates in order to keep up with the Germans, leading to higher unemployment. Moreover, sterling was different from other Community currencies, not least because we were a net oil exporter and they were substantial oil importers. Finally, she made the point that, given the absence of exchange controls, there could be massive speculation against the pound in the run-up to a general election, requiring a politically embarrassing rise in interest rates.

I replied that it was clear from the events earlier that year that the exchange rate was already having a powerful influence on interest rates, and ERM membership, by stabilising the exchange rate, could actually reduce the volatility of interest rates. As for the oil factor, the extent to which the markets regarded sterling as a petrocurrency had greatly diminished. The problem of pressure on the pound in a run-up to an election, I pointed out, could occur whether we were inside or outside the ERM, and might actually be easier to handle within it; were we to join in 1985, we would have fully established the credibility of ERM membership and the parity we had chosen by the time the election came. In the last resort, I added, we could take the *congé* route I have already described.

Perhaps the most depressing aspect of Margaret's response was the renewed evidence that, despite her reputation for sound money, in practice she was too ready to allow sterling to depreciate rather than raise interest rates. Geoffrey's remark that ERM membership would actually strengthen the MTFS had been very much to the point. As I said to her, the significance of the MTFS was that it represented a public commitment to the pursuit of an anti-inflationary policy. Linking the pound to the Deutschmark via the ERM would represent exactly the same sort of public commitment to an anti-inflationary policy, and one that would by that time carry greater conviction.

Margaret concluded that she had not been convinced that the balance of argument had in fact shifted in favour of joining the ERM. There would need to be a further discussion, to which other colleagues should be invited. She would circulate a list of questions which needed to be answered which could form an agenda for that meeting. She no doubt felt that, with the Treasury and the Bank both now solidly ranged against her on the issue, supported by the Foreign Office, she was becoming dangerously isolated, and that she needed to bring in other colleagues (whom she would, of course, choose) to redress the balance. I for my part welcomed the wider ministerial discussion she had proposed, since, given her own scepticism, at the end of the day it might be through a collective decision of this kind that ERM membership could be obtained.

The meeting had lasted a little over two hours. Afterwards I told officials that in addition to providing the answers to the Number 10 questions, it was essential that we circulated a very persuasive paper of our own to all those who were going to attend the meeting, and that we should involve the Bank fully in the preparation of that paper. A joint Treasury and Bank team was put together to draft both this paper and the answers to the questions, which I asked to be done in a coherent and logical way of our own choosing, rather than in whatever sequence they happened to emerge from next door. Over the next few weeks I held a succession of meetings on the papers, which went through a number of drafts before I was satisfied.

When the Number 10 questionnaire arrived, it proved to contain no fewer than twenty-three questions, and read rather like a rag-bag of every objection to ERM membership that anybody could come up with. In so far as there was an underlying theme, it was that sterling would be subject to greater pressure inside the ERM than if it remained a non-member, and that the economy was not strong enough to sustain a fixed parity against the Deutschmark. There were also practical questions, such as the Deutschmark parity at which sterling should join. Curiously, about the only objection that was not included in the list of questions was that dubbed (by Alan Walters) the 'Walters' critique'. Because of the importance he and some others attached to it, I deal with it later in this chapter; but it was never raised by Margaret herself.

THE MEETING OF 13 NOVEMBER

The ministerial meeting was fixed for 9 o'clock in the morning of Wednesday, 13 November, the day after the Autumn Statement. Less than a month earlier, at the Mansion House Banquet, I had announced the suspension of the £M3 target, an occasion on which neither Robin nor I had been able to conceal the fragility of the presentation of the Government's existing monetary policy. The colleagues Margaret had invited to the meeting were Willie Whitelaw, Geoffrey Howe, Norman Tebbit, who had recently been moved from Secretary of State for Trade and Industry to Party Chairman, Leon Brittan, Norman's successor at Trade and Industry, John Biffen, the Leader of the House of Commons and John Wakeham, then Chief Whip.

Of these six, three – Willie, as Deputy Prime Minister, Geoffrey, and Leon as head of the second economic Department of Government – were there because she could scarcely exclude them. The other three had been chosen largely because she felt sure they would support her, either on political grounds or, in John Biffen's case, on economic grounds. Apart from Geoffrey and myself, none of them had given any previous indication of support for ERM membership. Biffen was a committed free-floater of long standing, and I regarded him as a lost cause. All the others I saw individually, before the meeting, to go over my paper with them, and answer any doubts they may have had about any of the arguments it advanced.

The meeting was not a formal Cabinet committee meeting, but an *ad hoc* gathering to which others besides Cabinet colleagues had been invited. I myself was accompanied by Peter Middleton and Terry Burns while Robin Leigh-Pemberton was also, of course, present, accompanied by Eddie George. Margaret was once again flanked by Brian Griffiths and a private secretary. None of us, however, was in any doubt of its importance.

As someone wholly outside the Government machine, Alan Walters clearly could not be present at a meeting of this kind. But Margaret had a short letter from him among the papers in front of her. He was evidently concerned that we were now on the brink of joining the ERM, since his chief point was that the oil price was clearly weakening and would weaken still further, and that we should therefore defer entry until the following Easter, by which time the oil price fall would have been completed and we would then be able to join, should we wish to do so, at a lower and more realistic parity. He was, of course, quite right about the oil price; but equally he knew full well that, if a November 1985 meeting towards which I had taken so much trouble and time in working were to decide against entry, it was most unlikely that I would be able to get the horse to jump the fence at a second attempt the following Easter.

I opened the meeting by summarising the main points of my paper. The paper was not of course intended as an exhaustive analysis of the pros and cons of ERM membership, but was much more specifically designed to meet the particular concerns that Margaret had raised with me in our earlier conversations on the subject. It recalled that the Government's clearly stated policy was to join the ERM when the time was right, and argued that that time had now come. It pointed out – and I elaborated this in my opening remarks – that the position was not one of deciding whether, on balance, we would be better off with a fixed or a floating pound in the abstract. The plain fact was that the ERM existed, and thus the question asked by the markets was why we refused to join it; and I pointed out that this led them to the inevitable conclusion that it was because we sooner or later wished to see sterling depreciate, which in general made the conduct of economic policy harder than it would otherwise be, and in particular required interest rates to be kept higher in the longer run than would otherwise have been necessary.

My paper also went into the potential pre-election problem, and floated the *congé* option. It concluded with these words:

> My judgement that the advantages of joining now outweigh the risks is shared not only by the Governor of the Bank of England, but also by senior officials in both the Treasury and the Bank. They all believe that it makes operational sense to join, and that they can now deliver our policy objectives more effectively in the EMS than if we remain outside it.

From then on the discussion did not go as Margaret had expected. Geoffrey, of course, spoke in favour, along the lines that he had done at the 30 September seminar. But then Leon Brittan said that while he had been opposed to ERM membership in the past, because of the problems of sterling's petrocurrency status, since the importance of this factor had diminished and given the declining credibility of the monetary aggregates, he now believed we should join. Norman Tebbit, who was to turn against the ERM later when it was seen as part of the essentially political argument about European monetary union and the single currency, also declared himself in favour if I thought it would be helpful economically; and added that, as Party Chairman, he felt that it would be easy to carry the Party and that a decision to join now might silence some of the back-bench critics of our economic policy.

A nettled Margaret promptly asserted that what it would do would be to split the Party in Parliament right down the middle; to which John Wakeham replied that as Chief Whip, he had no worries on that score: there would be very few rebels and he was in fact surprised that so far there had been relatively little back-bench pressure to join, but he expected this to increase. John Biffen unsurprisingly declared himself very doubtful of the merits of ERM membership. Robin Leigh-Pemberton then had his say arguing that the difficulties of sterling outside the ERM were greater than they would be inside the ERM.

Margaret then weighed in. She recited what had become a familiar litany of objections. The United Kingdom had low foreign-exchange reserves and a more open capital market than anyone else. The Government would be left with no discretion on interest rates; and the UK could not pull out of the ERM, even on a very temporary basis, in advance of an election, without looking as if it had lost all faith in its own policies. A 'rigid grid' would deprive the Government of all freedom of manoeuvre.

Willie, as was his custom, had held himself back to the end. Unless he disagreed with it, it was his habit to formulate what he thought was the clear consensus of any meeting (equally, if there was no consensus, he would make that plain), as an aid to Margaret in her summing up. On this occasion, having listened attentively to the discussion he declared, 'If the Chancellor, the Governor and the Foreign Secretary are all agreed that we should join the EMS then that should be decisive. It has certainly decided me.' I suspect he was as surprised as the rest of us when Margaret instantly replied, 'On the contrary: I disagree. If you join the EMS, you will have to do so without me.' There was an awkward silence, and the meeting broke up.

There is just one other point to be made about that fateful meeting. Whatever differences there might have been in the extent of their own personal enthusiasm for ERM membership, both then and at the earlier meetings, all my officials fully, loyally and competently backed my position. Despite Margaret's attempts to drive a wedge between them and me, she completely failed to do so.

At the end of the meeting Margaret swept out, with Griffiths trotting behind her. I asked Willie, Geoffrey and Norman to accompany me next door to Number 11 to discuss what had happened. I was extremely depressed, and told them that, in the circumstances, I saw little point in carrying on and probably ought to resign. Willie, too, had clearly found it a depressing as well as an embarrassing occasion, but urged me not to resign, as did both Geoffrey and Norman. Norman said he was convinced that she would eventually come round, and Willie agreed.

In a sense, they were right; but no-one could have foreseen the sequence of events which took her there. Given the emphasis that she had laid on the political arguments – despite a warning from Willie, among others, that the political pressure was likely to stem from not joining rather than joining – it was clear that it would be difficult, to say the least, to reopen the issue before the next general election, which was at least eighteen months away. An historic opportunity had been lost, when the time really had been right.

SECRET MISSION TO GERMANY

Having, after much reflection, decided to accept the advice of Willie, Geoffrey and Norman not to throw in the towel, I gave the green light to a secret mission I had planned in advance in the hope of a favourable outcome of the meeting. Accordingly on, 7 December, Peter Middleton, Geoff Littler and (from the Bank) Anthony Loehnis went on a highly confidential visit to Bonn to discuss contingency planning in the event of Britain deciding to join the ERM. The two key figures on the German side were Leonhard Gleske, the Bundesbank board member in charge of external affairs, and Hans Tietmeyer, then a top Finance Ministry official who was both Stoltenberg's Deputy in the G5 context and Chancellor Kohl's 'sherpa' for the annual economic summit. Although something of a rough diamond for an official, Tietmeyer is a highly competent and agreeable man, who in 1991 was appointed Vice President and President-elect of the Bundesbank.

The Germans made it clear that they would welcome sterling's membership of the ERM, which in their view would help to maintain the soundness of the system despite the weakness of its southern members (they were particularly concerned about Italy). They also found British thinking about the further development of the EMS very close to their own and 'sensibly pragmatic'. Two days later Loehnis had a separate talk with Gleske about possible swap arrangements with the Bundesbank – that is to say a substantial line of short-term credit – to support British entry, and reported back that 'the reaction was unexpectedly favourable'.

In his report to me on his secret talks, Geoff Littler said that in his opinion, after the coming French elections, there was likely to be an ERM realignment, particularly if the Right under Chirac won. (This proved accurate in every respect.) One possibility would be for the UK to wait until the system had settled down following the realignment, and then join. While, in a purely rational world, there would have been much to be said for this, I could not see Margaret changing her mind so soon after the drama of 13 November.

For their part, the Germans were more interested to hear our views on the parity at which sterling should enter the system than to suggest a figure of their own, but they made it clear that they regarded somewhere in the region of DM3.50 to DM3.75 as reasonable. They believed that if the UK were to join from strength on a credible basis there would be an inflow of funds into London and upward pressure on the sterling exchange rate – something which we did indeed experience when I subsequently shadowed the Deutschmark, albeit at the appreciably lower rate of DM3.

I was able to confirm the German view for myself when I discussed the matter privately with Gerhard Stoltenberg in the margins of the next Ecofin meeting early the following year, 1986. He greatly welcomed my desire to see sterling in the ERM, which he believed would strengthen the system as well as benefiting the UK. He saw no problem whatever with the kind of practical co-operation the Treasury and Bank officials had discussed on their visit.

RETROSPECT

Looking back with hindsight on all this, the saddest event of my time as Chancellor and the greatest missed opportunity, I believe that my handling of the issue was about the best I could have done. I had waited until the time was right, and chosen a moment when Margaret's misplaced faith in free floating had been shaken by events. I had replenished the reserves, and demonstrated how painlessly this could be achieved. Although the Plaza agreement was, of course, primarily Jim Baker's doing, I had been urging something of the sort on him ever since he was first appointed Treasury Secretary in February 1985, and this had provided the right international context. And I had secured a meeting of senior Ministers on the issue, on which the line-up was what should have been a decisive 6 to 2 in favour of joining (5 to 1 excluding Margaret and myself).

Perhaps, constitutionally, the most extraordinary aspect of all was that the Government's official and collectively agreed position on the ERM of the EMS was that it was in favour of, and indeed committed to, joining, as soon as the time was ripe – a position that Margaret herself had publicly stated and repeatedly restated. Yet here was a Prime Minister allowing herself to be guided on the issue by someone who made no bones about the fact that, in his opinion, the ERM was the work of the devil and that we should never, in any circumstances, join it. Had Margaret come to that conclusion, too, she could at any time have sought Cabinet's endorsement of this fundamental change of policy.

Had she done so, I would of course have opposed it; and had Cabinet been persuaded by her I would have been faced with the choice between giving up my repeated attempts to secure ERM entry and resigning. It is hard to say with honesty which of the two it would have been – probably the latter – but it would have had to be one or the other, and in either event there would subsequently have been a greater degree of harmony in the conduct of policy than in fact, towards the end, proved the case. But she never once sought Cabinet's endorsement of a fundamental change of policy of this kind. Until after my resignation at the end of October 1989 she simply acted as if Government policy were different from what she herself repeatedly avowed it to be.

IF THE UK HAD JOINED IN NOVEMBER 1985 ...

At the time of the November ministerial meeting, the ERM was not in practice a completely rigid system. During its first eight years, from its inception in March 1979 to March 1987, there was an average of one major realignment against the Deutschmark a year (defining a major realignment as one involving either the French franc or the Italian lira, and usually both: there were also three involving only the Danish kroner, the Belgian franc or the Irish punt over the same period). Subsequently, the system hardened: up to the middle of 1992 there was only one, involving the lira – and that was a special case, being a consequence of Italy's decision to move from the wide band to the narrow band in January 1990. Given the downward pressure on the pound in the wake of the oil price collapse in the first quarter of 1986, sterling would almost certainly have moved down with the franc in the realignment of April of that year. Had we entered the ERM, as I had recommended in November 1985, at a parity of DM3.70, this would imply a move to some DM3.50 in April 1986.

This puts into perspective Walters' claim in his curious book *Sterling in Danger* that an attempt to hold the pound at DM3.75 would have involved interest rates of 17-20 per cent when sterling came under pressure as a result of the oil price collapse – quite apart from the fact that the particular way in which he reaches his estimated interest rate is wholly spurious. But I readily accept that some increase in interest rates would almost certainly have been required to maintain a parity of DM3.50 in 1986 – and a good thing, too. It would have been a small price to pay to prevent the collapse from DM3.45 in March 1986 to DM2.85 in December 1986 that actually occurred. Those who wish to criticise me for not taking sufficient action soon enough to curb the credit boom, cannot complain about the higher interest rates a more restrictive stance would have entailed.

I am not, of course, suggesting that Margaret's veto on ERM entry in November 1985 absolves me from responsibility for any mistakes I may subsequently have made. But it undoubtedly made the conduct of economic policy more difficult, and thus errors more likely. In particular, it was very difficult, outside the ERM, to handle the effects of the 1986 oil price collapse and prevent sterling from falling too far. Moreover the advantage of rules over discretion in the conduct of economic policy is not merely that this can save policy-makers from their own mistakes. It also – and this is equally important, although usually overlooked in discussion of the subject – affects decision-makers in the private sector, persuading them to conduct their affairs in a more prudent way.

It is hardly an extravagant exercise in hypothetical reasoning to claim that ERM entry in November 1985 (or indeed soon after it) would have put a dampener both on pay and price increases in the internationally exposed sector of the UK economy – most importantly on the prices of products sold at home and subject to competition from imports – and, through higher interest rates, on the credit explosion and the housing boom, thus moderating the excessive spending by businesses and consumers alike which those developments fuelled.

Not the least of the advantages is that Margaret would not have been able to prevent me from raising interest rates in 1986, as in practice to some extent occurred. Margaret was right in arguing that what I was advocating would constrain the freedom of Governments to do whatever they like. But a constraint of this kind is highly desirable, and should be welcomed by all true 'Thatcherites', even though it was evidently anathema to Margaret herself.

Although I was not aware of it at the time, there would have been two further advantages in ERM entry in November 1985, rather than five years later as eventually occurred. The first is that it would have been unequivocally an act of economic policy, clearly distanced from the wider political argument over the future of Europe which later threatened to split the Conservative Party. The second is that, in those days, German reunification was nothing more than a distant and eccentric dream. In other words, we would have enjoyed a clear run of five or six years during which the Deutschmark would have served us, as it served the other member nations, as a very satisfactory low-inflation anchor, without the strain of the relatively high interest rates that unification was eventually to impose on the system as a whole.

CHAPTER TWENTY-NINE

FROM THE PLAZA TO THE LOUVRE

The Dollar Peaks · The Road to Plaza · From Secrecy to Ballyhoo
Exchange Market Follow-through · Common Cause, Different Aims
Another Oil Shock · The G5 in London · The 'Spirit of Gleneagles'
The Road to the Louvre

THE DOLLAR PEAKS

My abortive attempt to put sterling into the ERM in November 1985 took place in parallel with wider moves to introduce some order into the pattern of world exchange rates.

On 17 January 1985 members of the G5 had announced in Washington a landmark agreement to undertake co-ordinated intervention when necessary to achieve greater exchange monetary stability. The first practical results were seen in February 1985. During that month the dollar advanced again to new record highs against all the major currencies, in line with rising American interest rates and in the wake of an unfortunate remark by President Reagan on 21 February that he opposed attempts 'artificially' to depress the currency. This clearly breached the spirit of the January agreement, a point made to the Americans particularly forcefully by Karl Otto Pöhl. On 26 February, the dollar reached its peak against the Deutschmark at over DM3.47 (the same day that the UK came nearest to the 'one dollar pound').

The European central banks, led by the Bundesbank, supported by the Bank of Japan, sold dollars aggressively in the markets the following day, and for several days thereafter. The intervention amounted to at least $10 billion, including a modest contribution from the UK. Coupled with a more sober assessment of US economic growth, which clearly could not continue at the unsustainable 1984 rate of between 6 and 7 per cent and a change in financial market sentiment, this caused the dollar to fall sharply for the first time in over four years. In the seven weeks to mid-April 1985 it dropped 20 per cent against the pound, 15 per cent against the other European currencies and over 6 per cent against the yen. At the time, it was widely felt that this could well be merely a short-term correction, and not the long-awaited change of trend.

THE ROAD TO PLAZA

It was Jim Baker who initiated the negotiations which led to the Plaza agreement of 22 September 1985 on international agreement to reduce the excessive value of the dollar. Having first sounded out the Japanese, he telephoned me at my home in Stoney Stanton in the middle of August and suggested a meeting of the G5 Finance Ministers to agree on a co-ordinated strategy. He was extremely worried by the protectionist legislation Congress was threatening to pass on its return from the summer holidays, and believed that its passage into law would be facilitated by any further strengthening of the dollar. The best he could hope to do, he said, was prevent the legislation securing the two-thirds majority support needed to override a Presidential veto. He asked how I felt about this, and mentioned that he would be speaking to Gerhard Stoltenberg next. He also swore me to secrecy, saying that he had not yet broached the matter with the Fed chairman, Paul Volcker – even though he enjoyed a far better rapport with the Fed chairman than the awkward arm's length relationship which had existed between Volcker and Don Regan, his predecessor as Treasury Secretary.

I warmly welcomed the idea, and we discussed the broad outlines there and then. We agreed that there should be no prior announcement of the meeting, believing that an unexpected event would have a greater impact on the market. During late August and early September the G5 Deputies met amid conditions of great secrecy to draw up what became known as the 'non-paper'.

Initially Baker tried to put pressure on Germany and Japan – and to a lesser extent Britain – to take action to 'stimulate growth', and thus impress Congress. This we all resisted; but both Stoltenberg and I thought it should be possible to re-state our existing policies in a positive form in a communiqué. Coupled with the threat of concerted intervention, we reckoned it might suffice to depress the dollar. The resulting communiqué eventually reflected this. The crucial details were largely resolved at a meeting of the Deputies in London on 15 September, although they did not appear in the final communiqué. An extraordinary meeting of the Finance Ministers of the G5 was then scheduled for 22 September, at the Plaza Hotel in New York.

The 'non-paper' prepared by the Deputies before the meeting aimed at a '10-12 per cent downward adjustment of the dollar ... over the near term'. It envisaged a six-week blitz on the dollar, with the central banks jointly selling up to $18 billion of foreign currency reserves, mainly for Deutschmarks and yen. It was not lost on the British Press that the agreement came less than a week after the UK Government had raised $2.5 billion for the reserves on the Euromarkets.

The initial US plan had suggested that the United States, Germany and Japan should each assume a quarter of the intervention burden, and France and Britain an eighth apiece. This was amended at the meeting itself, following an agreement between the three European members, in favour of the United States and Japan being responsible for 30 per cent each, Germany (claiming in effect to speak also for other EMS members not in the G5) 25 per cent, France (which wanted a relatively large share on prestige grounds) 10 per cent and the UK (I was conscious of the still relatively low level of our reserves) 5 per cent. The overall European contribution thus amounted to 40 per cent rather than 50 per cent of the total, a scaling-down amply justified by the fact that the misalignment causing most concern was between the dollar and the yen – indeed, it was explicitly agreed at the meeting that the yen needed to rise more than the Deutschmark against the dollar.

After a five-hour meeting in the White and Gold Room of the Plaza Hotel, the communiqué was issued. They key passage read:

> The Ministers and Governors agreed ... that in view of the present and prospective changes in fundamentals, some further orderly appreciation of the main non-dollar currencies against the dollar is desirable. They stand ready to co-operate more closely to encourage this when to do so would be helpful.

It was Paul Volcker who insisted on the word 'orderly' to guard against a free fall of the dollar. He was supported by Pöhl and myself. The full communiqué was, at Jim Baker's urging, inordinately prolix and ranged far beyond the foreign exchange markets, with each member of the G5 giving specific policy commitments; all of which, however, reflected existing known policy intentions.

The United States undertook to reduce the Federal Budget deficit, although President Reagan remained adamantly opposed to any commitment to raise taxes; the Japanese to open their markets to foreign imports, increase public spending and allow the yen to appreciate; and the Germans to continue their programme of tax reduction and reform. For the UK, I cobbled together a series of pledges to operate an anti-inflationary monetary policy, to pursue a prudent fiscal policy, to reduce public spending as a share of GDP, to undertake further privatisation, to reduce the burden of taxation, to improve the working of the labour market and to liberalise the financial markets. All of the signatories pledged themselves to co-ordinate macroeconomic policy and to resist protectionism. This last point was regarded as very important by all of us, although it was inevitably overshadowed by the unprecedentedly specific words about exchange rates.

The word 'intervention' was not explicitly mentioned. But it had been in the January communiqué which was quite enough to leave no doubt as to the meaning of the last sentence in the extract quoted above. Few of us, of course, imagined that exchange rate stability could be achieved by intervention alone. Interest rate policy, in particular, would need to be consistent with our objective. But that was far too politically sensitive a matter to feature in any communiqué, even in code.

FROM SECRECY TO BALLYHOO

By the standards of the G5, which normally met in secret and had never issued a communiqué at all until the January meeting in Washington, the publicity that came after the Plaza agreement was astonishing. Although I recognised the immense pressure the Reagan Administration was under from the protectionist lobby in Congress, I had not realised the extent to which Jim Baker had envisaged the Plaza agreement as a great domestic political event in the United States. At the conclusion of the meeting all the US media were summoned to a hastily convened televised press conference in the slightly shabby gilded grandeur of the ageing Plaza Hotel. In order to impress Congress that there was an alternative to protection as a way of solving the world's and especially America's problems, the hitherto secret society of the G5 went public in a big way.

There is no doubt that Jim Baker hoped to derive some personal and political advantage from the Plaza agreement, as well as to silence the protectionist lobby. He was a very close friend of George Bush, who was then Vice President and the front-runner to succeed President Reagan. Baker would almost certainly have shared the Presidential ticket with Bush in 1988, were it not for the fact that both were Texans, and he explained to me the convention that the Vice President should come from a different State than the President. Nevertheless, Baker's association with an important agreement to avert a potential domestic and international economic catastrophe clearly contributed to his becoming Secretary of State under Bush in 1989.

There was another and more important benefit from the Plaza agreement. The extremely well co-ordinated publicity did not end at the Plaza Hotel. I gave a large press conference as soon as I got back to London, and most of my opposite numbers did the same on their own return.

What was evident to the world's Press, and to the financial markets, was that for the first time in many years the Finance Ministers of the major nations had genuinely got their act together, had reached an agreement of substance, and were all speaking about it in much the same terms. This gave a new credibility to the idea of international financial co-operation in general and to the G5 (and its successor) in particular. This in turn gave a boost to financial and economic conferences throughout the world – that unquantifiable but essential ingredient of economic success.

This needs to be set against the less happy consequences of the ballyhoo at the Plaza. Meetings of the G5 were never the same again. Press knowledge of a meeting increased the pressure on us to issue a communiqué, if only to prevent journalists speaking to Finance Ministers individually and – if they found that Ministers were not all singing from the same hymn book – circulating stories of discord among them. Secret meetings became impossible, and the expectations that built up ahead of meetings whose existence was publicly known were almost impossible to fulfil. If the communiqué was too bland, the Press judged the meeting a failure and the financial markets became nervous; but if it went beyond the familiar platitudes the Press would announce that the policy had changed, and the markets would take fright. The loss of privacy exacted its price. Today the only way Finance Ministers can have a genuinely secret meeting is by telephone – an innovation I suggested in 1987 and which was implemented in December of that year – but it is less satisfactory.

It was also the blaze of publicity at the conclusion of the Plaza meeting that effectively turned the G5 into the G7 that exists today. Bettino Craxi, the Italian Prime Minister at the time, found it intolerable that it should be exposed to the whole world that there was a top table to which Italy was not invited, and within a year he had found a defence issue over which he could threaten Reagan, who knew little about the G5 anyway, into promising to secure Italy's membership. This duly occurred, and inevitably Italy's inclusion meant Canada's too, thus replicating the Economic Summit membership, although thankfully no-one was so unwise as to suggest following in Jim Callaghan's footsteps and inviting the European Community to be represented. It was, however, agreed, as part of the deal among the G5 to submit to America's arm-twisting over the creation of the

Finance Ministers' G7, that the G5 should continue to have a shadowy existence alongside it. This was the cause of a great diplomatic row on the occasion of the Louvre agreement in February 1987; but with the passage of time the separate G5 became progressively more spectral.

Arguments about the Group of Seven and the Group of Five – let alone the economic summits, the Group of Ten (with its eleven members), the IMF Interim Committee and other gatherings – must remind the reader of a hastily guided tour of the splendid Gothic-Renaissance Doges' palace in Venice, where council chambers for a bewildering variety of combinations are to be found. But there were serious matters at stake. In particular, there was to my mind a real danger in the demise of the G5 and its *de facto* replacement by the somewhat unwieldy G7, with its seven Finance Ministers and seven Central Bank Governors, as well as seven Deputies. The real focus of co-operation could easily become an informal G3 consisting of the US, Japan and Germany, from which the UK would be excluded. The only reason why this did not happen after the Plaza was that the US was at least half-persuaded that it was better for it to deal bilaterally with both Japan and Germany, rather than risk being 'outvoted' in a G3. But that view could change, as it showed signs of doing under Nick Brady who took over as US Treasury Secretary towards the end of 1988. In any event the resort to bilateralism, with its counterpart on the trade front, carries dangers of its own.

EXCHANGE MARKET FOLLOW-THROUGH

The noise made by the Plaza agreement led some observers to conclude that it merely put a gloss on what was happening anyway. In retrospect, that might appear to be so. The dollar had peaked in February and was already declining, partly under the pressure of central bank intervention. But at the time, it was by no means clear that that decline would continue. Indeed there was evidence of a modest rise in the dollar shortly before the Plaza meeting. The experienced Karl Otto Pöhl was so convinced that the markets would be sceptical of our resolve that he warned us that they would test the agreement as soon as they opened on Monday morning. I suspected at the time that he was right, and it was agreed that the central banks should intervene jointly and decisively as soon as the markets challenged the agreement.

In fact the markets accepted the Plaza agreement at its face value, and by the end of the year the dollar had fallen by a further 15 per cent and more against both the yen and the Deutschmark. It went on falling throughout

1986, with sterling appreciating against the dollar and depreciating against the Deutschmark – arguably a better mix, even though the net depreciation went too far.

COMMON CAUSE, DIFFERENT AIMS

It is important to recognise, in the context of the Plaza and subsequent accords, that although I was able to make common cause with Baker most of the time, there was in fact a fundamental difference in our thinking. His objective, which he first mentioned to me in his August telephone call to me at Stoney Stanton, and which became a constant theme thereafter, was to get other countries, especially Germany and Japan, to give their economies a Keynesian demand boost in order to solve the US current account deficit and make a contribution to world growth. Baker was always terrified that high interest rates would push the United States into recession. There were clear echoes of the disastrous 'locomotive' approach of the 1978 summit in this line of thinking, despite the switch from Jimmy Carter to Ronald Reagan in the White House.

Unlike me, Baker believed in a 'real' rather than 'nominal' framework for economic policy, and his approach was essentially Keynesian. In other words, he believed that a monetary and fiscal stimulus would boost real activity rather than be frittered away in higher inflation. The fundamental change in the approach to macroeconomic policy described in my Mais Lecture, and implicit in the Medium Term Financial Strategy, never really took hold in the US Administration. The Americans continued throughout my time and afterwards to talk the old neo-Keynesian language and seemed incapable of accepting either the nominal framework or the reason for its adoption. The Administration left it to the Fed to deal with any inflationary dangers, which it did in a pragmatic way.

The earlier Regan-Sprinkel regime was in many ways much nearer to the UK Government's approach and to my own thinking; but a combination of its resolutely hands-off attitude to the dollar and its determination that US views should prevail at all costs – whereas Baker was always looking to do a deal – made it more difficult to do business with than was the case with the Baker-Darman regime.

In any event, the ideological differences that divided us mattered little so long as the dollar was clearly overvalued by almost any yardstick. Moreover the preoccupation with the US current account deficit was useful to the extent that it made the US Administration pay attention to the supposedly 'twin' Budget deficit. It would have been harmful only if it had succeeded in persuading the world's leading nations to give their economies an inflationary boost in order to help the US.

But the main reason why the process in fact developed on the whole more in the direction that I sought rather than the direction Baker sought, despite the immense power of the US, was that the Germans were simply not prepared to play ball and repeat the locomotive errors that followed the 1978 summit. When the secret Middleton-Littler mission went to Germany in December 1985, they were told that the inflation target for the next five years was an average of 2.5 per cent. In fact it averaged less than 1.5 per cent, and was slightly negative in 1986, the year oil prices plunged. Despite its refusal to follow the Americans' advice and stimulate demand, Germany still achieved a respectable growth rate of some 3 per cent a year between 1985 and 1990.

The Japanese were not too keen to stimulate their economy either, for much the same reasons. But they were always more inclined to defer to the Americans, partly because they relied on US military protection for their defence and partly because they feared US protectionism. So they placated the Americans by giving periodic boosts to their economy via grandiose plans for public works. They had the engaging habit of announcing the same programme several times, in order to make the Americans feel they were doing more than they were. But there was a genuine expansion of public works in Japan, not unconnected with the fact that the Japanese construction industry is the principal financial backer of the ruling Liberal Democrat Party, and the Japanese political system is money-based to a remarkable extent. Fortunately the Japanese economy was robust enough, at least until the early 1990s, to take these boosts in its stride. Moreover, given the chronic surplus that developed in the Japanese Budget and the country's inadequate public infrastructure, the relatively moderate boosts (after allowing for the repetition factor) were probably objectively justified.

ANOTHER OIL SHOCK

The first half of 1986 was dominated by yet another oil shock, but this time it was a price collapse rather than an explosion. After the fall from its previous peaks which occurred during my talks with OPEC Ministers as Energy Secretary the spot oil price had remained remarkably stable at $27 to $28 a barrel until almost the end of 1985. But all the time demand was being undermined by the search for energy saving and for oil substitutes triggered by the previous two price increases. And as happens in this sort of market, when the price fell, it dropped like a stone, the trigger being the failure of OPEC to agree on production quotas. Saudi Arabian light crude was selling in the first half of 1986 at an average spot price of $10 a barrel – below the level prevailing before the Iranian crisis of 1979. It recovered slightly afterwards. But apart from a brief flare-up when Iraq seized Kuwait in 1990, it remained in real terms well below the 'pre-Iranian' levels.

Just as the impact of the two oil price explosions had given an upward shove to inflationary expectations and a downward one to growth and employment, the plunging oil price was widely expected to have the opposite and much more desirable effect of ushering in a period of non-inflationary growth. The falling oil price did indeed have a beneficial immediate impact on the rate of inflation throughout the G7, which fell from just under 4 per cent in 1985 to just over 2 per cent in 1986. But just as we in the UK sadly failed to 'lock in' the oil-induced fall in inflation, the same failure was evident to some degree in the G7 as a whole, where inflation rates began to creep upwards, starting in 1987 and continuing up to 1990.

As for growth, the likely impact of lower oil prices had been greatly exaggerated by the economic forecasters. For the OPEC countries had by now learned how to spend their oil revenues (governments soon learn how to spend: it is how to refrain from spending that creates headaches); and the main impact of the lower oil price was simply a transfer of spending power and thus of demand from some countries to others. So far from boosting demand there may even have been a modest pause: for what they are worth, the official statistics show a temporary dip of half a percentage point in a very steady 3 to 3.5 per cent growth rate in the industrial world as a whole over this period.

But just as the Weimar inflation had given Germany a low toleration of inflation, so the slump of the 1930s had given the United States a low toleration even for the smallest degree of hesitation, pause or uncertainty – let alone recession. These underlying fears are magnified a thousandfold by the many very short-term analysts who live off the American financial markets. The perennial American tendency to lecture other countries about their over-restrictive policies and to call for a stimulus thus redoubled at the time of the largely mythical growth pause.

THE G5 IN LONDON

The resulting US pressure for co-ordinated international interest rate cuts was supported by France at a G5 meeting I chaired at Number 11 on 18 January 1986 – the first to be held in London for a very long time. Pierre Bérégovoy, then in his first incarnation as President Mitterrand's Finance Minister, was, with good reason, worried about the forthcoming French Parliamentary elections in March, which the Socialists lost – leading to the brief period of 'cohabitation' between a Socialist President and a Conservative Cabinet. But the rest of us were unmoved.

The advantage of holding the meeting at Number 11 was that even if the ballyhoo of the Plaza had made it impossible to hold meetings in secret any more, the barrier at the entrance to Downing Street would at least keep the Press at a reasonable distance. During the lunch I gave in the Soane dining room at the end of our discussions, however, the atmosphere took a marked turn for the worse when Jim Baker revealed that President Reagan had assured the Italian Prime Minister, Bettino Craxi, that Italy would be invited to all future meetings of the G5. It turned out that Reagan had made the offer, without consulting any of the other member governments, in response to a fierce Italian complaint backed by a threat to close American military bases in Italy. Both Gerhard Stoltenberg and I felt badly let down, and made this clear to an embarrassed and apologetic Jim Baker. But there was little we could do in the face of this *fait accompli*, apart from insisting that the old G5 should continue alongside the new arrangement.

The London meeting ended with no more than an expression of hope that interest rates might come down in the next twelve months – which to some extent they did, in response to the improved inflationary outlook – and was of historic significance only in being the last old-style free-standing meeting of the G5. It will, however, live in my memory as the occasion on which Paul Volcker went off with my navy blue Aquascutum overcoat, leaving his own behind: an amazing exchange to anyone who has seen a picture of the two of us together.

Not long afterwards the French Socialists duly lost the March election. But although I was pleased in political terms, and developed a warm personal regard for his Gaullist successor, Edouard Balladur, this did not prevent the customary exchange between Pierre Bérégovoy and myself going beyond the normal courtesies. In reply to my letter saying how much I had enjoyed working with him, he replied:

> Nous avons démontré, l'un et l'autre, qu'il était possible aux responsables des finances de nos deux pays de coopérer efficacement, bien que leurs conceptions politiques fussent différentes.[22]

[22] We have together shown that it is possible for the financial leaders of our two countries to co-operate effectively even though their political outlooks are different.

Bérégovoy, who became Finance Minister again in 1988, wrote me a warm letter after my resignation the following year; and I was delighted to see him appointed Prime Minister of France in 1992, as I made clear (to the best of my French-speaking ability) in an interview I gave French television at the time. A short, bespectacled man of working-class and trade-union background and simple tastes, he had not the slightest trace of a chip on his shoulder; and his cheerful demeanour gave no sign of the admirable toughness he displayed as a Minister. He was also one of the few active survivors of the generation whose formative years were during the war, which left him with a warmth towards Britain which is not universally shared among the French political classes today.[23]

It was at an informal Ecofin at Ootmarsum in Holland in April 1986 that I first met his successor, Edouard Balladur, a true product of the French establishment, as dignified in appearance as Bérégovoy was not, and in political terms a kindred spirit. His first task was to negotiate the devaluation of the franc against the Deutschmark at the EMS realignment meeting held in the midst of the Ootmarsum Ecofin, and he carried it off well. I felt it would be helpful to get closer to him, so I invited him to private talks in London a couple of months later. The meeting ended with lunch in the Soane dining room at Number 11, for which the Government Hospitality Services produced a claret of such splendour that Balladur talked longingly about it whenever he saw me for months afterwards.

Our political fellow-feeling was cemented by his passionate espousal of privatisation. He changed his own official Ministerial title from the traditional 'Minister for Finance and the Economy' to 'Minister for Finance, the Economy and Privatisation', and was determined to have an even larger privatisation programme than ours. There was certainly great scope for surpassing the British, since the French public sector was among the largest in Europe.

'THE SPIRIT OF GLENEAGLES'

Britain assumed the Presidency of the European Community for six months from 1 July 1986, which meant that it fell to me to host the September informal Ecofin Council. There are a number of differences between the normal monthly Ecofin Council meetings and the so-called informal meetings, of which there is one in each Community Presidency, making two a year. Whereas the regular

[23] [2010 note] Sadly, Pierre Bérégovoy committed suicide a few months after these words were written, following electoral defeat and under heavy media pressure in connection with a financial scandal.

meetings can be fitted into a normal working day, the informal ones stretch over an entire weekend. This gives time not only for relaxation and entertainment, to which wives are invited, but for more work to be done as well. The two other main differences are that Central Bank Governors attend the informal Ecofins, but not the regular meetings of the Council; and whereas the regular meetings are always held in Brussels or Luxembourg, each informal Ecofin is held in the country of the Presidency for the time being.

In my case I decided to hold the informal Ecofin of 19-21 September 1986, at Gleneagles in Scotland – the first time the Council of Ministers of the European Community had ever met in Scotland. It proved to be a popular venue, particularly among the central bankers, who have more time than Finance Ministers do to spend on the golf course.

We met at a time when the dollar was diving, largely because Jim Baker was deliberately talking it down, threatening that he would not stop doing so until the Germans gave their economy a boost by cutting interest rates. Talking a currency down is, of course, very much easier than talking it up; and Stoltenberg was not amused. There was no case in terms of German domestic policy for them to cut their interest rates, nor was there any substance to Jim Baker's belief that the world economy was flagging and in need of a boost. I was very much on Stoltenberg's side over this – as was Edouard Balladur, the French Finance Minister – and felt that Jim's behaviour was verging on the irresponsible.

I called a private breakfast meeting on the Sunday morning of my European G5 colleagues, Stoltenberg and Balladur, and our Central Bank Governors, to discuss the problem of the dollar and what our response should be. Balladur and I agreed to support Stoltenberg against Baker in return for a promise from Karl Otto Pöhl that the Bundesbank would step up its intervention in the foreign exchange market with a view to supporting the existing pattern of parities.

This agreement subsequently became known as 'the spirit of Gleneagles', and it was agreed that I should communicate our joint views by telephone to Baker. I duly did so, adding to Baker that in my opinion megaphone diplomacy of the type he was conducting was something that Finance Ministers would do better to eschew. Jim did not particularly welcome the advice, but he could see that for once his diplomatic skills had deserted him: the Germans were not going to move, and all he had achieved was a united European front against him on the issue. I then gave a rather windswept *al fresco* press conference in the bracing Highland air.

THE ROAD TO THE LOUVRE

My first meeting with Jim Baker after Gleneagles was over breakfast at the US Treasury on the morning of Saturday, 27 September 1986. I had flown to Washington for that year's Fund/Bank annual meeting. Baker was prepared to abandon his policy of talking down the dollar, and told me that the United States was in principle prepared to enter into an international agreement to stabilise exchange rates. He was prepared to discuss two versions: preferably a 'hard' one, which would include an interest rate understanding, but failing that a 'soft' one, in which the understanding would be confined to intervention. It was abundantly clear, however, that the interest rate understanding he sought concerned exclusively European, and in particular German, interest rates, rather than US rates. Indeed, either way he wanted an undertaking from the Germans at the G5 meeting that afternoon that they would cut their discount rate by half a point. I met Gerhard Stoltenberg later the same morning. He was content to see a half-point cut in the German discount rate, but said that Pöhl would not budge. Any hopes of a deal between the Americans and the Germans eventually foundered, thanks to Pöhl's opposition. This was only partly because he believed that an interest rate cut was not objectively warranted. What concerned him more was the failure of the Americans to recognise the importance of the independence of the Bundesbank, which he felt obliged to assert.

The deadlock was not broken until the Louvre Accord, some five months later. In essence, the well-prepared G5/G7 meeting in Paris over the weekend of 21 and 22 February 1987, and chaired by Edouard Balladur in that corner of the Louvre in which, as Finance Minister, he still had his office, was the sequel to the 'spirit of Gleneagles'. The French, the Germans and ourselves had agreed there that something needed to be done to arrest the plummeting dollar, and we had also agreed that Jim Baker should cease his megaphone diplomacy – and on behalf of the three of us, I had told him so. It followed that we needed to have a private meeting with Jim, where we could count on Japanese support.

Since the Plaza meeting less than eighteen months earlier, the dollar had fallen almost 50 per cent against the Deutschmark and more than that against the yen. The situation had become absurd. It was not simply a matter of German and Japanese concerns about American competitiveness. That was the least of my worries. The real problem, as I saw it, was different, and more fundamental. Not surprisingly, given the 'J curve' phenomenon (a devaluation initially causes a deterioration in a country's trade balance, before there is any improvement, since prices adjust before volumes do, rather like the shape of the letter 'J'), the US current account was still in substantial deficit.

This was causing many Americans who should have known better to argue that the dollar should continue to decline until the current account deficit was eliminated. At the same time, the foreign exchange markets were happily selling dollars on the way down in the same spirit as they had been buying them on the way up. In other words, we were headed for a dollar overshoot in the downward direction which could well prove as massive as the earlier upward overshoot had been. If nothing was done, there was no reason why this violent switchback – wholly unrelated to economic fundamentals – should not become the norm, causing severe dislocation to the world economy.

In these circumstances, it did not require a genius to discern the need for the G5 to reach an agreement to stabilise the dollar, at least for a time. Nor was this disputed by Jim Baker (still less by Paul Volcker). But Jim was determined to get something in return for his agreement: an undertaking by the Germans and the Japanese to boost their economic growth. They duly obliged – the Japanese modestly, the Germans entirely cosmetically; but it was enough to save Baker's face, which was important. There remained only the precise details of the concerted intervention scheme to be worked out and the wording of the communiqué to be agreed; both of which, after prolonged discussion, were achieved.

Once the meeting was over, a press conference was arranged at one of the grander rooms in the Louvre, all chandeliers, gilt and mirrors, at which it was agreed that all the Ministers present should make a short statement. Baker, Stoltenberg and I were the only ones who had also taken part in the Plaza agreement; and when it came to my turn I was anxious to promote the thought that this was not an ephemeral response to an immediate crisis but part of a continuing process of international financial co-operation. Accordingly, I described the Louvre agreement (somewhat to Balladur's dismay, I suspect), as

> Plaza 2 ... I see this meeting as the lineal descendant of the Plaza meeting ... Then we all agreed that the dollar should fall; now we all agree we need stability.

There was another reason why I wished to link the two. The markets knew that the dollar had indeed fallen following the Plaza, and I wanted them to expect a similar success following the Louvre. For sterling, an agreement to peg the three main world trading currencies offered the prospect of a welcome respite from the pressure the pound had been under for most of the previous year. For that reason, as well as for the contribution it could make to currency stability in the world as a whole, I was a strong supporter of the Louvre Accord.

The communiqué issued by the G6 on 22 February 1987 contained a great deal of routine prose pledging the signatories to eradicate current account imbalances, fight protection and co-ordinate economic policies. The Germans agreed to a package of tax cuts (mostly the bringing forward of measures which were already part of Stoltenberg's policy) and the Japanese to reform taxes, raise public spending and cut their discount rate by half a point. For their part, the Americans undertook to stabilise the dollar and once again promised to cut the Federal Budget deficit. The key paragraph in the communiqué was the tenth and last:

> The Ministers and Governors agreed that the substantial exchange rate changes since the Plaza Agreement will increasingly contribute to reducing external imbalances and have now brought their currencies within ranges broadly consistent with underlying economic fundamentals, given the policy commitments summarised in this statement. Further substantial exchange rate shifts among their currencies could damage growth and adjustment prospects in their countries. In current circumstances, therefore, they agreed to co-operate closely to foster stability of exchange rates around current levels.

The unpublished central rates agreed for the dollar were 1.825 Deutschmarks and 153.5 yen. There was no explicit range for sterling, but it was understood that sterling would conform to the spirit of the agreement. Needless to say, it suited me to let the market think there was a floor under the pound, which had been having a rough time. Indeed, in effect I put one there at my press briefing immediately following the Louvre Accord, when I declared, with deliberate asymmetry that I did not wish to see sterling fall any further or rise significantly, from its then level.

There was an inner range of 2.5 per cent either side of these central rates within which intervention would be discretionary and an outer range of 5 per cent on either side beyond which it would be obligatory.

A modest war chest of $4 billion was established for intervention, with the US, Japan, and Europe contributing a third each. Much scholastic argument was devoted to what to call these ranges: the agreed jargon was 'reference ranges'.

These ranges would have 'soft edges'. This was partly a reference to the inner and outer ranges. But it also meant – although this was much less explicit – that if the outer ranges came under pressure there would be consultations on whether to continue defending them or to move the centre point.

The Louvre Accord worked reasonably well for a time, after an upward adjustment of the yen central rate to Y146 to the dollar at the G5 held in Washington in April 1987 on the eve of the IMF spring meeting. The weakness of the Accord, which eventually undermined it, was its failure to bolster the pledge to intervene in the foreign exchange markets with an undertaking to adjust domestic monetary policies to validate the agreed ranges.

There was in fact much discussion and general agreement on the need to be prepared to validate the ranges by interest rate changes, although nothing about interest rates appeared in the official declaration partly because of American political sensitivities (shared to a lesser extent by others), partly because of the Bundesbank's insistence that nothing could be allowed to derogate from its independence, and partly because the agreement in principle on interest rate differentials did not in practice solve the problem of how any change in differentials should be shared between the country whose interest rate needed to rise, in relative terms, and the country whose interest rate needed to fall in relative terms.

In itself, the absence of any explicit reference to interest rate changes was in line with historical precedent, and thus scarcely surprising. Bretton Woods was a highly formal exchange rate system, and it contained no express provision for accompanying domestic monetary policies. But Bretton Woods contained a key currency or numeraire, the dollar, which in effect told everyone what they had to do – that is, to adjust their policy to maintain the dollar parity. The Louvre lacked this. As a result, when the dollar weakened against the Deutschmark (or the Deutschmark strengthened against the dollar), the Germans were convinced that the US should raise interest rates, something the Americans refused to do; while the Americans for their part were equally convinced that the Germans should reduce *their* interest rates, something to which the Germans were equally adamantly opposed.

The resolution of this dilemma might have been helped had I been able to persuade Baker to agree a global nominal framework, since this might have indicated whether a net loosening or a net tightening of global monetary conditions was appropriate. As it was, while my relationship with Baker worked well in personal terms and on the basis of immediate deals and strategies, there was a very practical disagreement on whether the main dangers facing the world in 1987 were recession or incipient inflation, which could not be papered over so easily.

Later that year, in September, Jim Baker made no effort to conceal his irritation at a German decision to raise interest rates shortly after the Federal Reserve had done the same, thereby nullifying its effect. When the dollar slipped outside its Louvre trading range against the Deutschmark the following month he refused to support an increase in interest rates, arguing that it would tip the American economy into recession. This fear was manifestly unfounded – the American economy at that time was growing strongly – and may have mainly reflected his exasperation with Pöhl. Unfortunately, his very public dispute with the Germans erupted at a time when Wall Street had enjoyed a particularly large and substantial rise and was ripe for a correction. By undermining market confidence in G7 co-operation, he undoubtedly helped to precipitate the stock market crash of Black Monday, 19 October 1987, a few days later.

PART FOUR

POLICIES AND PEOPLE

CHAPTER THIRTY

THE STORY OF THE POLL TAX – 1

Prologue · Basic Issues · Early Reform Efforts · Alternatives to Rates
Scottish Revaluation · Lord Rothschild Lights a Fuse

PROLOGUE

In retrospect, it is clear that all the elements which were to bring down Margaret Thatcher five years later had emerged in embryo in 1985: the row over ERM and the dawn of EMU; the Poll Tax; the Prime Ministerial ambitions of Michael Heseltine; and the quasi-presidential aspirations of Margaret herself. But on the most comprehensible of these issues – that of the Poll Tax – many of the charges against Margaret Thatcher are unfair. It was a colossal error of judgement on her part to seek to turn a form of taxation which had been notorious throughout the ages into the flagship of her Government. Yet it is quite untrue to say that her Cabinet colleagues were 'bounced' into accepting it.

Despite her profound personal commitment, she observed the proprieties of Cabinet government throughout. For month after month in 1985 she chaired innumerable meetings of the Sub-Committee of the Economic Committee of Cabinet known as E(LF), the 'LF' standing for Local Finance. In view of the wide range of local government responsibilities, the membership of that Committee comprised two thirds of the entire Cabinet, including such politically aware colleagues as Willie Whitelaw, Douglas Hurd, Norman Fowler and Norman Tebbit; and because of its obviously political nature the Chief Whip, John Wakeham, also attended.

So far from the tax being a product of haste and inadequate preparation, it was preceded by the most detailed Departmental studies, by no less than two and a half years of intensive ministerial discussion, and by a Green Paper which ushered in a period of public consultation. Nor is it true that Ministers were uninformed about how the tax would work in practice. We were all provided with a very full 'Specification Report' by the Department of the Environment. Having failed to persuade the Prime Minister in private of the folly of what she had in mind, I had no alternative but to table a dissenting Cabinet paper, which I did in May 1985, drawing on that report and explaining precisely what the consequences would be.

Unfortunately, I received no support from any of my colleagues on the 1985 Cabinet Sub-Committee – with the exception of my two Chief Secretaries, Peter Rees until the 1985 reshuffle and, more vigorously, John MacGregor thereafter; but inevitably they were not heard as independent voices. The main blame for this lies not with Margaret Thatcher, who certainly made clear her impatience with dissent (on one occasion, when I was unavoidably absent and left it to John MacGregor to carry the torch, he had his head well and truly bitten off for his pains), but with a general characteristic of Cabinet government in practice.

Ministers too often see themselves first and foremost as departmental chiefs with their own departmental battles to fight. When an issue arises, as it did with the Poll Tax, where the Prime Minister of the day and the responsible Minister (in this case Kenneth Baker) are wholly and indeed enthusiastically at one, their colleagues – who have causes of their own over which they are either seeking Prime Ministerial support or resisting Prime Ministerial pressure – are disinclined to raise objections. That the Poll Tax was a disaster is beyond dispute; but it is important to learn the right lessons and not the wrong ones from this sorry story.

BASIC ISSUES

The battle between central and local government for control of local authority expenditure was one of the perennial themes of the Thatcher years. Its persistence reflected the failure of the Government to resolve satisfactorily the two fundamental problems which bedevilled dealings between central and local government. One was the unsatisfactory constitutional position of the local authorities. Throughout my time as Chancellor local authority spending accounted for a quarter of total public expenditure, of which roughly half was funded by the Treasury. Overspending by local authorities could thus have a pronounced effect on the public finances. Yet central government had in practice very little control over local government spending.

The second and closely related problem was the inadequacy of the rates as a tax base for fulfilling the many responsibilities either imposed upon or voluntarily assumed by local authorities. The rates were invented in 1601, but extended rapidly during the nineteenth century. At that time most local authority services – refuse collection, roads, gas, water and electricity – were supplied to properties. A property rate, based on the rental value of the house, was a sensible way of paying for such services. Moreover, in those days the franchise was restricted to property owners; so those who did not own property were unable to vote to receive services at the ratepayers' expense.

By the 1970s most of the original local authority services had long since been nationalised and councils were obliged to provide a variety of other services, of which education and personal social services were only the most obvious and the most expensive. Successive Governments responded by substantially augmenting the rates with grants from the Exchequer. The principal mechanism for this, the Rate Support Grant (RSG), was calculated according to an incomprehensible formula designed to take account of local needs and resources, and there was a variety of other, more specific, grants from central government.

EARLY REFORM EFFORTS

A succession of devices was introduced during the 1980s to enhance central government's influence over the amount of local spending. These included taking a tough line on the overall sise of central government grants, a complicated system of allocating grants which penalised overspending, abolition of the power to levy supplementary rates, compulsory tendering to provide certain services, scrapping the Greater London Council and the six metropolitan authorities, the establishment of the Audit Commission for Local Government and, via the Rates Act of 1984, taking powers to cap excessive rate increases. According to one count, the Government passed roughly fifty separate acts affecting local government in its first decade, almost all of them designed to restrain council spending. Every measure was easily caricatured as an affront to local democracy.

Throughout this saga there were always two distinct perspectives within the Government. The Department of the Environment, which dispensed central government grants to local authorities, maintained throughout the tenureship of several different Secretaries of State that, unless the local authorities were treated generously by central government, they would raise the rates and alienate local businessmen and voters from the Government. The Treasury view, on the contrary, was that a generous central government grant would only encourage the local authorities to spend even more.

In fact, both sides were right. Faced with a smaller grant than it would have liked to receive, the typical council would respond partly by trimming back its spending plans, as the Treasury always maintained, and partly by increasing the rates. Given our muddled constitution and muddled system of local government finance, part of the blame for any large rate increase would be laid at the council's door and part at the Government's, as the Environment Department claimed. The strength of the Treasury's case was that, given the overriding need to curb the growth of public spending, its truth was a more important truth than the Environment Department's was. Moreover the Government had a reserve power to cap the rates.

The annual battle within Government over the size of the rate support grant invariably exposed Margaret's ambivalence. Her low regard for local government, particularly that large part of it under Labour control, made her unsympathetic to the Environment Department's case for generosity; while her fixation with the evil nature of the rates made her reluctant to endorse the Treasury's case for parsimony. In the event, the Government did take a tough line over central government grants to local government, but probably not tough enough.

Although the relationship between central and local government had started to turn sour during the latter part of the previous Labour Government, when the then Environment Secretary, Anthony Crosland, uttered his celebrated warning that 'the party is over', it was during the Thatcher Government that it degenerated into something close to open warfare. The reason for this was the collapse of the traditional understanding that, irrespective of the colour of the Party in power at local level, a local authority would conduct its affairs in more or less conformity with the economic policy of the Government of the day.

This understanding broke down for two main reasons. The first was the arrival in office, for the first time within living memory, of a Government committed to imposing severe curbs on public spending, and this at a time when local councillors – Conservative almost as much as Labour – had come to believe that their sole *raison d'etre* was to improve the services for which they were responsible by spending ever more public money. The second was the emergence of a new breed of Labour councillor, of which the Militant Tendency group which for some years controlled Liverpool were only the most extreme example, dedicated to pursuing a policy diametrically opposed to that of the Government.

As a result, the tendency of local government to exceed the spending forecasts the Government made and on which its grant disbursements were based, became endemic. It was this that led to the gradual decline in the share of local government spending financed by central government grants from 57 per cent in 1979/80 to 48 per cent in 1989/90. Had the overspending been validated by the Government maintaining the share unchanged, public expenditure control would clearly have disappeared out of the window altogether. This was particularly acute because of the differences between the behaviour of different councils. At one end of the scale there were still some councils that sought to abide by the traditional understanding. At the other end there were those whose ambition was to establish a high-spending Socialist republic. In these circumstances, to validate overall overspending would have meant rewarding the worst overspenders, which would have been as counterproductive politically as it was unthinkable in economic terms.

Indeed, as it was, the annual battle between the Treasury and the Environment Department was accompanied by a separate but parallel battle between the Government and its back-benchers. The Government, conscious of the acute problems of the inner cities, distributed a large amount of grant to those areas (even if it was considerably less than they sought). Tory back-benchers tended to consider this as the sacrifice of their own constituents' interests in favour of the irresponsible extravagance of doctrinaire socialist authorities. Parochial though the back-benchers often were, they had a case; which increasingly led the Government to seek more effective and imaginative ways of dealing with the inner city problem, involving a larger role for the private sector and the sidelining of unco-operative local authorities. This is clearly a field in which there is still much to do.

ALTERNATIVES TO RATES

It may be a surprise to some readers that rates and their successors' taxes were not under the control of the Chancellor of the Exchequer. Unfortunately, although all forms of local taxation are undoubtedly taxes, they have always been seen as an aspect of local government, and thus fall within the responsibility of the Secretary of State for the 'Environment' (a trendy version of the more accurate earlier title 'Housing and Local Government'). The Chancellor has his say, as he does in all matters affecting public finance, but his unique personal responsibility for national taxes does not extend to the local level.

As Chapter 2 records, the centrepiece of the housing section of the Conservative Manifesto for the second 1974 general election had been a pledge to replace rates by 'taxes related to people's ability to pay', although no-one in the Party had the slightest idea what the replacement would be. When the Conservatives lost the October 1974 election the whole package automatically lapsed. Moreover, the election-winning 1979 Manifesto clearly stated: 'Cutting income tax must take priority for the time being over abolition of the domestic rating system.' But Margaret Thatcher did not forget the promise she had made to the voters in 1974. She was determined to return to the issue at some stage.

The rating system attracted a variety of criticisms. Because domestic rates were levied on the basis of houses, irrespective of the number of occupants, a widow living alone on a pension complained that she paid the same amount as four adults in paid employment living in exactly the same kind of house next door. People who improved their home, and thereby increased its notional rental value, had to pay higher rates – something that Margaret considered particularly reprehensible. Local businesses, which paid more in rates than did householders, had no vote at all in local elections and were therefore suffering from taxation without representation. To cap it all, the egalitarian grant system was so complicated as to be completely incomprehensible.

By 1981 the difficulties the Government was experiencing in controlling local authority expenditure, and increasing complaints that excessive rate increases were driving firms out of business, had reawakened Margaret's interest in the iniquities of rates. Michael Heseltine, then the Environment Secretary, published on 16 December 1981 a Green Paper entitled *Alternatives to Domestic Rates*, which explored a wide range of options. It remains a valuable summary of the three main alternatives to some sort of rating system – a local sales tax, a local income tax and a poll tax – and of the reasons why none of them would work.

A sales tax, it pointed out, would merely encourage people to shop in neighbouring areas where the sales tax was lower. A local income tax was the solution favoured by most local government professionals; and the Layfield Committee of Enquiry into Local Government Finance, set up by the Labour Government, had recommended supplementing the rates with a local income tax collected via the national PAYE system. But the Green Paper was lukewarm both about this idea and about local income taxes in general, warning of additional staffing needs at the Inland Revenue, of delays in introducing it and of a variable yield. Moreover, as part of the PAYE system, it would merge imperceptibly into the national income tax, defeating the goal of making councillors more accountable to their electorates. It was in any event of little attraction to a Government pledged to reduce the overall burden of income tax.

The 1981 Green Paper was also unenthusiastic about a flat-rate poll tax, calculating it would cost every adult in Britain the politically unacceptable sum of about £120 a head, or more if there were significant exemptions. It concluded: 'The Government believes that a flat-rate annual capitation charge of this order of magnitude would almost certainly not be a practical proposition.' In fact, the Poll Tax averaged roughly £400 when it was introduced in 1990, or more than twice the level the Green Paper judged impractical, even after allowing for inflation since 1981.

SCOTTISH REVALUATION

The consultations on the Green Paper, which were formally concluded in March 1982, led to the conclusion that there was no satisfactory alternative to the rates. This was greeted with relief by almost everybody in the Cabinet, and the issue went to sleep for the remainder of the parliament. But although asleep, it was not, alas, dead. Patrick Jenkin, who succeeded Michael Heseltine after the 1983 Election, and whose desire to seek after truth invariably exceeded his political judgement, felt he ought to launch yet another review of local government finance which, with Margaret's enthusiastic support, he duly announced at the 1984 Party Conference. Even so, this might not have come to anything had it not been for the problems raised by the 1985 Scottish rating revaluation.

Under English law, which also covers Wales, rating revaluations are meant to occur periodically, but it is left to the Government of the day to decide exactly when. They are obviously highly unpopular, and there had not been one in England and Wales since 1973. The delay was not entirely cynical. The private rental sector had been virtually eliminated, and there was scarcely any evidence on which to base a revaluation. It was for this reason, among others, that the Layfield Committee had recommended in 1976 that the next revaluation be carried out on the basis of sale prices rather than on notional rental values. Although evidence of sale prices was plentiful, a revaluation on that basis would, as the Heseltine Green Paper demurely put it, lead to 'some redistribution of the rate burden between households.' It therefore recommended banding to reduce the extent of the changes which were bound to take place. This, ironically, was the essence of the system which Michael Heseltine, once more Environment Secretary a decade later, was to announce in April 1991 as the replacement for Poll Tax.

In Scotland, however, revaluation was unavoidable, since Scottish law explicitly required it every five years. All revaluations are unpopular, since there are bound to be losers, but the Scottish rating revaluation of 1985 was particularly explosive, since commercial properties gained at the expense of the domestic ratepayer. Household rates rose by an average of 20 per cent, and in many cases, of course, the increase was substantially greater than this. The politics were uncharacteristically badly handled by George Younger, who was then Secretary of State for Scotland. The new valuations were announced without any transitional arrangements to ease the shock, and many Scottish voters, particularly in the more prosperous areas represented by the twenty-one remaining Conservative MPs north of the border, found themselves facing massive rate increases overnight.

A huge political row broke out in Scotland and George Younger had an exceptionally rough reception at the Scottish Conservative Party Conference in May 1985. I was obliged to shore up his position and eventually agreed to make the best part of £100 million available in transitional relief to ease the burden of the revaluations, of which more than half was spent on domestic ratepayers. This put the rates issue right at the forefront of the political agenda. George Younger argued passionately in Cabinet that quinquennial revaluations were political suicide for the Conservative Party in Scotland and that the Government had to abolish the rates before the next one was due in 1990. Margaret added that a revaluation could not be put off indefinitely in England and Wales, either, and that would be far worse. She was adamant that the rates had to go.

LORD ROTHSCHILD LIGHTS A FUSE

Patrick Jenkin, asked by Margaret to devise an alternative to the rates, was at a loss to know what to do. He asked his two junior Ministers on the local government side of the Environment Department, Kenneth Baker and William Waldegrave, to re-examine the territory covered by the 1981 Green Paper to see if they could come up with anything. Waldegrave in turn asked his hero, the late Lord (Victor) Rothschild – the former head of Ted Heath's Central Policy Review Staff, in which William had served in the early 1970s – to let him have a paper on the principles of local taxation.

This was a fatal invitation. Rothschild prided himself on having no political judgement: he was above that sort of thing. Unfortunately, William Waldegrave seemed to consider it an advantage that Rothschild would examine the issue with a mind uncluttered by political preconceptions. The central proposition of the paper Rothschild eventually produced was that a poll tax was the best solution. William added his gloss to it and submitted the paper to Patrick Jenkin, who passed it without much further reflection to the Prime Minister, who in turn convened a meeting to discuss it at Chequers on Sunday, 31 March 1985, to which I was of course invited. I never liked giving up a Sunday in this way; and having been assured that this was simply a preliminary discussion at which no decisions would be taken, I foolishly decided not to go and to send Peter Rees, then my Chief Secretary, in my place. Before leaving for the weekend, I briefed him to register my firm opposition to a poll tax, and gave him the arguments to use.

In fact, the Chequers meeting moved the discussion on much further than I had been led to expect. It apparently began with a description by Kenneth Baker of the existing state of affairs in local government. He argued that many councillors and voters were extremely unhappy with the rating system and its lack of accountability, which he defined as the absence of any strong connection between local expenditure and local taxation. Any solution, he said, must act on that central issue. One option was to bring local expenditure and taxation into line by shifting the cost of education to central government. Perversely, he rejected the idea as failing to improve local accountability: in fact the reverse was the case.

William Waldegrave then presented the preferred alternative of the Environment Ministers. This was the creation of a national business rate to replace non-domestic rates, coupled with the abolition of domestic rates and their replacement by a local residents' charge falling equally on all adults in each local authority area. He maintained that only this idea achieved true local accountability, by making local voters responsible for local spending and bringing home to them the real cost of local authority services. There would be rebates for those on low incomes, but not so generous as to insulate them completely from spendthrift councils. In this way a 'graduated residents' charge' would gradually replace the rates. He also recommended a move over the long term towards single-tier local authorities.

The discussion which followed these two presentations was a lengthy one, during which the immense political disadvantages of a poll tax became apparent but were ignored. The meeting evidently agreed that the case against the rates was a strong one, both politically and financially. (In fact, in England and Wales it was a sleeping dog that could perfectly well have been allowed to lie.) But it was also recognised that the proposed residents' charge would be much more difficult and costly to collect, and that the effects of an increase in the tax would be felt much more keenly and immediately by the voters than increases in rates. That, of course, was meant to be part of the attraction of the scheme. Margaret, summing up, congratulated Waldegrave and his officials on their proposal and invited them to develop the idea, by drawing up illustrative examples of the effect of a poll tax on particular authorities and individuals.

She rejected outright the idea of single-tier authorities, perhaps because it would only delay the rapid timetable she was already formulating in her mind. The aim was to publish a White Paper in the autumn of 1985, and to introduce legislation in the 1986–87 parliamentary session. A second ministerial discussion was scheduled for the second half of May.

Once I found out from Peter Rees what had happened at the Chequers meeting I was horrified. There were some aspects of the Waldegrave proposals – like the national business rate – which I could support, but it was clear to me that the idea of replacing domestic rates with a poll tax would be a political disaster. I asked William Waldegrave to come round and see me privately at Number 11 and told him as much. He noted my dissent but defended his ideas vigorously, apparently confident that there was considerable Prime Ministerial momentum behind them. This prompted me to explain the political dangers as I saw them to Margaret directly at one of our regular bilaterals. She played down the advanced state of the discussion, assuring me that I would be a member of the Cabinet committee responsible for the reform of local government finance and that I could lay all my objections before it. This led to the memorandum of dissent which I circulated ahead of the committee's initial meeting on 20 May 1985. It was the most strongly worded attack I launched on any policy proposal throughout my time in Government.

CHAPTER THIRTY-ONE

THE STORY OF THE POLL TAX – 2

'Unworkable and Politically Catastrophic' · The Steamroller Rolls
'Everyone Pays' · The Death of Dual Running · The Disaster Unfolds
Operation and Outcome

'UNWORKABLE AND POLITICALLY CATASTROPHIC'

In drafting my memorandum of 16 May 1985, I was able to draw much of my ammunition from the exemplifications of the Poll Tax in practice which had been drawn up by officials at the Department of the Environment (who were privately astonished that the tax had been taken seriously) and circulated to the Committee in the Specification Report:

> I agree that our system of local government finance cannot be left as it is, and that radical change is needed ... I believe it is well worth pursuing further the proposals which Kenneth Baker and William Waldegrave have made to enhance local accountability by making radical changes both in the system of Exchequer grants to local authorities and in the way revenue is raised from non-domestic properties ... I am also attracted by the subsidiary proposals for annual elections, for the greater use of fees and charges, and for overhauling local authorities' budgetary framework ... Fixed needs grants and per capita grants also have clear attractions ...
>
> It is only when we come to the question of what local tax we should have that I have to depart altogether from the proposals in the Specification Report. The report recognises that a flat-rate poll tax would be politically unsustainable; even with a rebate scheme the package would have 'an unacceptable impact' on certain types of household.
>
> The biggest gainers would be better off households in high rateable value properties; the losers would be poorer households, particularly larger ones. Tables 3 (a) to 3 (e) give a horrifying picture of the impact. A pensioner couple in Inner London could find themselves paying 22 per cent of their

> net income in poll tax, whereas a better off couple in the suburbs would pay only 1 per cent. We should be forced to give so many exemptions and concessions (inevitably to the benefit of high spending authorities in Inner London) that the flat-rate poll tax would rapidly become a surrogate income tax. That is what a 'graduated residents' charge' is. The Introductory Report, for very good reasons, rejects local income taxes ...
>
> Whatever system we adopt, we should learn from this year's experiences in Scotland: we should always ensure that revaluations – and other changes – are phased in over a reasonable period. The problems of an old-style revaluation upheaval would, of course, be magnified many times during the period of transition from rates to poll tax. This is not simply a hideous political problem: local authorities would seize the opportunity to bump up their spending and revenue and blame it all on the imposition by the Government of an alien system of taxation ... The proposal for a poll tax would be completely unworkable and politically catastrophic. A radical reform of the rating system seems a more attractive option.

My paper was unequivocal in its condemnation of a poll tax, not least because even if it were transformed into a surrogate income tax it would have exactly the same disincentive effects as an increase in national income tax. The radical reform of the rating system I proposed in its place had the following features:

- There would be a shift to capital values as the basis of reformed rates.
- The change could be simplified and the redistributive effects reduced by 'banding': that is to say, houses within a particular price range would be taxed on the basis of the bottom of the range.
- Shocks caused by revaluation would be much reduced by 'rolling revaluations' in which the new valuation would be phased in very gradually over a period of, say, ten years, or when the property changed hands, whichever was sooner.
- The most deeply felt injustice of the rating system would be met by a fixed percentage reduction for pensioners living alone.
- The problem of accountability would be met by central government taking over complete responsibility for the financing of, and key aspects of the management of, education – desirable in itself on educational grounds.
- The educational expenditure taken over would be financed either by the Government retaining the proceeds of business rates as a national tax or by

eliminating the bulk of the Rate Support Grant, which local authorities, relieved of the cost of education, would no longer need.

These proposals would have greatly improved local accountability by substantially reducing councils' reliance on central government funding and producing a much closer link between local spending and local revenue. Moreover, as I pointed out, taxes on property are cheap to collect and difficult to avoid. They have a clear local base and have a rough-and-ready relationship to ability to pay.

My proposals would also have had the bonus of acting as a dampener on the great housing boom that was to make the conduct of economic policy so difficult in subsequent years. But even without any such boom, a tax on property values is abundantly justified as it reduces the fiscal privilege attaching to home ownership over alternative investments. Indeed a Treasury economist's paper might well have started with this point. The interaction of extended fiscal privilege (due to the prospective demise of the rates, superimposed on mortgage interest relief) with the effects of credit liberalisation was undoubtedly a potent and aggravating force in the boom of the late 1980s. Kenneth Baker's own 1986 Green Paper acknowledged that abolishing domestic rates would raise house prices by about 5 per cent. Most outside economists put the figure at around 20 per cent.

THE STEAMROLLER ROLLS

To my intense disappointment and some surprise, since the case seemed to me so clear, my objections received no support at all at the meeting of 20 May. Margaret invited Patrick Jenkin to develop the Waldegrave proposals further, but I was asked merely to circulate further details of my modified property tax proposal. The Poll Tax was then given fresh momentum by the removal of Patrick Jenkin as Environment Secretary in the first week of September 1985 and his replacement by Kenneth Baker, who as Minister of State in charge of local government was part-author of the original proposal. This was Kenneth's first Cabinet post.

Partly because he had managed Ted Heath's leadership campaign in 1975, Margaret had not had much time for Kenneth. When the Government was first formed in 1979 he languished on the back benches until he wrote his own job specification by persuading her in January 1981 that the Department of Industry needed a Minister for Information Technology. In that post he presided over such wonders as 'IT Year' in 1982. These essentially presentational skills commended him to her in the autumn of 1985, when the Government was trailing badly in the opinion polls. Kenneth sought to secure his new status as a Cabinet Minister by outdoing Margaret in his enthusiasm for the proposed new tax. His performances for Cabinet and the Press, using slides and charts and blackboards, clearly demonstrated his talent for presentation. It was only the policy that was wrong.

At a two-and-a-half-hour meeting of the Cabinet Sub-Committee on 23 September 1985, I again voiced my grave misgivings about the Poll Tax, and was loyally and effectively supported by my new Chief Secretary, John MacGregor. Kenneth, to my relief, said he now proposed to supplement a flat-rate poll tax with a property tax along the lines I had suggested. But the meeting was inconclusive, and a second meeting of the committee had to be convened before Cabinet on 3 October, to clarify what Kenneth could tell the Party Conference the following week. I lobbied some of my senior colleagues on the committee; but they tended to view the matter very much from a departmental perspective rather than a political one. The Poll Tax seemed unstoppable and was the centrepiece of the new Green Paper *Paying for Local Government*, unveiled by Kenneth Baker on 28 January 1986.

At this stage, the proposal was to freeze domestic rate bills in 1990 and introduce a 'residents' tax' on everyone over eighteen to make up the amount of local authority income lost to inflation every year. The new tax would rise gradually as frozen rate bills produced falling real income for councils, until by the turn of the century domestic rates would have disappeared altogether. This became known as 'dual running'. It was hoped that, by phasing the rates out and the Poll Tax in, the voters would gradually become accustomed to the Poll Tax as the primary source of local authority revenue.

While this made sense on its own terms, I saw an additional advantage in dual running. If the Poll Tax were to prove as counterproductive and as big a political liability as I had warned my colleagues it would, it would be a relatively simple matter to 'stop the clock' as soon as this started to become apparent, leaving us with a hybrid system consisting largely of the rates, but with a small poll tax superimposed on them. This might not be very elegant, but it would be in every way preferable to a state of affairs in which rates no longer existed and the Poll Tax was the sole form of local government taxation.

The Green Paper estimated that the average Poll Tax bill might rise from £50 a head in 1990 to £250 a head in the year 2000. A rebate system would vary the level of the charge from 20 per cent for the least well off to 100 per cent for the wealthiest individuals. The non-domestic rate was to be abolished altogether and replaced by a uniform business rate levied on all commercial and industrial property, which would have been revalued by 1990. Indexed to inflation, it was designed to rescue business from the swingeing rate increases levied by local authorities on a sector which, as such, had no vote.

The Green Paper was well received on the Conservative benches, where there was no love for the rates, and they accepted Kenneth's sales patter without wishing to probe too deeply – as indeed, to their discredit, did the Press. It was greeted, rather more ominously, with universal hostility among the local authorities, Conservative as well as Labour, who would have to operate the new system. The consultation period was due to expire on 31 October 1986. By then Kenneth had moved on to the Department of Education, where Margaret hoped his presentational skills would help to solve the teachers' pay dispute. Nick Ridley, who as Transport Secretary had served on the Cabinet Sub-Committee on the Poll Tax, replaced Kenneth as Secretary of State for the Environment in the same reshuffle, which was prompted by the resignation of Keith Joseph, on 21 May 1986.

At the time, I greatly welcomed the change, partly on public spending grounds – since for Kenneth no level of spending was too high, whereas Nick was thoroughly sound on that issue at least – but partly, too, because it seemed to offer the last chance to draw back from the Poll Tax. And, indeed, initially Nick did not feel at all comfortable with the Poll Tax. However, he soon recognised Margaret's enthusiasm for it, and became a convert himself. Sadly, Margaret had lost all her usual political judgement about the issue. By 1986 it had become a matter of principle to her to abolish the rates, about which she had developed a phobia rivalling her sentiments towards the ERM. By that time, too, it had acquired its official name of the 'Community Charge', and at informal lunches, on completely different topics, she would become very agitated if the 'Poll Tax' was mentioned, drumming her fingers on the table as if it were a piano, and saying that it must *not* be called a poll tax but a 'Community Charge'.

'EVERYONE PAYS'

Supporters of the Poll Tax – and even some opponents – were mesmerised by its supposed great merit that, unlike the case with the rates, 'everyone pays'. This was one of the arguments stressed most strongly by Kenneth Baker, when he first presented the tax to his Cabinet colleagues, and it was eagerly taken up by Margaret. In this, as so often, I found myself marvelling at her inconsistency.

While eloquent on the 'everyone pays' argument for the Poll Tax, she welcomed increases in personal tax allowances which took people out of the income tax net altogether. And of all the imposts on the statute-book, the one she detested most was the television licence fee, the closest approximation to a poll tax in the entire system, with precisely the same regressive characteristics.

But in any case the distinction between the rates and the Poll Tax, on these grounds, was largely spurious. While it was true that only one rate bill was sent to each household, the vast majority of the alleged non-payers of rates were the wives of householders, few of whom can have been unaware that the family had to pay rates. The only other sizeable class of adult non-ratepayers consisted of those at the bottom of the income scale, whose rate rebates (later subsumed into housing benefit) were large enough to exhaust their liability to rates altogether. But this problem had already been dealt with, before the advent of the Poll Tax. In time for what was to prove the last year of the rating system, the law had been changed to ensure that rate rebates could not exceed 80 per cent of the rate bill.

THE DEATH OF DUAL RUNNING

Nick Ridley initially recognised some of the problems inherent in the Poll Tax, which I had spelled out in my 1985 memorandum, and came to see me at Number 11 for a heart-to-heart talk about them. He was particularly concerned about the politics of the duke paying the same as the dustman, and we discussed how the tax might be changed to make it less regressive. Following our meeting, he wrote to me saying that he would be working up an alternative to the Community Charge along the lines we had discussed, but would bring it forward only if the issue went badly at the Party Conference in October.

Despite these doubts, Nick was opposed from the start to the Green Paper's proposal that there should be dual running – on the grounds, as he later put it, that it 'never seemed to me right to have two taxes in operation at once, and the accountability advantages of the Community Charge would be completely obscured'. This was apolitical to the last degree. Even though it was costly in administrative terms, 'dual running' was the one safeguard against disaster that Kenneth's Green Paper had incorporated.

Initially I won the argument. The merits and demerits of 'dual running' were debated exhaustively in the Committee over two Parliamentary sessions, and I succeeded in July 1987 in securing agreement to a five-year transitional period. This was duly announced. Nick Ridley and his new number two, Michael Howard, who had become Minister of State at the Department of Environment thereupon began an energetic lobbying campaign to persuade parliamentary colleagues that 'dual running' was an abomination and that a clean switch from the rates to the poll tax was preferable. At the Party Conference in October 1987 they contrived a succession of speakers from the floor – led by the then recently unseated MP for Aberdeen, South, Gerry Malone – who called for the immediate abolition of the rates, with no transitional period. Margaret, who was on the platform with Nick, was duly impressed. According to his account, she whispered in his ear: 'We shall have to look at this again, Nick.'

When the Committee reassembled in London after the Conference, Nick formally announced that, in the light of the views expressed at the Party Conference, he wished to reopen the decision to retain dual running. This seemed to me the height of folly, and I wrote to Margaret on 10 November 1987:

> We should stick to the policy which we agreed and announced in July. It is a complex area, but we should do ourselves no good in 1990 if we change our minds now on the basis of what is, I have to say, generally, if understandably, ill-informed pressure.

The Committee duly met to discuss the issue, and once again the case on both sides was argued long and hard. This time, however, at the end of the day the majority on the Committee, including Margaret, was against me. Nick was delighted, and felt he had won a famous victory. In fact, it sounded the death knell of the Community Charge. It repeated precisely the blunder of the Scottish rates revaluation of 1985, despite the fact that it was in order to avoid such horrors that the reform of local government finance was being carried out at all.

Meanwhile, as a last desperate attempt to salvage something from the wreckage, I had urged that the Poll Tax be introduced in Scotland a year earlier than in England and Wales. This was welcomed by the new Secretary of State for Scotland, Malcolm Rifkind. There had to be separate Scottish legislation in any case, and he was keen to forge ahead. The Scottish Bill received Royal Assent before the 1987 election. As I saw it the Scottish tail had been wagging the English dog for far too long; and there was an outside chance that, if implementation of the Poll Tax in Scotland demonstrated its horrors, there might still be time for the Government to have second thoughts about its introduction in England and Wales. In the event, however, despite all manner of trouble when the Poll Tax was introduced in Scotland in April 1989, Margaret was by that time far too committed to the tax, which had figured prominently as a 1987 Manifesto commitment, to contemplate drawing back.

THE DISASTER UNFOLDS

The events that followed had a grim inevitability about them. As late as 1988 the Department of the Environment envisaged a poll tax averaging £200 a head rather than the £400 or so which eventually emerged in 1990. Nick Ridley attributes the doubling of the charge to local authorities using the occasion to increase their spending and staffing and blaming the consequences on the Government – precisely what I had predicted would happen. It was, indeed, a rich irony that a measure designed to curb local government spending led directly to the biggest increase in local government spending of the entire Thatcher period. In May 1991 the Government admitted that 10 per cent of budgeted revenues from the Poll Tax, or some £2 billion, went uncollected in its first year of operation. This, too, could scarcely have been a surprise to anyone who had glanced at my original 1985 memorandum.

Meanwhile, before the 1988 Budget, Nick had the gall to try and persuade me to abandon my tax-cutting plans, in order to offset the regressive effects of the Poll Tax; going so far as to draft a mock statement in pseudo-Treasury language. He must have known there was no chance I would fall for this. The reduction in the higher rates of income tax had enormously important incentive and supply-side effects, whereas the windfall gain to the better off from the switch to the Poll Tax brought no economic benefit whatever, and merely added further distortions to the housing market.

After this, one expedient followed another, most of which had the effect of reducing the distinctive characteristics of the Poll Tax and moving it towards a clumsy, arbitrary and ill-drafted caricature of an income tax, as I had warned would be the case. Chris Patten, who succeeded Nick Ridley at Environment in July 1989, characteristically sought far larger injections of public money than Nick had ever done. With considerable misgivings, I agreed in 1989 an unprecedented increase of £2.6 billion in the total central government grant to local authorities for the following financial year – an increase far in excess of the rate of inflation. Yet what the Press described as 'sources close to Patten' suggested I was deliberately trying to kill the Poll Tax by providing inadequate financial lubrication.

Not content with the £2.6 billion, Patten then pressed, in the autumn of 1989, for a further £2 billion, which he must have known was unacceptable. But what astonished me most about Patten's behaviour was that, while he was well aware that the Poll Tax was a political disaster, he made no effort whatsoever to abort it, even though he was in a strong position to do so.

The overall impact of the new system of local government finance involved, *inter alia*, a switch in the tax burden from richer to poorer councils. The switch was so great that a 'safety net' had been set up to phase in the change over four years. The safety net in turn led to an outcry from Tory back-benchers representing the more affluent areas, who objected to their constituents having to pay an extra amount of Poll Tax – even for a transitional period only – in order to cushion the blow for those living in the less affluent areas. They pointed out that many of those adversely affected in this way were not themselves particularly well off.

But although this was the focus of the discontent on the back benches, the really sensitive political problem concerned not different local authority areas and the safety net, but the effect of the Poll Tax on those – generally of modest means, and often pensioners – living in low-rated property, wherever they happened to be. It was clear that we had to address both these shortcomings. It was equally clear, and here Margaret was in full agreement with me, that there could be no question of spending anything remotely approaching the £2 billion that Patten had demanded to deal with it. Time was pressing, and Margaret was busy preparing for the Party Conference, so she asked Geoffrey – exceptionally – to exercise his role as Deputy Prime Minister and chair a meeting with Patten and myself to work out a detailed solution.

The meeting began in a somewhat ill-tempered way; but thanks to Geoffrey's soothing chairmanship we eventually reached a reasonable agreement within the overall figure I had set myself, a package of help for the hardest hit costing, in all, an estimated £345 million; and this was put to Cabinet, and endorsed, the next day. The amount involved was by no means a derisory sum, but just about modest enough for Margaret to be able to stipulate, without testing the bounds of realism too much, that it should come wholly from the Reserve, leaving the overall spending plans for 1990/91 unaltered.

OPERATION AND OUTCOME

At the time these discussions were taking place, the Poll Tax had been in force in Scotland for some six months, and stories of disaffection and non-payment were widespread. But since the Scots had made a practice over the years of complaining bitterly about every initiative the Government had ever taken, this occasioned little surprise, let alone alarm. In any event, we were regularly assured by the then Scottish Secretary, Malcolm Rifkind, who had inherited his enthusiasm for the tax from his predecessor George Younger, that in reality it was all working out pretty well. No doubt he was keenly conscious of the key role the Scottish Conservatives had played in bringing the Poll Tax about in the first place.

Six months later, in April 1990, the tax was duly introduced into England and Wales. By then, of course, I was no longer a member of the Government. All I could do was watch from the sidelines, with mounting horror, as all that I had warned about five years earlier came to pass. Whatever theoretical arguments may be advanced in its support, no new tax can be introduced and sustained that is not broadly acceptable to the majority of the British people. The Poll Tax failed this basic test in the most fundamental way imaginable. There was, of course, an organised hard Left 'can't pay – won't pay' campaign against the tax, with all the usual demonstrations and one particularly violent riot in Trafalgar Square, the television pictures of which, beamed round the globe, convinced half the world that the UK was on the brink of bloody revolution. But opposition of that kind was something the Government could have taken in its stride.

What was insupportable was the anguish caused to millions of ordinary people, with no political axe to grind, up and down the land. In all my years as a Member of Parliament, I had never encountered anything like it. Constituents of modest means would come to me, asking me why they should suddenly be faced with this huge increase in their local tax bills; and there was no convincing answer I could possibly give them. We had asked people, on numerous past occasions, to accept tough decisions because they were part of the only route to economic salvation. I had found no great difficulty in explaining the case, and the British people by and large accepted it. But the Poll Tax was another matter altogether.

There may be some surprise that I did not resign over the Poll Tax. This would, in fact, have been extraordinary conduct, which was given retrospective credibility only by my subsequent resignation in October 1989 over the conduct of economic policy. Senior ministerial resignations are few and far between – I was the first Chancellor to resign for more than thirty years – and there are good reasons for this. If Cabinet Ministers resign whenever they disagree with a policy being pursued, Cabinet Government would be impossible. You certainly fight for your own corner, but you can never expect to win every battle. In this case what was at issue was a proposal that did not lie within my own range of ministerial responsibilities, and which was not a matter of high principle but simply a grotesque political blunder. When I did resign, it was because a situation had arisen which made it impossible for me to carry out my job successfully. Whatever other troubles the Poll Tax may have caused, it did not do this.

Some back-benchers had seen the Poll Tax disaster coming, and had staged a revolt, on an amendment designed to relate Poll Tax liability to the individual's income, thus converting it into a form of income tax, when the Local Government Finance Bill which introduced the tax was in the later stages of its passage through the House of Commons; but they were too few in number to win the day. The amendment had been moved by Michael Mates, a close associate of Michael Heseltine.

Once the tax had been in operation for a short time, however, the number of back-benchers who had become thoroughly alarmed far exceeded those who had supported the Mates amendment. They did not need the opinion polls to tell them that the Poll Tax had become the issue of greatest concern to the voters, and the issue most likely to determine how they voted at the next general election. They noted, too, that they were stuck with the hated tax so long as Margaret remained leader. Within seven months of its introduction in England and Wales, she was leader no longer. In the subsequent contest for the succession, the appeal of Michael Heseltine's pledge to review the tax – and his position on it was well known – forced his two opponents, John Major and Douglas Hurd, to promise that they, too, would review it.

The Poll Tax was without doubt Margaret Thatcher's greatest political blunder throughout her eleven years as Prime Minister. I pointed out to her very early on the many dangers it posed; but without any support from Cabinet colleagues I was unable to persuade her that they were real. Indeed, at the time of its initiation in 1986, she had openly boasted to her favourite journalists about how she had 'seen me off'. Ironically, in the end it played a large part in seeing *her* off as Prime Minister.

Nor was that all it did during its relatively brief and dismal existence. It was also one of the roots of the gradual loosening of public spending control that characterised the period from my resignation up to the 1992 election, and in particular after the departure of Margaret. For the concessions I had been obliged to make in 1989 marked only the beginning of the subsidisation of the Poll Tax. Michael Heseltine, who succeeded Chris Patten as Environment Secretary after John Major became Prime Minister in November 1990, felt obliged to supply a further £3 billion of central government support in January 1991, to fund the so-called 'Community Charge Reduction Scheme'. This was financed in the 1991 Budget by a 2.5 per cent increase in VAT, which was used to reduce every Community Charge bill in the country by £140.

Finally, at long last, at the end of April 1991, the Major Government published its plans for replacing the Poll Tax with a new Council Tax, based largely on banded property values – not dissimilar to the scheme I had put forward, as the desirable alternative to the Poll Tax, some six years earlier.

CHAPTER THIRTY-TWO

REFORMING SOCIAL SECURITY

A Finger in Every Pie · The Fowler Review · The Age of Retirement
Priorities and Politics · Benefits and Taxes

A FINGER IN EVERY PIE

The Treasury is not simply a Finance Ministry. It is also, both in name and in reality, the central Department, with a finger in pretty well every pie that the Government bakes. While this stems principally from the fact that there is a financial dimension to everything, it is entrenched in the UK by the conventions and procedures of Government. How much time a Chancellor spends on matters outside the field of economic policy proper depends partly on the extent of his own interest in these matters and partly on the degree to which the Government of the day is engaged in reform. For the issues involved in reform are clearly very much more important than those involved in the effective operation of the status quo. On both these counts, my involvement was, I suspect, well above average.

It would be foolish to imagine that my colleagues welcomed this interference. But they would have been wrong if they imagined that my sole concern was to ensure that whatever they were proposing did not cost too much. That was obviously one of my concerns: if the Treasury fails to keep a beady eye on cost, then no-one will, and all is lost. But in addition, I was keenly aware that many of these other matters, from social security to education, could have a profound bearing on economic performance, at least in the long run. And even where that was less obviously true, such as health care or the legal system, there was always the political dimension, which should in theory engage the interest of every member of Cabinet, irrespective of his or her departmental responsibility.

THE FOWLER REVIEW

The social security system is of profound concern to the many millions of people who to a greater or lesser extent rely on it, and represents far and away the biggest item of Government spending, costing more than the *total* yield of income tax. From every point of view, Norman Fowler was right, as Social Services Secretary, to decide in 1984 that this was far too important an area of Government to escape the searchlight of reform.

Norman set about his task in an admirably thorough way. He had been Social Services Secretary for over two years before he did anything at all, which gave him ample time to make up his mind about the weaknesses of the existing system. In early 1984 he set up four separate reviews of different parts of the system, which made recommendations to a Cabinet Committee on which I sat in the first part of 1985. Legislation was passed the following year.

The review of pensions was the most important of the four, and it was over pensions, and more particularly SERPS – the State Earnings-Related Pension Scheme – that Norman and I had our only serious disagreement. SERPS was the creation of the last Labour Government, providing a generous second State pension, over and above the basic old age pension, based on the individual's earnings (up to a limit). Like the basic State pension, it was unfunded, and given the increasing size of the pensioner population and the irresponsible generosity of its provisions, it should have been clear to anyone who took the trouble to analyse the scheme that it was a potential doomsday machine.

Quite rightly, Norman wished to abolish SERPS. While the provision of an adequate basic pension was a legitimate responsibility of the State, any further pension provision over and above that should be entirely a private matter. That is to say, each individual should be free to purchase from the private sector whatever level of additional pension provision he or she wished to possess. To make this possible, Norman was anxious to develop personal portable pensions, wholly independent of whatever company scheme an employer chose to operate. I was willing for my part to provide them tax relief – without which they were unlikely to get far – although the immediate impact on the PSBR would be adverse. But it was a price worth paying to close down the doomsday machine.

All sorts of alarm bells started to ring, however, when I discovered at the eleventh hour that one of the options being considered was that of *compulsory* private provision. My officials should have entered a Treasury reservation on this point until I had had time to come to a view, but in a rare lapse had not done so. Worse still, I was told that the various options had not been costed. A crash analysis conducted over the weekend produced sufficiently alarming results for me to fire off a minute to the Committee stating that I could not accept compulsory private provision at the level envisaged.

I had never seen Norman so cross. He was furious at what he saw as a last-minute attempt to sabotage his plans, and claimed that I had no right to act in that way. I had considerable sympathy with him. It was pretty intolerable to have a fundamental objection raised at the eleventh hour. But he was wrong to imply that I was reopening matters that had already been fully discussed and agreed. Through no fault of his, the key issues had never even been put to the Cabinet Committee. However late in the day, it was clearly important that they *were* put to the Committee before the final decision was taken.

In general, I have nothing but praise for the high standard of service I received as Chancellor from my officials. Of course I was served up erroneous advice on occasions – the most obvious example, perhaps, being the serious forecasting errors of the late 1980s – but these were honest errors of judgement which are bound to occur from time to time. Examples of sheer incompetence were very few and far between. In all my time as Chancellor, this was the worst.

Ironically, Norman's position had originally been the same as mine. It was the abolition of SERPS, coupled with the availability of private provision through personal pension schemes which he sought. It had been Margaret – backed by the majority of the Committee – who had argued that there would be no political support for the abolition of SERPS unless an adequate replacement private sector scheme were made compulsory. I disagreed, pointing out that we were the Party of individual freedom; that different people had different views about how much pension provision they required; and that to make the taking out of a particular level of private provision compulsory was wholly contrary to our political philosophy. Margaret replied that compulsory private provision had long been the practice in Switzerland. 'But Prime Minister,' I countered, 'it is well known that in Switzerland everything that is not forbidden is compulsory' – a pardonable exaggeration in the circumstances. At least I never had Switzerland thrown at me again.

Eventually, after much discussion and a Green Paper putting forward the compulsory private scheme, which hit heavy opposition from business, we ended up with the compromise that I had put forward earlier, of no compulsory private scheme but a drastic scaling down of SERPS. This found its way on to the statute-book the following year.

As for the rest of the social security review, this produced no comparable drama. I failed in my bid to secure significant immediate savings out of the reform of this massive programme, but the changes Norman made, with my full support, undoubtedly checked the escalation that would otherwise have occurred.

THE AGE OF RETIREMENT

Curiously, however, the more obvious way of reducing the cost to future generations of workers, not only of SERPS but of the basic State pension, too, was never even considered. I refer to raising the age of retirement. Norman was never prepared to propose it, and Margaret, whenever I raised it with her informally, was strongly against it. She seemed to identify with the women involved, who would inevitably be particularly affected by this, since any change in the age of retirement would be bound at the same time to remove the anomaly of women reaching pensionable age a full five years earlier than men – currently sixty rather than sixty-five. But it was evidently a wholly disinterested identification, as her own dismay at having to retire from arguably the most demanding job in the country at the age of sixty-five in 1990 was to testify.

Norman's successor, John Moore, did however take up the charge. He minuted Margaret in June 1989 arguing the case for a common retirement age for men and women of sixty-five, to be phased in from the year 2010 so as to ensure that no woman then (in 1989) over forty would be affected. I promptly sent Margaret a minute strongly supporting John, adding only that in my opinion the common pension age should be sixty-seven rather than sixty-five. Margaret refused to have anything to do with the issue. But given the steady deterioration in the ratio of pensioners to working population that is bound to occur over the next forty years unless something like this is done, coupled with the indefensibility of the difference between the male and female age of retirement, I have no doubt that this change must come, and the sooner the better. Whether it is accompanied by the introduction of a so-called decade of retirement, according to which a pension can start to be drawn at any time within five years either side of the central retirement date, the size of the pension rising the later it starts to be drawn, is – however sensible – very much a secondary consideration. It is the central State retirement age that is crucial.

PRIORITIES AND POLITICS

There was one important area, however, where I believed Norman to be mistaken. As he puts it in his memoirs:

> My view was that we should examine whether the money was reaching those that most needed it and whether the priorities of the system laid down in 1945 were still the same. In the 1940s the elderly, often totally without pensions, were the first concern. More and more, I became convinced that the priority for the 1990s should be families with children.

The case for this switch had long been an article of departmental faith, where officials had been exposed to years of effective lobbying by that most professional of all social security pressure groups, the Child Poverty Action Group. It also appeared justified, as Norman demonstrated to us, by a simplistic one-dimensional analysis of the incidence of poverty. He duly achieved it by making means-tested benefits less generous to the elderly and more generous to 'families with children', to use the jargon. But it was a major political blunder; and I was surprised that someone as politically shrewd as Norman undoubtedly was should have swallowed the fashionable case for the switch so uncritically.

I recalled Dick Crossman, when he was the first ever Secretary of State for the Social Services in the 1960s, telling me how he had discovered to his surprise that an increase in Family Allowances – the then name of the social security benefit for poor families with children – was invariably unpopular with the electorate at large. Whereas the DHSS sees things in terms of the children, the electorate sees them in terms of the parents (or parent) to whom, after all, the benefit (whatever its name) is actually paid, with no guarantee that it will be spent on the welfare of the children. Moreover, the parents who receive the bulk of means-tested benefits for families with children tend to be either those with large numbers of children or unmarried mothers, who of all the categories of social security beneficiaries tend to evoke least sympathy among the public at large – the feeling being, rightly or wrongly, that to a large extent they are the deliberate authors of their own misfortune.

By contrast, the category of social security beneficiary which evokes the greatest degree of sympathy among the general public are the poorer pensioners. No-one can accuse them of having brought their misfortune upon themselves, they suffer other disabilities besides low incomes, and they lack the ability that the able-bodied possess to increase their income by their own efforts. There is a general moral sense, too, that those in the last phase of their lives, who may have contributed a great deal to society over many decades, should not have to suffer poverty on top of the infirmity and loneliness that is their unavoidable condition. Perhaps there is a sense of guilt, too, among the increasing numbers of the able-bodied who choose not to have their elderly parents living with them.

Whatever the reason, Norman's switch of support, at the very sensitive margin, from the elderly to 'families with children' ran clean counter to the moral sense of the nation. It was bound to be unpopular – which it was, massively, when the reforms came to be implemented by Norman's unfortunate successor, John Moore, in April 1988; while the emasculation of SERPS caused no trouble at all. It was also bound to lead to irresistible pressure both to moderate the withdrawal of benefit from the losers and to do more for the elderly poor – which, again, it did. But that was not my main worry. Any upsurge of popular feeling about pensioner hardship was bound to lead to renewed pressure for a general increase in the basic state pension, over and above indexation; and this – given the vast and growing size of the elderly population – would be inordinately costly.

I have to confess that, while I was aware at the time that Norman was making a mistake, I kept quiet about it. Priorities within the social security budget were pre-eminently a matter for him; and had I raised the matter he would undoubtedly have responded that he was obliged to take money from the elderly to finance improved support for poor families with children, which he was determined to do, only because I was not prepared to allow him to increase his budget overall: indeed, I was urging him to reduce it. Since my immediate bone of contention with Norman was SERPS, I had no wish to open a second front; but I subsequently regretted not having spoken up. Whether it would have made any difference if I had is more doubtful.

BENEFITS AND TAXES

There was one fundamental issue, where, to his chagrin, I felt obliged to baulk Norman right from the start. He announced that he wished to look not only into the social security system, but into the tax system as well, in so far as it affected the clients of the DHSS. I refused, holding fast to the hallowed Treasury doctrine that taxation is a matter for the Chancellor and must not be put into commission. Towards the end of April 1985 he came back to me again, and suggested that we announce the setting up of a joint Treasury-DHSS study group on the links between the tax and social security systems. Again I refused. There was thus no discussion of either a tax-credit scheme of the kind that had been advocated by the Heath Government, and which enjoyed considerable sympathy among Conservative back-benchers, or of any of the so-called 'basic income' schemes that had more recently been advocated.

My objection to Norman's superficially sensible proposal was not simply an obscurantist defence of my own turf, although the Treasury is entirely right to believe that for any Chancellor to agree to put tax into commission would be disastrous. I had enough trouble as it was with Margaret, who was always urging me to introduce special tax concessions for anything she wished to promote or protect. My objection was based on a careful assessment of the issues involved.

I subsequently published that assessment in my March 1986 Green Paper, *The Reform of Personal Taxation*, chapter 6 of which is devoted entirely to an analysis of the pros and cons of bringing together the tax and benefit systems. This lucidly demonstrated the overwhelming practical case for keeping the two systems apart – a case which, significantly, no-one even attempted to rebut.

The key point is that the tax and social security systems are not simply mirror images of each other, with social security payments a form of negative taxation. Whereas liability for tax is measured over a period of twelve months, which makes life simpler for the taxpayer and Inland Revenue alike, income-related benefits have to be assessed on a weekly basis to ensure that poor families can always meet their basic needs. Again, tax liability is based on individual income; whereas means-tested benefits are based on the finances of the household, which is essential if benefit is to flow where the need is greatest. Moreover, income-related benefits look at circumstances, such as the capital resources of the claimants, which the income tax system does not and should not do. It may be that the social security authorities pry too far; but the features of a system for taxing income to pay for public spending can hardly be the same as those of a system of payments to relieve poverty.

In any event, even if these practical difficulties could be overcome, which they manifestly cannot be, it is hard to see what great gain would arise. The problem that worries many people is the disincentive effect that there is at the bottom of the income scale, as people discover that, by earning more, they are very little better off. By basing eligibility for means-tested benefits on post-tax rather than pre-tax income – one of the most useful of the changes which flowed from the Review – Norman removed the possibility of people being actually worse off by earning more; but even after this reform, the amount by which they were better off could be very small indeed. The illusion, however, is to suppose that this could be prevented by some kind of amalgamation of the income tax and social security system. Indeed, the problem has nothing whatever to do with income tax as can be readily seen by imagining a world in which income tax did not exist at all.

Suppose the Government of the day has a fixed sum of money to apply to the relief of poverty (raised, for example, from VAT). The choice before it is whether to spread the money evenly among the population at large, which would be manifestly absurd and would not relieve poverty, or whether to concentrate it on the poor. The latter course is the only one that relieves poverty; but equally it means that as the poor become less poor – essentially as they earn more – their eligibility for benefit is reduced. It is this withdrawal of benefit, and not the tax system, which creates the inevitable consequence that the poor are little better off from earning more. The only practical way of mitigating this debilitating disincentive effect is to embrace the US concept of workfare, in which the payment of benefit is contingent on doing work for the local community.

The 'basic income' concept, too, becomes less attractive the more it is studied. The essence of this is that every adult should be paid a basic income from the State, sufficient to live on, which is then progressively clawed back through the income tax system as the individual's other income rises. The idea is to overcome the problem of the poor not availing themselves of their entitlement to means-tested benefits. But a heavy price would have to be paid for this advantage. A large part of the population would be saddled with the disincentive effect of a significantly higher marginal rate of tax than they suffer at present. And the critically important distinction between what individuals earn by their own efforts and what they receive from the State would be blurred.

Indeed, at bottom, it was the inability to grasp the importance of the fundamental philosophical difference between tax and social security which worried me most. It may have been the Thatcher Government's passionate desire to curb public spending that led Norman to support Margaret's unsuccessful attempts to persuade me to reintroduce the old child tax allowance. For here was a way of helping a large number of his Department's clients without incurring any extra public spending at all, even though it would have meant complicating the tax system in order to give maximum relief to the better-off parents who needed it least. Even that excuse does not apply to the simple failure to recognise the fundamental difference between the tax and social security systems.

The tax system enables the State to take money in the simplest, least economically damaging and fairest way it can devise in order to finance necessary Government spending, with no 'social' dimension of any kind. This is a wholly different activity from that of the social security system, which is the State *giving* (other people's) money to alleviate poverty. The distinction may seem obvious. But any Minister who seeks to use the tax system, rather than public expenditure, to achieve social objectives, is failing to observe it. So, too, is any Opposition spokesman who describes tax cuts as 'hand-outs' (whether to the rich or any other undeserving group); for taking less can never be the same as giving, whether it is a benign Government that is doing the taking or the meanest protection racketeer. So, too, is any Chancellor who boasts how much money he has 'given away' in tax reduction: it is not his to give. I trust that, whatever other mistakes I may have made, I was never guilty of this elementary political and philosophical howler.

CHAPTER THIRTY-THREE

DEREGULATION AND THE CREDIT BOOM

The Effect of Deregulation · Building Societies Unleashed
The English Language Disease? · Banking Fever · Too Much Optimism
Not So Permanent Income · Appendix: The Building Societies Act, 1986

THE EFFECT OF DEREGULATION

When the Thatcher Government first took office in 1979 it inherited an economy beset by all manner of government controls and regulations. We judged these controls and regulations to be among the causes of Britain's economic weakness, and we wished to be rid of them – to get the Government off people's backs. The same applied to monopolistic restrictions imposed by the private sector.

The programme of deregulation thus needed to be, and was, a comprehensive one, and one embarked on without delay. In the financial area the Bank of England was a strong supporter of deregulation on the practical grounds that the controls were ineffective, produced their own distortions, and diverted business from reputable financial institutions to fly-by-night operations.

Any radical reform, even if it achieves its objectives, as I believe deregulation did, was also likely to bring about unforeseen side-effects.

This proved particularly true in the case of financial deregulation. Moreover, given that deregulation in general and financial deregulation in particular became part of a continuing worldwide trend, the subject is one of more than parochial relevance.

Although financial deregulation is a somewhat imprecise term, it is possible to identify at least ten specific events, of varying degrees of importance, that qualify as acts of financial deregulation, most of which occurred during the early part of the Government's term of office. In chronological order, these were:

- The unannounced ending, virtually as soon as the new Government took office in May 1979, of the restrictive guidelines on building society lending.
- The abolition of exchange controls in October 1979.

- The abolition of the so-called 'corset', the Supplementary Special Deposits Scheme designed to curb bank lending, in June 1980.
- The abolition of the Reserve Assets Ratio requirement, under which banks had to hold at least 12.5 per cent of their deposits in a specified range of liquid assets, in August 1981.
- The abolition of hire-purchase restrictions in July 1982.
- The collapse of the building societies' cartel in October 1983.
- Some aspects of the Building Societies Act, 1986.
- The ending of the restrictive practices of the stock exchange in the so-called 'Big Bang' of October 1986.
- The withdrawal of mortgage lending 'guidance' in December 1986.
- The effective abolition of the Control of Borrowing Order in March 1989.

Two of these events stand out as being of particular importance. The first, and most important of all, was the abolition of exchange controls. At the time a radical and highly controversial act, it became the norm throughout the major industrial nations of the world – partly because of a genuine belief in freedom and deregulation, partly because the information technology revolution made controls on capital movements increasingly difficult to police. As a result we were returning to a degree of economic freedom last seen in the early years of this century, before the First World War – but with international capital flows on a very much larger scale.

The consequences of this for the conduct of economic policy were considerable. In the first place, it transformed the foreign exchange markets. Whereas for well over half a century the movement of currency across the exchanges had been largely associated with trade flows, and the external value of currencies largely determined by the state of the balance of payments on current account, this ceased to be the case in the 1980s. But in the second place, and of greater relevance to the events considered in this chapter, the ending of exchange control rendered ineffective any form of direct national controls on credit. For in a world in which capital can flow freely across the exchanges, the effect of such controls would merely be to drive lending offshore.

BUILDING SOCIETIES UNLEASHED

This bears directly on the second of the two main acts of financial deregulation in this country: the collapse of the building societies' cartel. Unlike exchange control abolition, this was not brought about by the Government – indeed, although I was philosophically in favour of it, I always feared the short-term consequences. That was why, as Financial Secretary, I resisted official advice to take Government action to break the cartel; believing also that in any event market pressures would sooner or later cause it to disintegrate. That was what duly occurred, shortly after I became Chancellor.

Until 1981 the building societies, and to a lesser extent the local authorities, had almost a monopoly over housing finance. Building societies took in funds on retail terms – that means they were easily withdrawable in small quantities – and lent them to homebuyers at rates of interest fixed by the Building Societies Association. The cartel broke up as a result of a burgeoning of the competitive instinct among the bigger building societies themselves, followed by the massive invasion of the mortgage lending business by the banks, who were growing increasingly disenchanted with the joys of lending to Latin American and other governments overseas.

Competition for mortgage business was further increased in the second half of the 1980s by the entry of specialist mortgage lenders, many of them American, who raised finance in the wholesale capital markets – in other words, they borrowed large sums of money from the financial markets to lend in smaller packages to householders.

The collapse of the building societies' cartel, under which mortgage rates were kept well below market clearing rates and advances were rationed by a queuing system, thus occurred in a new world in which direct credit controls were out of the question; and the only checks on excess were the price of credit, which the Government remained able to control, and prudence, which it could not. Moreover the previous existence of the cartel had created a pressure of pent-up mortgage demand of unknowable size until it unleashed itself following the cartel's collapse. But the adjustment from regulation to deregulation took some years fully to work through.

The consequent explosion of lending, and of spending financed by lending, for both consumption and investment, by both consumers and business, was thus on a wholly unprecedented and unforeseen scale – despite UK interest rates which both in nominal and real terms were consistently well above those of the other major economies. This is now a generally accepted explanation of the switchback course the UK economy followed in the late 1980s and early 1990s.

Compared with the two principal acts of financial deregulation just identified, the other eight had little real impact, since the restrictions they abolished were either ineffectual (particularly, in the case of the corset, following exchange rate control abolition), or purely technical, or (as in the case of Big Bang) not directly connected with bank and building society lending at all.

Arguably, the one exception to this is Big Bang, which had one important and unpredictable, or at least unpredicted, side-effect. Against the background of the huge worldwide rise in equity prices and turnover – until it came to an abrupt halt on Black Monday in October 1987 – Big Bang clearly contributed to the massive rise in investment spending by the financial services industry in the UK. This in turn was probably one of the major contributors to the unforeseen scale of the surge in domestic demand in the late 1980s.

THE ENGLISH LANGUAGE DISEASE?

In looking at this period, it is important not to be too parochial. Of the seven major industrial nations that comprise the G7, three – the United Kingdom, the United States and Canada – underwent a recession at the beginning of the 1990s of a remarkably similar nature. It is hard to believe that the economic consequences of the English language provides the common thread. What seems a far more likely explanation is that these were the three economies that travelled furthest along the road to financial deregulation. A similar phenomenon occurred in Japan.

There always has been, and always will be, an economic cycle. But with credit in all its forms facilitated by financial deregulation, these three economies experienced a particularly virulent form of credit cycle. In other words, individuals and companies alike came to borrow excessively. And while this was bound to be a self-correcting process – which the authorities could by their monetary policy to some extent expedite – it was not surprising that the correction involved a period of recession as individuals and companies alike reined back their spending in order to correct their over-extended balance sheets.

Clearly, with hindsight, I greatly underestimated the demand effect that financial deregulation, a supply-side reform, was to have. But borrowers and lenders alike also made their mistakes. Hence the hardships of many of the former and the unprecedented bad debts reported by the latter.

If the switchback was somewhat sharper in Britain than across the Atlantic, that is perhaps not too surprising, since the extent of deregulation was significantly greater here – chiefly because we started from a greater degree of regulation in the first place. There was subsequently an interesting parallel, among a number of the smaller economies in Scandinavia. In the words of a 1991 *Financial Times* article on the region:

> The banking crisis has its origins in the financial deregulation that swept the region in the 1980s ... The banks, breathing the heady air of liberation, vastly expanded their lending – and their risks. But risks appeared minimal during the 1980s ... as property prices rose sharply. Since then, however, the recession that began in Norway and has spread to Finland and Sweden has exposed the weaknesses of the banking system.

Happily, the UK banking system, although battered, was incomparably stronger than its Scandinavian counterpart. But the echoes were striking.

BANKING FEVER

What were the respective responsibilities of the building societies and banks for the 1986/8 credit boom? Building societies remained the largest source of mortgage finance for housing. A substantial proportion of that finance leaked into consumer spending – a process known as 'equity withdrawal'. The societies still accounted for nearly a third of all lending by the banks and building societies to the private sector in the peak year of 1988; and they certainly went beyond the bounds of prudence in their lending policies in the second half of the 1980s.

They lent an ever higher proportion of house valuations – in some cases over 100 per cent. They also lent an unusually large multiple of people's earnings. Instead of the traditional maximum loan of two and a half times earnings, they went up to three and a half and even four times earnings. Moreover the loan was usually based on the applicant's own estimate of his or her income. This was often exaggerated and seldom checked – quite apart from the numerous cases of straightforward mortgage fraud by deliberate lying.

Even so, the building societies were not as imprudent as the banks. Most of the societies insured against default – which is why the insurance companies subsequently found themselves in such trouble. Nor were the building societies able, under the Building Societies Act, to follow the banks into Maxwell-type lending. Mortgage lending is, other things being equal, the least risky form of lending – which is why the Bank of England refused my request to it to intervene on prudential grounds.

The combination of artificially stimulated demand for housing and some of the tightest planning controls on land use in Europe puts a long-run upward pressure on house prices. But the upsurge is unsteady and characteristically takes the form of a series of heady booms punctuated by downturns when people have difficulty in selling their homes at all. Between the start of the housing boom in 1985 and its peak in 1989, average house prices in the UK more than doubled: in real terms they rose by 70 per cent. Moreover, with the increase in home ownership, this had an even greater effect on the economy than previous housing booms.

The banks, for their part, only dimly recognised the extent of their vulnerability to the credit cycle, and in particular to the fact that, as interest rates rose, homebuyers would inevitably cut back on their purchases in the high street in order to keep up with their mortgage payments. Thus by fuelling the housing boom with easy lending against the apparently reassuring security of bricks and mortar (which they continued to do even after interest rates had begun to rise sharply in response to emerging inflation), they were not only taking bigger risks than they imagined on their housing business. Far more seriously, they were inadvertently undermining the quality of their lending to the smaller and more vulnerable end of the corporate sector.

We are left with some key questions: was the Government responsible for the banks taking leave of their senses? Were the banks, by contrast, largely responsible for the excesses of the credit binge? The point here is not that the banks should put the public interest above profit. The point is that by acting in the imprudent way they did, they inflicted terrible damage on their own profit-and-loss accounts and balance sheets. The 'authorities' cannot fine-tune bank lending. That is one of the reasons why the economic cycle cannot be avoided. Had I been able to foresee how excessive the lending would become, my only useful weapon, whether some call it 'one-club golfing' or not, would have been to have raised interest rates sooner and even more sharply than I did.

There are at least three conclusions to be drawn from our first experience of a world in which freedom of capital movements and an uncartelised lending industry are facts of life. The first is that a financially deregulated economy, while more efficient and dynamic, is also probably less stable, by virtue of an amplified credit cycle. The second is that, recognising this, borrowers need to exercise prudent self-discipline and lenders to develop a far more sophisticated risk analysis than they have hitherto found necessary. It is clearly not good enough for a bank to look at a potential corporate borrower – his accounts, his track record, his business plan, his management and so on – in isolation. The industry risk also needs to be assessed, including its links with other industries and their risks. Above all, its vulnerability to changes in economic conditions has to be fully taken into account.

The third conclusion, and the most reassuring, is that what Britain went through in the later 1980s was to a considerable extent a once-for-all occurrence: the change from a financially regulated to a financially deregulated economy. Others may still have this pleasure in store.

TOO MUCH OPTIMISM

The most important acts of deregulation and increased financial market competition – the ending of exchange control and the building societies' cartel – took place respectively in 1979, when I was Financial Secretary (although heavily involved: see Chapter 4), and in 1983, not long after I arrived at Number 11. Yet inflation did not start to take off until the second half of 1988, after I had been Chancellor for five years, and did not reach its peak until the autumn of 1990, a year after I had departed. This is an example of 'long and variable lags' in the financial system, extending far beyond anything Milton Friedman had in mind when he promulgated the phrase.

An increase in the ratio of debt to income was only to be expected as householders and businesses adjusted to the end of credit rationing; and the timing of both the adjustment and its effects were inherently unpredictable. Borrowing as a proportion of disposable income rose to new peaks in 1986 for the corporate sector and in 1987 for the personal sector. Companies borrowed on a larger scale to finance takeovers and overseas investment; but also to purchase capital equipment made in the UK, which while itself desirable, added to the pressures on productive capacity. In the personal sector, much of the increased investment was in land and housing already in existence, pushing up the price of land and housing, which made households feel wealthier and thus able to borrow more. This played a large part in the fall in the personal savings ratio (saving, less borrowing, as a proportion of income) from an average of 11.5 per cent between 1979 and 1984 to 8 per cent in 1986 and a low of 5 per cent in 1988.

But was there not something more? One of the most balanced and comprehensive treatments of the forces behind the credit boom which I have so far seen is by Dick Sargent (a former economic adviser to the Midland Bank and an academic economist in his own right). His main stricture on my policies and statements is that I encouraged excessive optimism – a point to which I return when I discuss the 1988 Budget. As Sargent writes:

> The scale of the credit increase is larger than seems plausible to attribute to credit liberalisation alone. There was also an increase in the extent to which the private sector was willing to incur debt at given levels of income and interest rates. This increase was a direct result of a climate

> of over-optimistic expectations which developed in the 1980s about the economy's performance. This hypothesis is consistent with the fact that the boom in the second half of the 1980s was characterised, to a much greater extent than most previous booms, by inflation of asset prices as distinct from producer prices, wages or retail prices.

NOT SO PERMANENT INCOME

One of Friedman's early pioneering works was his *Theory of the Consumption Function* in which he related consumer spending to two variables: a person's 'transient' income in a particular period and the 'permanent' income he thought he was likely to obtain in a normal year of his or her working life. In the mid to late 1980s, there was a substantial upward revision of this permanent element, particularly if we include capital gains, notably from home ownership. In part this was wholly justified, given the undoubted supply-side improvements that had occurred. But it clearly went too far.

In the six years from 1982 to 1988, the only one in which output growth fell below 3.5 per cent was 1984, when it was artificially depressed by the miners' strike. This was a considerably stronger performance than either I had expected or the Treasury had forecast at the time. The Central Statistical Office commented in a 1991 post-mortem in *Economic Trends* that growth was exceptionally steady for many years in the mid-80s, with much smaller cyclical variation than in the past. This phenomenon, coupled with the exceptional duration of the upswing, led too many borrowers and lenders to believe that it would go on for ever, and that the economic cycle, with its alternation of upswing and downswing, was a thing of the past. This was the fatal error.

With hindsight, however, I must accept my share of responsibility for the excessive optimism that characterised the climate of the time. Given the all-pervasive defeatism that was the grimmest aspect of our 1979 inheritance, I regarded the creation of a climate of confidence as a major objective of policy, and the tone of my speeches tended to reflect this. And of course my speeches on the economy set the tone for those of my colleagues, from Margaret downwards. But, while these things are difficult to calibrate, I probably overdid it. There is a link here, too, with my tax-cutting Budgets. Those who, in retrospect, argue that those Budgets (notably the 1988 Budget) caused the overheating, are on any quantitative analysis clearly wrong. But in psychological terms they did contribute to the climate of optimism – which does not invalidate the Budgets, but reinforces the case for more measured speech-making.

A similar but more abstract analysis has been provided by Mervyn King, an economist who is more sympathetic to the supply-side revolution. He demonstrates, with a command of algebra which makes me nostalgic for my former self, that even a moderate change in underlying growth, if it is suddenly perceived, can lead to a very sharp temporary rise in both investment and consumption, which would subside after a short period once the adjustment had been made. As he writes:

> Any successful attempt to raise the rate of growth of a small open economy will, in a world of integrated liberal financial markets, lead to a rise in investment, and a step-jump in consumption which will have all the appearance of an unsustainable Government demand stimulus, including a swing into deficit in the balance of payments.

A question worth considering is whether we could have ridden out a temporary rise in investment, consumption and imports, which was the once-for-all effect of a shift to a higher growth path, without applying the monetary brakes in the way that I did. Theoretically, we might have been able to do so if, per impossible, the economy had been 100 per cent open to international trade instead of 50 or 60 per cent open. In that case a temporary increase in consumption and investment could readily have been supplied from abroad, without any rise in prices at home. But since some goods and services, such as new construction, can come only from home suppliers, overheating inevitably appeared.

Nevertheless, analysis underlines the usefulness of a current account deficit as a safetyvalve.

APPENDIX: THE BUILDING SOCIETIES ACT, 1986

The building societies, which had lost a substantial slice of their core business to the banks in the early 1980s, complained that they were unable to counter-attack effectively while they were barred from raising money on the capital markets or from offering services such as cheque books. They successfully lobbied the Treasury to liberalise the regulatory regime. They had a legitimate desire for a level playing field with the banks, at least where their business overlapped.

The building societies had been pressing for fresh legislation for a considerable time. They pointed out that the statute under which they operated dated back to the nineteenth century and was wholly out of date. It also happened to be at odds with European Community legislation in this field, something which sooner or later would have to be rectified. Indeed, Treasury officials urged me to persuade Geoffrey to legislate on all this when I was Financial Secretary, with delegated responsibility for the building societies, but I declined to do so, telling them that it would have to wait.

When I returned to the Treasury as Chancellor in 1983, it was clear to me that it would be wrong to procrastinate any longer. But I had to wait until the 1985–6 session before I could persuade my Cabinet colleagues to give me a slot for it in the busy legislative timetable. I had entrusted responsibility for the Bill to Ian Stewart, the Economic Secretary, who had issued a Green Paper in July 1984, which eventually became the immensely complex Building Societies Act of 1986. This enabled societies to issue cheque books and cheque guarantee cards, make personal loans and carry on a number of other quasi-banking activities.

The societies had sought even greater powers to compete with the banks, but I was unwilling to go the whole hog. Under the new Act they still had to raise the bulk of their funds from retail deposits, and put most of their assets into straightforward home mortgages. A new supervisory authority, the Building Societies Commission, replaced the Registrar of Friendly Societies.

There was some criticism that the Government was being unreasonably restrictive; but those societies which found the restrictions unduly irksome were given the option of converting themselves into joint stock banks, provided that borrowers and investors approved by a large and complex majority. As banks. of course, they would come under the supervisory authority of the Bank of England and, more important, be subject to the capital adequacy requirements applicable to banks. Up to the time of writing, only the Abbey National has chosen to exercise this option and convert itself into a bank. It is proving an effective and low-cost competitor in the field of retail banking.[24]

[24] [2010 notes] Subsequently most of the other building societies chose to demutualise and convert themselves into banks, with mixed results. However, the increased competition in retail banking I had hoped to see was largely frustrated by the consolidation that occurred within the banking sector, with many of the ex-building society banks in particular being absorbed into larger banking groups.

CHAPTER THIRTY-FOUR

FROM GROWTH PAUSE TO OVERHEATING

Rewriting History · A False Dusk · Fallible Forecasts

REWRITING HISTORY

There are three further questions about the credit boom. When exactly did it begin? Why were its effects not diagnosed earlier? And what was – or could have been – done about it?

The Bank of England's June 1986 *Bulletin* stated that 'there is little indication that liquidity is unwillingly held at current real interest rates or that monetary conditions are loose'. By December it had moved no further than the neutral 'Monetary conditions continue to be difficult to assess ... on account of far-reaching structural changes in the financial system'. A closer analysis of the housing component of bank and building society lending might have given a clue that something was afoot. Net advances for house purchase rose from £19 billion in 1985/86 to £27 billion in 1986/87, a jump of almost 50 per cent. Too many economists were satisfied that house prices were essentially relative prices and not a symptom of general inflation.

This was unfortunate, since it turned out that, during this period, rising house prices were an important part of the transmission mechanism from credit creation to inflation – namely the effect of a sharp rise in house prices in increasing perceived personal wealth, and the increase in personal wealth in leading to an upsurge in consumer spending. I myself, however, was reassured at the time not merely by the arguments of my advisors both at the Treasury and the Bank, but also by the observation that a similarly sharp rise in domestic property prices was occurring in Japan, and there was no sign there of it spilling over into general inflation. It was not until the summer of 1987 that the Bank began to worry that monetary conditions may not be tight enough; a concern that I then shared and met by raising interest rates by one percentage point on 7 August, which at the time was regarded as a bizarre move by most monetarists and the financial Press.

The Bank's concern started to re-emerge in the autumn, but it was once again met, this time by the Wall Street crash of 19 October 1987, which the Bank believed, like almost all other commentators at the time, implied 'a tightening of monetary conditions', to quote its own *Bulletin*. The only occasion in all my years as Chancellor when the Bank can be interpreted as having wanted a tighter policy than I was pursuing, was in the difficult period subsequent to that event when Eddie George argued that sterling should be allowed to rise in the autumn of 1987. Everything else that has emerged from some Bank quarters since my resignation amounts to an attempt to rewrite history with the benefit of hindsight; an understandable activity, but scarcely a commendable one. It is, I suppose, theoretically possible that the Bank from time to time believed that monetary policy should be tighter, but refrained from telling me – even at the markets meetings I regularly held with the Governor and his senior officials. But this would have amounted to a dereliction of duty so grave as to be unthinkable.

A FALSE DUSK

A failure to foresee the consequences of financial deregulation in a climate of unusual optimism, the consequences which were greatly exacerbated by the follies of the lending institutions and in particular the banks, was not the only reason for my slowness and that of my advisers to recognise the full significance of the credit boom. There was also an apparent marked slowdown in the growth of the real economy at a crucial period in the first half of 1986. Indeed, when the official statistics were first published the public perception was that the upswing that had begun in 1981 was drawing to a close – it had already lasted if anything longer than the average of previous upswings – and that a period of recession lay ahead.

Shortly after the original figures for the first quarter of 1986 were published, purporting to show that, after adjusting for the coal strike, growth had virtually come to a standstill, I felt it necessary to use the occasion of a lunchtime meeting of the Association of Economic Representatives in London on 28 May to give a robust, confidence-boosting speech. The mood of the time, which is seldom remembered today, can be gauged from the following extract:

> Some are even asking whether the British economic recovery – whose end has been regularly predicted every year since the recovery began in 1981 – may at long last really be petering out. I am confident that it is not. Some pause in growth was to be expected, if only because fluc-

> tuations are a fact of life. But I see no reason to change the analysis of the effect of lower oil prices I set out in my Budget Speech. What is happening – here as elsewhere – is that we are getting the inflation benefits of the oil price fall before the output benefits ... I can see a number of forces which, before many months have passed, will sustain a vigorous resumption of growth in this country as well as in the major oil-consuming nations – growth in the private sector, not an artificial and short-lived stimulus provided by the public sector. Critics have been caught out in the recent past by underestimating the current strength of the British economy, and they look like being caught out again.

The speech was received by industry and the Press with ill-concealed scepticism. No doubt the fact that I was suffering at the time from one of my infrequent bouts of laryngitis, and could summon up only an apology of a voice, did not assist me to carry conviction. But even those who were not aware of this, and only read the speech – which I had distributed as a handout in its entirety – felt that it was one of the most contentious I had made.

Given the figures as they appeared in 1986, there was particular alarm that the upturn seemed to be coming to an end before unemployment had even stopped rising. At the time I made my speech to the Economic Representatives, unemployment had been increasing for seven years without a break; and although the rate of increase had previously been slowing down, in the spring of 1986 it started to accelerate again. On 8 May the Government had lost the ultra-safe Yorkshire seat of Ryedale in a by-election caused by the death of the sitting Member. Even committed supporters of the Government's economic strategy were insisting that reducing unemployment should now have priority.

In fact it was in July 1986 that unemployment at long last peaked, at well over three million (11.2 per cent), although this was not yet apparent in early September, when I made one of my visits to Scotland to test the temperature there. It was a perfect late summer's day, and the Highlands had never looked lovelier. But as I flew to Inverness the rows of mothballed oil rigs clearly visible in the Moray Firth seemed to give the pause a palpable form.

The first clear-cut evidence that the pause was over did not emerge until the GDP figure for the third quarter of 1986 was published on 19 November. At the same time it was now clear that unemployment had started to turn down after its July peak, and it was to fall without interruption for the next three and a half years. In fact, while commentators were still arguing about whether we faced recession, slowdown or merely pause, the upturn was if anything becoming uncomfortably vigorous. But I had not waited for the November GDP figure to act against the danger of inflationary excess. Certainly, inflation was gratifyingly low in 1986; but I was aware that the figures were flattered by the oil price collapse, as I made clear in speeches at the time. I had already been alerted to the risks by the renewed weakness of sterling, which was in part a symptom and in part a cause of growing inflationary pressures. Indeed, I would have done more had I been allowed to do so, as the next chapter explains.

My conviction, even when the misleading first quarter GDP figures were published in May, that the recovery would resume of its own accord, was indeed largely based on the low inflation we were enjoying in 1986. This worked through two different channels. First, other things being equal, low inflation makes people confident enough to save less and spend more. Second, with the rate of growth of earnings still stubbornly stuck at the 7.5 per cent to which it had fallen in 1984, real incomes were growing unusually fast. This last phenomenon was not, of course, something I welcomed. It would clearly have been better if pay per head had risen less, in which case the same increase in overall national earnings could have been spread among more people, bringing forward the fall in unemployment and reducing the inflationary pressure at any given level of unemployment.

FALLIBLE FORECASTS

I cannot, however, claim to have foreseen the full extent of the boom that began to develop. Moreover, I was not helped by the Treasury's economic forecasts, which despite being regularly castigated by Labour as ludicrously optimistic, in fact seriously and consistently underestimated the strength of the upturn. In each of the three years 1986, 1987 and 1988, growth was forecast at 3 per cent – only some half a percentage point at most above the best guess of the underlying growth of productive capacity. In the event, growth in those three years averaged over 4 per cent a year; which was too much to be borne without inflationary consequences. As I showed in the last chapter, the outside forecasts underpredicted the boom by an even greater margin than the Treasury did.

Still greater errors were made in forecasting the strength of domestic demand. This inevitably led both to a strong growth in imports and the diversion of exportable goods to the home market. Hence the extreme inaccuracy of the current account balance of payments forecasts in each of the three years, which transformed what I called 'a readily financeable current account deficit' into the

£15 billion and £19 billion current account deficits we experienced in 1988 and 1989. I was right in one respect, however: even these unexpectedly high deficits proved, in the new world in which we now lived, to be 'readily financeable'.

It was in 1986 that the forecasters, both within and outside the Treasury, started to get domestic demand seriously wrong. With hindsight, however, it is clear that there were two important clues that something was amiss. The first was the weakness of sterling, which at the time was seen by the Treasury as for the most part an inevitable and acceptable consequence of the oil price collapse. The second was the behaviour of house prices. These began their stratospheric climb in 1986, when they rose by over ten percentage points more than inflation. Yet few foresaw in 1986 that this was but the prelude to a rise of 12 per cent more than inflation in 1987 and no less than 22 per cent more than inflation in 1988. Certainly, neither I nor my advisers, either at the Treasury or at the Bank, did.

Contrary to much that has been written since, the rapid increase in domestic demand in the second half of the 1980s was not just a consumer boom. Indeed, whereas the average annual increase in consumption in the three years 1986, 1987 and 1988 is now reckoned to have been around 5 per cent a year, investment rose by more than 8 per cent a year.

Exports of goods continued to grow strongly in 1986 and 1987, at over 5 per cent a year. But by 1988 the pull of the home market had become so great that exports did not grow at all. Import growth, on the other hand, shot up from 7 per cent in 1986 and 8 per cent in 1987 to almost 13 per cent in 1988. The strain of excess demand at home was taken mainly on the balance of payments in the boom years themselves, and relatively little was reflected in higher prices. The underlying rate of inflation averaged only 4.5 per cent in 1988: the inflationary peak came in 1990, after the boom in spending had at last come to an end and had given way to recession.

On the basis of the information that was available to me at the time, it would have been thought highly eccentric to have pursued a tighter policy than I did. Inflation, however measured, was down to 3.5 per cent in 1986 – reflecting of course the impact of lower oil prices. (Indeed, the headline rate went below 2.5 per cent in July 1986.) Producer price inflation was also at the lowest level for decades. House prices did, as I have already remarked, start to take off; but this followed several years in which there had been virtually no increase in real terms at all. Moreover, at this stage the housing boom seemed confined to central

London, and around the turn of 1986/87 the Bank advised me that it was probably petering out.

The domestic monetary indicators also showed a high degree of tightness. Real interest rates were around 7 per cent in 1985 and 1986 – probably the highest level experienced since the 1920s and some 2.5 percentage points higher than the G7 average. The growth of M0, at 4.2 per cent (year on year), was well within its target range. Even the growth of the broader aggregate, M4, dipped slightly compared to the previous year.

Interestingly enough, the Treasury's inflation forecasts were almost spot on, predicting a rise in the headline RPI in 1986 and 1987 very near the actual outcome of 3.4 per cent and 4.1 per cent respectively. The serious deterioration in the Treasury's inflation forecasts did not take place until 1988 and 1989, showing the importance of time-lags. It also shows the value of the current account balance of payments deficit as a safety valve, so long as underlying policies are sound and errors unhesitatingly corrected. A failure to grasp the long time-lags between excessive demand growth and its inflationary consequences is one reason why most of my critics have focused on minor errors in the winter of 1987–88 rather than the more serious errors of 1986. Another reason why critics play down the errors of 1986 is their ideological reluctance to recognise the value of the exchange rate as a warning signal.

At the time, the relationship of any measure of the growth of money to either the national income or to the price level seemed highly unreliable. M4 rose by a cumulative total of 50 per cent in both the first and second halves of the decade 1975–85. In the first half it was accompanied by a rise in nominal GDP twice as great as this, whereas in the second half it was accompanied by a rise in nominal GDP only half as great. So whatever people may say today, and whatever technical adjustments are made to the series, it did not appear to be a reliable indicator. Indeed, for the first half of the 1980s, the Bank of England's analysis seemed to fit the facts perfectly. Extra money balances were willingly held, and the increased bank credit did not stimulate excess spending on goods and services.

The fact is that throughout our period in office we suffered from the operation of Goodhart's law,[25] the financial equivalent of the better-known Murphy's law, which states that any monetary aggregate ceases to be reliable the moment it becomes a target for policy purposes.

---

[25] So called because it was first enunciated by Professor Charles Goodhart of the London School of Economics when he was adviser on monetary policy to the Bank of England from 1969 to 1985.

There were some other warning signals, of varying significance. It was worrying that pay increases got stuck at 7.5 per cent a year, despite falling inflation and seven years of steadily rising unemployment, right up to the summer of 1986. And I have already referred to the evidence of house prices, for what that was worth in 1986. But the warning signal which influenced me most was the fall in sterling, which I instinctively did not like and which I tried to halt at various times in 1986, with little support from most of those who subsequently blamed me for the upsurge in inflation. That is a story for the next chapter.

CHAPTER THIRTY-FIVE

AN UNWANTED DEVALUATION

The Hidden Sterling Crisis of 1986 · Base Rate Cuts, Spring 1986
The ERM Again · The Sterling Crisis Surfaces

THE HIDDEN STERLING CRISIS OF 1986

The earliest and clearest warning that policy might be too lax came from the behaviour of sterling, which during the course of 1986 – that is, from December 1985 to December 1986 – plunged by some 12.5 per cent as measured by the official exchange rate index. This was the largest fall of any year during the lifetime of the Conservative Government, and towards the end of it, in November, the pound reached what at the time of writing remains its lowest level ever recorded on this basis. Yet curiously it gave rise to little of the hysteria that had accompanied previous sterling crises, and featured scarcely at all in the political debate at the time.

There were two main reasons for this: oil and the dollar. It had been the dramatic collapse in the oil price in the first half of 1986 that had triggered the sterling plunge in the first place. Between December 1985 and June 1986, the oil price dropped like a stone from about $28 a barrel to only $10 a barrel. During the second half of the year it then staged something of a recovery, reaching over $14 a barrel in December 1986. But what should have set the alarm bells ringing was that, of the overall fall of 12.5 per cent in the sterling index during the year, less than half occurred in the first half of 1986 when the oil price was plummeting. The greater part occurred in the second half of 1986 when the oil price was recovering.

The fact that, by and large, it did not, can be explained partly by the belief, then widely held, that the fall in the second half was essentially a delayed reaction to the oil price collapse. But it also owed much to the false comfort derived from the behaviour of the dollar. Since the Plaza meeting of September 1985, the dollar had been declining sharply from the stratospheric heights it had earlier reached, as indeed the G5 participants had hoped and intended; and this continued throughout 1986. As a result, the 12.5 per cent fall in the sterling index over the year was composed, *inter alia*, of a small *rise* (of some 2.5 per cent) in sterling against the dollar, and a fall of almost 20 per cent against the Deutschmark. In those days the focus of attention still tended anachronistically to be the sterling/dollar rate, which had caused Margaret such panic when it looked as if the pound might actually fall to below parity against the then mighty dollar in the wake of the Ingham crisis of January 1985.

Even so, it was disturbing that, once again dividing the year into its two halves, sterling's rise against the dollar was entirely confined to the first six months: in the second half of the year it even fell slightly against the dollar, too.

When the sterling plunge began, the political and public debate, in so far as it was not distracted by the Westland affair, focused not on the pound at all but on the damage that the collapse of the oil price would do to the UK economy as a whole. The Labour Party had convinced itself that anything good that had happened to the economy, notably the recovery from the recession, which the Opposition had gradually and grudgingly admitted had to some extent occurred, had happened solely as a result of the windfall of North Sea oil. The media, too, were convinced that the prospect for tax cuts depended entirely on the tax revenues from North Sea oil, which had now gone down the drain. In general, it is difficult today to recall how widespread was the absurd view that the British economy depended entirely on oil, as if we were some Gulf state, and that with the collapse in the value of our North Sea oil the UK ship – as a *Daily Telegraph* cartoon of the time graphically portrayed it – was heading straight for the rocks.

While I was aware, of course, that all this was nonsense, that did not help with the problem of perceptions – particularly the perception of overseas holders of sterling, who even more than domestic holders tended to believe it. I was deeply worried that, as a result, the slide in sterling would turn into a rout. Nor was confidence assisted by the Government's evident disarray over the Westland affair. On the morning of Wednesday, 8 January, I asked Robin Leigh-Pemberton to come over to the Treasury, with his key officials, to discuss the situation at one of the frequent markets meetings I used to hold. We rapidly reached the conclusion that interest rates should be raised by a full percentage point, from 11.5 per cent to 12.5 per cent, forthwith.

I was under no illusion about Margaret's likely reaction. It would be the first rise in interest rates for almost a year, the first since I had hoisted them to 14 per cent in the aftermath of the crisis of January 1985. Given the certain prospect of a sticky meeting, I decided to take Robin and Eddie George with me to Number 10 to acquaint her with the decision I had reached. I pointed out to her that the markets were clearly expecting us to raise interest rates, and that if we did nothing at all the prospect for sterling could be very ugly indeed. She took it every bit as badly as I feared. She argued that the markets were being their usual hysterical selves, and that if we succumbed to their pressure they would simply try it on again the following week. Eventually, after prolonged resistance, she conceded with a conspicuously bad grace, insisting that any further pressure for higher interest rates should be firmly resisted.

For a time the 1 per cent increase seemed to have done the trick, but the position of the pound was still a precarious one. The oil price continued to crumble; the very day after the interest rate hike Michael Heseltine resigned from Cabinet over Westland, plunging the Government into a political crisis; and the mood could not have been worse. It was not long before sterling was under severe pressure again, and on 23 January I took the unusual step of getting the Treasury press office to distribute to all and sundry a one-page 'Factsheet on oil and the UK economy'. This pointed out that, at its peak in 1985, North Sea oil and gas represented only 8.5 per cent of our total tax revenues, only 8 per cent of our total exports, only 5.5 per cent of GDP, only 5 per cent of UK capital investment, and less than 0.5 per cent of UK employment. Having attempted to put the UK's alleged total dependence on North Sea oil into perspective, it concluded that: 'The overall effects [of the oil price collapse] on both output and inflation in the UK are expected to be broadly neutral – if anything, slightly beneficial.'

The intention, of course, was to steady the markets. My great fear was that the counter-inflationary benefits of lower oil prices would all be lost in an excessive depreciation of sterling, which Margaret's refusal to allow me to take the pound into the ERM the previous November made it particularly difficult to avoid.

The following morning, Friday, 24 January, against a grim background, I held a further markets meeting with my top Bank and Treasury advisers. Once again, I concluded that interest rates should be raised a full percentage point, this time to 13.5 per cent. On this occasion I took just Robin with me to Number 10 to see Margaret. I told her that the pound was under severe pressure, and I was afraid that if we did not act that day the bottom might fall out of the market. She was even worse than on the previous occasion, insisting that it was quite unnecessary, that it would be a positive disaster, and much else in the same vein. Eventually, after a particularly unpleasant harangue, she concluded, 'Go ahead if you insist, but on your own head be it'. After we had left her room, the small study on the first floor, Robin said to me 'I don't know how you put up with this sort of thing'. I explained that she had a great deal on her mind. By then she was fighting for her own political survival over Westland (Leon Brittan was to resign later that day). But that did not excuse her intolerable behaviour.

Robin returned to the Bank to implement the interest rate increase so bruisingly agreed, only to discover that the pressure on sterling, on which I had largely based my case, had suddenly eased, and even to some extent reversed. He telephoned me to acquaint me of this unexpected and, in the circumstances somewhat embarrassing, turn of events. With considerable reluctance, I felt honour bound to rescind my earlier decision. I then went to see Margaret, to tell her that we would not be going ahead with the interest rate rise after all: she was suitably pleased. I have regretted doing so ever since.

The difficult analytical question we now faced throughout 1986 was how far the exchange rate should be allowed to fall in response to the sharp fall in oil prices, without weakening monetary policies.

I myself had accepted the need for some real depreciation of sterling in the speech I had made at Cambridge in 1984 when speculating about 'What happens when the North Sea oil runs out?' But I had hoped that a fall in the real exchange rate would be secured via a UK inflation slightly below the international average over a period of years, rather than by a depreciation in the nominal exchange rate, which, quite apart from its inflationary dangers, might well, on the basis of recent experience, not even bring about a real depreciation at the end of the day.

The view of officials, both Treasury and Bank of England, was that an oil price fall would lead to higher interest rates, a lower exchange rate, a higher PSBR and relatively little effect on output or inflation. The official Treasury had produced a set of ready reckoners based on their expectations of what might happen following an oil price fall. They had been reworked each year for some time as there were constant rumours of a sharply lower oil price.

Based on this work, they had developed the concept of the oil-adjusted exchange rate. This was designed to show changes to the exchange rate that would leave the inflation rate unchanged following an oil price fall. It was at no time challenged by the Bank.

The oil adjusted exchange rate was often mentioned as a point of reference in the Monthly Monetary Reports I received. In the early months of 1986 it suggested that the exchange rate had in fact fallen rather less than would have been needed to compensate for the fall in the oil price in terms of its implications for future inflation. It was not until August that it was suggesting that the exchange rate had dropped to a level where it was putting upward pressure on inflation.

I was never convinced by this sophisticated analysis, which seemed to me too clever by half. While I accepted that a halving of the oil price made some exchange rate depreciation inevitable and necessary, I soon came to feel that sterling was falling too far and too fast.

BASE RATE CUTS, SPRING 1986

The economic strategy paper Terry Burns presented to the pre-Budget Chevening meeting, in January 1986, argued against any further tightening of monetary or fiscal policy and maintained that further downward pressure on inflation could be combined with a respectable increase in output if policy was left unchanged. The official Treasury view throughout 1986 was that allowing the pound to fall in line with oil prices would not only restore the competitiveness of exports but also allow interest rates to be lower – which would in turn give a further boost to investment, growth and employment. They maintained that the adverse impact of a lower pound on domestic inflation would be offset by lower oil prices, which indeed it was in the short term.

When the Budget of 18 March was well received in the markets and sterling strengthened slightly I took the opportunity the following day to reverse the January increase. Over the following two months, with the rise in unemployment, already over 3 million, apparently accelerating again, with the oil price appearing to have bottomed out and sterling reassuringly steady, I concluded that the pound was now safe and gradually reduced interest rates further, half a point at a time, to 10 per cent in May.

I now regret this far more than anything focused on by my critics. For my confidence that sterling had weathered the storm was distinctly premature. Not only had I acquiesced in the relatively modest depreciation that had already occurred, but the second half of 1986 was to see a much more serious sterling slide. As a result, I lost the opportunity to lock in the marked fall in inflation that the oil price collapse had temporarily secured, and allowed policy to become looser just when the credit boom was starting to take off. Needless to say, I disliked intensely sterling's depreciation in the second half of 1986; but there was a limit to what I could do, outside the ERM, particularly given Margaret's profound hostility to raising interest rates or maintaining any kind of sterling target. The net result was that the exchange rate exerted no downward pressure on inflation in 1986; and interest rates, although high in real terms – they averaged over 7 per cent in real terms in the second half of 1986 – were, with the benefit of hindsight, clearly not high enough to stifle at birth the excessive growth of credit which was to lead to the resurgence of inflation in 1988/90.

THE ERM AGAIN

The collapse of the oil price should have had one beneficial effect: it removed what remained of the petrocurrency argument against joining the ERM, as Leon Brittan, by then a back-bencher, pointed out in his contribution to the Budget debate. Support for membership was growing. A survey of CBI members showed some 85 per cent declaring themselves in favour, and support also came from the Institute of Directors, the quality Press and numerous other bodies. But with the possible exception of the Institute of Directors, these were not names to conjure with so far as Margaret was concerned.

She could in any case have responded by pointing out the apparent lack of support for ERM membership from any eminent academic economists. It was certainly striking how Alan Walters' periodic blasts in the newspapers, though invariably flawed, seldom if ever elicited an academic counterblast. One reason for that was that those who favoured free floating tended to be fired with purist zeal, whereas those who favoured ERM membership on economic grounds did so (as I did) for pragmatic reasons, as probably the least bad alternative in a wicked and imperfect world. The only pro-ERM zealots were those who wanted it on political ('European') grounds.

Be that as it may, in my Lombard Association speech in April 1986, I myself dropped a broad hint. After expressing my misgivings about the various definitions of the money supply I went on to say:

> In the right circumstances membership of a formal fixed exchange rate system can itself provide a very effective framework for monetary policy. Indeed, the gold standard was the earliest and most durable form of financial discipline. Modern fixed exchange rate systems are more flexible. But the exchange rate can still provide a very clear and tough discipline, obliging the authorities to take timely action when domestic policies are out of line with other low-inflation countries. Of course the exchange rate will not signal the right policy action every time, any more than the monetary aggregates. But, over the medium term, maintaining a fixed exchange rate against countries who share our resolve to reduce

> inflation is a pretty robust way of keeping domestic monetary policy on the rails.
>
> But I see no role for an exchange rate target outside a formal exchange rate system, shared by other countries, and supported by a co-ordinated approach to economic management and intervention. And that, for the UK, means outside the exchange rate mechanism of the EMS.

So far as the phrasing of this last paragraph is concerned, it has to be remembered that, at the time I gave my Lombard Association speech, the Louvre Accord had not even been envisaged, let alone signed. In any event, not wishing to mislead the market into thinking that I was signalling sterling's imminent membership of the mechanism, I added that 'the Government does not believe the time is yet right for us to join the ERM'. The use of the expression 'the Government' rather than the word 'I' was, of course, deliberate. It so happened, however, that on the very same day Geoffrey Howe made a speech to the Conservative Group for Europe saying that 'a decision cannot be postponed indefinitely'; adding that it should be left to the Chancellor. Meanwhile Margaret took the opportunity of congratulating herself in the House for refusing to join the ERM at the relatively high sterling/DM rate that had prevailed before the oil price collapse. But for me the ERM realignment earlier that month was a good illustration of how the system, when working normally, engendered market expectations that any realignment would be small.

Geoffrey was keen to follow up our speeches with more private pressure on Margaret. I told him that I thought it best to wait a little before returning to the charge. Not that I would have objected in the slightest had I thought that his proposed approach would have been productive, but unfortunately it was far more likely to prove counterproductive. Geoffrey had been one of the principal architects and most articulate expositors of Thatcherism, but his relationship with Margaret had never been a particularly close one, and even by 1986 the signs of tension were beginning to become apparent.

This was largely a matter of personal chemistry: he for his part never sufficiently treated her as a woman, while she found his quiet, dogged manner intensely irritating. Increasingly, over the years, she felt compelled – to the acute embarrassment of everyone else present – to treat him as something halfway between a punch bag and a doormat. At least while he was Chancellor they were at one on most issues of policy. Even this bond steadily weakened after he became Foreign Secretary, and was taken over, as she saw it, by the Foreign Office, a

Department she deeply distrusted as being congenitally 'wet' and always on the foreigners' side rather than ours, even though she admired individual Foreign Office officials, sometimes excessively. Towards the end, matters went from bad to worse, as Geoffrey became steadily more pro-European Community while she moved violently in the opposite direction.

THE STERLING CRISIS SURFACES

As I have mentioned, the foreign exchange markets reacted well to the Budget in March and the pound remained firm for the next three months. It then began to slide again, this time at a more alarming rate, with the pressure becoming intense by September. In the three months from June to September, 1986, it fell a further 10 per cent on the index, and considerably more than this against the Deutschmark, for the first time ever threatening to fall below DM3.

I was rather more concerned than my advisers by sterling's depreciation. No doubt some depreciation compared with the previous autumn's DM3.7 was inevitable given the fall in oil prices. But the oil price was by then well off the bottom and the further depreciation late in 1986 simply risked an upsurge in inflation. I had become convinced that the time had come to act, initially through intervention, but standing ready to raise interest rates if intervention alone was not enough. My intention was to defend a floor of DM3 – an interesting figure in the light of subsequent events.

The week before I had to fly off to Washington for the annual Bank and Fund meetings, I asked Peter Middleton at our regular weekly bilateral on 19 September what he thought the implications for interest rates were of 'tracking' the Deutschmark at around that level. He replied that the prospects for interest rates had deteriorated, but that no-one had suggested an increase. Nevertheless, when I saw Robin the following day I remarked that we were hanging on by our fingertips.

The pound came under further pressure with the publication on 23 September of a then record monthly current account deficit of £886 million for August. I instructed the Bank to use the reserves unstintingly to defend the pound, and to sell Deutschmarks in particular, given the agreement at Gleneagles that it was desirable to halt the fall in the dollar.

The markets not unreasonably concluded that the Government was trying to avoid a politically damaging increase in interest rates before the (very likely pre-election) Conservative Conference in the second week of October, which indeed I was. Gerhard Stoltenberg, however, was persuaded by an angry Karl

Otto Pöhl, the President of the Bundesbank, to telephone me the following day to complain that by selling dollars at all the Bank of England was contravening 'the spirit of Gleneagles'. By this he meant that it was acting in opposition to the Bundesbank's purchases of dollars to prop up the US currency. I pointed out that I had explicitly instructed the Bank to sell more Deutschmarks than dollars, which was (in my interpretation) fully in accord with the 'spirit of Gleneagles'. This was something of which Pöhl had evidently omitted to inform him. As I flew to Washington on 25 September, sterling had closed in London at just under DM2.94, ominously below the Bank's objective.

In September 1986 the mood of the media was particularly hysterical; but even discounting media hysteria it was clear that interest rates would have to rise. The question was how much, and when. Nevertheless, market sentiment had not been helped by Robin's remark to a journalist who had taken him unawares in the spacious atrium of the Fund building. Asked whether we would be raising interest rates, Robin replied that we had no intention of doing so 'today'. On 28 September I held a meeting with Robin and his and my senior officials in Washington in the office of Tim Lankester, the admirable Treasury official who was then the UK's executive director of the Fund and Bank and economic Minister in Washington. I had not yet made up my mind whether or not more than one percentage point was required, and in any case I wanted to defer the move at least until I was back in London and fully in control of events, and if possible until after the forthcoming Party Conference. What we needed to do now, I concluded, was to buy a small amount of time.

Accordingly, the same day I took Robin with me to see Stoltenberg and Pöhl to ask for their help in supporting sterling on the foreign exchange markets. Stoltenberg was sympathetic, but Pöhl said there was nothing he could do. It was Bundesbank policy to hold nothing but dollars in their foreign exchange reserves, which meant that they could not buy sterling on their own account, but only as an agent acting on behalf of the Bank of England. I overcame this problem with some hurried diplomacy and an early morning phone call to the Prime Minister, who was livid at German unhelpfulness and threatened to pull out the British Army of the Rhine. In the end I secured us a standby swap arrangement similar to that already existing between the US and Japan, under which the Bundesbank would lend us the money which it would use to intervene on our behalf. Needless to say, the money was repaid well before the due date.

Meanwhile, it was understood in the markets the following day that the Bank of England and the Bundesbank were acting in concert, and the pressure on sterling immediately subsided. As one City analyst put it: 'It is always more impressive if the Germans are buying sterling because the markets know that they have more ammunition in their locker'. The concerted intervention also revived speculation that Britain was about to join the ERM and that the Government was already pursuing a covert exchange target for the pound. This was premature. Although the Bank of England was now aiming to stop sterling falling too much below DM3, this was purely a matter of short-term tactics. It was not until the framework of the Louvre Agreement was in place, five months later, that I started to see it differently. At my Washington press conference – a regular annual event – I made a light-hearted allusion to Robin's earlier gaffe when I replied to the inevitable question by saying that the UK had 'no intention of joining the ERM ... today'.

Before leaving Washington I decided to take some time off to go on a shopping expedition, using the amazingly long black stretched limo which the Ambassador always kindly hired for my use when in Washington. Taking Alex, Terry and Robert Culpin with me, I bought presents for Thérèse and the children. On our return to the Fund building Robert discovered that the Press, noting my disappearance, had concluded that I had been so overcome by the crisis I had hidden away in some bunker.

As soon as I had returned to London, I called a meeting on 2 October with Robin and the usual cast of senior Treasury and Bank officials. Terry was struck by the change of mood, remarking that only a few weeks earlier the Treasury had been thinking that industrial confidence was fragile and monetary policy too tight. By now, however, I reckoned that the increase in interest rates that was clearly necessary could wait until after the Party Conference the following week. Before going off to Bournemouth for the Conference on 6 October, I held one further meeting with Robin and the others. Pressure on sterling had re-emerged, and the position was undoubtedly uncomfortable with the pound now below DM2.90. The only real subject for discussion was whether, after the Conference, interest rates should rise by one percentage point or two. I suggested that we should decide that in the light of conditions at the time.

CHAPTER THIRTY-SIX

POLITICS AND INTEREST RATES, 1986

Conference Success at Last · Another Seminar · The Row Goes Public · Looking for a 'Trigger'

CONFERENCE SUCCESS AT LAST

I was determined to make an impact at what promised to be the last Party Conference before the election, and with some help from an autocue (and an excellent peroration from Tony Jay) delivered my most successful speech to date. I was rewarded with an embarrassingly long standing ovation for pledges of a 25 pence basic rate of income tax, more privatisation, and zero inflation (final score: two out of three). More important than my speech, however, the entire 1986 Conference was an outstanding success, and marked a turning point in the Government's fortunes so marked that you could sense it at the time. We had started the year in the shadow of the Westland affair, which had not only cost two prominent Cabinet resignations but left Margaret herself so badly wounded that at one point it looked mortal. The economy appeared to be faltering badly after seven successive years of inexorably rising unemployment, and we were losing safe seats in by-elections. Even as late as September, the month before the Conference, when Westland had already receded into a distant memory, we were still five points behind Labour in the polls. Immediately after the Conference, we leapt into a lead which continued right up to the 1987 general election.

Meanwhile, as soon as I got back to London on the Friday I called a markets meeting with Robin and the customary cast and decided without much difficulty to raise interest rates by one percentage point, deferring the implementation until the following Tuesday to prevent it from being indecently close to the end of the Conference. The markets had recovered sufficiently from the fevered mood of the Washington meetings to enable that to 'stick', and Margaret was sufficiently relieved that I had not gone for a two-point rise to agree to it with relatively little resistance. For myself, I disliked going up by more than one point at a time partly because it looked like panic and partly because I wanted to educate the markets that this was the norm. Recorded inflation was just 3 per cent and real interest rates were already at their highest level ever. I had no wish to confirm the incipient market view that interest rates always rose by 2 per cent when the pound was under pressure.

The Mansion House speech on 16 October was a far more difficult hurdle to negotiate than the Party Conference. The rise in base rates had obviously been triggered by the fall in the exchange rate, and I saw no point in denying it – although I gave a somewhat unconvincing mention to M0 as well. But I was determined that, if I could possibly avoid it, there should be no further fall. Against the strong advice of the mandarins, who felt I was being rash to the point of insanity, I said:

> Given the precipitate collapse of the oil price, it was inevitable and indeed necessary that the exchange rate should fall ... But there are clearly limits to the necessary and desirable extent of that fall.

Sterling was still not out of the woods, however, especially after the OPEC meeting broke up on 22 October without reinstating firm oil production quotas. The dismissal of my old opposite number Sheikh Zaki Yamani on 29 October, who was regarded the best hope for their restoration, added to the uncertainty. Fortunately, the so-called Baker-Miyazawa accord of 31 October, in which Jim Baker agreed to stabilise the dollar in return for a pledge from the Japanese to cut their discount rate and undertake a fiscal boost, took some of the pressure off the pound. Following the Gleneagles agreement among the European members of the G5, this paved the way for the multilateral currency stabilisation agreement reached at the Louvre in Paris the following February.

ANOTHER SEMINAR

On Sunday, 19 October, Margaret decided to hold one of her occasional economic 'seminars' at Chequers. Those present included, in addition to John MacGregor, the Chief Secretary, and myself, Peter Middleton, Terry Burns and Brian Griffiths. She began by expressing deep concern at the underlying economic position. She said that the combination of shrinking savings, high consumer spending, booming retail sales, growing current account deficit and the falling pound, smacked of another 'Barber boom'.[26] Stop there and Margaret

[26] A reference to Anthony Barber (later Lord Barber), Chancellor of the Exchequer from 1970 to 1974, who was widely blamed for the lax policies which led to record inflation in the mid-1970s, but which were in fact largely instigated by the then Prime Minister, Edward Heath.

looks impressively prescient. But in fact she was far more wrong than right; and it was hardly surprising that I chose not to alter course as a result of the seminar. She had called the gathering in the wake of the very necessary sterling-induced one per cent base rate hike of 14 October, which she had not liked. Her three main complaints were:

1. That the current account was swinging from surplus into deficit for the first time since she had become Prime Minister.[27] Like the Labour Party, Margaret never managed to emancipate herself from the early post-war belief in the current account balance as a key indicator of economic success. A pure monetarist would have paid little attention to the current account, leaving it to a market-determined floating exchange rate to balance all movements, current and capital, across the exchanges. Even an 'exchange rate monetarist', as I became, would know that, in a world without exchange controls, a current account deficit in itself revealed little beyond the fact that the country was a net importer of capital.
2. That the pound had been falling. Yet she herself had insisted, only a few months earlier, on rejecting what was then clearly the best means of preventing this slide – membership of the ERM – and had opposed interest rate increases designed to stop the pound falling.
3. That fiscal policy was too lax, and more specifically that the £7 billion PSBR set at the time of the last Budget was too large. Here she was simply ill-informed: the 1986/87 PSBR was in fact running well below the Budget estimate and turned out to be £3.5 billion, equivalent to only 1 per cent of GDP, the lowest level for a very long time.

Indeed, the conclusion she drew, that fiscal policy ought to be tighter and monetary policy looser, was wholly perverse and if anything the reverse of the truth. It represented her perennial harking back, whenever she was uneasy, to the 1981 formula, which was appropriate to a special situation when the Budget deficit was in excess of 5 per cent of GDP and sterling had soared to an unsustainably high rate. Now the whole situation had gone into reverse. The Budget deficit was well under control, but sterling was weak.

[27] This was, however, entirely a consequence of the collapse of the oil price and should not have been a cause for concern at that time even for those who took the recorded current account figures at face value. The current account went back into surplus during the last quarter of 1986 and the first quarter of 1987.

As the autumn of 1986 went on and my political and personal standing started to rise, I remained worried about the low level of sterling. I did not see how it could be stabilised at a reasonably satisfactory level on the basis of any politically feasible interest rate changes in the run-up to an election – or even on the basis of a level of interest rates justified by the state of the domestic economy as we saw it at the time. I was convinced that we needed to bolster the effect of interest rate policy by a public commitment to a stable exchange rate system, such as the ERM, not the least of whose virtues was an obligation to engage in short-term intervention on the part of the central bank of the strong currency as well as that of the weak currency. It was true that this obligation meant less than met the eye, since it came into effect only when a currency was right up against the limit of its parity range, which in practice seldom occurred. But the knowledge that this rule existed was itself a stabilising force, which was intended to be further fortified by the Basle/Nyborg changes agreed the following year.

Fortunately (as I mistakenly thought at the time), the day after the Chequers seminar, Karl Otto Pöhl, the Bundesbank President, was due to visit London to deliver a lecture. While in London he had arranged to see not only Robin and myself, but also Margaret. Short, bespectacled, well-built and usually sun-tanned (his holidays in South Africa saw to that), Pöhl, with whom I always got on well although he was never the friend that Stoltenberg became, was one of the most powerful and most colourful characters on the international financial scene. He and his deputy (and successor) Schlesinger formed a well-balanced combination; with Schlesinger, the archetypal central banker, quietly providing the technical grasp and Pöhl, the flamboyant former sports journalist, the international awareness.

Pöhl was affable, highly articulate (in English as well as German), intelligent, quick-witted, vain, and somewhat too talkative to the Press. He was also extraordinarily volatile – at one moment a confirmed sceptic about intervention in the foreign exchange markets, for example, and a prominent advocate of it the next. (There may have been some consistency in this instance, however: he tended to favour intervention when the dollar was strong vis-à-vis the Deutschmark and to be philosophically opposed to it when the dollar was weak.) He has two outstanding achievements to his credit. The first was to persuade the world outside Germany that it was his outstanding qualities that made the Bundesbank the force it was. Only inside Germany was it understood that in fact the reverse was the case: it was the Bundesbank which gave Pöhl the stature he so enjoyed. The second was to know when to quit: just before reunification (the dangers of which he had warned against in advance) was to throw the German monetary scene into turmoil.

For some time Pöhl had been arguing in public in favour of British membership of the ERM, and I knew that Margaret held him in high – perhaps exaggerated – regard. I hoped he might persuade her of the desirability of the move where I had so far failed to do so, and I said as much to him when I saw him at Number 11. I was later told that she began the meeting (which was with Pöhl alone) by making it clear that she did not wish to discuss the EMS, and that as a result they never did.

The newspapers the next day mentioned Pöhl's visit. They also carried a story, clearly emanating from Number 10, to the effect that the UK had no intention of joining the ERM before the next general election. When I sought to raise the matter with Margaret at my bilateral with her later that day, she brusquely declined to discuss it with me. I was feeling increasingly frustrated. I was also becoming somewhat isolated, since my senior officials had come to take the view that the Prime Minister had vetoed entry, and that was that – at least for the forseeable future.

THE ROW GOES PUBLIC

What could not be postponed until after the election were immediate decisions on interest rate policy and how to respond to the continuing downward pressure on sterling. By now Margaret was becoming sufficiently careless to allow the disagreement between us to emerge into the open. In an interview she gave to the *Financial Times*, which was published on 19 November, she conceded that, after the election, 'I will expect to have to reconsider membership'; but the hostility she showed towards the ERM was so extreme that it was difficult to imagine her doing so objectively. She also came out in the open about her threat to 'do another 1981' – that is, to raise taxes. She seemed curiously unable to believe the massive improvement in the public finances I had told her about at the Chequers seminar the previous month.

Much more serious was her refusal even to hint that there might be any limit to the downward movement of sterling against the Mark. Asked about my statement at the Mansion House to the effect that the pound had fallen far enough she said:

> I do not think there are a great many consequences of that statement. We may believe it has gone far enough, but it is what the market believes

> [that matters] and you know what the market is: 95 per cent of the movement is speculation and the other 5 per cent is trade.

It is indeed precisely the febrile and anchorless nature of a freely floating exchange rate which make it both possible and desirable for national monetary authorities to give a lead. Even more dangerously, after seven and a half years in Number 10 she was clearly coming to see loyalty as a one way street: something her Ministers owed to her but not she to them – a mistake which the old Margaret Thatcher would never have made. Despite this public rebuff I held my ground and told the Treasury Committee the following day that the 'step change' in the exchange rate due to the sharp collapse of the oil price had now come to an end:

> So we are back to the policy of having an exchange rate which is exercising a financial discipline and that means I do not want to wish to see it fall further ... I think there is clearly a case for being a part of an explicit regional fixed exchange rate system.

LOOKING FOR A 'TRIGGER'

But sterling could not simply be talked into stability, and the pound was under constant pressure during both November and December. My worries about sterling were reinforced by the growth of M0. This had been rising on a seasonally adjusted basis for some months, almost certainly reflecting the strength of consumer spending.

On Thursday, 20 November, the day on which I appeared before the Treasury Select Committee, I warned the Bank that I would probably want to raise interest rates by one percentage point to 12 per cent the following Monday (24 November). It was disappointingly resistant to the idea. Whereas I was now convinced by the evidence both of sterling and of M0 that monetary policy was in danger of becoming too lax and should be tightened forthwith, the Bank was above all concerned to avoid surprising the markets, which were not expecting an interest rate hike, given my firm declaration at the time of the October increase that one per cent was enough.

I accordingly convened a full-scale markets meeting for Wednesday, at which I argued that if it was necessary in the Bank's view to have a 'trigger' before raising interest rates, we should use either the publication of the next M0 figures or the next bout of pressure on the pound, whichever was the sooner. On a seasonally adjusted basis, M0 was growing at a rate slightly above the top of the range I had set in the Budget. The Bank which was always hostile to using M0 as a trigger for an interest rate change, agreed in principle that we were likely to need to raise rates, but maintained that we should wait until the pound began to fall sharply from its already low level.

I felt I had little option but to accept this advice. It was hard enough to persuade Margaret of the need to raise interest rates when I had the Bank with me. If she were to get wind (as she almost certainly would) of the fact that the Bank were against the idea, it would be impossible. If there is one thing I learned about the timing of pressure on the pound, it is its innate perversity. It comes when you want it least; but now that I did want it, it failed to materialise. However, anxious to avoid the risk of enabling Margaret to exploit a rift between the Bank and myself, I eventually persuaded Robin that we should take the unusual step of sending her a joint note making the case for an interest rate rise.

At my weekly bilateral with her on 9 December, I told her that I was concerned that monetary conditions were too loose and believed that interest rates ought to go up by a further one percentage point. I promised her a note on the matter that evening, on the basis of which we could have a proper discussion the next day. The key passages of the joint Chancellor-Governor note I sent across to her that evening read as follows:

> We have been considering our stance on interest rates in the light of the latest monetary indicators, with an eye also on the pressures which have beset us in the past two Januaries ... There is considerable advantage in moving well before our hand is forced by the market. Last January the fact that we were prepared to raise interest rates promptly by 1 per cent enabled us to avoid the sort of drastic action we had to take in July 1984 and January 1985 ... The consequent improvement in market sentiment will also enable us to replenish the reserves ... The next set of money numbers to be published on 18 December could provide a suitable opportunity; but in any event we need to be prepared to move quickly should financial confidence start to deteriorate.

This was drafted a good deal more tentatively than I would have liked, but I wrongly assumed that it would not be long before sterling came under pressure again. Moreover, as I saw it, the need was to tighten policy, and it was absurd to allow the technicality of the trigger to get in the way of it.

The meeting to discuss this took place the following evening, 10 December. Brian Griffiths was present. Margaret was every bit as resistant as I had expected. After I had put my case, along the lines of the note, which I pointed out represented the considered opinion of both Robin and myself that monetary conditions had become too lax, she reeled off all her objections. Nothing had changed since we had decided to raise interest rates by 1 per cent rather than 2 per cent in October. Raising interest rates now would hit people with mortgages. So far from bringing down inflation it would increase it (this was a reference to the RPI effect), and it would also increase public expenditure. She suspected, too, that the seasonal adjustment of M0 was defective (a point she had no doubt got from Brian Griffiths) and would like the Treasury to prepare a note on this – a palpable delaying tactic.

Most bizarre of all, she argued (as she had done at the Chequers seminar in October) that in so far as we were experiencing any problems at the present time, they all stemmed from the PSBR having been set too high in the 1986 Budget, and the right answer was therefore not a rise in interest rates, but a 'very prudent' Budget in 1987: she suggested that I should aim for a PSBR 'as low as £5 billion', even if that left no room for tax cuts.

It was difficult to decide which was the more perverse: her refusal to accept that inflation had to be fought by the use of monetary policy, or her persistent misunderstanding of the fiscal position. The 1986 Budget may have set a PSBR of £7 billion, but the out-turn for 1986/87 was only £3.5 billion. Thus in urging me to aim, in the 1987 Budget, for a PSBR 'as low as £5 billion' she was unknowingly knocking at an open door: I was to aim for a PSBR for 1987/88 considerably less than £5 billion, even after cutting taxes by some £2.5 billion, and to achieve a surplus.

I duly countered all her various points, and reiterated the importance I attached to taking no avoidable risks with inflation. After a long discussion, she concluded that everything should be done to avoid a rise in interest rates in advance of a Budget which, she reiterated, would need to be prudent enough to obviate any conceivable need to raise interest rates (indeed, it might make possible a reduction in interest rates). However, she conceded with the utmost reluctance that it might nevertheless be right to raise interest rates – but if, and only if, there was 'a clear trigger' for an increase.

We left it at that. However unconvincing most of the arguments she had used, her final conclusion was so similar in substance (if very different in tone) to the Bank's position, that to have pushed it any further would merely have destroyed the common front I had taken so much trouble to construct. And I was of course unaware that the clear (exchange rate) trigger was not to materialise until the run-up to the Louvre Accord of February 1987, by which time I was thinking in terms of a different way of keeping sterling strong.

These two occasions in 1986 – one towards the start of the year, the other towards the end of it – were the only occasions during my time as Chancellor on which Margaret actually prevented an interest rate increase I sought. Conceding an interest rate rise with ill grace was, most of the time, par for the course. There were, needless to say, no occasions when she made any attempt to stand in the way of a proposal of mine to reduce interest rates; and there was one important time when, as we shall see, she foisted on me an interest rate cut I had not wanted.

No doubt every Chancellor has experienced the same difficulties as I did in persuading the Prime Minister of the day that interest rates should be increased. Some may have encountered even greater difficulty. Essentially, Margaret was no different from the others so far as this was concerned. The picture she liked to present of herself as a uniquely doughty fighter against inflation was, in this sense, largely mythical. Where she was unusual was in her courage and resolve, most of the time, to see a tough policy through, once it had been embarked upon, irrespective of short-term unpopularity. This was highly commendable. But it was not the same thing.

CHAPTER THIRTY-SEVEN

A SURFEIT OF RESIGNATIONS

Prelude to Westland · The Westland Affair · The Resignation of Michael Heseltine The Resignation of Leon Brittan · The Bunker Beckons · A New Policy for the Pound

PRELUDE TO WESTLAND

In November 1985 Margaret's former PPS, Ian Gow, resigned as Treasury Minister of State in protest at the Anglo-Irish Agreement. The resignation of a middle-ranking Minister is not normally a matter of great political significance: Ian's resignation was of unusual interest at the time because none of her Ministers was closer to Margaret than he was. But it was soon eclipsed by the much greater disaster of the Westland affair. An essentially trivial matter, it exploded into a major political crisis at the turn of the year, which Margaret survived only by the skin of her teeth. Looking back, there were two events early in 1985 that had an important bearing on it.

Margaret had inherited Michael Heseltine from the Heath Shadow Cabinet, and had initially been very wary, not to say distrustful, of him. But as her first Environment Secretary she had become rather impressed by him, in particular by the businesslike way in which he ran his Department, which she felt was an object lesson to those of us who appeared to be interested only in policy. Indeed, during this time it was Willie who took against him far more than Margaret did, as Michael brought modern gimmicks like massive computer print-outs to the Cabinet table and generally tried to blind us with science. She, by contrast, was sufficiently impressed to appoint him Secretary of State for Defence in January 1983, replacing John Nott who had announced his intention of leaving Parliament at the next general election.

This was only partly because she saw in Michael a flamboyant campaigner against the folly of Labour's then policy, under the quixotic leadership of Michael Foot, of unilateral nuclear disarmament – a task he performed admirably. It was also because she felt that the Ministry of Defence could do with the businesslike approach that only Michael could bring to it. Michael, however, saw it differently. As someone whose sole ambition other than the premiership was to be Trade and Industry Secretary – an ambition eventually realised under John Major's premiership in 1992 – and organise what he saw as a Japanese-style industrial policy, the defence procurement budget offered him the chance to achieve this from another Department.

As Margaret began to realise what was afoot, relations between them deteriorated rapidly, with her old distrust of him once again in full bloom, while he became increasingly frustrated by what he saw as her excessive interference in his departmental business. The first portent of the Westland crisis occurred very early in 1985, when the question came before the Economic Affairs Committee of the Cabinet, which Margaret almost always chaired herself (I did so only when she was unable to), of whether an order for a Type 22 frigate should be given to Cammell Laird of Merseyside or Swan Hunter of Tyneside. Michael urged the former, but Margaret, backed by a clear majority of the Committee, of whom I was one, preferred the latter. Margaret hurriedly closed the meeting, and then asked Willie and me to come with her upstairs.

There she told us that Michael had indicated to her that, if the decision did not go his way, he would resign. She would rather avoid that; and since the issue was such a minor one she hoped Willie and I would agree to letting him have his way at a subsequent meeting. Despite the emotional commitment to Merseyside that Michael had developed at Environment in the wake of the Toxteth riots of 1981, I was astonished that he could seriously contemplate resigning over so trivial a matter. I had not previously realised the extent of his frustration with Margaret. The further meeting was duly held, and Margaret blithely opened by announcing that we had had a preliminary discussion at the previous meeting; now we had to reach a decision. Willie nobly did his bit, and Cammell Laird duly got the Type 22. She did not show it, but she was seething. Michael had humiliated her: from then on, she was as determined to do him down as he was determined to run his own Department in his own way.

The second portent came a little later in 1985, when the same Cabinet Committee had to decide on a replacement for the RAF's ageing Phantoms. The Treasury official advice, with which I entirely concurred, was against any replacement at all, failing which we should buy the next generation of American fighters off the peg. As I had expected, I could get no support for either of these propositions: the Committee was persuaded that we had to have a fighter and we had to keep the technological skills alive in the UK.

Margaret then characteristically proposed that we went into partnership with the Americans, only to be told by Michael that he had sounded them out and they were not interested: not altogether surprisingly, since they had already embarked on their own project. The choice then came down to either the UK going it alone, favoured by Margaret, or a European joint venture, favoured by Michael. At this point I supported Michael: going it alone would have been absurd. That led to the decision to go for what was to be known as the European Fighter Aircraft (EFA).

In the event, the French were outmanoeuvred. They refused to participate in the agreement unless a cheaper and less sophisticated aircraft was specified than that envisaged by the UK. They were confident that the powerful Franco-German special relationship that dominated the European Community would ensure that Germany would never dare participate unless France did, thus frustrating the entire venture unless something closer to the French specifications was agreed. They may well have been right about the specifications, but – partly thanks to Michael's negotiating skill – they were wrong about the Germans. To their immense chagrin, the agreement was signed in August 1985 by the UK, Germany, Italy and Spain, with the French left out in the cold. Michael was seen as having pulled off a coup – and had acquired a taste for European joint ventures.

THE WESTLAND AFFAIR

Meanwhile, in the early summer of 1985, I received a message one weekend that Margaret was calling an urgent meeting about Westland on the Sunday evening and she would like me to come. All I knew about Westland at that time was that it was Britain's only helicopter manufacturer, based in Yeovil, and very badly managed. The only others present were Michael Heseltine and Norman Tebbit, then the Trade and Industry Secretary. Michael said he felt we should know that Westland had informed his Department that unless they were given Government assistance they would have to go out of business. Michael said he was not prepared to divert any of his existing budget to Westland, since its survival was of no strategic importance to the UK. Norman was not prepared to divert any funds from his much smaller budget and I made it clear that I was not prepared to make any new money available. Michael said that he now knew what answer his people must give the company, and that was that. Norman and I were left wondering why, if Westland was of no strategic importance, it was necessary to have had a sudden Sunday evening meeting at all.

Westland, *in extremis*, then acquired a new chairman, John Cuckney, a very able businessman and financier whom I had known off and on for a fair number of years, who set about finding a private sector solution; and by the autumn had emerged with a wealthy suitor in the shape of the American helicopter firm, Sikorsky. This perfectly satisfactory solution galvanised Michael, who sought the permission of the Economic Affairs Committee of the Cabinet, on Monday, 9 December, to see if the various European National Armaments Directors, as government defence procurement chiefs are known in NATO-speak, could cobble together a European alternative. It was clear that he had already been actively exploring this informally, and was fairly confident they could.

I was wholly opposed to Government intervention of this kind. Rescue operations were bad enough when the alternative was closure; when there was not even, as in this case, a threat of closure any longer – indeed the intervention had only been suggested when the closure threat was removed – it was absurd. The moral hazard involved was enormous: a European consortium which had emerged not spontaneously but at the prompting of the National Armaments Directors would inevitably expect government orders to keep it in business; and governments could scarcely 'rescue' a company one day and let it go to the wall the next.

Margaret, too, was opposed to the idea, and sought to condition the Committee by, most unusually, holding the meeting in two parts. In the first part John Cuckney and his managing director were present. They explained why they believed the Sikorsky deal was best for the company, and answered questions. They then withdrew, and we had the Committee meeting proper. Although Cuckney was a very polished performer, Margaret's ploy was predictably counterproductive. Cabinet Ministers dislike being told by outsiders what conclusion they should reach. Although there was still a clear majority in favour of the perfectly coherent line that the Government should stay out of it altogether, Margaret was visibly shaken by the degree of support, which included Norman Tebbit, for Michael's plea to be given a chance. While the balance of argument was clearly against Michael, sentiment was with him. Unwisely, I think, she changed the summing up she had intended to give and instead gave him the green light, coupled however with what she may have imagined was an impossible deadline: four o'clock on the afternoon of Friday the thirteenth – in other words, only four days away.

THE RESIGNATION OF MICHAEL HESELTINE

Michael has subsequently claimed that it was agreed that the Committee should meet again then. As I recall it, the understanding was simply that we might need to, not that we would. In any event, Michael did succeed in getting a somewhat vague European alternative together just before the deadline, but the next Ministerial discussion was not until Cabinet the following week, on 19 December, the last Cabinet meeting of the old year. Margaret now realised she had got herself into difficulties; and the discussion in Cabinet hinged on the question of whether it was a matter for the shareholders to decide which offer they preferred, or (as Michael insisted) for Ministers, given the nature of Westland's business. Cabinet decided it should be the shareholders, and Michael's blood was up.

Throughout this saga, Leon Brittan, although still smarting from his loss of the job of Home Secretary in the September 1985 reshuffle, when he was made Trade and Industry Secretary instead, loyally supported Margaret. But I had the sense that his normally clear judgement had been affected. His brother Samuel, the *Financial Times* assistant editor, told me he was going to stay with Leon for Christmas and had bought him a toy helicopter as a Christmas present. 'I wouldn't, if I were you', I told him, 'this is no laughing matter.' After Christmas he could not wait to tell me that I had been quite wrong, and that Leon had thought it an excellent joke.

But if Leon was losing his judgement, Michael had by now thrown caution to the winds. Over the Christmas recess, while the rest of us were taking a break (or at worst quietly reading the papers for Chevening), Michael was busy campaigning for the European consortium, in open defiance of the Cabinet decision that Ministers should stay out of it and leave it to Westland's shareholders to decide; while Number 10 was equally busy campaigning against Michael. The extraordinary climax came with the leaking, on 6 January, of a Number 10-inspired warning letter to Michael from the then Attorney General, Patrick Mayhew. The letter turned out to be ill-founded, having been based on incorrect information; but the real scandal was the leaking of confidential advice from a Law Officer, which by strict convention is never made public. Mayhew was furious, and threatened to resign unless there was an inquiry into the source of the leak.

None of this was mentioned, however, when Westland came up as the first substantive item on the agenda at the first Cabinet meeting of the new year, on 9 January. By then Margaret realised she was in a desperate position, and that desperate measures were called for. Having gone out of her way to prevent his resignation over the absurd issue of the Type 22 frigate only a year previously, she now set out to humiliate Michael, in the full knowledge that this would almost certainly lead to his resignation over an issue on which he could cobble together a colourable case. Indeed, she had already decided whom she would appoint Defence Secretary in his place. The issue before Cabinet, Margaret said, was quite simply the restoration of the doctrine of collective Cabinet responsibility (not something of which she was at all times the most devoted adherent herself). To that end Michael would have to be gagged, by the requirement that he could say nothing on the issue without first clearing it with Robert Armstrong, the Cabinet Secretary.

Michael objected that this was wholly impracticable, and that in any case collective Cabinet responsibility could scarcely apply since she had not permitted a proper collective discussion of the issue. He spoke quietly, and not at all aggressively, and sought to find some compromise arrangement. But Margaret was adamant. She could see that Michael was now isolated in Cabinet. The general view of the colleagues was that Michael had become obsessed with the issue, and had lost all sense of proportion; while as for gagging, it was a great pity that everyone had not been gagged a good deal earlier. She pressed home her advantage; whereupon Michael slammed his Cabinet folder shut, saying 'If this is the way this Government is going to be conducted, I no longer wish to be part of it', picked the folder up and strode out of the room. It was the most dramatic moment in any Cabinet I have attended. In the stunned silence that followed, Margaret announced that there would be a short break for coffee (to enable her to brief Bernard Ingham) after which Cabinet resumed with the rest of its agenda. When we were once again in our places, Margaret announced that the new Defence Secretary was George Younger.

THE RESIGNATION OF LEON BRITTAN

The Opposition wanted Margaret's blood. The back-benchers, too, felt that they had been badly let down by the Cabinet, as indeed they had been, and wanted blood. Some of them wanted Margaret's, but most of them wanted Leon's; as it emerged that it was he who had authorised the leak of the Mayhew letter, having been given the clear impression that that was what Margaret wanted him to do. There was an unpleasant whiff of anti-semitism, and Leon resigned on 24 January.

Once again, I was amazed by his uncharacteristic lack of judgement. No doubt he was frustrated by the fact that, in the unorthodox and improper political game that had been played during the Christmas and New Year break, Michael had outsmarted him. But for any Minister to leak a confidential Law Officer's letter was amazing enough; for a lawyer of Leon's distinction to agree to do so, whether

Margaret wanted him to or not, was mind-boggling. Yet once again his lack of judgement was equalled only by his amazing loyalty to Margaret. Had he made public all he knew, she could not possibly have survived; but he chose not to do so. As it was, he meekly accepted the role of scapegoat. It was a ghastly time for him. Despite having to a considerable extent brought it on himself, I felt deeply sorry for him.

Margaret was at the lowest ebb I had ever seen her. Leon had resigned on the Friday. Thérèse and I had invited her round to Number 11 the following Sunday evening, so that, after Thérèse had withdrawn, I could outline to her my plans for the 1986 Budget. It was pretty hopeless: she was totally exhausted and unable to focus or concentrate on anything. Never the best of listeners, that evening she simply did not appear to be able to hear what was being said to her, and when she spoke it was like the automatic responses of a zombie. When Emily, then four years old, entered the room, Margaret said in a tired voice, 'What a pretty dress.' Emily replied 'Yes, it comes from Marks Expensive'. Thérèse explained that Emily was under the impression that that was the name of Marks and Spencers. Margaret, completely missing the point, replied a trifle tetchily, 'Yes, I know little girls' dresses are expensive.'

THE BUNKER BECKONS

In some ways Margaret's period of acute weakness, while her own job was on the line, was helpful to me. Not that it lasted very long: she was nothing if not resilient. But it was during that patch that the oil price collapsed. The Saudi royal family started leaning heavily on my successor as Energy Secretary, Peter Walker, to persuade us in effect to become an honorary member of OPEC, by agreeing to restrict production so as to support the oil price. Peter was initially undecided how to respond.

Had Margaret, with her soft spot for the Saudi royal family, been in a condition to intervene, we might well have acceded to their request, which was certainly what the Foreign Office would have liked. As it was, it was left to Peter and me to determine our response. As in 1983, I was clear that there could be no question of our joining forces with OPEC. Peter agreed and duly made this known to the Saudis.

A few months later, King Fahd dismissed his very long-serving Oil Minister, Zaki Yamani, for having (as he saw it) badly mismanaged things. I felt I had now played a part in seeing off both the energy tsars who had sought to dominate the scene when I was Energy Secretary: Scargill and Yamani. While I was delighted with the political castration of Scargill, I was sorry to see Yamani, whom I liked, go. Both had made the mistake of imagining that they could dictate terms to the British Government.

The longer-term effects of the Westland affair, however, were wholly adverse. The lesson Margaret took from it was that her colleagues were troublesome and her courtiers were loyal. From then on she began to distance herself even from those Cabinet colleagues who had been closest to her – certainly those who had minds of their own – and to retreat to the Number 10 bunker, where the leading figures were Charles Powell and Bernard Ingham.

I have already written of Ingham, against whom she would not hear a word said. On the occasions when I complained about his activities, she roundly denied that he could possibly have been guilty of what I was alleging, even though it was well known to the Press that that was exactly what he had been doing. Other Ministers met precisely the same response. Charles Powell, the Foreign Office man who had become her foreign affairs private secretary, and for most of the time the dominant force in her private office, was as polished as Ingham was blunt. Highly intelligent, he wrote the best and wittiest notes of meetings of anyone in Whitehall. His closeness to her was reinforced by the unlikely friendship Margaret developed with Powell's vivacious and somewhat less polished Italian wife, Carla. He never saw it as his role to question her prejudices, merely to refine the language in which they were expressed. And like Ingham, he stayed at Number 10 far too long – despite all Whitehall's efforts to persuade her to make a change and the Foreign Office's repeated attempts to lure him away with the promise of ever more attractive Ambassadorial posts.

With things drifting in this undesirable direction, I was both surprised and immensely heartened when, on the flight back from the May 1986 Tokyo Summit, Margaret took me aside and said she was considering forming an inner Cabinet: what did I think? It was, of course, what I had for some time felt to be the crucial missing ingredient in the Thatcher Government, and I told her I thought it an excellent idea. Soon afterwards she asked Geoffrey to join us, and we discussed the membership. It seemed to boil down to herself, Willie, Geoffrey, Norman Tebbit, John Wakeham and myself. But no sooner had she arrived back in London, than the plan changed. Perhaps she changed her mind unaided, perhaps she was persuaded against it by the courtiers, whose role would have diminished. There was no point in asking her, as she would inevitably have replied that it was her unaided decision.

A NEW POLICY FOR THE POUND

As I have already recorded, 1986 had been a terrible year for the pound. Essentially, what had happened was that, as the dollar fell from the stratospheric height it had reached in 1985, sterling fell with it, dropping very nearly 20 per cent against the Deutschmark. But sterling had not been grossly overvalued in 1985 as the dollar had been. And Margaret's veto of the interest rate rise I had sought in December 1986 made the prospect for the foreign exchange markets in the run-up to the 1987 general election even more worrying.

The slide continued into January 1987. But by then relief was at hand. For we had agreed to hold meetings of the G5 and G7 at the Louvre in Paris in February, with a view to ending the dollar's long decline and ushering in a period of stability. And just as the pound had been falling with the dollar, so there was a reasonable prospect that stabilising the dollar would also stabilise the pound – just what was needed in the approach to a general election, when markets always tend to be nervous. Before going off to the Louvre, I discussed all this with Margaret, who was in full agreement with my objective. On my return I sent her a minute, explaining what had been agreed. After setting out the 'readiness to engage in concerted intervention' to defend the key parities specified in the Accord – the dollar/Deutschmark rate and the dollar/yen rate – I added:

> No limits of this kind were suggested for the pound or the Canadian dollar, but I indicated that I would expect sterling to fit into the general climate of stability, and should we need to intervene we would endeavour to avoid doing so in a way which was contrary to the spirit of the overall agreement ... We can be well content with an outcome which does not involve us in onerous commitments, and which if successful could helpfully provide a more stable external background for us in the coming weeks.

I also attached to my minute – since, contrary to much subsequent insinuation, I was scrupulous in keeping Margaret fully informed about the Louvre – a transcript of my brief press conference, at which I said:

> The agreement applies to all currencies, though the principal focus, as with Plaza, is the dollar, and the key rates are the dollar/Deutschmark and dollar/Yen. So far as the UK is concerned, I have said many times

> that I do not want to see sterling fall further. By the same token I have no desire in current circumstances to see a substantial rise.

The asymmetry of the last two sentences was of course deliberate, as was appreciated at the time. And the Louvre duly did the trick, causing a sudden resurgence of confidence in sterling. I sat back while the pound rose from DM2.79 on the eve of the Accord of 22 February to DM2.94 on 10 March – an increase of more than 5 per cent in just over a fortnight – before trimming interest rates by half a point to 10.5 per cent. The Budget a week later was well received in the financial markets, and I shaved interest rates by a further half point to 10 per cent, with the pound at DM2.95. It was clear, both to me and to the financial markets, that the Louvre framework had for the first time made a policy of exchange rate stability credible. So far as the pound was concerned, the markets started to infer that my intention was to keep it below DM3. At the markets meeting I held on 18 March, at which the reduction to 10 per cent was agreed, I told the senior Treasury and Bank officials present that this market view was useful, and that we should validate it, by being ready to intervene as and when necessary, making sure that the intervention was sterilised in order to neutralise any monetary consequences. This should be a simple matter, given the very low PSBR; while the intervention would be useful in enabling us to rebuild our reserves, which had been severely depleted in the previous year. Thus it was that the policy of shadowing the Deutschmark, at DM3 to the pound, was born.

Unexpectedly there now emerged strong upward pressure on the pound, as the confidence created by the Louvre was augmented by the markets' conviction that we were going to win the general election – an astonishing turnaround compared with only a year before. This meant intervention on a much larger scale than anything previously experienced, leading to a strengthening of the reserves that my predecessors would have given their eye teeth for, as well as two further half-point cuts in interest rates on 28 April and 11 May, this last on the very day the general election was announced, taking rates down to 9 per cent. It was a helpful prelude to the election itself, but I saw it as essentially an interim measure. My hope was to replace the policy with full membership of the EMS, as soon as practicable once the election was out of the way.

CHAPTER THIRTY-EIGHT

1987 – A PRE-ELECTION BUDGET

My Own High Noon · Two Pence Off …

… But Still Cautious · 'Yes; Of Course I Do'

MY OWN HIGH NOON

My 'unassailable' period began in the late autumn or early winter of 1986. The Autumn Statement on 6 November had been badly received by the financial markets. As described earlier, John MacGregor's success in limiting public spending in a pre-election year was largely disguised by the shift to a more realistic projection and presentation. The disappearance of the misbegotten autumnal 'estimated fiscal adjustment' did not prevent gloomy reports from appearing of the likely fiscal outlook for the present and coming financial year.

But then quite suddenly the atmosphere changed. To be fair, the lead was taken by the City analysts – not always my favourite scribes – who suddenly concluded from the monthly Exchequer returns that the PSBR outlook was much better, rather than much worse, than the Treasury had thought. Recorded unemployment had at long last peaked in July (at some 3.1 million) and the subsequent fall provided helpful mood music. Those of the chattering classes in more contact with business and industry were beginning to accept that some things had changed for the better. It was the time when the left-wing intelligentsia, in organs such as the briefly influential *Marxism Today*, began to talk seriously of 'Thatcherism' and how to learn some of its lessons.

Too much talk of 'economic management' has obscured the fact that the reputation of a modern Chancellor is to a substantial extent dependent on much the same factors (with many more noughts added) as those on which a Chancellor's reputation in Gladstone's time depended. If public spending is under control, revenue is coming in well and there is a margin to divide between tax reductions and judiciously targeted public spending measures, he will be riding high. If not, not. The big difference from Victorian times is that a good fiscal prospect is now a necessary, but not a sufficient, condition of perceived success. Other factors are needed, such as the absence of uncomfortable increases in interest rates, or too much recession gloom and doom. But spending and revenue are still the key. Nor will this ever be changed by sophisticated (and speculative) cyclical correction of the figures.

TWO PENCE OFF ...

I did my best to dampen expectations of a pre-election Budget bonanza. At the time of the Autumn Statement in November 1986, for example, I told the House that 'Clearly the same pound cannot be used twice. A pound which is used in higher public expenditure is not available for a reduction in taxation.' This was in the context of my pledge to stick to the 1987/88 Budget deficit indicated in the previous year's Red Book.

Since the commentators at that time were convinced that the PSBR was spiralling out of control, dampening expectations was not too difficult. But it was clear to me that the commentators had got it wrong. On 23, November 1986, I scribbled on the back of my diary card eight items I hoped to include in the 1987 Budget. They were to cut the basic rate of income tax, simplify the higher rates, introduce tax relief for profit-related pay, allow cash accounting for VAT, raise the Inheritance Tax threshold, reform corporate and individual Capital Gains Tax (CGT) and levy either a credit card tax or a consumer credit tax. The date of the card shows that, unlike the case with the 1986 Budget, the 1987 decision to cut the basic rate was there from the start. Four of the other measures listed on the card were wholly or partially effected in the 1987 Budget. Two of those left undone or half done – simplifying the higher rates and reforming CGT for individuals, as well as businesses – were merely postponed until the immediate post-election Budget. The consumer credit tax was the only failed candidate, for reasons I have already explained.

Not surprisingly, the Chevening meeting of 10 and 11 January 1987, was one of the easiest and pleasantest of any during my time as Chancellor. The house was snow-bound, which added to the happy atmosphere – marred only by Norman Lamont's wife, Rosemary, slipping on the ice and breaking her wrist. We provisionally agreed to raise the income tax allowances and thresholds strictly in line with inflation and to cut the basic rate by 2p to 27p, which is exactly what happened.

The Treasury mandarins never sought to prevent me from cutting income tax, since they accepted that it was the Government's clearly stated policy; and, with Government borrowing coming down faster than taxes were, they could scarcely argue that I was being imprudent. None the less, there was no disguising the fact that they disliked it, and hoped that I would do it as little as was consistent with Government policy. The ethos of the official Treasury – and for all its quirks, I retain both respect and affection for the Department – is unremittingly austere. They disapprove of tax cuts almost as much as they dislike increases in public spending. They cannot imagine what the public have done to deserve tax cuts, which will inevitably be put to frivolous use. Interest rates were a different matter altogether.

Curiously enough, though for rather different reasons, Margaret's views on all this were closer to those of the official Treasury than mine were. She was positively soft on interest rates. Indeed, what with that and her opposition to the ERM, it always seemed to me that, so far as the battle against inflation was concerned, she willed the end without being prepared to will the means. Her softness on interest rates was primarily dictated by her overriding concern to promote home ownership and to look after those who were buying their homes with a mortgage. But she also saw her Government's finest hour, her equivalent of the Battle of Britain, to which in her mind she was always harking back, as having been the 1981 Budget, in which taxes were increased and, as a trade-off, interest rates (although admittedly not for long) reduced. This was the turning point, as she saw it, in the battle against inflation, and the event which finally confounded her critics.

As a result, throughout most of my time as Chancellor, I found myself favouring both lower taxes and higher interest rates than either the Treasury mandarins on the one hand or the Prime Minister on the other.

But to return to 1987. After Chevening, Margaret pressed me to raise the £30,000 mortgage interest relief ceiling – she had successfully induced Geoffrey to raise it from £25,000 in the pre-election Budget of 1983, and had wanted to go considerably higher – but when I made it clear that I was prepared to do so only as part of a package in which the relief was restricted to the basic rate, she quickly desisted.

... BUT STILL CAUTIOUS

When I presented my Budget on 17 March 1987, it looked as if the PSBR for 1986/87 would be a little over £4 billion, some £3 billion less than originally forecast. According to the Treasury's projections, it was possible to reduce taxation by getting on for £3 billion and still bring the Budget deficit below the £4 billion the MTFS had indicated for 1987/88. The result was much better still:

a deficit of little more than £3.5 million in 1986/87 and – what I christened a Public Sector Debt *Repayment*, or PSDR – that is, a Budget surplus of almost £3.5 billion in 1987/88.

There was nothing in the 1987 Red Book economic forecast to indicate inflation or overheating. It was thought by the forecasters at the time that GDP had risen by 2.5 per cent in 1986 and would rise by 3 per cent in 1987, if anything falling back slightly in early 1988. These rates straddled the then estimated growth of productive capacity and were expected to be accompanied by a small current account deficit. Unfortunately, this was the period when both the statistics for the recent past and the projections of the future started to go seriously off the rails. The 1986 growth rate was subsequently revised upwards to 3.9 per cent, and growth in 1987 came to no less than 4.8 per cent – a very substantial difference in each case. Not surprisingly, a large part of the excess demand spilled over into imports, leading inevitably to a greatly enlarged current account deficit.

Despite the reassuring forecasts, I decided to err on the side of caution. First, there was my decision to aim for a very low deficit. Second, and more controversially, anxious about the inevitable rebound in recorded inflation as the effects of lower oil prices passed out of the year-on-year comparison, I decided to refrain from revalorising the excise duties. Thus, for once, there was none of the usual x pence on a pint of beer or packet of cigarettes in the Budget speech. Instead, after telling the House about some very minor changes, I simply said: 'I have no further changes to propose this year in the rates of excise duty', and passed on. It was some time before anyone realised what had happened.

My failure to revalorise the excise duties shocked senior Treasury officials, who regarded it as 'tinkering', if not worse. They also argued that I would find it impossible to present, certainly so far as cigarettes and alcohol were concerned – a view shared by some of my ministerial colleagues. I saw no great difficulty. The man in the street was unlikely to protest about the failure to increase the price of cigarettes and drink. And by doing nothing at all (rather than, say, merely increasing the duties by less than inflation) there would be no need for any clauses in the Finance Bill, and thus no occasion for a parliamentary debate. The fundamental belief of the official Treasury is that the Chancellor should never knowingly give away revenue which might be difficult to recover. They have a point. But I was worried about the likely consequences of the depreciation of sterling in 1986. Not that I thought, of course, that leaving beer and tobacco duties unchanged was a barrier against the forces of inflation. But I was anxious to do what I could to prevent a rekindling of inflationary expectations, and to buy time while more fundamental measures – which I saw increasingly in terms of ERM membership – were put in place.

'YES; OF COURSE I DO'

Naturally, I was beginning to think of my future after the election. I did not believe in going 'on and on'; but the likelihood of a 1987 election meant that some of my most cherished tax changes had to be postponed. So quite apart from any hopes I may have harboured on the EMS front, I still wanted to present at least one more radical Budget.

I therefore took the opportunity of my usual informal pre-Budget discussion, this time unusually held in the Long Gallery at Chequers, on 1 February, to ask Margaret if she wanted me to continue as Chancellor after the election. Her reply was unequivocal: 'Yes; of course I do.'

CHAPTER THIRTY-NINE

AN ELECTION WON ON THE ECONOMY

The Date Chooses Itself · The Campaigns Compared · Costing Labour's Pledges Divided Counsels · Of Lice and Fleas · My Freelance Election Campaign The Tide Rolls On

THE DATE CHOOSES ITSELF

By 1987 it was clear that an election was imminent. Not only would we soon be in the final year of the parliament, but having won in May 1979 and June 1983, Margaret was convinced that May and June were her lucky months. There was thus a strong presumption that the election would come in June 1987, and the Budget had provided the ideal launching pad. All that remained was to take the political temperature by analysing the results of the local elections held throughout England and Wales on 7 May. Margaret asked me to come to Chequers on the morning of Sunday, 10 May, by which time all the analysis would have been done and we could choose the election date.

I duly arrived at Chequers that sunny Sunday morning. In addition to me, she had invited Willie, Geoffrey, Norman Tebbit (then Party Chairman) and David Young, who had been allotted a somewhat ill-defined role in Central Office once the starting pistol had been fired. What it really amounted to was that Margaret was becoming uneasy about Norman's growing popularity, and suspected that he was using Central Office to build up for himself a rival power base. David's job, essentially, was to keep an eye on him: an unhappy augury. Norman presented his analysis, which showed that we ought to win a June general election quite comfortably. We then fell to discussing dates, and had very soon settled on 11 June. It was the easiest choice of election date in which I have ever been involved. It was announced the following day.

THE CAMPAIGNS COMPARED

The Labour campaign undeniably began well, with the smoothly professional filmed 'profile' of Neil Kinnock, by Hugh Hudson of 'Chariots of Fire' fame, showing him in various photogenic settings, notably walking hand-in-hand with his wife, Glenys, on the cliff tops with the birds circling above them. It was also the only election broadcast I can recall which did not close with the Party's name. Instead of 'Labour' the film ended with the screen filled with the one word 'KINNOCK'. Sentimental and corny though it was, it made the Conservative TV broadcasts look old-fashioned and amateurish by comparison, and was said to have raised Kinnock's personal opinion poll rating by no less than 19 percentage points overnight – although if it did it was too ephemeral to affect voting intentions.

The Labour campaign did not really start to unravel until 25 May, when Kinnock told David Frost in a television interview that if the Russians invaded a non-nuclear Britain they would be resisted by guerilla bands who had taken to the hills. The Conservative poster depicting a soldier with his hands up in the surrender position above the simple slogan 'Labour's Policy on Arms' was the most memorable image of a less than vintage campaign for political posters. The Alliance campaign, initially regarded as a great threat, never really took off, largely because neither David Owen nor David Steel could trust each other, let alone agree on a single leader.

It was just as well that we entered the election comfortably ahead, as demonstrated by the local election results, since the Conservative Party campaign was in every way the most incompetent in which I have ever participated – and my participation dates back to 1964. The manifesto, crammed with pledges which caused considerable difficulty in the early days of the campaign, was launched at Central Office on 19 May. Margaret highlighted the three 'flagships', as she called them, of the Poll Tax, education reform and housing. This, I felt, was a mistake. The key strategy in fighting a general election is to determine the territory on which the main battle is fought. The most favourable territory for the Tories in 1987, as in most years, was defence, central government taxation, and the economy in general.

As for the three 'flagships' themselves, the only saving grace of the Poll Tax was that, as it had not yet been introduced, the full extent of its horrors was not widely appreciated. Nevertheless, we were extremely lucky that Labour unaccountably ignored this juicy target altogether. As for the education and housing reforms, these had been cobbled together so hastily to get them ready in time for the manifesto that a number of details had still not been finally worked out; and even where they had been they were not wholly familiar to those fighting the campaign, not least to Margaret herself.

COSTING LABOUR'S PLEDGES

A major contribution made by my Treasury team to the campaign was the careful costing of the policies proposed by the Labour Party. Labour was still lumbered with all of its historical commitments to reverse pretty well every spending cut and multiply every benefit. As far back as the summer of 1986 I had asked John MacGregor, the Chief Secretary, to supervise an exercise in which Treasury officials would cost specific policy proposals put to them by the Special Advisers, who had taken these proposals from commitments made by Labour frontbench spokesmen, resolutions passed at Labour Party Conferences and the proposals made in various *ad hoc* policy papers produced by the Labour Party. The sums were then added up, and it was calculated what they would mean in terms of the extra taxation needed to finance them.

There was some criticism at the time that it was improper to use officials for party political purposes, but the Cabinet Secretary ruled that it was entirely proper for Ministers to ask officials to cost alternative policy proposals, as indeed the previous Labour Government had done. The 'costings' rose as new Labour commitments were made. After Labour's social security spokesman Michael Meacher, added a raft of new and uprated benefits at the 1986 Labour Party Conference, they reached a grand total of £34 billion, which implied a basic rate of income tax of no less than 56p in the pound or VAT at almost 50 per cent, or some combination of the two. In reality it was of course more likely that had Labour been elected, the pledges would have been dishonoured; but that was not the most impressive of defences. Right from the start, the Shadow Chancellor, Roy Hattersley, had considerable difficulty in sustaining his claim that only those earning more than £25,000 a year, or the top 5 per cent of the population, would pay more tax under a Labour Government.

To my astonishment, I discovered that those responsible for organising the campaign had made no plans to use this meticulous work. Fortunately I had my own personal campaign team, in the shape of the three Treasury special advisers. I based Peter Cropper in Central Office to keep an eye on what was happening there and to keep me informed; Andrew Tyrie remained at the Treasury to be my link man there; while Alistair Ross-Goobey travelled with me wherever I went. Using Peter as an intermediary, I managed to organise an unscheduled Central Office press conference on the morning of Saturday, 23 May, at which, with whatever visual aids Peter could get them to rustle up at short notice, I introduced the John MacGregor costings of Labour's spending plans. Saturday morning is not a very good time (that was why no press conference had been scheduled for then); but at least it helped to get the issue into orbit.

DIVIDED COUNSELS

It was, in fact, extremely difficult to discover just who was running the campaign. As Party Chairman, it should have been Norman Tebbit; but as I have indicated, even though Norman had been one of her closest colleagues, both personally and politically, Margaret had come to distrust him and fear him as a future rival for her job. She was particularly worried that he would take the credit for an election victory. Hence her decision to put David Young in Central Office, too; reporting directly to her. The effect was predictable. Central Office, throughout the campaign, was divided into two warring factions, who spent far more energy trying to get the better of each other than they did in fighting the enemy.

As if the idea of divided leadership were not bizarre enough, the choice of David Young as Norman's *alter ego* was unbelievably perverse. David had many excellent qualities. He was a genuine believer in the enterprise culture, had useful business experience, and had a particularly fertile mind, which was always coming up with ingenious ideas and schemes, all of which, given his business background, were practical, and many of them had merit. But David was a businessman who had gone straight into the House of Lords and the Cabinet via a back-room advisory role and the chairmanship of a quango, without ever having stood for political office or even been a local Party worker. As a result, he knew less about election campaigning and had his finger further from the public pulse than any other Cabinet colleague.

He was, however, a great believer in the power of advertising. As Employment Secretary he had spent copious amounts of public money on promoting the advertising campaign 'Action for Jobs'. He seemed to believe that it was the choice of advertising agency which would determine the outcome of the election. Margaret, who was always inclined to think that if a policy was unpopular it could only be because of poor presentation, had a weakness for this line of thinking. Norman had retained the Party's usual advertising agents, Saatchi & Saatchi, for the 1987 election. Margaret, however, had turned against them when Norman presented the results of opinion research they had done which suggested that the public found her 'bossy' and 'fussy'. He had presented it, too, at the very time when her own relations with him were at their lowest ebb, and it certainly did nothing to improve them.

David decided that the solution was to bring in a new advertising agency (Tim Bell, with a walk-on part for Young and Rubicam), initially behind Norman's back. This introduced yet further tension at Central Office, which came to a head on the so-called 'wobbly Thursday', a week before polling day, when a rogue and clearly faulty adverse opinion poll caused David Young to panic completely, a panic which he succeeded in communicating to Margaret Thatcher. It was in fact abundantly clear, to anyone who had any sense of what was actually happening on the ground, that there had been no change in electoral intentions at all. However, according to David's own account, he got Norman 'by the shoulders and said 'Norman listen to me, we're about to lose this f--- election! You're going to go, I'm going to go, the whole thing is going to go. The entire election depends on her doing fine performances for the next five days – she has to be happy, we have got to do this.' By 'this' he meant the campaign that the second agency had come up with.

OF LICE AND FLEAS

So far as the battle of the advertising agencies, which dominated David's account of the 1987 election, is concerned, I am inescapably reminded of Dr Johnson's remark: 'Sir; there is no settling the point of precedency between a louse and a flea'. Politics and the media always tend to exaggerate the importance of election campaigns. In most elections – and 1987 was one of them – the overwhelming majority of people have already made up their minds how they are going to vote before the campaign starts; and then wait more or less patiently for polling day to arrive. But in so far as the campaign does matter – and obviously the closer the election the more important it can be – the least important aspect of the campaign is that of paid advertising. The relative contributions to the ultimate victory of the two agencies concerned were, in Johnsonian terms, those of a louse and a flea.

I cannot recall a campaign in which both public and business opinion was better disposed to the Government of the day than it was in 1987. I was particularly struck by the enthusiastic welcome I received from those youngsters, particularly in the Midlands and the North of England, who had started their own businesses. Irrespective of their backgrounds, they all instinctively identified with the Conservative Party. Much of that enthusiasm and support will inevitably have been destroyed by the recession of the early 1990s; but it would be a tragedy if none of it has survived.

I always asked the Party workers wherever I went what their canvass returns were showing. They had been greatly impressed and therefore worried by the

Hugh Hudson film on Kinnock, and were relieved to find on the doorsteps that it had not led to any loss of Conservative support. If anything, while no doubt reinforcing existing Labour support, it seemed it had also fortified existing Conservative support. As for wobbly Thursday, they were totally mystified. There had been no wobble in their constituency.

The time I was able to spend touring marginal constituencies was in large part a consequence of the decision made at the start of the campaign to keep me out of sight (and off television), in case I frightened the voters or stole the limelight – the first being the ostensible reason given. It was, from the outset, a particularly foolish decision. This judgement says nothing about me personally. It is simply that the economy is always a major issue in any election, and it is invariably in the Tories' interests that it should be a major issue. Given all the exposure he receives during the course of the year, year in year out, the public comes to know the Chancellor as the man who talks about and takes decisions about the economy. Thus to try and hide the Chancellor – any Chancellor – during an election campaign is a folly that can only harm the Government.

MY FREELANCE ELECTION CAMPAIGN

My principal frustration about the campaign, however, was not my lack of television exposure, absurd though that was in an election in which the economy was (as it frequently is) the most important factor. It was rather the persistent failure of the official campaign to highlight the implications of Labour's tax and spending plans, where I was convinced they were highly vulnerable. After making no headway with several telephone calls to Norman Tebbit, and after Peter Cropper had reported to me that he had been unable to get Central Office interested at his level, either, I decided to forget about the official Party election campaign and run a separate one of my own in parallel. This meant using to the full my three special advisers, who were all first class; with Andrew Tyrie in particular playing a key role.

Up to the point at which I intervened, at the beginning of June, Labour spokesmen had been instructed to stick to the line that no-one who earned less than £25,000, or some £500 a week, would be worse off. This worked well enough to start with. I then fired my first salvo, with a couple of press releases from a tour I had been making of marginal constituencies in Yorkshire on 1 June. This was essentially to prepare the ground for the Central Office press conference which Norman Tebbit had at last decided I should give on the economy, and Labour's threat to it the following day, 2 June, only nine days before polling day. I focused hard on the tax issue. The Press at long last began to sense that there might be a good story in all this.

Two days later, on 4 June, Labour's position started to crumble, when friendly journalists who had been well-briefed by Andrew Tyrie forced Neil Kinnock to admit that Labour's plans to abolish the ceiling on employees' National Insurance contributions meant people earning between £15,000 and £17,000 a year would have to pay a 'few extra pence a week'. He further conceded that the abolition of the married man's tax allowance and its replacement by higher child benefit (another Labour policy which I had been vainly trying to get Norman Tebbit to exploit) would hurt married couples without children earning as little as £10,000 a year. Labour had also admitted – they could scarcely deny it, having voted against it in the House of Commons – that they would, if elected, reverse the two-pence reduction in the basic rate of income tax in my 1987 Budget.

It was the exposure of Labour's plan to abolish the married man's tax allowance which really destroyed their credibility. The abolition of the upper earnings limit for employees' National Insurance Contributions was at least something to which they were openly committed. But when it came to their earlier proposal to abolish the married man's tax allowance in order to finance an increase in child benefit, they had decided to put in their manifesto only the increase in child benefit. Very carelessly, however, they had stated that the increase in child benefit would be not £7 a week, or £8 a week, but the extraordinarily precise figure of £7.36 a week – which happened to be the value of the married man's tax allowance in 1986/87 prices. Apparently Roy Hattersley and John Smith had removed the abolition of the married man's tax allowance from the Labour manifesto at the last minute, but had forgotten to amend the child benefit pledge, which was in a different chapter. It was this tell-tale figure which gave the game away, and obliged them to admit – under cross-examination – that they were proposing what amounted to a substantial tax increase for millions of married couples without children under eighteen. This came as a revelation to the Press.

The meticulously reliable Peter Cropper then made a series of calculations illustrating the total increases in taxation and National Insurance contributions that would be payable by married couples in the event of a Labour victory, and compared the outcome with the Government's plans. The extra taxes ranged from £6.80 a week for a husband earning £70 a week to £29.75 for one earning £400 a week. On 5 June, the *Daily Mail*, carefully briefed by Andrew Tyrie, and supplied with a suitable quote from me, led with 'Labour's Lies over Taxation'.

A similar Tyrie/Lawson operation caused the *Daily Express* to run a story headed 'Exposed: Labour's Tax Fiasco' the following day, 6 June. At last those responsible for organising the Conservative campaign realised that we had Labour on the run; and that same morning I gave yet another unscheduled Saturday press conference at Central Office, on the tax cost of voting Labour, and made public the full figures. As events had turned out, I was able to mount an attack on two fronts: Labour's would-be tax increases themselves, and their deceit in attempting to hide the fact. The broadcasters then took up the story for the first time.

Labour's response to this barrage was gratifyingly muddled. On the day of the press conference, Neil Kinnock reiterated his admission that 'some people' earning less than £25,000 a year would be worse off under a Labour Government, but Bryan Gould and Roy Hattersley stuck to the original line. It was easy for me to accuse Roy Hattersley of, as I delicately put it, 'lying through his teeth' – a charge he was unable to rebut when we appeared on the *Today* programme together. The Labour campaign was in shreds. One account described those three days as the turning point in Labour's fortunes.

> In the course of that Saturday before polling, Labour lost its initiative. It was not merely a matter of fading away: by the evening Labour's campaign had broken into several pieces, cracked apart by a Tory attack on Labour's precarious tax policy ... The newspapers were telling Labour's target voters that they would be clobbered for tax if they succeeded in earning what seemed a relatively modest income. That would have been damaging enough. But it was immediately compounded by muddle among Labour's senior politicians over what the Party policy actually meant.

Peter Mandelson, the highly professional Labour Party official who masterminded the 1987 campaign, has himself admitted that his plans were disrupted only twice during the campaign. The first was Neil Kinnock's defence gaffe; the second was the exposure of the incoherence of the Party's tax and spending plans in the final week. The subsequent 1992 campaign, which included John Smith's maladroit 'Shadow Budget', showed that Labour had still not fully learned the lesson.

The exposure of what I called Labour's 'deliberate deceit' had finally placed the economy and taxation at the centre of the campaign. Norman Tebbit later acknowledged that:

> It was not easy to get the economic issue going ... Nigel Lawson, by sheer persistence and the strength of his personality, finally focused attention on the economy just as our heavy advertising campaign did the same. Labour were in a mess, as Hattersley's figures clearly did not add up and in the last few days – unlike 1983, when we lost several points – our support remained rock solid.

THE TIDE ROLLS ON

Even before the polling stations closed on the evening of Thursday, 11 June, it was clear that the Government had won an overwhelming victory, despite the BBC making themselves look foolish by giving great publicity to a final poll they had done which purported to show the two Parties neck and neck. The eventual Conservative majority over all the other Parties was 101, with my own share of the traditional three-cornered poll at Blaby going over 60 per cent for the first time ever.

It was a remarkable achievement for the Government to have won a third term by such a handsome margin, and marked the intellectual ascendancy of the market economy even more surely than the Labour landslide of 1945 had marked that of socialism. 'Never underestimate the tide of ideas,' I had told the Scottish Party Conference at the start of the campaign:

> No British Government has ever been defeated unless and until the tide of ideas has turned against it. And so far from turning, the tide of ideas that swept us into office in 1979 is flowing even more strongly today. And that, after all, is what will sweep us back into office on the 11th of June.

It was a theme to which I was to return, at greater length, in a major speech at the Carlton Club in January 1988, published by the Centre for Policy Studies the following month as a pamphlet entitled *The New Britain: the tide of ideas from Attlee to Thatcher.*

By April 1992 the tide had still not turned.[28]

[28] [2010 note] Nor did the tide turn when the Conservative Party was eventually defeated in 1997 in a Labour landslide, with the victorious Labour leader, Tony Blair, proclaiming that he would govern as 'New Labour', abandoning socialism and absorbing most of the ideas embodied in the so-called Thatcher revolution. This is further discussed in the new final chapter.

CHAPTER FORTY

PUBLIC SPENDING REVISITED

The Treasury Team · The Child Benefit Drama · Still Fresher Faces
Public Spending in Retrospect

THE TREASURY TEAM

I had no fixed date in mind for leaving Number 11. There were two things I wanted to achieve in my second parliament as Chancellor – income tax reform and full EMS membership. Given that, I saw myself laying down the burden amicably, at the time of a reshuffle. This meant that the earliest date would be the summer of 1988, after the tax reforming 1988 Budget was on the statute-book – and the very latest the summer of 1990. If I stayed on any further I would inevitably be stuck for the rest of the parliament. Leaving it until the summer of 1990 would have made me the longest-serving Chancellor this century. But although this had some attraction, it was not a major consideration, and an earlier date – such as the summer of 1989 – was more the sort of thing I had in mind when I was reappointed in 1987.

In retrospect I should have gone immediately after the 1988 Budget, as Thérèse urged me at the time; but I was sufficiently conventional to leave it until the summer of that year, that being the customary season for reshuffles, by which time the current account deficit had soared, overheating had become apparent, and I felt I could not honourably leave my post until I had dealt with it.

Where would I like to have moved if things had gone according to plan? The only other senior offices of State, apart from the Exchequer, are those of Foreign Secretary and – more arguably – Home Secretary. The latter never held any appeal for me. Foreign Secretary, although nothing like as important a job as Chancellor in today's world, had compensating attractions which did appeal to me. But even if there had been a vacancy, I would probably have been too unconventional an appointment for even Margaret to make. It was perhaps just as well that the job of Chancellor kept me too occupied to spend time brooding on all this.

But such questions were not at the front of my mind when, the day after the 1987 general election, I joined Margaret at No. 10 to discuss the membership of the new Cabinet, along with Willie Whitelaw. Later Norman Tebbit and John Wakeham, the Chief Whip, joined us. My presence at such a gathering underlined the fact that, at that time, despite our differences over the ERM and the Poll Tax, and our tiffs over interest rates, Margaret and I remained politically very close, as we had been since the Government was first formed in 1979. But almost from that moment on, to my intense regret, our relationship started to deteriorate.

The trouble began when she discovered that I was widely seen in the Party as the man who had won the 1987 election. For the first time, she started to see me in a completely new light, as a potential rival. I have already explained why, rightly or wrongly, this was never the case; but it was her perception, and not the reality, which counted. Our relations then took a further turn for the worse in the wake of my IMF speech that September, of which she disapproved and her acolytes disapproved even more. But even then Willie was still at hand, a voice of sanity to calm her down whenever the need arose. It was only after his sudden departure at the end of the year that the rift became irreparable. Indeed, after his going the Thatcher Government, which for more than eight years had been such a great and glorious adventure, was never the same again.

I was at least well placed to influence the successor to John MacGregor as Chief Secretary, since it was always clear that he would be given a Department of his own after the election. John Wakeham was my first choice, but he told me he did not want the job. Failing him, my preference was for John Major, of whom I had formed a high opinion since his time as Finance Whip in 1985. He had a relatively unusual combination of mastery of detail and likeable manner which would, I felt, make him an excellent Chief Secretary. Margaret had originally wanted him to be Chief Whip, but with Willie's support I persuaded her to send him to the Treasury. I was greatly relieved at this outcome.

Thus it was that John Major entered the Cabinet, as Chief Secretary, in June 1987. This event influenced the course of future history, because had he instead become Chief Whip, as Margaret had intended, he could never have been a candidate to succeed her when she stepped down in 1990.[29]

For a time after the 1987 election I was concerned that I might have made the wrong choice of Chief Secretary after all – a view I suspect was shared by John Major himself. He found the job far more difficult than anything he had

[29] *Pace* Mr Michael Dobbs, and his entertaining political fantasy, *House of Cards.*

ever done before, and had to work very hard to try and master it. He would come and see me at Number 11, ashen faced, to unburden himself of his worries and to seek my advice. Before too long, however, he was thoroughly on top of the job. But throughout his two years in the post, which were to constitute the greater part of his total Cabinet experience before becoming Prime Minister, he made a point of sticking to his last. Apart from the Budget-making process, and of course the political matters we discussed at ministerial prayer meetings, he chose not to contribute to the discussion of any Treasury matter which did not have a public expenditure dimension.

He was assisted in his public spending task by the fact that he had the good fortune to become Chief Secretary at the start of the new parliament. This helps in several ways. For one thing, there is not the pressure from colleagues to increase spending for electoral reasons that always emerges in the second half of a parliament. For another, the large scale reshuffle that follows a general election means that a great many spending Departments have new Ministers in charge who do not know the subject at all well, and moreover do not feel bound by the aspirations of their predecessors.

Spending control was further helped in 1987 by three other factors. First, strong economic growth meant that less money was needed for those social security benefits which are related to unemployment – which was falling fast – and for the nationalised industries, whose profits were looking very much healthier. In addition the proceeds of council house sales, which count as negative public spending, had risen significantly. Secondly, there was a helpful trend of debt interest as the public finances moved into substantial surplus.

Thirdly, Margaret had appointed to the DHSS, the biggest spending Department of all, John Moore, who was determined to be more Thatcherite than his predecessor, Norman Fowler. Indeed it soon became clear that the problem with John Moore was not the normal one of overbidding, but the fact he had not asked for enough. This was to cause a number of problems; but the great gain was that John Moore's helpful attitude enabled John Major to secure a freeze in the rate of the indiscriminate and untaxed child benefit, in return for a substantial rise in the means-tested Family Credit for poorer families. This switch, which saved a large sum of money, had been a long standing ambition of the official Treasury. Moreover, we were able to maintain this policy, not without some difficulty, throughout the rest of my time as Chancellor.

Thus it was that it proved possible in 1987 for the first time in many years to secure a public spending outcome in line with the summer remit, without even requiring recourse to the Star Chamber. This was helped by the fact that, when John Major had succeeded in whittling down the non-settlers to a hard core of three, I decided to see each of them privately myself. At these tête-à-têtes I indicated that everyone else had either settled or was on the brink of settling except my interlocutor, suggesting that I could not believe that he would want to incur the odium of having the whole apparatus of the Star Chamber activated simply to deal with him. That seemed to do the trick.

THE CHILD BENEFIT DRAMA

Although membership of Cabinet Committees took a surprising amount of my time, much more central to my job as Chancellor were my last three public expenditure rounds. I have already outlined my general approach to Government expenditure and my earlier efforts to bring public spending under control in Chapter 17.

The 1987 public spending round, John Major's first, had proved a highly successful one. The plans in the Autumn Statement showed general Government expenditure (excluding privatisation) falling from the equivalent of 42.5 per cent of GDP in 1987/88 to 42 per cent in 1988/89. The reality turned out to be a very much greater decline, from 42 per cent to 39.5 per cent of GDP. This represented an overall fall of 7 percentage points from the Thatcher Government's peak of 1982/83, and the lowest ratio achieved since 1966/67. I fear that it will also be the lowest ratio for several years to come. While the scale of the reduction in 1988/89 was obviously in part a consequence of the unsustainably rapid rise in GDP, that was by no means the whole story. Government spending, in real terms, actually fell, for the second year in succession. Other countries, whose economies were also forging ahead in 1988, achieved nothing comparable on the public spending front.

However, two successive years in which public spending, in real terms, actually declined, as the economy grew rapidly, made it impossible to avoid some let-up in the 1988 public spending round. I announced in the 1988 Autumn Statement an increase in real public spending of 1.25 per cent, which I expected would lead to a further modest decline in the public spending ratio. In the event things did not turn out quite so well: there was a real increase in spending of 3 per cent and a modest rise in the public spending/GDP ratio from 39.5 to 40 per cent. There was mounting pressure throughout 1988, by no means confined to the Opposition benches, for still further increases in spending on the National Health Service, in particular.

Nevertheless, all in all, the 1988 spending round was satisfactorily uneventful until very near the end, when there were two hiccups. The lesser of the two concerned Nick Ridley, then still Environment Secretary, who refused to settle his housing budget with John Major, then Chief Secretary. Nick wanted more public money over a wide front, and contended that the Treasury should permit him to use some of the excess receipts from council house sales, which had been exceptionally buoyant in 1988, for this purpose. John, rightly, insisted that the proceeds of council house sales had no bearing on the merits of spending more money on the housing programme.

In the normal course of events an impasse of this kind would have been resolved by Star Chamber. But in this case both of them were anxious to avoid this. John was proud that he had succeeded in achieving a good result in the 1987 spending round without recourse to Star Chamber. He was determined to maintain his record if he possibly could. With Nick the problem was a different one. Willie's departure had, among other things, left a vacancy as chairman of Star Chamber. I had suggested to Margaret that Geoffrey, as her most senior Cabinet colleague now that Willie had gone, and a former Chancellor, would make the best replacement. I had already seen Geoffrey, then still Foreign Secretary, to make sure that he had no foreign trips during the brief but intensive Star Chamber period. Margaret, however, was by that time already in no mood to confer any mark of preferment on Geoffrey, even when it was in the Government's interest to do so. It had been bad enough that she had felt obliged to reappoint him as Foreign Secretary; she was certainly not going to let him think that he was a second Willie, a *de facto* deputy Prime Minister. She therefore gave the Star Chamber job, to the astonishment of many, to Cecil Parkinson – which incidentally led to unfounded speculation in the Press that she was planning to make him Chancellor.

This had an unexpected consequence. A number of colleagues, who had regarded a Star Chamber presided over by Willie as part of the natural order of things, could not adjust to the idea of having Cecil sitting in judgement over them. All of these had settled bilaterally, except Nick. There was only one solution. I saw Nick privately at Number 11, with no officials present. We went over his programme together, and I offered him a number of modest concessions – which I had discussed with John in advance. We soon reached what was from the Treasury's point of view a very satisfactory agreement on all the outstanding issues between us.

The other, and much more serious, hiccup was over child benefit. In 1987, for the first time, this had been frozen in cash terms instead of being uprated in line with inflation. The argument was that help should be concentrated on the poorest families – which meant that what mattered was not the indiscriminate child benefit, but the means-tested Family Credit. This had long been the Treasury's position, but it was not until 1987 that the DHSS had, in John Moore, a Secretary of State sufficiently in favour of selectivity to accept it. John defended the decision very effectively at the despatch box, and there was no serious back-bench revolt.

Needless to say, having established the principle, John Major, with my strong backing, was anxious to consolidate it with a further child benefit freeze, accompanied by a further large increase in Family Credit, in 1988. When the 1987 freeze had been announced, the Press had characteristically described it as a defeat for John Moore at the hands of the Treasury. This was something John could have taken in his stride, had it not been for Margaret's decision in July 1988 to split the DHSS in two, adding insult to injury by giving him the Social Security job, the political inferior of the two jobs created from the one he had previously held. Feeling his political position on the slide, and knowing full well how a further child benefit freeze would be interpreted by the media, he became determined to resist it, and unwisely let this be known to the Press.

He was rapidly painting himself into a corner, and as he did so he felt driven to raise the stakes still higher. As the impasse between John Major and himself over the issue continued, he saw David Waddington, the Chief Whip, and told David that unless child benefit were increased he himself would resign from the Government. David immediately informed Margaret, who, on the afternoon of 18 October 1988, hastily arranged a meeting in her first-floor study at Number 10 with John Moore, John Major and myself. It was a tense and difficult occasion. John Moore was quiet, but highly emotional. The arguments on both sides of the child benefit case were gone into in considerable detail. His case became no better as the argument developed, but at the end he said that he had not changed his mind about resignation. He simply could not carry on with his job unless child benefit were increased.

Margaret wisely asked him to sleep on it, and he left the room, as did John Major. I stayed behind for a bit, and told Margaret that, in my judgement, his Department had been of no help to him over this. It was repeating the mistake that had been the source of so much trouble over the Fowler reforms, but in an even more foolish way. It had become obsessed – a tribute, perhaps, to that tireless pressure group, the Child Poverty Action Group – with the problem of child poverty. Yet although child benefit had a strong following among supporters of the middle-class welfare state, not least among Tory back-benchers, the greatest sense of grievance, so far as the level of welfare benefits was concerned, was felt by the poorer pensioners whose average age was well above that of pensioners generally; and it was their plight that evoked the greatest public sympathy, too.

If I had not been aware of this before it had certainly been borne in on me while campaigning in the 1987 election. If John wanted to make a stand, it should have been over these people. Margaret agreed, and said she hoped that John would not be so foolish as to resign. I warmly endorsed that. John was an old friend, who for five years had worked for me, first at Energy and subsequently at the Treasury, with energy, enthusiasm, commitment and total loyalty. The last thing I wanted was to see him resign, particularly over such a wrong-headed issue. I told her I would do what I could to talk him out of it.

I managed to get a message to him that evening that I would like to see him, completely privately, at Number 11 at 8 o'clock the next morning. When he called round his mood had changed. He was less emotional, clearly did not wish to resign, and was looking for a way out. After explaining to him how much I personally wanted him to stay in the Government, and what an impossible position he would be in if he were to resign over a policy which he himself had defended so robustly only a year earlier, I offered him something for the poorer, older, pensioners as a way out. He rejected it, insisting that it was child poverty that the argument was all about. I then offered him what the official Treasury had had in mind all along: a freeze in child benefit, but extra money for Family Credit. This he accepted; and after he had left I sent a message to Margaret to let her know that the crisis was over. On 27 October 1988, John announced the child benefit freeze and Family Credit increase to the House of Commons, defending it with all the verve he could muster. At the next reshuffle, some nine months later, she sacked him.

It was a sad, unnecessary, heartless and foolish act; for apart from that one aberration over child benefit, John had been loyal to a fault throughout his ministerial career, one of the few unwavering free-market Ministers in the Cabinet. It was true that he had not been a great success as Secretary of State at the DHSS; but the mistake was Margaret's in appointing him in the first place. On top of all that, he had to grapple – as his more politically nimble predecessor, Norman Fowler, had not – with the question of reforming the National Health Service. Small wonder he was slightly out of his depth.

STILL FRESHER FACES

For what was to prove my final public expenditure round in 1989, I had once again a new Chief Secretary, my fourth, in Norman Lamont. For in the first of his astonishing leaps, Margaret had made John Major Foreign Secretary in place of Geoffrey Howe, in the same fateful reshuffle of July 1989 that had seen the dismissal of John Moore.

Margaret suggested to me three possible successors, all of them undoubtedly able: Peter Brooke, Michael Howard and Michael Portillo. For different reasons, I felt that none of them was quite right for the job. But my reservations would not have been decisive, had it not been for the fact that I felt it would be very unfair to Norman Lamont. Norman had been a Minister since the Government was first formed in 1979, and after a disappointing start had been serving me loyally and well as Financial Secretary, a post he had held for the past three years. I did pass him over in favour of John Major in 1987. But to have passed him over yet again in 1989 was something he would have taken very hard, and understandably so. It had come to the point where he felt that this was his last chance of making it into the Cabinet. I felt that he deserved to be given that chance.

Margaret did her best to talk me out of it; but in the end, and with considerable reluctance, she conceded that her Chancellor should be allowed the Chief Secretary he wanted. Thus it was that, little more than a year later, Norman was in a position to run John Major's leadership campaign following Margaret's enforced departure, and to succeed John as Chancellor of the Exchequer. If politics does nothing else, it develops an appreciation of irony.

I do not recall the precise details of the 1989 public spending round so well, since it was a particularly traumatic time for me, coinciding as it did with the events leading up to my resignation. Indeed, although little of substance remained to be done, I did not quite see it through to the end. In the circumstances, it was just as well that my Chief Secretary, Norman Lamont, was someone who had been working for me for a considerable time. Although the pressures were beginning to build up as they always do in the second half of a parliament, the outcome was not at all bad. Two factors made large contributions to this satisfactory result. First, 1990/91 saw the fourth successive Budget surplus – or public sector debt repayment – which helped greatly so far as the burden of debt interest was concerned. And second, it was the third year in succession in which child benefit was frozen; in return, as John Major had negotiated in the two previous years, for a substantial rise in Family Credit for the poorest families. This caused much less furore than on either of the two previous occasions. To all intents and purposes, the Government had won the argument.

Sadly, it was John Major himself, who, as one of his earliest acts as Prime Minister, was to overrule his Chancellor at a time when the new policy had at last been widely accepted, and caused it to be announced in March 1991 not only that child benefit would be increased, but that it would henceforth be increased every year in line with inflation. This was a big mistake. Child benefit, the overwhelming bulk of which goes to people who do not really need it, was estimated to cost some £5.75 billion in 1992/93 money. Compared with that, the cost of a substantial advertising campaign to overcome the problem of inadequate take-up of Family Credit, which concentrates help on poor families, is chickenfeed. Moreover, not only is the untaxed child benefit a straight addition to the income of better-off parents, but in the normal course of events any increase in it is of no help to the poorest families who suffer a pound for pound deduction from their means-tested benefits. The difficult task was to break the habit of the annual child benefit uprating. Once that had been accomplished, and the ground had been consolidated, giving it up again – unnecessarily and irrevocably – has made the task of curbing the growth of public spending, which has once again become one of the main challenges facing the Government, very much harder.

PUBLIC SPENDING IN RETROSPECT

The accompanying table shows the record of public spending since the mid-1960s. Under both the Wilson Labour Government of the 1960s and the subsequent Heath Conservative Government it was growing much faster than any conceivable rise in the national income. It slowed down under the Wilson-Callaghan Government of the 1970s, at the behest of the IMF, but only enough to make a very small dent in the public spending ratio, since economic growth had also declined.

Under the first three Conservative parliaments following the 1979 election, public spending rose only slightly more slowly than under the previous Labour Government, but economic growth was a great deal faster and the spending ratio fell by two percentage points – an unusual achievement. A worrying acceleration of public spending is officially expected in the period up to 1996, which cannot all be put down to recession. This is a clear danger signal, particularly since there is a tendency for the out-turn to be worse than the plans.

I trust that it will not be considered unforgivably immodest to look in particular at my own period as Chancellor. Of course it was somewhat easier for me than for Geoffrey Howe, who initially had to cope with a recession. Even so, the table, which excludes all benefit from privatisation proceeds, shows that the unprecedented fall of up to 8 percentage points in the public spending ratio during my stewardship of the Exchequer, cannot be written off as simply a boom phenomenon.[30] The very low growth in public spending in real terms clearly demonstrates that this was a time of genuine public spending restraint.

THE GROWTH OF PUBLIC SPENDING (GENERAL GOVERNMENT EXPENDITURE EXCLUDING PRIVATISATION PROCEEDS)

	Average annual percentage growth (real terms)	*Overall change as % of GDP*
Labour (1964–70)	4.7	+4.2
Conservative (1970–74)	4.9	+2.4
Labour (1974–9)	1.8	-0.6
Conservative (1979–92)	1.7	-2.1
of which		
Howe (1979–83)	2.3	+3.5
Lawson (1983–9)	0.6 (0.9)	-8.0 (-7.6)
Howe/Lawson (1979–89)	1.3 (1.4)	-4.5 (-4.1)
Major/Lamont	2.0 (1.4)	+2.4 (+2.0)

NB. The figures refer to the financial year ending in the year in question. The figures in brackets show the effect of taking 1989 to refer to the financial year 1989/90 rather than 1988/9.

[30] [2010 note] Considerable effort was made to update this table to 2010, but sadly official data series have been modified over the years in ways that have made it a very difficult task reliably to marry past and present.

CHAPTER FORTY-ONE

'MANAGED FLOATING'

A Promise Broken · From Europe to the World · My 1987 IMF Speech
Reactions to the Speech · The Poorest of the Poor · The Toronto Terms

A PROMISE BROKEN

Towards the end of Chapter 37, I pointed out how the Louvre Accord of February 1987 created a framework which for the first time made a policy of exchange rate stability credible. My decision to take advantage of this to embark on a period of what later became known as 'shadowing the Deutschmark', arose from my desire to put a floor under sterling, which had fallen more or less continuously from its somewhat artificial peak of over DM5 to the pound in January 1981 to a low of DM2.75 in January 1987. But a floor would not be credible without a ceiling. If the markets saw a 'hands off' policy on the way up, they would take it for granted that there would be a 'hands off' policy on the way down, too – at least until a very low point indeed had been reached. Hence the DM3 ceiling. Moreover I had no wish to inflict on British industry the unnecessary trauma of an appreciation of sterling which would in the event prove unsustainable. The sterling overshoot of 1980 had provided a much-needed shock. But since then the Government had fully established its credentials and the economic climate – and expectations – had changed completely. There seemed to me to be no cause for a repeat dose of the same medicine seven years later.

Shadowing the Deutschmark (and nudging up interest rates when I had an opportunity to do so) provided both a welcome period of exchange rate calm in the run-up to the election, and a practical demonstration of sterling's ability to keep station with the Mark. But I saw it essentially as a short-term expedient which would keep the show on the road until after the election. Despite earlier setbacks, I had not lost hope of securing my long-term objective of full EMS membership.

Within that framework, I wanted to err on the side of caution. Towards the end of July 1987, the Bank, supported by the Treasury, began to urge a base rate rise. I had no hesitation in agreeing; and a slight weakening of sterling provided me with an opportunity to raise rates by 1 per cent to 10 per cent on 9 August, thus reversing the two pre-election reductions. The markets were taken completely by surprise. But I had little doubt at the time that the next move in interest rates would also be upward – as it almost certainly would have been had it not been for the stock market crash two months later.

Margaret had explicitly indicated to me that she felt the right time to consider the EMS was after the election, at the start of a new parliament, so that ERM membership was fully bedded in by the time of the subsequent election campaign. I reminded her of this at my bilateral with her on 27 July, some seven weeks after the election. I went on to point out that the reserves were now very much stronger, and that ERM membership would provide a stability that would help business confidence and reassure the financial markets. Moreover the Treasury was engaged in negotiations to improve the technical working of the ERM and their fruition would be a good opportunity to announce British membership.

Margaret responded as if our earlier discussions had never happened. She attacked the ERM with every debating point that occurred to her (or to whomever had written her brief). I said I was not prepared to let the matter drop: it was too important for that. I told her I would want to discuss it further in the autumn, after the summer break. She dissented insisting the autumn was too soon: she would not be prepared to hold a further discussion on ERM membership with me until the New Year. Finally, she was adamant that, whatever happened, she would not be prepared to hold meetings of the kind she had held in the autumn of 1985 – when she had found herself heavily outnumbered in a meeting of senior Ministers and had to threaten to resign herself.

I was dismayed. It was clear that she had simply been stringing me along in everything she had said before the election, which obviously had not been uttered in good faith. Perhaps I should have resigned then and there. Rightly or wrongly, I did not do so, since I could not see what good it would do. There was no way in which I could force her to join the ERM at that time against her will. It was true that my political position was stronger than it had ever been before: I had been widely credited, much to her annoyance, with being the true author of the 1987 election victory. But by the same token Margaret, as the leader who had just won a third election victory in succession – an unprecedented achievement – was at the peak of her authority.

FROM EUROPE TO THE WORLD

In any event, I felt I could never trust her completely again. She complained afterwards that I played my cards close to my chest. There is something in this – even if it was a case of the pot calling the kettle black. For by then it was the only alternative to either resignation or confrontation. For the time being, I decided to shift the focus of my exchange rate efforts to the wider international field. Since the Plaza and Louvre Agreements I had been reflecting on how to take further the informal G5/G7 accords on exchange rates. Partly because G5/G7 currency management had been enshrined in international agreements to which we were a signatory, and partly because the process had been initiated by the US Administration, Margaret was not inclined to make a full-frontal assault on it, or prevent my co-operating in its working, on which I had duly briefed her at every stage.

That summer we took our August holiday in Sardinia (much needed after the election campaign), where I worked my way through some rather unusual holiday reading – a pile of academic articles on exchange rate policy from all points of view, supplied by Terry Burns. There I sketched the main points of my subsequent IMF speech on 'managed floating', sitting by the pool.

Immediately prior to the IMF was an Ecofin meeting at Nyborg in Denmark, where I backed French efforts to persuade the Germans to adopt a more communautaire approach to intervention in support of other EMS currencies. We had partial success, issuing in what were catchily dubbed the 'Basle-Nyborg Changes'. The meeting also began the process that led, in July 1990, to the final removal of all exchange controls within the Community, thus knocking down another stock objection of Margaret's to the ERM.

As usual, the G7 (as it by then firmly was) met in Washington on the eve of the annual Bank and Fund meetings, and on Saturday, 26 September issued a worthy communiqué reaffirming the adjusted Louvre currency ranges, but remaining silent on the accompanying interest rate moves necessary to underwrite them. The dollar continued to be under pressure, and the row about whether the Americans should increase their interest rates or the Japanese and Germans reduce theirs continued to rumble on, and could not be papered over by the indicator exercise. While I saw little case for a rise in *average* world interest rates, I had no sympathy for the US refusal to contemplate any increase in their interest rates.

In my address to the IMF Interim Committee, I focused for the first time on the so-called problem of the trade imbalances. This had long been (in my view mistakenly) a major preoccupation of international gatherings in the context of the US trade deficit and the German and Japanese surpluses, but I had largely ignored it, preferring to focus on genuine problems. With the UK now moving into current account deficit, I was conscious that this was likely to re-emerge as an issue in the UK, and I decided to break my silence, saying:

> It is easy to overstate the problem. There is no iron law that dictates that the current accounts of the major industrial countries should always be in balance. We have an integrated world economy and we encourage the free flow of capital and goods. Investment opportunities and savings propensities inevitably differ from country to country and it is natural for this to produce substantial, and often sustained, capital account flows. These flows are bound to have their counterparts in current account surpluses and deficits. But ... there are clearly limits to the accumulated external liabilities or assets that can be sustained without creating major anxieties for capital markets.

I was to develop this thesis much more fully in my main address to the annual Bank/Fund meeting in both 1988 and 1989.

MY 1987 IMF SPEECH

The major event of my Fund/Bank visit of September 1987 was my formal address to the Joint Annual Meeting on Wednesday, 30 September. Fortunately I had a little time to do further work on it. The traditional reception given by the British Ambassador on the Monday evening in honour of the Chancellor of the Exchequer and the Governor of the Bank of England was not very taxing. The American bankers present tended to be figures from the past – more likely the product of an out-of-date Embassy guest list than anything else. The informal lunch given the following day by Tim Lankester, the Embassy's Economic Minister, was much more useful, but left the rest of the day free. This was needed. Although a draft speech had been prepared for me, with a considerable input from Terry Burns, on the basis of my Sardinian notes and subsequent briefings, it was not quite what I wanted and I decided to rewrite it completely.

The main section of the speech discussed the evolution of exchange rate policy since the breakdown of the Bretton Woods system in the late 1960s and early 1970s, with particular reference to our experience in the 1980s. I went on to sketch how, based on that experience, I thought the world's exchange rate regime should develop in the years ahead.

So far as the past was concerned, I pointed out how the period of free floating had in practice led to wild gyrations in exchange rates, especially for the dollar, which still dominated the world's money markets and accounted for 97 per cent of all transactions on the London foreign exchange market. The problem with 'global 24-hour foreign exchange markets' was the absence of players who 'take a longer view and so provide a stabilising influence'. As a result, exchange rate movements 'have often acquired a momentum of their own, which has not been reversed until they have reached extreme levels of over-or under-valuation'. These gyrations were harmful to the growth of world trade, caused businesses to divert scarce management time and skills to coping with currency fluctuations rather than improving company performance, inhibited risk-taking, and required shifts in resources from the home to the export market and back again, at a pace that was wholly unrealistic.

It was in response to this unsatisfactory state of affairs that the major nations, first at the Plaza and then more fundamentally at the Louvre, had moved to a regime of what I called 'managed floating'. (I thought at the time that I had invented the term myself, but subsequently discovered that, unknown to me, it had been used before, albeit in a rather different context.) This had proved possible in the 1980s, whereas it would not have been in the 1970s, essentially for two reasons: first, the fact that we had moved from a world of high inflation to one of low inflation; and, second, because a new consensus had emerged over the conduct of economic policy – broadly speaking, greater reliance on market mechanisms within the framework of a firm monetary and fiscal policy.

On the basis of my account of the recent past, I then turned to the future, and I quote that section of the speech in full since it was to prove somewhat controversial:

> I believe that we can and should use the experience we have gained to build a more permanent regime of managed floating. I do not see the past two years as a temporary phase. Our objectives should be clear: to maintain the maximum stability of key exchange rates, and to manage any changes that may be necessary in an orderly way.
>
> Let me make it clear that I am not suggesting that we can or should return to Bretton Woods. That system was undermined by its rigidity; the margins were too narrow; it required a predictable and mechanical

response from the authorities that made them an easy target; necessary realignments were postponed too long, and consequently, when they came, they were inevitably large.

For the future, it is important, therefore, that we continue to keep an adequate degree of flexibility in terms of the width of the bands within which currencies are able to fluctuate. And, if and when the time comes to adjust one of the rates, that adjustment should be made by moving the midpoint within the confines of the existing range. This means that the markets are not given a one way bet, and the authorities retain tactical flexibility.

As I have already emphasised, what made the Plaza and Louvre agreements possible was that the countries participating were, and remain, in effect, members of an anti-inflationary club, with a clear commitment to taking whatever steps are necessary to curb their own inflation. It is vital that that commitment continues, individually and collectively. A resurgence of inflation in any individual country would make it difficult for that country to remain within the club.

At the same time, we must also ensure that there is no persistent inflationary (or for that matter deflationary) bias for the group as a whole.

REACTIONS TO THE SPEECH

Much of the subsequent press comment said that I had come out in favour of target zones, a perennial French proposal for the conduct of exchange rate policy and something with which the US Treasury team, notably Jim Baker's number two, Dick Darman, had been flirting. Indeed Baker, whose own speech immediately followed mine, spoke (without any collusion) in remarkably similar terms – although in his case Press comment largely latched on to his proposal to add the gold price to other commodity prices as the anchor for the system.

In a sense it was true that I had come out in favour of target zones, although with important qualifications and accompaniments. But what I myself thought was important about the speech was its analysis of what had actually happened and why, of where we found ourselves as a result, and what its essential logic was. Beyond that, what was 'new' in the speech – apart from the fact that it was the first time it had been uttered by a British Chancellor – was the thesis that it was not a matter of proposing a new international monetary order: that we were already three quarters of the way there.

In this I was much too optimistic. Within a matter of weeks the Wall Street crash of Black Monday, 19 October, had thrown everything into confusion. There were even those who contrived to claim that it was the Louvre Accord that had caused the crash – claiming bizarrely, that there was somehow a fixed quantum of instability in financial markets, and that stable exchange rates channelled all the instability to the stock market. By the time the world had recovered from the crash, Jim Baker had resigned as Treasury Secretary to organise his old friend George Bush's 1988 Presidential campaign, taking Dick Darman with him; and when he returned to office after the election it was as Bush's Secretary of State. At the same time, Darman was appointed to head the Bureau of the Budget, which is concerned solely with public spending.

Given the uniquely important position of the dollar, a necessary (although not a sufficient) condition of international financial co-operation, particularly on the exchange rate front, is American leadership. Baker's successor at the US Treasury, Nick Brady, had neither the desire nor the capacity to exercise international leadership in this or indeed any other field, and the situation degenerated into one of *ad hoccery* and drift. There was neither the ideological belief in free floating that characterised the Regan period, nor the commitment to a structured form of managed floating that characterised Baker's term of office.

Meanwhile my speech was well received by the more thoughtful observers on both sides of the Atlantic, with one important exception. Although she never said a word to me herself, I learned indirectly that Margaret had been complaining that my speech had not been 'cleared' with her in advance – the implication being that she would have stopped it if it had been.

I also learned, again indirectly, through friends in the City and in the Press, that Brian Griffiths, whose capacity for causing trouble was considerable, had been letting it be known that my speech did not represent Government policy. It appears that he did not consider that the Louvre Accord, to which the UK was a signatory, and which had been formally endorsed by the seven Heads of State and Government at the Venice Summit, represented Government policy, either.

Needless to say, and contrary to what some of her apologists have subsequently sought to maintain, Margaret knew all about the Louvre agreement and about my understanding of how sterling fitted into it, since I had made a point of keeping her well informed at every stage. She also knew all about the intervention in the foreign exchange market to implement the policy, receiving a market report every evening showing *inter alia* the full extent of that day's intervention.

Indeed, until September 1987 she welcomed not merely sterling's stability and strength (for while remaining steady against the Deutschmark, the pound was rising against the dollar), but the intervention itself. Whenever she saw Robin Leigh-Pemberton during this period she would greet him with the question 'how much have you taken in today, Mr Governor?' (that is to say, how much foreign exchange had been added to the reserves that day through sales of sterling on the foreign exchange market), and the larger the answer the happier she would be.

But around September 1987 (perhaps during a visit to the United Nations in New York, when she may have seen Walters) she turned against the intervention involved in shadowing the Mark, seeing it as the UK almost single-handedly financing the US deficit, but above all as somehow inflationary. It was against this background that she reacted so badly to my IMF speech – although, as I have already mentioned, saying nothing about it to my face. Then, before I had fully appreciated the extent of her *volte face*, the focus of attention switched abruptly with the irruption of the Wall Street crash of Black Monday, 19 October.

THE POOREST OF THE POOR

Fortunately there was more to life and even to international economics than arguing about exchange rate policy. Before the 1986 Fund and Bank Annual Meetings in the Autumn of 1986 I asked my officials to let me have an up-to-date analysis of the international debt situation, with a view to launching a UK initiative. The picture they came up with was a remorselessly realistic one, and very gloomy reading it made. It was clear that the position of most of the debtors was not improving but deteriorating, and that the assumption that they would ever be in a position to repay their debts in full was pure moonshine. Any UK initiative, the official paper concluded, would have to start from a recognition of this reality.

It was impossible to dissent from either the analysis or the conclusion. Nevertheless, I shied away from making any move so far as Latin American and similar sovereign debt was concerned. This was owed largely to the commercial banks, and I felt it was for them to come to terms with reality in their own way, just as they have to do with bad loans to industrial customers. Government intervention could easily do more harm than good. But it was a different matter so far as the poorest countries, largely in sub-Saharan Africa, were concerned. By Latin American standards, the sums involved were small. But in terms of what their enfeebled economies could actually withstand, the Africans were in a far worse position than their Latin American counterparts. Their GNP per head was typically less than $350, and their overseas debt per head averaged $250.

These countries faced a heavy burden of debt service at a time when their ramshackle economies were going from bad to worse, with many of their people close to starvation. Those that were simply unable to service their debts found that the capitalisation of unpaid interest meant that their indebtedness was steadily increasing. Straightforward debt rescheduling (there had been eighty-eight rescheduling agreements in the previous decade) was clearly leading nowhere. These countries were so poor that even the banks had refused to lend to them, with the result that, in contrast to Latin America, the money was owed to Western governments (not least to their export credit agencies) and, to a lesser extent, to international financial institutions. This meant that the problem was clearly one where direct official action was appropriate.

I abandoned my idea of an initiative at the imminent Annual Meetings, and asked my officials to work up a scheme to help those whom I termed the poorest of the poor, which I could launch in the spring of 1987, after the Budget was out of the way. The plan they came up with had three parts. These were, first, to convert official aid loans into grants; second, to allow longer repayment periods (of up to twenty years) for other types of official loan; and third (the only really new element, and one that was absolutely critical) to reduce the rate of interest on the outstanding debt to well below market rates. These concessions were to be confined to those debtors which were pursuing sensible economic policies.

Some commentators found my interest in helping the countries of sub-Saharan Africa out of character. I was not known, for good reason, as a bleeding heart. But that was not out of any lack of sympathy for black African suffering, as anyone who recalled the campaign I had waged as Editor of the *Spectator* on behalf of the Ibos of 'Biafra' during the appalling Nigerian civil war of the 1960s would have recognised. It was rather because government, for me, was not about fine-sounding words but about achieving practical results. It was clear, on a straightforward practical basis, that there was no prospect of the governments who had lent the money to these desperately poor countries ever getting it back.

It was, I reckoned, more sensible to recognise this fact, and use it to manoeuvre the governments of those countries into pursuing sensible economic policies for the benefit of their own people, than to pretend for cosmetic budgeting reasons that the loans were good. But it was also clear that I would have to secure the agreement of all the creditor nations, which would not be easy, since unilateral action by the UK, although it might be emulated by some other countries, would benefit not the debtors, but the remaining creditors.

I decided to broach my plan first, privately and in the most general terms, at the informal Ecofin at Knokke, on the Belgian coast, on 5 April 1987. This was not a matter of canvassing support: it was essentially a courtesy to my Community colleagues, since my intention was to launch the plan officially at the spring meeting of the IMF Interim Committee in Washington, a few days later, when I would have the wider world audience I needed. On the eve of the Interim Committee meeting, again as a courtesy, I mentioned that I would be launching an initiative to help the poorest of the poor to my G5/G7 colleagues.

It was clear that the main practical effect of these two advance warnings would be to alert the French, who always looked on sub-Saharan Africa as their own sphere of interest (even though there were at least as many anglophone as francophone black African countries that were likely to qualify) and would not wish to be upstaged by the UK. I therefore took the precaution of informing the Press, immediately after the G5/G7 meeting, of the broad outline of the initiative I would be putting forward at the interim committee meeting the next day, at which I managed to ensure that I was called to speak before my French opposite number, the estimable Pierre Bérégovoy. I am afraid the French did not relish being beaten at their own game in this way.

Not surprisingly, my initiative was extremely well received by the black African Ministers present. But it quickly ran into formidable American and West German opposition over the question of offering sub-Saharan debtors sub-market interest rates. They believed that it would encourage the so-called 'middle income debtors', mainly in Latin America, to press for a similar concession, deter commercial lenders and give the Africans no incentive to pursue more realistic economic policies. This kind of thinking was either confused or self-serving.

From the April 1987 Interim Committee meeting onwards, it became a matter of drumming up support from the rest of the world outside the United States, Germany and Japan (the last of which could be counted on to drop its objections if and when the United States did so), and wearing the United States and Germany down by a mixture of persistence and their unease at their increasing isolation.

The cause was helped by the fact that the IMF, sensing the way the wind was blowing, developed a different but complementary initiative of their own to help the poorest of the poor. This was formally communicated to the Economic Summit held in Venice in June 1987, in the midst of the UK election campaign.

As a result, and at the strong urging of the UK, it was accepted in principle, for the first time at one of those gatherings, that the problems of the poorest countries, chiefly in sub-Saharan Africa, were different in kind from, and warranted different treatment from, the general international debt problem.

Clearly, however, I needed to make further progress at the Annual Fund and Bank meetings in September. But I decided first to make a rare appearance at the preceding Commonwealth Finance Ministers' meeting, which in 1987 was held in that most English of all the Caribbean islands, Barbados. My speech there was warmly received, and I won the endorsement of the Commonwealth for my plan, although not without some carping from some of the countries that realised they would not qualify for assistance under it, and hesitation right up until the last moment from the Canadians. Getting Canada on board was one of the main purposes of the exercise, since the United States tended to count on them to support the US position on international financial issues. The other main purpose was to keep up the momentum, and to secure a backing I could quote and use when I got to Washington.

The overall atmosphere at Barbados could scarcely have been more different from that which had greeted me at my first Commonwealth Finance Ministers' meeting in Port of Spain four years earlier. The ritual denunciations of Britain, coupled shamelessly with pleas for additional aid, had given way to boasting about the free-market policies which they were now pursuing. It was a most encouraging change.

THE TORONTO TERMS

Patience and persistence are the two main requirements of any successful international initiative. I had first launched my plan in April 1987. It did indeed gain further momentum of a kind at the IMF in September. Even so, it was far from being in the bag. The crucial breakthrough did not occur until the summer of 1988, on the eve of the Economic Summit which that year was to be held in Toronto. Up to that point Margaret had tolerated my initiative, without showing any great enthusiasm for it, although it had been agreed that it should be one of the UK's objectives to secure the plan's endorsement at the Summit. Then President Mitterrand, out of the blue, announced with a great fanfare a French initiative which he proposed to put to the Summit. This was similar to the UK initiative (of which he made no mention), save that instead of an interest rate reduction on all debt there would be a complete write-off of one third of the debt, with full market interest rates continuing to be payable on the rest.

This seemed like a clear attempt to steal the UK's thunder, and it transformed Margaret's attitude. She was determined that Toronto should be the scene of a successful UK initiative rather than a successful French one. Meanwhile Jean-Claude Trichet, who as *Directeur du Trésor* was Bérégovoy's deputy and, even more important in this context, chairman of the Paris Club, the forum at which the policies of the various national export credit agencies are co-ordinated, not least in respect to bad payers, sought to defuse the situation by working out a synthesis of the British and French plans.

At Toronto my first task was to have a private talk with Jim Baker, who at last said he was prepared to do something, simply to get me off his back; but for budgetary and Congressional reasons this could not be either the interest rate reductions I had proposed or the partial debt write-off the French were pressing. The best he could offer was ultra-long rescheduling – up to twenty-five years – with a very long period of grace before any interest would be payable at all. After considerable discussion, it was clear that it was not possible to push him any further.

Thus it was that, in June 1988, the Heads of State and Government agreed to what was to become known as the Toronto terms. This was a package in which every creditor country would offer the poorest of the poor, in addition to the conversion of aid loans into outright grants (or the equivalent), one of three items from a menu which consisted of an interest rate reduction as proposed by the UK, a partial write-off of principal as proposed by France, and an ultra-long rescheduling, with a very long period of grace, which the Americans had made clear was the best they could do. The Paris Club was charged with working out the details, and the intention was that the resulting scheme would be agreed by the entire world financial community at the forthcoming Bank and Fund annual meeting in September.

Trichet, who exemplified, both professionally and personally, the French Civil Service at its impressive best, duly worked out a matrix in which the details of the various options made each of them, in theory at least, of equal value to the recipient. By the time we arrived at the Annual Bank and Fund meeting, all the details had been fully worked out, and the only country of any significance not to have agreed was Germany. Since, however, the annual meeting that year was in Berlin (it takes place in Washington two years out of every three, but rather absurdly becomes peripatetic in the third), Stoltenberg had little choice, as host, but to give in gracefully. At long last, eighteen months after I had first launched my initiative, full international agreement was finally secured.

It did not, of course, transform the appalling position of the debt-laden countries of sub-Saharan Africa, but it was the best that could be agreed at that time. It was, moreover, a breakthrough, which could be built upon subsequently. Among the Africans, no-one was in any doubt that, despite the 'Toronto terms' appellation, it was a UK initiative that had started it all off. The episode earned the UK quite remarkable goodwill from those benighted countries, at a cost which, however it appeared in the official accounts, was in reality almost nugatory.

PART FIVE

TWILIGHT, EXIT AND BEYOND

CHAPTER FORTY-TWO

THE WALL STREET CRASH

Blackpool Parade · Black Monday · Policy After the Crash
Base Rates After the Crash · The US-German Row
International Co-operation Survives · An Important Non-Meeting

BLACKPOOL PARADE

The Conservastive Party Conference in Blackpool in the second week of October 1987 was more or less a victory parade, and my own speech was tailored to the triumphal mood of the Party. In it I coined the phrase 'a nation of inheritors'. There seemed no point in pretending that all personal property was the result of lifetime personal savings. An element is inherited: and a good thing, too, in giving people a cushion to fall back upon, a capital base with which to start their careers or take a few risks, and a stake in the capitalist system. But I was keen that inherited wealth should be diffused and not confined to a few. The notion of a nation of inheritors was not merely, as I saw it, the logical sequence to the property-owning democracy. It was also an essential means of entrenching the political, economic and cultural changes we had sought to bring about – an objective that increasingly preoccupied me.

BLACK MONDAY

Less than a fortnight after I had spoken, the triumphal mood of the Party Conference was abruptly shattered by what came to be known as Black Monday.

The Wall Street crash of Monday, 19 October, cannot be described as a bolt from the blue. The New York stock market had been falling quite steeply in the two weeks before the crash, as had London. The crash was essentially a reaction to an earlier excessive stock market boom. At its peak in September the New York equity market was no less than 44 per cent above its level at the start of the year, and the Tokyo market 42 per cent up. The London market had peaked in July, some 46 per cent above the level at which the year had begun.

In England, nature provided a suitably Gothic overture to the cataclysm which followed. During the night of Thursday 15 October, southern and south-eastern England were devastated by a freak hurricane. (Among the many victims was the Governor of the Bank of England, Robin Leigh-Pemberton, whose Kent estate was stripped of many of its finest trees.) Blocked roads and railways prevented more than a handful of people getting to work in the City on the Friday morning, and the stock exchange and the money markets were both officially closed. This postponed any further downward pressure on the London market until Monday morning.

On Black Monday itself the Dow-Jones fell by 23 per cent – an unprecedented fall in a single day – taking the index to 34 per cent below its early October level. The fall in London was of similar dimensions but less concentrated into a single day. Continental bourses fell by equivalent amounts, but Tokyo fell much less. There were then modest rallies and further falls to strain the nerves. The equity markets eventually bottomed out in early December. After the large correction markets resumed their more normal fluctuations. By the second half of 1989 London was back at pre-crash levels. Other markets regained their pre-crash levels somewhat sooner. So there should have been no lasting damage to the cause of wider share ownership. And if investors had a spectacular lesson in the fact that security prices can move in both directions, no harm was done.

Such phlegm may be all right after the event. Indeed by 1988 I was publicly calling the crash an economic 'non-event'. But at the time it seemed to many the end of financial civilisation as we had known it.

Because the Wall Street crash of 1929 had been the prelude to the Great Depression, every subsequent major stock market setback tended to be followed, like a conditioned reflex, by predictions of 'another 1929'. But there had never been a setback as sharp as that of 1987. For a few days, sheer panic reigned.

Even after I had modestly reduced interest rates, the Labour Party called for still more cuts. At the end of December 1987, after rates had come down by one and a half percentage points, their spokesman still accused me of 'fiddling', of 'staggering complacency' and of 'wringing my hands ... while continuing to saddle industry with excessively high interest rates.'

The mood in the boardrooms was, to say the least, alarmingly fragile. I remember a morale-boosting dinner Margaret hosted at Number 10 for David Nickson, the President of the CBI, Denys Henderson, the chairman of ICI, and a number of other business leaders. Their deep gloom and despondency bore no relation to the roaring economic boom of 1987 which the statistics subsequently conveyed.

POLICY AFTER THE CRASH

While I myself did not share the general crash hysteria, for the first and only time during my period as Chancellor I judged the risk of serious recession as greater than the risk of inflation. On the Tuesday after Black Monday I spent most of the day giving television and radio interviews trying to spread reassurance. I told the Stock Exchange Conference for Industry exactly one week after Black Monday:

> One well-known characteristic of financial markets is their tendency to overshoot ... It was neither unexpected nor in any way unprecedented that sooner or later there would be a sizeable correction ... It is abundantly clear that market corrections of this kind do not require there to have been any change in economic fundamentals. Still less do they imply that the world's economies are fundamentally unsound.

Inevitably, I devoted the major part of my Mansion House speech that year to the stock market crash. I said the fact that share prices were actually at much the same level as a year ago was 'something that needs very much to be borne in mind when assessing the likely scale of the economic effects of the stock market falls.' I added that the effect in the 'UK may not be very large and should reduce any risk of overheating there may have been'.

It seemed nevertheless likely that there would be some real effects from the crash, if only because of the collapse of financial and business confidence. There was also some concern that the US, where the stock market impinges most on personal wealth and the public mood, might by its sheer size lead the world into recession. In the regular economic forecast which accompanied the Autumn Statement on 3 November 1987 the growth prospects for 1988 had to be revised in a rough-and-ready way. They showed growth falling by almost a half, from 4 per cent in 1987 to just 2.5 per cent in 1988. In the event, the crash had very little impact on the real economy at all, which expanded all too vigorously.

There was one thing I was determined not to do: that was to abandon my budgetary guidelines. If the crash had been followed by a recession the Budget would have moved automatically into temporary deficit. This I would have been prepared to accept, since it was consistent with underlying balance over the cycle as a whole. But I did not see anything on the horizon which would justify discretionary anti-slump spending increases, despite all the advice showered on me to institute emergency public works programmes from the Opposition front bench and even from some of my own senior back-benchers.

BASE RATES AFTER THE CRASH

The crash had a significant effect on the conduct of domestic monetary policy. Until then I had regarded it as almost certain that the one percentage point increase in base rates to 10 per cent in August would soon be followed by another. During September and the early part of October evidence of overheating had gradually been growing. Once the immediate trauma of the crash had passed, it seemed as if it had been a blessing in disguise – a douche of cold water just when it was needed. In the words of the November Bank of England *Bulletin*, 'the sharp fall in equity prices ... implies a tightening of monetary conditions, by raising the cost of equity capital to firms and, through the effect of wealth reduction, by depressing consumption demand by households. It is far from easy ... to judge just how powerful these last effects will be ... but they are unlikely to be negligible.'

There was another way in which developments at the time of the crash eased some policy problems. It was never my practice to look only at the sterling-Deutschmark rate. I always kept a weather eye on the sterling index too. Because of the weakness of the dollar, sterling strengthened against the currency basket, even when it was up against the DM3 ceiling. There was a particularly strong rise in the sterling index in November; and in the whole year of shadowing the Mark – up to March 1988 – it rose by 5 percentage points, thus tightening the policy stance.

Indeed, whereas before the crash I had been discussing with senior officials at the Treasury and the Bank whether, and if so when, interest rates should rise further, discussion after the crash turned to the question of interest rate reductions. I called a meeting of the usual cast – with the exception of Robin Leigh-Pemberton, who was abroad – to assess the situation the day after Black Monday, 20 October. There was a general concern that normal forecasting methods might not take sufficient account of the effects of the stock market crash on personal and corporate wealth. This was stressed especially by Terry Burns. He was supported by the Bank, which warned that if the US was dragged into recession the British economy would follow. At the end of the week there were further meetings, and I decided to make a half per cent cut in base rates 'for psychological reasons only', in order to bolster business confidence. It was also agreed to have a short funding pause to ease any liquidity problems, which lasted only a few days.

Alan Greenspan, who had succeeded Paul Volcker as chairman of the Fed, declared on 20 October:

> The Federal Reserve, consistent with its responsibilities as the nation's central bank, affirmed today its readiness to serve as a source of liquidity to support the economic and financial system.

These words were widely thought to have stabilised market sentiment. But I saw no need for them to be repeated in the UK.

I cut interest rates by a further half per cent on 4 November, after a further plunge of eighty points in the London equity market that morning had touched a raw nerve, coming only a fortnight after Black Monday. At the same time sterling was rising against all currencies. Thus both external and internal considerations argued for a cut, which was concerted with similar action in most other financial centres. As I told the City bankers – who were for once probably listening carefully – at the Mansion House that evening:

> I fully understand – and sympathise with – the hesitations of those who are fearful of the risks of inflation. I have made it clear in the management of the UK monetary policy that I am as conscious as anyone of such risks. But if interest rates were the right levels three weeks ago, then it is unlikely that those levels are still right after all that has happened since ... What is needed in the world today, above all, is the avoidance of any major blow to industrial confidence. It was not the 1929 crash that caused the depression of the 1930s, but the policy response to it: the failure to provide adequate liquidity to the system, leading to a rash of bank failures, which in turn led to further monetary tightening; and of course the lurch into beggar-my-neighbour trade policies ...

The third and final half per cent cut in base rates in response to the crash was made as part of a co-ordinated move by European countries to stem the falling dollar, and to encourage the US to commit itself to a hands-on policy. The Germans cut interest rates on 3 December, accompanied by the Benelux countries, France, Switzerland and Austria. On 4 December, British base rates came down from 9 per cent to 8.5 per cent, implying a real interest rate of a shade under 5 per cent, comfortably above the G7 average. The co-ordination, which required a large number of telephone calls, was also intended to boost confidence by demonstrating that international financial co-operation remained alive and well.

Throughout this difficult and somewhat fraught phase, there was no rift whatever between the Treasury and the Bank. A few days after the 1987 election I had received a note from George Blunden, the Deputy Governor in which he wrote that 'I don't think there has been a time since the war when Treasury Ministers, the Treasury staff and the Bank have worked so well together.'

Even with several years' hindsight, I cannot regret the action which we took, along with our partners, to avert the risks from the Wall Street crash. One does not regret a fire insurance policy because there has been no fire. Nor, indeed, can we be absolutely sure (and here the analogy breaks down) that there would not have been a fire had we all simply sat on our hands and done nothing. It might well have been one of those relatively rare occasions on which there was no 'right' course to take: it was rather a matter of choosing the lesser of two evils. If so, however, this emphasises that the real mischief occurred in 1986, when the sharp fall in the exchange rate, exacerbated by my inability to secure the interest rate increases I sought, created an excessive degree of laxity. On 5 November, the day after the second of the three half-point reductions in interest rates I made in the wake of Black Monday, the Labour Party moved a motion in the House of Commons urging the Government, *inter alia*, 'to significantly cut interest rates [and] to target increases in public expenditure in order to prevent an economic downturn'.

The Liberal Democrats also urged me to bring interest rates down further, as did a number of Conservative back-benchers, echoing the almost universal message of the Press and other commentators. If, in the event, I overreacted to the 1987 crash, it is clear that matters would have been incomparably worse had I heeded the advice that was being showered upon me from all sides.

THE US-GERMAN ROW

The Wall Street crash had a diplomatic prelude and postlude. I have alluded more than once to the simmering row between the Americans and the Germans as to whether the former should tighten monetary policy or the latter loosen theirs to maintain the Louvre ranges.

Intervention had been taken almost as far as it could go in 1987. The American authorities possess a great deal of gold, but are remarkably short of foreign currency. The Germans, and the Bundesbank in particular, were concerned that under their system, endless intervention to sustain the dollar was inflationary. The subsequent German inflation figures did not bear this out in Germany itself; but evidence does suggest that the average G7 policy stance was too inflationary, not because of intervention but because average short-term interest rates were not high enough. In any case the 1987 position – when the greater part of the US current account deficit was financed by overseas monetary authorities acquiring dollars – was highly abnormal, and could not and did not recur.

In the US both growth and inflation were rising to unsustainable rates and the Federal Reserve had perfectly good domestic grounds for raising its discount rate at the end of September. Baker had pressed Greenspan to use his contacts with the Bundesbank to dissuade them from negating the American increase by raising their own interest rates. But the Bundesbank went ahead and raised its discount rate a few days later, thus necessitating a second rise in American rates towards the end of September. In the second week of October – the week before the crash – Baker publicly expressed his exasperation, saying that the German monetary tightening 'violated the spirit of our consultations' and that the Louvre accord did not require further increases in US interest rates to stop the dollar depreciating.

However understandable Jim Baker's annoyance may have been, this was a doubly unwise statement to have made. Indeed, the standard study by Destler and Henning described it as 'the greatest mistake Baker made as Treasury Secretary'. In the first place, the financial markets' confidence in international financial co-operation was bound to be seriously damaged by a public row between two of the main participants. And in the second place, Baker appeared once again to be threatening to let the dollar go into free fall. To his credit, the US Treasury Secretary repented of his remark very rapidly, and flew to Germany from Sweden where he happened to be at the time, to meet Stoltenberg and Pöhl in the immediate wake of the crash. In a joint communiqué released that day both sides reaffirmed their commitment to a 'flexible application' of the Louvre Accord with a view to 'exchange rate stability at around current levels'. The agreement was understood to provide for an easing of German monetary policy.

Ever since then a controversy has rumbled between those who maintain, somewhat implausibly, that the Louvre Accord was the cause of the Wall Street crash and the rival view that it was the failure to observe the Accord that was the culprit. A third school, following the Brady Commission, places emphasis on various technical innovations in the New York stock exchange such as automatic computerised programme selling, which magnified any incipient downturn.

As I saw it, some market correction was overdue and probably desirable, and the US-German row may have provided the trigger for something that would have occurred sooner or later anyhow. As for computerised programme selling, this did not so much magnify the downturn but rather sped it up, telescoping what might have taken a week into a single day. While it was the unprecedented rapidity of the decline that caused the panic at the time, there is nothing intrinsically wrong with a rapid correction; and now that we have safely survived the first of these it must be more likely that the next time it occurs the refrain will be not the alarmist 'remember 1929' unless the conditions genuinely warrant it, as they did not in 1987.

INTERNATIONAL CO-OPERATION SURVIVES

There is a myth that monetary and exchange rate co-operation collapsed in the wake of the crash. In fact it continued, and did not evaporate until 1988 brought new problems and a new US Treasury Secretary.

I was in constant touch with my opposite numbers in the other G7 countries from the day of the crash onwards. Indeed, during the fortnight following Black Monday, I was on the telephone to my fellow-G7 Finance Ministers at what seemed to be all hours of the day and night. Until then I had supported German resistance to American pressure for more expansionary policies. But I now thought that a new situation called for a new attitude; and in my speech to the Stock Exchange industry conference on 26 October I remarked:

> What is not required in current world circumstances is either a lurch into protection or undue monetary tightening. It was this which quite unnecessarily turned the 1929 Wall Street crash into the Depression of the 1930s. I believe the lesson has now been widely learnt. But it would certainly be helpful if the German authorities were to show more obvious awareness of this.

Jim Baker's main priority, however, was to secure agreement with the Democrat-controlled Congress on a package of policies to reduce the American Budget deficit, which was then a main concern in the financial markets. He secured this on 20 November, the deadline set by the Gramm-Rudman-Hollings legislation for supposedly automatic deficit cuts. The US Budget deficit had in fact already started to fall in 1987 and on nearly all measures shrank substantially in 1988 and 1989, only to balloon again with the subsequent Savings and Loan Rescue Operation and the onset of recession.

Meanwhile, the Americans, nursing what was at that time an unwarranted fear of recession, were happy to let the dollar slide for a while after the crash, and Louvre ranges were set aside. By early December UK businessmen were starting to complain to me about the effect on their competitiveness of the falling dollar exchange rate. Other European Finance Ministers and central bankers were similarly concerned about the falling dollar and were looking for firm evidence that the Americans were prepared to stabilise it. In view of the US Administration's continued preoccupation with recession, it seemed to me the only feasible move was a co-ordinated cut in European interest rates. It was something the Americans had frequently called for, but this was the first time in my Chancellorship that it had seemed appropriate. Robin Leigh-Pemberton told me that Karl Otto Pöhl was prepared to cut the Bundesbank's discount rate by half a point on the understanding that other countries would follow suit.

A co-ordinated cut in European interest rates was intended to entice the Americans into committing themselves to a stable dollar. There was much talk of whether there should be a meeting of the G7. Indeed, in the UK the Opposition had been calling for one ever since Black Monday. I took the view that it would be better to have no meeting at all than one at which the Americans refused to accept such a commitment. I told the American Chamber of Commerce in London on 24 November that a get-together would be useless 'unless all those involved were prepared to contribute wholeheartedly to the stabilisation of the dollar'. On 3 December, I wrote to Jim Baker setting out the conditions I felt essential to a successful G7 agreement. After some flattering remarks about the 20 November US budgetary agreement, I got to the point:

> We must address the two basic and linked problems of exchange rates and the financing of the US fiscal and current account deficits ... Official intervention has in effect financed the major part of the US external deficit this year. Though intervention has an important part to play, it obviously cannot be the sole or major source of external funds. Spontaneous private flows have to meet this need. I believe it is unrealistic to hope to restore sufficient private capital flows to the US as long as the market harbours

> expectations of dollar depreciation which could be self-fulfilling. Unless we can co-operate to prevent this, I see a real risk of further dollar depreciation spiralling out of control ... I cannot see how the US could then avoid serious inflationary consequences, and sooner or later the market would inevitably drive up US interest rates.

I suggested that the G7 should endorse prevailing exchange rates and demonstrate its ability and willingness to support them with all measures including interest rate changes.

AN IMPORTANT NON-MEETING

Baker eventually agreed to commit himself to dollar stabilisation. But the question then arose of where we should meet. Baker felt he had to remain on American soil while the budgetary legislation was grinding through Congress; and Japan's Kiichi Miyazawa claimed that parliamentary obligations made it difficult for him to manage the long trip to Europe. Baker eventually suggested Anchorage in Alaska, a godforsaken place whose sole claim as a venue (apart from the fact that it was US soil) was that it was more or less equally inconvenient for all of us.

This did not appeal to me at all, nor were my European counterparts very much keener. It occurred to me that in the circumstances, we did not really need to meet at all. What we needed was a communiqué that would steady the markets. It so happened that an Ecofin meeting was due to be held in Brussels on 7 December. I got in touch with Stoltenberg, Bérégovoy (who had returned as French Finance Minister) and Amato, and fixed a meeting between the four of us and our deputies at the office of the British Ambassador to the European Community an hour before the Ecofin was due to begin.

I put it to them that we had got into the habit in the G7 of meeting and issuing communiqués, and pointed out that in the good old days the G5 used to meet without issuing a communiqué. Why should we not avail ourselves of the remaining option, a communiqué without a meeting? The telephone had, after all, been invented some time ago; it would avoid an inconvenient trip to Anchorage; it would serve the purpose of having the US signed up; and it would be a useful shot in our locker for the future, since the markets could never be sure when we were going to do it again.

The others were attracted by the idea, and Stoltenberg, as the senior European Finance Minister, undertook to sell the idea to Baker, which he did. The

Japanese then had no option but to concur. An agreed text was hammered out by telephone. It took a number of lengthy calls; but the reason for the delay in issuing it was Jim Baker's understandable desire to postpone it until Congress had finally ratified the US Budget reduction programme.

The communiqué, which was published on the evening of 22 December, US time, or 23 December, European and Japanese time, reaffirmed the 'basic objectives and economic policy directives agreed in the Louvre Accord'. The key paragraph was Number 8, which read – with deliberate asymmetry – as follows:

> The Ministers and Governors agree that either excessive fluctuation of exchange rates, a further decline of the dollar, or a rise of the dollar to an extent that becomes destabilising to the adjustment process, could be counter-productive by damaging growth prospects in the world economy. They re-emphasised their common interest in more stable exchange rates among their currencies ... In addition they agreed to co-operate closely on the exchange markets.

Predictably, the communiqué was disparaged by the Press when it was released. The Press hate being taken by surprise, and on this occasion they were. Not only was no-one expecting a communiqué without a meeting, but no-one was expecting anything at all on the day before Christmas Eve. The markets were equally taken by surprise, and on the first day of trading in the New Year, 1988, the central banks of the G7 were able to spring a highly successful and large-scale 'bear trap'. Expecting a continuing dollar decline, the markets had gone short of dollars over the Christmas and New Year period – that is to say, their obligations to supply dollars exceeded their holdings of dollars. The central banks then went into the market to purchase dollars on a large scale, forcing it up, which meant that the market had to square its position at a heavy cost. Worldwide intervention during the first few weeks of January exceeded $3 billion. The dollar may not have responded to a communiqué alone, but it certainly responded to the combination of a communiqué followed by well-timed intervention, and revived strongly in 1988/89.

It is notable that throughout all the turbulence of the five years that followed the Louvre Accord of February 1987, the dollar stayed largely within the DM1.50 to DM2 range and during that period the wild currency gyrations of the mid-1980s were not repeated. No doubt convinced floaters could argue that the markets were at last beginning to operate floating rates as the textbooks had expected. Believers in currency co-operation could retort that the diplomacy and intervention of the years 1987/8 had their effect; and the markets were aware of a strong possibility of official action if they went to absurd extremes in either direction. There may be something in the first of these views; but, given the nature of the foreign exchange markets in the real world, there is, I believe, a great deal more in the second. However, in the absence of any further initiative, by the second half of 1992 the stabilising effect of actions taken several years ago had inevitably waned, to the general detriment. The torch will have to be taken up again.

CHAPTER FORTY-THREE

SHADOWING THE DEUTSCHMARK

Exchange Rate Policy After the Crash · The Financial Times Interview
The Switch to Marks · A Near Realignment

EXCHANGE RATE POLICY AFTER THE CRASH

The relief provided on the sterling front by the Wall Street crash was short-lived. Indeed, the problem of the inflow into London re-emerged as early as 30 October. The very fact that interest rate cuts were internationally co-ordinated meant that the comparative attractions of holding money in London and other centres had not changed very much.

It cannot be emphasised too strongly that, although I was obviously interested in demonstrating that sterling was fully ready for ERM membership by giving it a dry run, the main purpose of the policy of shadowing the Deutschmark was to arrest the fall in sterling which, both in terms of the index and against the Mark, had been going on, intermittently but inexorably, since the peak in 1980/81, and about which I had already become worried both in 1984 and 1986. My original post-Louvre policy was to secure sterling stability at a level higher than the pre-Louvre rate of some DM2.8, but with no specific parity in mind. The markets, however, assumed that we must have had a desired parity and tried to guess what it was. Their guess was DM3. As I have already recorded, this occurred well before the 1987 election. As a result, the market started to do much of the stabilising for us, selling sterling when it approached DM3 and buying sterling whenever it dipped below it. So we decided to ride on the back of that.

As for the scale of the intervention required by the policy, I was anxious at least to recoup the sizeable loss of reserves that had been incurred in the defence of sterling in the closing months of 1986. The official monthly reserve figures, so conscientiously quoted and commented upon by the financial Press and by analysts, are in fact a far from accurate indicator either of the amount of intervention over the month or of the true level of reserves at the end of it. This is so even if the figures are adjusted for special borrowing to replenish the reserves, annual revaluations, the proceeds of privatisation offers (the large ones always had an overseas component) and many other complications.

Far more important is the fact that the published figures relate solely to the spot book and not to the forward book, the size of which is never revealed. (The forward book consists of foreign exchange already acquired or sold, but for delivery at a later date.) During 1987, when money was flooding into London, I understated the size of the inflow by tucking some of it away into the forward book – that is to say, by getting the Bank to resell part of the foreign exchange inflow before the end of the month with a matching repurchase for delivery some months later. This was partly to avoid the danger that a large inflow might make the market so optimistic about the pound that still more foreign money flowed in. But it was also in part so that when sentiment turned, as I had little doubt one day it would, I would be able to offset much of the cost of intervention to support the pound by taking delivery of some of the hidden reserves in the forward book, thus minimising the reduction in the published reserves.

The idea of making use of the forward book to conceal the true position was not an innovation of mine. I believe that, during the acute run on sterling in 1976 under Labour, the true reserves were completely exhausted and actually became negative; and that this was concealed from view by selling dollars the UK did not possess in the forward market and buying them back spot, relying on IMF funds to save the Government from the day of reckoning when the time came to deliver the dollars that had been sold in this way. Be that as it may, whatever was concealed from the Press or the financial commentators, it goes without saying that the Treasury's own market report, which was sent to Margaret every evening without fail, always gave the full and true figure of UK intervention.

Her own view of all this underwent an astonishing transformation. During the first half of the period of shadowing the Mark, up to my September 1987 IMF speech, she positively loved the steady accumulation of reserves. Alan Walters, however, who deeply disapproved of my IMF speech, got on to her about it and thoroughly put the wind up her; as a result of which she completely changed her tune.

It is worth underlining that the rows I had with her at the end of 1987 and in the early part of 1988 were entirely about intervention. She had convinced herself that this was inflationary, even though it was fully sterilised. She at no time suggested that interest rates should be higher, which she should have done if she had really wanted a stronger counter-inflationary stance. Indeed, she made it clear that, if we stopped intervening and let the pound rise, one of the attractions for her was that this might enable interest rates to come down. I vividly recall, too, how cross she was as late as May 1988 when the main article in the Bank of England *Bulletin* that month suggested that a better policy mix, if achievable, would be to have a lower exchange rate and higher interest rates.

There was, of course, an international dimension. Although there was no specific Louvre range for sterling, the purchase of dollars clearly fitted in with the agreed G7 policy of preventing any further fall in the dollar. But my chief concern was the defence of sterling. The foreign exchange market may appear at times to be a one-way street, but nothing could be more unwise than to assume it will stay that way. By resisting *upward* pressure on the pound I sought to create credibility for a commitment to resist renewed *downward* pressure. Although I was no longer a believer in the old orthodoxy that exchange rates always moved in line with the current account of the balance of payments, I still expected that the UK's swing into current deficit, which had taken place in the second quarter of 1987, would sufficiently unsettle the financial markets that they would be reminded that the underlying UK inflation rate remained stubbornly above that of our main competitors, and start to sell sterling. The fact that UK short-term interest rates were more than 5 per cent above German rates in late 1987 (they were also more than 2 per cent above German rates in real terms) seemed to me a reasonable assessment of the relative risks of holding the two currencies.

Neither in our regular weekly bilateral meetings nor on any other occasion did Margaret make any complaint to me about the exchange rate policy I was pursuing until December. But it is clear in retrospect that she was getting more and more worked up about it. She was increasingly seeking advice from other sources and biding her time to act.

THE FINANCIAL TIMES INTERVIEW

A portent of the wrath to come was another interview Margaret gave to the *Financial Times* published on 23 November 1987, when she categorically and repeatedly denied that there was any exchange rate target for the pound. She rejected completely the notion of the pound being tied, even unofficially, to a rate of just under or around DM3. 'There is no specific range,' she said. 'We are always free.'

The objection she gave to both shadowing the Deutschmark and to joining the ERM gives the lie to the notion that she saw the inflationary dangers ahead and wanted a tighter policy. On the contrary, she argued that the 'DM at the moment is slightly deflationary. That means that the whole of Europe is geared to a slightly deflationary policy. Now, we have not been so geared and we have had a degree of freedom in relation to both the dollar and the D-Mark and I just think that I am grateful for that.'

Her interlocutors reminded her that a year previously she had told the paper that Britain could not become a full member of the EMS because the domestic economy was still too weak. In her reply she shifted, as she had done in our conversation in July, to opposing ERM entry outright, even though it was Government policy to join. She also expressed scepticism about the possibility of a more managed international system.

Opinions such as those she expressed on the record to the *Financial Times* could have been elicited from her at any time had the Opposition been more alert. Although she was ultra-scrupulous about Budget secrecy, on currency questions Margaret indulged in a stream-of-consciousness response, apparently oblivious to the sensitivity of the foreign exchange markets to her words. At the time I was thankful that no-one else did press her. My attitude, when publicly questioned about the apparent contradictions between us, was to point out that 'actions speak louder than words', a formula I first used before the 1987 election and was still using when I was questioned by the Treasury Select Committee on 30 March 1988.

THE SWITCH TO MARKS

The first rumblings of trouble on the operational front came in the early days of December 1987. The co-ordinated European base rate cut of 16 per cent had been agreed on 2 December and implemented on 4 December. Between these two events, on 3 December, there had been further upward pressure on the pound, and the Bank had intervened heavily to hold the rate, acquiring a further $1 billion. When I held a meeting on Friday, 4 December, to review the situation in the immediate aftermath of the 16 per cent cut, the pressure had abated somewhat, but the position was still uncomfortable. The pressure might flare up again at any time, and I was clear that we would not be justified in cutting interest rates any further – indeed, I would not have considered the 4 December cut had it not been a concerted European move designed, as I indicated in a previous chapter, both to demonstrate to the markets that international co-operation was still alive and well and to meet the American terms for their active participation in stabilising the dollar.

The main purpose of intervention, from the UK's point of view, had been to maintain the DM3 parity. Yet the intervention hitherto had consisted entirely of purchases of dollars. This was partly because the Bank preferred it, since the dollar market is far and away the largest and easiest to deal in, and partly because we had committed ourselves under the Louvre agreement to participating in the stabilisation of the dollar. But by that time I reckoned we had already (admittedly for our own purposes) contributed more than our fair share to supporting the dollar and fulfilling our Louvre obligations. It would be far more logical and effective, in the event of any resurgence of pressure, for us to buy Deutschmarks, which was clearly possible, whatever the Bank felt about the size of the market.

Indeed, in a sense the smaller the market the better, since it might mean that a given amount of intervention would have greater immediate effect. I therefore told Robin that, from then on, should there be further upward pressure on sterling, we should buy Deutschmarks and not dollars. The ownership of, and responsibility for, foreign exchange reserves as between the Government and the central bank varies from country to country. In the UK the reserves belong to the Treasury, and policy for the reserves is a Treasury responsibility. The Bank acts in the foreign exchange markets explicitly as the Treasury's agent.

What I was not aware of, however, when I told Robin of the change of policy, was that one of the clauses of the March 1979 agreement setting up the EMS, which had been concluded shortly before we took office, stated that no member country would purchase the currency of another member country without first securing the permission of that country's central bank. And, although sterling was not in the ERM, we were of course technically a member of the EMS – a perfect example of the British art of compromise securing the worst of all worlds. My officials, who did know of this, had not sought to trouble me with it since there was a clear understanding that the necessary permission would normally be granted, and there would need to be a compelling reason for its not being, which they did not see in this case.

But when Robin returned to the Bank and telephoned Karl Otto Pöhl to inform him that we would be purchasing Deutschmarks, he received a flea in his ear and was told in no uncertain terms that we could not do so. In Germany, unlike in the UK, the foreign exchange reserves are owned by the Bundesbank and policy for the reserves is the responsibility of the Bundesbank. The Finance Ministry's only statutory right is to receive a substantial share of any profits the Bundesbank makes from its reserves. The Bundesbank was strongly averse to the Deutschmark becoming a reserve currency, believing that this caused problems far greater than any offsetting reward, and in particular that the more Deutschmarks were held overseas, the harder it would be for it to exercise monetary control. But it was generally accepted that this was not a sufficient ground for withholding consent. Instead, Pöhl's ostensible objection was that the purchase of Deutschmarks was contrary to the Louvre Accord.

Robin reported Pöhl's refusal to me, which seemed to me wholly unreasonable, and I undertook to take the matter up with Stoltenberg, whom I would be seeing the following Monday, 7 December, at the Ecofin meeting in Brussels. There is a strict protocol in the conduct of international financial relations, requiring that, outside joint meetings such as the G7, Finance Ministers speak only to Finance Ministers, and Central Bank Governors only to Central Bank Governors. When I saw Stoltenberg I was armed with the figures showing the amount of dollars we had purchased since the Louvre Accord, an amount far greater than the Bundesbank's purchases of dollars, for which I also had figures. Given that, I suggested that it would require far larger purchases of Deutschmarks than anything I had in mind for the UK to be vulnerable to the charge of breaching the Louvre Accord. Moreover, we were not selling dollars, but pounds. Stoltenberg replied that he would have a word with Pöhl, but it was all very difficult. I concluded that we should go ahead regardless.

The following day, 8 December, I had my regular weekly bilateral with Margaret. I found her in an extremely agitated and aggressive mood. She told me that she was deeply concerned about the continuing large-scale intervention required to hold sterling below DM3, which already amounted to some $27 billion since the beginning of the financial year. (This information was one of the items contained in the evening report which the Treasury sent her every day.) She argued that the resulting extra liquidity would lead to renewed inflation. I pointed out that there was no increase in liquidity at all, since the intervention was always sterilised (that is, the equivalent amount of liquidity was removed from the system by the sale of gilt-edged securities).

I had, in fact, sought to explain the position, in my Mansion House speech the previous month, when I said:

> To prevent there being excessive liquidity in the economy, our policy is to ensure that, over time, any net intervention is sterilised – in other words fully funded, and that will be done, as and when appropriate although not necessarily entirely within the financial year in which the intervention takes place ... Nor should there be any doubt about commitment to

> maintain a stable exchange rate, with the rate against the Deutschmark being of particular importance. It gives industry most of what it wants, and provides a firm anchor against inflation. And we now have very substantial reserves with which to maintain a stability in the future.

I reiterated the point, at my bilateral, that not only was there no problem of increased liquidity, but we were gaining the advantage of a significant strengthening of our foreign exchange reserves, something she had earlier agreed was needed. She then changed tack, arguing that we were losing money by acquiring dollars which depreciated in value. This gave me the cue to suggest that, if this was her fear, the answer was to intervene to maintain the DM3 ceiling by purchasing Deutschmarks instead, which in any case seemed to me the sensible thing to do. The problem, however, was Pöhl's invocation of the March 1979 EMS agreement, to which the Bank of England was a signatory (it was technically an agreement between the central banks of the member states). This made Robin very reluctant to buy Deutschmarks.

Margaret was attracted by this. She said that although she was still worried about the scale of the intervention, she agreed that it would be worth attempting in the first instance to hold sterling below the DM3 ceiling by intervening in Deutschmarks, not least because she very much hoped that considerably less intervention would be required. She told me to instruct the Governor that, as from the next day's opening, the purchase of dollars should cease, and all intervention should be done in Deutschmarks – irrespective of the 1979 agreement.

The whole nature and context of this discussion, incidentally, gives the lie to the extraordinary suggestion, put about by her acolytes after the event, that Margaret was somehow unaware of my policy of shadowing the Deutschmark. It was always an implausible insult to her formidable intelligence to suggest that she could possibly have been unaware of it, even if I had wished to keep her in the dark, which, of course, I did not. In fact, we discussed it openly on a number of occasions, of which the 8 December bilateral is merely one instance. What is true is that there was no meeting at which the DM3 ceiling was formally agreed. That was because, as I have already explained, it evolved gradually over a period of weeks from the Louvre Accord, of which she was also fully aware.[31]

[31] In an interview with Simon Jenkins in *The Times* of 29 June 1991, Margaret publicly admitted that she had known about my policy of shadowing the Deutschmark, claiming however that her decision to allow it was her 'great mistake'. Despite this, the myth that she did not know about it continued to be peddled by some of her supporters.

Following the decision to confine intervention to Deutschmarks, I telephoned Robin and confirmed that this was to be the policy from now on. I added that Margaret, too, was clear that this was what we should do, despite the 1979 agreement, of which I had made her fully aware. This was clearly most unwelcome to Robin, who said that he could carry out this policy only if he were given clear instructions in writing to do so. This would enable him to explain to Pöhl that the Bank had no choice in the matter. I agreed to do this, and first thing the following morning, Wednesday, 9 December, sent him a letter by hand, the key section of which read as follows:

> From now on all intervention ... should be in Deutschmarks and not in dollars. Where it is necessary to intervene in markets where the direct sterling/Deutschmark market is thin, and hence for technical reasons intervention has to be in some other currency, the proceeds should be switched into Deutschmarks as soon as possible ... We have bought enormous amounts of dollars since the Louvre Accord, far more than the Bundesbank: our market intervention in dollars has totalled some $25 billion, compared with intervention by the Bundesbank of under $3 billion. In these circumstances it is wholly unreasonable for the Bundesbank to object to what we shall be doing.

Later that day, Robin telephoned me to say that he had received the letter, but was still very unhappy. He had now heard from Jacques de Larosière, who had clearly been approached by Pöhl. De Larosière urged Robin very strongly not to buy Deutschmarks, since this would put strains on the ERM which could be very dangerous for the franc. Robin felt he could not carry out the new policy without first having the opportunity to put his case to Margaret himself. This was fair enough, and I arranged for Robin and myself to see Margaret about it the following morning, 10 December. I felt that de Larosière was on to a much better point than Pöhl, although it was, of course, the Bundesbank's permission that was formally required, not that of the Banque de France. It obviously was possible that sizeable purchases of Deutschmarks could put upward pressure on that currency, making it harder for the French to maintain the Deutschmark/franc parity. I concluded that we should accommodate de Larosière's point by amending the policy to one of purchasing Deutschmarks and francs in equal quantities. This would avoid any conceivable strain being put on the Deutschmark/franc parity; and although it formally meant that the

Bank of England would need to secure the permission of the Banque de France to purchase the francs, they could scarcely object, since it was being done for their benefit.

Robin and I accordingly went to see Margaret the following morning, after Cabinet. Robin made his case. I then chipped in with my suggestion for meeting the French objection, and Margaret agreed that the policy should be amended in this way. There was a brief further discussion, at which it was agreed that other currencies might also be purchased: Margaret's chief concern at this point was that we should purchase no further dollars. Robin then pointed out that he still had a letter from me instructing the Bank to purchase exclusively Deutschmarks. I undertook to let him have a new letter which would supersede the earlier one, which I sent him later that same day. The key passage read as follows:

> I am writing to confirm what we agreed at our meeting with the Prime Minister this morning ... It was agreed this morning that intervention in French francs should broadly match intervention in Deutschmarks, and that intervention in Swiss francs and yen would also be permitted. But details of intervention should be settled between the Treasury and the Bank.

The letter then went on to cover various other details, including the fact that the Bank could make purchases of Ecus (the artificial currency created from a basket of all the Community currencies) as and when feasible. The main argument for buying Ecus, which it was not easy to do in large quantities at that time, was that it was to some extent a means of buying Deutschmarks through the back door, since the Deutschmark was far and away the largest component of the Ecu basket. But it was not covered by the 1979 agreement – even though Pöhl at one point had the gall to argue that implicitly it was and that no European Community central bank could buy Ecus without the Bundesbank's permission.

Meanwhile the upward pressure on sterling was continuing. By the following day, Friday, 11 December, it stood at DM2.997 – only a whisker below the DM3 ceiling. I arranged to have a meeting with my three key Treasury advisers on the Monday morning. Sterling was still under heavy pressure, despite renewed intervention, this time under the new policy guidelines. As a result, on Thursday, 17 December, Stoltenberg telephoned me to protest about our purchases of Deutschmarks. It was clear that the originator of the protest was Pöhl who had been told by Robin that there was nothing he, Robin, could do: he was acting under instructions from me; and protocol prevented Pöhl from speaking to me himself: he had to go through Stoltenberg.

However, Stoltenberg added his own four penn'orth by arguing that what we were doing would make it much more difficult to get a satisfactory section on intervention in the G7 'communiqué without a meeting' which, as I explained in the previous chapter, we were at that very moment engaged in drafting. I told Stoltenberg that I understood the problem, but that what we were engaged in was essentially a temporary expedient to overcome an immediate problem with which we were faced. I did not envisage it being a permanent feature of our policy. This seemed to satisfy him: Stoltenberg and I knew each other well, trusted each other, and had been working together closely for the past four and a half years.

A NEAR REALIGNMENT

What I had in mind when I assured Stoltenberg on 17 December 1987 that what we were engaged in was only a short-term expedient was that it was clear to me that intervention on this scale could not continue very much longer – not least because it was becoming subject to the law of diminishing returns. Before long, either the sterling tide would turn, or else, if the upward pressure continued, we would have to 'realign'. Indeed, we had come very close to a realignment only three days previously.

I had opened the meeting with my three key Treasury advisers on 14 December by asking 'Have we run out of road?' For the decision I had to take was whether the time had come to abandon the DM3 ceiling and allow the pound to rise – and, if so, how the policy change was to be presented to the markets. A number of views were expressed. One was that we should not abandon the DM3 ceiling. Another that any uncapping should be accompanied by a cut in interest rates, in the sense that a modest cut would not be taking great risks with inflation, as it would merely offset the contractionary effect of sterling appreciation. Yet another was to cut interest rates sharply, to break the bullish mood by leaving markets in no doubt that the next interest rate move would be upward. The consensus was that if it really was impossible to hold the line, it would be better to uncap the pound and cut interest rates afterwards, with a view to restoring the DM3 ceiling as soon as possible.

Listening to the discussion, I came to a clear conclusion. We should not rush into anything. But if the status quo became unsustainable, we would allow the pound to rise through the DM3 ceiling and then seek to stabilise it at a new, slightly higher level. We would, in short, have an informal realignment. Quite apart from the drawbacks to all the other courses, this seemed to me to be the least difficult to present as essentially a continuation of the existing policy, while avoiding taking any risks with inflation. It was agreed that this was what we would do.

However, as it happened, my caution about doing anything straight away proved justified. The upward pressure on sterling abated that very week and the pound, in fact, fell slightly against the Deutschmark. At the time, it seemed like a last-minute reprieve. In the light of subsequent events, it might have been better to have had the realignment.

CHAPTER FORTY-FOUR

FROM SHADOWING TO SHOWDOWN

Sterling Uncapped · 'No Way One Can Buck the Market' · Griffiths Tries to Draft Shadowing the Deutschmark: a Post-Mortem

STERLING UNCAPPED

By the beginning of March 1988 sterling had returned to virtually DM3, a level last seen in mid-December. In forty-eight hours on Wednesday and Thursday, 2 and 3 March, some $1.8 billion of intervention had been required in the effort to hold the pound. Sudden movements in the reserves are always inclined to cause a panic, even when, as in this case, the movement was in an upward direction; and the advice of Bank and Treasury officials on the morning of Friday, 4 March, was that I should uncap the pound forthwith.

I told my officials I would think about it over the weekend and let them have an answer first thing on Monday morning. It was not that I failed to recognise the inevitable. It was simply that we were by then only eleven days from the Budget, and I very much wanted to hold the line until then. I felt that an orderly realignment would be easier to achieve in an orderly setting, on a day on which I clearly held the initiative. Moreover, I was planning to leave London at 2.30 that afternoon for Stoney Stanton to work on the Budget speech. It was an important Budget, and I wanted to focus my mind on that. I then received a message that Margaret would like to see me at two o'clock.

I found her in a highly agitated state. She said she was deeply worried by the scale of the intervention in the foreign exchange markets needed to suppress the pound over the previous two days. She argued that it was adding to the inflationary pressure in the economy, and that the defence of the DM3 ceiling was attracting speculators to sterling, so adding to the upward pressure on the pound. I explained to her once again that there was no question of the intervention being inflationary, since all the excess liquidity was being 'sterilised' by sales of gilt-edged securities. I added, 'The time will come when you will be very grateful we have acquired all these reserves.'

I explained to her my intention to try to hold the position until Budget Day and then, if the pressures had not abated, make an informal upward realignment.

But she had the bit between her teeth and would not hear of it. I told her I would discuss the situation with my officials, and come back to her. I returned to the Treasury to discuss with Treasury and Bank officials the best means of uncapping the pound. My intention was still to lift the informal range rather than to leave sterling to its own devices. Robin was away, but the rest of the normal cast was present. It was agreed to uncap the pound from Monday morning, and to try and brake its rise through intervention and, if necessary, interest rate cuts, once it breached DM3.08. As for presentation, I decided that the least bad course was to insist that policy was unchanged, and that stability had never meant immobility.

I then returned to Number 10 at half past four. I told Margaret that, as she wished, the pound would be uncapped from Monday morning, but that intervention would continue in London and New York that evening because it would be unwise to let the pound breach the ceiling just before the weekend. I also explained that further intervention might be necessary to prevent the pound rising too sharply the following week. This greatly upset her. She insisted that sterling should be left to find its own level without any intervention at all. I told her that it would be absurd to abstain from intervention altogether.

After a heated discussion, she agreed to allow some limited intervention to smooth market movements and mentioned the sum of $50 million. This was a ridiculously small amount in the circumstances, and I told her that I could not possibly accept this constraint. She replied that my private office should contact Number 10 every half hour during the course of Monday and that she reserved the right to convene another meeting at short notice to review developments if she did not like the way policy was unfolding. It was an unpleasant meeting, and I particularly resented her manner on the eve of a Budget that was to achieve so many of the objectives we shared. Equally, there was no way in which I could contemplate resigning then: I was determined to introduce the 1988 Budget for which I had laboured so long and so hard. And Margaret knew this.

What was striking was that Margaret's entire concern in all this was with the level of intervention – and the fact (although she did not say this in terms) that I was using it to circumvent, in an informal way, her ERM veto. Not once did she suggest that interest rates needed to be higher, monetary policy tighter.

The uncapping of the pound in March 1988, coupled with her adamant refusal to contemplate British membership of the exchange rate mechanism of the EMS, removed a major plank of my counter-inflationary policy. A substantial current account deficit was already looming, and I could see sentiment in the markets turning against sterling before long. The massive reserves the Government had acquired during the previous year were bound to be useful, but the fact that the authorities had been driven off their declared policy of stabilisation would not be forgotten in the markets. So it proved.

The credibility earned in resisting upward pressure, so important when it came to resisting downward pressure, was largely dissipated. By denting the already wavering confidence among businessmen that the Government was committed to exchange rate stability, the uncapping of the pound, as David Nickson, the CBI President, was to point out, represented a major threat to British industry since it lowered the resistance of his members to high pay awards.

I was also irritated by the style in which Margaret had conducted the meeting. I was particularly outraged by her claim that I had misled her about the conduct of exchange rate policy, and reminded her very firmly during the meeting that she had been fully briefed by me both before and after the Louvre Accord – when the policy of shadowing the Deutschmark was initiated – and that she had received every evening a report of daily intervention in the markets in pursuit of it.

I detected in her allegation that I had misled her about the policy – which she knew to be untrue – the influence of Alan Walters. He knew nothing of the Louvre agreement, except what he had read of it in the newspapers, and I suspect that she was articulating his ignorance of what was going on rather than her own. I knew also that he contacted her fairly regularly, usually by letter, and that the British Embassy in Washington passed him information on Margaret's instructions. His advice was never copied to me, although I would sometimes find out through informal official sources. Coming so soon after her disparagement of my IMF speech five months earlier, it was increasingly clear that Margaret preferred the advice of an academic economist observing the British economy from 3,000 miles away to that of her Chancellor of the Exchequer.

'NO WAY ONE CAN BUCK THE MARKET'

Some journalists subsequently reported to me that she had been particularly incensed by my evidence to the Treasury Committee on 9 December when I had said: 'Obviously interest rates are something I watch carefully all the time and when I think they ought to go up they go up and when I think they should come down they come down.' It may not have been the most felicitous formulation, but, as the context made clear, I was simply emphasising the point that interest rates could not somehow be left to the market, or determined by a formula: they were an inescapable responsibility of the authorities, and in the last resort the buck stopped with the Chancellor. Perhaps she felt it stopped with her. Margaret had a habit of talking in the first person singular about every aspect of policy, as if no other Cabinet Minister existed. But when I once slipped into a similar usage in an area which, in the absence of an independent central bank, was unquestionably my own, it was evidently too much for her.

Not surprisingly, on Monday, 7 March, the pound rose to DM3.05. The Treasury Press Office was still talking along the lines that 'stability does not mean immobility' and I still wanted the policy to be seen as some sort of realignment. But Margaret was evidently determined to sabotage even this hope by saying at Question Time the next day that she ruled out action to hold down the pound through either intervention or interest rate cuts:

> The only way to deal with that is either to have excessive intervention ... or to deal with the matter by interest rates, which would not be in the interests of inflation at the present time.

In the circumstances, this could only be construed as an encouragement to the market to run the pound up still further.

This was the last thing either industry or the economy wanted; and during Treasury Questions in the House of Commons two days later I countered with the opinion that any further appreciation of the pound against the Deutschmark was 'unlikely to be sustainable'. Treasury Questions are always followed by Prime Minister's Questions, and Margaret lost no time in making a bad situation worse. Under pressure from the Labour leader, Neil Kinnock, to explain the apparent difference of opinion between us, she said:

> My Right Honourable Friend the Chancellor and I are absolutely agreed that the paramount objective is to get inflation down. The Chancellor never said that aiming for greater exchange rate stability meant total immobility. Adjustments are needed, as we learnt when we had a Bretton Woods system, as those in the EMS have learnt that they must have a devaluation from time to time. There is no way in which one can buck the market.

Up to that last sentence she was sticking reasonably closely to her prepared position, and it would have caused no comment had she stopped there. But it was that simplistic last sentence, which she added on the hoof, that was all that was remembered, and which did the damage. There may indeed be circumstances in which one cannot buck the market. But in the context Margaret's remark was inevitably taken to mean that any policy for sterling was being thrown out of the window.

As it happened, in the short term we got away lightly, in that the pound closed that week at DM3.0775, still short of the level at which I had thought further intervention would be justified a week earlier. But the unprecedented and highly damaging public spat between Prime Minister and Chancellor threatened to overshadow the Budget itself.

GRIFFITHS TRIES TO DRAFT

There was one further argument between us before the Budget, although this time, thankfully, it was at least in private. It was over the passage on monetary policy and the exchange rate in the Budget speech. I sent the final draft of the speech to Margaret, for her to read and let me have her comments, on the morning of the Friday before the Budget (which by tradition is always on a Tuesday). That afternoon Brian Griffiths, the head of the Number 10 Policy Unit, came to see me at Number 11 with a fresh draft he had done of that section of the text. It was wholly unacceptable, describing monetary policy without any reference to the exchange rate at all; a formulation we had abandoned as far back as 1981, and one which bore no relation to the way in which policy was in practice conducted. I rejected it out of hand. But it was equally clear that Margaret would not swallow my original draft, and there was no time to thrash out the underlying issues ahead of the Budget. With Terry's help, I drafted a compromise version, and sent it to Number 10 with a message saying that I had gone as far as I could to accommodate the Prime Minister's views, taking the Griffiths version into account. I then went off to Dorneywood, saying that I looked forward to receiving her comments on the rest of the speech over the weekend.

The essence of the exchange rate section of my compromise version, which she did not challenge, and which I duly delivered, read as follows:

> The objective of greater exchange rate stability [has been] given an explicit role in the process of international co-operation ... for well over two years now. I can assure the House that we shall continue to play our full part ... Exchange rates play a central role in domestic monetary decisions as well as in international policy co-operation. I believe that most businessmen have

welcomed the greater exchange rate stability over the past year. It is important that they also accept the financial discipline inherent in this policy.

Margaret wasted no time, and sent the speech back to me, with a number of minor comments, some of which I accepted, on the Saturday. She attached a fulsome note in her own hand: 'Marvellous – extremely clear ... Congratulations – I am sure it will be a great success.' I was irked that she thought I could be mollified so easily. It was never praise that I sought from her: just trust, honesty, and the loyalty she expected of others.

Meanwhile, I recall telling the Queen, the one person to whom I could unburden myself in complete confidence, during my usual pre-Budget audience with her the following Monday, that I thought the 1988 Budget would be my last, because the Prime Minister was making the conduct of policy impossible.

SHADOWING THE DEUTSCHMARK: A POST-MORTEM

Whatever may have been said subsequently, by the autumn of 1987 senior Treasury officials were fully supportive of the policy of shadowing the Mark, particularly following the stock market crash. They believed that the real policy dilemma would come when sterling started to weaken again, and that economic policy needed both an intellectually coherent framework and to be something that could be presented to the outside world. By that time it was clear to them that the £M3 doctrine with which we had started was no longer viable; and we now had something which was both viable and actually working. They feared that if we were to lose that, we would be without any anchor at all, floundering about in no-man's land.

The only objection any official raised to shadowing the Mark came, as I have already recorded in Chapter 34, from Eddie George in the autumn of 1987. This was partly because he did not like fighting the market, but also because Margaret Thatcher had been getting at him. To be fair, he did worry about domestic inflationary pressures more than most other officials at the Treasury or the Bank. Nevertheless, his main concern was with the level of intervention. At a meeting just before the internationally concerted half-point cut in interest rates of 4 December 1987, he said that, although he was still concerned about domestically generated inflation, he preferred another small cut in base rates to yet more intervention.

Over a year after the March 1988 uncapping I asked the Treasury to let me have an honest post-mortem on the policy of shadowing the Deutschmark.

Most of what they came up with represented common ground. Because of lags, we had, they said, to look back to the conduct of policy from mid-1986 onwards. In retrospect we had failed to spot both the extent of the decline in the savings ratio and the strength of the investment boom. They believed that the assessment of events in 1986–88 had been complicated by the oil price collapse of 1985/86 and the stock market crash in 1987. Further distractions were the mythical 1986 growth pause and the IMF's unfounded economic pessimism in the spring of 1987. They believed that, as a result, the shadowing of the Deutschmark had probably taken place at too low a parity.

Their main conclusion, however, was that the shadowing of the Deutschmark had no bearing whatever on our underestimation of the strength of the boom. Both the size of the decline in the personal savings ratio and the strength of private sector investment were unprecedented. (They might have made more of how they were both affected by financial deregulation.) They did not believe that the intervention had been inflationary. The problem, with hindsight, was simply that the overall stance of policy – taking both exchange rates and interest rates into account – was not tight enough. Had we made the right diagnosis from 1986 onwards, it was possible that on average interest rates might have been around 2 per cent higher and the exchange rate some 10 per cent higher – say DM3.30: a remarkably similar level to that at which I suggested earlier we would have eventually settled for, had my 1985 bid for ERM entry succeeded.[32]

[32] [2010 note]: The technically minded might like to consult the original edition of this book at this point, where they would find a lengthy appendix to this chapter, titled 'Intervention and Inflation'. I noted that the closest thing to an agreed position on this topic among economists was that intervention did not cause inflation when it was successfully 'sterilised' – i.e., offset by sale of government securities on the part the central bank or government intervening – but the sterilisation would render it ineffective. I had reservations about this semi-orthodoxy. Certainly in Britain and the US the authorities invariably acted to sterilise intervention and, in my view, therefore, it indeed had no inflationary effect. But I had little doubt that sterilised intervention *could* be effective in the short to medium-term, particularly when countries acted in concert to alter market expectations and the weapon of interest rates was also clearly available.

CHAPTER FORTY-FIVE

BACKGROUND TO THE 1988 BUDGET

The Overheating Debate · The Prospects at Chevening
Forecasting: The Moral · A Tight Budget · A Balanced Budget

THE OVERHEATING DEBATE

In the summer of 1987, roughly a year after unemployment – that most lagging of indicators – had peaked, a debate began in the economic and financial Press about whether the economy was overheating. There were two aspects to it. How much of a supply-side improvement had taken place in the British economy? And was demand increasing excessively?

On the first of these issues I stuck my neck out when I told the Edinburgh Chamber of Commerce on 23 June:

> As this upswing goes on, more and more people, at home and abroad are realising that what we are seeing is much more than a recovery from recession, or than the operation of the normal cyclical pattern ... Instead of wondering whether the recovery will last, people are asking what has caused this transformation.

In the immediate aftermath of the election optimism was rampant. City economists were revising their growth projections upwards, and both the OECD and the IMF were forecasting higher growth in the United Kingdom than in any other industrial country. Business surveys by the CBI and the DTI predicted continuing increases in output and investment.

Did I, in fact, mistake an unusually long cyclical upswing for a permanent supply-side improvement? When the two are occurring simultaneously it is never easy to apportion the contribution each has made, and I probably exaggerated the extent of the latter. But I remain convinced that the massive supply-side changes that occurred have produced a fundamental long-term improvement in the performance of the British economy. It was, however, never my intention somehow to use 'growth' as a substitute for the proper control of monetary demand. I have already recorded how the extent of the upturn was vastly underestimated not only in the forecasts, but also in the statistics of the recent past which were afterwards revised heavily upwards.

There were some warning signs from business surveys, particularly the CBI survey of capacity utilisation, and from house prices. The monetary data were, however, reasonably reassuring. £M3 was rising particularly rapidly, but that was now so distorted and had performed so misleadingly in the recent past that its predictive success in this one instance must be considered something of a freak. The growth rate of the best indicator of broad money, M4, was in double digits, but no greater than for many years past. The narrow measure of money, M0, which we did target – as an indicator and not as a cause of inflation – was well within its target range.

Most economists were dismissive of the dangers of inflation at this time, and the Bank of England was also reassuring. The author of a lengthy article in the Bank's May 1987 quarterly *Bulletin* was not worried about any inflationary threat, pointing out that rising personal indebtedness was more than offset by increased holdings of financial assets like bank and building society deposits, life policies, pensions and stocks and shares. 'To some extent,' as the Governor put it in the Mais Lecture which he delivered the same month, 'the personal sector's monetary behaviour ... may reflect simply a redistribution of its portfolio of assets and liabilities without serious implications for future inflation.'

THE PROSPECTS AT CHEVENING

The economic prospects were still far from clear when we met for the Budget planning meeting at Chevening in January 1988. The growth of credit and the consequent fall in the personal savings ratio were pointers, but they were not conclusive. The personal savings ratio was already well below its historic norm: it clearly could not go on falling for ever. At some point people would decide that they did not wish to get any further into debt. The difficult, if not impossible, question was to forecast when that would be. One Treasury economist's paper, circulated before the Budget, was entitled 'Are we about to experience a cyclical downturn in demand?' Life was relatively simple for the Treasury forecasters in the days when personal spending rose more or less in line with personal incomes. But the credit revolution, which allowed people, to an unprecedented and unknown extent, to bring their spending forward, ahead of their incomes, left the forecasters fumbling in the dark. There were of course other indicators of buoyancy, too – most notably the state of the housing market. Although that was in part simply another aspect of the same credit phenomenon, that was not all it was.

Towards the end of 1987 Gordon Pepper warned me privately of the imminence of a severe recession – indeed he excused himself for leaving early to give a talk on that very subject. The danger to the financial system which so alarmed him was not mythical. He simply got his timing wrong and was ahead of the game.

There is some similarity here with my own error in believing the Treasury forecasts which indicated a slowing down in the economy in 1987 and again in 1988. Clearly, although the forecasters did their best, they let me down badly. But I believed them not because I had any faith in Treasury forecasts as such, but because they reinforced my own instinct. That instinct was based on the fact that, while the banks and many others seem to have believed that the economic cycle had been abolished and that the upswing would go on for ever, I believed nothing of the sort. I was convinced that it would be followed by a downswing, and felt that the upturn had gone on for so long already that the downswing must be imminent. Moreover, I fully expected the payments deterioration and the early signs of a rise in inflation to put downward pressure on sterling which would need to be checked by higher interest rates. In all this I was not so much wrong as premature; for the downward pressures I feared were to emerge in 1989 in a big way.

Nor was this false reassurance confined to the Treasury. Robin Leigh-Pemberton, speaking on 29 January 1988, was doubtful whether credit expansion had been too fast. He told the annual luncheon of the Newspaper Conference that day that the rise in borrowing:

> ... has much to do with more intensive competition between financial intermediaries, particularly in the mortgage field, which has made it easier, for example, for home-owners to borrow against the accumulated equity in their houses. Not all of this increased borrowing has fed through immediately into higher consumer spending. Much of it has gone into a parallel increase in the personal sector's holdings of financial assets, including deposits with banks and building societies ... We need to be wary of over-simple and over-hasty conclusions ... There could be a danger of overreaction if we simply took the credit figures at their face value.

Indeed, as late as May 1988, the lead article in the Bank of England *Bulletin* had sub-headings saying 'Rapid growth of the economy continued to the end of 1987 ... But signs are gathering of a more sustainable pace'.

FORECASTING: THE MORAL

There is, I suspect, a moral in all this – probably several – which may be of interest and possibly even of some help to my successors. The first is that the nature of a modern economy is such that, while there will always be turning points, it is impossible to predict when those turning points will occur. Thus when speaking in a timeless sense about the economy, one should *always* forecast a turning point, while when speaking about the year immediately ahead, one should *never* forecast a turning point – since in any given year the odds are that it will not occur. The second is that the absurd 1975 Industry Act requirement that the Treasury must maintain a forecasting model and use it to make and publish forecasts should be repealed, as I unsuccessfully sought to persuade Geoffrey Howe to do when we first took office in 1979.

The third is that, unless and until this is done, Treasury forecasts should in practice be replaced by what is explicitly a conventional assumption that the immediate future will be a repetition of the immediate past (as has long been done, incidentally, in the case of the exchange rate implicit in the forecast).[33] The fourth, following on from this, is that the effort and skills of the economists and statisticians should be concentrated on establishing what in fact *has* been happening in the recent past. Unlike the future, the past is at least in principle knowable; yet the greatest source of error in assessing the economic situation has in practice been a misperception of the recent past. Fifth and finally, economic policy decisions should be based as little as is humanly possible on short-term forecasts, or even on conventional assumptions about the future: that is one of the principal reasons for steering by the exchange rate instead.

I was aware of most of this at the time, but there were other reasons, besides the mistaken advice I was receiving, that led me for a time to be more relaxed about monetary conditions than I should have been. In the first place, when we met at Chevening, the growth of the targeted monetary aggregate, M0, was still comfortably around the middle of its target range of 2-6 per cent. This proved to be another illustration of Goodhart's Law – exacerbated, in this instance, by

[33] By a repetition of the immediate past, I have in mind the same inflation rate as in the previous year and the same (positive or negative) real growth rate. To repeat, this would be a conventional assumption, and in no sense a true forecast; even though in practice it might well be no further from the actual outcome than most self-styled forecasts.

the fact, which did not emerge until some time later, that the Bank of England had got its seasonal adjustments wrong. Second, the exchange rate was strong, which is seldom a sign of lax monetary conditions.

Third – and this is frequently forgotten – the underlying rate of inflation (as measured by the RPI excluding mortgage interest payments) was below 4 per cent. Not only that, but it had been below 4 per cent consistently for the previous year and a half, with scarcely any sign of acceleration. To be precise, it had risen from a low point of 3.3 per cent in the second quarter of 1986 to 3.9 per cent in the fourth quarter of 1987 – and was to fall back to 3.7 per cent in the first quarter of 1988, when I presented my Budget.

This, then, was the mixed background to the January 1988 Chevening discussions. Before the Budget I had become concerned that monetary conditions were not tight enough for comfort, and on 2 February I took advantage of a modest weakening of sterling to raise interest rates by half a point. At that time the strengthening of the dollar and disputes in the motor industry kept sterling slightly subdued. But by mid-February overseas funds were once again being attracted by the relatively high level of UK interest rates, compared with German rates; by market perception of the UK's political stability and economic strength and, in the words of the Bank of England *Bulletin*, by 'the growing perception of the strength of the UK fiscal position'.

A TIGHT BUDGET

That strength was in no way dissipated by the 1988 Budget itself. Indeed, it is not sufficiently realised that it was a tight Budget in overall terms, and the occasion on which I re-established the target of a balanced Budget to be achieved in a normal year. How could a Budget that reduced taxation by £4 billion in the coming financial year and by £6.25 billion in a full year be regarded as prudent and tight? That this could be seen as an outrageous suggestion is a reflection of the nonsensical post-war habit of judging the fiscal stance, and thus the appropriateness of the Budget, entirely on the tax side, omitting all consideration of expenditure. Even on the tax side the outraged commentators ignored the effects of 'fiscal drag' in increasing the tax burden so that rates have to be cut simply to stand still.

Few critics of this supposedly irresponsible Budget have noticed that general Government expenditure, even excluding privatisation proceeds, did not rise at all in real terms in 1987/88 and actually fell in 1988/89. As a percentage of GDP it fell between 1987/88 and 1988/89 by 2.5 percentage points, having fallen as much in the previous financial year, too.

The result of these favourable trends was that, instead of the small Budget deficit the Treasury had predicted for 1987/88, there was a Public Sector Debt *Repayment*, or Budget surplus, of £3.4 billion. For 1988/89 the Treasury projected another Budget surplus of £3.2 billion. In the end the surplus came to £14.7 billion, or £7.6 billion even without privatisation proceeds. The more thoughtful commentators, well outside the Conservative ranks, realised that the 1988 Budget was very far from a reckless giveaway. Hamish Macrae, writing in the *Guardian* the following day, said: 'The final thing to get clear about this Budget is that it is not a tax-cutting Budget ... In its big numbers it is quite a cautious Budget.'

As we now know, the Budget arithmetic was based on notoriously bad economic forecasts. By then the Treasury and CSO realised that they had greatly underestimated the expansionary forces at work in 1987 – when by the time of the final revision, GDP was seen to have risen by 4.5 per cent. The forecasts, however, as is their wont, showed a return to a more sustainable growth rate – 3 per cent in 1988 and 2.5 per cent in the year to the first half of 1989. In fact, growth stayed well above trend, at 4.5 per cent, in 1988; and the *level* of demand remained above trend in 1989. As a result, a further 2 per cent of demand was deflected into the balance of payments – that is, into extra imports or goods diverted from exports to the home market – making well over 6 per cent overall growth in domestic demand in 1988.

Suppose I had had both a perfect forecast and a completely free hand from Margaret to manage the economy – two extreme counterfactuals – would my Budget judgement have been very different? I hate to disappoint the unreconstructed Keynesian reader, looking for a *mea culpa*. But (and it is fiscal policy that we are discussing here) the answer has to be 'no'. Innate caution led me to budget for a substantial surplus for 1988/89 rather than anything approaching balance. I find it difficult to imagine that even the most unreconstructed Keynesian Chancellor would have budgeted for a still higher surplus for 1988/89 than the unprecedented £14.7 billion or 3 per cent of GDP actually achieved – especially at a time when sterling was experiencing upward rather than downward pressure.

According to estimates published by the OECD – which puts every country's Budget on the same standardised basis – UK fiscal policy was strongly tightened in the calendar year 1988 even on a cyclically adjusted basis. According to other reputable estimates made by Goldman Sachs, the fiscal tightening was even greater, namely a reduction of the PSBR on a *cyclically adjusted basis* in each of the four financial years from 1985 to 1989 – amounting in total to over 4 per cent of GDP. As for the Public Sector Financial Deficit, which excludes privatisation proceeds, there was an even larger cumulative tightening on this basis.

I did not rely overmuch on such calculations, but generally aimed to keep public borrowing as low as practicable, and eventually zero, over the medium term, and not be deflected by shocks and windfalls in particular years.

With foreknowledge and a completely free hand, the main difference in my policy decisions would have been on the interest rate and exchange rate side. The difference on the budgetary side would essentially have been one of tone rather than substance – that is, a different speech rather than a different Budget. I would probably have dwelt much more on the sentence 'It will not be possible in this Budget to reduce taxation as a share of GDP'.[34] I would have dwelt on the inevitability and the nature of the economic cycle. And I might have engaged in a homily on savings, much as such exhortations go against the grain. The idea would have been to talk down exaggerated expectations of real income growth. In other words it would have been a less buoyant and very much more boring 'economic' speech.

When all is said and done, I must stress what I made clear at the time. The Budget was in no way an attempt to give the economy a boost. Nor, in any strict economic sense, did it. Taxation and public spending have to be seen together, and the expenditure side in those days was under the most rigorous and effective control. As the OECD table above shows, in orthodox fiscal policy terms the 1988 Budget, even cyclically adjusted, was the tightest since 1981. To put things further into perspective, the scale of the growth in consumer credit in the ensuing year was ten times as great as the reduction in taxation. The purpose of the 1988 Budget was simply and solely to improve the supply-side performance of the economy through tax reduction and reform, which is what Budgets ought to be about. The long-term benefits of that will become apparent in the recovery from the recession of the early 1990s. But in the short term, it may have unintentionally contributed to a climate of excessive optimism and dangerously unrealistic expectations.

[34] In the event, there was a slight and unintended 0.75 per cent reduction in the tax taken as a proportion of GDP in 1988–89, due probably to the lag of tax receipts in the boom. But that hardly counts as a relaxation of fiscal policy, given the sharp swing to surplus in the overall balance. Throughout my whole period as Chancellor the tax burden, as defined in terms of the revenue from non-oil taxes as a proportion of non-oil GDP, never moved outside a range of more than half a percentage point either side of 38 per cent. I would, of course, have liked to see a steady decline, but this would have to be earned by continuing to keep public spending growing more slowly than the economy as a whole.

INDICATORS OF FISCAL STANCE

Change in general government financial balance as a percentage of GDP

	Actual	*Cyclically adjusted*
1980	-0.1	+1.3
1981	+0.7	+2.2
1982	+0.2	+0.8
1983	-0.9	-1.2
1984	-0.6	-0.6
1985	+1.1	+0.7
1986	+0.5	-0.3
1987	+1.0	0.0
1988	+2.4	+1.7
1989	+0.1	0.0
1990	-2.0	-1.4
1991	-1.4	+0.2

+ = tightening; – = loosening
Source: OECD

A BALANCED BUDGET

I took advantage of the strong fiscal position in 1988 to reinstate the doctrine of a balanced Budget. As I said in the Budget speech:

> At one time it was regarded as a hallmark of good Government to maintain a balanced Budget; to ensure that in time of peace, Government spending was fully financed by revenues from taxation with no need for Government borrowing. Over the years this simple and beneficent rule was increasingly disregarded, culminating in the catastrophe of 1975/76, when the last Labour Government had a Budget deficit, or PSBR, equivalent in today's terms to some £40 billion.[35] This profligacy not only brought economic disaster and the national humiliation of a bail-out by the IMF; it also added massively to the burden of debt interest, not merely now but for a generation to come.

[35] Equivalent to some £55–60 billion in 1992–93 terms.

Before my time as Chancellor, a balanced Budget had been achieved on only one isolated occasion since the early 1950s. But now that it was achieved, it represented

> ... a valuable discipline for the medium term. It represents security for the present and an investment for the future. Having achieved it, I intend to stick to it. In other words, henceforth a zero PSBR will be the norm. This provides a clear and simple rule, with a good historical pedigree.

My prime difference from the Gladstonians was in being consciously medium term. I warned that 'In the very nature of things, there are bound to be fluctuations on either side from year to year'. It was no part of my doctrine to raise taxes in a recession, if the underlying balance was sound (as it was not in 1981), or in the face of a temporary deterioration due to, say, a war or a strike. Equally I had no intention of dissipating purely cyclical surpluses achieved in periods of boom.

The discredited neo-Keynesian idea of cutting the Budget deficit by raising tax rates to curb a boom, and increasing the deficit by lowering them to counter a recession, did not, in practice, stabilise the economy but merely destabilised tax rates. By the same token, I had no wish to inflict the supply-side damage caused by volatile tax rates in order to balance the Budget in fair weather and foul alike. But this in no way detracted from the importance of the doctrine of the balanced Budget as the norm – that is to say, over the cycle as a whole, or when the economy was growing at its normal trend rate.

While senior Treasury officials, over-impressed perhaps by the degree of arbitrariness inherent in the definition of the PSBR, would never have rehabilitated this doctrine if left to their own devices, they were happy to go along with my decision to espouse it. For they saw in it a useful weapon in the unending battle to control public spending particularly as the alleged connection between public borrowing and the level of short-term interest rates became increasingly implausible. Moreover the fiscal side of the MTFS clearly had to have some terminus – an ever-increasing Budget surplus was manifestly absurd – just as the monetary side, in its heyday, had as its terminus the rate of monetary growth consistent with stable prices.

Of course, the new doctrine was a departure from my previous objective of a PSBR of 1 per cent of GDP, which I had described at the time as 'the modern equivalent of a balanced Budget'. But why bother with the complications of a 'modern equivalent' which could not in any case stand up to rigorous examination as a scientific doctrine, if balance was within reach? Leaving aside the problems of the transition, it is a delusion to suppose that economic activity will be any lower if the medium-term objective is a balanced Budget than if it is a 1 per cent deficit as I had previously suggested – or an ill-defined 3 per cent ceiling, as in the Maastricht Agreement of 1991.

Nor does the choice between such medium-term goals have any direct bearing on the control of inflation. Where it does make a difference is, first, in providing a readily comprehensible rule of thumb which is less likely to be fudged than any other more complicated rule which would mean nothing to the average voter; second, in reducing the burden of debt service and therefore the tax level in years to come; and third, if one day it could be the basis of a global agreement, in reducing the demands made by governments on the savings of the private sector.

One detail needs to be clarified. My objective of zero borrowing was for the PSBR as conventionally defined. But proceeds from privatisation – and for that matter council house sales – were bound to dry up once all saleable assets had eventually been realised. So in the long term – say by the end of the century – the balanced Budget would have to be achieved without asset sales.

CHAPTER FORTY-SIX

1988 – A PROVOCATIVE BUDGET

Reforming Personal Taxation · Cutting Tax Rates
Uproar in the House · Aligning Capital Gains
Restricting Mortgage Interest Relief
Ending Tax Breaks · A Triumph Marred

REFORMING PERSONAL TAXATION

During my time as Chancellor, I developed two overriding ambitions, to which I devoted considerable time and thought. These were international monetary reform and tax reform. Having been largely frustrated in the first, I came to give priority to the second.

I had always intended the 1988 Budget, like that of 1984, to be a major tax-reforming Budget, this time focusing on personal rather than company taxation. Indeed, my desire to be reappointed Chancellor after the 1987 election was principally in order to introduce just such a Budget; just as my failure to have a real showdown with Margaret in early March 1988, over the issue of shadowing the Deutschmark and her subsequent disloyal remarks in the House, which in other circumstances might well have led to my resignation then, was caused by my determination to introduce the tax reforms.

I was clear, too, that a key element in the tax reforms should be a reduction in the higher rates of income tax. Controversial changes to the tax system are best implemented in the first Budget of a new parliament, to allow time for the inevitable opposition to die down and for the benefits to become apparent – as in 1984 with Corporation Tax. I told the House in my Budget speech on 15 March, 1988, that I was guided by four basic principles: 'First, the need to reduce tax rates where they are clearly too high; second, the need to reduce or abolish unwarranted tax breaks; third, the need to make life a little simpler for the taxpayer; and, fourth, the need to remove some manifest injustices from the system.' The objectives had hardly changed since 1984.

CUTTING TAX RATES

The centrepiece of the 1988 Budget was the establishment of a single higher rate income tax of 40 per cent, in place of the previous sliding scale going up to 60 per cent, coupled with the fulfilment of our manifesto pledge to reduce the basic rate of tax to 25 per cent.

The reduction and reform of personal tax rates had become more necessary than ever before in the light of the changes that were occurring elsewhere in the world. Most conspicuously, the United States had cut personal taxes and eliminated a series of tax breaks in 1986. But major reforms were also taking place in countries as diverse as Australia, New Zealand, Canada, Ireland, Japan, Sweden, France, the Netherlands, Germany and Denmark. There was increasing recognition throughout the industrialised world of the importance of tax reform and low marginal rates in raising economic performance through improved incentives and encouraging enterprise – and in maintaining revenue by containing avoidance and keeping talented individuals within the jurisdiction. In a world in which the international barriers to capital and labour mobility were steadily diminishing it would have been folly to ignore what was happening abroad. But my ambition was not merely to keep up with the Joneses: I wished to see the UK reap the advantages of being, if possible, ahead of the Joneses.

The income tax reductions of 1988 were not confined to the basic and higher rates. With some misgivings, but in order to improve the 'social' balance of the Budget, and thus its presentation, I increased the personal allowances by twice as much as the inflation rate, bringing the tax thresholds to a level 25 per cent higher in real terms than where Labour had left them in 1979; and, in the case of the still-existing married man's allowance, to its highest real level for nearly half a century.

Having at last achieved the 25 per cent basic rate which Geoffrey had first advocated in 1979, which I had revived as an objective in 1986, and which had become a Manifesto pledge in 1987, I persuaded a reluctant Margaret that I should announce in the Budget speech a new objective of reducing the basic rate to 20 per cent 'as soon as we prudently and sensibly can'.

Some people, even among those sympathetic to my general objective, regarded the new target as appallingly crude, and could think of many more reformist and radical changes to make if there were scope for reducing tax revenue. They overlooked the politics and the psychology. The basic rate is the flagship of the tax system. A public commitment to reduce it sends the right signals about the commitment of a Conservative Government to continue to reduce both taxation and the share – not the level – of public spending in GDP. Without this kind of commitment it is extremely difficult for a Chancellor and a Chief Secretary to hold the line against spending pressures.

Moreover, I was keenly conscious of the fact that the tax burden even by the middle of a third Conservative term was still virtually unchanged from when I first became Chancellor in 1983 (and still above what we had inherited from Labour in 1979, when the tax burden was artificially kept down – not that it felt like that at the time – by an unsustainably high level of public borrowing). The rate reductions I had been able to make had been almost entirely absorbed by so-called fiscal drag. If we were to show that we were in earnest about reducing taxation and to move the centre of debate away from how much to increase public spending, we had to keep the basic rate of income tax at the centre of the political debate.

UPROAR IN THE HOUSE

By long-standing tradition, the Budget Statement is listened to without interruption (although sedentary mutterings are by no means unknown). But that tradition was flouted, in the most lamentable way, in 1988.

The first interruption occurred well before I reached the higher rates, when I had just announced the cut in the basic rate. The Scottish Nationalist Member Alex Salmond began shouting: 'The Budget is an obscenity. The Chancellor cannot do this.' He would not stop when the Deputy Speaker (who always occupies the chair for the Budget speech) 'named' him. The motion was then put that Mr Salmond be suspended 'from the service of the House' for five days. This was then voted on, with the Labour front bench voting with the Government in support of the Deputy Speaker's decision. A handful of the Labour left joined the Scottish and Welsh Nationalists in the No lobby. But the voting figures – 354 to 19 – for the suspension show that most Labour Members abstained. I could not help wondering what kind of democracy the Nationalists would establish in Scotland if ever they had the opportunity.

All this however, was no more than a curtain-raiser compared to what occurred when I came to the higher rates. Here are the supposedly provocative, not to say obscene, words:

> It is now nine years since my predecessor, in his first Budget in 1979, reduced the top rate of income tax from the absurd 83 per cent that prevailed under Labour to 60 per cent, where it has remained ever since.

> At that time this was broadly in line with the European average for the top rate of tax. It is now one of the highest. And not only do the majority of European countries now have a top rate of tax below 60 per cent, but in the English-speaking countries outside Europe – not only the United States and Canada but in Labour Australia and New Zealand too – the top rate is now below 50 per cent, and sometimes well below. The reason for the worldwide trends towards lower rates of tax is clear. Excessive rates of income tax destroy enterprise, encourage avoidance, and drive talent to more hospitable shores overseas. As a result, so far from raising additional revenue, over time they actually raise less.
>
> By contrast, reduction in the top rates of income tax can over time result in a higher, not a lower, yield to the Exchequer. Despite the substantial reduction in the top rate of tax in 1979, and the subsequent abolition of the Investment Income Surcharge in 1984, the top 5 per cent of taxpayers today contribute as much again in real terms as they did in 1978/79, Labour's last year; while the remaining 95 per cent of taxpayers pay about the same in real terms as they did in 1978/79.
>
> After nine years at 60 per cent I believe that the time has come to make a further reduction in the top rate of income tax. At present there are no fewer than five higher rates of income tax: 40 per cent, 45 per cent, 50 per cent, 55 per cent and 60 per cent. I propose to abolish all the higher rates of tax above 40 per cent ...
>
> This major reform will leave us with one of the simplest systems of income tax in the world, consisting of a basic rate of 25 per cent and a single higher rate of 40 per cent, and indeed a system of personal taxation in which there is no rate anywhere in excess of 40 per cent.

Although I had to resort to it in my Budget speech for reasons of brevity, comparing top rates of tax is a manifestly inadequate way of comparing different tax systems. Just as important is where the rates tend to bite. Japan had a top rate of 93 per cent in 1979 which was reduced in the 1980s to 65 per cent. But this top rate came in at such a high level of income that it was much less penal on the top executive earners and professionals than the apparently lower British rates. It is possible that, had I kept a top rate of 60 per cent, but reserved it for incomes in excess of £1 million a year, the reaction would have been less extreme. But this would have made it very difficult indeed to align the income tax and capital gains tax rates – an important reform in its own right.

The ellipses before the last paragraph of the quotation from the Budget speech cover some of the most amazing scenes ever to have taken place on Budget Day. Dave Nellist, the Labour MP who was subsequently expelled from his Party because of his close involvement with Militant Tendency (a group of far Left anti-parliamentary extremists within the Labour Party), not to be outdone by the Scottish Nationalists, started shouting and interrupting. Other Labour Members, to their great discredit, joined in. In the words of *Hansard*, 'grave disorder having arisen in the House, Mr Deputy Speaker suspended the sitting for ten minutes'. If all income belongs to the State, then my reliefs were indeed outrageous handouts to the rich. But if it does not, then the Labour explosion was nothing but a particularly loutish display of the politics of envy.

The tax reductions in the 1988 Budget were a vital part of the Government's sweeping reform of the supply side of the economy, to which privatisation, trade union reform and employee share ownership were also central. The actuality and expectation of cuts in tax rates were part of an important cultural change, which fuelled business confidence and economic growth in the 1980s, and benefited the population as a whole. Few doctrines are more insidious than the view that poverty is relative. None of this means that we can ignore the hardships of the homeless or the increase in the number of beggars on our streets. But the prosperity of the many, which is to be welcomed, is not the cause of the poverty of the few.

ALIGNING CAPITAL GAINS

Reducing top rates of tax to 40 per cent enabled me to introduce a further radical tax reform. This was the alignment of capital gains and income tax rates. Instead of the special 30 per cent tax on capital gains which had existed since the tax was first introduced in 1965, I legislated to tax capital gains, after deduction of the exempt amount and the exclusion of purely inflationary or paper gains via the indexation provision, as if they were income – that is, at either 25 per cent or 40 per cent as the case may be. Not surprisingly, this change was, and remains, very unpopular with many Conservative back-benchers, who saw it as an increase in the Capital Gains Rate from 30 per cent to 40 per cent – although they were in no position to complain too loudly in a year in which the higher rates had been significantly reduced.

But the case for the reform was overwhelming. Before 1988 anyone paying tax at the higher rate paid less – often much less – on capital gains than on income. A whole tax avoidance industry had therefore grown up whose sole purpose was to dress up income as capital gains. I had been reinforced in my desire to bring this unproductive activity to an end by the US Tax Reform Act of 1986, which had similarly provided for capital gains to be taxed as income. (A so-far unsuccessful campaign to reverse this has been raging ever since.) There is little genuine economic difference between income and most capital gains, and no obvious reason why one should be taxed more heavily than the other. With the reduction in the basic rate below 30 per cent, we had reached the bizarre position in which some people were being taxed more heavily on capital gains than on income, while others were being taxed more heavily on income than on capital gains. Moreover, contrary to popular supposition, the new UK capital gains tax regime was less onerous, even at low levels of inflation, than its American equivalent, in which there was neither indexation nor a separate capital gains tax threshold.

At the same time, I converted the capital gains tax system from a partially indexed to a fully indexed regime. The indexation provisions introduced by Geoffrey Howe in 1982, which I had extended in 1985, applied only to future, i.e. post-1982 gains. Gains made between the introduction of the tax in 1965 and 1982, many of them purely paper gains reflecting the high inflation of the 1970s, remained untouched by the indexation relief. I removed this injustice in the only way practicable: by exempting pre-1982 gains from tax altogether. This would bring the added economic advantage of unlocking those assets, particularly land, where the unindexed capital gains tax liability had been so great that the owners would never dispose of them during their lifetime – knowing, of course, that on death the liability would disappear altogether.

Yet a further 1988 reform was to the Inheritance Tax I had introduced in 1986 to replace Labour's Capital Transfer Tax. In place of the ascending scale of rates inherited from the Capital Transfer Tax (and before that the Estate Duty) I introduced a single flat rate of 40 per cent, after raising substantially the (indexed) threshold for the tax. This reduced the number of estates liable to tax by a quarter, allowing many more people to inherit the family home free of tax. It was only the impending and misguided abolition of local authority rates, to be replaced by the disastrous Poll Tax, that made me unwilling to go even further in this direction. As it was, the change not only helped to realise the ideal I had set out at the 1987 Party Conference, of making Britain a nation of inheritors; coupled with the income tax changes, it also meant that no personal tax anywhere in the system would be levied at a rate higher than 40 per cent. In other words, every taxpayer in Britain would remain the majority shareholder in his or her own income and capital.

RESTRICTING MORTGAGE INTEREST RELIEF

There were many other clear-cut reforms, some discussed in earlier pages. In particular, I restricted mortgage interest relief to £30,000 per property, instead of (as previously) £30,000 per borrower, thus ending the practice by which a group of 'sharers' could secure very substantial relief on the purchasing of a large property – and also the unfairness and perversity of enabling an unmarried couple to draw a £60,000 double ration of relief, whereas the married couple were confined to a single ration. The complete removal of interest relief on home improvement loans stopped the most notorious abuse of mortgage interest relief to finance consumer spending.

Unfortunately, the effect of the first of these two restrictions – the ending of multiple mortgage interest relief – was perverse in the short term, and added further fuel to an already booming house market. The Inland Revenue, whose advice was normally of a very high quality, insisted that the restriction should not come into force until 1 August: more than four months after the Budget announcement. They maintained that the lending institutions, whose responsibility it was to collect the mortgage interest due to them net of tax (under the so-called MIRAS – Mortgage Interest Relief At Source – system) could not reprogramme their computers any sooner than this.

After the meeting at which this was provisionally agreed, Terry Burns mentioned to me that he was worried that it would lead to a wave of additional borrowing to take advantage of the relief while it lasted. I told him that I shared his concern – so much so that I would hold a further meeting with the Revenue and press them on this specific point. This I did; but they remained adamant, arguing that any earlier date would lead to a shambles, and the Government would be left with a large amount of egg on its face. As I am no computer expert myself, I felt obliged to accept this advice.

The result fulfilled my worst fears. Foolishly, considerable numbers of people pushed house prices up still higher in their rush to secure the extra income tax relief, despite the fact that this could not possibly recompense them for the excessive price they were having to pay for the house in the first place – and thus the excessive sum they were having to borrow. What this, in practice, did was to add froth to an already heady housing boom, which made the subsequent inevitable downturn all the more painful. It was inevitable both in the sense that excess always ends in tears – every binge is followed by a hangover – and because multiple mortgage interest relief, did, of course, come to an end on 1 August.

I have no regrets over the end of multiple mortgage interest relief. It was clearly the right thing to do: what was wrong was the long delay between announcement and implementation. It was scant consolation that the Revenue subsequently concluded that perhaps their firm advice had been wrong, and that the institutions possibly could have reprogrammed their computers more quickly had they been requested to do so.

It would have been better, of course, if multiple mortgage interest relief had been ended much earlier, as I had wished. It had first emerged as a proposal in my March 1986 Green Paper, *The Reform of Personal Taxation*, in the context of independent taxation (since the logic of this was either that husband and wife would each have to be given their own £30,000 ration of relief, as already occurred with unmarried couples, or the whole basis of the ration would have to be changed from the individual to the property, which was indisputably preferable). But it was clearly a free-standing proposal, desirable on its own merits, which could be introduced well in advance of the rest of the package.

Although I had sought to do this in both the 1986 and 1987 Budgets, on each occasion I ran up against the brick wall of Margaret's passionate devotion to the maximum amount of mortgage interest relief the Exchequer could afford. Indeed, it was only because the 1988 Budget was such an exciting one overall that Margaret reluctantly agreed to my going ahead with the announcement of independent taxation,[36] and it was only the logic of independent taxation that persuaded her that this restriction on mortgage interest relief was unavoidable.

ENDING TAX BREAKS

There were other measures, too, which the overall scale of the tax cuts made possible, and which otherwise Margaret would have resisted. I felt strongly that the sharp reduction in tax rates on cash incomes should be accompanied by an increase in the tax on benefits in kind, or 'perks'. I had a great deal of work done on a general fringe benefit tax; but both the political and practical problems proved far more daunting than I had hoped, and the likely yield at the end of the day was limited. So I decided to cut the Gordian knot, and concentrate on company cars, which had a value far in excess of all other perks put together, and which were still, despite the increases I had introduced in each of my four previous Budgets, manifestly undertaxed. I decided to double, with immediate effect, the tax on the benefit conferred by the possession of

[36] This major reform is dealt with fully in Chapter 50.

a company car, as measured by the so-called scale charges. This brought in a healthy £300 million.

I also ended all tax relief on covenants, apart from charitable covenants, which (once the inevitably complex transitional arrangements had been worked through) greatly simplified the system as well as ending an indefensible tax avoidance device. I similarly simplified the tax treatment of maintenance payments. Both these changes, but especially the latter, raised complicated legal questions. I decided to take James Mackay, the Lord Chancellor, into my confidence. He was characteristically helpful and constructive.

One of the most blatant tax shelters I closed concerned forestry. The previous system, (as I explained in the Budget speech) enabled 'top rate taxpayers in particular to shelter other income from tax, by setting it against expenditure on forestry, while the proceeds for any eventual sale are effectively tax free'. Forestry, of course, genuinely is different, given the long time that elapses between the initial planting and the production of saleable timber. Moreover, the Government, for a mixture of political, agricultural and environmental reasons, had foolishly made a public commitment to a specific level of tree planting. Nevertheless the existing system gave top rate taxpayers such a ludicrously generous tax break that the overall yield from the taxation of forestry was negative – the Inland Revenue was giving more in tax relief than it raised in tax revenue.

I decided that the most elegant solution was to remove forestry from taxation altogether – a measure that could scarcely be portrayed as unduly harsh – and, given the Government's pledge, to use the money thus saved on improved planting grants, which at least could be given with environmental considerations uppermost. Thus not only was a long-standing tax break eliminated, and the system greatly simplified, but rural Scotland (in particular) was saved from having its environment further ruined by the eyesore of plantations of Sitka spruce, that unattractive but previously tax-efficient conifer. Indeed, my action on forestry, coupled with a further twist in the taxation of petrol in favour of unleaded petrol (I had originally introduced this uncharacteristic departure from neutrality in my 1987 Budget), was the main reason why Jonathan Porritt, at that time Director of the high-profile environmental pressure group, Friends of the Earth, was moved to declare that my 1988 Budget had done more for the environment than any action by any other Minister – a most unexpected bouquet.

The Inland Revenue had wanted me to go for perks in a much more detailed way. Shortly before the 1987 pre-election Budget they came to me with a long list of allegedly taxable benefits, ranging from corporate Christmas presents (diaries, calendars and the like) to the provision of car parking spaces for employees on the company's premises. They warned me that unless I legislated explicitly to exclude these from tax, they would have to pursue each and every one of the beneficiaries for tax. I told them to go away and come back to me after the election, which they did. The 1988 Budget accordingly took some benefits (such as car parking) out of tax altogether, and simplified the tax on others above a *de minimis* level. It was a very tedious business. The Revenue was always a rich source of odd and usually counterproductive revenue proposals which would have required large numbers of extra staff to monitor for little revenue and at the cost of considerable annoyance to the taxpayer.

I even found yet another tax to abolish. This was Capital Duty, of which most people had never even heard. It had to be paid at a rate of 1 per cent when companies raised new capital or sold shares to the public. It was an understandable irritant and a further deterrent to equity finance as distinct from debt finance. At a cost of £100 million a year it was well worth abolishing.

A TRIUMPH MARRED

The 1988 Budget completed what I then thought was more or less the maximum politically feasible transformation of the British tax system, certainly so long as Margaret was Prime Minister. The Cabinet, when it first heard of it the morning of Budget Day, was enthusiastic. I ended my Budget speech with the following peroration:

> I have announced a radical reform of the taxation of marriage, which for the first time ever will give married women a fair deal from the tax system. I have eliminated the long-standing injustice of taxing inflationary gains, and abolished a fifth tax. I have radically reformed the structure of personal taxation, so that there is no rate anywhere in the system in excess of 40 per cent.
>
> After an Autumn Statement which substantially increased public spending in priority areas, I have once again cut the basic rate of income tax, fulfilling our manifesto pledge of a basic rate of 25 pence in the pound and setting a new target of 20 pence in the pound.
>
> And I have balanced the Budget.

I sat down to tremendous cheers and waving of Order Papers. Conservative back-benchers were genuinely ecstatic, and they were determined to outdo the earlier hostile disturbances I had endured. I received an equally warm reception at the back-bench Finance Committee.

But it is a general rule that when something really angers the Labour Party there will be timid Conservative Members who think the Government has gone too far. And this rule was reinforced by my anxiety about how the Budget changes would square with the implementation of the Fowler social security reforms due to come into force in the following month, which although expenditure-neutral, introduced a marked tightening-up of entitlement to some benefits.

Inevitably, the Press reception tended to divide along standard Left–Right lines, which had not on the whole been a feature of my earlier Budgets. The *Guardian*'s political commentator, Hugo Young, wrote that it marked 'the final disappearance of the last vestiges of the postwar consensus ... Fairness and social justice, as registered through the tax system, have ceased even to be the pretended aspiration of the Conservative Party'. My favourite headline from the popular Press was 'Nigel The Tax Terminator' in *Today*, which borrowed from the cover of *Punch* the week before the Budget a portrait depicting me as the sword-wielding Conan the Barbarian, poised to cut taxes. A few months later the editor of *Punch* kindly invited me to lunch, where I was presented with the framed original.

Given that a Budget as controversial as this was hardly likely to be welcomed by those of a contrary political philosophy, my 1988 Budget must be accounted a signal success, in terms both of the reception it secured and, more importantly, of the amount of radical reform it embodied. But for me personally the triumph was marred by the continuing row with Margaret over the exchange rate.

CHAPTER FORTY-SEVEN

THE BATTLES OF DOWNING STREET

After the Hat-Trick · Hammering Out the Concordat · 'You'll Pay for This'
The Four-to-One Rule · Ghosts from the Past

AFTER THE HAT-TRICK

To the political activist on either side, the aftermath of the 1988 Budget must have seemed extraordinary. The Government had achieved the hat-trick – higher spending on public services, lower tax rates and a Budget surplus. Moreover, contrary to what unhistorical commentators assumed, such a hat-trick was not normal in the boom phase of the economic cycle. The missing element in the past had been a Budget surplus, which had last been achieved by Roy Jenkins in 1969/70 with the aid of a good deal of pressure from the IMF following devaluation. Normal UK experience since the mid-1950s was for public expenditure to rise faster than GDP, with control being effected only by periodic sterling crises such as those accompanying the 1967 devaluation or the 1976 borrowing from the IMF. The unusual element in the 1980s was the maintenance of very firm public expenditure control in the absence of any crisis imperative. This, rather than the boom alone, was what made the hat-trick possible.

Yet although the Budget itself was met with widespread acclaim, the passage in the Budget speech dealing with the exchange rate was obviously a compromise, which left a number of options open. The multiplying tribe of City analysts – and even bankers and holders of sterling – were demanding a resolution. In the circumstances, nothing short of ERM membership would have been accepted as a resolution, and that looked further away than ever. Sterling soared after the Budget and looked like breaking above DM3.09. Contrary to City gossip that Margaret had forbidden all intervention, there was a sizeable amount of intervention on Budget Day. Nevertheless the City view was substantially correct. In accordance with my undertaking to Margaret on 4 March, there was to be no further large-scale intervention (not that 'large scale' was ever defined) and any further actions to restrain the pound had to be through interest rates. She had got what she wanted – an end to intervention on any significant scale, and a bias towards unduly low interest rates. But her victory was to prove Pyrrhic.

At the markets meeting I called immediately following the Budget there was universal agreement that the Government could not be seen to be indifferent to the exchange rate. As I had accepted Margaret's veto on any further shadowing of the Deutschmark, there was no point in pretending that there was another hard ceiling at, say, DM3.10. But we did have to demonstrate that sterling was not a one-way bet. The pressure was so strong early the following day, Thursday, 17 March, that I authorised a half-point cut to 8.5 per cent. It did not help relations in Downing Street that the media reported the decision as a defeat for the Prime Minister – which was far from the case, as she never objected to lower interest rates.

HAMMERING OUT THE CONCORDAT

Until the row in March 1988 my personal relations with Margaret had remained generally harmonious; but once she had disowned me in public things could never be the same. All the pundits said that open warfare between the Prime Minister and Chancellor could not be allowed to continue – which meant that they assumed that it would. But an agreed policy clearly had to be hammered out. To this end, Margaret called a meeting in Number 10 for 25 March, ten days after the Budget. Meanwhile the stakes were getting higher. David Young, the Trade and Industry Secretary, made some remarks about the ERM in which he came down rather ineptly on Margaret's side, while the day before the meeting at Number 10 Geoffrey Howe gave me unsolicited support in a speech he made in Zurich, in which he said 'exchange rates have necessarily come to play a more significant role in both domestic monetary decisions and international policy operations'. The same day I received from Peter Brooke, by then Chairman of the Party, and still a Treasury Minister, a letter offering help, encouragement and the assurance of support, but also expressing his concern at the impact of the dispute on the Government. 'I am very conscious', he wrote, 'of how trying it must be at the moment; and that your friends feel for you is, I admit, as much because of your centrality to this Administration and its success as it is because of their profound liking, respect and admiration for you personally.'

It was an extraordinary situation: a private policy meeting between the Prime Minister, the Chancellor, the Governor, and various advisers was treated in the media as if it were a truce meeting between warring generals with trumpets blazing off-stage. As the basis for the discussion, I asked Terry Burns to produce a paper analysing the role of the exchange rate and setting out the options for the future conduct of policy. He made a good job of it. It was, of course, written in full consultation with me, and thus expressed my views as well as his own. But within that context it bent over backwards to try and accommodate Margaret's.

The paper began by explaining how an appreciating exchange rate tightened monetary conditions – for example, by putting pressure on the profit margins of companies that made internationally traded products, whether for the home market or for export. It argued that it also had significant 'secondary effects' in restraining wage negotiations in this sector and reducing inflationary expectations more generally. A depreciating exchange rate had the opposite effects. The paper contained a chart showing clearly the strong connection, over a long period, between exchange rate and interest rate moves. It also cited the increasing role of the exchange rate as an anti-inflationary anchor for many other countries – such as Switzerland, of which Margaret was a great admirer, where the Swiss franc was at that time closely linked to the Deutschmark. It also rebutted the notion that the Louvre Accord had caused the Wall Street crash, citing Paul Volcker in support.

The paper then went on to discuss the problem of speculative capital movements that had caused periodic exchange rate misalignments. The actions of the authorities in such circumstances were important, since they formed part of market expectations. The paper accepted that on rare occasions a conflict could arise between the needs of internal monetary stability and those of exchange rate stability: indeed, one such occasion provided the background to the meeting. In such cases domestic stability should come first. But the paper argued that the resulting exchange rate change should be presented as a realignment and not as abandoning the long-term policy of currency stability.

The paper then listed the three broad options for the future conduct of policy. These were:

1. To take sterling into account in formulating monetary policy, as we had during most of the 1980s.
2. To announce an explicit commitment to exchange rate stability, but within an unpublished band.
3. To join the ERM.

It deliberately did not include the theoretical but, in my judgement, wholly unrealistic option of untrammelled free floating. The last of the three options listed was the easiest to explain and, once credibility had been established, would be a powerful bulwark against inflation. If this at any time produced insufficiently tight domestic monetary conditions, the solution would be an upward realignment rather than abandoning the whole policy.

It is worth noting that this presentation of the ERM was very much geared to the conditions and mood at the time. Thus it did not consider the possibility of a situation in which ERM membership produced excessively tight domestic monetary conditions. Nor did it canvass the so-called 'hard' ERM, in which realignments are eschewed in all but the most extreme and unlikely circumstances, relying on the fact that, if sterling were to be tied more or less irrevocably to the currency of a low-inflation country such as Germany, any period in which domestic monetary conditions in the UK were looser than they ought to be must of necessity be short-lived. But there was no point in exploring the ERM case in depth since there was no chance at that time of persuading Margaret to accept it. The immediate purpose of including the third option was to try and persuade her to reinstate the second option, an informal target range supported by both interest rates and intervention.

After considerable discussion, Margaret and I accepted what the Press began to call a concordat. She conceded the desirability of a measure of exchange rate stability, subject to the overriding importance of sound policies to control inflation. She also conceded a role for intervention, but insisted that it be a much smaller one than before, and said that we should avoid commitments to specific levels of sterling. Her main point was that, however desirable exchange rate stability might be, it should never be an *objective* of policy, or presented as such. This, however, begged the question, which concerned the role of the exchange rate in securing and maintaining the agreed objective of near-zero inflation.

Although clearly better than conflict, a concordat between the Prime Minister and her Chancellor was a pretty rum notion. Rather more seriously, it had been reached by a process of compromise and fudge, which meant that even if it was just about workable as a basis for policy decisions, it was incapable of explicit articulation in the way the markets sought.

When sterling rose above DM3.12 on 8 April the Bank and I agreed that, in the circumstances, there should be a further half-point cut in base rates to 8 per cent. Needless to say Margaret was happy to go along with this. But although I had not yet appreciated the full extent of the boom, it was a cut that ideally I would not have made. I would have preferred a higher interest rate to damp down domestic demand offset by a lower exchange rate to reinforce business expectations of exchange rate stability. But my ability to achieve this combination was fatally undermined by the foreign exchange market's conviction that Margaret favoured leaving sterling to its own devices.

When I went to Washington for the spring meeting of the IMF Interim Committee in early April the international outlook was little better. There had been intervention to support the dollar, but with the Presidential elections looming the Americans were unwilling to support it with higher interest rates. I made a further plea for exchange rate stability, but without going into the sort of detail that I had the previous September. I flew home to find the concordat already starting to fall apart.

'YOU'LL PAY FOR THIS'

On the financial front, sterling was continuing to rise, as the markets now believed there would be no appreciable intervention to restrain it. Politically, too, the situation was getting out of hand. The rift between Number 10 and Number 11 was getting headline and feature treatment by journalists who would normally have walked the other way if anyone had so much as mentioned interest differentials or the policy mix. When I was pressed on the matter on the BBC television programme *This Week Next Week* on Sunday, 24 April, I repeated that I did not want to see the exchange rate appreciate further: 'It would be an unsustainable appreciation. That does nobody any good and is damaging for business and industry.'

I also observed somewhat pointedly that it was 'unfortunate' and 'not sensible' that the question of the exchange rate 'was discussed as much as it was in public, because these are very sensitive matters'. I added, however, that this problem was now 'behind us' and that both the Prime Minister and I were interested in securing 'the maximum possible exchange rate stability within the context of a sound anti-inflation policy'.

I had weighed my words carefully; but perhaps it was inevitable that when, the following evening, in the division lobby of the House of Commons, Margaret beckoned me over for a brief and perfectly amicable discussion of the row that had erupted over the social security reforms which had been implemented a fortnight earlier, some troublemaker told the Press that she had been seen angrily wagging her finger at me. The myth duly appeared in most of the newspapers.

But the real mischief did not occur until Prime Minister's Questions in the House of Commons on Thursday, 12 May when at last Neil Kinnock seized the opportunity that had been staring him in the face for so long. The Labour leader asked Margaret whether she was content to see the pound going on rising against the Deutschmark. She gave an evasive reply, complimenting me on the way in which I had been running the economy. Kinnock then quoted at her my observation that I did not want to see the pound rise further, and believed that any such rise would be unsustainable. 'Does the right hon. lady agree with the point the Chancellor made?' he asked. Once again Margaret was evasive, replying that 'The Chancellor runs the economy extremely well.' Kinnock then rose a third time, asking with uncharacteristic brevity 'That is all very interesting. Can the right hon. lady give us a straight answer? Does the Prime Minister agree with her Chancellor of the Exchequer?' Yet again, Margaret conspicuously refused to say 'Yes', and gave a complete non-answer about the Government having achieved low inflation, excellent growth, high living standards and a high standard of social services.

It was an astonishing and immensely damaging performance. All she had to do was to reply 'The Chancellor and I are in full agreement about everything', which the conventions of Cabinet Government and collective responsibility required, and she would have defused the situation without in any way compromising herself. No doubt few, if any, would have believed her; but Kinnock could not have called her a liar, which, apart from anything else, is an unparliamentary and therefore impermissible expression. But she simply could not bring herself to defuse the situation in the conventional way – and, as a result, made it infinitely worse.

She nevertheless realised that the exchange had, to say the least, not gone well. At the end of Prime Minister's Questions we left the Chamber together, and went straight to my room – the Chancellor's room in the House of Commons is almost immediately behind the Speaker's chair, and the nearest Ministerial room to the Chamber. She was accompanied by the bevy of officials and advisers who helped her over Question Time. 'Was that all right?' she anxiously asked me. She was trying to pretend to herself that her praise of my handling of the economy had somehow saved the day. 'I only hope so,' I replied, grimly; 'but I doubt if we have heard the last of it.' Needless to say, it was manifestly not all right, with the Press buzzing about her pointed refusal to say that she and I were in agreement over the exchange rate; and it was hardly surprising that the following day the pound rose to DM3.18, its highest level since the end of 1985.

That day I had to travel to Travemunde, on the Baltic coast of Schleswig-Holstein, Stoltenberg's political base – the Germans had the European Community presidency at the time – for an informal Ecofin Council. No sooner had I got there when I began to receive reports that Geoffrey Howe had just made a speech to the Scottish Conservative Party Conference at Perth, in which he had departed from his prepared and press-released text to say that the Government could not go on for ever repeating the formula that sterling would join the ERM when the time was right. Needless to say, I had known nothing about this in advance; but coming on top of Thursday's damaging episode in the Commons, Geoffrey's apparent challenge to Margaret on the Friday led to an orgy of speculation in the weekend Press. One story was that she would move me to the Foreign Office and Geoffrey to some other job, thus silencing two turbulent Ministers at a stroke.

I returned from Schleswig-Holstein on the Sunday, and called in my Private Secretary, Alex Allan. It was clear to me that Kinnock, having scored a bull's-eye beyond his wildest dreams, was bound to return to the subject at the next opportunity, which meant Prime Minister's Questions on Tuesday, 17 May. With Alex's help I drafted an answer for her to give to Kinnock's inevitable question. It was carefully designed to indicate that she did agree with me, but in a way that was within the terms of the 25 March concordat. Alex then telephoned his opposite number at Chequers to tell him that I would like to see the Prime Minister privately at Number 10 as soon as she returned that evening.

I went next door to see her after dinner. We met in her upstairs study, alone. I explained that developments both in the financial markets and on the political front had made it clear that her answers to Kinnock on the Thursday had not had the desired effect, and that the Government was now in serious trouble. The only way to save the situation was for her to make it quite clear on Tuesday, when Kinnock would inevitably return to the charge, that she did agree with me. I then handed her the draft answer to read, pointing out that it was fully in line with the concordat.

Amazingly, while she recognised that there was nothing for it but for her to remedy on the coming Tuesday the damage she had done the previous Thursday, she still could not bring herself to indicate that she agreed with her Chancellor. It was conspicuous how, during her last three years in office, she was always eager to claim that her Ministers agreed with her, but found it extraordinarily difficult to say that she agreed with her Ministers.

Rejecting my succinct draft on the grounds that it would not sound right from her, she took up her pen and a piece of paper and embarked on a fresh draft of her own. The atmosphere was calm and businesslike. Her draft was considerably longer than mine, and went into the details of policy much more. We then went over it carefully together, with my making a number of suggestions for changes, some of which she accepted. After a prolonged drafting session – we went over it several times, altering it each time – she called in a private secretary to get it typed. While we were waiting for the typed version, I said that her draft would undoubtedly help – she had made an unexpectedly positive reference to intervention, a subject which my draft had not mentioned at all – but I still felt that the simple affirmation that she and I were in agreement would be far safer.

To my astonishment she suggested that the best way to strengthen the effect of her proposed reply to Kinnock on Tuesday was not to alter the draft we had agreed but to accompany it by a half-point cut in interest rates, from 8 per cent to 7.5 per cent. The May Bank of England *Bulletin* had just infuriated Margaret by declaring that:

> The combination of a stronger currency and lower interest rates does not represent an ideal response to current concerns and a different balance would be desirable if it could be achieved.

It may be that Margaret was determined to snub the Bank's implicit call for higher interest rates. But whatever her reasons, to my eternal regret, I accepted this poisoned chalice. While nothing had been farther from my mind than a further interest rate reduction, I could see when Margaret suggested it that it would clearly demonstrate that we took sterling into account in our interest rate policy; and I was confident that I could reverse it fast enough to prevent it from bringing about a reduction in mortgage rates. And this indeed is what came to pass: I allowed the 7.5 per cent base rate to persist for only a fortnight before reversing it, and mortgage rates never went down at all.

When I returned to Number 11 I gave Alex a copy of the revised draft answer and asked him to keep closely in touch with Number 10 the next day in case Margaret, having slept on it, had second thoughts. I also asked him to fix a markets meeting for the following day, with the usual cast, explaining to him that Margaret and I had decided that interest rates should go down another half point to 7.5 per cent, and that I felt that this could do no harm provided it was a purely temporary move to deal with the current difficulty. The markets meeting was duly convened on the Monday morning, and the temporary half-point cut agreed. The following day, 17 May, the reduction was implemented around midday and then, in the afternoon, came Prime Minister's Questions, with me sitting beside Margaret on the front bench. Kinnock asked the inevitable question, but in terms which filled me with foreboding as soon as he uttered them:

> May I warmly welcome today's cut in interest rates and the Chancellor's victory over the Prime Minister? Does this cut mean that the Prime Minister has changed her position and now wholeheartedly agrees with the Chancellor that further rises in the pound would be unsustainable and would damage British business and industry?

After a short impromptu response on the interest rate cut, Margaret got down to reading the response she had drafted during my meeting with her on the Sunday evening:

> I am sure that he [Kinnock] would like a detailed reply. My right hon. Friend and I entirely agree [interruption] that we must maintain a firm monetary policy and a downward pull on inflation. I agree completely with my right hon. Friend's Budget speech, every bit of it, which is more than the right hon. Gentleman the Leader of the Opposition does.
>
> The right hon. Gentleman asked about exchange rate policy. It is a part of overall economic policy. As I indicated a moment ago, he will note that we have taken interest rates down three times in the last two months. That was clearly intended to affect the exchange rate. We use the available levers, both interest rates and intervention, as seems right in the circumstances, and *[interruption]* it would be a great mistake to think at any time that sterling was a one-way bet.

Our back-benchers were delighted by what seemed an unequivocal endorsement of my policy and the end of the rift between Margaret and myself. William Clark, the long-serving chairman of the back-bench Finance Committee, who had been among those most concerned by the rift, asked her 'Does not today's reduction [in interest rates] prove beyond peradventure that there is complete and utter unanimity in the management of our economy under the capable management of the Chancellor?' Margaret replied with the single word 'Yes'.

If only she had been able to bring herself to utter that single monosyllable five days earlier, there would have been no need whatever for the prepared answer on 17 May – and the question of an interest rate cut would not have arisen. I do not believe for a moment that Margaret had deliberately proffered me a poisoned chalice: it was just that, whereas the thought of saying that she agreed with me was repugnant to her, she was always keen on an excuse to cut interest rates. But there was no doubt that – even though, ironically, it was at Margaret's instigation and not mine – the fact that I had reduced interest rates (albeit for only a fortnight) to 7.5 per cent, the lowest level ever reached during the entire Thatcher era, and that I did so at the height of a boom, was subsequently to do considerable damage to my reputation.

But that was not the only damage the half-point cut inflicted. Kinnock's response that it was a victory for me over Margaret – particularly ironic given the true origin of the interest rate cut – was inevitably, personalities being so much more interesting than economics, the theme of all the newspaper headlines the following morning. It was something that Margaret had never before experienced, and I knew she would hate it. So did Thérèse. 'You'll pay for this,' she said to me. We all did.

THE FOUR-TO-ONE RULE

The official Treasury, understandably anxious to find some firm policy bedrock among all these shifting sands and political turbulence, fell back on a rule of thumb which had apparently emerged from the Treasury's computerised economic model. This was that a 4 per cent rise in the exchange rate was roughly equivalent in terms of its restrictive effect on demand and inflation to a 1 per cent rise in base rates. The equation was based on the sterling index, but it was so rough and ready that it could almost equally well be applied to the DM rate. This had risen by just over 6 per cent since the March uncapping, conveniently equivalent to the 1.5 point cut in base rate which we had made in total since the Budget.

I myself never went overboard for the 4-to-1 rule. Interest rate and exchange rate changes worked their way through the economy by such different channels and through such different sectors that to treat them as equivalent with this degree of quantification was too great a violation of reality even for macroeconomic policy.

But the real problem was not the precise nature of the interest rate/exchange rate trade-off. It was that the overall combination was not tight enough. My critics have subsequently alleged either that I lost interest in the battle against inflation, which is demonstrably untrue, or that I took my eye off the ball. There may be some truth in this latter charge for the brief period of April and May 1988, when I became so absorbed in my battle with Margaret over exchange rate policy that I was unable to devote the attention to the state of the economy that I should have done. But it was soon remedied.

Critics who have focused on the 17 May half-point cut in base rate to 7.5 per cent have got it wholly out of proportion. Because I had never sought it in the first place I was determined to reverse it as soon as practicable. As a result, as I have said, it lasted a mere two weeks, during which it had no influence whatever on mortgage rates. Nor, of course, did I stop there. As the bullish sentiment towards sterling began to falter, as I had expected it would, I raised interest rates by a rapid series of half-point steps to 11 per cent by 5 August. The purpose of doing it by half-point steps was to demonstrate that this was a tightening of monetary policy for its own sake, and not a macho move designed to impress the foreign exchange market in order to protect the pound. The pound did not, in fact, recover its mid-May level against the Deutschmark until late July.

By 22 June I had reversed all the post-Budget base rate cuts, and by 4 July, when base rates were back at 10 per cent I had reversed all the post-crash reductions. By 8 August, I had raised base rates to 11 per cent, their highest level since 1986. Moreover, mortgage rates never fully followed base rates down, reaching a low point of 9% per cent in May, which lasted for less than three months before they were on their way up again. In 1988 as a whole, UK *real* short-term interest rates averaged well over 5 per cent, compared with 3.5 per cent in the US and 3 per cent in Germany – not high enough, but hardly the degree of laxity with which some have charged me.

The monetary tightening in the late spring and summer of 1988 was a relatively harmonious process, with Margaret, for once, in agreement with the interest rate increases I proposed. By this time, moreover, I had become worried about the massive expansion of mortgage lending on prudential grounds. It did not seem to me conceivable that lending growth at this rate, and in the indiscriminate way anecdotal evidence made it clear was occurring, could possibly be prudent. I was confident that I could prevail upon the Building Societies Commission, headed by the former Treasury official Michael Bridgeman, with whom I had worked closely when I was Financial Secretary, to lean on the building societies; but this would work only if the Bank of England could be prevailed upon simultaneously to lean on their competitors in the mortgage market – the clearing banks, whose supervisory authority was the Bank.

Astonishingly, the clearing banks had totally failed to recognise that the relentless interest rate increases in the summer and autumn of 1988 presaged difficult times ahead. Just as management exacerbated the cost of defeating inflation by obstinately continuing to negotiate excessive pay awards, so the banks worsened the pain of disinflation for themselves and their clients by imprudent expansion of their loan books. My particular concern with mortgage lending derived from the key role the housing boom was playing in the overheating process. This was not least because of its effect on public psychology – in effect, the excess of optimism, to which I referred in Chapter 33.

Accordingly, in May 1988 I convened a meeting in my room at the Treasury with Robin and his key Bank of England officials, including the head of banking supervision, Brian Quinn, to encourage them to lean on the clearing banks on prudential grounds. I pointed out that, if they did, I was confident that the Building Societies Commission would do the same with the building societies. They declined to make any serious attempt to do so. I tried, on more than one subsequent occasion to persuade the Bank to ask the clearers to be more prudent in their mortgage lending, but with similar lack of success.

The reason the Bank gave, at my May meeting, for its refusal to act was essentially threefold. First, the Bank's duty as supervisor was the protection of depositors, and in its judgement there was no risk to bank depositors. Second, there was no threat to the banking system as a whole, in the sense of a core bank getting into serious difficulties, even though some loans were bound to turn sour. In particular, there was no danger in the UK of a collapse on the lines of the Savings & Loan debacle in the United States. (The spectacular UK failures of the early 1990s were in the commercial property sphere.) Third, mortgage lending was probably the safest form of lending in which the banks engaged, secured as it was on domestic bricks and mortar: it would not make sense to caution the banks about this form of lending, when much of their lending to business and industry was less well secured or even unsecured.

While there was undoubtedly substance in all these arguments, I believe that at the more fundamental level at which central bank thinking ought to be pitched the Bank was both unimaginative and misguided. In the first place, the grossly imprudent bank lending which took place in 1988 and 1989 may not have led to the collapse of any core bank, let alone the collapse of the banking system as a whole. But it gravely weakened it – something which ought to have been of concern to the Bank of England. And in the second place, while it is true that mortgage lending is in normal times the safest form of lending, there are three important qualifications to be made.

The first is that when it leads to the sort of house price bubble that occurred at the end of the 1980s, which at some point was bound to burst, this type of lending is less secure than it seems. Second, the credit-based house price bubble of the late 1980s, by creating an exaggerated impression of personal wealth and prosperity, led to a great deal of other borrowing and lending of a less secure nature. And third, it was inevitable that at some point the burden of rising mortgage payments would mean that other forms of spending would be cut back, thus making much other lending even less secure. A central bank needs to be aware of these connections, and of their implications.

The Bank's strongest argument for inaction was probably the one that it left unsaid: that the commercial banks, driven by a desire to maintain and if possible increase their share of the mortgage market, come what may, would have taken no notice of a call for greater prudence and caution from the Governor of the Bank of England. But although it was true that the Bank's authority had diminished over the years, I very much doubt if it had vanished completely. And if the worst came to the worst, it would have been better to have tried and failed than not to have really tried at all.

GHOSTS FROM THE PAST

The summer of 1988 was a time for the return of two ghosts from the past. The first of these was our old friend the current account balance of payments deficit. This took a marked turn for the worse in 1988. I was giving a press conference in support of the Conservative candidate at the Kensington by-election that had been caused by the death of the sitting Member, the redoubtable if lonely back-bencher, Brandon Rhys-Williams. I had said my usual piece about the fundamental strength of the British economy, when one of the journalists present asked me how I could possibly claim that the economy was strong when the May current account figures, which had just been published, had shown an unexpectedly large deficit, and all the City pundits were preaching doom and gloom. I light-heartedly replied that I would not advise him 'to take too much notice of the teenage scribblers in the City who jump up and down in an effort to get Press attention'.

There are, of course, a very small number of economists of distinction and perception who work for various City firms. But, allowing the element of polemical exaggeration in the adjective 'teenage', so far as the generality is concerned my remark was as accurate as it was unwise. Not only was it deliberately misconstrued as an attempt to dispute the accuracy of the analysts' revised forecasts of the current account for the year as a whole; but I was seen as belittling the entire self-important tribe of City analysts. For the rest of my time as Chancellor, they were determined to get even and were unremitting in their hostility towards me – something I could have done without.

However, the more threatening ghost from the (more recent) past was Alan Walters. In July 1988 I got wind of the news that Margaret was negotiating with him for his return as her personal economic adviser, the post he had held between 1981 and 1983 before leaving to take up a couple of academic posts in the United States. This caused me considerable concern. Between 1981 and 1983 he was a relatively little-known figure who worked quietly behind the scenes. But once he had escaped from the conventions of the civil service he had traded heavily on his self-proclaimed importance as Margaret's economic *éminence grise* and became a minor celebrity, giving his forceful views to the Press at the drop of a hat. All this had rather gone to his head. The fact that, by 1988, he was writing articles in the UK Press attacking me and my policies, made matters considerably worse; but it could not make sense, as I saw it, for a Prime Minister to have as a special adviser anyone as opinionated as Alan Walters, when their opinions have been widely publicised and become so well known, and when they continue to feel free to utter them irrespective of Government policy.

I went to see Margaret privately to express my concern. We met in the white state drawing room of Number 10. I told Margaret that I did not for one moment dispute her right to have her own personal economic adviser if she felt she wanted one. But I foresaw serious trouble ahead if she gave the job to Walters. His hostility to various aspects of Government policy was well known; and he had become far too high-profile to be able to reassume the conventions of civil service discretion. She replied that he had done an excellent job when he had worked for her before; and she had never wanted him to leave. Now he had accepted her request to him to return, and she could not go back on that. I repeated why, in my judgement, to reappoint him would cause considerable trouble for the Government, which we could well do without; and for the Government's sake, I begged her to think again. But she had clearly made up her mind.

For good measure, however, I went to the Whips' Office and told a more or less complete gathering of the Government Whips of my concern and foreboding: they were entirely sympathetic; but, so far as I am aware, David Waddington, the Chief Whip, took no action of any kind. The mandarins for their part, appeared to be under the illusion that Walters would do less damage 'inside' Whitehall than outside, as his views would be properly circulated and rationally discussed, instead of creeping through the back door into Margaret's personal brief. They did not realise how much he had changed since his departure from full-time Government service in 1983. In his second incarnation, he attended only a small number of meetings and when he did he kept very quiet, giving the impression he was keeping his real opinions for his tête-à-tête talks with Margaret, and was there merely to gather ammunition.

In the short term the political fall-out from Walters' activities was entirely favourable to me. This was the third time that Margaret had appeared to disown me within a few months – first by torpedoing my exchange rate policy in early March, then by conspicuously failing to back me over the 'unsustainable' rise in sterling in mid-May, and finally by refusing to disown Walters' remarks and by taking an unconscionable time before getting her Number 10 staff to tell him to desist from further public pronouncements.

Parliamentary colleagues who had no interest in monetary or exchange rate policy – and even some who did not particularly like me personally – were enraged that a non-resident economist should be treated, in John Smith's words, as an 'unelected Chancellor' and allowed to rock the boat in the way he was doing. On the evening of 19 July I was given a resounding vote of confidence at a packed meeting of the Party's back-bench Finance Committee, at which the back-benchers banged their desk to show their approval of me and disapproval of the way Margaret was treating some of her Cabinet colleagues. Ian Stewart, my former Economic Secretary, who since the 1987 election had been Minister for the Armed Forces, wrote to me on 20 July:

> I have been appalled (and astonished) at the circumstances to which you have been subjected these last few days. I had hoped and thought that things had got back to a reasonable working relationship with next door after the previous bout of public angst. Anyway, you have my profound sympathy and I know you have the same from most of our colleagues.

One back-bencher told *The Times* after the Finance Committee meeting that I was 'unsackable'. William Clark, the chairman of the Committee, wrote to me a few days later to say that 'there was no question as to your standing in the Party'. Margaret herself did not respond to this unaccustomed display of back-bench concern until Prime Minister's Questions on Thursday, 21 July, when she fell back on the usual generalities that I was pursuing 'excellent economic policies'. Later, at the final meeting of the 1922 Committee of all Conservative back-benchers before the 1988 summer recess, she declared that I had 'handled the Crash marvellously' and that the Budget was 'quite the best Budget we have seen. Brilliant in concept, brilliant in drafting and brilliant in delivery.' 'Unassailable' could not be far away.

CHAPTER FORTY-EIGHT

MY LAST STRUGGLE WITH INFLATION, 1988/89

Locked into Number 11 · On to 14 per cent · The Ludicrous RPI
Why Not Overkill? · Mythical Golf Clubs · My Balance of Payments Heresy
A Self-Correcting Mechanism?

LOCKED INTO NUMBER 11

Margaret had no intention of making it easy for me to resign in the summer of 1988, when my standing within the Party was still high. It was not that, however, which kept me at Number 11, but the increasing signs of overheating in the economy. I had a word with Peter Brooke, whose disinterested and shrewd political judgement I valued, one evening when we were both stuck at the House just before the July reshuffle. I told him that I was fed up with Margaret's behaviour, and was thinking of telling her that she should use the occasion of the reshuffle to find a new Chancellor. We went round and round the subject, in my room at the House, and the next day he sent me a note summing up his view:

> Your friends (and our benches) would reject outright a charge of 'cut and run', but Smith (who has touches of Asquith about him) would lend it a gravitas not available in Sparkbrook.[37] I am conscious this is more a Treasury and Party view, but it does have a personal component too: I recognise it would not be decisive against any new class of cruiser (HMS Intolerable, HMS Impossible etc.) but it should weigh.

I took the point; but was still wondering whether I had taken the right decision when, on 22 August, I was given advance warning of the trade figures for July which were due to be published three days later. The current payments

[37] The constituency of Roy Hattersley, John Smith's predecessor.

deficit for the month was put at a staggering £2.2 billion; as large as that for the previous two months, which had been bad enough, taken together. It was clear to me that demand in the economy was pressing against the limits of capacity to a much greater degree than I had previously realised, and that decisive action was required. It was not the current account deficit itself which concerned me: quite apart from its changed significance in the new global economy, our foreign exchange reserves stood at all-time record levels. It was the message it conveyed.

I had already surprised the financial markets with my half-point increase in base rates to 11 per cent on 8 August. On learning of the July trade figures I immediately drove from Stoney Stanton to Downing Street to see Margaret and told her that I believed we should raise interest rates by a further full point to 12 per cent on 25 August, the day the figures were due to be published. She was even more shocked by the figures than I was, since she attached importance to them in themselves rather than, as I did, as a symptom of something else. I informed my officials, asked them to arrange a markets meeting with the Bank on 25 August to decide the nuts and bolts, and returned to Stoney Stanton to resume my summer break. Fortunately, confidence in sterling was still robust.

In retrospect the August trade figures and the consequent rise in base rates marked the turning point in my Chancellorship. It was then that it finally became clear just how strong the boom was, and the difficulties I would have in curbing it if inflation was not to get out of hand. It was then that my colleagues realised that I was no longer the miracle worker that some had imagined me to be. It was then that I recognised that there could be no thought of resignation: I owed it to the Government and myself to see the thing through.[38]

ON TO 14 PER CENT

Needless to say, I was far from alone in hoping that 12 per cent base rates would do the trick. Indeed, with real interest rates at 6.5 per cent, the prevailing view both in business and industry and among my parliamentary colleagues was that they were already too high. Some economists took a similar view. I recall the domestic monetarist, Patrick Minford in autumn 1988 inveighing against the 'savagery' of a four-point rise in interest rates in under three months. But by the late

[38] Later revision of these figures showed a rather different picture, with a sharper deterioration in the first quarter – and on a rising rather than falling trend. Had these figures been available at the time, sterling would likely have been weaker and policy tightened that much more quickly. The shock figure for July was also substantially lower on revision (£1.4 billion rather than £2.2 billion). And even in their revised form the figures included a £6 billion 'balancing item'. In truth, the official statistics had a large fictional component.

autumn there was uncomfortable evidence that domestic demand was continuing to increase too rapidly.

The recorded current account deficit had initially subsided somewhat after the then all-time record of July. Indeed, by September it had apparently fallen back to some £600 million. But then came the next bombshell: towards the end of November I was informed that the current account deficit for October had come out at £2.4 billion, larger even than that of July. Moreover, other indicators – such as retail sales, underlying inflation, mortgage commitments, manufacturers' margins, house prices and earnings – were by then telling a similar story. There had also been an acceleration in the growth of M0 to 7.75 per cent, well above the 1 to 5 per cent target range. It was clear that interest rates would need to be raised again. At the markets meeting I held, my advisers were divided, but I settled for a further one-point increase to 13 per cent.

As in August, I timed the interest rate increase to coincide with the publication date of the trade figures – which also happened to be the day I was due to travel to Birmingham to present the Midlands Businessman of the Year Award, under the auspices of the Variety Club of Great Britain. In the circumstances, my audience was remarkably civil and good-natured. But it was a reminder of the unwisdom of agreeing to undertake commitments of that kind on a day on which significant economic statistics were scheduled for publication.

The interest rate rise also took place in the middle of the six-day debate on the Queen's Speech which, at the start of each session of Parliament, sets out the Government's programme for the coming parliamentary year. By tradition, the opening speaker for the Government on the final day of what is technically known as the Debate on the Address is the Chancellor. Not surprisingly, I had a pretty sticky time when I spoke on 29 November. The only memorable contribution that day came from Ted Heath, not normally a great phrase-maker, when he said:

> In golfing terms, the Chancellor could be described as a one-club man, and that club is interest rates. But if one wishes to take on Sandy Lyle and the rest of the world one needs a complete bag of clubs. The Chancellor flatly refuses to have that. He has turned down any other measures to influence the economy.

The accusation that I was a 'one-club golfer' stuck. It was an excellent example of how a good phrase can transfigure a bad point. As the contents of this book amply demonstrate, I was engaged in implementing a whole range of measures, not least tax reform, to 'influence the economy'. But interest rates are the essential means of curbing inflation, just as a golfer confines himself to the use of his putter for putting.

As it happened, after six months during which I had felt obliged to raise interest rates by almost as many percentage points, there then followed six months during which they remained unchanged at 13 per cent. But in the second half of May 1989, there were clear signs that sentiment towards the pound, which I had expected to turn sour considerably earlier, had at last begun to do so. There was nothing dramatic about sterling's weakness, but there was no mistaking the change in the market climate; and it was a change across the board, not simply against the Deutschmark, since the early months of 1989 had witnessed a modest recovery in the dollar. At the same time, evidence that the steady monetary tightening that I had embarked on as far back as the beginning of June 1988 was cooling the economy down adequately was disappointingly thin on the ground. In particular, bank and building society lending in May 1989 was still growing at an annual rate of over 23 per cent – precisely the same explosive rate of growth as when I began the tightening about a year earlier.

I was due to fly to Spain for an unusually important informal Ecofin Council meeting on Friday, 19 May. That morning, I called a markets meeting with a view to increasing base rates by a further percentage point to 14 per cent – the highest level since the sterling crisis of January 1985. In addition to the usual cast I invited Alan Walters, who had just arrived back as Margaret's personal economic adviser. Curiously, the Bank, which the previous November had toyed with the idea of moving straight from 12 per cent to 14 per cent, was now in two minds as to whether we should move to 14 per cent at all. Walters, who arrived late for the meeting, said that in his opinion 13 per cent was quite high enough. My senior Treasury advisers, like me, felt uneasy at the prospect of leaving things as they were.

I decided to defer a final decision until my return, when on Tuesday, 23 May, there was a further run on the pound. So far as I was concerned, that clinched it. The following morning Margaret reluctantly went along with my proposal to move base rates up a further point, from 13 per cent to 14 per cent. Politically, the timing could scarcely have been more awkward: I was due to address the annual Conservative Women's Conference that afternoon; and for the first and only time that normally well-mannered congregation gave me a rough ride.

WHY NOT OVERKILL?

Looking back, it may be argued that I should have deliberately gone in for shock treatment, and raised interest rates much more sharply in the early stages. This might have led to a more pronounced recession; but it might well have started to bite much sooner and lasted less long. Hindsight is a wonderful thing. At the time, even what I did do was considered pretty severe. Moreover, the real problem, for which I had not bargained, was the extraordinary slowness of borrowers and, even more, of lenders to react to the tightening. My interest rate moves represented a sharp change of policy fully backed by tough talk. Had I foreseen the inability of the credit markets to grasp the inevitable consequences of this – and I vividly recall spelling out some of them in radio interviews at the time – I would indeed have gone in for a greater degree of shock treatment.

The figures tell the story. Bank and building society lending had been growing at a steady rate of between 16.25 per cent and 18.25 per cent from the first three months of my Chancellorship in 1983 up to and including the third quarter of 1986.[39] It then rose to an annual rate of growth of 19.5 per cent and stayed in the 19.5–20.5 per cent range until 1988, when it surged further ahead. The peak annual growth of 24.75 per cent was in the first quarter of 1988. Lending then continued at a remarkably high rate, despite the very high level of interest rates, right through to the middle of 1990: it did not fall below an annual growth rate of 19.25 per cent until the third quarter of that year. From then on, of course, it fell rapidly, as the economy slid into recession.

The extraordinary and unforeseen continuation of the rapid expansion of bank and building society lending, right through to the middle of 1990, two years after the sharp monetary tightening began, is a major reason why the boom went as far as it did; why the banks and so many of their customers subsequently got into difficulties; why the subsequent recession was as bad as it was and lasted as long as it did; and why the recovery was as delayed as it was. In other words, my own misjudgements were enormously compounded by the mistakes of the private sector in general and of the banks in particular.

Throughout this period I was not helped either by the composition of the generally accepted measure of inflation in the UK, the Retail Price Index or RPI, which ludicrously and perversely included mortgage payments. Not only are mortgage interest payments not a retail price in any normal sense of that term, but their inclusion meant that the principal means of fighting inflation – raising

[39] The quarterly figures are the growth over the same quarter of the previous year.

interest rates – showed up as an increase in the rate of inflation, with knock-on effects (particularly to pay negotiation) that made the cost of fighting inflation higher.

Few other countries followed Britain in this respect, understandably enough. But changing the measure proved impossible, not least because when index-linked gilts were first introduced in 1981, the Treasury and the Bank of England had agreed that the prospectus for each issue should contain an undertaking to the effect that, if the RPI were materially changed in any way which was disadvantageous to holders of the bonds, the holders had the right to demand immediate repayment in full at par. Most were well below par at this point.[40]

MYTHICAL GOLF CLUBS

The advocates of shock treatment were few and far between, and would almost certainly have melted away had it been put into effect. More serious politically were those who urged me to find other weapons, apart from interest rates, to use against inflation. A refrain that has frequently punctuated this narrative has been the desire of those who should have known better for a painless technical gimmick to secure low inflation, a call that came from left and right alike. I gave this wishful thinking no quarter, telling the House on 7 June 1989 that there was no alternative to setting interest rates and holding them at the level needed, and for the time needed, to do their work.

It was not difficult to rebut the simple-minded advocates of direct controls, who tended to be chiefly concerned about credit cards and hire purchase. I needed only to point out that some 85 per cent of total household debt consisted of mortgages. Credit card and hire purchase lending taken together amounted to only a little over 5 per cent of total household debt. So it was absurd to imply that introducing controls on hire purchase or credit cards would do anything significant to reduce the growth of consumer credit, or to allow interest rates to be one whit lower. In any event any such controls would have been simplicity itself to get around in a deregulated financial market without exchange control. As for direct controls on bank lending; these had proved increasingly ineffective even before exchange control was abolished. By the late 1980s they would simply have provided a field day for foreign lending institutions.

---

[40] [2010 note] In 2003 the UK abandoned the RPI as its principal official measure of inflation, and aligned with the rest of the European Union in adopting the Consumer Price Index (CPI). Subsequently, in December of that year, the Bank of England's monetary policy remit was also redefined in terms of CPI inflation. For legal reasons, index-linked gilts remained linked to the RPI, even though they had recovered to well above par. The CPI contains no reflection of house price inflation at all, and has been frequently criticised on that account.

The novel feature of the 1989 debate was the alliance between left-wing financial columnists and right-wing City critics who both supposed that there must be sophisticated methods of controlling the money supply which would slow down monetary and credit growth without having to ration credit by interest rates. The devices usually suggested had been aired for a very long time, such as Monetary Base Control, attractive to Margaret for that very reason and much discussed when I was Financial Secretary. Although I did not share the Bank's abhorrence of MBC, I had no doubt, either at the beginning or the end of the 1980s, that it was essentially just another way of generating the level of short-term interest rates needed to curb inflation. It was in no sense an alternative to high interest rates – as the Americans discovered during Paul Volcker's experiment with MBC in 1979/81, when short-term interest rates at times exceeded 20 per cent.

Another frequent variation on the same theme, which was taken up both by the Labour Opposition and within the Cabinet by Peter Walker, then Welsh Secretary, was a variable assets ratio for the banks. I explained to him that his proposal reflected a common misunderstanding about the way in which monetary policy operated in Germany, and in some other countries as well. In normal circumstances, the German banking system was short of reserve assets and the Bundesbank operated regularly in the course of each month to provide the required reserves, normally by means of repurchase agreements against the banks' holdings of public debt. The key to the system was the price at which the Bundesbank provided reserves. This set the level of short-term interest rates in the economy, and it was changes in the level of interest rates which represented the mechanism for monetary control. What the Bundesbank system did not do (and still does not do at the time of writing) was to operate a direct quantitative control on credit. There was no question of the Bundesbank refusing to supply the quantity of reserves that banks needed.

Thus in essence the German system was little different from that operated in the UK by the Bank of England. As in Germany, the banks normally needed assistance from the central bank to build adequate reserve holdings. It was the price at which the authorities provided the cash that they needed, by way of money market operations, that set the level of interest rates. The only substantive difference between Britain and Germany was that in Germany there were mandatory, and much larger, reserve requirements – idle balances so far as the banks were concerned. The high German reserve requirement did not make German interest rates any lower: it merely encouraged the Frankfurt banks to escape the impost by channelling business through offshore centres such as Luxembourg, to the annoyance of the Bundesbank. This explanation had, in fact, been given numerous times in the Bank of England *Bulletin*. But the myth was so much more attractive than the bleak reality that it seemed indestructible.

Yet another technocratic attempt at a painless short cut was overfunding. I have already chronicled the Government's unhappy experience with this in the early 1980s. The only effect of overfunding – insofar as it has any effect at all – is to make long-term interest rates slightly higher relative to short-term rates; which is scarcely a solution to anything. I told the *Weekend World* Sunday lunchtime television audience that unless we were to bring back mortgage queuing, which would soon be circumvented and would be grossly unfair on first-time buyers in the meantime, people had to adjust to the new climate of freedom and borrowers had to learn self-discipline. Until they did, interest rates, at whatever level was necessary, would have to hold the balance.

MY BALANCE OF PAYMENTS HERESY

I have mentioned earlier that I always sought to make my speech to the annual Fund and Bank meeting more interesting by developing some original thinking on a topical economic issue. At the 1988 meeting, which was held in West Berlin, I chose as my heretical theme the thesis that the balance of payments on current account did not have the central importance as an indicator of success or failure that popular comment supposed. This thesis did not, in fact, come as a bolt from the blue. I had touched on it at the spring meeting of the Interim Committee in 1987 and had discussed it on several subsequent occasions, most fully in my IEA lecture in July 1988 on the 'State of the Market'.

As the title of that lecture suggests, it was a serious if broad-brush account of my thinking on a number of prominent issues, including the superiority of the market economy, privatisation, deregulation, tax reform, monetary policy and the exchange rate, as well as the current account of the balance of payments. Needless to say, the popular Press concentrated exclusively on the passage dealing with the exchange rate, where their interest was in perpetuating the story of the rift between Margaret and myself. On the exchange rate I had the temerity to state the following:

> With separate national currencies in an international financial marketplace, it is inevitable that the exchange rate plays an important part in determining monetary conditions. So governments have to come to

> terms with the behaviour of the foreign exchange market. Left entirely to its own devices, we have seen in recent years how destabilising and disruptive that behaviour can sometimes be.

The journalists could not wait to tell Margaret's Press Secretary, Bernard Ingham, that I was once again attacking the Prime Minister; and he did nothing to discourage them from the most troublemaking interpretation possible. This duly enabled him to describe my speech in his press summary for Margaret the next morning in these terms:

> While you defend the Chancellor and praise his Budget and handling of the stock market crash, he makes a speech to IEA which is interpreted as yet another 'declaration of independence'.

This interpretation was then backed up by selective extracts from various newspapers, starting with one from Ingham's favourite organ, the *Sun*:

> I'll do it my way – Lawson puts job on line in row with Maggie. But he receives a pat on the back from you. His speech is an amazing challenge to your authority and a massive gamble over his future.

Since Margaret never read the daily newspapers herself, and relied entirely on the daily press summary Ingham prepared for her, the effect of this sort of poison, week in, week out, month in, month out, on Margaret's attitude towards me is not hard to gauge.

But to return to my balance of payments heresy: my proposition was not that the current balance of payments could be ignored. No piece of economic information should be thrown away. My point was that the current balance of payments deficit was not like a company running at a loss – 'Britain in the red', as the headlines were inclined to put it. As I explained to the IEA:

> A better analogy is with a profitable company raising funds externally either by borrowing or by raising new equity. A company with greater investment opportunities than it could finance from retained profits would look for additional funds from outside. A country in a similar position will draw on the savings of the world, which is particularly easy in today's global markets.

I accepted that part of the UK current deficit was a symptom of an excessively rapid boom at home, but went on to say:

> But that is only part of the story. For there is no iron law that the private sector's finances must be in balance, in any given year or indeed any given period of years. Sometimes savings will exceed investment; sometimes investment will exceed savings. If domestic savings exceed domestic investment, there will be a capital outflow and a current surplus; if domestic investment exceeds domestic savings, there will be a capital inflow and a current deficit.
>
> Looked at like this, it would in fact be very surprising if the current accounts of the major countries were always in balance. Net capital flows are inevitable and indeed desirable, given differing propensities to save and differing investment opportunities. And a country whose investment opportunities are sufficiently attractive to generate a net capital inflow will by definition have a current account deficit.

The dethronement of the current account balance as a sensible objective of policy can also be seen as a consequence of financial deregulation. In a world of rigid foreign exchange controls, a current account deficit could be financed only by a country running down its foreign currency reserves, which was clearly something that could continue only for a very short time. It was this state of affairs which justified the IMF emphasis on the balance of payments in the post-war world, and its continued preoccupation with the balance of payments of its clients in the Third World and the former Soviet bloc, whose enterprises do not have a sufficient credit rating to borrow on the private international capital market.

In today's world, by contrast, an advanced industrial country that can maintain a reasonable degree of confidence in its currency can finance a current account deficit for a considerable number of years – as for example the United States did – by importing capital from overseas. This in turn can be seen in terms of the relationship between savings and investment. For a mixture of cultural, historical, institutional and economic reasons, countries differ in their savings ratios. Similarly, profitable investment opportunities vary from country to country. While these things, of course, change over time, at any given period those countries whose capacity to generate savings exceeds their indigenous investment opportunities will experience a capital outflow, which will finance the current account deficits of those countries whose capacity to generate savings falls short of their indigenous investment opportunities.

I concluded this section of my IEA address by saying that, given a firm financial framework, a period of private-sector-induced current account deficit should give no cause for concern. But the proviso about a firm financial framework is crucial. It has a number of facets. As I explained:

- It depends on the public finances staying in balance. The current account deficits of the 1970s reflected excessive Government borrowing and spending, which it was certainly the Government's job to correct.
- It means remaining vigilant for signs of inflationary pressure, whatever the source, and standing ready to tighten monetary conditions by raising interest rates whenever such pressures emerge.
- And it implies not accommodating increases in costs by a depreciation of the exchange rate.

These provisos are frequently forgotten both by critics of my balance of payments thesis and by those who accept it too readily.

A SELF-CORRECTING MECHANISM?

The IMF staff – not surprisingly in view of the history of the organisation – were initially sceptical of what I was saying. However, a remarkably similar analysis crept into the IMF's *Economic Outlook* in the following year. In a sense all I was doing was harking back to the assumptions of an earlier age. No Chancellor of the Exchequer in the days of the classical gold standard before the First World War – the only previous occasion when complete freedom of capital movements existed – lost any sleep over the balance of payments. Indeed, since the only figures available then were for visible trade, and these were even less accurate than those we have today, he had little idea of what the size of the UK current surplus or deficit was. It is, incidentally, interesting that six out of the eight economies for which reasonable data for that era are available ran current account deficits averaging more than 2.5 per cent of GDP – that is, in terms of the UK and the money of 1992, more than £15 billion – in the years prior to 1914.

Treasury officials, notably Terry Burns, continued to defend the downgrading of the current account at hearings of the Commons Treasury Committee after my resignation in October 1989. But in the absence of a Ministerial lead, efforts to develop the Lawsonian heresy further – at least for public consumption – inevitably lapsed. Be that as it may, a number of practical questions clearly arise from my thesis. For example, how does one distinguish between a current deficit that is a symptom of domestic overheating and one that reflects merely the normal international flow of borrowing and lending? Domestic overheating apart, when – if ever – is a current deficit excessive? When is a currency depreciation the right answer?

So far as the first question is concerned, there is no foolproof way of deciding if a deficit is a sign of overheating. But a clue is provided by changes. A deficit that has been running for several years without much change and been readily financed is unlikely to be a symptom of inflationary pressure. But a sudden increase, such as that experienced in the UK when it went from zero in the early part of 1987 to some 4 per cent of GDP in 1989, is indeed likely to be a sign of such pressure. The second question, whether a purely private sector deficit can ever be too great, is more difficult. The answer I suggested in my September 1988, IMF speech was in two parts. I mentioned first:

> ... the arithmetic of debt accumulation and debt service costs. Persistent large imbalances do become a problem as flows compound and therefore by definition become unsustainable. But even for deficits of the size we have seen recently in the major countries, this problem emerges quite slowly. As the OECD has suggested, the effective constraint is not so much the size of the current account imbalance as the country's overall creditworthiness, in which net overseas assets play an important part.

But this was clearly an extreme and unlikely constraint; and in general I was sceptical of the case of Government action even when the deficit was due to low net private sector savings. Here I came to the most controversial part of my speech, the 'self-correcting' doctrine:

> The main source of fluctuations in net savings is changes in the amount of borrowing by the private sector. There is a limit to the amount of debt which the private sector will be willing – or can afford – to undertake. Once that limit has been reached, the savings ratio will rise again. Moreover higher debt means higher interest payments in the future, which will reduce disposable income and consumption ... It is only in the unlikely event that the self-correcting mechanisms threaten to stretch over so long a period that the

> creditworthiness constraint to which I have alluded comes into play that it would be appropriate for the Government to run a large budget surplus in order to offset the lack of private sector savings.

The heart of the matter was that the obsession with the current balance of payments was a hangover from the period when the Government was expected to manage the whole economy. A corollary of the switch to market ways of thinking in the 1980s should have been that the Government was responsible for its own finances and the private sector for its finances. If the Government's finances are in order, then excessive borrowing, whether at home or overseas, is a private sector matter, which will be automatically corrected. For the non-bank private sector does not have access to a lender of last resort and cannot get out of its debts by depreciating the currency. As for the self-correcting thesis, the UK experience of the early 1990s showed clearly that it does indeed operate. The savings ratio, after falling very sharply, did indeed rise again as borrowing was cut back severely. But it can be a painful process. And meanwhile the Government's finances went into sizeable deficit.

Needless to say, my IMF speech was not intended as a purely theoretical dissertation. I had a number of practical objectives, of which probably the most important was to question the automatic assumption that a country which was running a deficit of, say, 2 per cent of GDP was an automatic candidate for devaluation, and one running an equivalent surplus was an automatic candidate for revaluation. In the first place there might not be a problem at all. But even if there were, it is the savings/investment balance which should be tackled in the first place.

It is when a normal stabilisation programme would require a country urgently to deflate costs and prices that depreciation should be considered. It is probably most appropriate for a country such as Poland, re-entering the world market economy after a period of rigid controls during which its cost levels had been allowed to lose touch with the rest of the world. In a normal Western economy, persistent unemployment is much more likely to be a symptom of labour market failure than an overvalued currency; and frequent devaluations will serve only to entrench a high inflation mentality without improving job prospects at all.

CHAPTER FORTY-NINE

TOWARDS AN INDEPENDENT BANK OF ENGLAND

An Accident-Prone Month · The Tape that Never Was
An Independent Bank of England · Margaret Thatcher's Response

AN ACCIDENT-PRONE MONTH

November 1988 was the most accident-prone month of my Chancellorship. The day before the Queen's Speech I had a late night at a charity gala. Unfortunately, I had to get up at six the next morning, as usual, to go through my boxes, and got very little sleep. As we all stood there in the House of Lords listening to the Speech, my eyes momentarily closed. It was only for a split second; but with the whole thing recorded live on television it was a simple matter for that particular frame to be frozen and the photograph published in all the papers alongside one taken at the gala, with a 'morning after the night before' story.

The much more serious gaffe had occurred a little earlier that month. It had always been my general policy to avoid mass briefings on 'lobby terms', a phrase that means that full use may be made of what is said provided that both direct quotation and direct attribution are avoided. Obviously I had private conversations with individual journalists, but press conferences in which journalists are expected to restate one's words in lobbyspeak ('senior Ministers are concerned that ... ') seemed a recipe for misunderstanding and trouble. If I had something to say, it was better to put it in my own words and take the responsibility.

However, there had been four annual exceptions to this: the meeting with the journalists who composed the parliamentary lobby proper after both the Budget and the Autumn Statement, and the meetings with the political correspondents of the Sunday papers, who called themselves the Sunday lobby, on the Friday after the Budget and the Autumn Statement. When Robert Culpin became Press Secretary we agreed on two important but unrelated innovations. The first was that the two briefings of the parliamentary lobby paper would be entirely and explicitly on the record: the status of my two Sunday lobby briefings would be clearly established at the time. The second innovation was that all my on the record conferences at the Treasury and at Number 11 would be openly – indeed ostentatiously – taped. This was partly so that the Treasury knew exactly what I had said, but partly for my own protection against misquotation or misrepresentation.

Despite these sensible precautions, the briefing I gave the Sunday lobby after the 1988 Autumn Statement, on Friday, 4 November, proved a total disaster. Margaret was on her travels, and most of the senior political correspondents were with her, so it was for the most part a rather less experienced second eleven who attended my briefing at Number 11. Robert Culpin had just ceased his long and successful stint as my Press Secretary, and this was the first lobby briefing at which his new and at that time inexperienced successor, John Gieve, had officiated. There was confusion over whether the briefing was on the record or on conventional lobby terms: he had said nothing at the meeting itself, but when he was asked afterwards he said it was on the record, believing this to be my wish. When he reported this to me, I told him that, on the contrary, I had been speaking on lobby terms. He agreed to telephone those who had been present to explain the position. This was embarrassing for him and sounded very suspicious to them; but I was not too concerned because (as I thought) I always had the tape transcript to fall back on.

The reader will recall that the main purpose of the Autumn Statement was to set out the Government's public expenditure plans, and that the main drama in 1988 had been over the continued freezing of child benefit. It was no great surprise, therefore, when the journalists' questioning concentrated on social security issues, particularly since there had been a Tory back-bench revolt over charges for eye tests that very week. What was a great surprise, and shock, was the banner headlines in the Press the following Sunday, alleging that I was planning to do away with universal benefits for pensioners, in particular, in favour of means testing; and to cease uprating a number of benefits in line with inflation. These highly coloured scare stories were backed by leading articles, of which the worst was probably that in the *Mail on Sunday*, which pontificated 'The Government's determination to 'means test' every single benefit available from the State to the ordinary citizen will be met with predictable cries of outrage.' Even the *Sunday Mirror*, no friend of the Government's, had conceded that 'the state pension is safe'.

What, in fact, I had said, according to one of the journalists' shorthand notebooks that subsequently came to light, was that 'We have to see in the evolution of the social security system whether we can do better, so that we can help the minority of pensioners who genuinely do have difficulty in making ends meet.' My purpose in all this was to head off the pressure for a general increase in pensions, over and above inflation; and I made my remarks in the knowledge that John Major (as Chief Secretary) and I were already engaged in discussion with the Social Security Secretary, John Moore, about a targeted scheme to provide additional help to the oldest and neediest pensioners.

THE TAPE THAT NEVER WAS

When this damaging travesty appeared in the Sunday papers, I got hold of John Gieve as soon as I could and told him to publish the full transcript of the meeting as the best means of killing the story. It was only then that he revealed, to my horror, that – due to his own inexperience – he had failed to set the tape-recorder properly, as a result of which nothing had been recorded at all: there was no transcript. Furious though I was at this, the real villains were clearly the members of the Sunday lobby; and when I agreed to appear on the radio programme, *Today*, on the Monday morning, I laid into them for their fevered imagination and deplorably low standards, which led them to publish stories that bore no relation to what I had said.

The Opposition clearly thought they were on to a winner. The same day, Monday, 7 November, Neil Kinnock tabled a Private Notice Question to me asking me to make a statement on my intention to introduce further means-tested benefits for pensioners. This was the first occasion in more than thirty years that a Leader of the Opposition had asked a Private Notice Question of anyone other than the Prime Minister: the normal convention is for a Minister to be asked a Private Notice Question by his opposite number. I replied simply that:

> I have no such intentions except in one respect. I have been discussing with my right hon. Friend the Secretary of State for Social Security a scheme to give special help to poorer pensioners. This would be over and above the existing level of benefits. We shall announce the outcome of this consideration in due course.

This did not prevent the mild-mannered and normally sensible Labour back-bench social security expert, Frank Field, from saying 'We in the Labour Party have rarely got our teeth near an election winner. We have one today and we do not intend to take them out.'

However, one of the journalists who had been present at my briefing, Jack Warden of the *Sunday Post*, had taken full shorthand notes of the meeting, and had decided there was nothing worth publishing on the Sunday. He made his notes public in the *Daily Telegraph* and *Evening Standard* early the following week. They entirely corroborated my own version of the incident. I was reminded of the true story of a distinguished political correspondent I knew who, many years previously, when he had first become a member of the lobby, was telephoned by his editor one night to demand why he had not got a story which, as the first editions showed, the other papers were all running. My friend explained that he had not filed the story because he happened to know that it was not true. 'That doesn't matter,' his editor replied, 'if the others have all got it, we must have it too.'

That does not mean that Governments cannot make good use of the lobby system: they can and do. The prime example is the Number 10 press secretary – in Margaret's time, Bernard Ingham; but other Prime Ministers' Press Secretaries before him had done much the same, albeit in a very different style. This works, however, because the Number 10 Press Secretary is such a regular source of information that no journalist is likely to risk biting the hand that feeds it. By contrast, a Minister whose contacts with the lobby are few and far between has no such leverage.

But by the time the full account – with which I had no quarrel – of what I had actually said came out, the Press had changed the subject. The new issue that transfixed them was the mystery of the missing tape. The following Sunday the *Sunday Times* ran the banner headline 'Lawsongate' – a reference to Nixon and Watergate – strongly implying that I had been guilty of suppressing the tape because of its incriminating nature, and by implication lying about it. A number of other papers took a similar line, despite the fact that, as the full account had shown, I had no motive whatever to suppress it: indeed, its absence was a severe handicap to me. As a result of my November 1988 experience I never gave another briefing on lobby terms, nor did I ever again speak to the Sunday lobby.

AN INDEPENDENT BANK OF ENGLAND

But for me the most important event of November 1988 was my submission of a five-page memorandum to Margaret on 25 November setting out a carefully worked-out proposal for an independent Bank of England – a proposal I first revealed publicly in my resignation speech to the House of Commons eleven months later. I had first thought seriously of the idea during the summer recess of 1988. When I returned from holiday in September of that year I amazed and horrified my officials by asking them to devise a concrete proposal for an independent but accountable Bank of England. When they realised that I really meant it, a small but high-level group was formed, which worked with the utmost dedication and in the greatest secrecy throughout the autumn, with periodic meetings with me. The Bank of England was not told: it was important that the Government should make up its own mind itself.

The purpose of my proposal was to entrench the use of monetary policy to fight inflation and secure price stability. This would be a far more useful constitutional reform than any advocated by lobbyists. Part of the background to it was the repeated rejection by Margaret of ERM membership. An independent Bank was to some extent an alternative way of entrenching the commitment to stable prices and, as I put it in my paper, 'making it a permanent feature of UK economic policy, while at the same time assisting us in the completion of our present task'.

An independent Bank would not, of course, have had the merit of ERM membership of replacing discretion by rules. But it would at least, in the words of my paper, 'be seen to be locking a permanent anti-inflationary force into the system, as a counterweight to the strong inflationary pressures which are always lurking'. In particular, it would do something to 'depoliticise interest rate changes'. I also sought to persuade Margaret that an incidental advantage of creating an independent national central bank, with a proper statutory framework, would be to demonstrate that we did not envisage the absorption of the Bank of England into a European central bank.

The advantages I envisaged sprang not from the illusion that the Bank of England possesses any superior wisdom, but from the logic of the institutional change itself. I was certainly not proposing to hand over responsibility for monetary policy to the Bank of England for it to interpret in any way it liked. I had in mind a Bank working under a completely new statutory framework, with an explicit statutory obligation to preserve the value of the currency. Three important consequences would flow from this. First, monetary policy decisions would be taken not by a Government, which has a number of objectives, but by a central bank statutorily charged with the achievement of one sole objective. Second, unlike Ministers, who are subject to political and electoral pressures, central bankers would be largely immune to such pressures. An incidental consequence of this is that international financial co-operation is likely to be very much easier between independent central banks, all charged with the same task, than it is between governments with different domestic electorates to appease.

But third, and in many ways most important, even if there were to be a Government genuinely committed to put the conquest of inflation above all other objectives, and genuinely determined to ignore all political and electoral pressures to stray from the path of virtue, it would never enjoy the same degree of market credibility that an independent central bank has. And this extra market credibility is what would make the successful conduct of monetary policy less difficult. It is no accident that it was the independent Bundesbank, and not the German government, that possessed the market credibility to be the anchor authority for the ERM.

At first sight, without a written constitution, it might seem that the independence of the Bank of England would be pretty flimsy. But I argued that there would in practice be powerful market sanctions against the repeal of the legislation by a future Government: the mere announcement of the intention to do so would be so damaging to confidence that a future Government would be extremely reluctant to attempt it. The longer and better the independent Bank's track record, the more powerful this sanction would be.

Despite its deep dislike of the loss of power involved, the official Treasury, on investigating the matter, had to concede that the change was technically feasible. The Bank would be responsible for setting short-term interest rates and monetary targets, while the Government would remain responsible for the exchange rate regime. The Bank would then carry out monetary policy within that framework. Of course, all sorts of examples can be constructed in which there is a tension between the two assignments. Yet there is a similar division of responsibility in both Germany and the US, which works better than the UK arrangement under which, so far as monetary policy is concerned, the Bank of England takes its marching orders from the Chancellor of the Exchequer. Anyone looking for perfection will not find it in this world.

I concluded my minute by saying that the proposed change 'would provide a beneficial jolt to inflationary expectations and would help lock into the body politic of this country a permanent anti-inflationary force'. My plan was to publish a White Paper on Budget Day of 1989 and have the necessary legislation introduced in November of that year.

MARGARET THATCHER'S RESPONSE

When, a few days later, I discussed my paper with Margaret, I was disappointed but not surprised to find her wholly unreceptive. She did not ostensibly reject it out of hand, but argued that it was something that could be considered only when inflation was low and coming down. At the time of our discussion the latest headline rate of increase in the RPI was a shade under 6 per cent, and edging higher; and although the more reliable underlying rate was lower, at 5.25 per cent, it too was edging higher. In those circumstances, she contended, an announcement that the Government proposed to hand over the responsibility for monetary policy, and thus for the fight against inflation, to an independent Bank of England would look as if the Government were admitting that, after all, it was unable to bring inflation down itself, which would be highly damaging politically.

There was undoubtedly something in this, although at the time I did not myself consider it a decisive argument. No-one at that time expected inflation to go on rising as much as it did or for as long as it did. The Treasury forecast in the Autumn of 1988 was that headline inflation would peak at under 7 per cent in the summer of 1989; and by November 1989, when I had suggested the Bill be introduced, the forecast suggested that headline inflation would be back to around 5 per cent and edging lower. I saw no problem in introducing a Bank of England (Independence) Bill in those circumstances. In the event, of course, headline inflation in the autumn of 1989, when I revealed my proposal in my resignation speech, was some 7.5 per cent, and the underlying rate a shade over 5 per cent. Moreover, even then few expected that – partly thanks to the effect of the Poll Tax, and partly to the temporary effect of the Gulf War on oil prices – it was not to peak for a further year, at a shade under 11 per cent on the headline basis and a true underlying rate of 7.5 per cent.

Nevertheless, a long historical look suggests that the 1990 bulge in the rate of inflation was indeed a blip rather than a change of trend. Yet it did not seem so at the time, and might not have remained so without the firm and unpopular, if belated, action I took on interest rates in 1988/89. Indeed in October 1988, when I discussed the proposal with Margaret, base rates were already at 12 per cent, implying almost 7 per cent in real terms, on the basis of the underlying RPI – and, of course, the rate for borrowers is always appreciably above base rate. I certainly did not feel that I was running away from the measures needed to bring inflation down, and proposing to pass the baton to an independent Bank of England as a gesture of defeat. On the contrary, I was anxious above all to entrench our counter-inflationary commitment and policies against the vagaries of future governments, possibly of a different political complexion.

Even so, I would have been content for my proposal to have been put on the back-burner until not merely the Treasury forecast of inflation, but inflation itself, was coming down, had I believed that that was Margaret's sole concern.

However, I strongly suspected she was using the unripe time argument over an independent Bank of England just as she had used it over the ERM. And as the discussion developed I became increasingly convinced that her opposition to the idea went far beyond the question of timing.

She seemed quite incapable of accepting the possibility that there might be another Government some day, and that it was in the national interest to entrench counter-inflationary policy against that eventuality. So far as she was concerned, she really was going to go on and on and on, as she had told a television interviewer she would. While she was there, she was not going to give up the levers of power which the control of interest rates, as she saw it, represented.

It was, in a sense, the ERM argument all over again. Unlike the ERM, however, there was at least no problem of losing face, even though by that time this undoubtedly told against any proposal, at least in the monetary policy and exchange rate area, that emanated from me. I concluded that my best bet was indeed to come back to it later, but in the meantime to choose a good moment to get the proposal into the public arena, in order to secure a groundswell of back-bench support – which I felt was, on this issue, a considerably better bet than my Cabinet colleagues. In the event, the preoccupations and problems of my final year in office prevented me from getting round to this; and it was indeed to make up for my failure to do so when in office that I launched the proposal publicly in the most high-profile way, in my resignation speech of 31 October 1989.

It appeared to have the desired effect. Support for the proposal from senior back-benchers was considerable, and the serious Press began to take up the issue. The Labour Party was predictably hostile; but the Liberal Democrats, in order to differentiate their product, duly espoused it. So, more significantly, did Michael Heseltine, who made it one of his policy planks in his campaign to succeed Margaret in 1990. However, despite the fact that Margaret had departed, and Michael was once again a senior Cabinet Minister, the Government formed by John Major after the election victory of 1992 showed no sign of movement on this issue. I sense that its time will come – as indeed it should.[41]

It is, incidentally, sometimes forgotten that the Conservative Party, under Margaret Thatcher, stated in its 1977 policy document *The Right Approach to the Economy* that 'we favour a more independent role for the Bank of England'. Although that was only some eighteen months before we took office for the first

---

[41] [2010 note] And indeed it did, in 1997. See new final chapter.

time, nothing became of it. In fact, it is not difficult to see why. A close reading of the text shows clearly that what was envisaged was a Bank of England with an independent voice but with no independence of action – the sort of ill-considered if well-intentioned compromise that Oppositions, who are themselves condemned to voice without action, tend to espouse. A moment's reflection reveals that this would achieve the worst of all worlds. Whereas a genuinely independent Bank of England, responsible for setting interest rates in the context of a statutory obligation to promote price stability, could greatly enhance credibility, a central bank empowered only to criticise publicly the economic policy of the Government of the day would, in fact, diminish credibility. All the same, the 1977 policy document could be a foundation on which to build.

In Heathite terms, it may be argued that what I proposed would turn the Chancellor of the day from a one-club golfer to a golfer who has to remain in the clubhouse because he has no clubs at all. But this serves only to demonstrate the folly of the original analogy. With responsibility for monetary policy transferred to an independent Bank of England, a future Chancellor would still have everything that a Finance Minister in a country with an independent central bank has to do.

That is no sinecure, including as it does the control of public expenditure; tax reform; the whole of the rest of the supply side, from labour market measures to privatisation; and a whole raft of international financial issues, both within the European Community context and in the wider world – to name but a few of the non-monetary matters that occupy a large part of this book.

For good or ill, however, there was a limit to how much I could brood over these issues at that time. Within a very few weeks of presenting my proposal for an independent Bank of England I was fully occupied with the 1988 Autumn Statement, after which I had to get down to preparing what was to prove my last Budget.

CHAPTER FIFTY

1989 – MY LAST BUDGET

Down to Earth at Dorneywood · Colleagues Against Alcohol
The Search for Savings Incentives · Envoi: A Fair Deal for Married Women

DOWN TO EARTH AT DORNEYWOOD

Since I now had the use of Dorneywood, it would have been absurd to have decamped to Chevening for the traditional January Budget planning weekend. Because of its modest size, however, there was no possibility of providing overnight accommodation at Dorneywood. This meant no wives, and concentrating on getting through the business in a single day – Saturday, 7 January. The Dorneywood staff rose to the occasion magnificently, and everyone was well looked after. We made an early start, and succeeded in finishing by dinner time; leaving those who wished to do so to stay on after dinner for snooker and bagatelle.

The Dorneywood bagatelle book, in which anyone who makes a score of a thousand or more is invited to record the event for posterity, goes back quite a long way, with Churchill's one of the earlier signatures. A little application enabled me to add mine to the long and distinctly mixed list.

The background to the 1989 Budget was clear: the overriding need to ensure that the inflation blip remained only a blip. This meant that interest rates, which at the turn of the year stood at 13 per cent, would have to be kept high enough for long enough to put inflation on a firm downward track, whatever the short-term cost.

The usual pre-Budget economic paper warned that the struggle could be harder and longer than the official forecasts envisaged. Consumers might choose to borrow even more to sustain their standard of living through what they might imagine would be a temporary monetary squeeze. The net wealth of the personal sector was still sufficient to allow banks and other lenders to churn out yet more credit. That would postpone the adjustment in behaviour, and necessitate higher interest rates for longer, increasing the eventual agony by raising the overall level of indebtedness. That is more or less what happened. All forms of personal borrowing continued to increase sharply in 1989 and even in the first half of 1990.

The official forecasts for once slightly overstated the growth of output; but they continued to understate its *level* and therefore the pressure it was putting on resources. However their biggest flop by far was the inflation forecast. The rise in the headline RPI, which had reached 6.5 per cent in the last quarter of 1988 was expected to decline steadily to 4.5 per cent by the second quarter of 1990. In the event it rose unsteadily to 9.75 per cent in that quarter before peaking at not far short of 11 per cent in September and October of 1990. The error was due to the failure to forecast the momentum of the rise in underlying inflation, which required further interest rate increases not expected by the forecasters, thus magnifying the rise in the headline RPI, thanks to the absurd inclusion of mortgage interest payments in the index. On top of that, the Whitehall machine failed to foresee either the full impact of the Poll Tax on the index, or (with considerably more excuse) the short-lived rise in oil prices following Saddam Hussein's seizure of Kuwait in August 1990.

So far as the Budget itself was concerned, I consciously aimed at a surplus – of no less than £13.75 billion, similar to the latest estimate of the outcome for the previous year. This still allowed me to reduce taxation by almost £2 billion in the coming financial year. Half of that – rising to four-fifths in a full year – went on a National Insurance reduction for the lower paid.

Nevertheless, I did not want the 1989 Budget to be called a 'Budget for the Poor'. To do so would be inviting the 1988 Budget to be indelibly labelled a 'Budget for the Rich', with 1989 as a penance for it. More fundamentally, such a label would have entrenched just the sort of confusion between the tax system and the social security system from which I was trying to get away: that is to say, the misconception that tax cuts are handouts, like benefits, but differ from them because they are usually given – with immoral perversity – to the rich. In fact the tax system, as I saw it, was about how much was taken from people and how it was taken, with a view to what was best for the economy. It was the purpose of the social security system to help the poor. Indeed, I never liked the idea of budgets 'for' any particular section of the population. They were intended to benefit the economy and thus the country as a whole.

As it happened, the 1988/89 Budget surplus turned out, at £14.75 billion, to be even higher than expected, while that for 1989/90 eventually came out somewhat lower at just under £8 billion. Such variations are to be expected given the vagaries of the economic cycle, interest rate changes and so on. But I was still well on target for the medium-term aim of a balanced Budget.

Because of my deliberate policy of allowing surpluses to accumulate in years of above-trend growth, the Government repaid in the three years to the end of March 1990, as I told the House of Commons, 'roughly a sixth of the public debt that had accumulated over more than two centuries'. But I was anxious to scotch the idea of repaying the whole National Debt as an objective of policy, which had attracted Margaret and which Cecil Parkinson had misguidedly promoted in public speeches. I specifically rejected the idea as 'deferring for a long time the benefits of a reduction in the burden of taxation'.

In 1989/90 the economy actually slowed down somewhat faster than the official forecasts envisaged; but the starting point was a higher level of activity and of pressure on resources than was realised; and both the current account balance of payments deficit and the inflation rate continued to rise and did not start to turn down until the following financial year. As in 1987 I omitted to revalorise the excise duties, at a cost of just over £1 billion. At a time of large Budget surplus this temporary way of shaving the top off what was then forecast to be a brief blip in the RPI seemed worth trying. But the recrudescence of inflation proved to be a rather more substantial blip than that of 1985.

COLLEAGUES AGAINST ALCOHOL

My failure to revalorise the excise duties was despite the fact that I had received – as in the previous year – a solemn deputation from a group of colleagues Margaret had asked to look at all aspects of the problems of alcohol, particularly among the young. It was headed in 1989 by the then Home Secretary, Douglas Hurd, and came to Number 11 to plead the case for an increase in the excise duties on alcohol on grounds of social policy. Though deeply unpopular with the general public, increases in the duties payable on alcohol always meet with almost as much approval among the *bien pensants* of Parliament and the serious Press as do increases in the tobacco tax.

This perennial puritanism was lent additional weight in 1989 by the fact that Margaret had become greatly concerned about football hooliganism the previous summer, and had set up a committee to explore methods of combating it. It led, *inter alia*, to the launch in January 1989 of the ill-fated Football Spectators Bill, which aimed to establish a national football club membership scheme. The committee also concluded that alcohol consumption by football hooligans might be reduced if its price were increased through higher excise duties. This was unlikely. If experience was anything to go by, hooligans would simply consume less of the more highly taxed drinks and more of the less highly taxed ones. For that reason, raising the excise duty on alcohol – unlike petrol, the demand for which is almost completely unaffected by an increase in the duty – rarely raises the tax yield. However, it does have a disproportionate effect on the Retail Price Index, as the Hurd delegation was well aware.

THE SEARCH FOR SAVINGS INCENTIVES

Savings incentives were at the time much in vogue. I learned on the grapevine that Margaret had held an informal seminar at Chequers on the subject the previous autumn without inviting me – an instance of her growing desire to keep me at a distance. If any good practical ideas had emerged I would presumably have been made aware of them, so it was clear they had not.

Despite that, as previous chapters have made clear, I was interested in the idea of fiscal incentives to increase savings in the long run. The problem was that most such incentives simply substituted the transfer of existing savings from one medium to another at the expense of the Exchequer. What I did not believe was that fiscal incentives of this kind could help in reducing inflationary pressure in the short term. I was in no doubt that the best short-term deterrent to borrowing was a sufficiently high interest rate. As I was to say in my Budget speech, 'inflation is a disease of money; and monetary policy is the cure. The role of fiscal policy is to bring the public accounts into balance and to keep them there and thus underpin the process of re-establishing sound money.'

Base rates were already 13 per cent and I reaffirmed that interest rates 'will stay as high as is needed for as long as is needed'. I also said, in a passage which bears on the depth of the recession of the early 1990s:

> The question of just how 'soft' or 'hard' the so-called landing will be is not in the hands of Government alone. The Government's task is to reduce inflation by acting through monetary policy, to bring down the growth of national income in money terms. The task of business and industry is to control their pay and other costs. The more successfully they do so, the less costly in terms of output and employment the necessary adjustment will be.

I did, in fact, take the opportunity to increase the attraction of PEPs, as outlined earlier. In addition I raised the annual limit on employee share schemes and on SAYE share option schemes as well as trying to encourage employee share ownership plans (ESOPs). Deterrents to unit trust investment were removed.

I also introduced the cap on occupational pensions, whose long-term effects I have already discussed and which led to a vitriolic pamphlet from the National Association of Pension Funds, entitled *Truth, Honour and Democracy*. The most awkward resistance, however, came from within the official machine. The cap on tax relief applied to public sector pensions as well as private. The Treasury mandarins made a determined – but unsuccessful – attempt to persuade me to exclude them. I am sure they have subsequently secured adequate compensation for this setback.

ENVOI: A FAIR DEAL FOR MARRIED WOMEN

Although it has nothing whatever to do with the 1989 Budget, ostensibly the subject of this chapter, it is fitting to conclude my accounts of the tax changes for which I was responsible during my six years as Chancellor with the reform which, I believe, is least likely to be reversed by any of my successors. I refer to the independent taxation of married women.

Income tax law, as it stood when I first entered Number 11, made no bones about married women being second-class citizens. In a form of words unchanged for the best part of two centuries, it roundly declared that 'A woman's income chargeable to pay income tax should be her husband's income and not hers.' However simple this made life for the Inland Revenue, in the 1980s it was, I felt, an unacceptable anachronism, completely denying married women either independence or privacy in their tax matters. It is true that the system had been, to some extent, mitigated in 1914 by the introduction of the option of separate assessment, which allowed a wife to file her own separate tax return and receive her own separate assessment for tax. But the basis for that assessment remained unchanged: her income was still taxed as if it were her husband's.

The old system was indefensible in pecuniary terms, too. Under it a husband enjoyed a married man's allowance amounting to rather more than one and a half times the single person's allowance. A wife who was earning enjoyed the wife's earned income allowance, which was the same as the single allowance, while a non-earning wife had no allowance at all. Thus a couple with two earners would have a combined allowance equivalent to roughly two and a half times the single allowance, compared with roughly one and a half times the single allowance for the couple where only the husband was an earner.

This seemed to me manifestly unjust. A couple where the wife ceased paid work to have, and look after, a baby suffered a double blow at that point: not only did the wife's income disappear, but the tax system turned against them, too. Moreover, because there was a wife's earned income allowance but no allowance at all for savings income, the system was particularly harsh on a wife who had managed to accumulate some savings of her own. This, coupled with the fact that the wife had to reveal the full details of her savings to her husband, since the income from them was taxed as if it were his, was an increasing source of resentment. Finally, in most cases the old system meant that there was a financial penalty on marriage, as distinct from living together unmarried.

There had already been one Green Paper on the subject of the taxation of husband and wife, produced by Geoffrey in 1980, but the response had been inconclusive. It certainly showed that the status quo had very few friends, but as so often, there was no agreement whatever over the various options for change that were clearly set out. Despite Geoffrey's strong desire to right this wrong, the unhelpful response to his Green Paper, coupled with Margaret's pronounced hostility to doing anything at all (partly, I suspect, because she believed it was all inspired by Geoffrey's wife, Elspeth), ensured that no further action was taken.

It therefore fell to me, when I became Chancellor in 1983, to pick up Geoffrey's baton. It seemed to me that the next stage should be a White Paper, setting out the Government's preferred option. After careful study, I came to the firm conclusion that this should be a system of independent taxation, with the allowances freely transferable between husband and wife. This would remedy all the grievances created by the old system.

When I discussed this with Margaret, however, she made it clear that she did not like the idea at all, and felt that there was nothing really wrong with the status quo. She was emphatic that a White Paper was out of the question. Although my officials had warned me of her views, I had expected a woman, and a married woman at that, to be more receptive to the strong sense of grievance felt by so many married women about the old system. But it was clear that, despite her oft-pronounced and no doubt deeply felt belief in the importance of the family, in practice she strongly identified with the two-earner couples, who (in financial terms) were the beneficiaries of the old system. I suggested that there was a long-term electoral bonus to be secured from being the party that emancipated married women so far as the tax system was concerned. She countered by claiming that all we would do was alienate working wives, on whose votes we depended.

En passant, I have to say that I have never liked this distinction between 'working' and 'non-working' wives. There are, of course, idle married women, but they are very few. Most of the wives who are described as 'non-working' are so described because they work at home (frequently very hard) and not outside it, have no employer and receive no wage. Moreover, among a very large number of pensioner couples, it is often the so-called non-working wife (and pensioner wives were bound to be particularly numerous among the beneficiaries of any move to independent taxation) who works the harder of the two.

Be that as it may, I clearly had my work cut out if I was to get anywhere on this issue; but I was disinclined to give up. Following the success of my 1984 Budget, in which I radically reformed company taxation, Margaret accepted my proposal that I should have a go next at reforming personal taxation, and that this should be preceded by a Green Paper.

Although the Green Paper procedure is not one to which I was often attracted, least of all in the field of tax, my 1984 Budget had propelled tax reform into the centre of the political debate, certainly within the Conservative Party. As a result, there were a number of reforms being floated (or re-floated), such as a tax credit scheme, involving a degree of integration of the tax and benefit systems, along the lines that had been proposed, but never enacted, by the Heath Government, and the amalgamation of the National Insurance Contribution and income tax systems, which had been exhaustively studied within the Treasury (under the unattractive acronym NICIT) during Geoffrey's last year as Chancellor.

Both these proposals were superficially attractive, and could not be dismissed lightly; on the other hand, I had pronounced reservations about both. A Green Paper seemed to me the best means of getting the disadvantages as well as the advantages of these schemes into the public arena – which should then give me a freer hand to introduce those reforms I wished to bring about. Moreover, I pointed out to Margaret that, if we were going to have a Green Paper on the reform of personal taxation, we could not avoid a chapter on the taxation of husband and wife, which we had left hanging since Geoffrey's 1980 Green Paper. On the clear understanding that this was a Green and not a White Paper that is to say, a basis for discussion without any commitment on the part of the Government – she consented to this, and agreed to my announcing the Green Paper in my 1985 Budget speech.

This I duly did, and took the opportunity to make the case for a system of independent taxation with transferable allowances. I explained it in these terms:

> Everyone, man or woman, married or single, would have the same standard allowance. But if either a wife or a husband were not able to make full use of their allowance, the unused portion could be transferred, if they so wished, to their partner.
>
> This reform would produce a more logical and straightforward system. Far more people would be taken out of the poverty and unemployment traps, and indeed out of tax altogether, for a given sum of overall tax relief, than is possible under the present system. It would end the present discrimination against the family where the wife feels it right to stay at home, which increasingly nowadays means discrimination against the family with young children.

Under the scheme I had in mind, the revenue for providing the wife with her own personal allowance under the new system would in essence have come from phasing out the 'bonus' enjoyed by the two-earner household. I proposed to move gradually to the new system, on the 'no cash losers' principle. This is always possible so long as there is inflation: while I would far rather have seen inflation eradicated, if one is suffering all the evils it brings, it is folly not to put it to good use when one can.

At the time of the Budget I had planned to publish the Green Paper in the autumn of 1985. I entrusted the work of drafting it to Frank Cassell, a senior Treasury official (and Kent cricket fanatic) who had originally been a financial journalist and was a master of good, clear English: he did an excellent job. But any thoughts that I was home and dry were soon disabused when Margaret insisted that that particular chapter would have to be cleared by an *ad hoc* Cabinet Committee which she would chair. It required a large number of meetings, at which I was ably supported by John Moore, then Financial Secretary, and was quite a struggle.

Margaret showed herself to be out of sympathy with the project altogether. A number of spending colleagues, in particular Norman Fowler, then in charge of the DHSS, saw it as a plot by me to outflank Cabinet by pre-empting for tax cuts resources that otherwise might have been available to increase public spending. This was not, fortunately, an argument that had much resonance for Margaret; but she insisted that what I was proposing was the wrong kind of tax cut: the right way to help families with children was by reinstating the old child tax allowance – a proposal of singularly little merit which I knew to be a hobby-horse of hers (she was always proposing it).

I was rather more surprised to find it enthusiastically supported by Norman. Fortunately I was able to head it off, with the help of David Young, whom I had seen privately and demonstrated to him the benefits of my proposed scheme in terms of the so-called unemployment trap. In addition, although not of course on the Committee, the formidable Emma Nicholson, whom Margaret had made women's chairman at Central Office, was a strong supporter, and I persuaded her to lobby Margaret with her customary vigour.

In the end, Margaret reluctantly agreed to authorise the publication of the Green Paper on Budget Day in 1986 – insisting yet again that she was doing so only because it was a Green Paper and therefore did not commit the Government to acting on it – despite the strong preference it expressed for independent taxation with transferable allowances.

I had hoped that the response to the Green Paper would be so strongly favourable that I could use this as the clinching argument for action at long last. Unfortunately, it was nothing of the sort. Very few ordinary people responded at all – although those who did were generally in favour. Response came for the most part from the various women's lobbies and pressure groups, many of which had their own pet scheme they wished to promote. Moreover some women, whose support I had hoped for, argued that transferable allowances would destroy all the gains to privacy that they and I both sought, since husbands and wives would still have to reveal their incomes to each other to decide which of them should have the allowance. This surprised me, since the wife for whom privacy was important could always purchase it cheaply enough by letting her husband keep the transferable allowance.

What I plainly lacked was the mandate for action for which I had hoped. There was a real risk that, as a result, we would be left with the status quo – the one thing that almost everyone agreed they did not want. Still determined to find some way out of the maze, I drafted a holding statement for Norman Lamont, who had taken over from John Moore as Financial Secretary in the 1986 reshuffle, to make in the course of the 1987 Budget debate. The key passage went as follows:

> The Government do not yet feel that there is sufficient support to take a decision now to go ahead with so far-reaching a reform ... We will be considering the matter further and will be exploring whether there is any satisfactory halfway house to the approach in the Green Paper.

At the time, I had not the faintest idea what any 'halfway house' might be; but there the matter rested until after the 1987 general election. Reconfirmed as

Chancellor, I resumed discussions with the Inland Revenue. By now the earliest I could act was in the Budget of 1988, and the Revenue warned me that the implementation of a system of transferable allowances was so complex that, with the computerisation of income tax still being bedded in, there was no way my preferred scheme could start before 1993. That was the other side of the *next* general election, and I was determined to have a scheme up and running during the lifetime of the parliament that had just begun.

So a halfway house it had to be, and one without fully transferable allowances. When I got down to it, it did not take too long to work out the specification of the new system. There would be genuine independent taxation, with everyone, man or woman, married or single, having the same standard allowance, being legally responsible for their own tax return, and being taxed at the rate appropriate to them as individuals. The allowances would not be transferable.

On top of that, however, all married couples would have an additional married couple's allowance (equivalent, initially, to the difference between the single allowance and the married man's allowance, but which ideally should be allowed to wither on the vine). This would, for administrative simplicity, initially go to the husband; but in the event of his not having the income to make use of it, he would be able to transfer it to his wife. On this basis, the Revenue assured me, they could have a scheme legislated for in 1988 up and running in 1990.

I decided to go ahead. Although inferior to independent taxation with fully transferable allowances, it was so superior to the old system, and went so far towards remedying all the existing grievances, that it would have been folly not to go ahead. But there was still the matter of persuading Margaret. I decided that, for once, I could make good use of the Party Conference. I was due to reply to the debate on the economy and taxation on 8 October 1987, and the chairman for that session was to be Joan Seccombe, then vice chairperson of the National Union (the organisation representing the voluntary Party workers), and an ally on this issue. I invited Joan to Number 11 before the Conference, and she agreed to call in the debate a number of women speakers who were likely to be in favour of independent taxation. She did, and they were; enabling me to begin my reply to the debate with some ostensibly impromptu opening remarks:

> I was struck by the number of speakers today who raised the question of the tax treatment of married women. Let me say to them, and to

> you, Madam Chairman, that I agree that the traditional tax treatment of married women is no longer acceptable, and that change will have to come.

Margaret, who was on the Conference platform alongside me, heard for herself the tremendous cheer that pledge evoked. When we returned to London, I told her that I had revised my plans for independent taxation in the light of the views she had expressed, and remarked on the strength of feeling expressed at the Party Conference. I gave her a persuasive outline of the 'improvements' I had made, and said that I wished to announce the reform in the coming Budget and legislate in the 1988 Finance Bill, with a view to embarking on the new system in 1990. She asked to see a paper on it, but agreed in principle.

Thus it was that, at long last, independent taxation came into being, and for the first time married women were given a fair deal by the tax system. The announcement in my 1988 Budget received a warm welcome on all sides, and the Revenue kept to their side of the bargain with implementation in 1990. In both his 1991 and 1992 Budgets, Norman Lamont sensibly refrained from indexing the Married Couple's Allowance, and attracted no criticism for so doing. Moreover, he was able to announce in 1992 that the one discriminatory feature I had been obliged to leave in the system, the payment of the Married Couple's Allowance in the first instance to the husband, which at that time was all that the Revenue could administratively cope with, would as from 1993 be removed. The couple would opt to which one of them it should go, with it split down the middle if they were unable to agree.

Throughout the rest of my time in the Commons, I could still get a cheer among an audience of women whenever I wished by referring to independent taxation. Yet it came to pass only after the best part of five years' struggle by me, built on the foundations of four years' battle by Geoffrey. The moral is clear. The achievement of worthwhile radical reform requires the continuity in office of a single Party for a considerable period of time, and preferably a similar continuity among its senior Ministers, too.

CHAPTER FIFTY-ONE

EUROPE AND THE DAWN OF EMU

1985 and the Single European Act · The Role of Jacques Delors
My Opposition to Monetary Union · The Road to 1992
Margaret Thatcher Unites Europe

1985 AND THE SINGLE EUROPEAN ACT

In writing this account of my time as a Minister, and in particular my unusually long time as Chancellor, I have tried to inject a degree of coherence by dealing with different issues in different chapters in a broadly logical sequence. But in one sense this gives a false picture of the job, since the overriding reality is that, to a considerable extent, everything is happening at the same time. Perhaps the abrupt leap from the independent taxation of married women to the issues of Europe in general and Economic and Monetary Union in particular serves at least to give a flavour of the true nature of Chancellorial life.

I observed in an earlier chapter how, in retrospect, 1985 was in many respects a watershed year: it was then that all the elements that were to bring about the downfall of Margaret Thatcher five years later originally emerged. This was certainly the case with Europe. I refer here, however, not to the ERM, although it was indeed in November 1985 that I made my first and most substantial unsuccessful attempt to persuade Margaret that the time had come for sterling to join the mechanism. That, although of the first importance, was never something I saw primarily in European terms. Certainly, I was conscious that our self-imposed exclusion from the ERM greatly diminished our authority and influence within the Community. But that was never why I wanted to see sterling within the ERM. My case, as readers will be aware, was wholly in terms of the balance of economic argument: the assistance that ERM membership could provide in the conduct of economic policy in general and the fight against inflation in particular.

The important event on the European front in 1985 was the meeting of the European Council in Luxembourg at the beginning of December, where

Margaret agreed to the first ever substantial amendment to the Treaty of Rome, known as the Single European Act. It was a fateful step.

The Single European Act covered a wide range of issues, but three stood out as being of particular importance. The first was an explicit target for the completion of the European common market, rechristened, to make it sound as if it were a new initiative, the Single Market, by the end of 1992. The legal obligation to bring into being a genuine common or single market within the Community was, of course, enshrined in the original 1957 Rome Treaty; but once internal tariff barriers had been removed and the common external tariff established, progress had more or less ground to a halt. The second was a substantial extension of majority voting on matters where previously unanimity had been required by the Treaty, in order to make it less difficult to meet the end-1992 deadline. Indeed, in the economic field, majority voting was extended to cover almost everything, the most conspicuous exception being taxation.

Margaret had originally been opposed to any extension of majority voting, since the requirement for unanimity gave her a precious blocking power, which she was more than happy to use, over any new Commission proposal in any of the areas where the unanimity rule applied. When she grudgingly allowed herself to be persuaded that a major move to majority voting was essential if the single market was ever to be achieved, she consoled herself by assuring the House of Commons, in her Statement announcing the outcome of the Luxembourg European Council, that 'The Luxembourg compromise, whereby a member state can invoke a very important national interest to prevent a decision being taken, is unaffected.'

Whether this unwritten article of the Community's constitution, a legacy of de Gaulle, could in practice amount to anything was never put to the test, thanks to the bizarre policy the Foreign Office had developed over the compromise. It had been invoked by the UK just once during the Thatcher years, by Peter Walker when he was Minister of Agriculture. What Walker had done, however, was to make it quite plain that he had no serious reservation about the matter concerning which he had threatened to invoke the Luxembourg compromise, but that he would carry out his threat unless he received satisfaction on another front. This was, of course, a wholly illegitimate use of the compromise, and the others quite properly ignored it altogether, leaving Walker with egg on his face.

The Foreign Office was horrified and, believing that the Walker episode had severely, if not mortally, wounded the Luxembourg compromise, developed a policy designed to ensure its survival. This consisted of two principles. The first was that if any other member country sought to invoke the compromise, the UK should always support it so as to prevent the compromise from being undermined – which indeed we did, even when this was contrary to the UK's interests in the particular issue at stake. The second was that the UK should never invoke the compromise itself, since it could not risk having it overridden a second time. When I discovered that the Foreign Office had developed this bizarre doctrine, and had persuaded Margaret that it was necessary if the compromise was to be preserved, I wrote to Geoffrey, with a copy to Margaret, pointing out that this more or less guaranteed that the compromise could be used only in a way that was harmful to the UK, which did not seem particularly sensible.

In fact, I had to write more than once to Geoffrey pointing out how unsatisfactory the current policy was, and that it clearly needed to be reviewed and changed. Eventually even the Foreign Office had to recognise elementary logic, and Geoffrey agreed that our policy towards the Luxembourg Compromise should be reviewed. The outcome of the review was still unclear at the time of my resignation in October 1989.

The third key provision of the Single European Act was what was clearly understood by both our major partners and the Commission to be a commitment to the achievement of Economic and Monetary Union (EMU). The preamble to the Act explicitly recalled the European Council's 1972 commitment to the objective of 'the progressive realisation of Economic and Monetary Union'. This was a commitment which, over the intervening thirteen years, had certainly fallen into desuetude and had arguably expired, since the 1972 commitment was to the final achievement of Economic and Monetary Union by 1980 – which made its revival in 1985 particularly significant. Moreover, the Act itself contained a chapter providing for closer economic and monetary co-operation in Europe – which would have been perfectly acceptable had it not been headed 'Co-operation in Economic and Monetary Policy (Economic and Monetary Union)'.

THE ROLE OF JACQUES DELORS

The plan to include in the Single European Act – which in effect created a new Treaty superseding the original Rome Treaty – a reference to EMU as an agreed objective had first surfaced early in November 1985, when Luxembourg, which at that time held the six-monthly rotating Community presidency, tabled a proposal to that end. They had been put up to it by Jacques Delors, who had become President of the European Commission in January 1984 – an event, incidentally, that should never have occurred. It had been agreed informally by all the member governments of the Community that when the Commission Presidency became vacant at the beginning of 1984, it was Germany's turn to fill it. Late in the day, however, Helmut Kohl, the Federal German Chancellor, pathetically announced that Germany could find no candidate of sufficient stature for the post, and that he had therefore agreed with President Mitterrand that it should go to France instead.

Until then, Delors had been my French opposite number as Mitterrand's first Finance Minister, so I had got to know him quite well. Slight, bespectacled, studious and unprepossessing in appearance, he was one of the cleverest men in Mitterrand's administration and one of the toughest, too. An intellectual, he compensated for not having made it to France's intellectual elite – he was not an *Énarque* or even a *Polytechnicien*, let alone an *Inspecteur des Finances* – by becoming a workaholic. Indeed, when I first came across him he had made himself ill by going without a holiday altogether, until he was forced to do so.

Like many intellectuals from a deeply Catholic background, he had a profound need to believe in some ideal. From an early age there had been two candidates for this role: socialism, reflecting to some extent his modest social origins, and Europe, where he had been inspired by working for Jean Monnet. His socialism had always been more social than economic in character; nevertheless the disaster over which he had to preside, and courageously steer a way out of, when the Mitterrand government entered office in 1981 committed to a socialist economic policy which proved so disastrous that it had to be completely abandoned within eighteen months, undoubtedly took some of the bloom off his belief in socialism and made the European star shine brighter.

His other main characteristic was a single-minded appetite for power. I remember his telling me in the autumn of 1983 that Mitterrand had tried to persuade him to accept the job of Prime Minister, but that he had declined because under the French system, when the President was of the same Party, the Minister of Finance enjoyed more real power than the Prime Minister. Of course, all sensible politicians want power, since it is only through power that anything can be achieved; but with Delors this trait was particularly well developed. The trappings of power interested him not at all: it was power itself that mattered to him.

So when he agreed to leave the job of Finance Minister to become President of the Commission I was under no illusion as to how he was likely to behave. Indeed, it was a particularly happy niche for him; for it did not take a great deal of ingenuity to promote the notion that anyone who questioned the transfer of power to the Commission in Brussels was *ipso facto* a bad European. Regrettably, as he came to identify the sacred cause of Europe with himself, he became increasingly thin-skinned and intolerant of criticism.

MY OPPOSITION TO MONETARY UNION

My own opposition to the idea of a single currency for Europe went back a long way. In June 1970, the Conservative Party, led by Ted Heath, took office and almost immediately embarked on negotiations to secure the UK's belated membership of the European Community, an objective I strongly supported. I had been a believer in closer European unity ever since my days as an undergraduate at Oxford in the early 1950s, well before the European Community had come into existence, when I had been President of the Strasbourg Club, a student society dedicated to that then unfashionable end. But my idea of Europe was that of de Gaulle's *Europe des patries*, a Europe of nation states, rather than the single federal superstate, or United States of Europe, which some espoused. Then, when the European Community came into being, and showed that it could work, I welcomed it as an inspired constitutional innovation far more intimate than any alliance, but less than a federation, providing a framework in which independent nation states could work together as never before.

Then, a few months after the Heath Government had opened negotiations for UK entry to the Community, the Werner Report on Economic and Monetary Union was published, recommending a common European currency. The implications appalled me, since it clearly implied doing away with the Community in favour of a single European superstate. As I wrote in *The Sunday Times* on 22 November 1970:

> ... a national currency lies at the very heart of national sovereignty. A common currency is something that can only properly follow political union: it cannot precede it. It is significant that whereas the Zollverein or customs union paved the way to the German Federation a century ago, it was only after Prussia and Bismarck had achieved a political union, with blood and iron, that a common German currency could be born.

The heads of government of the Community member states, without any analysis of either the political or the economic consequences of what they were doing, and in most cases without the faintest understanding of what those consequences might be, duly committed their countries in 1972 to the goal of full Economic and Monetary Union by 1980, as the Werner Report had recommended; and promptly turned their minds to other things. When this sleeping dog was at last woken up by the Luxembourg proposal of early November 1985, I lost no time in minuting Margaret to warn her about it. On 14 November I wrote to her in these terms:

> The inclusion of EMU as a Treaty objective would be a political commitment going well beyond previous references to EMU, which have been non-binding European Council resolutions or solemn declarations. It would be perceived in political terms as a major change.
>
> Our objective in my view should be to avoid any amendment to Article 107 [this was the article in the Rome Treaty concerning exchange rates]. The Delors proposal is unacceptable both politically and in substance. So also is any reference to EMU.

Margaret took the point; but I remained concerned. At that time it was still the rule – as indeed it remained throughout my time as Chancellor – that, irrespective of the matters under discussion, Finance Ministers were not permitted to attend meetings of the European Council. The only colleagues the heads of government were able to take with them were their Foreign Ministers. This had originally been inspired by a patronising pronouncement of the first President of the Commission, Walter Hallstein, that 'The business of the Community is politics, not business' – which, translated, meant that the European ideal must not be impeded or debased by contact with awkward realities – and had been perpetuated by the desire of Europe's Foreign Offices to protect their privileged position.

Yet despite the fact that when, in the 1970s, Giscard d'Estaing and Helmut Schmidt inaugurated the annual summits of the industrialised world, it was taken for granted that Prime Ministers would be flanked by their Finance Ministers as well as by their Foreign Ministers, the absurd and unhelpful exclusion of Finance Ministers from European Councils was something that Margaret never once challenged. Since I was not to be present at the Luxembourg Council, and the Foreign Office would inevitably be soft on the issue, I minuted Margaret again on Thursday, 28 November 1985, just ahead of the Council which was due to start on the following Monday:

Your line might be:

> 'There should be no reference in the Treaty to EMU, since this – which implies progress towards a common currency and a common Central Bank – would be no more credible to outside opinion than the commitments entered into in 1971 and 1972, and is in any case politically unacceptable to the UK.'

In the event, she was able, with German support, to get the Treaty reference to EMU watered down, but not removed altogether; and, preferring the on-the-spot advice of the Foreign Office, who told her that what remained was little more than hot air, to the counsel I had proffered in advance, she signed up. The great prize was allegedly the target of completing the single market by the end of 1992 and the facilitation of this by a large-scale move from unanimity to majority voting. I was sceptical about the wisdom of the deal she had struck. I felt that we had embarked on a dangerous slippery slope towards EMU; whereas the move to majority voting, which had been strongly urged by Delors as essential if Europe was to regain the momentum it had latterly lost, would have been agreed even without EMU.

THE ROAD TO 1992

Certainly, it was necessary to inject a new dynamic into the stalled progress towards the completion of the common or single market, and the 1992 deadline was to assume considerable importance both in maintaining the momentum and in changing for the better the perception of Europe overseas. Moreover, although the target was, in the event, not to be met, the progress made was impressive. But in achieving this, enshrining the 1992 target in a new Treaty was less important than two other factors that had already occurred. The first of these was the appointment, at the beginning of 1985, of Arthur Cockfield as the senior UK Commissioner and his securing of the internal market portfolio, as it was called. His formidable intellect, mastery of detail and above all his drive soon made a profound impression. He had published his seminal Community White Paper *Completing the Internal Market* which included the 1992 target date, early that year, and had had it endorsed at the June 1985 European Council in Milan; and having got his teeth into this bone he was not going to let go of it.

The second critical breakthrough which ended the log-jam, that had hitherto caused progress towards a genuine common market to grind to a halt was the acceptance by the Commission of the so-called passport principle established by the *Cassis de Dijon* case. Ever since its inception, the Commission had been busily trying to create the common or single market by the typically bureaucratic and absurd method known as 'harmonisation': the process of imposing a common European standard for every conceivable product, satirised in the *Yes, Minister* episode about the Euro-sausage. Not surprisingly, progress became completely bogged down.

Then came the European Court's decision in the *Cassis de Dijon* case. This is an agreeable French blackcurrant liqueur, best added in very small quantities to chilled dry white wine to make the excellent summer drink, Kir. The import of this drink was banned in Germany because it did not conform to any of the German standards of alcoholic strength, and no common European standard had been agreed. The Court decided that since it was permissible under French standards, it must be accepted anywhere else in the Community. This was the great breakthrough: the recognition that harmonisation was unnecessary for the completion of the single market. All that was needed was the principle that any product that conformed to the standards of one member state, must be free to compete throughout the Community. The only common European standards that needed to be established were those covering a limited number of matters such as safety, financial prudence, and some forms of pollution.

MARGARET THATCHER UNITES EUROPE

Hitherto, I had frequently been embarrassed by the way Margaret conducted herself within the Community; but it was the argument about harmonisation of indirect taxes in the single market (renamed 'approximation') that first fully opened my eyes to just how counterproductive and damaging to the UK's interests her tactics were. In early 1989 she insisted on rejecting a perfectly sensible resolution of the Commission's long and fruitless campaign to set minimum rates and ranges for VAT and excise duties, a solution which would have preserved our essential interests – and which represented, indeed, a negotiating triumph for her Government. For her, unanimity meant she had a veto; and if you had a veto you used it. It was as simple as that. For everyone else, unanimity gave them a card that could from time to time be played to secure a national objective. Once the others realised that Margaret was playing by quite different rules, there ceased to be any reason, in any of the fields where unanimity prevailed – or in any other field for that matter – to make any concessions to the UK, since nothing could be secured in return.

Moreover, this, along with other aspects of her style and tone of voice, came to irk the others so much that they instinctively sank their differences and joined forces against her. Ironically, by 1989 she had become the Community's great unifying force – and the unity she had forged was a unity against the UK. Partly as a result of her undoubted triumph in the Community Budget negotiations of her early years as Prime Minister, she believed that only head-on confrontation yielded results in Europe; and she revelled in being one against eleven. But on most issues this approach was foolish and threw away many opportunities to build alliances and exploit differences among the others. In particular, we had major differences with our partners over both EMU and the so-called social charter. It was useless to expect any support from any of them over these major issues if we were never prepared to yield anything in return over matters which concerned us less. Yet another unhappy relic of her budget confrontation was a dangerous concentration on detail, at the expense of the underlying trend of events.

Had she proposed withdrawal from the Community altogether, at least there would have been some intellectual coherence. But she knew that was not possible: it would have provoked the biggest split in the Conservative Party since Tariff Reform, which had played a large part in the Party's crushing electoral defeat in 1906 and in keeping it in the wilderness until it was rescued by the need to form a coalition government during the First World War. So she pursued a policy which ensured that, while remaining in the Community, the UK's objectives were least likely to be secured.

In many ways my view of Europe was remarkably close to Margaret's. A great struggle was under way between two rival visions of Europe. As I was to put it in my Chatham House speech of 25 January, 1989, one vision was that of:

> ... an over-regulated, bureaucratic, protectionist Europe, where uniform standards are enforced by new directives and new regulations from Brussels, where outsiders are excluded, and where competition is seen as a threat, rather than a challenge to greater efficiency; a Europe in which 'regulate and protect' might be the motto. On the other hand, there is the vision of a deregulated, free-market, open Europe; one where competition is seen as the key to improved economic performance; one driven by consumer choice, by transferring sovereignty not to Brussels but to the people.

I was as determined as Margaret was that it should be that second vision that prevailed. Moreover, I shared her conviction that the political constitution of Europe must remain what it had so successfully become, a Community of nation states, rather than be transformed, contrary to the profoundest instincts of most of its people, into a single European state, albeit of a federal nature. But I departed from her not only in my judgement of tactics most likely to secure these ends and achieve Britain's objectives more generally. Our gut sentiments were just as far apart.

For Margaret, the special relationship with the United States was all-important, and she regarded the continental Europeans with distrust and, in private, with undisguised distaste and hostility. Germany, in particular, increasingly became the butt of the visceral sentiments she had developed during the war. I have no doubt that the reason why Nick Ridley felt it was safe to make the anti-German remarks in his *Spectator* interview, which were to lead to his enforced and reluctant resignation in 1990, was that he had many times heard Margaret utter precisely the same sentiments in private – as, indeed, had I. Margaret was, of course, at all times a politician; and I was never entirely sure how much the saloon-bar xenophobia of her later years represented her own uninhibited feelings and how far she saw it as a potential vote winner. Both elements were present.

But to return to the vexed question of tax approximation. My successor, John Major, discovering the deal that was there to be done on this issue, raised it very early on in his Chancellorship, only to have his head bitten off by Margaret. This so shook him that when, as Prime Minister in 1991, the deal was still on the table – although by then the minimum standard VAT rate had risen from 12 per cent to 15 per cent – it was not until the general election was out of the way and the UK had assumed the Community Presidency, that he eventually accepted it in July 1992. As a result of this long delay and evident reluctance, what was in fact a UK success was made to appear almost a capitulation.

But a success it was. The Community agreed to move to the elimination of VAT checks at national borders on 1 January 1993, a system of indirect tax approximation based on the setting of minimum rates only, at levels which cause no problems for the UK, the acceptance of the UK's zero rates of VAT, and an increase in travellers' allowances with a view to the eventual abolition of any limit at all by July 1999. These are more or less exactly the terms I had privately agreed with the Commission and proposed to Margaret in February 1989, and involve no change whatever in any of the UK's indirect tax rates. Nor, indeed, do they prevent us from making any changes we are conceivably likely to wish to make. But all this was merely a prelude to the far greater problems we were to find ourselves in over the much more important issue of EMU.

CHAPTER FIFTY-TWO

EMU MOVES TO CENTRE STAGE

Mixed Motives · Mishandling Hanover · Bad Blood · The Delors Committee
My Chatham House Speech · EMU Facts and Fallacies · The Delors Report
Disaster with the Dutch

MIXED MOTIVES

Having succeeded, at the Luxembourg European Council of December 1985, in getting the objective of EMU clearly written into the Community's constitution via the Single European Act, it was only a matter of time before those responsible for this coup would launch the process of achieving that objective. Its three main proponents formed a powerful trio, although their motives were rather different.

For Jacques Delors, the position was clear: EMU, and in particular monetary union, was the most promising route to the full European integration he had set as his goal. For François Mitterrand, the perspective was a different one. The political and intellectual leadership of Europe which France regarded as her birthright was threatened by the superior economic strength of Germany and in particular by the unquestioned dominance of Germany's central bank, the Bundesbank, in the crucial field of monetary policy. The only way the French could see of trumping the Bundesbank was to subsume it into a European central bank responsible for a single European currency. For Helmut Kohl, acting very much under the influence of his long-serving Foreign Minister, Hans-Dietrich Genscher, a strong Germany aroused too much fear for it to be able to exercise the political power and influence beyond its borders that its economic strength warranted. The solution was for it to allay that fear by exchanging its German clothing for European attire.

Nor was it hard for the big three to find allies – again, for different reasons. For example, of the other member states of the Community, leaving aside the UK, the largest – Italy – had been a nation state for little more than a hundred years. Indeed, my 1906 Harmsworth Encyclopaedia observes that, even then, 'the consolidation of Italy into one nation cannot be said to be yet complete'. Moreover, not only were the roots of its nationhood shallow, but despite its considerable success in a number of fields, it suffered from an underlying lack of confidence in its ability to govern itself. Handing over the task to some greater European entity, both politically and economically, might be a better bet.

What was most striking about the three main advocates was not only that their motives were different, and at least in the case of France and Germany to some extent conflicting, but that they had committed themselves to achieving this immensely ambitious, highly complex and historically unprecedented act of fusion without any serious attempt to analyse and assess the far-reaching political and economic consequences. It was an astonishingly rash and dangerous way to proceed.

MISHANDLING HANOVER

The launch of the next step came with the assumption of the Community presidency by Germany on 1 January 1988. In the spring the Germans let it be known that their objective at the European Council to be held at Hanover on 27 and 28 June would be the setting up of a committee of experts to recommend the best way of creating a European Central Bank. Margaret had by then become worried at the genie she had allowed out of the bottle by agreeing to sign the Single European Act with its commitment to EMU; and was determined to block the German proposal. In front of the Luxembourg Council I had warned her about EMU, but she had chosen to accept the Foreign Office advice rather than mine. By the spring of 1988, however, as the reader will be aware, relations between us had sadly worsened, and in front of the Hanover Summit she did not even seek my advice, choosing to rely almost entirely on Charles Powell.

Between them they settled on a most extraordinary negotiating objective. Margaret realised that she would have to agree on some sort of study group. So she decided that her objective should be, first and foremost, to get any mention of a European Central Bank expunged from the terms of reference. Her secondary objective was to prevent the study group from being a committee of so-called experts. She always distrusted 'experts', whom she felt produced airy-fairy ideas unrelated to political realities; and believed that any post-Hanover study group should be composed of Central Bank Governors, who not only possessed the expertise required but could be relied upon to keep their feet on the ground. This would also mean that she had her own man on the group, in the shape of the Governor of the Bank of England, Robin Leigh-Pemberton.

The others, when they discovered where she stood at Hanover, must have been amazed at her innocence. At any rate, after a sufficiently long argument to enable her to feel that she had scored a signal success, they agreed that the study group should essentially be a committee of the Community's Central Bank Governors, albeit appointed in their personal capacity, but that the chairman should be, of all people, Jacques Delors – something that so far as I was aware had never even been canvassed prior to the Hanover Council itself: it may have been a Franco-German plot of which the Foreign Office had failed to get wind. Delors had just been given, exceptionally, a second term as Commission President. They also agreed that there should be no reference to a European Central Bank: instead, its terms of reference would be to 'study and propose concrete stages towards the progressive realisation of Economic and Monetary Union (EMU)'.

The European Council had met, as usual, on the Monday and Tuesday. On the Wednesday, 29 June 1988, I had my regular weekly bilateral with Margaret. My tact extended to talking about other matters instead. But then she mentioned, as if it were some sort of triumph, her achievement in getting 'them' to drop all mention of a European Central Bank. 'Prime Minister,' I said, 'I'm afraid you've achieved nothing. There is no way that a committee with those terms of reference can possibly do anything else than recommend the setting up of a European Central Bank.' She abruptly changed the subject, no doubt feeling that I was being awkward yet again.

In fact, far from Hanover being a success, it was a disaster so far as anyone with her views or mine was concerned – and the irony is that this was an issue on which our views were very similar. Not that she had an easy task: having sold the pass over EMU and the Single European Act in 1985, the committee set up at Hanover could scarcely have had terms of reference that led to a different destination. But at least she could have avoided the disaster of having Jacques Delors as the committee's chairman, or even as one of its members. Any number of independent experts would have been better than that, and nothing could have been worse than that.

This was not simply because of his well-known dedication to EMU, the whole EMU, and nothing but EMU. It was rather that with the President of the Commission, newly renewed in office, as its chairman the committee's report would inevitably enjoy an authority within the Community that it could never otherwise have secured. At the same time, it was assured of securing the uncritical backing of the Commission to an extent that a report from a group chaired either by the chairman of the Community's long-established Committee of

Central Bank Governors (at that time Karl Otto Pöhl), or even by a distinguished independent chairman, might well not have enjoyed.

I claim no great prescience in recognising the reality of Hanover as I did. What amazed me was that Margaret, and those to whose advice she chose to listen, could have got it so wrong. It may be, I suppose, that she did not care because she was confident that, at the end of the day, nothing would come of it. That might have been a tenable position; but nothing she ever said to me suggested that she held it herself. On the contrary, she took the threat of EMU very seriously indeed. She simply failed to understand what she was about.

Her confusion became apparent when she made her Statement to the House the following day, 30 June. Having announced the formation of the committee, she said:

> The committee's task will be to study and propose concrete steps towards the progressive realisation of Economic and Monetary Union. That goal was, of course, set out in the preamble to the Single European Act, which was approved by this House.

This was, incidentally, so far as I am aware, her first tacit admission that the pass had been sold in 1985. Kinnock then observed:

> It is well known that the Prime Minister ... has said that a European Central Bank is 'not on the cards'. However ... as it is obvious, as President Mitterrand has pointed out, that a central bank follows from monetary union, is it not clear that the Prime Minister is facing both ways?

To which she responded:

> With regard to the European Central Bank, we have taken part in the Single European Act, which went through the House and which said that we would make progressive steps to the realisation of monetary union, and we have set up a group to consider that. Monetary union would be the first step, but progress towards it would not necessarily involve a single currency or a European Central Bank.

The last sentence was positively mind-boggling. Unlike economic union, monetary union had a clearly defined meaning, which had been established in the Community context by the Werner Report as far back as 1970, and which I had spelled out to her on the eve of the 1985 European Council. Now she appeared to be implying that it meant something completely different and relatively trifling, even though she had not the slightest idea of what that might be.

BAD BLOOD

The Delors Committee began its deliberations in September 1988. Both Margaret and I saw the working papers which emerged from it on a *sub rosa* basis, and it soon became clear that the Delors Committee and the UK Government were set on a collision course. As if this were not troublesome enough, bad blood was being created in other ways, too. I doubt if Jacques Delors had deliberately set out to inflame Margaret, but if he had he could not have done it better. He first boasted to the European Parliament that, in ten years time, 80 per cent of all the key economic and social decisions would be taken in Brussels rather than in the member states. Then, in September, he travelled to Britain to address the annual conference of the Trades Union Congress, where he said:

> It is impossible to build Europe only on deregulation ... It is essential to strengthen our control of our economic and social development, of technology and our monetary capacity.

The theme of control rather than deregulation could not have been more clearly expressed, nor a more explicit rejection of the British Government's vision of Europe.

The idea for the Delors visit to the TUC had come from the Foreign Office, who thought it might help to make the unions and the Labour Party less hostile to the Community. So far as that was concerned it succeeded beyond their wildest dreams, and did more than anything else to bring about Labour's Damascene conversion over the European Community. But it was scarcely a triumph of diplomacy to have been instrumental in greatly widening the already dangerous rift between the British Prime Minister and the President of the European Commission.

Later that same month it was Margaret's turn to put the boot in, with her famous Bruges speech of 20 September 1988. In fact, in the form in which she delivered it, it said a number of things that needed to be said, in a perfectly reasonable manner. Her five main principles were a Europe of nations working closely together, without any concentration of centralised power in Brussels; a preference for the practical over the grandiose; an emphasis on deregulation and market economics; free trade; and a defence based on NATO. The best-known sentence in the speech, 'We have not successfully rolled back the frontiers of the State in Britain only to see them reimposed at the Community level', also expressed a perfectly valid sentiment. But the newspaper reports, which reflected the gloss Bernard Ingham had given when briefing the press, few of whom bothered to read the text, were very different in tone and truer to her own feelings: intensely chauvinistic, and particularly hostile to the Community.

THE DELORS COMMITTEE

The practical question, however, was whether anything could be done, via Robin, to secure a report from the Delors Committee that the UK Government would not be obliged to repudiate out of hand. To this end, on 14 December, 1988, Margaret called the first of a series of meetings at Number 10 with Robin, Geoffrey and myself; with Charles Powell and usually Brian Griffiths in attendance. Robin told us that the report was likely to fall into three parts. The first would be a straightforward description of the current working of the ERM. The second would attempt to define economic and monetary union, and outline the institutional changes necessary to achieve it. The third section would examine the case for early constitutional change as a first step towards EMU. This last section, which was clearly crucial, had not yet been properly tackled by the Committee; and the greater part of our meeting was spent discussing the tactics that might be employed to make this section as modest and as tentative as possible.

We were agreed, so far as analysis was concerned, that the report ought to make it quite clear that a single currency was not essential for the completion of the Single Market. It was clear to us, too, that Robin's tactics should be to assemble the widest possible opposition within the Committee both to any early treaty amendment required to achieve the full EMU objective espoused by Delors, and to anything that smacked of a recommendation to take any particular course of action: the Committee's role should be confined to saying that *if* you wanted to achieve x, *then* you would need to do y. Robin was understandably anxious not to become isolated within the Committee, but at that stage he felt he could count on the support of Pöhl.

Pöhl, indeed, was the key. He was known to have doubts about EMU, nor did the Bundesbank relish its own extinction. Moreover, if Robin and Pöhl stood together, there was a good chance that some of the others would join them, notably the long-serving Governor of the Danish Central Bank, Erik

Hofmeyr. This meant that any alternative ideas we put forward on this front should not be ones that might alienate Pöhl – for example, the idea, which I had for some time been urging, that European monetary co-operation could be improved by each country holding the currencies of the other Community countries in its reserves, something to which the Bundesbank, which held only dollars, was resolutely opposed. So while it was decided that we ought to prepare a contingency paper mentioning distinctively British proposals for improved monetary co-operation in Europe which would not involve any amendment of the treaty, it should for the time being be kept in reserve and not tabled.

But Pöhl proved a broken reed. Despite telling Robin privately about his grave doubts about EMU, and promising Robin his support in toning down the Committee's report, true to form he did not stand firm. He made a number of sceptical interventions in the Committee's deliberations, but he never really engaged himself; at the end of the day shrugging his shoulders and going along with Delors and de Larosière. This made a complete nonsense of the tactical plan we had evolved.

The draft of the Delors Committee report was circulated in February 1989. We discussed it at one of our Number 10 meetings. It was clear to both Margaret and myself that it was wholly unacceptable. It was equally clear that there was no possibility of Robin, on his own, securing a redraft that would be acceptable to the UK. I suggested to him that he might submit a free-standing statement of his own objections for inclusion in the final Report, emphasising the need for practical co-operation between member States and stressing that the massive shift of political sovereignty implied by full EMU went far beyond the competence of a Committee of Central Bankers to pronounce upon. But at the end of the day he decided that he did not wish to be seen as a minority of one among his peers in any way, and contented himself with trying to get some of the wording in the draft Report toned down.

MY CHATHAM HOUSE SPEECH

By the middle of January it was already plain that our plan to influence the Committee's conclusions from within had foundered on Pöhl's failure to live up to his promises to Robin, and I felt the time had come to speak out in public on the issue. The Royal Institute for International Affairs, better known as Chatham House, had long been asking me to address them; and this seemed the ideal forum for a pre-emptive strike against what the Delors Report was likely to recommend. I arranged to speak to them on 25 January 1989.

I had three objectives in mind. First and foremost, it was time I set out exactly where I stood on an issue of the first importance that was likely to be at the forefront of the political debate for some years to come. Second, there was an outside chance that it might exercise some influence on the final draft of the Delors Committee's Report – and even if it did not, it would prepare the ground for what seemed Britain's inevitable rejection of the Report. And third, it would be a way of demonstrating to Margaret both the grounds on which EMU, as I saw it, ought to be rejected, and how this fundamentally differed from the ERM. Unlike most of my speeches, my Chatham House speech was subsequently published in pamphlet form, where I was able to add a foreword relating it more closely to the Delors Report, which by that time had been published.

The greater part of my Chatham House speech was devoted not to currency issues, but to the Single Market, and some of the problems we were then encountering, for instance in the banking and financial areas. Indeed I voiced the suspicion that:

> This divisive and intensely difficult new issue [EMU] has been propelled into the forefront of European debate at this time either out of culpable carelessness, or as a smokescreen to obscure a lack of sufficient progress towards the Single Market – or, worse, as a means of running away from taking the practical but difficult steps the Single Market requires, running away from the challenge of freedom. For it is an observable fact that those nations which are most vocal about their support for EMU now, tend to be those that are most assiduous in preserving barriers to free trade within the Community.[42]

France was one country that sprang to mind in this context. As I have already indicated, one of my three key objectives at Chatham House was to distinguish between membership of the ERM and full-scale monetary union. It could not be more fundamental – a point echoed, incidentally, by the Delors Report itself. As I put it at Chatham House:

> The ERM is an agreement between independent sovereign states ... Economic and Monetary Union by contrast, is incompatible with independent sovereign states with control over their own fiscal and monetary

[42] [2010 note] Even now, 18 years since this was written, and more than eight years since EMU came fully into being, there remain a number of significant barriers to free trade in services within the European Union.

> policies. It would be impossible, for example, to have irrevocably fixed exchange rates while individual countries retained independent monetary policies ... Thus EMU inevitably implies a single European currency, with monetary decisions – setting of monetary targets and of short-term interest rates – taken not by national Governments and/or central banks, but by a European Central Bank. Nor would individual countries be able to retain responsibility for fiscal policy. With a single European monetary policy there would need to be central control over the size of the budget deficits and, particularly, over their financing ... What organisation would really be the Government? It is clear that Economic and Monetary Union implies nothing less than a European Government – albeit a federal one – and political union: the United States of Europe. That is simply not on the agenda now, nor will it be for the foreseeable future.

EMU FACTS AND FALLACIES

There were some, I knew, who disputed this, arguing that a single European currency was essentially no different from the classical gold standard, under which dollars, pounds and Reichsmarks were different names for an essentially metallic common currency. I pointed out, however, that the gold standard was far from a monetary union. 'Co-operation was informal and not institutionalised; and although countries could see advantages for themselves in maintaining their parities against gold, they were free to change if it seemed in their national interest to do so.'

The UK went off gold during the Napoleonic Wars, and then again in the First World War, not returning in the latter case until 1925. In addition, Peel's Bank Charter Act of 1844, which put convertibility into gold on a legal basis, could be temporarily suspended in a severe financial crisis – as indeed it was on three occasions in the seventy years between 1844 and 1914.

Yet none of this prevented the classical gold standard from providing an invaluable financial discipline; and it did not occur to those setting pay and prices in any major country in the half century and more before the First World War that a currency depreciation would bail them out if they went too far. By contrast, a full monetary union normally followed the establishment of a central political power. The German Customs Union or *Zollverein* of 1834 neither required nor led to monetary union. That did not come until more than forty years later, when Bismarck founded an all-German political union under Prussian hegemony.

I also voiced my suspicion of the structural and regional policies which the Delors Committee believed would be required once the poorer member countries had lost the right to devalue. This, I said, was 'quite simply a bid for ever larger awards of taxpayers' money to be placed in the hands of bureaucrats in Brussels, to be used for the sort of interventionist policies that failed [in the UK] so decisively in the 1970s.' Such policies were no more likely to be successful at the Community level: 'Subsidising industry and subsidising regions destroys their will to compete and their ability to compete.'

EMU was an issue of growing importance on which I had not previously pronounced – indeed, very few at that time had – and the views I expressed in my Chatham House speech of January 1989 I have seen little reason to change since. It was also worth drawing attention, in less strident terms than those that were later to be used by Margaret, to the major political implications of EMU, which were at that time underplayed, if not ignored, by those, especially in the City, who saw it in exclusively financial terms.

The City supporters of EMU could not be expected to understand the politics. It was the politicians whom I felt were particularly culpable. The blame attached not to those who openly sought a federal Europe, a perfectly reputable objective which I happened not to share; but rather to those who maintained that there was no real political issue at all, and that talk of sovereignty was simply a matter of semantics. It was hard not to conclude that the many politicians who fell into this camp were either deceiving themselves or, if not, deliberately deceiving the people.

I also felt it was worth trying to prevent the depressing polarisation of opinion on Europe between, on the one hand, the chauvinistic anti-Europeans who opposed all forms of entanglement, and, on the other hand, the knee-jerk Eurofederalists who in practice believed in a strong concentration of power at the European centre. I was not worried that, as a result, the speech left me isolated from both the two warring camps. I am neither a Europhobe nor a Eurofanatic and have no wish to ingratiate myself with either group. Had my political standing not been damaged by the need to raise interest rates so much, my Chatham House speech might have come to be seen by the bulk of the Tory Party – and by many non-Tories too – as a standard around which to rally.

Although she did not relish my favourable mention of the ERM, Margaret was delighted with my Chatham House speech, citing it frequently and indeed remembering it long enough to refer to it in favourable terms in her very last and unforgettable speech as Prime Minister, in the House of Commons on 20

November 1990. But it was not her praise that I sought. What I needed from her was trust – or, at the very least, for her to refrain from undermining me.

THE DELORS REPORT

It was the custom to conduct the formal business at Ecofin Council meetings during the morning and afternoon sessions, leaving the trickier, more important, and more interesting matters for informal discussion over lunch, when no minutes were taken and to which no reference would normally be made afterwards, not least to the Press. Thus it was over lunch at the April 1989 Ecofin Council at Luxembourg that Jacques Delors first unveiled his Committee's Report.

It mapped out the achievement of EMU in three stages. In essence, these were:

> Stage One: Completion of the financial aspects of the Single Market; all Community members to join the ERM within the narrow band; the development of the Ecu; and closer European monetary co-ordination.
>
> Stage Two: Rather vague, but essentially a transitional phase during which the new institutions required for Stage Three would be developed. In addition, ERM realignments would become few and far between, and it was implied that the various national central banks would become independent, as a prelude to their fusion into an independent European Central Bank in Stage Three.
>
> Stage Three: The Community's exchange rates would become irrevocably fixed. The European Central Bank would take over responsibility for monetary policy and eventually establish a single currency. The arrangement would be buttressed by binding conventions on national Budget deficits and by enlarged subsidies to offset regional imbalances.

In the discussions Margaret, Geoffrey and I had had in London it had been agreed that we could accept Stage One, but that there was no way in which we could accept Stage Three. For myself, I saw no fundamental problems, and indeed some attractions, in Stage Two, particularly as it ultimately emerged from the subsequent intergovernmental negotiations, provided it could be changed from a transitional phase to a final destination. But Margaret was wholly opposed to Stage Two in any shape or form. Be that as it may, over lunch at Luxembourg Jacques Delors gave us a brief and lucid exposition of the merits of his Report, as he saw them; only to be followed by an awkward silence. It was clear that most of my colleagues did not see it as a matter for genuine debate, something that was to cause increasing problems as the saga unfolded over the years that lay ahead.

I brought the silence to an end by making it clear, after elaborate courtesies to Delors, complimenting him on the lucidity of the Report and so on, that the UK could not accept the massive transfer of sovereignty over fiscal and monetary policy implied by the Report. Pierre Bérégovoy then responded with a defence of Delors, arguing that for France sovereignty was a matter of having an independent defence capability, and was unaffected by the matters dealt with in the Delors Report. No-one else uttered a word. Bérégovoy subsequently told me that he had initially been very sceptical about EMU, but had been talked round to it by Jacques de Larosière, who as Governor of the Banque de France had been a key member of the Delors Committee.

DISASTER WITH THE DUTCH

So far from causing the issue to go away, the Delors Report affected the question of sterling's membership of the ERM in two important if conflicting ways. On the one hand, it gave it a new lease of life, since the inclusion of all Community currencies in the ERM was an integral part of Stage One of the process outlined in the Report, which Britain was formally to accept. But it also fatally confused the essentially economic question of the ERM with the fundamentally political argument over EMU; and linked the hard-earned credibility of the ERM, which had by then been in existence for a decade, to the speculative and uncertain EMU.

Meanwhile, Geoffrey Howe had come to the conclusion that if anyone could persuade Margaret of the merits of the ERM, it would be the Dutch Prime Minister, Ruud Lubbers. Lubbers was a Conservative and the closest thing to an ally Margaret had within the Community. She was also attracted to his rugged good looks and personal charm. Despite the sharp contrast between his relaxed and benign style and her own strident and confrontational one, she undoubtedly had a soft spot for him. Geoffrey had therefore been trying for some time to persuade Margaret to hold what he called a mini-summit with the Dutch.

The UK had long held annual bilateral summits with the Germans, French and Italians. Having participated in these, and discovered that their only useful purpose was to provide attractive photo opportunities for the host premier, I tried whenever I could to find a legitimate reason why I could not take part. Given that the dates were chosen to fit the diaries of the two Prime Ministers and Foreign Ministers, this was not usually too difficult. The idea of a mini-summit with the Dutch did, by contrast, have a real purpose; but I told Geoffrey it would never work, since Lubbers had nothing to gain from browbeating Margaret on the issue of the ERM. I had, in any case, sometime earlier had a private word with Lubbers myself, and he told me he regarded her as a lost cause on the ERM. Geoffrey was characteristically undeterred, and eventually found a good excuse to convene the mini-summit when Margaret wanted to secure Dutch support for the modernisation of nuclear weaponry prior to an important NATO meeting.

Lubbers accordingly turned up at Chequers on Saturday, 29 April 1989, accompanied by his Foreign Minister, Hans van den Broek, and his Finance Minister, Onno Ruding. Margaret was accompanied by Geoffrey and myself, with Charles Powell as note-taker. I arrived, as requested, at four o'clock in the afternoon. It was only subsequently that I discovered that Margaret had met Lubbers privately in the morning and discussed EMU as well as the NATO summit with him. Lubbers apparently told Margaret that the Dutch had found membership of the ERM highly beneficial. He also endorsed the eventual goal of full monetary union. But he had serious misgivings about the passage in the Report that insisted that embarking on Stage One implied a commitment to the process as a whole. The Netherlands preferred, he said, to proceed step-by-step and gauge exactly what was needed at each stage rather than opt at the outset for amendments to the Treaty of Rome.

This was an obvious basis on which to build an Anglo-Dutch alliance against the Delors Report. But Margaret threw the opportunity away and instead told Lubbers that the UK's experience of stable exchange rates was much less happy than the Dutch one, and that it was in shadowing the Deutschmark that excessively loose monetary conditions had been allowed to develop. It was an unpromising curtain-raiser for the afternoon 'plenary' session.

Most of that session was taken up by Margaret berating the Dutch for not taking a sufficiently hard line over NATO modernisation, at a time when the Germans had gone soft and even the Americans were wavering.

I found her manner distinctly embarrassing, and was surprised that the Dutch took it as well as they did. As the tirade went on, I began to suspect that she was deliberately postponing the EMU discussion because I had told her before the meeting that I would have to leave early to collect Thérèse from hospital, where she had undergone a minor operation. Unwilling to be outmanoeuvred quite so easily, I slipped out of the room to arrange for someone else to pick up Thérèse.

Eventually, and very belatedly, the discussion moved to the Delors Report. I said that the British Government was happy to discuss practical steps towards closer economic and monetary co-operation within the framework of the existing Treaty, but did not see any need for the Treaty to be amended. Ruding said that The Netherlands had an equally pragmatic outlook, and also preferred a step-by-step approach, even though the Dutch entirely accepted the eventual goal of full EMU. He added that the effectiveness of Britain's resistance to the recommendations of the Delors Report would be greatly enhanced by membership of the ERM.

The last point, although perfectly true, predictably aroused Margaret's wrath. She brusquely interjected that sterling differed from the guilder and that exchange rate stability was secondary to the defeat of inflation. For the first time she said to my face that it was shadowing the Deutschmark that had caused Britain's inflation to pick up again. I immediately intervened, saying that with hindsight it was arguable that the Mark should have been shadowed at a slightly higher rate; but that it was not the case that the shadowing itself had been inflationary. It was very embarrassing having to argue with Margaret in front of the Dutch, but I simply could not let the charge pass unchallenged.

Ruding then weighed in, saying that membership of the ERM would provide a stern anti-inflationary discipline if sterling entered at the right parity. He also suggested that, while the weakness of the British economy had made entry unthinkable when the system was first set up in 1979, the transformation of the supply side over the past ten years made it infinitely easier for the British authorities to sustain an exchange rate target. He then tried a different tack. He said that he was not advising Britain to join immediately but merely to give an undertaking to join on the completion of the Single Market by January 1993. Margaret was unpersuadable, claiming that membership of the ERM added nothing to monetary policy and took a great deal away. Ruding – with whom I had not had any prior discussions – re-emphasised his belief that it was only by joining the ERM that Britain could expect its objections to EMU to be taken seriously at the forthcoming European Council at Madrid.

It was at that point that Lubbers, who had received such a battering on the NATO issue – over which the Dutch had not in fact been at all 'wet' – that he found it hard to summon much enthusiasm for the EMU discussion, made his only contribution to the argument. He said: 'Well, you can drive a car without a seat belt, but on the whole it is better to have one.' He warned that if Britain stayed out of the ERM, it would be much harder for Britain and the Netherlands to co-operate in a whole range of areas unconnected with EMU. With Margaret hectoring her Dutch guests and my contradicting her in mid-stream it was a ghastly and embarrassing occasion, and I was eventually glad to make my excuses and depart to see how Thérèse was, before the proceedings had formally ended.

CHAPTER FIFTY-THREE

'I MUST PREVAIL'

A Battle of Wills · Margaret Tells the World ...
... and Apologises to Me · The Euro-Elections of June 1989
A Formula for Ripe Time · New Light on Monetary Union

A BATTLE OF WILLS

The Anglo-Dutch mini-Summit had proved as useless for the purpose for which Geoffrey had intended it as I had warned him it would. Nevertheless, there was no point in pretending that it had not happened; and when I next saw Margaret in private, at my weekly bilateral the following Wednesday, 3 May 1989, I asked her how she thought it had gone.

She replied by saying what nonsense Ruding, the Dutch Finance Minister, had talked about the ERM. I said that, on the contrary, I thought the idea of setting a date by which we would enter the ERM had much to be said for it: it would establish the good faith of our repeated assurances that we would join when the time was right, which was beginning to be questioned. We had to keep our eye on the ball, and the ball, in this context, was the grave danger posed by the Delors Report and EMU. Our official position on that was that we could accept Stage One of the Report's recommendations, which involved sterling joining the ERM, within the standard narrow band, but that we could not accept Stages Two and Three. But this position, and our contention that the Community's monetary arrangements should remain the ERM, was unlikely to carry much conviction so long as we remained resolutely outside it.

Margaret would have none of it. Setting a deadline by which we would join the ERM would be 'particularly damaging'. Joining the ERM would in no way strengthen our hand against EMU. In any case it was shadowing the Deutschmark that had led to the resurgence of UK inflation. We should never have 'given up control of monetary policy' by adopting a parallel objective of exchange rate stability. 'You cannot serve two masters,' she declared: what we had to do now was to concentrate on re-establishing our counter-inflationary credentials. I replied that it was not a question of serving two masters: downward pressure on inflation was obviously the paramount objective. However, there was a clear link between the internal and external value of a currency – something I could never get her to accept.

It was evident to both of us that the discussion was getting nowhere; but the terms in which she brought it to a close were particularly revealing. 'I do not want you to raise the subject ever again,' she said; 'I must prevail.' It was those last three words that said it all. The economic and political arguments had become an irrelevance. Joining the ERM, as she saw it, had become a battle of wills between her and me; and it had to be her will that prevailed. The humiliation, as she clearly saw it, of May 1988, when the Press interpreted her prepared parliamentary answer on exchange rate policy – and, ironically, the half per cent base rate cut – as a defeat for her, still rankled.

Of course, she was quite right; in the sense that matters had now reached the pitch where there was a good chance that any decision to put sterling in the ERM would have been presented in the Press as a victory for me and a defeat for her. That was one of the malign consequences of her habit of personalising every issue and exposing every difference; but it was no basis on which to determine a matter of such importance to our country. I contented myself by saying that, while I would certainly cease discussing the subject then and there, I could give her no assurance that I would not come back to it again when it seemed right to do so. But it was the ominous 'I must prevail' that was still ringing in my ears as I left the room.

MARGARET TELLS THE WORLD ...

It was clear to me that handling the EMU challenge was going to be far more difficult than Margaret apparently realised. The first substantive discussion of EMU was scheduled to take place later that month, on Saturday, 20 May 1989, at the informal Ecofin Council to be held under the first Spanish presidency of the European Community, at the coastal resort of S'Agaro.

Before then a number of events were held to mark the tenth anniversary of the formation of the first Thatcher Government in May 1979. One I particularly recall was a dinner Margaret gave at Number 10 on 4 May for Cabinet Ministers and their wives, marred in my case only by the fact that Thérèse could not be there as she was still recovering from her operation. Geoffrey Howe, as the senior of the few remaining survivors of Margaret's first Cabinet, spoke on behalf of us all; and in addition to an elegant tribute to Margaret he succeeded in evoking the camaraderie that had kept us going during those difficult early years. I could not help reflecting how much that spirit had changed. Elspeth Howe, sitting next to me, was quietly fuming throughout Geoffrey's well-judged speech. Evidently she felt that he was being a touch too fulsome to someone who treated him so badly.

The Press always love anniversaries: anything that can be portrayed as a major event and which can be prepared for well in advance is an obvious boon. The coverage of Margaret's tenth anniversary was therefore predictably lavish. Margaret herself, however, was shrewd enough to seek to play it down as much as she could. She recognised that, once it was over, the harsh realities of life would appear even harsher. It was a pity that she did not have the further insight to recognise that it was the ideal time for her to step down gracefully of her own free will.

I was in the car on the way to Northolt on Friday, 19 May, to catch the RAF plane to Spain for the informal Ecofin, accompanied by my G7 deputy, Nigel Wicks, when Thérèse rang through to ask me if I had heard what Margaret had said on the one o'clock news bulletin on BBC Radio. I told her I had not. To my horror, she told me that Margaret had given an interview in which she had blamed me for causing the upsurge in inflation. I thanked her for alerting me, and telephoned Alex at the Treasury, asking him to procure a transcript of the interview and fax it to me at the hotel I was heading for at S'Agaro, to await my arrival.

The fax was duly waiting for me at the hotel when I arrived, and I asked Nigel Wicks to come to my room so that he could read it, too. It was appalling. It turned out to be an extract from an interview she had originally given to the BBC World Service, in which she told the interviewer that we had 'picked up our inflation tendency' as a direct consequence of the intervention in which we had engaged in order to shadow the Deutschmark. The accusation was not, of course, new to me; but she had never before made it in public. What made it even more intolerable was that she chose to make what the BBC rightly interpreted as a personal attack on me just when I was on my way to represent Britain in a complex and difficult set of international negotiations on what was widely seen as a closely related issue. I told Nigel Wicks that I felt that this was the last straw, and that I would be telephoning Thérèse to discuss with her whether I should resign.

This was not a manoeuvre: I meant it and did indeed telephone Thérèse, who advised me to do nothing until I had got back to the UK. But Wicks was sufficiently alarmed to telephone Peter Middleton in London off his own bat, and Peter had evidently got straight on to Number 10 to ensure that Margaret was aware of my state of mind. Fortunately I was spared the attention of the UK Press, who were at S'Agaro in force. So as to enable us to conduct our discussions in complete privacy. Carlos Solchaga, the Spanish Finance Minister, had arranged for there to be a *cordon sanitaire* around the hotel where we were meeting and staying, which was very effectively policed; and there was to be no contact with the Press until the meeting was over.

This also enabled me to refocus my mind on the agenda for the Council, of which the most important item was EMU. Given that I was in a minority of one over EMU, the meeting did not go too badly from the UK's point of view. The agreed communiqué issued by Solchaga at the end of the discussions, which had not been easy, conspicuously stopped short of endorsing the Delors Report, stating merely that the Ecofin Council saw it as a 'valuable and comprehensive basis for further work'. I also succeeded in getting Stage One, which the UK could accept, detached from Stages Two and Three, which we could not. While, in my opinion, it was Stage Three, which created the single currency, which was wholly unacceptable, Margaret, as I have already mentioned, was not prepared to accept the somewhat nebulous Stage Two, either.

This separation was marked in the communiqué by the agreement that, while preparatory work for launching Stage One should be set in hand 'as a matter of urgency.' So far as Stages Two and Three were concerned, it was a matter of 'defining the operational elements' so that 'a decision can be taken in due course' on whether an intergovernmental conference should be called to consider amendments to the Treaty. Jacques Delors, who was, of course, an active participant at the meeting, made no secret of his displeasure with the outcome, and of his determination to secure a very different outcome from the European Council itself, which was due to discuss EMU at Madrid the following month. For my part, I felt that the outcome gave Margaret a useful foundation on which she might, with skilful handling, build at Madrid.

... AND APOLOGISES TO ME

The discussions had, in fact, only just begun when I was passed a telephone message asking me to ring Margaret in London. I waited until the coffee break and then did so. She was at her most emollient, apologising profusely – a phenomenon so uncharacteristic as to have been almost unique – for the way her BBC interview had turned out. She had not intended any attack on me at all, she said, but had been provoked into saying what she did by the idiocy of the interviewer who had spoken as if joining the ERM were some magic solution to all our problems. I replied that it was clearly most unfortunate, but I was glad to hear her explanation. I then went on to let her know how the Ecofin meeting had begun.

When it had ended, and I crossed the *cordon sanitaire* to the hotel where the Press were billeted, to give an *al fresco* press conference beside the swimming pool, all they were really interested in was, of course, Margaret's attack on me in her radio interview on the Friday. I told them that the Prime Minister had telephoned me to assure me that the interpretation that had been put on her words was incorrect. After establishing that the telephone call had been initiated by her and not by me, I was then asked whether she had rung up in order to apologise. I replied, rather stuffily, that it was a private telephone conversation and I did not propose to say anything further about it.

Whether the Press simply put two and two together, or whether they had been told more by someone else, I do not know; but the story in the Press on the Monday morning was of her having apologised to me – something which, although it happened to be true, she could not have relished. But, once again, she had brought it on herself. Presumably, the purpose of her call had been to prevent my resignation – not that either of us had so much as hinted at the possibility. In any event, by the time I landed at Northolt I had decided that, despite the problems I was having with Margaret, I would stick to my earlier resolve to soldier on. The fact that almost the first thing I had to do on my return was to raise interest rates a further point to 14 per cent, their highest level since the sterling crisis of January 1985, did not make life any easier.

THE EURO-ELECTIONS OF JUNE 1989

The following month, June, was the scheduled date for the fixed-term four-yearly elections to the European Parliament. While of little importance except to the candidates themselves – the European Parliament was the least powerful of all the Community's institutions and the majority of the British electorate recognised this by not even bothering to vote – the political parties took them seriously as an indication of their general standing with public opinion. Moreover, with Europe having once again elbowed its way to the forefront of the political debate, there was rather more interest than usual in the 1989 elections.

Margaret opened the Conservative Party's campaign with a Euro-manifesto press conference on 22 May. Predictably, she was asked about the Government's attitude to the ERM, and lost no time in departing from the agreed compromise wording that we would not be joining until we had got inflation back under control, by adding 'and maybe not even then', followed by various gratuitous sidesweeps at fixed exchange rates in general and the ERM in particular – which, when all was said and done, it was the Government's official policy to join. The press inevitably interpreted this as yet another snub to me, and our back-benchers once again expressed concern at the re-emergence of a public split between the Prime Minister and the Chancellor. Walters' presence was clearly making itself felt.

But my concern was by no means confined to Margaret's attitude to the ERM. Under her instructions, the Conservative campaign for the Euro-elections was characterised by a crude and embarrassing anti-Europeanism which had never before played any part in the Party's stance on this constellation of issues. The new tone and nature was well encapsulated by the ubiquitous poster which simply asked 'Do you want to live on a diet of Brussels?'

Leaving aside the merits of the case, this seemed to me appallingly bad politics. One of the great strengths of the Thatcher Government had been that, unlike the case with many of its predecessors, whether you liked what it was saying and doing or not, at least you knew where it stood. This clarity had a considerable appeal. But over Europe, the public was totally confused. It had been the Conservatives under Macmillan that had first applied to join the Community, the Conservatives under Heath that had secured UK entry, and the Conservatives under Margaret Thatcher that had solved the problem of the budgetary injustice and, on that basis, reaffirmed the UK's position within the Community. Compared with the hesitancy and bitterly divided counsels of the Labour Party, it was the Conservatives who had always appeared as the Party of Europe. Yet suddenly the voters were presented with an election in which the Conservative Party appeared to be campaigning not against the Labour Party but against the European Community.

Needless to say, in addition to completely confusing the public, the Conservative campaign brought to the surface the conflicting views on Europe that had always existed in the Party but which had hitherto been largely quiescent. It was no surprise that the results of the elections, held on Thursday, 15 June, were an unmitigated disaster for the Government. While the unpopularity caused by the inexorable rise in interest rates had probably been the main factor, the nature of the Euro-campaign itself had clearly not helped.

Yet Margaret did not see it that way at all. I suddenly realised, with a shiver of apprehension, that she saw the Euro-campaign as a trial run for the next general election campaign; and that, with the short-term economic outlook unpromising, she saw a crude populist anti-Europeanism as her winning strategy. It was a strategy that would undoubtedly have evoked a considerable response: xenophobia always does. But it would have been a disaster for the Party, splitting it from top to bottom and making no sense to the voters, who would not have understood what we stood for and, indeed, why we wished to remain within the Community at all if that was how we saw it.

I was, as I have said, never either a Eurofanatic or a Europhobe, and had become resigned to being caught in the crossfire between these passionate warring minorities within the Conservative Party, whose discordant and numbingly predictable views used to dominate every European debate in the House of Commons. It was always clear to me that the Conservative Party could be successfully led only by someone who took their stand in the centre of the spectrum on this issue, where the silent majority dwelt. Margaret's evident determination to lead the Party from one of the two extremes of that spectrum spelled nothing but trouble.

A FORMULA FOR RIPE TIME

On Monday, 12 June, I was scheduled to appear before the House of Commons Select Committee on the Treasury, to give evidence to the Committee's inquiry into the Delors Report on EMU. I played to a full house, which must have stimulated the adrenalin. The meeting had to be shifted to the Grand Committee Room off Westminster Hall, the largest room the House could provide; and long before I arrived a queue of spectators had formed, consisting not only of journalists and curious members of the general public, but dozens of City analysts and a discreet sprinkling of more senior figures from Whitehall and the City.

The questioning inevitably covered the ERM as well as EMU. It is a tribute to the tradition of lively political debate in the UK that in no other European country could these subjects have had such appeal. The German Press, for example, did not wake up to the threat to the Deutschmark implicit in EMU until after their Government had already signed the Maastricht Treaty of December 1991.

I recalled Jacques Delors observing to me, when we were sitting together at an Ecofin lunch, that he received cuttings from all the European papers; and, although he did not welcome all he read in the UK Press, he was impressed by the fact that there was more lively debate about European issues in the UK than in the rest of the Community put together. This *de facto* conspiracy of silence over Europe on the Continent is, I believe, storing up serious trouble for the future; and in this context the Danish people's rejection of the Maastricht Treaty in a referendum in 1992 fired a healthy warning shot. But in the short term its main effect was to make the UK Government's task, particularly in relation to EMU, considerably harder.

As for the ERM, I put the case for it in a single sentence:

> It would reduce exchange rate fluctuations and we would be able to use it to assist us in our anti-inflationary policy.

I also dissented from the view that ERM members had to have identical interest rates. The market, I explained, had to take into account two currency risks: the possibility of a realignment and the scope for change within the existing bands. To achieve a successful domestic monetary policy, 'you have got to be prepared to make use of both elements of flexibility'.

But the most newsworthy item consisted of the essential conditions, which I specified for the first time, which needed to be satisfied before Britain could join the ERM. These were, first, a reduction in British inflation and, second, a lifting of exchange controls in the major Community countries, especially France and Italy. Community Finance Ministers had already agreed to do the latter by mid-1990 and, in fact, France was to move at the beginning of that year. Like the inflation condition, the exchange control condition was one on which I had reason to believe that Margaret and I would be able to agree.

It was the voicing of this condition which dominated the Press headlines the next day, although there was less than complete agreement on quite how to interpret it. *The Times* had 'Lawson Gives Hint of Early British Move to Join EMS'; the *Financial Times* 'Lawson Signals 1990 as Probable Date for Full Entry into EMS'; and the *Independent* 'Lawson Calls for Truce in Row over EMS'. I certainly believed that this was a formula that might heal the rift in an acceptable way.

As for the inflation condition, the official published UK forecasts showed a strong decline in inflation throughout 1989 and onwards. This was indeed in the pipeline, despite the events which knocked the RPI off course and delayed the big reduction until 1991. (Despite my scepticism of official forecasts, I publicly supported the decision taken by my successor as Chancellor, John Major, to join at last in October 1990, when inflation was at a statistical peak, but clearly poised to fall dramatically.) As I said at the time, it was a far less favourable time than the opportunities I had been obliged to miss, notably in 1985; but there seemed nothing to be gained from waiting still longer.

NEW LIGHT ON MONETARY UNION

In some ways, what I said about European Monetary Union was more radical, if less newsworthy, than what I said about the ERM. At Chatham House I had followed Delors in accepting that monetary union required some central control over the size of fiscal deficits. But I had subsequently reflected on it further; and told the Committee, as I had told my opposite numbers at the S'Agaro informal Ecofin, that even a common currency did not in theory require either the control of the budgetary and fiscal policies of members, or a great enlargement of regional policy.

To make a monetary union work, I said, 'What you need is basically a simple rule that, if any member country gets itself excessively into debt, then there will be a clear understanding of no bailing out; but there is nothing further you need.'

I added that there was no federal system in the world, with the possible exception of Australia, where provincial government budgets were subject to the control of the federal government. 'There is no more reason for having central control of European deficits than there is to have central control of the borrowings of ICI.' I subsequently came to believe that both views on this tricky issue were probably correct: my second thoughts were certainly right in theory, but my first thoughts were probably closer to the mark in practice. As I was to put it in my 1990 Stamp Memorial Lecture:

> There is the minimalist position which holds that the market can be left to exercise a discipline on excessive borrowing by member states, just as it does on borrowing by individual companies within a single national currency area, provided there is a clear rule that no member country that gets into difficulties would be bailed out by the Community as a whole. Whether this would be enough would depend, *inter alia*, on whether such a rule could be made credible. The parallel is whether, say, if New York were once again to become bankrupt, it is credible that the US Federal Government would stand aside and allow it to default on its debts.[43]

[43] [2010 note] This scepticism proved well-founded when the EMU crisis, triggered by the threat of Greece defaulting on its public debt, erupted in 2010. See also the new final chapter.

Continuing, in what was to be described in the Press as an unscripted virtuoso performance, I described the Delors Report as 'totally flawed' in saying that there had to be 'a huge transfer of resources from the centre to the periphery ... What you need for adjustment is flexibility of wage rates, of land prices, of the various factors of production ... It is a complete illusion to suppose that if you devalue you are somehow gaining resources. You are not ... There is no reason why you should be compensated for it [i.e. the inability to devalue].'

But even in a pure monetary union, without unnecessary paraphernalia, the crucial dimension of democratic accountability would still be missing. The Bundesbank itself was constitutionally subject to German law. To achieve accountability for a European Central Bank 'you would have to have a genuine European parliament'. National parliaments would become like county councils – a comparison which Norman Tebbit later took over. There would have to be a genuinely democratically elected European government to balance a European Central Bank. A small but crucial passage in my exchanges with the Treasury Committee concerned the relationship between ERM and EMU. I indicated the indirect linkage I had already raised with Margaret:

> Influence in these matters would be greater when the time has come that we are within the Exchange Rate Mechanism, or even if it were clear that we were going to be within the Exchange Rate Mechanism within a reasonable period of time. I think that would help us in the discussions that are to come on this matter. That cannot be decisive; but I think it is true.

Sadly, by joining the ERM as late as we did, the influence we secured, although by no means negligible, was far less than it could have been. Moreover, by the time we did join, a more direct and malign linkage had begun to emerge. For the first ten years of its existence, the ERM had stood on its own merits and had steadily gained in credibility as the years went by. But when EMU appeared on the horizon, and the ERM began to be seen as merely the first stage towards full monetary union, as soon as doubts about the prospects for EMU began to be widely entertained in 1992, the credibility of the ERM began to be questioned, too.

Throughout this period, sterling was being put under strain by the habit of financial analysts of treating Alan Walters' views, which had not only been widely publicised before his return but continued to be aired to groups of outsiders on both sides of the Atlantic at supposedly private gatherings, as representing the views of Margaret herself, and thus expecting that the pound would be allowed to sink freely without much preventive action. Paradoxically, Margaret's unwillingness to back me publicly on sterling added to the level of base rates required to maintain the pound at any particular level. During the first half of 1989, despite a further increase in base rates to 14 per cent, sterling had fallen by 6 per cent against the Mark and 7 per cent on the index. There was a real risk of a sterling crisis precipitating yet further increases in interest rates in late summer or autumn, particularly if Margaret mishandled negotiations at the Madrid summit later that June. The Walters problem was also starting to cause me – and the Government – considerable trouble in the House of Commons.

CHAPTER FIFTY-FOUR

THE ROCKY ROAD TO MADRID

To Resign or not to Resign? · Geoffrey Howe Enters the Picture
The First Thatcher/Howe/Lawson Meeting
The Second Thatcher/Howe/Lawson Meeting · Movement at Madrid
Geoffrey Howe Pays the Price

TO RESIGN OR NOT TO RESIGN?

John Smith, my Labour opposite number, was an effective parliamentary debater with a particular talent for mockery. He was a likeable and successful Edinburgh advocate, one of the few Labour front-benchers who had the capacity to earn more outside Parliament than he did within it. Smith's jokes, which were often very successful – he has a good, dry, sense of timing – were invariably better than his speeches, which were entirely predictable. They were always about the importance of training and of manufacturing industry, accompanied by allegations of Government misuse of North Sea oil – to which, as a Scottish Member, he characteristically attached grossly exaggerated economic importance. After Labour's fourth successive election defeat in 1992, he was to succeed Neil Kinnock as his Party's leader.[44]

Prior to Walters' reappearance in May 1989, Smith's poor understanding of economics and obvious reluctance to engage in serious economic argument had meant that I had very little difficulty dealing with him across the floor of the House. But once Walters was there Smith was able to ignore the economic policy issues with which he felt so uncomfortable and concentrate exclusively on the evident split between Margaret and myself, and in particular on Walters' role in this: a soft target which made the going very much more difficult. It was after a telling example of this in an Opposition Day debate in the House of Commons on 7 June that I began to think once again that it might be better all round if I were to resign. Margaret would be having her

[44] [2010 note] He died in office in 1994 and was succeeded as Leader of the Labour Party by Tony Blair.

annual reshuffle the following month, and if I were to go that would probably be the best time to do so. However, I needed to talk it over with someone first. I telephoned Willie Whitelaw at his home in Cumbria and asked him when he next planned to be in London, since I would value a private word with him. He said he would, of course, see me at any time, and we made a date for him to come to Number 11 at six o'clock on the evening of Tuesday, 13 June.

When we met it was clear that he was well aware of the acute difficulty of the position I was in and clearly felt that Margaret had become impossible. I told him I was contemplating resignation. He was not surprised, saying that although he hoped I would not resign, it was clearly a matter for me and that he would fully understand it if I did. He repeated what he had told me on an earlier occasion, that although he had made clear that he was always available, Margaret never consulted him on anything. We talked for some time; and although it resolved nothing, I felt a little better to have got it all off my chest.

GEOFFREY HOWE ENTERS THE PICTURE

My agonising was to be overtaken by events. Despite the disastrous mini-summit with the Dutch on 29 April, Geoffrey was anxious to keep up the pressure, and suggested that we might send Margaret, jointly, an analysis of the economics and politics of the ERM, in the context of the new situation created by our need to respond to the threat of EMU. We had, of course, been working together on the EMU issue, under Margaret's chairmanship, since the previous December; but had clearly got nowhere. I was sceptical; but said that I was happy to have our respective officials work something up, to see what it looked like.

Headed 'EC Issues and Madrid', the draft minute, which was of considerable length, argued that if we simply said 'no' to EMU at Madrid, the others would go ahead without us, creating a two-tier Europe, which would be very damaging for the UK in a number of specified ways. Our objective must therefore be to build on the S'Agaro formula of going ahead with Stage One of the Delors plan and postponing progress towards Stage Three until further work was done on what it really entailed, including notably its political implications; and there was some evidence that the Spanish presidency were prepared to work for an outcome along these lines (the Spanish Prime Minister, Felipe Gonzalez, subsequently confirmed this to Margaret when he saw her in London on 19 June). If it could be achieved, this would head off the intergovernmental conference and the subsequent amendment to the Treaty on which the French were so keen. But we could turn this trick only if we convinced a sufficient number of the others of our sincerity.

This was partly a matter of 'tone of voice', and partly of substance. The ERM issue, the paper argued, would inevitably arise at Madrid, given its central position in Stage One, and we would need to go beyond reiteration of the time-worn formula of entry when the time was right. It concluded that this should take the form of a 'non-legally binding' undertaking that sterling would join the ERM by the end of 1992 (the proposal that the Dutch Finance Minister, Ruding, had made at Chequers: a point the minute forebore to point out). Any such undertaking would be explicitly subject to the condition that all the major member states had abolished all exchange controls well before that date – as indeed the Community's Capital Liberalisation Directive already required them to do – and an understanding that the pound could enter with the wider margins pioneered by the Italian lira and emulated by the Spanish peseta. As for UK inflation, that was a matter for us and not the Community, but we were, in any event, determined that it must be on the way down again well before the end of 1992. The minute concluded by asking for a meeting with Margaret to discuss all this.

Geoffrey explained that he was deeply concerned that Margaret would badly mishandle the Madrid European Council which was now less than a fortnight off. Her manner at these meetings had become increasingly strident and confrontational, something that was no longer bringing any useful results; and the issues at stake were, thanks to EMU, more important than ever. I replied that, while I did not go along with everything in the minute, I agreed with him about the dangers we faced at Madrid, the risk of Margaret mishandling the Council, and the desirability of underlining the genuineness of our commitment to join the ERM by giving a latest date by which we would enter the mechanism. But I had some doubts about the desirability of a joint minute, and its likely effectiveness. I said that I would sleep on it and let him know my verdict in the morning.

THE FIRST THATCHER/ HOWE/ LAWSON MEETING

When I got back to Number 11 I told Thérèse of this conversation. There was much about it that left me feeling uneasy. I had an innate distaste for cabals and plots, and had never been part of one; and while a minute to Margaret, drafted by senior Foreign Office and Treasury officials, and copied to the top officials in both Departments, could hardly be called a cabal or a plot simply because it was signed by two Ministers rather than one, her growing bunker mentality might make it seem to her that way.

On the other hand, although there was in fact a very considerable difference between my view of the Community and Geoffrey's, I shared his apprehension at Margaret's likely handling of the Madrid Council. Moreover, although my reasons may not have been exactly the same as his, I could hardly dissociate myself from a move designed to promote sterling's membership of the ERM. The notion of setting a self-imposed deadline was something I had warmed to, as Margaret knew, when Ruding had suggested it at Chequers the previous month; while the proposed conditions effectively reiterated the line I had taken with the Treasury Select Committee the previous day.

The next morning I telephoned Geoffrey and told him that I would sign the joint minute subject to a number of amendments, none of a fundamental nature, and to his agreeing that the minute was sent to Margaret on Foreign Office paper, since the nature and tone of the minute, even amended as I sought, made its origins blindingly obvious and it would be foolish to try and conceal this. Geoffrey agreed, accepting all my amendments – which, although they somewhat shortened the minute, still left it the best part of twelve pages long – and the paper was sent to Number 10 that evening, Wednesday, 14 June.

Margaret's reaction was extraordinary. I could not imagine any other Prime Minister considering it in any way objectionable to have a meeting with her Foreign Secretary and Chancellor before embarking on an international politico-economic negotiation of the first importance. Indeed, most would have taken the initiative themselves. Not only had Margaret not done so, but – so great had her hostility to ERM entry become, even when the suggestion was of a deadline more than three years off and well into the next parliament – she was reluctant to hold a meeting even when her Foreign Secretary and Chancellor had sought one. Grudgingly, she agreed to see us at five o'clock in the afternoon the following Tuesday, almost a week ahead.

Geoffrey and I duly went to see her on the afternoon of 20 June. Geoffrey spoke to our joint paper, and she then waded in, saying that she disagreed completely with both our analysis and our conclusions. She was totally opposed to any commitment to join the ERM by any particular date, which would put an unwelcome constraint on economic and monetary policy as the date approached; it would in any case take no EMU tricks at all and we would simply have made a significant concession for no return; any departure from the 'when the time is right' formula, so soon after we had fought the Euro elections on that platform, would be seen by the Europeans as a sign of weakness; and the right course was not to decide any tactics now but for her to decide what to do when she was in Madrid and had heard what line the others were taking.

I argued that the EMU threat was very real indeed, and that, with such high stakes, simply playing it by ear was very dangerous; and that we were committed to joining the ERM – which I believed to be very much in our economic interest – anyway, so we had nothing to lose by playing that card at Madrid. Geoffrey came in again; but it was clear that we were getting nowhere, so I asked her not to close her mind but to reflect further on what we had written and said. She said she would, and trusted that we would reflect further on what she had said.

Her further reflection did not take nearly as long as she had taken to see us in the first place. Geoffrey telephoned me the following day, Thursday, 21 June, asking me if I could come across for a further word. When I arrived, he showed me a lengthy letter his office had received from Charles Powell, dated the previous evening. Purporting to be a note of our 20 June meeting, which for the most part it was, it also contained 'an alternative way of proceeding' to that which Geoffrey and I had suggested. Building on the approach I had taken with the Treasury Select Committee of indicating the conditions that would need to be fulfilled for sterling to join the ERM, it added to the exchange control abolition and inflation improvement conditions which I had suggested, both the creation of a 'level playing field' in Europe on the monetary *(sic)* front and the final completion of the Single Market – both of which, moreover, would have to be in effect long enough for us to be able to judge that they were being genuinely implemented by all member states.

This was palpably absurd. It had nothing whatever to do with securing an acceptable outcome from Madrid, and everything to do with postponing sterling's entry into the ERM as long as possible, if not indefinitely. The hand of Walters was all too visible.

THE SECOND THATCHER/ HOWE/LAWSON MEETING

Geoffrey understandably felt we could not leave the matter there, and that we should seek a further meeting. On the morning of Friday, 23 June, we sent Margaret a further joint minute, this time very much shorter. It gave a crisp restatement of the main thrust of the earlier minute, and responded to the 'alternative way of proceeding' by pointing out that this would take no tricks whatever at Madrid, which was the object of the exercise. Indeed, by inventing further, largely irrelevant, reasons to delay for a considerable number of years sterling's entry into the ERM, it would if anything be counterproductive. The minute concluded by asking Margaret for a further meeting before she and Geoffrey flew to Madrid on the Sunday evening, particularly since I would not be at Madrid myself.

After we had agreed the text of the minute, Geoffrey, who had clearly been thinking further about his future, told me that if the Powell letter really reflected Margaret's planned position at Madrid, and she was totally unwilling to make any forward move of the kind advocated in our original minute, then he would feel obliged to resign. This took me by surprise, as I had (wrongly as it eventually turned out) never thought of Geoffrey as the resigning type. But I told him that we were both in this together, and if he went, then clearly I would have to go, too.

Margaret was very angry indeed that we had returned to the charge. She first said she had no time to see us at all, as she would be working on the papers for Madrid. She then tried to fob us off by offering to talk to me on the telephone at midday on Sunday and to Geoffrey Howe afterwards on the flight to Madrid. This was a transparent divide-and-rule tactic, increasingly characteristic of her premiership. She had long believed that Geoffrey and I were plotting against her, but this was, in fact, the only instance in eight years as Cabinet colleagues when we combined to promote a particular course of action. Very grudgingly, she eventually agreed to a meeting at Number 10 at nine o'clock in the morning of Sunday, 25 June, a time which she knew would cause us both the maximum inconvenience.

On the Sunday morning we left Dorneywood and Chevening respectively and met briefly at Number 11 before going next door to see Margaret. We made it clear that, this time, we wished to see her alone, with no official present. The atmosphere was unbelievably tense. As before, Geoffrey opened, and spoke briefly along the lines of the minute. Margaret was immovable. Geoffrey then said that if she had no time whatever for his advice, and was not prepared to make the sort of forward move at Madrid necessary to avoid the disastrous outcome he feared, then he would have no alternative but to resign. I then chipped in, briefly, to say 'You should know, Prime Minister, that if Geoffrey goes, I must go too'. There was an icy silence, and the meeting came to an abrupt end, with nothing resolved.

MOVEMENT AT MADRID

On the aeroplane to Madrid that evening, Margaret refused to utter a single word to Geoffrey. When they arrived at the Ritz Hotel in Madrid, she immediately repaired to her room with Charles Powell to work out her line for the following day's meeting, ostentatiously excluding Geoffrey from the exercise. But in the short term it proved to be the storm before the calm. At the European Council meeting the next day the other heads of government, not to mention Geoffrey, were pleased and surprised to discover an apparently new Margaret Thatcher, and lost no time in informing the Press. Where she had previously been strident she was now conciliatory. That was – to quote the Howe/Lawson minute – largely a matter of 'tone of voice'. But there was a change of content, too.

This concerned the sensitive issue of sterling and the ERM. In place of the hackneyed formula of joining 'when the time is right', she sought to spell out more precisely what this meant, in terms that were very much more forthcoming than those set out in the Walters-inspired 'alternative way of proceeding' contained in the Powell letter. She subsequently conveyed this to the House of Commons in an uncharacteristically obscure way. In her Statement to the House of 29 June on the outcome of the Madrid European Council she said:

> The Council agreed that the measures necessary to achieve the first stage of progressive realisation of economic and monetary union will be implemented from 1 July 1990. These include completion of the Single Market, abolition of all foreign exchange controls, a free market in financial services and strengthening of the Community's competition policy by reducing state aids ... I reaffirmed our intention to join the ERM, but we must first get our inflation down. We shall look for satisfactory implementation of other aspects of the first phase of the Delors report, including free movement of capital and (sic) abolition of foreign exchange control.

It had been explained to the Press that what this meant was that there were five so-called 'Madrid conditions': lower inflation and the abandonment of exchange control – the two conditions I had stipulated to the Treasury Select Committee – plus *further progress* towards completion of the Single Market, free competition in financial services, and the strengthening of European competition policy.

Irrelevant though these last three conditions were to the objective question of ERM membership, it was clear that they were as long as a piece of string: they could be interpreted as having been satisfied at any time. By contrast, the original Walters/Powell formulation had implied that there could be no ERM membership for some four years at the earliest – the single market was not due for final completion until the end of 1992, which meant that even in the unlikely event of everything going according to plan, it would have been well into 1993 before the monitoring period had been completed.

Margaret clearly felt that she had stood her ground. She had refused to give a deadline for ERM entry, and had produced a new formula which, although very different from the old one, would, she believed, give her almost as much freedom to decide that the time for entry had not yet come. She also believed Walters' assertion that the ERM would, in any event, collapse as a result of the removal of exchange controls. But despite all Ingham's efforts to sell the new formula as only a minor change, the Press, perhaps influenced in part by her new tone of voice, universally interpreted it as a major new development and a big step towards ERM membership. And a particular interpretation of the Madrid conditions did indeed assist my successor, John Major, to persuade a Margaret Thatcher weakened by my resignation to assent to ERM membership some sixteen months later. But that was not what she had in mind at the time.

Whether the original Howe/Lawson proposal would have succeeded in arresting the Treaty changes required to implement a single European currency managed by a single European central bank is something we shall never know. Certainly Margaret's contrary approach failed to do so. The Madrid Council went far beyond the S'Agaro Ecofin, agreeing to embark forthwith on the preparations for an Intergovernmental Conference to determine the Treaty changes required to implement Stages Two and Three of the Delors plan for a single currency, a process which was to culminate in the Maastricht Treaty of December 1991.

GEOFFREY HOWE PAYS THE PRICE

The Madrid Council ended on the afternoon of Tuesday, 27 June. I saw Geoffrey in his room at the House of Commons after the ten o'clock vote that evening, to discuss with him where we stood on the resignation question. The media, rightly or wrongly, were without exception hailing Madrid – which Margaret was felt to have handled with unaccustomed skill – as a major breakthrough on the ERM, and our back-benchers, particularly those in the pro-ERM camp, were echoing the chorus. He understandably felt that, although she had rejected our deadline proposal, a resignation in those circumstances would have been bizarre and incomprehensible. But the events that had preceded Madrid were a profound shock to Margaret, and relations between the three of us were never the same again. I have little doubt that, whether or not she was actually planning to do so, our joint resignation warning in June 1989 ensured that she removed Geoffrey from the job he loved above all others in her summer reshuffle the following month. No doubt she would have removed me, too, had she felt strong enough to do so.

Not that Geoffrey expected it. Right up to the last moment, David Waddington, the Chief Whip, was consulting him about the reshuffle, asking him whom he wished to have as his junior Foreign Office Ministers. It was in a state of considerable shock that he telephoned me at Number 11 on the morning of Monday, 24 July, to tell me that Margaret had told him that she was relieving him of the Foreign Office and that he could have the choice of being either Leader of the House or Home Secretary, a post then held by Douglas Hurd. If he chose the latter, Douglas would become Leader of the House. He said he would think about it and let her know later that day. He asked me what I thought he should do – he was clearly planning to consult a number of friends and colleagues – and told me he was thinking of accepting neither offer, and resigning.

I said that whether he resigned or not was a matter for him, on which I could not advise him. But if he chose not to resign, I had no doubt that he should choose the Home Office, which when all was said and done was a major Department of State and the only one of the 'big three' which he had not himself held, rather than be Leader of the House, which in my view was simply a second-rank job which provided no departmental power base at all. I also urged him, if he did want to stay, to insist on being nominated as Deputy Prime Minister. In the event, he did do the latter; but to my surprise opted for Leader of the House – a big mistake.

Later on he told me that he should have resigned. I was not surprised. Not only was his ministerial post a poor one, but Margaret went out of her way to humiliate him at every turn, berating him in front of colleagues and conspicuously excluding him from *ad hoc* meetings of senior Ministers. It was extraordinary conduct, since even if she had invited him – which she should have done, given his seniority and experience, leaving aside the empty title of Deputy Prime Minister she had reluctantly accorded him – she had no need to accept his advice. It was yet another example of her recklessness which one senior official, a particularly shrewd and close observer, described to me as the outstanding characteristic of her long-drawn-out final phase. She had become reckless over Europe, reckless over the Poll Tax, reckless over what she said in public, and reckless over her colleagues.

On the afternoon of the Cabinet reshuffle, after Geoffrey had decided he was not going to resign, Margaret asked to see me. She explained that Geoffrey would have to hand over the occupancy of Chevening to his successor as Foreign Secretary, my former number two, John Major, whom I had met emerging from her room in a daze as I arrived. John had of course expected promotion to a Department of his own, had always hoped to succeed me as Chancellor in due course, and had ultimate aspirations to Number 10; but never in his wildest dreams had he seen himself as Foreign Secretary.

Margaret told me that the reason why she wanted to see me was that, deprived of Chevening, Geoffrey would need to have Dorneywood instead. Did I mind handing it over to him? It was not, of course, a question, but an instruction. It was also a considerable, if not entirely unexpected, blow. We had grown to love Dorneywood; and it had been the tranquillity of that idyllic retreat, and the pampering I had enjoyed from its admirable staff, that had kept me going despite the stresses and strains of my problems with Margaret over the previous year and more. But Geoffrey was formally Deputy Prime Minister, and that was that. Margaret must have enjoyed the irony. I told her that we had planned to spend the children's summer holiday there, but that I would, of course, vacate it after that.

I happened to be in the Chamber when Geoffrey first rose to speak in his new capacity as Leader of the House. A loud and prolonged spontaneous cheer rose from the massed Conservative benches of a kind that is rarely heard. It was a tribute to the affection in which Geoffrey was held within the Party. But more than anything else, it was a clear warning to Margaret. No experienced Tory Member could have failed to get the message – except perhaps one: Margaret Hilda Thatcher.

CHAPTER FIFTY-FIVE

FROM MADRID TO ANTIBES

A Cabinet for the Election · Policy on the Hoof · Competing Currencies
Ecofin at Antibes · Posthumous Publication

A CABINET FOR THE ELECTION

Margaret behaved little better to her colleagues after the July 1989 reshuffle than she had before. The press briefings by Ingham became ever more presidential and Margaret's trust in – and dependence upon – her kitchen cabinet ever more pronounced. Yet seeing her at close quarters it seemed clear to me that she had in fact been quite shaken by the turbulence created by the reshuffle. At the first subsequent Cabinet meeting she surprised us all by announcing, out of the blue, that she now had the Cabinet with which she planned to fight the next election, and that there would therefore be no further Cabinet changes for the remainder of that parliament. She had never before vouchsafed anything to Cabinet about her future reshuffle intentions: yet this statement was volunteered and clearly premeditated.

Meanwhile, after the drama of Madrid at the end of June, both Margaret and I began independently to start worrying about the domestic economy again. She asked for a meeting with me to discuss the situation, at which I was to bring along Peter Middleton and Terry Burns. This was fixed for 5 July. Two days earlier, I held a meeting of my own, to which I invited Robin Leigh-Pemberton and his senior colleagues from the Bank. I expressed concern at the slowness of bank lending and consumer credit, and the spending they were financing, to decelerate in response to the monetary squeeze. The narrow measure of money, M0, remained well above its target range. I was told that it was the considered view of the Bank that monetary policy should not be tightened further for the time being. So far as I was concerned, the operative words were 'for the time being'.

At Margaret's meeting of 5 July she expressed considerable concern at the outlook for inflation. The underlying rate of inflation, which in the first quarter of 1988 had still been well below 4 per cent, where it had stood for the previous two years, had since then risen steadily to within a whisker of 6 per cent. I told her I shared her concern, and felt that the time was fast approaching when we should raise interest rates by a further 1 per cent. Predictably, this did not attract her at all. Arguing that any further rise in interest rates would raise mortgage rates, and hence the headline RPI, which in turn would add to wage pressure and upset the financial markets, and might tip the economy into recession, she said she would rather see interest rates held at 14 per cent until the RPI started to fall, when they could be brought down again.

I gave a full warning of the risks in my annual 'end-of-term letter' to all Conservative MPs on 26 July 1989, when I said I would keep interest rates 'as high as is necessary for as long as is necessary', a formula I had been using for some time. As usual, I included a positive element, pointing out that business investment as a share of national income was higher than at any time since records began, and that the UK had moved from the bottom to the top of the European investment league. Not only had investment surged ahead, but its quality had improved out of recognition. Indeed despite the severity of the subsequent recession, investment remained much higher as a share of GDP than had occurred in previous downturns.

POLICY ON THE HOOF

My other main preoccupation during the summer of 1989 was with developments on the EMU front. At her first pre-Madrid meeting with Geoffrey and me on 20 June 1989, Margaret had expressed the view that it would be more sensible to play the Summit by ear than to agree tactics in advance. This was of course a transparent device to explain her unwillingness to discuss tactics with either of us. But, amazingly, it was also how she did in part behave. In the middle of the discussions at Madrid she announced that the UK would be putting forward its own proposals for monetary union, as an alternative to the Delors plan which we rejected.

In itself there was much to be said for this sort of approach. It was clearly more positive than the 'No, no, no' which had hitherto been her preferred negotiating stance, and was more likely to bring out the underlying issues. But suddenly to announce this at a European Council without any prior discussion with her Chancellor, and without the faintest idea of what the UK alternative might be, was, to say the least, an unusual way of proceeding.

The first I and my senior officials knew of this proposal was a report on the radio from Madrid which stated that the Treasury was already working on alternatives to Delors. Peter Middleton subsequently told me that he heard the news when driving his car, and was so astonished that he nearly crashed into a tree. About twenty-four hours later came the request from Number 10 to validate the Prime Minister's promise. My officials gave me a submission setting out every possibility they could think of – there were not very many – including a return to the gold standard.

COMPETING CURRENCIES

I soon decided that only one was really worth pursuing. The great economist and political philosopher, Friedrich Hayek, had some years previously come up with the idea of removing the monopoly of issuing currency from the Central Banks, privatising it, and opening it up to competition. Hayek's idea was that as in other private markets, so with currencies: competition would ensure that the best currency – that which kept its value best, and was thus the most sought after – would steadily increase its share of the market.

I had long been interested in Hayek's analysis – and had, indeed, referred to it *en passant* in my IEA lecture the previous summer. I told Peter Middleton that the alternative form of monetary union we should propose should be based on the Hayekian idea of competing currencies, but with the fundamental difference that currency creation would remain in the hands of the national Central Banks, which in turn would act within the framework of the ERM. The element of competition would be achieved by removing all barriers to the use in any one Community country of the currencies of other member states, in the true spirit of the single market. With complete interchangeability and no legal impediments, good currencies would threaten gradually to drive out the bad, in a happy reversal of Gresham's law, until eventually Europe might theoretically find itself with a single currency, freely chosen by the people.

Certainly, Central Banks would have a clear incentive to compete, if only to collect the profit from the note issue, or seignorage as it is technically known, and if the competition failed to lead to a single currency – and competition does not normally lead to monopoly – that would be either because two or more currencies were considered more or less equally desirable, or simply because the people of Europe did not want a single currency. But even then the removal of all barriers between the different European moneys was something that could just about be considered a monetary union. But no new institutions, no treaty amendment, and no massive transfer of sovereignty would be required.

Peter then commissioned a Treasury paper along these lines, and I went off to enjoy my last summer holiday at Dorneywood with Thérèse and the children.

ECOFIN AT ANTIBES

When I returned in the latter part of August and found the paper waiting for me, it was clear that it would have to be completely redrafted. This was duly done, but the hiatus was sufficient to ensure that the paper could not be properly vetted by me and cleared with Margaret – who accepted the general idea, when I put it to her – in time for the informal Ecofin Council to be held on the French Riviera on 8 and 9 September at the Hôtel du Cap/Eden Roc at Cap d'Antibes.

This was one of the few informal Ecofins to which Thérèse decided to accompany me, and she certainly chose well. Only a Socialist government would have contemplated putting up twelve Finance Ministers and their wives, twelve Central Bank Governors and their wives, twelve 'deputies' and their wives, various European Commissioners and their wives, and assorted hangers-on, at a hotel whose cheapest room cost £800 a night (our own suite was priced at £2,000 a night). If any hotel was worth that extraordinary price, however, that was: the setting, the comfort, the food – they produced what in my opinion was the best Mesclun salad in the world – the wines, the service and, so far as I had time to enjoy them, the facilities, were unbeatable.

When we got on to the subject of EMU and the Delors Report, I told my fellow Finance Ministers and the Central Bank Governors that we would soon be publishing the paper that Margaret had effectively promised at Madrid, and proceeded to give a resumé of its contents. Delors himself was, inevitably, extremely hostile, but few others were. The prevailing attitude was one of polite scepticism and of reserving final judgement until they had read the paper. I had no overt support, even though Karl Otto Pöhl said to me, shortly after I had spoken, as he passed me on his way out of the room, 'I agreed with every word you said'. I was far too old a hand to believe that that would lead to anything: I was much more interested to discover the doubts that were beginning to dawn in the minds of my fellow Finance Ministers at the private discussion we had over lunch, and the strong desire of most of them to adopt a more cautious, step-by-step approach than the Commission's.

Predictably, the British Press reported the UK proposal as having been greeted with total hostility and derision. During Margaret's time, the Brussels-based Press corps, who for the most part covered these events, had become accustomed to writing 'UK isolated' stories and could think in terms of little else. They had also got into the habit of taking their cue from the Commission, with whom they had a continuing close relationship. But I was myself remiss in not briefing selected journalists privately in advance. As it was, they had difficulty in understanding what the proposal meant, and scoffed at the idea of a tobacconist in Aberdeen being obliged to accept payment in Greek Drachmas. In fact, of course, he would have been no more obliged to take Greek Drachmas than he is to take credit cards – the true international money, in many ways, as it happens – since the idea was essentially permissive rather than mandatory.

My proposals were, of course, disappointing to those who were interested in European money only as a means to political union. Some officials in the Foreign Office, Bank of England and even the Treasury were worried that the paper simply proposed an intensification of Stage One, and that no new international body was elaborated. That, however, was one of its great virtues.

In any event, I had no qualms about putting the emphasis on the twin pillars of a genuine single market and the fuller development of the ERM. It was not as if my proposals pointed to inaction. Even with the abolition of exchange controls there was a long way to go before currencies were freely interchangeable in the fullest sense. One example of the remaining restrictions related to the currency and geographical location of the assets of long-term savings institutions such as pension funds. Another was legal impediments to the simplification of international cheque-clearing systems. Some of these obstacles exist even in single currency areas such as the US, and are worth removing for their own sake.

POSTHUMOUS PUBLICATION

The press of events meant that it was not until October that the paper, which I called *An Evolutionary Approach to Economic and Monetary Union*, was in a final form with which I was content. It began by pointing out the flaws in the Delors approach, including *inter alia*, the fact that:

> By eliminating both competition and accountability ... the Delors version risks producing a higher inflation rate in Europe. The administratively imposed changes that are required would inevitably fail to foresee future developments. And they involve major constitutional and institutional changes which are wholly unnecessary.

Its main argument was that the removal of exchange controls and the creation of a single financial area, together with the ERM, the possibility of currency substitution, and the influence of capital and labour mobility, would all exert a powerful influence towards stable prices and exchange rates. The emphasis was on the financial integration of Europe emerging from Stage One rather than from any new Brussels-type institutions. The currency basket known as the Ecu could come into wider use, first for financial, but perhaps eventually for everyday, purposes. The paper also suggested freezing the composition of the Ecu basket permanently – a step eventually incorporated into the Maastricht Treaty.

The evolutionary route to what might just be called a sort of monetary union was summarised in paragraph 23:

> Realignments would become rarer, fluctuations within the ERM band would become smaller, and the EMS could evolve into a system of more or less fixed exchange rates. Concurrently with minimal exchange rate uncertainty and reduced costs of switching between currencies, all Community currencies would become effectively interchangeable. In this way a practical monetary union would be achieved as a result of a gradual evolutionary process.

After I had sent the paper to Margaret, she decided that it would have to be formally cleared for publication by a small group consisting not merely of herself, myself and the Foreign Secretary, now John Major, as had been her practice on similar occasions hitherto, but also of Nick Ridley. Nick had become her strongest supporter over the ERM, and had already seen me privately to voice his disagreement with the policy I was pursuing.

Margaret of course well knew of Nick's views, and her inclusion of him in the meeting to clear the paper was not intended to make my task any easier. The meeting eventually took place on the afternoon of Wednesday, 25 October – ironically, the day before my resignation – and the paper was cleared for publication with only the most trivial of amendments. My officials, who had been apprehensive of Margaret's reaction to a paper whose proposals assumed sterling's membership of what would ultimately become an unequivocally 'hard' version of the ERM, felt that I had achieved something of a coup.

Certainly, it was never likely that the paper's proposals, particularly launched so late in the day, would deflect the rest of the Community's political leaders from the Delors path on which they had already embarked. Its long-term merit was that it set out a series of measures, desirable in themselves, to which the Community could return if and when the momentum for full-blooded monetary union faltered for other reasons. In the short term the paper's value was largely domestic. It contained, for the first time, a firm Government commitment that sterling would join the ERM when the Madrid conditions, which were clearly spelled out in a perfectly acceptable form, were satisfied. This definitive statement meant that, when Margaret subsequently sought to add further conditions as and when they entered her head, it was easier to ignore them as apocryphal.

My paper was eventually published, by my successor, John Major, on 2 November, the week after my resignation. Subsequently the Government shifted its allegiance to a new and much more complex alternative to Delors, the so-called 'hard Ecu' proposal. A highly ingenious but fundamentally unworkable proposal which included an unwise Euro-institutional component, it was understood by few and served chiefly as a talisman: for some time any Minister asked where the UK stood on EMU could reply, 'We favour the hard Ecu'. The scheme had been sold to Margaret by the irrepressible Michael Butler, a former UK Ambassador to the Community who, in 1979, had sold the previous Labour Government the idea of being in the EMS while outside the ERM. Very few outside the UK showed the slightest interest in it, and John Major quite rightly abandoned it well ahead of the negotiations over the Maastricht Treaty.

CHAPTER FIFTY-SIX

COUNTDOWN TO RESIGNATION

A Sticky Wicket · Bad Timing by the Bundesbank · 15 Per Cent
The Siege of Stoney Stanton · Party Conference Success · The Iceberg and its Tip
The Die is Cast · On the Brink of Resignation

A STICKY WICKET

Returning to London from a visit to Washington on Thursday, 28 September, I had to turn my mind to my speech for the Party Conference, which was due to begin some twelve days later. The economic background had changed markedly for the worse since the previous year's Party Conference; but at least I could make something, if only as a peroration, of the remarkable events that were unfolding in Eastern Europe, with the collapse of Socialism and the first faltering moves towards a genuine market economy. The tide of ideas, which I had first invoked in my 1986 Party Conference speech, was flooding into areas that I had never then envisaged.

But there was no point in deluding myself that there was going to be an easy wicket on which to bat; and to add to the problem sterling was looking far from healthy. The big fall had been in the first half of the year, when the pound had dropped from DM3.21 at the start of 1989 to DM3.02 by the end of June, and from $1.81 to $1.55 over the same period. Then there had been a brief recovery in the course of July, but since then it had drifted down again to DM3.02 and $1.62. Market sentiment was not at all good, and in that context its proximity to the psychologically important DM3 level was particularly worrying. It was when sterling was weak that the Walters view, which was widely taken by the markets to be that of Margaret, too, that sterling should be free to 'find its own level', was most damaging. I set up a stocktaking meeting, with the usual cast, for the following Monday, 2 October.

BAD TIMING BY THE BUNDESBANK

The news that Robin Leigh-Pemberton brought to the meeting could not have been more inconvenient. With the Party Conference due to start on Tuesday, 10

October, it appeared that there was a strong chance that the Bundesbank Council, at its regular fortnightly meeting on Thursday, 5 October, would raise German interest rates. I had believed for some time that a further one-point rise in UK interest rates would probably be needed on purely domestic grounds. It was true that the underlying rate of inflation had fallen back slightly from the 6 per cent level reached in May, but the inflationary evidence that had worried me in the first week of July had in no way abated three months later. The timing, however, was diabolical: the last thing I wanted to do was to raise interest rates on the eve of the Party Conference. I asked Robin to find out more about the Bundesbank's intentions and to let me know.

On the Wednesday, 4 October, Robin informed me that the Bundesbank would definitely be raising their interest rates the following day. The only unresolved question was whether the increase would be half a point or a full point. I arranged to see Margaret at five o'clock that afternoon, to tell her the unpalatable news, and the consequences as I saw them. I told her that if the Germans moved by half a point, I was prepared to hold the line with the aid of large-scale intervention. But if they moved by a full point, then I saw no alternative but for us to follow, uncomfortable as it was on the eve of the Party Conference – and I was well aware of the sort of reception I could expect for my speech in the circumstances. Not to do so would be to risk a full-blown sterling crisis and the possibility of being forced to raise interest rates in the middle of the Conference itself.

Margaret very reluctantly agreed that following the Germans immediately, in the event of a full point increase, would in the circumstances probably be the lesser evil, but expressed the fervent hope that they would do only half a point.

I called a markets meeting, again with the usual cast, for half past eight the following morning, Thursday, 5 October. There was no dissent from my proposition that, if the Bundesbank moved a full point that day, we should follow. Not to do so would have sent a signal to the markets either that short-term political considerations now weighed more heavily than our anti-inflation resolve, or that we were no longer concerned about the level of sterling – or probably both. Even so, there was likely to be pressure on the pound and we agreed that we should not defend the DM3 benchmark regardless of cost, but that it would be better if it were not breached. We then went on to discuss the nuts and bolts of the actions we might well have to make.

15 PER CENT

At lunchtime that day the Bundesbank announced that its interest rates would indeed be raised by a full point. We immediately followed, as did most other

European countries, including a number of those, like us, outside the ERM. This meant base rates of 15 per cent, the highest they had been for very nearly eight years. I presented the move as part of an international attack on inflation, which had indeed been rising worldwide. In economic terms, I had no doubt that the move was correct; but the politics could not have been worse. It was clear to me that I would have to recast my Conference speech completely, taking the interest rate issue head on, and make a virtue of having put economic rectitude above short-term political advantage.

The Conservative Party Conference was, by tradition, held in the North of England and the South of England in alternate years. There were a number of different venues in the south, of which Brighton was the most popular; but in the north there was only one: Blackpool, a holiday resort unique in the world, which everyone should visit once in their lives, even if many may choose not to repeat the experience. In fact, the wonderfully old-fashioned gilt and plush interior of Blackpool's Winter Garden, where the Conference itself was held, made it my favourite venue, with an atmosphere no modern hall could match. It was Blackpool's turn in 1989, and I went home to Stoney Stanton on the Friday evening to start thinking about how I would rewrite my speech, as well as catching up on the rest of my workload, which was always particularly heavy at that time of year.

I was telephoned there on the Saturday evening and informed that the following day's *Sunday Times* was carrying a story that claimed that Walters had opposed the rise in interest rates, and that Margaret had 'reluctantly sided with her Chancellor'. The paper went on to describe this as 'another damaging disagreement on policy between Lawson and Walters', and the clear implication for the markets of Margaret's alleged 'reluctance' was that there would be no further increase in interest rates, whatever happened to the pound.

Through the good offices of the unfailingly cheerful and efficient Number 10 switchboard, I telephoned Walters at home, who professed complete mystification about the story, swearing that he had not spoken to anyone. But he refused to issue a denial. Similar suggestions had in fact appeared over the previous few days from some writers of City circulars and a group of journalists who considered themselves to be Margaret's praetorian guard; but *The Sunday Times* story was by far the most serious one, as that paper has a wide circulation among the business community.

To this day, I do not know how the paper came by their story. Nor do I much care. The point was that Number 10 allowed *The Sunday Times* story to pass without an explicit denial: any dissociation was so feeble that the markets were left to draw their own conclusions. Not surprisingly, sterling, which had rallied at the end of the previous week following the base rate increase, plunged on the Monday morning, taking it below the DM3 benchmark for the first time since the March 1988 uncapping.

THE SIEGE OF STONEY STANTON

One of the advantages of Stoney Stanton when the Party Conference was at Blackpool was its geographical location, almost exactly halfway between Blackpool and London. I had planned that year to write my speech, which was bound to be a difficult one, in the peace and quiet of the Old Rectory on Tuesday and Wednesday, following a flying visit to a pre-conference dinner on the Monday.

I duly arrived at Blackpool on the Monday evening, and Margaret suggested that I call in at her suite in the Imperial Hotel *en route* to the dinner, so that we would be seen arriving at the dinner together as a show of solidarity. While the appearance was no substitute for the reality, I could see that the appearance was better than nothing, particularly so far as the media and the financial markets were concerned, and we were accordingly televised descending the staircase of the Imperial Hotel together, somewhat awkwardly, and to a distinctly sceptical massed Press. As I left Blackpool for Stoney Stanton after the dinner, as planned, I had no inkling of the horrors in store.

The next morning, Tuesday, 10 October, I was assailed by the worst Press I encountered throughout the whole of my political career. Almost the whole of the front page of the *Daily Mail*, and much more, was devoted to a scurrilous personal attack on me, headlined 'This Bankrupt Chancellor' and accompanied by a large and grotesque cartoon. I was accused of betraying my Party, my Prime Minister and the British people, and there was much else in a similar vein. Margaret telephoned me at home very early in the morning to tell me how horrified she had been to read it in her hotel suite at Blackpool – Party Conference week being one of the few occasions when she actually read the papers rather than Ingham's carefully drafted summaries.

But while that was the worst of the Tuesday Press, it was the rest which caused the greater problem. To my astonishment, the other papers were all running a cock-and-bull story that I had fled from Blackpool because I could not face the wrath of the Constituency representatives and that I might never return, resigning with my tail between my legs instead.

Before long, I found myself under siege. The garden of the Old Rectory was walled on three sides, with the fourth open to the old churchyard. Reporters, Press photographers and television cameramen turned up in the churchyard in large numbers, clambering over the graves to try and get a view of me inside the house – my study overlooked the garden – and to catch me should I venture outside. When a few tired of waiting in the churchyard and invaded the garden to try and get a better look through the window, and to ring the front doorbell in an attempt to get me outside, I was obliged to telephone the Leicestershire Special Branch, who looked after me splendidly whenever I was out and about in the county, to get them ejected. I had told the intrusive media people right at the start that I was working on my speech, that I would be returning to Blackpool the next day, and that I would appreciate it if they left me alone to get on with it. But they insisted on keeping a noisy vigil in the churchyard. The oasis of calm to which I thought I had repaired to write my speech turned out to be anything but that.

PARTY CONFERENCE SUCCESS

I returned to Blackpool the following afternoon, Wednesday, 11 October and walked into the Imperial Hotel to a battery of waiting television cameras and young girls holding out microphones, yelling at me, 'When are you going to resign Mr Lawson?' It was clearly even more important that my speech at the end of the economic debate went down well. Fortunately, it did, from the very beginning:

> I warmly welcome this motion, with its emphasis on the paramount need to fight inflation. Indeed, that is why I raised interest rates to 15 per cent last week. It was not a decision I took lightly. But it had to be done. Of course, I knew it wouldn't be popular. But anyone who becomes Chancellor in order to be popular has chosen the wrong job. I have only one ambition in politics. That is the long-term well-being of the British people. There is no greater threat to that well-being than inflation.
>
> Inevitably people ask whether there is an alternative to high interest rates at the present time. And whether they can be sure that the policy will work. Bluntly, the answer is that there is no alternative and the policy will work. I realise the problems high interest rates cause to homeowners, particularly those with large mortgages, and to many small businesses. But the damage caused by high inflation would be far, far worse.

This led to my message to the markets and to Margaret alike: 'Nor is there any salvation in the rake's progress of perpetual devaluation ... The Conservative Party never has been, and never will be, the party of devaluation'; then to my reminder to the Party that the Thatcher Government had faced economic problems in the past and surmounted them all; and financially to the 'Eastern Europe' peroration – almost all that remained of my original speech.

I was no doubt helped by a feeling amongst my traditionally loyalist audience that, whatever their own reservations about the level of interest rates, the *Daily Mail* had gone way over the top in its hatchet job on me, and that the Party was not to be pushed around by the tabloid Press. At any rate, the speech, according to a somewhat nonplussed Press, was punctuated by more than thirty rounds of applause and greeted at the end by the longest and most enthusiastic standing ovation of any speech at that year's conference – apart, of course, from the ritual hysteria reserved for the Leader.

Indeed – something I would not have thought possible a week earlier – it turned out to be one of the few high spots of a generally lacklustre Conference. The theme of the Conference, too, was to prove ill-fated. Kenneth Baker, by then Party Chairman, and uncomfortably aware of Margaret's growing unpopularity in the country, decided to build on her post-reshuffle announcement to Cabinet that she had the Cabinet with which she planned to fight the next election, and make the Conference theme 'The Right Team', with omnipresent photographs of various members of what was by then for the most part a highly experienced Cabinet. Within little more than a year, one-third of 'The Right Team' – Geoffrey Howe, Norman Fowler, Peter Walker, Nicholas Ridley, Cecil Parkinson, Margaret Thatcher herself and, of course, myself – were, for one reason or another, no longer members of it.

There was no time, however, to savour my political success at Blackpool. The following Thursday, 19 October, I had to satisfy the financial markets at the annual banquet given by the Lord Mayor at the Mansion House. But before then, Margaret was off to Kuala Lumpur for the Annual Commonwealth Prime Ministers' meeting.

THE ICEBERG AND ITS TIP

No sooner had Margaret left for Kuala Lumpur the following day than the Walters problem erupted once again. The *Financial Times* of Wednesday, 18 October carried extracts from an article by him scheduled to appear in due course in an obscure American academic journal. In it he reiterated his familiar view that the ERM was 'half-baked' and that the case for sterling joining the ERM had never 'attained even a minimum level of plausibility', adding that 'my advice has been for Britain to retain its system of flexible exchange rates and stay out ... So far, Mrs Thatcher has concurred'.

So much, evidently, for the British Government's recently reaffirmed commitment to join, once a number of readily fulfillable conditions were met. Walters subsequently complained that he should not be criticised for an article he had written well before he returned to Number 10. That was disingenuous, to say the least. Certainly, the unpublished article had been written many months before. But it was well after he had been re-installed as Margaret's personal economic adviser that he had brought its existence to the attention of the *Financial Times* and sent them a copy with explicit permission to quote from it.

In fact, this particular Walters article was among the least serious of his hostile activities. As I was to remark in my resignation speech:

> It was of significance only inasmuch as it represented the tip of a singularly ill-concealed iceberg, with all the destructive potential that icebergs possess.

Walters' activities were well known on both sides of the Atlantic. To cite just one piece of evidence, Peter Riddell, the highly respected American Editor of the *Financial Times*, wrote that:

> Alan Walters ... has recently told US bankers and policy-makers that sterling needs to fall to avoid a severe recession in the UK ... His comments concerned some of his American listeners, according to participants, who felt they contradicted the message from Mr Lawson about trying to secure a stable pound.

I received independent corroboration of this episode in a letter from an eminent British economist who happened to be present. Although the report appeared two days after my resignation, the event to which it referred occurred, of course, while I was still Chancellor and Walters was still personal economic adviser to the Prime Minister. It was the iceberg that concerned me; not the minor, if clearly visible, tip.

All the same the article was yet another gift to the Opposition, who made it the focus of their attack on the Government at Treasury questions the following day, Thursday, 19 October. I replied frostily that Walters' views on the ERM were 'clearly not the view of the Government'. Kinnock, too, made the apparent confirmation of the gulf between Margaret and myself contained in the Walters article the core of his assault at Prime Minister's questions, which immediately follow Treasury questions; to which Geoffrey Howe, deputising for the absent Margaret Thatcher, responded almost as dismissively.

That evening I made what was to be my last Mansion House speech. I made the customary restatement of the Government's monetary policy, stressing the unavoidable reliance on interest rates and the spurious nature of the suggested alternatives, announced some minor technical improvements to funding policy, took the opportunity to reaffirm the Madrid formula for sterling's entry into the ERM in a positive light, and trailed my forthcoming paper on competing currencies as an 'evolutionary and market-based' route to a form of EMU, in preference to the Delors Report's 'centralist and bureaucratic agenda that poses grave threats to any known form of democratic accountability' – which, I added, if attempted, was likely to 'end in tears'. I concluded my last Mansion House speech with these words:

> In the perspective of history, what will stand out about this period is not the short-term vagaries of the economic cycle, which will always be with us, but the long-term improvement in the supply performance of the British economy. An improvement so clearly shown in the quantity and quality of business investment, and the greatly improved productivity and profitability of British industry. The people of Britain may have temporarily forgotten the habit of thrift. That is undoubtedly a short-term problem. But at the same time they have rediscovered the spirit of enterprise. And that is the greatest prize of all.

Some journalists read that as a valedictory: they were not entirely unperceptive. As to the people of Britain having temporarily forgotten the habit of thrift, which some had argued was not temporary at all but a permanent behavioural change, they were subsequently to return to it with a vengeance.

THE DIE IS CAST

The next day, Friday, 20 October, I asked Mark Lennox-Boyd, Margaret's PPS, to come and see me at Number 11. I told him that Walters' activities had reached the point where they had become so damaging to the Government that I could tolerate them no longer, and that I felt he ought to know that straight away so that he could inform Margaret. I had never before spoken to him in these terms. Nor had I ever before asked him to see me at Number 11, rather than speak to him when we happened to bump into each other at the House.

Moreover this was against a background of growing concern among Conservative back-benchers about the political difficulties Walters was causing: both William Clark, then chairman of the back-bench Finance Committee, and Cranley Onslow, then chairman of the 1922 Committee of all Conservative back-benchers, had been to see Margaret about it; and the Whips, too, were inevitably well aware of the mood. Even most of those in the Party who disagreed with my policy felt Walters to be a troublemaker to whom Margaret would be well advised to bid a fond farewell.

Mark must have known the score and, having been for four years my own PPS, should have known me too. In particular, I assumed he would have realised that, in the normal course of events, I would have waited for Margaret's return from Kuala Lumpur the following week to say what I wanted to say to her face to face: the fact that I was asking him to pass the message to Margaret then and there showed that the situation had become ominous. Perhaps I should have been more explicit: in any event, Mark misread my message and state of mind, merely informing officials at Number 10 that I was irritated by Walters' latest intervention and ensuring that the full text of his American article was faxed to Margaret in Malaysia.

The problem, as I saw it, was not the difference between Margaret and myself over sterling's membership of the ERM. I had been living with that during most of my six years as Chancellor, and although it was far from ideal, I could have continued to do so.[45] What made my job impossible was Number 10 constantly giving the impression that it was indifferent to the depreciation of sterling. I cannot recall any precedent for a Chancellor being systematically undermined in this way.

This could be resolved, it seemed to me, in one of two ways. The first way would have been for sterling to join the ERM without further ado; but that was manifestly not on. The only other way was for Walters to go; quite apart from the fact that that was what, for sound political reasons, the Party wanted, it would have been a clear sign to the market that the exchange rate policy with which he was so publicly associated had been unequivocally repudiated.

---

[45] Hence my decision not to mention the ERM in my resignation letter: see next chapter.

ON THE BRINK OF RESIGNATION

My last speech as Chancellor outside the House of Commons was on Monday, 23 October at the Institute of Economic Affairs, which had decided to hold a dinner to celebrate the tenth anniversary of the abolition of exchange control. The two invited speakers were Geoffrey Howe and myself, the two Ministers who had been responsible for that historic step. I spoke off the cuff, and no record survives; but it was a happy, if piquant, occasion. Here were the two Ministers who, of all Margaret's Cabinet colleagues, had probably done most over the previous ten years to roll back the frontiers of Socialism, very often against Margaret's own cautious hesitation; yet we were now at the top of her blacklist. Earlier that day, at one o'clock, I had arranged for Geoffrey to see me briefly at Number 11, where I had told him that as things were I felt that there was no point in my continuing as Chancellor.

My last speech in the House of Commons as Chancellor was the following day, Tuesday, 24 October. Inevitably, the Labour Party, whose day it was, had chosen to hold a debate on the economy, and, equally predictably, the focus of their attack – for they could not have been given an easier target had we tried – was what John Smith, in a witty speech, described as 'the confusion and disarray in the formulation and explanation of Government economic policy', a charge backed by copious references to Walters. I replied that Walters was 'a part-time adviser and his views on the ERM are not the views of the Government' – adding, in a television interview later that afternoon, that 'I think it is right that advisers do not talk or write in public. It is a good convention that should be adhered to'. But, to repeat, the problem was not Walters as such; nor was it even the difference between Margaret and myself over the crucial question of exchange rate policy. It was her persistent public exposure of that difference, of which Walters was the most obvious outward and visible symbol.

Margaret returned from Kuala Lumpur at four o'clock in the morning of Wednesday, 25 October. I saw her for my usual bilateral at half past three that afternoon. I could see that she was absolutely exhausted. She had had only two or three hours sleep on the flight back and I felt it would have been unfair to tackle her in those circumstances. I gave her a run-down of the main economic and financial events while she had been away, and we had a brief discussion. As the meeting drew to a close, I simply said, 'I do not want to talk about Alan Walters now, but we must have a talk about him very soon. There is a problem there.' She replied that she saw no problem. I assured her that there was one, and that we would need to talk about it very soon. At that point John Major and

Nick Ridley were shown in, and we embarked on the meeting that approved my competing currencies paper.

That evening I talked my position over with Thérèse and one or two close friends whom I could trust implicitly. I told them I felt that, unless she wished to get rid of Walters, which would transform the position in the financial markets, but which I was sure she would not be prepared to do, I had no real alternative but to resign. My position had become completely impossible. I had no wish to give up the Exchequer, and realised that, so far as my own reputation was concerned, I would be doing so at the worst possible time; but at least I could leave knowing that I had tightened monetary conditions sufficiently to bring inflation down again. One reason why, despite immense provocation, I had not resigned earlier, was that I wanted to do everything necessary to undo the inflationary surge over which, regrettably, I had presided, rather than leave any of that task to others. With the rise in interest rates to 15 per cent earlier that month, which I expected would be the peak – as, indeed, it proved to be – I felt confident that I had done what needed to be done and could resign with a clear conscience.

There was no dissent from the conclusion that I had, with much sadness, reached. Ministerial resignations on political grounds are few and far between, and I would be the first Chancellor to do so since Peter Thorneycroft in 1958. But I saw no other course that I could with integrity, and sensibly, pursue, much as I hated having to do it. I sat down to draft a resignation letter.

CHAPTER 57

'UNASSAILABLE'

26 October 1989: Resignation ... · ... and its Aftermath · Retrospect

26 OCTOBER 1989: RESIGNATION ...

My first scheduled meeting on the morning of Thursday, 26 October, was at a quarter to ten, with Margaret, the Defence Secretary Tom King, and the industrialist Frank Tombs, with the Cabinet Secretary, Robin Butler, in attendance, to discuss the changes required at the Atomic Weapons Establishment at Aldermaston, where inefficiency had reached the point where it was causing serious problems. Early that morning I told John Gieve, my Principal Private Secretary, that it was essential I saw Margaret privately, before that, with no Private Secretary present, which of course made clear to her that it was a very serious matter I had to discuss. He got on the phone to Number 10, and came back with the message that she could see me at nine o'clock.

I went next door and up to the first-floor study and came straight to the point. Reminding her of the fears I had expressed the previous year when I had first learned of her intention to bring Walters back to Number 10 as her personal economic adviser, I had to tell her that the reality had proved worse than my worst fears. His disagreement with Government policy and actions over a range of issues, in particular the highly market-sensitive question of the exchange rate, had been well known before his return; and despite everything possible being done to gag him, his views continued to seep out by one means or another, as indeed they were bound to do. Given his position as the Prime Minister's personal economic adviser, this made my job as Chancellor impossible. The markets heard two voices, and did not know which to believe.

Not only was this confusion giving aid and comfort to the Opposition, but it was doing great damage to the economy. It was impossible for any Chancellor to conduct economic policy successfully, unless he enjoyed authority in the eyes of the financial markets, and my authority was being almost daily undermined. I stressed that this was nothing to do with any personal desire on my part for unchallenged authority: any Chancellor would be in exactly the same position.

I had therefore come to the firm conclusion that, for the Government's sake, Walters would have to go. I realised, I said, that this would be difficult for her; for that reason I would understand if she did not want him to go immediately. It would be just about tolerable if he were to stay until the end of the year, and leave then, with whatever face-saving formula seemed appropriate. If not, my position as Chancellor would be untenable.

I spoke quietly and Margaret listened intently. When I had finished speaking, she said she had always thought I would want to stay and see the job through. Moreover, was I not close to becoming the longest-serving Chancellor of the twentieth century?[46] Did I not want to stay to achieve that record? As for my position, so far from being intolerable, it was very strong indeed. She then said something that I found more revealing than everything else taken together: 'If Alan were to go, that would destroy my authority.'

I told her that that was absurd: her authority owed nothing whatever to Walters. I reiterated my conclusion that, if she were not to get rid of Walters by the end of the year, I did not see how I could possibly remain as Chancellor, for the reasons I had already set out. She begged me not to go, and asked me to take no decision straight away but to reflect on what she had said. I said I would indeed reflect, and let her have my reply by two o'clock that afternoon; but warned her that it was most unlikely that I would change my mind. I added that, meanwhile, I very much hoped that she, for her part, would reflect on what I had said.

Back at Number 11, I found a glum and dejected Peter Middleton waiting for me. John Gieve was there too. He had clearly guessed what was afoot, and had alerted Peter. I told John that I had arranged to see Margaret again at two o'clock, and that in the meantime he had better stand down the RAF plane that was to have flown me to Germany – I was due to take off from Northolt at half past twelve – and telephone the office of the German Finance Minister, Waigel, to cancel the meeting we had planned for that afternoon, using any excuse he could think of. As soon as he had done that, I told him to get all Treasury Ministers and special advisers over to Number 11 for an important meeting.

I had gone to Margaret not to tell her I wished to resign, but to ask her to wave goodbye to Walters – making clear to her, however, what the consequences

[46] The longest-serving twentieth-century Chancellor was David Lloyd George (1908-15), with a tenure of seven years and one month. When I resigned I had been Chancellor for six years and four months.

would be were she not to do so. She had made it clear she would not do so. There was really nothing for me to reflect on. Whether she actually wanted me to go, or was indifferent to whether I stayed or went, or whether she simply assumed that if she stood firm I would back down, was neither here nor there. I had issued no public ultimatum to her, and told none of my colleagues of my intention. Although, knowing her as I did, I never expected her to agree to get rid of Walters, I did everything I could to make it easy for her to do so. I wrote out, in longhand, a clean copy of my draft resignation letter.

By then it was time for me to inform my Treasury team of my imminent departure. We met for the last time in the room I used for meetings on the ground floor at Number 11. They urged me to change my mind. They said that what I was proposing to do would be bad for the Government, bad for the Party and bad for me. I thanked them for their kindness. But my mind was made up. Norman Lamont, then Chief Secretary and subsequently to be Chancellor himself in the Major Government, stayed behind afterwards to remonstrate with me in private but nothing he said raised any considerations that I had not already thought about. Shortly after he had left, a handwritten letter arrived from him, as a final attempt to get me to desist, before my two o'clock meeting with Margaret. In it he wrote:

> You have always been a very good friend to me over the years and often when I have least deserved it. My main concern in all this is for you. Leaving aside, for the moment, the effect on the Party and the Government, I am concerned that you would do yourself an immense injustice ... Your position has in the past year certainly been made more difficult – and it should not have been allowed – but it has not become impossible. A resignation would be widely misunderstood and no doubt unkindly it would be noted you had left when there were problems ... I believe you would do yourself and your reputation harm ... Lastly, I do beg of you to think of the blow it will be to the Party. No-one you say is irreplaceable. There are not many true believers left. It is not just your technical skill as Chancellor, it is the coherence, clarity and self-confidence you give us all. No-one else would do that. Please don't do it. It isn't necessary.

Norman was wrong about whether my position was impossible – something, I suspect, that his subsequent experience as Chancellor may have enabled him to understand more clearly than he could from the perspective of Chief Secretary – but he was of course right about my reputation. Once I had departed, it was inevitable that I should become the convenient scapegoat for every ill with which the economy was afflicted. I knew that it would be unpleasant for me; but although the experience was to prove even worse than I had expected – as is invariably the case – it would not have affected my decision had I fully realised what I was to endure.

When I returned to Margaret's first-floor study at Number 10 shortly after two o'clock, I told her straight away that I had reflected on our earlier discussion, and had not changed my mind. I handed her my resignation letter, telling her that I proposed to publish it as soon as practicable. At first she refused to take it; but then she took it and popped it into her handbag, unopened, saying that she did not wish to read it. She begged me not to resign, heaping extravagant praise and flattery on me. She reminded me of a private conversation we had had some two years earlier – she said she had 'squirrelled it away in her mind' – when she had asked me about the Governorship of the Bank of England when Robin Leigh-Pemberton's term came to an end, and I had told her that I would be interested in the job myself; to which she had responded favourably, without of course committing herself. Did I want to give that prospect up, too?

In fact, she said everything except the one thing that would have persuaded me to stay; namely, that she agreed that Walters should go. She then said that she had no time to discuss the matter any further as she had to prepare for Prime Minister's questions. She suggested we continued our discussion as soon as she returned from the House: her office would let me know when she was back at Number 10. I realised that my resignation, however welcome to her in many ways – despite what she had been saying to me – had come as a shock, and agreed.

Her return from the House was delayed, no doubt to enable her to confer briefly with her kitchen cabinet, but eventually, at about half past four, I went to see her for the third and last time that day. Once again, she begged me to stay, heaping praise on me, but this time she was simply going through the motions. She knew the die had been cast, and was already thinking of her next move. I agreed to defer the announcement of my resignation and the release of my letter until six o'clock, to enable her to announce my successor – and release her reply – at the same time. I was in any case anxious that the Treasury and Bank should have time to decide how to handle the likely effects on the financial markets.

We had a short and civil discussion, during which she thanked me for all I had done, and asked me whom I would suggest as my successor. I told her that it was entirely a matter for her. She then said she would miss me, and we parted in an atmosphere of suppressed emotion.

The text of my resignation letter, and of her reply, read as follows:

> Dear Margaret,
>
> The successful conduct of economic policy is possible only if there is, and is seen to be, full agreement between the Prime Minister and the Chancellor of the Exchequer.
>
> Recent events have confirmed that this essential requirement cannot be satisfied so long as Alan Walters remains your personal economic adviser.
>
> I have therefore regretfully concluded that it is in the best interests of the Government for me to resign my office without further ado.
>
> I am extremely grateful to you for the opportunity you have given me to serve in the Government, particularly over the past six and a half years as Chancellor; and I am proud of what we have achieved together.
>
> I shall, of course, continue to support the Government from the back benches.
>
> Yours ever
> Nigel

> Dear Nigel,
>
> It is with the most profound regret that I received your letter. We have spoken since and, as you know, it was my most earnest hope that you would continue your outstanding stewardship as Chancellor of the Exchequer at least for the rest of this Parliament. There is no difference in our basic economic beliefs, and Britain's economy is vastly stronger as a result of the policies which you and I and the Government have planned and pursued together.
>
> You took a key part in preparing our party for Government before 1979. Your work at the Treasury, as Financial Secretary, on the Medium Term Financial Strategy, and at the Department of Energy in overseeing the privatisation of Britoil were landmarks in the Government's success. You have been responsible for possibly the most far-reaching reform of our tax structure this century, as well as for a period of unprecedented

> growth and prosperity. It is a matter of particular regret that you should decide to leave before your task is complete.
>
> I know you will continue to support the Government vigorously from the back benches, but all in Cabinet will miss the great ability and breadth of understanding which you have brought to our deliberations.
>
> Please thank Thérèse for her splendid support.
>
> Yours ever
> Margaret

While all this was happening, Thérèse was at Stoney Stanton with our two children, Tom, then thirteen and Emily, then eight. It was their half-term holiday. I had, of course, been on the telephone to Thérèse several times throughout the day, letting her know the state of play. She was half expecting Margaret to choose to keep me rather than Walters, and it was only when I telephoned her after my third and final meeting with Margaret, to tell her that my resignation would be announced on the six o'clock news, that she made arrangements to join me at Number 11. Telling them simply that she had to make an urgent trip to London, Thérèse left Emily with Jim Bradley, the local village newsagent, and his wife, Lilly, who had been such good friends to us over the years, and drove up to London with Tom.

They were still on the M1 when they heard the announcement on the six o'clock news, which revealed that my successor was John Major, with Douglas Hurd replacing him as Foreign Secretary – both of them thus acquiring the jobs they had always wanted – and David Waddington, surprisingly, becoming Home Secretary. Events then followed thick and fast. On the financial markets sterling plunged and gilts took a tumble. The pound fell two cents against the dollar in the first ten minutes, and was a further two cents down by the New York close. There was a similar dive against the Deutschmark, taking the pound once again through the DM3 barrier, this time as far as DM2.90. The collapse would have been considerably greater had there not been massive intervention by the Bank of England. The reserves I had accumulated were being put to good use.

That side of things, however, was no longer my responsibility; but other equally pressing matters were. I had to make plans to vacate Number 11 while requests for me to speak to the Press and television, not merely from the UK media but from all over the world it seemed, were flooding in. Resignation from high office, particularly in the sort of circumstances surrounding my departure, is a trauma unlike any other. Moving house can be surprisingly traumatic too.

It is the misfortune of the tenant of a tied cottage to experience both at once. I telephoned Alex Allan, who had been my longest-serving Principal Private Secretary, and Robert Culpin, who had been my longest-serving Press Secretary, and asked them to come over to Number 11 to help me deal with everything.

We moved temporarily to a mews house generously lent us by my constituency chairman. Finding something more permanent was easier said than done: we had sold our London house when I became Chancellor in 1983, since when London property prices had rocketed. I had resigned with no other job lined up, and the only certainty was that my ministerial salary had disappeared overnight.

But to return to that 26 October: before long Thérèse and Tom turned up at Number 11 – just in time before Downing Street was surrounded by the media hordes. So far as the media bids were concerned, I clearly had to state my case, but equally clearly had no wish to rock the Government's boat. I decided straight away that I would do nothing until I had explained my resignation to the House of Commons. Thereafter, I would do one television programme and then hold my peace. It was not difficult to decide which television programme to accept. Margaret was due to be interviewed by Brian Walden, at that time probably the most formidable and serious political interviewer in the business, on the Sunday immediately following my resignation; and the *Walden Interview* people had offered me the same slot the subsequent Sunday. The programme with Margaret had, of course, been agreed well before I resigned; but it was bound to go into my resignation at some length, and I accepted the invitation to state my own case the following Sunday.

John Major telephoned me to say how bad he felt about inheriting my job in the circumstances in which it had come about, even though it was the job he had always wanted. I told him that there was no need for him to feel bad at all. It was my own decision, made in circumstances which he had had no hand in creating. I added that Thérèse and I proposed to vacate Number 11 that evening, and that I would remove all my private papers and other belongings from the official part of the building before doing so; but that we would need a few days to make the arrangements to move all our stuff from the private flat upstairs. This he readily accepted.

We had barely started on the process of sorting out and packing my private papers into assorted cardboard boxes, assisted by Alex and Robert, when the bittersweet news came through that Walters had been a casualty of the fall-out from the explosion caused by my resignation, and had resigned as Margaret's personal economic adviser. If she was to be believed, her object had been to keep both her Chancellor and her guru: yet she had chosen the one course of action that had caused her to lose both. I reflected that, however painful it was to me personally, I had performed a signal service to my successor and to the Government in general.

Alex discovered from the police that, by that time, the Press were keeping vigil outside the Old Rectory too, waiting for me to arrive there. He made arrangements for us to leave Number 11 via the basement that runs underneath both Number 11 and Number 10, into the Number 10 garden, and out through the garden gate into Horseguards Parade, where Thérèse's car would be waiting. The Leicestershire Police were informed of our estimated time of arrival at Stoney Stanton, and would ensure us trouble-free access to the Old Rectory. At about half past eleven on that very dark October evening we left Number 11, escorted by Alex, for the last time, and Thérèse drove us and Tom in her Metro back to Leicestershire. Two hours later, with the help of the Police, we drove into the Old Rectory without stopping, and locked the gates behind us.

... AND ITS AFTERMATH

As usual, I slept well that night, but poor Thérèse could not sleep at all. I woke up to discover that the Old Rectory was once again under siege. Not surprisingly, the media men and women who had been waiting outside the house when we arrived in the small hours of Friday morning had not been all that numerous. By daybreak their numbers had swollen enormously, with the police patrolling the unwalled side of the garden to prevent access from the churchyard. I told the police I would make a brief statement to the Press and television people in the garden, after which they should leave. With Thérèse by my side, I walked out of the front door, stated my full and unqualified support for John Major, whom I regarded as a first-class choice as my successor, and declined to answer any questions. They then left the garden, but continued to lay siege to the property, back and front. Indeed, so far from going away, they erected tall gantries so that their television cameras, equipped with what looked like satellite dishes, could see over our high stone walls and through the upstairs windows – a fact that we discovered only when a friend telephoned to say she had just seen Thérèse, on television, in the bedroom.

The Press that day, Friday, 27 October, concentrated primarily on Margaret's position in the wake of my resignation, but there was inevitably comment on the resignation itself. The tabloids showed that Ingham's black propaganda machine was already fully cranked up, the most succinct example being, as ever, the *Sun*, with its simple headline, 'Good Riddance'. At the other end of the scale, the *Economist* came up with a different verdict, stating that I

> was a main architect of the Thatcher Government's economic success; if there have been the beginnings of a British economic miracle they are in large measure Mr Lawson's. In his tax reforms he was the most radical Chancellor this century, if never as radical as his own instincts may have inclined him.

The article ended prophetically with the words:

> The day Nigel Lawson said 'enough' may be the day that Mrs Thatcher's term of office started to draw to its close.

Pretty soon, the letters started flooding in, in their hundreds, the bulk from ordinary members of the public, unknown to me. Although some were hostile, the overwhelming majority were supportive – and came predominantly from Conservative voters. There were also a huge number of letters from friends and colleagues, many of which greatly moved me, since they went far beyond the normal courtesies. They came from considerable numbers of Treasury officials most of whom, in addition to paying generous tribute, stressed how much they had *enjoyed* working for me or with me, which pleased me.

I was particularly touched by one very senior official, who wrote, 'It is harder for officials when they see Ministers go whose judgement they admire than is sometimes realised.' They also came from parliamentary colleagues, both back-benchers – even a small number from the Labour benches – and ministerial colleagues, past and present. Ian Gow wrote in characteristically generous terms, including the statement, 'The lady really did want to keep you – and so did I.' As for the first part of that statement, it seemed to me that Willie Whitelaw was, as usual, the most perceptive when he wrote, 'She could so easily have got rid of Walters, but increasingly I fear that she simply cannot bring herself to be on the losing side in any argument. That failing may ditch us all.'

There were also a large number of generous letters from abroad, particularly from fellow Finance Ministers and former Finance Ministers with whom I had worked. The French were particularly courteous; I received letters not only from Pierre Bérégovoy, the then Finance Minister, and his predecessor, Edouard

Balladur, but also, in particularly generous and characteristically French terms, from Jean-Claude Trichet, the permanent head of the French Treasury, and Jacques de Larosière the Governor of the Banque de France.

In an attempt to capitalise on the situation, the Labour Party had initiated an economic debate on Tuesday, 31 October, five days after my resignation. It was the obvious occasion on which to make my resignation speech to the Commons, and the Speaker called me, as is customary on these occasions, immediately after the two opening speeches – on this occasion, from John Smith and John Major, the latter's first as Chancellor. I knew exactly what I wanted to say, and kept it uncharacteristically brief, less than ten minutes. Speaking from the traditional place for such speeches – just below the gangway, one bench up from the front, the place normally occupied by the Father of the House – I made it clear that the 'cut and run' smears that were already being peddled by the black propaganda brigade were wholly untrue. My resignation, I pointed out,

> was not the outcome I sought. But it is one that I accept without rancour – despite what might be described as the hard landing involved.

The key economic issue I highlighted was whether the exchange rate was

> to be part of the maximum practicable market freedom or ... a central part of the necessary financial discipline. I recognise that a case can be made for either approach. No case can be made for seeming confusion or for apparent vacillation between these two positions.

I went on to emphasise that systems such as the EMS were not 'panaceas or soft options. Tough decisions still have to be made.'

The speech was listened to with rapt attention and clearly went down well in the House. It received a better press than any I had made as Chancellor.

The previous Sunday, 29 October, I had watched with particular interest Margaret being interviewed by Brian Walden, knowing that I would be in her shoes a week later. It was not one of her better performances. Depressingly, she appeared to be adding to the Madrid conditions, unilaterally, as she went along. She insisted that 'Nigel was Chancellor, Nigel's position was unassailable, unassailable' – and altogether used the word 'unassailable' about me so many times that it acquired a new and ironic meaning in Westminster parliamentary discourse. But what made me almost fall off my chair was when, asked by Walden, 'Do you deny that Nigel would have stayed if you had sacked Professor Alan Walters?', she replied, 'I don't know, I don't know.' When Walden persisted, she stuck to the 'I don't know' line until, exasperated, she expostulated, 'I'm not going on with this.'

I had, of course, made it perfectly clear to her that in those circumstances I would have stayed, but she presumably realised that admitting it would have got her into even deeper trouble, particularly with Walters having departed too. My main concern for my own interview, the following Sunday, 5 November, was how to explain clearly, calmly and truthfully the reasons for my resignation, without appearing to brand Margaret a liar, which I had no wish to do, when Walden asked me about her extraordinary answer, as he was clearly likely to do. My interview with Walden had not been going long before he was asking why Margaret had said that she did not know why I had resigned – a slight variation on the same point. I gave the reply I had decided to use, 'The only conclusion I can come to is that she found it impossible to believe that I meant it ... or she thought that I would back down.' The interview went well and I received another large mailbag of favourable letters; but I felt 'so what?'. The depression that inevitably follows a trauma of that kind was already beginning to set in.

RETROSPECT

There was some surprise that I could have resigned over, as some saw it, anything as minor as a part-time adviser to the Prime Minister. Indeed even some well-wishers felt that I had demeaned my high office by phrasing my resignation letter in the way that I did. It was quite true that Walters was in one sense simply a symptom of a growing rift between Margaret and myself, not just over the ERM, but over exchange rate policy more generally. But even that has to be set against the fact that over most other aspects of policy, I was, ironically, closer to her than was almost any other senior member of her Cabinet. What made it a resigning issue was the way in which she handled that difference of view over the exchange rate.

Essentially, the point is that Prime Ministers have an unfettered right to dismiss any Cabinet Minister, however senior – including the Chancellor – for whatever reason they like. That I always accepted. What is unacceptable conduct in a Prime Minister, however, is to recoil from sacking a Minister, and systematically to undermine him instead. Walters was a principal instrument of that undermining process, a process that made my job impossible.

The parting of the ways came over a genuine difference of opinion on exchange rate policy, which Margaret handled badly in personal as well as policy terms. It also arose from suspicions of me she began to harbour when I received much of the credit for the 1987 election result, and which did not diminish after my popularity began to wane. As to the substantive issue of policy, the plain fact is that no British Chancellor concerned with halting inflation has ever been able to turn a blind eye to the value of the pound on the foreign exchange markets. 'Benign neglect' may or may not be an option for a large continental power like the US – although I fear that even the US may still bear a heavy cost for neglecting the value of the dollar. But it is not an option for a British government; and all previous attempts to adopt it have ended in a humiliating U-turn and a screeching of the economic brakes.

Looking back, however, I have no doubt that the substantial achievements of the Thatcher era will survive its sad and messy disintegration – and indeed, in the perspective of history, will become even more apparent. It was a great adventure on which we embarked in 1979; an adventure to rescue Britain from economic and political decline of a kind that is now barely remembered, but which stank to high heaven at the time; the adventure of charting a radically new way forward and – despite universal doubt and cynicism – seeing it through. It could not have been done without Margaret Thatcher, who will go down in history as one of the greatest Prime Ministers this country has known. But equally, Margaret could not have done it without her core team, who translated her strong will, courage and conviction – wayward and self-contradictory though it could be – into a coherent and consistent course of action. This has been an account of the stewardship of one who was fortunate enough to be a member of that core team.

CHAPTER FIFTY-EIGHT

RETROSPECT FROM 2010

Politics 1989–1997 · New Labour · The Economic Crisis 2008–10
Global Warming · Conclusions

POLITICS 1989–1997

Almost exactly a year after my resignation as Chancellor, Margaret Thatcher herself was forced out of office by the members of her own Party. Convinced, however reluctantly, that she had become an electoral liability, they had come to the conclusion, almost certainly correctly, that the only way in which the Conservative Party could win the coming general election would be under new leadership. Thus ended what Andrew Marr (no Tory) has described in his *History of Modern Britain* as 'the most extraordinary and nation-changing premiership of modern British history'.

That was twenty years ago. Looking back now, with the benefit of hindsight and mature reflection, to what extent have subsequent events caused me to modify the views I held at the time and the thinking set out in the main body of this book?

Certainly, the world has changed greatly since the 1980s.

On the political front, the greatest change has been the collapse, first, of the Soviet empire in central and eastern Europe, and, subsequently, of the Soviet Union itself, these countries' abandonment of communism, and the end of the Cold War. The pre-eminent cause of this relatively bloodless collapse was the unmitigated failure of the command economy. It is a nice paradox that the events which finally and irrevocably demonstrated the bankruptcy of both Marxist economics and Marxist historicism at the same time conspicuously vindicated Marx's emphasis on the crucial importance of economics in the understanding of history.

Meanwhile, back in the UK, Margaret's somewhat improbable successor as Conservative leader and Prime Minister, John Major, lost little time in abandoning the misbegotten and deeply unpopular Poll Tax (as indeed any other successor would have done). Relieved of this incubus, he was able to secure victory in the general election of 1992 against all the predictions of the pundits and the polls. That election marked something of a changing of the guard at the top of the Conservative Party, with Margaret and most of her former senior Ministers, myself among them, deciding to stand down from the Commons and accept elevation to the civilised but politically peripheral benches of the House of Lords.

In his engaging autobiography, John speculates on what might have happened if, following the 1987 general election, I had failed (as Chancellor) to persuade Margaret Thatcher to make him Chief Secretary to the Treasury, and she had instead stuck to her original plan to appoint him Chief Whip. He plausibly suggests that, in that event, he would probably never have become Foreign Secretary, Chancellor or Prime Minister, but instead, as an astute Chief Whip, he would have been able to secure Margaret the extra few votes she needed to win on the first ballot against Michael Heseltine in 1990 – in which case she would have held on, as Prime Minister, until being ejected by the electorate in 1992.

Would this have been a good thing? Certainly, from many points of view, 1992 was a good election to lose. But on balance the Conservative victory served Britain well, because the really important consequence of the 1992 election – a personal triumph for John Major which was to prove the high water mark of his seven-year premiership – was the trauma for the Labour Party of suffering its fourth successive election defeat: a failure without precedent. When, two years later, the sudden and sadly premature death of its affable leader, John Smith, created a vacancy at the top, the party gritted its teeth and chose Tony Blair as the man most likely to end this seemingly interminable period of Conservative government.

Blair made it clear that the Party he now led would be not Labour, but New Labour. It was never entirely clear what New Labour was (or indeed is – if it still is), but it was clear what it was not: it was not old Labour. It accepted, indeed embraced, the capitalist system and the market economy (including privatisation), and abandoned socialism in any recognisable sense. Indeed, so far as economic policy was concerned, it ostensibly accepted the bulk of the Thatcherite revolution, including even a commitment, of totemic significance, not to increase the 40 per cent top rate of income tax which I had introduced in my (at the time) highly controversial 1988 Budget.

I warmly welcomed this transformation. It was, in the first instance, a clear if tacit acknowledgment by the Labour Party that, whatever they liked to say in public, our radically new policy approach had been broadly successful. But it was more than that. I had always hoped, not merely that we would successfully challenge the failed economic consensus of the post-war past, but that we would establish a new and more productive consensus. This was partly because I wished to see a cultural change embedded in the official Treasury, which would be greatly assisted by the existence of common ground between the two main parties. But it was also because I was reluctant to envisage all that we had worked so long and so hard to do being undone. A reforming government understandably wishes its reforms to become entrenched and to endure.

It was, of course, in my judgement very much in the public interest that this transformation should have occurred. But there is no doubt that it severely disoriented the Conservative Party, unable to decide whether Blair's abandonment of socialism was merely pretence, or – if not – how to come to terms with an apparently non-socialist opponent. The fact that there had long been a vigorous and healthy political battle in the United States between a party broadly on the right and another broadly on the left, but within the context of a common acceptance of the capitalist market economy, did not seem to register.

But if the repositioning of Labour under Blair was to prove surprisingly disconcerting for the Conservatives for many years to come, the disintegration of the Major Government of 1992–7 owed much more to developments in Europe. In October 1990, John Major, at that time my successor as Chancellor, had persuaded a by then greatly weakened Margaret Thatcher (she was ejected from office the following month) to agree at last to sterling joining the ERM.

The timing could not have been worse. Following the collapse of communism, the West German government had seized the opportunity in July 1990 to achieve the long-standing dream of German reunification. Fearful, however, that the result would be a hugely unpopular mass exodus of poor East Germans to find jobs in the much richer West, the Kohl government decided to lavish massive subsidies on East Germany, financed by running a ballooning budget deficit. Unsurprisingly, this greatly alarmed the Bundesbank, afraid of a resurgence of inflation, and German interest rates were raised to levels that were painfully high for its ERM partners, by then grappling with the problems of recession, not least in the UK.

Nor was this the only malign aspect of the timing. In December 1991, at Maastricht, the European Union had concluded yet another in its seemingly endless series of treaties designed to promote the sacred cause of ever closer union.[47] In fact, with one exception, the integrationist content of the Maastricht Treaty was modest – more modest, certainly, than the Single European Act, which Margaret had, against my misgivings, signed up to six years previously. That exception was the agreement in effect to replace the EMS/ERM with full-blown monetary union – a new single European currency, later to be known as the euro, and thus a single European monetary policy.

Very commendably, John had successfully negotiated a UK opt-out from membership of the monetary union, although in an attempt to preserve Party unity (the divisions over the issue were deep and rancorous) he declined to rule it out altogether. Be that as it may, these two events – the consequences of German reunification and the Maastricht Treaty – conspired to create a burgeoning crisis in the ERM, leading to sterling's departure from the system in particularly messy and humiliating circumstances on 16 September 1992, 'Black Wednesday'. A similar run on the French franc came close to destroying the system the following year.

As I record in the main body of this book, I had always been wholly opposed to European monetary union, not merely so far as UK participation is concerned, but indeed for Europe as a whole. In particular, I quote in Chapter 52 the major speech I made as Chancellor in January 1989 setting out the case against it (the first time this had been done by any Minister), and I continued to do so after I had left office – most fully at an EMU conference in London in July 1995.

In the first place, it is always a mistake to undertake a major economic initiative for political rather than economic reasons. It is no secret that European monetary union is a political and not an economic project, designed to achieve a further major step on the road to a fully integrated Europe. In an age of globalisation, the economic context is in any event global rather than regional, while in purely economic terms there can be little dispute that the imposition of a single monetary policy over an area as large and diverse as the European Union, with its many different languages, cultures and traditions, is undesirable.

I have consistently warned that monetary union, if it is to work at all satisfactorily, requires a high degree of fiscal union; and that, in a democracy, fiscal union inevitably demands a much greater degree of political union than the peoples of Europe – let alone the people of the UK – desire, or is indeed desirable. It is no

[47] The most recent, the Lisbon Treaty of 2007, enables new powers to be transferred from individual member states to the Union without any further treaty amendment.

historical accident that the evolution of the nation state and the evolution of the market economy coincided. For the market economy rests on a non-economic infrastructure, of which a vital component is the rule of law. And in a free society, the rule of law will work satisfactorily only if the people feel that, in the last resort, it is *their* law.

European monetary union nonetheless duly came into being when participating currencies – sterling, happily, not among them – were locked together at fixed rates on 1 January 1999. The formal birth of the euro came exactly three years later. The unresolved but far from unpredictable Eurozone crisis of 2010 has, I fear, underlined the misgivings I have repeatedly expressed.

Bitter Conservative divisions over Europe, coupled with the Party's inability to come to terms with the brutal (if necessary) rejection of Margaret, and sterling's inglorious departure from the ERM, (which lost the Party its reputation for the competent conduct of economic policy), greatly helped Blair in his campaign to overcome the electorate's resistance to Labour. All this perhaps unsurprisingly led to a Labour landslide victory in 1997 and, considerably assisted by Conservative incompetence in Opposition, secured them a full thirteen years of Government.

NEW LABOUR

To a considerable extent, except towards the end, they *did* govern as New Labour, and conducted economic policy very much along the lines set out in this book. Their best and most important decision was taken right at the start: to confer independence on the Bank of England for the conduct of monetary policy, very much along the lines that I had unsuccessfully proposed to Margaret some nine years earlier. The Bank was given the single objective of meeting an inflation target, initially set at 2.5 per cent, then from 2003 – when RPI was replaced by CPI – at 2 per cent. While the immediate purpose may have been chiefly to disabuse any fears that the financial markets may have otherwise had that the incoming Labour Government might – like its 1970s predecessor – be soft on inflation, the decision was a momentous one. It in effect institutionalised the proposition, which we had had such difficulty in sustaining in 1979, that the control of inflation was exclusively a matter for monetary policy, and not for either incomes policy or anything else, since monetary policy was the Bank's sole instrument.

The Conservative Opposition's initial hostility to this move, a move which I publicly welcomed (Gordon Brown, the new Chancellor, asked me to do so;

but I would have done so in any event), was exceedingly foolish, and fortunately soon abandoned. The Bank's remit was considerably easier than it would have been when I had advocated the move in 1988, since by 1997 inflation was already down to 2 per cent, with the result that its task was not that of getting inflation and inflationary expectations down, but the much less difficult one of keeping them down.

There was, of course, the practical question of what its guiding star should be. In Chapter 23 I listed the four candidates: a nominal GDP objective, a money supply target, a price level objective and an exchange rate objective; and I described the practical problems with the first two of these. As between the second two, I had chosen the exchange rate, commenting that 'a price-level rule works best when there is some authority removed from day-to-day political pressure, such as an independent central bank, which is free to choose its own method, but which is held strictly to account for the results achieved in terms of price stability'.

The newly independent Bank duly opted for this latter course of direct inflation targeting. Quite rightly in the circumstances. As the present Governor of the Bank of England, Mervyn King, has explained on a number of occasions, an important aspect of the conduct of monetary policy is influencing inflationary expectations, which requires market credibility. When inflation was as high as it was when we took office in 1979, with inflationary expectations rampant, and indeed for a considerable time thereafter, a 2 per cent inflation target would have had little if any market credibility, which is where the exchange rate came in. By 1997, with inflation already within the target range, it clearly did. And the Bank has carried out its task with considerable skill, establishing a valuable track record.

On the tax front the Labour Government's record was mixed. While the UK did become a more highly taxed nation, particularly compared with our principal competitors, the increase was considerably less than under previous Labour Governments; and income tax rates were further reduced, until right at the end, in 2008/9, when the top rate, which had remained at 40 per cent for more than twenty years since my 1988 Budget, was – contrary to an explicit manifesto pledge – regrettably increased to 45 and then 50 per cent for income over £150,000. Discussion of the economic effect of taxation, incidentally, is too often in terms of the tax *burden* – tax as a percentage of GDP – rather than tax *rates*. While both are important, changes in the tax burden require considerable interpretation. A reduction because the corporate sector has become unprofitable, for example, and therefore pays no corporation tax, is not a sign of economic health. In general, it is the level of tax rates which has the greater economic effect, for good or ill, and which is an unequivocal indicator.

But Labour's greatest departure on the tax front was its complete abandonment of the tax simplification agenda to which I had been committed. Gordon Brown, the Chancellor from 1997 until his elevation to Prime Minister in 2007 (thus incidentally taking from me, by a considerable margin, the record of being the longest-serving Chancellor since the First World War), was a compulsive meddler and micromanager, in the cause of which he complicated the tax system to an inordinate extent, to no useful result, and with the usual harmful side-effects. It was the same story over regulation, where the Thatcherite deregulatory agenda (and I will turn to the specific issue of financial regulation later) was replaced by a damaging plethora of unnecessary and detailed regulations.

Elsewhere on the supply side of the economy the record was better. In particular, only one of the privatised industries – the rail network, but not the railway companies – was renationalised, and in some other areas privatisation was modestly extended (although the Government retreated under trade union pressure from its plans to privatise the Royal Mail). And the important reform of trade union law which we had put in place was essentially left untouched. Reform of public services was a professed goal and the focus of much activity, though it met deep and all-too-effective resistance from unions in the public sector, which exploited to the full their position as the principal donors to Labour Party funds.

New Labour's biggest single economic failure was on the macroeconomic side: its gross mismanagement of the public finances. It began well, with a strong commitment to financial discipline throughout its first term of office and a firm grip on public spending. That grip was loosened somewhat during its second term, and in the third and final term all caution was thrown to the winds, with a massive rise in public spending leading to a public sector deficit in its final year, 2009/10, of well over 10 per cent – an unprecedented figure, of which only a minor part was the consequence of the recession.

Tackling this problem was to be the overriding and necessary objective of the incoming Conservative–Liberal Democrat coalition Government which took office in 2010, following an inconclusive general election at which the country ejected a discredited Labour Government led by an unpopular Prime Minister, but an inept Conservative campaign denied the Conservatives under David Cameron an overall majority.

THE ECONOMIC CRISIS, 2008–10

The real challenge to what I have called the new consensus, which over the years – particularly following the election of Ronald Reagan to the US Presidency in 1981 – had become something of a global consensus, came not from New Labour but from the onset of the world recession of 2008–9. The most severe downturn since the slump of the 1930s, this had, at its heart, a global banking meltdown. The verdict of some was clear, and not only (and predictably) on the traditional Left. In the words of the chief economics commentator of the *Financial Times*, for example, 'The assumptions that ruled policy and politics over three decades suddenly look as outdated as revolutionary socialism ... The era of financial liberalisation has ended.'

To what extent, if any, is this true? The recession of the late 2000s occurred in a world very different from and, I would argue, very much better than that of the 1980s. Financial liberalisation, whose single most important component was the liberalisation of capital movements pretty well worldwide, had ushered in the second coming of globalisation, the creation to a considerable extent of a single world economy – the first coming having been the remarkably successful half-century between the end of the American Civil War and the outbreak of the First World War, which put an end to it: a period justly dubbed *La Belle Époque*.

When the new rulers of Communist China came to the conclusion that socialist economic policies were a disaster, a conclusion demonstrated by what they had observed in Russia as well as by their own disappointments, and that they should move to a version of the capitalist market economy, it was the fact of globalisation that enabled China to become a major player in the world economy in such short order, enjoying a breathtaking rate of economic growth which has been the outstanding economic phenomenon of the past twenty years. India, too, somewhat more cautiously, decided to shake off its protectionist socialist shell, to embrace the market economy and to take advantage of the opportunities afforded by globalisation, and has benefited greatly as a result. A similar evolution has occurred among many, although not all, of the smaller developing countries.

This has transformed the world economy, and transformed it for the better, allowing hundreds of millions of people in the developing world to improve their previously pitiful living standards to a degree that would not otherwise have been possible. Of course, it has not been a comfortable experience for some in the richer industrialised world. For globalisation in general, and the emergence of China in particular, has made the world economy a vastly more competitive marketplace than it was before. But this in turn has greatly assisted the virtual elimination of inflation worldwide (at least, for the time being).

There is nothing like an increase in competition to facilitate the task of preserving stable prices. Many monetarists do themselves no favours by moving from the correct observation that inflation is caused by the excessive creation of money to the false conclusion that monetary authorities engage in this out of stupidity, venality or just for the hell of it, rather than in response to pressures in the real world.

It is in this overwhelmingly benign context that the recent world recession and global banking meltdown has to be assessed. That liberal market capitalism has been shown, in practice, to be deeply flawed should come as no surprise. That is the nature of mankind. What is more important is that history, and notably the history of the post-war world, has demonstrated beyond dispute that every other system of economic organisation is very much worse. What the recent financial and economic crisis does underline, however, is that a recession associated with a collapse of the banking system is, by an order of magnitude, worse than the 'normal' cyclical downturn. So it is important to distinguish between these two aspects of the crisis: the cycle and the banking problem.

An essential part of the new policy framework we set in place during the 1980s was to set the conduct of economic policy, very explicitly, within a medium-term context. The most obvious formal expression of this was the Medium Term Financial Strategy (MTFS). But behind the MTFS there lay a more profound reversal of the old post-war consensus, according to which the overriding object of the Chancellor's policies was a largely vain quasi-Keynesian attempt to eradicate, or at least greatly diminish, the vagaries of the typical business cycle, about which policy-makers can in reality do very little (and certainly not without doing more harm than good). The focus instead was to be on creating the conditions for improved economic performance over the longer term, about which history, both in the UK and throughout the world, teaches us that a great deal can be done, even though it may take a while for the results to become apparent.

There are rival explanations for the existence of the business cycle; but the evidence of an inescapable cyclical pattern is painfully evident. For Keynes himself, who was a close observer of, and active participant in, the financial markets, and whose thinking was greatly influenced by this, the cycle was essentially a matter of collective (for mankind is at all times profoundly affected by the herd instinct) mood swings, from high optimism to deep pessimism and back again, *ad infinitum*. This was made to sound rather more scientific by being described in the *General Theory* as fluctuations in what Keynes called the 'marginal efficiency of capital'. But the 'marginal efficiency of capital', which sounds so objective in those terms, was defined by Keynes as the expected return on new investment; and what fluctuated, he explained, was expectations. So we are back to mood swings, an ineradicable aspect of human psychology – which means that the business cycle is itself ineradicable, and we should not waste our time vainly trying to prevent it.[48]

Moreover, a case can be made for the proposition that what might be termed the normal business cycle confers benefits as well as incurring costs. The superiority of market capitalism lies in particular in two areas: the freedom and encouragement it gives to innovation and risk-taking entrepreneurial activity generally, and the discipline that drives up efficiency and drives down costs. The former is stimulated most during the cyclical upswing, and the latter is compelled most during the downswing. It is at least arguable that if economies moved in a straight line rather than a cyclical pattern, there might, in the long run, be less of both these benefits of the capitalist market system. However, whether that is so or not is academic; for the cycle is ineradicable.

So it is banking meltdown and the associated problem of systemic risk, and not the cycle, that we must seek to prevent. It is here, rather than in the generalised critique of capitalism, that the presently fashionable rejection of financial liberalisation needs to demonstrate whatever merit it may possess. The accusation is made that Thatcherism – and I in particular – took deregulation, and notably financial deregulation, far too far; and the finger is frequently (and mistakenly) pointed at the 'Big Bang' reforms, with which I was closely associated, as the epitome of this. In a sense, I suppose, I should be flattered to be fingered (even if only in the UK) as the author of this massive, if malign, global phenomenon. It certainly attributes to me a power and influence I never thought I possessed. But it is misguided for a more fundamental reason: it does not accord with the historical facts, which point clearly in the reverse direction.

[48] Keynes' overriding concern, unlike that of the neo-Keynesians *de nos jours*, was not in fact the economic cycle, discussion of which he relegated to a self-contained chapter, 'Notes on the Trade Cycle', tacked onto the end of the *General Theory*, but what he saw as the problem of endemic demand deficiency. Over-influenced by the experience of the 1930s, he had come to the mistaken conclusion that slump was almost the natural condition of free economies. It was this error which provided much of the intellectual underpinning of the inflationary disaster of the 1960s and 1970s.

I invite the reader to look again at Chapter 22 of this book, which covers both Big Bang and the question of bank regulation, and not least its opening paragraph, not because it is the last word on this complex and important issue – far from it – but because it was first published some eighteen years ago, and thus enjoys no benefit of hindsight. I recount there my concern at the inadequacy of the system of prudential supervision and regulation of the banks which I had inherited, and how I took the initiative to strengthen it greatly through the 1987 Banking Act, superimposing over the Bank of England, then responsible for the prudential oversight of the banks, a high-powered Board of Banking Supervision.

Moreover, this followed the passage by the Thatcher Government of the 1986 Financial Services Act, to deal with the area known as 'conduct of business' regulation. A piece of regulation, rather than deregulation, it replaced a patchy and informal system which had been rendered obsolete by the rapid development of the financial services industry in an era of globalisation and the internationalisation of the City of London (to the great benefit of the British economy) in the wake of Big Bang.

Whether the prudential system I set up in 1987 would have proved adequate to the task we shall never know. Perhaps not, in the light of the evolution of the banking system, in the UK and elsewhere, that was subsequently to occur. I will turn to this shortly. But it was undoubtedly a substantial improvement on what came before, and – more significantly – compared with what was to come afterwards. For, as a *quid pro quo* for conferring on the Bank of England independent responsibility for the conduct of monetary policy, the incoming Labour Chancellor, Gordon Brown, abolished the Board of Banking Supervision, took responsibility for banking supervision away from the Bank, and handed it to the Financial Services Authority – thus disastrously muddling the very different tasks of conduct of business regulation and prudential regulation, to the great detriment of the latter.

A case can certainly be made for having an entity separate from the monetary policy authority responsible for the prudential supervision of the banks, as is in place both deliberately in Canada and consequentially (following the migration of responsibility for monetary policy to the European Central Bank) throughout the Eurozone; and indeed I make it in Chapter 22. But there is absolutely no case for folding it into the agency responsible for conduct of business regulation. The new Conservative-led coalition Government quite rightly decided to undo this, returning responsibility for bank supervision and regulation to the Bank.

There is no doubt that the dysfunctional system of bank supervision and prudential regulation put in place by Brown, a particularly culpable error given the huge importance of the banking and financial sector to the British economy, was a major reason for the UK being one of the countries which suffered most from bank failures, at massive cost to the economy and the taxpayer, obliged to rescue the failed banks. But while New Labour's system of bank regulation and supervision was a disaster, that is in no way to deny that the root cause of the crisis lay in the greed and folly of all too many bankers, in the broadest sense of the term. Greed and folly are not of course peculiar to bankers. But there are two interconnected reasons why they are more serious and more pervasive problems in banking. They are more serious because of the unique importance of banking to the health of the economy as a whole. And they are more pervasive because, in other walks of commercial life, the disciplines of the marketplace keeps them in check, which indeed is one of the great arguments for the market economy. In banking, however, this discipline is greatly weakened by the lender of last resort facility and the presumption that the taxpayer will ultimately be called on to bail out any significant bank that gets into serious difficulties – the so-called 'too big to fail' problem.

Moreover, the problem has probably increased as a result of cultural change. In former times, bankers' greed and folly was to a considerable extent kept in check by the fear of loss of reputation if things went wrong: a powerful spur to banking prudence. But we now appear to live in an age in which the acquisition of wealth counts for more than reputation, a fact which has undoubtedly served to increase systemic risk.

Ever since Walter Bagehot wrote about the issue in the nineteenth century, it has been accepted that banks must submit to a degree of supervision and regulation which is both unnecessary and undesirable in any other industry. But the growth and extraordinary complexity of modern banking have outstripped the supervisory capacity. It is this that leads to the conclusion that something akin to the improved system I set in place in 1987 needs to be reinforced by structural change.

In a nutshell, we need to return, in all major financial centres, to the separation of commercial banking from investment banking that was enforced in the United States under the 1933 Glass-Steagall Act, until it was repealed by President Clinton in 1999, and was the settled pattern in Britain until the end of the 1980s. Achieving this will not be either easy or particularly popular in banking circles, but it can certainly be done. And we have time to get it right: this is not firefighting, but fireproofing.

The overriding reason why this separation is essential is straightforward. It is only a commercial banking crisis that poses a systemic risk and can lead to the sort of mess we are in today. It is folly to allow core banks, with their responsibility for the economically vital payments system and their taxpayer-guaranteed deposits, to be in a position where they can be brought down by exciting but highly risky investment banking activities. But the idea that this can be prevented by judicious regulation of investment banking activities is a chimaera. In the real world, that is not possible: either the investment bankers will outsmart the regulators, or the regulators will respond with damaging overkill – probably both.

Thus investment banks (like hedge funds, which proved to have been managed more prudently than most banks in recent years) should be left largely to their own creative devices, and subject essentially to the discipline of the marketplace. This leaves a much more limited, and practicable, but still absolutely essential, role for bank supervision and regulation: namely, to ensure that the core commercial banking system is thoroughly sound and adequately capitalised at all times.

The structural change outlined above, which I have been publicly advocating for some time now, is not of course in itself a sufficient condition for the avoidance of systemic risk. An improved capital adequacy regime, and a supervisory system that is fit for purpose, are also important. But it is a necessary condition. (It is worth adding that it is the capital adequacy regime, and not primarily interest rate policy, which needs to be responsive to asset-price bubbles.)

There is, incidentally, a danger in many parts of the world, and certainly in the UK, to imagine that, since this is a global problem, it requires a global solution, so the overriding need is for a global agreement. This may sound statesmanlike, but it is in fact a dangerous delusion. The overriding need is for the authorities in each country to put their own house in order. The threat from terrorism is an instructive parallel. Terrorism is indeed a global problem, and international co-operation is clearly desirable. But that in no way diminishes the overriding duty of national governments to do what is necessary to protect their own people. The same applies to financial regulation.

All this is fully in line with the thinking that led me to strengthen bank supervision with the 1987 Banking Act, and – needless to say – so far from marking the end of the era of financial liberalisation it would support and entrench it. But does the onset of the worst world recession since the 1930s nonetheless require a policy rethink, and in particular a reversion to the neo-Keynesianism which I rejected when in office and which many are now calling for?

I do not believe it does. In the first place, as I have already explained, the problem is not the (in any event inescapable) business cycle, but a recession seriously aggravated by a banking meltdown; and I have discussed what needs to be done about that. But what if a depression does loom, whether because of a banking meltdown (as in 2008) or for any other reason? I discussed this in the final part of the original version of my memoirs, which this new chapter replaces.[49] In it I wrote:

> There is nothing in the foregoing pages to justify passivity in the face of genuine deflation or depression. The underlying argument, given more fully in Chapter [33], is for a nominal framework ... But the same nominal framework [required to deal with the problem of inflation and excessive demand] is also relevant if there is a danger of too little demand. The question then is whether, should this threaten to get out of hand, nominal spending is best maintained by a Keynesian budget deficit policy or by cheap money. The first point to make is that, in the global economy of today, stimulatory action is most unlikely to be warranted unless the threat itself is worldwide ... If, however, the threat really is of worldwide slump, then worldwide, and – if only to avert the serious threat of a relapse into autarky and protection – preferably co-ordinated, action would be warranted. As between the alternatives of a global expansion of budget deficits, or a worldwide reduction of interest rates, the latter is in my judgment to be preferred. It is more readily reversible – an important practical consideration – and less likely to lead governments into bad habits and to a bloated state sector.

Fortunately, outside the United States, that appears to be the broad policy consensus today. In the UK, my successor but five as Chancellor, George Osborne, quite rightly introduced, within seven weeks of taking office in May 2010 and despite the weakness of the economy, a Budget designed to eliminate the massive structural deficit the new Government had inherited, largely by severe cuts in public spending, within the lifetime of the parliament. Needless to say, the old neo-Keynesians re-emerged in their former colours to condemn it with bell, book and candle. Osborne, fully supported by the official Treasury, was no doubt aware that neo-Keynesianism is a beautiful theory wholly devoid

[49] See also p 186 of this abridged version.

of empirical support; indeed practical experience, not least the events of 1981 recounted earlier in this book, has clearly demonstrated the wisdom of the course on which he has embarked. But it will still require considerable resolve to see it through.

Meanwhile, it is encouraging that the world economy is steadily, if slowly, recovering from the global recession of 2008–9, after a setback which, however serious, has been of greatly diminished proportions, in terms of both severity and duration, compared with that of the 1930s – and without, crucially, the relapse into protectionism that did such damage then.

GLOBAL WARMING

But the threat of such a relapse is ever-present when times are hard. And a new dimension of that threat has emerged with the advent, since my time as Chancellor, of a wholly new and major policy challenge. I refer to global warming, a.k.a. climate change, and the Government's response to it. This is a complex and fascinating multidimensional issue which it would not be appropriate to discuss at any length here. I would refer the interested reader to my short book, *An Appeal to Reason: A Cool Look at Global Warming*.[50]

By way of brief autobiographical digression, the first tasks I set myself after leaving office were to write my ministerial memoirs, while my memory of the events in which I was fortunate enough to be able to play a large part was still fresh in my mind, and to seek remunerated employment. Members of Parliament, and in particular Ministers, enjoyed in my time nothing approaching the salaries they are paid today. Included in that employment, incidentally, was eight years on the board of Barclays Bank, an instructive experience which has helped inform the views on banking and bank regulation expressed above.

I also decided that the time had come – indeed, it was long overdue, but I had neglected to do anything about it – to lose weight. This proved sufficiently successful to enable me to write a book about it, which surprisingly became something of a best-seller.[51] It was only after all this, and after the passage of time since my period as Chancellor inevitably led to a gradual thinning out of my initially busy programme of worthwhile speaking engagements, that I became aware of the global warming challenge and the policy issues it involved.

The first occasion on which I broached the matter in public was in the course of a lecture I gave at the London School of Economics in 2004. Perhaps the greatest

[50] Duckworth, 2008; second edition with additional chapter, Duckworth, 2009.

[51] *The Nigel Lawson Diet Book*, Michael Joseph, 1996.

failing of Tony Blair as Prime Minister was his Messiah compulsion. It was this that led him to participate enthusiastically in the invasion and occupation of both Iraq, to save the world from the imminent threat from Saddam Hussein's (non-existent) weapons of mass destruction, and Afghanistan, to save the world from the threat of Islamic terrorism – a real threat, this one, but one that the Western military presence in Afghanistan has in no way diminished, and may well have increased. It was the same Messiah compulsion that led him to commit the UK to saving the planet from the catastrophe of global warming. In each of these three cases he made a vastly expensive (in every sense) commitment without the slightest understanding of the history and complexity of the issues involved.

The concern I expressed about climate change in my 2004 lecture was that the Treasury had, unaccountably, not been asked to make a dispassionate economic assessment of the issue before the hugely costly commitment to the rapid decarbonisation of the British economy had been made – not even the most elementary form of cost–benefit analysis. That would certainly not have been permitted in my day. I also suggested that, had such an assessment been made, decarbonisation might not have proved cost effective, whereas adaptation might well have been. Only years later did the then Head of the Government Economic Service, Sir Nicholas (now Lord) Stern, publish a 692-page 'review' purporting to show that rapid decarbonisation would indeed be a cost-effective policy. But that was designed to support a policy to which the Government was already deeply committed, and Stern's analysis, as shoddy as it was prolix, has been rejected by the great majority of serious economists, both in this field and outside it.

It was in 2004 too that I persuaded my colleagues on the Economic Affairs Committee of the House of Lords that the Committee's first inquiry of the new session of Parliament should be on the economics of climate change. This enabled me to begin seriously to educate myself about the subject, in the course of which I discovered, *inter alia*, that important aspects of the science were far from certain.[52] A few years later I became increasingly concerned as the threat of protection in response to the hardships of the world recession was intensified, particularly elsewhere in the European Union, where so-called climate policy was moving in the

[52] I had been appointed to the Committee by accident, at the start of the 2004–05 session of Parliament. The Conservative chief whip in the Lords found a piece of paper in his pocket on which he had scribbled 'NL wants to go on the Economic Affairs Committee'. He remembered that the request came from a former Chancellor, but he could not recall whether it was from me or from Norman Lamont, so he put us both on the Committee – to my considerable surprise, since it was Norman who had asked to go on. The Committee's report on 'The Economics of Climate Change' was published in 2005 as the 2nd Report of Session 2005–06, HL Paper 12-1.

same direction as in the UK. All too often there were calls for tariffs and other trade restrictions against imports from countries, China especially, which were understandably unwilling to bear the heavy cost of forswearing the use of cheap carbon-based energy in order to curb their carbon dioxide emissions.

Unfortunately, both the UK opposition parties decided to sign up to Blair's messianic climate change agenda: the Conservatives as part of David Cameron's rebranding exercise for the Party (in awe of Blair, whose heir he once claimed to be, he had coined the slogan 'Vote Blue, go green'), and the Liberal Democrats, always anxious to be greener than thou. And the UK, alone in the world, is now legally bound to the policy of rapid decarbonisation under the terms of the 2008 Climate Change Act, enthusiastically endorsed by all three parties, and an important part of the glue which holds together the Conservative–Liberal Democrat coalition which came into being in 2010.

According to the chairman of the new Government's so-called Green Investment Bank Commission, 'The total estimated cost of our current climate change carbon reduction targets is between £800 billion and £1 trillion. There's really been nothing like it since the post-World War II reconstruction programme.' This foolish commitment has been made all the more futile by the complete failure of the UN climate change conference at Copenhagen in December 2009, which conclusively showed that a binding global decarbonisation agreement is unattainable – largely because the major developing countries, notably China and India, are quite rightly not prepared to curb the economic development their people so badly need to achieve this (not that the recession-hit industrialised world is all that keen gratuitously to add to the genuine economic problems that beset it).

At some point the Government will have to find a way of getting itself off this increasingly uncomfortable and self-imposed hook. I will do my best to help it to do so.

Meanwhile, a great miasma of political correctness enveloped the issue, in which to express doubt could be career-threatening for anyone in either politics or science. As someone with his career well behind him, I felt a duty to speak out, and followed up the gratifying success of my book[53] by founding, in 2009, a think-tank, The Global Warming Policy Foundation (www.thegwpf.org), whose overriding purpose was and is to bring balance and reason to the debate on this important issue, with the emphasis (as the Foundation's name implies) on the policies pursued.

[53] At the time I had had the greatest difficulty in finding a publisher prepared to publish the book, so great was the intolerance of dissent on the issue. In fact it proved, in its modest way, a best seller, and there have so far been eight foreign language editions published.

CONCLUSIONS

Looking back both at my time in office and at the two decades that have passed since then, it is clear that in the implementation of policy I made my share of mistakes. In particular, I underestimated the strength and duration of the boom of the late 1980s, and should have tightened monetary policy sooner than I did. But the policy framework I set in place, and the economic principles on which it was founded, were the right ones; and despite some momentous subsequent events, they have stood the test of time.

Essentially, the framework of the new approach consisted of three interconnected principles, each of them a reversal of the post-war conventional wisdom, as I subsequently set out in my 1984 Mais Lecture, a year after I became Chancellor.

The first principle was that the recipe for economic success is the greatest practicable market freedom within an overall framework of financial discipline. By contrast, the approach that culminated in the debacle of the 1970s had in practice consisted in an ever-increasing erosion of market freedom, accompanied by the progressive abandonment of financial discipline. And the subsequent abandonment of the fiscal component of that discipline by Gordon Brown has produced a disastrous deterioration in the public finances with which the successor Con–Lib coalition Government is having painfully to grapple.

The second principle was that, instead of seeking to use macroecomic policy – which for much of the post-war period meant fiscal policy, since monetary policy barely existed – to promote growth and employment, and microeconomic policy (of which prices and incomes policy was the central component) to suppress inflation, we should do precisely the reverse. That is to say, the Government of the day should direct macroeconomic policy, pre-eminently now in the form of monetary policy, to suppress inflation, and microeconomic (or supply-side) policy, such as tax reform, labour market reform, deregulation, privatisation and the promotion of competition, to provide all the other conditions most favourable to improved performance in terms of growth and employment. The fact that inflation is for the time being under satisfactory control in no way undermines this reassignment.

And the third principle, as I have mentioned earlier in this chapter, was to set all this explicitly within a medium-term context.

Being as objective as I can, I believe that this framework and these principles worked pretty much as well as could be expected in this imperfect world. If I had to choose between the two main economic achievements of the Conservative Governments of 1979–1997 – getting inflation down and reforming the supply side of the economy, both of which were of course essential – I would, however, maintain that the second was the more difficult and thus the greater of the two.

I do so on the basis of a simple test. Throughout most of Europe, the 1970s were a worryingly inflationary decade. Yet although the details varied from country to country, every established member of the European Union succeeded in getting inflation down. The 1970s also saw the European economy become increasingly sclerotic and underperforming. Yet though our partners on the Continent gradually reached the same conclusion as we had done, or at least paid lip-service to it, namely that the essential remedy was a full-blooded programme of supply-side reform, to remove rigidities and enable the market to work better, to a considerable extent they have failed to get very far, finding it too unpalatable or else too difficult.

Given that the most striking economic phenomenon since I left office has been the astonishing success of China since it abandoned socialism and embraced the capitalist market economy, the case for the market economy should not need to be made. But since there are a number of voices, notably on the continent of Europe but also in the UK, claiming that the recent global banking meltdown and recession points to the need for at least some degree of retreat from the market economy, it is worth briefly restating the case.

There is nothing ideological about the market. I admit, personally, to placing a high value on individual freedom; but there are other important values, too. The dominance of the market economy in the world today is essentially Darwinian: a matter of the survival of the fittest, as rival systems have been tested to destruction.

There are good reasons why this should have been so. There is the great benefit of competition, which only the market can fully provide. There is the Hayekian point that the market is an unbeatable signalling system, providing and diffusing the information required for rational business and consumer decisions on a scale to which no other system can remotely aspire. These are both compelling reasons; but to my mind the most compelling of all is that the most fundamental fact of economic life – as indeed of other dimensions of life – is that we are all fallible.

We all make mistakes and we always will. Markets make mistakes, and so do governments. Businessmen make mistakes, and so do politicians and bureaucrats. Thus any attempt to construct an economic system which will eliminate mistakes, or even some kinds of mistake, is doomed to failure. All we can sensibly do is put in place a system in which mistakes are soonest recognised and most rapidly corrected. And that means, in practice, the liberal capitalist market economy. By contrast, experience shows that, whatever the political system, it is governments that find it hardest to own up to mistakes, still less to correct them.

But embracing the market economy did not mean in my time, and should not mean, embracing the absurdities of modern finance theory, which encouraged the world's bankers in their recent and damaging folly. By 'modern finance theory' I refer to the combination of the efficient market hypothesis and the rational expectations hypothesis, which enabled mathematically inclined economists to provide the banks with computer models based on equations which effectively purported to take the uncertainty out of risk assessment.

It is of course true that markets are less inefficient than any other form of economic organisation, and that expectations are on the whole rational most of the time. But to derive the mathematical equations and construct the computer models it is necessary to assume total efficiency and total rationality, which is absurd. Economics, after all, is about human behaviour. The notion that you can adequately capture human nature in a series of mathematical equations is inherently ludicrous.

Yet that is the premise of modern finance theory, on which bankers chose to rely. Modern finance theory, and the mathematisation of economics of which it is a part, are both absurd and – as we have seen – highly dangerous. Their attraction – and, despite their part in the banking meltdown, they are now dominant in the economics faculties of most British universities – derives from the fact that economists, at least since Marshall, have mistakenly sought to dignify their calling by describing it as a science, and increasingly chosen to add verisimilitude to this pretence by clothing their propositions in the language of science, that is to say, mathematics. Despite being a one-time mathematician of sorts myself, I doubt if any Chancellor of the Exchequer has ever been assisted in the slightest by a mathematical equation. For economics is not a science.

On scientific matters we rightly expect a high degree of certainty, and are ready to leave many important decisions to properly educated experts. By contrast, economic policy is more like foreign policy than it is like science, consisting as it does in seeking a rational course of action in a world of endemic uncertainty. Perhaps that is why I increasingly found economic history, which is scarcely taught at our universities, and then inadequately, to be a more useful guide to economic policy decisions than economic theory, which is taught to excess.

Finally, there is the political dimension, as important as the purely economic. Underlying the policies set out in the main body of this book was a willingness to extend the bounds of the politically possible.

There was, for example, widespread acceptance at the time that inflation was a major economic and social evil, that all attempts – by governments of both parties – to contain it by incomes policies had not only failed but brought significant political and economic disadvantages of other kinds, and that the problem was getting worse, as inflationary expectations became embedded. But it was equally widely assumed that the alternative approach of a fierce monetary squeeze would bring levels of transitional unemployment that made it politically impossible. In the event, transitional unemployment rose rather more than we had expected, and lasted slightly longer. But it did not make the policy, which was pursued to a successful conclusion, politically impossible.

Again, there was general agreement that nationalisation of a large and important sector of the economy had failed, having brought neither business efficiency nor industrial peace (as its original architects had hoped, by ending conflict between workers and their capitalist bosses), and that this was a significant part of the explanation for Britain's poor economic performance. But the obvious remedy of recognising this and embarking on a policy of denationalisation – or privatisation as it came to be known – was assumed to be politically impossible: a rupture of the post-war settlement which the people did not desire and the trade unions would not permit. And, of course, it had never been done – neither in the UK nor anywhere else. Yet we did it.

It was widely accepted, too, that the trade unions had become an over-mighty subject, more interested in exercising political power than in raising the living standards of their members, and had made the country almost ungovernable. But following the unsuccessful attempts of both the Heath Conservative and Wilson Labour Governments to deal with this problem, it was equally widely seen as politically impossible to achieve. Yet we did it.

Again, the 'savage cuts' on which we embarked to deal with an unsustainable budget deficit and a bloated and unaffordable public sector were widely considered to be politically impossible and a recipe for intolerable civil strife and unrest. Yet we persisted, albeit rather more gradually than we had originally intended, and the public finances were, in my time, brought into surplus.

At the time of writing there is a new Conservative-led Government in office which is faced with an even greater budget deficit than that with which we were confronted. Happily, the other dragons that were in our path have remained slain. But once again, in this area, it is a matter of extending the bounds of the politically possible. No doubt in an ideal world a Government would always persuade the people of the wisdom of a policy before implementing it. In practice, however, that is often not possible, and becomes simply a recipe for inaction. A sensible Government does what it believes to be right, explains why it is doing so, and stands to be judged by the results. That after all – and not a damaging change in the voting system – is the essence of what democracy is all about. I hope the historical account set out in the main body of this book will be of some assistance to the new Government today.

INDEX